Francis Day

Report on the Fresh Water Fish and Fisheries of India and Burma

Francis Day

Report on the Fresh Water Fish and Fisheries of India and Burma

ISBN/EAN: 9783337060657

Printed in Europe, USA, Canada, Australia, Japan

Cover: Foto ©Andreas Hilbeck / pixelio.de

More available books at **www.hansebooks.com**

REPORT

ON THE

FRESH WATER FISH AND FISHERIES

OF

INDIA AND BURMA,

BY

Surgeon-Major FRANCIS DAY, F.L.S. & F.Z.S.,
INSPECTOR GENERAL OF FISHERIES IN INDIA.

CALCUTTA:
OFFICE OF THE SUPERINTENDENT OF GOVERNMENT PRINTING.
1873.

INTRODUCTION.

1. The following report is the result of investigations made since 1867, into whether a wasteful destruction of the fresh-water fisheries is or is not occurring in India and Burma. It may be said to be composed of two elements, personal investigations and the result of enquiries made by European and Native civil officers in India and Burma.

2. When personally enquiring in different districts, I found that such a large amount of valuable local knowledge existed that I proposed circulating a series of questions and deferring the compilation of the full report until answers had been received.

3. The questions circulated were as follows:—*For Collectors*, (1).—Are breeding fish and very young ones destroyed in your district to any great extent? (2).—If they are destroyed, how, in what places, and at what seasons? (3).—What is the smallest size of the mesh of nets allowed or employed in your district? (4).—What difficulties are there against regulating the size of the mesh of the nets? (5).—What size between knot and knot of the meshes of nets do you consider advisable? (6).—What objections exist against prohibiting the sale of the fry of fish in the bazars? (7).—Are there any objections against prohibiting the capture of fish in hilly districts, as the Himalayas or Nilgiris, during the first two months of the monsoon season when they are breeding?

4. *Those for Tehsildars or Native Officials were,*— (1).—What number of fishermen are there in your range, and

are they only such, or do they pursue other occupations likewise? (2).—What are the names of the fishermen castes in your district? (3).—Are the local markets fully supplied with fish, or could more be sold? (4).—What is the price of large and small fish in the bazar, and also that of first and second sort of bazar mutton? (5).—What proportion of people eat fish? (6).—Have the fish increased, decreased, or remained stationary of late years? (7).—Are very small fish taken in any quantity during the rains; if so, how? (8).—What is the smallest size of the mesh of the nets employed? (9).—Are fish trapped in the irrigated field during the rains? (10).—Enumerate the various sorts of fishing, and give the native names of every form of net, trap, or snare used in taking fish in your range.

5. Many of the answers received have been most exhaustive, and afforded me the opportunity of drawing attention to certain facts that I otherwise might not have so prominently brought to notice. Whenever possible, I have rather given the opinions of others than my own, provided the two were identical. Where so many reports are excellent, it would be invidious to draw attention to any particular one, especially as all will be found collated in the appendix.

6. All returns received prior to November 5th have been included, whilst due to the delay in some localities it was found impossible to even commence this work in June 1872 as had been anticipated. The period during which answers were being waited for was employed in drawing up the last three papers in the appendix, which it is hoped will add to the completeness and utility of the report.

MADRAS,
December 5th, 1872.

TABLE OF CONTENTS.

	PAGE.
REPORT ON INDIAN FRESH-WATER FISHERIES	1

    Origin of enquiry—Previous workers on the subject of Indian fishes—Enquiries made in 1867—Where fresh-water fisheries exist.

RIVERS AND THEIR EXPANSIONS 4

    Rivers of the Indian Empire—Hill rivers of India, some having Alpine sources—Those destitute of Alpine sources—Rivers of the plains—How these rivers shallow during the hot season until only a succession of pools exist, and here large fish have to remain until the rains return—How some rivers have seasons of inundations, filling large lakes in the contiguous country—How lakes thus formed may be isolated or connected ones.

IRRIGATION WORKS 7

    Irrigation weirs or bunds—Undersluices, either narrow or wide, the weirs impassable to ascending fish—Narrow undersluices—Wide undersluices—Fish unable to ascend over weirs—Irrigation canals—Simple irrigation weirs—Irrigation and navigation canals. How fish are carried into irrigating canals and perish there, due to a want of water—Small rivers diverted for irrigation in Malabar—Mills worked by water destructive to fish.

TANKS USEFUL AS FISHERIES 14

    Tanks used as fisheries—Jhils—How a natural protection may be afforded to fish.

THE FISHES OF THE FRESH-WATERS 15

    Fresh-water fish—Migratory and non-migratory species, some polygamous, others monogamous—Breeding season—Spiny rayed fishes, divisible into purely fresh-water and partially marine forms—Physostomatous order—Scaleless family, those of hills and plains—Their respiration—Family of Scombresocidæ and Cyprinodontidæ—The carps, loaches—Sand-grubbers true carps—Carps of the plains, migratory or not so—Herring family, migratory or not so—Eels—Lophobranchiate fishes—Plectognathi—Cartilaginous fishes.

RESPIRATION OF INDIAN FISHES 24

    Respiration of fishes—Water and compound breathers.

ÆSTIVATION OF FISH 28

MIGRATIONS OF FISH 29

BREEDING OF FISH 31

    Breeding fish, migratory and non-migratory ones of the plains—Migratory and non-migratory ones of the hills—Breeding of migratory hill fishes—Non-migratory fish of the plains, some monogamous, others polygamous—Migratory fresh-water fishes of the plains—Migratory sea fishes.

THE FRY OF FRESH-WATER FISH 36

    Fry how destroyed instead of being protected.

		PAGE
FISH IN AN ECONOMIC POINT OF VIEW	. . . .	37

The proportion of persons who use fish as food—Local markets insufficiently supplied.

THE FRESH-WATER FISHERIES	. . . .	40

How wasteful injuries to fisheries commence—Breeding fish and fry wastefully destroyed—The supply of fish in the waters decreasing—To whom the fisheries belong—Why British rules and regulations have a disastrous effect on fisheries—How fisheries were worked under native rulers—How they are treated under British law.

THE FISHERMEN	. . . .	49

Who the fishermen are—How fisheries are worked.

FIXED ENGINES	. . . .	57

What fixed engines are—Those made of elastic materials—Those of non-elastic substances, and weirs—Fixed traps.

MOVEABLE FISHING IMPLEMENTS	. . . .	65

Composed of elastic or non-elastic substances—The smallest size of the mesh of nets employed—Seasons when different meshes are used—Effect of regulating the minimum size of the mesh of nets—Damming waters for fishing purposes—Diverting rivers or streams—Waters may be poisoned—Sometimes solely to obtain the fish—Minor modes of fishing.

VERMIN WHICH DESTROY FISH	. . . .	80

Crocodiles as vermin—The fish-eating crocodile—The common crocodile—Otters as vermin—Minor fish-destroying vermin.

OBJECTIONS TO LEGAL ACTION BEING TAKEN	. . . .	85

Primary objections—Divine reasons—General objections—Legal objections—Regulations deemed unnecessary—Zoological objections—Political objections—Social objections—Fishermen's objections—Trading objections—Result of want of regulations elsewhere.

SUGGESTIONS AS TO WHAT LEGAL STEPS ARE NECESSARY	.	94

Reasons why such are desirable—General reasons—Regulations proposed—A necessity for restricting the minimum size of the mesh of nets—Minimum size proposed—Prohibiting the sale of the fry of fish in bazars—Further proposals.

FISHERY LAWS OF GREAT BRITAIN	. . . .	101

Fishery laws of Great Britain—Right of fishing—Nature of right of fishing—Right of property in a fishery—Fishing weirs when legal—Fixed engines—Size of mesh of nets in England—Laws for the preservation of fry in England—Other illegal modes of fishing—Poisoning waters—Fish roe—Weekly close time—Close season and prohibition of fixed engines—Taking unclean fish—Spawning salmon—All fishing amenable to the general laws—Boards of conservators—Weirs and fish passes—Remedies that have been tried—Beneficial results that have ensued.

RESULTS OF THIS ENQUIRY	. . . .	110

PROPOSITIONS AS TO WHAT ACTION IS NECESSARY	.	112

Legal action required.

A GENERAL FISHERY ACT	. . . .	113

One necessary—Skeleton of Act.

BYE-LAWS OR LOCAL ACTS	. . . .	114

Local regulations—Fence months—Regulating the minimum size of the mesh of nets—Minor modes of fishing—Vermin—Who is to pay for regulations, if any are to be carried out?

APPENDICES.

PANJÁB i
Territory included and its physical geography—Its population—Enquiry on this subject in 1869 and 1870—Proportion of population who consume fish—Local markets insufficiently supplied—Present state of the fisheries and destruction of breeding fish in hilly districts—Fisheries Government property, and how the Rajahs let them—Fishermen not dependant on this occupation as a sole means of subsistence—Breeding fish and fry if destroyed, and the result of regulating the minimum size of the mesh of nets—Fish killed wholesale in canals constructed for working mills—Diverting hill streams—Irrigation weirs and canals destructive to fisheries—Suggestions respecting prohibiting the sale of the fry of fish in bazars—Fence months advisable in hilly districts—Some pools in hill streams should be protected during the dry months—Trapping fish objectionable—Neighbouring native states should be asked to co-operate in preservative measures—Present Panjáb fishing regulations—Additional ones proposed.

Reports from European Officials viii
Secretary to the Panjáb Government—Commissioner of Pesháwar—Deputy Commissioners of Pesháwar, Hazara, and Kohat—Commissioner of Ráwal Pindi—Deputy Commissioners of Ráwal Pindi, Jhilam, Shahpúr, and Gujrat—Commissioner of Derajat—Deputy Commissioners of Bánú, Dera Gázi Khán, and Dera Ismail Khán—Deputy Commissioners of Jhang, Muzaffargarh, Montgomery, and Multan—Deputy Commissioners of Lahor and Gujranwalla—Deputy Commissioners of Amritsar, Sialkot, and Gurdaspúr—Commissioner of Ambala—The Deputy Commissioners of Ambala and Ludhiana—Commissioner of Jalandar: Deputy Commissioners of Jalandar, Phillúr, Hushiarpúr, and Kangra—Commissioner of Hissár and the Deputy Commissioner—Commissioner of Delhi—Deputy Commissioners of Delhi, Gurgáon, Sarsa, and the Extra Assistant Commissioner of Karnal—The Revd. Dr. Carleton's observations on fishing as carried on in hilly districts.

Reports from Native Officials - xix
Pesháwar Division, from Pesháwar, Haripúr, Mausera, and Kohát—Ráwal Pindi Division, from Ráwal Pindi, Attock, Gujer Khán, Fathi Jang, Muni, Jhilam, Pind Dádan Khán, Chakwal, Talegang, Gujrát, Khárim, and Sahem—Derajat Division, from Bánú, Isakhel, Miamaoli, Lakki, Dera Gázi Khán, Sangarh, Rájanpúr, Jampúr, Dera, Liah, Bhakkar, and Kolachi—Multan Division, from Multan, Ala Dal Khán, of Khángarh, Darogah Shere Shah, Mian Mahbab, Muzaffargarb, Kot Adu, Montgomery, Gugaira, Pákpatan, Riaz Hossain, Multan, Shoojabad, Lodhran, Mailsi, Seraie Saidhu—Lahor Division, from Lahor, Kásur, Chunia, Sharkpúr, Gujranwalla, Wazirabad, and Hafizabad—Amritsar Division, from Amritsar, Reyah, Pasrur, Zaffarwál, Sialkot, Shakergarh, Batala, and Pathankot—Ambala Division, from Ambala, Jagadri, Raossur, Kharar, Náráyangarh, and Pipli—Jalandar Division, from Jalandar, Phillúr, Nawashahr, Nacodar, Hushiarpúr, Unah, Garhsankar, and Dasuha—Hissár Division, from Hissár, Hánsi, Fathiabad, Bhawani, and Barwúla—Delhi Division, from Delhi, Larsauli, Ballabhgarh, Gurgáon, Rewari, Palwal, Nuh, Fázilka, Sarsa, Kurnal, Pánipat, and Kaithal.

SIND xxix
Its fresh-water fisheries—River Indus—Tanks or dhánds, isolated or connected with the Indus, and their finny inhabitants—Canal fisheries, and proof that prohibiting the use of small meshed nets, small fish do not disproportionately increase over the larger sorts—Fishery in Indus mostly for Shad—Fresh-water fish, river and inundation descriptions—No preventive destruction of the immature fish appears to obtain—Fish universally eaten—Fisheries peculiar.

	PAGE
Reports from European Officials	xxxi

Commissioner of Sind—Collector of Shikarpúr—Collector of Karachi—Collector of Haidarabad.

Reports from Native Officials	xxxii

BOMBAY	xxxiii

Its fresh-water fisheries—Reason why some returns are omitted—Rivers and inland tanks suitable for fisheries—Proportion of people who eat fish—Local markets insufficiently supplied—Comparative price of large and small fish—The amount of fish have decreased—Fisheries mostly Government property—Fishermen, as a rule, follow other occupations as well—Mature breeding-fish trapped and otherwise killed—Fry destroyed to a great extent—Modes of capturing fish—Size of the meshes of nets—Fish how trapped—Waters poisoned—Angling and line fishing—Conclusions as to the fresh-water fisheries—Coast fisheries of less consequence than inland ones—Majority of people eat fish—State of the fisheries—Which are Government property—Number of fishermen—Fish trapped during the rains—Fry destroyed to a great extent—Minimum size of the mesh of nets employed—Modes of fishing—Conclusions respecting coast fresh-water fisheries—Whether advisable to mitigate the present evils or let them continue—Objections to action being taken—Propositions as to what steps are desirable—As to the proper minimum size of the mesh of nets—Opinions as to prohibiting the sale of the fry of fish in bazars—On the necessity or the reverse of fence months.

Reports from European Officials	xliii

Chief Secretary to Government—Revenue Commissioners—Collector of Ahmedabad, Collector of Broach, and Assistant Collector—Collector of Kaira and Assistant Collector—Collector of Surat—Secretary to Municipality and Assistant Collector—Collector of Khandeish, Major Probyn, and Assistant Collector—Extra First Assistant Collector, Punch Mahals—Collector of Nasik—Collector of Ahmednugger, Acting First Assistant, and Acting Second Assistant—Collector of Puna, Assistant Collector, and First Assistant Collector—Collector of Tanna—Collector of Colaba—Collector of Satara—Collector of Kaladgi—Collector of Sholapúr—Collector of Belgaum, First Assistant Collector, and Assistant Collector—Collector of Dharwar and the Assistant Collector—Collector of Ratnagiri, Deputy Conservator, and Assistant Collector—Collector of Canara.

Reports from Native Officials	lv

Ahmedabad Collectorate, from Mamlutdars of Duskroee, Gogo, Purantey, Sanund, Dhundooka, Dholka, Veerumgam, and Morassa—Broach Collectorate, from Broach, Jumboosur, Ahmode, and Hansote—Kaira Collectorate—Khandeish Collectorate—Nasik Collectorate—Ahmednugger Collectorate—Puna Collectorate—Colaba Collectorate, from Alibag, Penn, Roha, Mangam, and Mhar—Satara Collectorate—Kaladgi Collectorate—Sholapúr—Belgaum—Dharwar Collectorate, from Dharwar, Petta Moogud, Hooblee, Nowlgoond, Dumbul, Bunkapúr, Hangul, Ranebedume, Kurujghee, Rutghutghee, and Kode.

MADRAS—*(First Report)* lxiii
    Origin of answers—The fresh-water fisheries—Few perennial rivers—Rules suggested as only to affect perennial rivers—Majority of people eat fish—Inland markets insufficiently supplied—Fish in waters has generally decreased—Fisheries Government property—Fishermen, with but few exceptions, only follow this occupation in addition to their usual work—Breeding fish destroyed—Fry killed in large numbers—Minimum size of the mesh of nets and interstices in cruives—Fixed engines, damming and poisoning waters—Conclusions based upon reports—Measures of amelioration which have been proposed—Personal propositions in 1868—Orders of the Madras Government and the Revenue Board—Fresh-water fisheries in Madras prior to Government investigations—Personal observations in the Presidency—Reply to an observation that regulating the minimum size of the mesh of nets would be *cruel* to the poor—Further propositions—Proposal of Revenue Board to appoint two Inspectors of Fisheries.

Reports, &c., from European Officials lxx
    Proceedings of the Board of Revenue: their draft rules for fresh-water fisheries—Proposal for Draft Fishery Act—Circular orders in 1848—Instructions to Collectors—Collector of Ganjam, Collector of Vizagapatam, Collector of Godaveri, and the Revd. Dr. Murphy—Assistant Collector of the Kistna districts, Executive Engineer, Acting Collector, &c.—Collector of Nellur and Major Clay—Collector of Bellary and Acting Collector—Collector of Tanjur—Collector of Trichinopoly—Collector of Cuddapah—Collector of Kurnal, the Assistant Collector, the Acting Head Assistant, the Deputy Collector of Peapally, and the Deputy Collector of Kurnal—Collector of Madras—Collector of Chingleput—Collector of Salem—Collector of North Arcot and Acting Collector—Collector of South Arcot and Sub-Collector—Collector of Tinnevelli—Collector and Acting Collector of Madura and Mr. Nelson—Collector of Coimbatore—Collectors of Malabar—Collector of South Canara—Experimental trial of pisciculture in South Canara.

Reports from Native Officials xcii
    Ganjam Collectorate, the Tehsildar of Chicacole, Gumsur, and Berhampore—Vizagapatam Collectorate, no answers—Godaveri Collectorate, from Ramachendrapúr, Amalapuram, Narsapuram, Rajahmundry, Bhimavaram, Tanuku, Peddapuram, Ellur, Coconada, Tuni, Pittapúr, Yernagudem, and Coringa—Kistna Collectorate, from Tehsildars—Nellur Collectorate, from the Tehsildars—Bellary Collectorate, from the Tehsildars—Tanjur Collectorate, no replies—Trichinopoly Collectorate, from five Tehsildars—Cuddapah Collectorate, no replies—Kurnal Collectorate, from seven Tehsildars—Chingleput Collectorate, from six Tehsildars—Salem Collectorate, three replies—North Arcot Collectorate, no replies—South Arcot Collectorate, from one Tehsildar—Tinnevelli Collectorate, from eight Tehsildars—Madura Collectorate, from the Tehsildars—Coimbatore Collectorate, from ten Tehsildars—Malabar Collectorate, from one Sub-Collector—South Canara Collectorate, no replies.

MYSORE AND COORG ci
    Their fresh-water fisheries—At least half the people eat fish—Markets generally insufficiently supplied—Fish decreasing—Fishermen also follow other occupations—Breeding fish and fry extensively destroyed—Every poaching mode pursued—Conclusions from the reports—Localities where fishing is carried on—Fisheries which have no perennial supply of water—Those which possess a perennial supply.

Reports from European Officials ciii
    Officiating Secretary to the Chief Commissioner—Superintendent of the Nundidrug Division—Deputy Superintendent of Bangalur, Colonel Puckle—Nagar Division, Deputy Superintendents of Shimoga, Chituldrug, and Kadoor—Deputy Superintendent of Tumkur—Deputy Superintendent of Kolar.

Reports from Native Officials cv
    Nundidrug Division, from the Amildars—Astragam Division, from the Antildars—Hassan District, from the Amildars—Nagar District, from the Amildars—Coorg, from the Amildars.

HAIDARABAD cviii
    Fisheries in the assigned districts—Fish eaten by a large proportion of the people—Markets insufficiently supplied—Fish in the waters have decreased—Fisheries Government property—Fishermen, as a rule, have other occupations as well—Breeding fish and fry destroyed to a great extent—Smallest meshes of nets used—Trapping and snaring, damming, lading, and poisoning waters practised—There would be but little difficulty in prohibiting the sale of fry in the bazars—Opinions as to the necessity for protective measures—How rules would affect fishermen—Proposals respecting regulating the minimum size of the mesh of nets—Conclusions from the reports—Fence months.

Opinions of European Officials cx
    Second Assistant Resident—Officiating Commissioner of West Berar—Deputy Commissioner of Akola—Deputy Commissioner of Buldana—Assistant Commissioner of Bassim—Deputy Commissioner of Amraotee—Deputy Commissioner of Ellichpoor—Deputy Commissioner of Woon.

Opinions of Native Officials cxii
    Tehsildar of Akola—Tehsildar of Buldana—Tehsildar of Bassim—Tehsildar of Amraotee—Tehsildar of Mortizapúr—Tehsildar of Chandore—Tehsildar of Morsee—Of Woon District.

CENTRAL PROVINCES cxv
    Majority of people may eat fish—Markets how supplied—Whether fish in the waters have increased or decreased—Fishermen, as a rule, have other occupations—Breeding fish how destroyed—Fry killed wholesale—The smallest size of the mesh of nets—Other modes of fishing—Remedial measures proposed—As to regulating the minimum size of the mesh of nets—Whether the sale of fry in bazars ought to be prohibited—Fence months.

Opinions of European Officials cxvii
    Chief Commissioner. Nagpúr Division, Collectors of Nagpúr, Bhandara, Chanda, Wardha, and Balaghat—Deputy Commissioner of Jabalpúr—Narbada Division, Collectors of Betul, Chindwara, Hoshangabad, Narsinghpúr, and Nimar—Chhattisgarh Division, Collectors of Raipúr, Sambalpúr and Bilaspúr.

Opinions of Native Officials cxxii
    Nagpúr Division, from five Tehsildars—Jabalpur Divisions from five Tehsildars—Narbada Division, from five Tehsildars—Chhattisgarh Division, from three Tehsildars—Upper Godaveri District, from the Tehsildar of Siroucha.

	PAGE.
RAJPUTANA	cxxvi
Opinions of European Officials	cxxvi
Governor General's Agent and Commissioner of Ajmir—Deputy Commissioner of Ajmir.	
OUDH	cxxvii
Opinions of Chief Commissioner—Large proportion of people fish-eaters—Supply in markets unequal to demand—Fry largely killed during the rains—The smallest size mesh of nets—Breeding fish trapped in irrigated fields—Whether the sale of fry should be prohibited.	
Opinions of European Officials	cxxix
Commissioner and Deputy Commissioner of Faizabad—Chief Commissioners—Commissioner of Faizabad—Those of the Collectors—Collector of Lucknow—Collector of Unas—Collector of Bara Banki—Collector of Sitapúr and Captain Thompson—Collector of Hardui and of the Settlement Officer—Collector of Rai Bareli—Collector of Sultanpúr—Collector of Pratabgarh.	
Opinion of Native Officials	cxxxiii
Faizabad Division, from Tehsildars—Lucknow Tehsildar—Unas Tehsildar—Suffeepúr Tehsildar Purwah Tehsildar—Mohan Tehsildar—Kantha Rungit Singh Mara Wan, Ganga Sahib Bangermoro Gopal Singh—Nawabgunj Tehsildar—Futtehpúr Tehsildar—Samahi Ghát Tehsildar—Hydergurh Tehsildar—Sitapur-- Hurdui Tehsildar— Shahabad Tehsildar—Sundeela Tehsildar—Bilgram Tehsildar—Rai Bareli Tehsildar—Sultanpúr—Putti—Pratabgarh Tehsildar—Behar Tehsildar.	
NORTH-WESTERN PROVINCES	cxl
Area and population—Rivers, canals, and rainfall—Ganges and Jumna rivers how replenished—Fishes of North-Western Provinces—Impediments to fish-breeding, as canals, &c.—Fixed engines and damming streams—Majority of population fish-consumers—Markets insufficiently supplied—Fish decreasing in the waters—Fishermen, as a rule, also have other occupations—Breeding fish and fry destroyed—Modes of fishing pursued—Conclusions—Reasons given for inactivity—Advisable steps—Propositions for temporary measures.	
Opinions of European Officials	cxlviii
Lieutenant-Governor—Commissioner of Meerut—Superintendent of the Doon—The Collectors of Meerut and Mozuffernuggur—Commissioner of Rohilcund—The Collectors of Budaon, Shahjehanpúr, Bijnour, Moradabad, and Bareilly—Commissioner of Kumaon, Senior Assistant Major Fisher—Assistant Commissioner of Gurhwal—Superintendent, Terai—Commissioner of Benares—Magistrate of Goruckpúr—Collectors of Bustee, Mirzapúr, Benares, and Ghazeepúr—Deputy Collector of Ghazeepúr—Collector and Civil Surgeon of Azimgurh—Commissioner of Jhansi—Deputy Commissioners of Jalom and Lullutpúr—Assistant Commissioner—Commissioner of Allahabad—Collectors of Jompúr, Futtehpúr, Allahabad, Hunipúr, Banda, and Cawnpore—Commissioner of Agra—Collectors of Furruckabad, Etawah, and Agra—Mr. Adams—Collectors of Muttra and Etah.	
Opinions of Native Officials	clxxii
Meerut Division—Rohilcund Division—Benares Division—Jhansi Division—Allahabad Division—Agra Division.	
BENGAL (*First Report*)	clxxix
Province—Main rivers—Fish largely eaten—Local markets insufficiently supplied—Fish have decreased—The fishermen—Breeding fish destroyed—Fry wastefully killed—Stocking ponds—Modes of fishing—Conclusions—Remedies proposed.	

	PAGE.
Opinions of European Officials	clxxxii
Burdwan Division—Collectors of Midnapúr, Burdwan, and Hooghly—Cooch Behar Division—Deputy Commissioners of Darjeeling, Goalpara, and Garo Hills—Rajshahye Division—Commissioner of Orissa—Officiating Collector—Engineers of Irrigation Works—Assistant Magistrates at Bhudruk and Balasur.	
Opinions of Native Officials	cxci
Tehsildars of Burdwan and Hooghly—Assam.	

BRITISH BURMA cxciii

Its provinces—Native mode of letting the fisheries—River and tank fisheries—Its principal rivers—Tanks or Eengs—Burmese eaters of fish—Usually boatmen and fishermen—Markets how supplied—Whether fish have decreased—Fisheries Government property—Breeding fish and fry destroyed.

Opinions of European Officials cxcvii

Chief Commissioner—Personal observations—Moveable engines—Reasons fisheries are not depopulated—Letting fisheries chiefly useless to the consumers—Present propositions as temporary measures to obviate local objections—Answers to questions circulated in 1869 not yet received—Chief Commissioner's opinions and those of a committee of experienced officers—Commissioner of Arrakan, Deputy Commissioners of Akyab, Ramree, and Sandoway—Deputy Commissioner of Thyetmyo—Commissioner of Tenasserim, Deputy Commissioners of Amherst and Shwégyen—Commissioner of Pegu, Deputy Commissioner of Rangoon, Senior Revenue Settlement Officer.

Opinions of Native Officials ccix

Akyab District—Ramree District—Sandoway District, from three—Thyetmyo District, from one—Amherst District, from four Myo-okes. Executive Engineer of Amherst respecting poisoning the waters—Tavoy District, from one Myo-oke—Shwégyen—Mergui.

MADRAS (*Supplementary Report*) ccxiv

Opinions of European Officials ccxiv

Collector of Bellary, Subordinate and Head Assistant Collectors—Collector of Trichinopoly—Collector of the Kistna, Head Assistant and Sub-Collectors—Collector of South Canara—Draft Fishery Act.

Opinions of Native Officials ccxix

Trichinopoly Collectorate, from five Tehsildars—Kistna Collectorate—South Canara Collectorate.

BRITISH BURMA (*Supplementary Report*) ccxxii

Opinions of European Officials ccxxii

Chief Commissioner—Commissioner of Pegu, Deputy Commissioners of Rangoon, Bassein, Deputy Collectors of Myanoung, Prome, and Thayetmyo.

Opinions of Native Officials ccxxv

Pegu Commissionership, from Prome, Rangoon, Pantanaw, Myoung Mya, Theegwen, Tsabai-yoon, Yay-gyee, Lay-myet-hna, and Shwé-loung.

BENGAL (*Supplementary Report*) ccxxvii

Opinions of European Officials ccxxvii

Commissioner of Assam, Deputy Commissioners of Durrung, Nowgong, and Seebsagur—Assistant Commissioners of Golaghat and Jorehat, Deputy Commissioner of the Khasi Hills—Collector of Tipperah—Commissioner of Dacca—Civil Surgeon of Furreedpore—Commissioner of Chota Nagpore—Deputy Commissioners of Hazareebaugh, Singbhoom, and Maunbhoom—Commissioner of Chittagong, Collectors of Noakhally and Chittagong.

Fish as food, or the reputed origin of disease . . . ccxxxvii.
    On a fish diet—Deficiency of supply of animal food to natives of India—Various estimations in which fish is held by the different races—General effects of a fish diet—Does such affect the procreative powers—Fish diet more suited than that of mammals to natives of the East—Large fish more valuable weight for weight than small ones—Fish as food may set up poisonous symptoms due to several causes—Spiny rayed fish as food, those having accessory breathing organs most esteemed by convalescents—Scaleless fish as food—Carps in hilly districts may set up deleterious effects—Herring family, members of it may be poisonous—Eels as food—Sclerodermi as food, or poisonous—Cartilaginous fishes as food—Diseases attributed to a fish diet—Skin diseases and scurvy—Wounds from fish spines, especially of Siluroids—Wounds from spiny rays of fishes.

Fresh-water fishes of India ccxlviii
    What they consist of—Definitions of sub-classes, orders, families, genera, and species of fresh-water fishes of India and Burma.

Order Acanthopterygii, T ccxlviii
  Family Percidæ ccxlviii
    ,, Pristipomatidæ ccxlix
    ,, Sciænidæ ccl
    ,, Squamipinnes ccli
    ,, Carangidæ ccli
    ,, Mugilidæ cclii
    ,, Gobiidæ cclii
    ,, Nandidæ ccliv
    ,, Labyrinthici cclv
    ,, Ophiocephalidæ cclvii
    ,, Rhynchobdellidæ cclviii
    ,, Chromides cclix

Order Anacanthini cclix
  Family Pleuronectidæ cclix

Order Physostomi cclx
  Family Siluridæ cclx
    ,, Scombresocidæ cclxxv
    ,, Cyprinodontidæ cclxxv
    ,, Cyprinidæ cclxxvi
    ,, Clupeidæ ccxcviii
    ,, Notopteridæ ccc
    ,, Symbranchidæ ccci
    ,, Murænidæ ccci

Order Lophobranchii cccii
  Family Syngnathidæ cccii

Order Plectognathi ccciii
  Family Gymnodontidæ ccciii

		Page.
Sub-class Chondropterygii	. . . .	ccciv
Order Plagiostomata .	. . . . .	ccciv
Family Carchariidæ .	. . . . .	ccciv
,, Pristidæ .	. . . . .	cccv
,, Trygonidæ .	. . . . .	cccv
On preserving specimens of fish .	. . . .	cccvi

On making preparations—Preserving fish in spirit.

REPORT

ON THE

FRESH-WATER FISHERIES OF THE INDIAN EMPIRE.

I. In August 1867, the *Secretary of State for India*, in a despatch to the "Madras Government," directed their attention to a communication from *Sir Arthur Cotton*, wherein he had stated he "should suppose that the injury to the coast fisheries must be very great, now that seven of the principal rivers on the East Coast" are barred by irrigation works that had been constructed. On 27th May 1868, I received instructions to proceed to the anicuts or weirs in the Madras Presidency, in order to obtain more specific information than had up to that period been received. First, the districts to the south of Madras were inspected,* subsequently those to the north.† Having been directed to continue these enquiries, I went next to Orissa and Lower Bengal,‡ afterwards to British Burma,§ and at the end of 1869 the Andaman Islands.‖ Being compelled to proceed to Europe on sick leave in March of 1870, due to an accident received during these investigations, I availed myself of the opportunity of visiting a number of the fish ladders existing in England, returning at the end of the year to India. At the commencement of 1871 these enquiries were resumed; first, the North-Western Provinces¶ and the Panjab** were inspected. On September 17th a brief synopsis of the result of the enquiries already made was drawn up, and a set of definite questions submitted for promulgation to all European and Native officials in India and Burma, from which a considerable amount of the following

margin note: Origin and progress of the present enquiry into the state of fresh-water fisheries of the Indian Empire.

---

* Report, to the Madras Government.
† Reports dated 17th November 1868 and 4th February 1869.
‡ Report, 8th March 1869.
§ Report on Fresh-water Fisheries and another on the Sea Fisheries, 1869.
‖ Report, dated February 1870.   ¶ Report, dated July.   ** Report, dated July.

details have been collated. Finally, Sind was visited,* and now the whole of these enquiries are brought together as briefly as possible, in order that individual investigations may be tested to the fullest possible extent by the opinions of others, prior to any definite conclusions being arrived at.

II. Respecting those who have previously worked amongst the fresh-water fisheries of India, our literature is exceedingly scanty. *Dr. Hamilton Buchanan* in 1822 published "The Fishes of the Ganges," his investigations into which commenced in 1794. He considered the question of fish as one, if not the most important, which could be enquired into, and gave many interesting observations bearing on the subject. *Dr. McClelland* in 1839 drew attention to the great benefits which might accrue in looking after the fresh-water fisheries. *Cuvier*, when writing to a correspondent in India, observed that he did not know a more interesting and important question that could arise in the East, than an enquiry into the fresh-water fisheries of Hindustan. In 1849, the late *Dr. Jerdon* published papers upon the fresh-water fish and fisheries of Southern India in the "Madras Journal of Literature and Science." *Mr. Blyth* has given some description† of these fishes in the "Journal of the Asiatic Society of Bengal," 1859 and 1860. In the "Fishes of Malabar," published by myself in 1865, are a few remarks on the same subject, my attention, when collecting the fresh-water fish, having been drawn to the wasteful destruction then going on. (See para. 139.) *Mr. Grant, Collector of Malabar*, about this time suggested to Government the necessity of affording some protection to the fishes in the waters of his collectorate from the indiscriminate destruction to which he considered they were subject, but nothing was attempted. Two years subsequently, the late Colonel Haly revived the question, and since that period a mass of valuable information has accumulated.

Previous workers on the subject of the fishes in India.

III. In 1867, some enquiries were made by the Government of India, the replies to which may well be adverted to in this place. The *Natural History Secretary to the Asiatic Society of Bengal* (21st January 1868) replied "that the Council are fully aware of the great importance of the question at issue, and they consider

Enquiries made by the Government of India in 1867, and suggestions as to what information then unavailable was required.

---

* Report, March 1871.

† There are several authors who have written on the fresh-water fishes of India, but confined their remarks simply to descriptions with or without figures—*Bloch.*, *Russell*, *Sykes*, *Cuv.* and *Val.*, *Gray* and *Günther*, whilst *Hardwicke* only gave drawings.

that the statement made by Sir A. Cotton, together with the strong *a priori* arguments that may be adduced, render it in the highest degree probable that the effects of anicuts or weirs across large rivers leads to a rapid destruction of many kinds of fish, which may ultimately lead to their extermination, not only by interfering with their spawning in their accustomed localities, but by leading to their accumulating in large numbers below the weirs, where they are not only captured in large quantities by man, but are exposed in an increased degree to the attacks of crocodiles and predaceous fishes." *Dr. Jerdon* (9th November 1867) observed on " the necessity for adopting some restrictive measures for preventing the wholesale destruction of large fresh-water fish, such as the mahaseer, during the spawning season." *Mr. Grote, Senior Member of the Board of Revenue, Lower Provinces* (15th March 1868), considered—" very little is known of the habits of Indian fish." " It may be found advisable to legislate for regulating the exercise of the public right of fishing in all our navigable rivers. As yet we have been unsuccessful in our endeavours to curtail that right, or to enforce the claim of Government to levy a tax from those who have been in the habit of exercising it." *Colonel Strachey, Inspector General of Irrigation Works* (23rd June 1868), propounded the following enquiries:—" What are the fish which constitute a practically important portion of the food of the people? Of those fish, which are those which migrate for the purpose of depositing their spawn? Amongst the migratory fish, what are those which live entirely in the fresh-waters, and what are those which pass from the sea or brackish waters into the fresh river waters? What are the precise habits of each of these classes of fishes, as to their migrations, both in respect to their extent up the rivers and the season at which they occur? And what is the season at which the young brood of fish is developed, and when do they descend the rivers? With such knowledge, we should be in a position to form an opinion of some practical value on the question that has been put." I now propose taking up all these and some other questions in detail, before entering upon the result of the investigations which have been made by others as well as by myself.

IV. The fresh-water fisheries of India and Burma

<small>Where fresh-water fisheries exist.</small> extend from a sea level to almost every place in which water exists in any quantity, even to high up amongst the hill ranges.

They are to be found in rivers, irrigation or other *(chools)* canals, lakes, tanks and *jhils*, and are of various degrees of importance, not only as regards the amount of fish residing in them, but likewise in accordance with the character of the contiguous people, as to whether they are fish-eaters or reject this article of food; also as to the sparsity or the reverse of the population.

RIVERS AND THEIR EXPANSIONS.

V. The *rivers of India and British Burma* possess certain peculiarities which tell, to a greater or lesser degree, upon the fishes that inhabit them—some of these being due to the season of the year, others to the amount of rain-fall. There are those descending from the hilly regions, as the Irrawadi in Burma, and the Indus in the Panjáb and Sind. Besides which, there are certain differences to be observed when the rivers are in the hilly districts from what obtains in the plains, and these re-act upon the fishes which inhabit them.

<small>Rivers of the Indian Empire.</small>

VI. The hill rivers of India, or, more properly speaking, those which take their rise in the hill ranges, may be divided into (1) those which have, or (2) have not, Alpine sources. Generally speaking, the *rivers which have Alpine origins*, as those which descend from the Himalayas, have for their sources of replenishment (exclusive of springs) two most prominent ones. During the hot months, that derived from melted ice and snow is abundant, and a daily rise and fall in the amount contained in them may be observed at certain hours, corresponding to the distance from their snowy sources, and which is due to solar influence. Throughout the monsoon season, doubtless, the rains also assist in the melting of the snows : exclusive of this, however, they are sufficient to fill the rivers in what may be termed a spasmodic manner. Thus, in the commencement of March, the snow-floods begin in the Indus, the inundations of this river being more entirely due to the influence of the melting snows than to that of the rains, as in the Ganges and Jumna, owing to the rain-fall being greater in the upper regions of the latter rivers than in those of the former and its affluents. These hill rivers consequently form torrents, rising rapidly and as rapidly subsiding, more especially during the rains, whilst, having no contiguous tanks into which the fish could retire, their

<small>Hill rivers of India: those having Alpine origins.</small>

piscine inhabitants are peculiar, or have habits and means of support differing from what obtains in those residing entirely or nearly so in the rivers of the plains. During the cold season, these rivers, unreplenished by rains or melting snows, become in places exceedingly small. The beds of hill streams are more or less restricted into one or more sharply-defined channels, frequently passing over considerable heights, whilst they have become widened by casual changes of force and direction, insufficient, however, to form lakes or even tanks. The wider or larger these rivers are, which pass over vertical falls of a given depth, the greater are the chances of fish being able to ascend. Many of the species which inhabit these regions are provided with an adhesive sucker, placed behind the lower jaw or on the chest, in order to enable them to retain their hold against rocks, and thus prevent their being washed away.

VII. In *rivers destitute of Alpine sources*, as the Nerbudda, Kistna, Godaveri, and those taking their origin in the Western Ghâts, Nilghiris, and other hill ranges, where snow but rarely reaches and never remains for months, we have a very different state of affairs. Amongst these must also be classed the sub-streams or affluents of the larger snow-fed rivers; and it is in these places, where the water is warmer, that most of the hill fishes, excepting many of the loaches, breed. Rivers unreplenished by melting snows are naturally destitute of the daily rise and fall throughout the hot months which is perceived in snow-fed ones. In the rivers of the Malabar Coast, most have their rise in the Western Ghâts, receiving the full force of the south-west monsoon, which, commencing in June, rarely continues beyond three months, and it is only during this period that we see those sudden rises and falls which enable breeding-fish to ascend to the hill ranges, for the purpose of depositing their ova in localities suitable for the rearing of their young. After the monsoon is over, the waters gradually subside, and the breeding-fish descend to the plains, leaving many of their young to be reared in the small pools remaining in the hill streams.

<small>Hill rivers destitute of Alpine sources.</small>

VIII. The *rivers of the plains of India* are, of course, chiefly the continuation of those descending from the hills; but even in those having Alpine sources, the daily rise from melted snows becomes less and less apparent the further they are from their sources. These rivers may be divided into those (as the

<small>Rivers of the plains of India.</small>

Indus, Ganges, Brahmaputra and Irrawadi) which have always a fair supply of water in them : and others (as the Sone, Godaveri, Kistna, Cauveri, &c.) that become comparatively dry in the hot months, in some of which this deficiency is increased by water being abstracted from them by works of irrigation. Their relative value as fisheries depends on several causes—some natural, others artificial. During certain seasons of the year, as in the height of the rains, and in those with snowy sources in the hot months, these rivers form impetuous torrents, absolutely precluding fishing being carried on, excepting at their edges.

IX. Throughout the cold months, and generally until the setting-in of the south-west monsoon in June, rivers are at their lowest, whether examined in hill ranges or on the plains. Thus, in the hill streams in the Kangra District (see para. 30), as the cold months commence, the amount of water shallows until there appears a succession of pools united by a more or less insignificant stream; to these places all the fish that do not descend to the plains resort. In the cold months, they take refuge at the bottoms and under rocks, and are not easily netted, but as the warmer weather sets in (unless the river is snow-fed), easily fall a prey to the fisherman as the water steadily decreases. The same thing occurs throughout the length and breadth of Hindustan: thus on the western coast of India, about August or September, as the south-west monsoon decreases, the rivers gradually diminish in size until the downpour of rain commences in June the succeeding year. As they subside, pools are left, in which the larger fish congregate. "Though there may be many pools in a river, there are only a few at intervals of four or five miles that are specially resorted to by the larger kinds of fish. These are generally the deepest and longest; they are sometimes as much as twenty feet deep and a quarter of a mile long. They are generally cooler, from being overshadowed by trees, and more or less overhung with rocks. Their very depth also would keep them cooler than the wide shallows extending for miles together, and in the height of the hot season, of a few inches only in depth, under a tropical sun."*

How during the dry months in the majority of the rivers of India, the waters shallow until only a succession of pools exist, connected by a larger or smaller stream, and here the larger fish must continue until the river rises.

---

* H. S. Thomas, Esq., on "Pisciculture in South Canara," p. 4.

(7)

X. In some rivers, as the Irrawadi or the Indus, a rather different state of things is perceived. In the latter river its greatest height is about August, and this is the period of heaviest floods; in September its subsidence is usually very rapid, zero being commonly reached by November. As a large tract of country becomes inundated during these periods of floods, the tanks, to wherever they extend, receive a fresh supply of water: in Burma, where this occurs, due to the risings of the Irrawadi or Pegu rivers and the downpours of rain, these tanks are termed *Eens*, whilst in a portion of the Panjáb and in Sind, where the Indus extends, the local term *Dhánd* is employed.

<small>How rivers have their seasons of inundations, flood the country, and fill lakes or tanks termed *Eens* in Burma, and *Dhánds* in portions of the Panjab and in Sind.</small>

XI. These tanks or *dhánds* in Sind, that are useful to fishermen, are of two classes: the first are *isolated dhánds*, and in which communication with the Indus only occurs during periods of inundations, and mostly dries up prior to the next year's supply; whilst the second are *connected dhánds*, being expansions of a river, small stream, or canal into a tank, and which, throughout or for the most part of the year, are connected with running water. Some of these *dhánds* are without, others within, embankments, which have been constructed for keeping the inundation water within due limits, or bunding it in certain desired directions.

<small>Dhánds or tanks in Sind mainly divisible into *isolated ones*, in which connection with running water only occurs during inundations, and *connected* ones, which are extensions of running water into a tank, and their communication continues throughout or for the most part of the year.</small>

IRRIGATION WORKS.

XII. Amongst the artificial causes affecting fisheries are anicuts, weirs, or bunds constructed for the purpose of irrigation or working mills. *Irrigation weirs* have been erected across various rivers in the Panjáb, North-Western Provinces, Bengal, and Madras, in order to deflect a certain amount of water into canals constructed for its reception and dissemination. These weirs are usually built in the form of stone walls across the entire breadth of rivers, and consequently form an obstruction, arresting the upward and downward passage of fish that are endeavouring to migrate, whilst, should it be sufficiently high, it entirely prevents their passing. On the bed of the river in front of it, or on its down-stream face, there is generally a stone pavement termed "an apron," or this apron may be a gradual slope of rough or smooth stones extending from the summit of the walls to the bed of the river. Likewise on the upstream face of these weir walls is a bund of stones, of greater or lesser extent, sloping down to the bed of the river.

XIII. These irrigation weirs are of different forms, *Irrigation weirs, under-sluices either narrow or wide; no fish able to ascend through the former.* but all arrest the passage of fish, some temporarily, others entirely; and as a consequence those migrating down-stream often pass into the irrigation canals. These weirs have openings of varying sizes termed "*under-sluices*," constructed for the purpose of permitting the surplus water passing through the body of the weir, and on a level with the lowest bed of the river; when rushing through with great velocity, it was expected large quantities of silt would be carried with it, keeping the general bed of the river washed out to its proper level. These under-sluices or complete gaps through the weirs are of different widths, and may be classed under two divisions: *first*, the long narrow ones in Madras, the North-Western Provinces, and the Panjáb; and, *secondly*, the wide ones in use at Cuttack, Midnapur, and on the Sone River. These under-sluices are kept closed, except when there is an excess of water, as during the monsoon months: those of the *Madras pattern* are from six to nine feet in width and several yards in length; they close by means of boards pushed down vertically into large wooden grooves, and these boards can be elevated, when it is desired to do so, by means of a capstan and windlass. As these narrow under-sluices are of many feet in length, there are generally two sets of grooves, one at each end, so that either can be made use of. These narrow under-sluices carry such a rush of water through them that no Indian fish can ascend up when they are open. I thought this had been clearly established, but as I see this belief again advanced, I must here digress in order to explain that such never occurs. Fish, which are attempting to pass weirs in the course of their ascent up rivers, are chiefly those who are in a breeding condition, and are trying to reach their natural spawning grounds. Thus, when near the sea, the shad or hilsa is the most valuable sort which becomes stopped by weirs without practicable passes, so they are unable to reach the only localities wherein their spawn or ova could come to maturity if deposited; they consequently have to drop it in the water below these weirs, and here it cannot be fertilised, but inevitably perishes. The same occurs with some of the large carps in the more northern rivers (as of the North-Western Provinces and the Panjáb) that are weired not far from the base of the Himalayas, the hilly streams of which are the natural breeding-places for some, as the mahaseer, &c. They descend over them before the cold months, when the rivers above contain too little water or are unsuited for their residence; and when attempting to return up-stream, find this stone wall an insuperable obstacle: thus their reproduction is likewise prevented. These questions will have to be considered more fully further on, but are only introduced here to demonstrate that it is fish heavy in roe which must have a free passage, at least if the fisheries are worth conserving, and such a ruinous course is not checked by sensible measures of restriction, irrespective of the consideration that below these weirs or obstacles large accumulations of fish take place, and thus assist man and other predaceous animals in destroying them. Fish when heavy in roe are not so well able to jump any great heights as are some of the younger or barren ones. Standing at the period of freshes, on the bridge above one of the Madras weirs possessing these narrow under-sluices, it is interesting to see the numbers of fish, both large and small, which leap up against their walls: some strike against the piers of the bridge, others fall into the cascade descending over its summit; but though I have passed hours watching them, I never saw one clear these obstacles, although I have seen thousands attempting it. The only rational reason that I can adduce for the jumping against the insurmountable weir walls whilst the narrow under-sluices are open, is because they find such to be impassable. Could they ascend through these, why do they not? The truth is that they are unable to do so. When these fishes were netted, many, especially the large ones, were bruised and scaleless in places, evidently due to injuries caused during their frantic but unavailing efforts to surmount the wall, or ascend through the open but narrow under-sluices. Take the Coleroon River as an instance. Since the construction of the lower weir, the shad, which formerly ascended high up to breed, and are now extensively netted below it, have never been taken above it (unless a breach has occurred), and this although there is a second weir nearer its source, where netting was permitted, and which was a further obstacle to ascent. At this second weir indiscriminate slaughter of fish was being carried on when I was there; mercy was unknown; the amount of present spoil formed the only anxiety of the fisherman, whilst the injury being done to future years' supply was entirely unheeded.

XIV. Thus here was a weir with narrow under-sluices at which the shad were being detained endeavouring to ascend to their spawning beds, although these under-sluices were open during freshes, and the floods were so great that a mere ripple on the surface of the river only marked the presence of a weir. In spite of all this, no fish have been found to pass this obstruction, and surely did they do so, a solitary straggler might have been' taken. Even a barren fish, in fact, a shad of any sort, had not appeared at Trichinopoly during the whole period that this construction has existed and been intact. Shad, or rather large fish, have been taken in these under-sluices, but only when they were closed at the up-stream end. It is true that a good current is then coming down between the boards which close these vents or narrow passages, but it does not prevent strong healthy fish from ascending as far as the boards, but these very boards form an effectual bar to their onward progress. The very use of the sluices is to force the water down with such impetuosity that, during high freshes when they are open, no Indian fresh-water fish could possibly ascend when the weirs are several feet in height: the water shoots down the openings and across the apron, bubbling and boiling a hundred yards or more down-stream. This torrent of about six feet in width is like a mill race, or as if it were shot out of an engine, carrying down stones, sand, &c., in its course, and which of themselves would be sufficient to injure fish attempting to ascend. From personal observation I am satisfied no fish could pass up them: persons locally employed on these weirs assert the passage of fish to be impossible: above such constructions these migratory species attempting to ascend cannot be found; it must, therefore, be evident to any one who will consider the question, that weirs are effectual barriers to the ascent of fish, even although such possess narrow under-sluices that are left open during the periods of the freshes.

Weirs with narrow under-sluices, continued.

XV. The *wide under-sluices*, such as exist in the weirs at Cuttack and Midnapur, are constructed on an entirely different principle and pattern, forming free gaps of many yards in width, so that, when open, fish cannot have any difficulty in ascending through them.

Weirs having wide under-sluices no impediment to ascending fish when such are open.

XVI. These weirs likewise, it is stated, may be topped by fish during heavy floods, as then they may ascend over them, especially when the summit of their wall is several feet below the

Fish unable to ascend over weirs.

surface of the water. But they do not appear to do so, or why are the shad entirely stopped at the lower Coleroon one? In the Kistna the ascent of the fish usually occurs after the freshes have subsided, and when a wall of stone is built along the top of the weir, and through which water only trickles, this construction being indispensable for the irrigation of the second crop of rice: fish, however, attempting to ascend during the freshes, one would at first sight have thought, could easily pass over the Bezwada weir, as it forms a long slope on its down-stream face, from its summit to the bed of the river. But such is not the case:* it is asserted that not a single marine species is caught there, or has been, since its construction. Those which try to ascend up the rough stones, in the face of an impetuous current, apparently become so bruised and injured that they are unable to cross, and even could they do so, their ova would probably be irretrievably ruined. But these rough stones do not exist in front of the under-sluices; and as the river is frequently five feet above the level of the wall above them, it might be advanced that they could cross at that spot, but they apparently do not contrive to do so, which is most probably due to the great force of the current, for they would have to rise 16 feet at least to clear the wall. As they ascend along the river's bed they find a wall and ascend to surmount it, but as they rise the strong current must take them backward down-stream, and thus they never reach its summit which the muddy condition of the water prevents their seeing, for it is only during freshes that the wall is covered.

XVII. Besides the foregoing there are *irrigation canals* which have a bearing upon the fisheries of a district, and these may be divided (1) into those simply constructed for purposes of irrigation, or (2) those which are made for both irrigation and navigation. These canals in some places, as the Roree one in Sind, are mere artificial streams, which, in some portions of their extent, exist in lieu of natural water-courses which have silted up. Here no great falls occur, and references to such are unnecessary. But irrigation canals, as a rule, are given off from one or both sides of a river, which has a stone weir thrown across it for the purpose of bunding up the water to a given height. At the head of each of

Irrigation canals simple or for traffic as well.

---

* It is stated at Kurnal (p. lxxxi) that sable are taken at the weir there; if so, they must cross the Bezwada one. Having written to the Collector, he is unable to say if it is the sable or not, so I have requested, but not as yet received, a specimen.

these canals are head-sluices, where the amount of water entering can be regulated in accordance with local requirements, or entirely cut off if necessary.

XVIII. *Irrigation weirs constructed simply for irrigation* are those in which boat-traffic cannot be also carried on, due to one or more vertical falls existing which are too great to permit such. These falls, which are sufficient to prevent traffic, are mostly also sufficient to entirely obstruct fish, which have once descended over them, from ever re-ascending. These canals almost invariably have a high fall near their commencement, whilst below all overflows, and due to the action of descending water, are holes of a larger or smaller size in their bed, and being well adapted for feeding in, here large fish live and thrive so long as they are permitted. The further the distance from the canal head, and as the amount and rapidity of the flow of water decreases, the falls are usually less and these holes are smaller; still, even there they are present, but are not so suitable for providing food for large fish. It will thus be seen that these canals form large receptacles which may be turned into traps for all fish which once obtain an ingress, unless there are *tanks* connected with them into which they could retire when the water is cut off and they become dried, or else that the *holes* in their beds retain a sufficient supply during these periods, so that the fish may remain in safety until the water is re-admitted. For at certain times every year, it becomes necessary to dry off these canals to enable the engineer officers to ascertain what repairs are necessary, and unless the fish have a safe place to resort to they might be easily taken. But, unfortunately, in some canals it is, or has been, the custom to allow the employés to kill all the fish at this period, and thus a simple irrigation canal becomes a vast trap for destroying fish. (See para. 12, p. v.)

Simple irrigation weirs.

XIX. In *canals* which are constructed *for both irrigation and navigation*, there are lochs at every fall, that boats may be admitted and floated up to a higher level. At these lochs I have observed that fish can obtain a passage up or down stream, so they will not be further alluded to.

Irrigation and navigation canals.

XX. None of these canals contain gratings or other appliances at their commencement for preventing the ingress of fish, and an official in the North-Western Provinces (para. 334) observes upon having personally

How fish are carried into irrigating canals, and how they perish from want of water.

witnessed how, when water is re-admitted into these canals, shoals of fish are carried over falls up which none can re-ascend, and below which they are unable to breed. Thus, the water is cut off and the contained fish destroyed, the canal to be again replenished with a supply from the river, to be again and again exterminated several times during the year; and a surprise is expressed that the fisheries are deteriorating. The oftener the canals are closed, and the longer the periods at each closure, the greater is the mischief (see para. 315.) But from either side of these main canals are given off side ones for the purposes of irrigation; these, again, have no grating to prevent fish ascending them; they go up, but, as they are mostly only filled every alternate week on either side, all that have gone up them invariably perish. In other districts fixed traps are permitted in all these small water-courses.

XXI. Again, in Malabar (see para. 167), as the dry season commences and water is required to irrigate a second crop of rice, the rivers are of small proportions, and near their sources the farmers collect boulders of stones, lay them across a stream, and fill in the interstices with shingle, stopping up the crevices with bushes and mud. This lasts until the next south-west monsoon sweeps it away, and whilst it exists, it diverts an entire river stocked with fry into rice-fields. Thus the young fish pass with the water into the irrigated fields, which have been levelled and partitioned with shallow embankments so as to economise the water as much as possible. Here, though predaceous fishes are excluded, man can do as he likes; the water, if it does not return to the river, may be entirely exhausted in these fields, and if every drop has been turned on, nothing can escape destruction, or else some may rejoin the river as waste water, and thus the young fish regain a locality suitable for their growth; but at each outlet from every field exists a fixed trap which captures every one of the fry. Again, when the yearly rains naturally inundate the country, when rivers and tanks overflow, and fish move about to find suitable localities for breeding in, the small streams and outlets resemble the net-work of irrigation channels. Many species ascend up them to breed, but find appliances of destruction, invented by man, meeting them at every turn. Persons may be watching to catch them, or fixed engines and traps existing, and which are sure in their effects, or, should some breeding-fish contrive to ascend, they are usually trapped on their return: whilst the fry obtain no greater immunity,

Small rivers diverted for irrigation in Malabar.

and this is said not to be "waste" because they are eaten!

XXII. On the Himalayas grain is, in places at least, ground in mills moved by water-power (para. 33), which is effected by constructing small canals, into which the water of streams is diverted as in irrigation works. Into these canals, termed *kools*, numbers of fry and even large fishes find their way, as there are no obstructions at the mouths of these *kools* to prevent their entrance. The mill-owner cuts off the water at his pleasure, and all the contained fish are left dry.

<small>Mills worked by water-power: small fish destroyed there.</small>

Tanks useful as Fisheries.

XXIII. Of *tanks* (see para. XI), there are those which are always in connection with such running water as rivers and works of irrigation; or those in which this communication only exists during the monsoon time: whilst others are entirely unconnected. *First*, there are those which are always in connection with running water, which are generally useful as breeding-places for the non-migratory forms of fishes, and merely require a little care to be taken as to how they are worked, in order to render them exceedingly valuable as fisheries. The *second* sort of tanks, or those in which communication with running water only exists during the monsoon time, are of two distinct forms: in the first, they always, or nearly always, contain water, whilst in the second, they are dry, or almost so, except during the rains. Fish obtain access to both these forms of tanks during the monsoons and breed there; but in the last, so soon as all communication with the running water has ceased, they become practically isolated, and unless they happen to be of such varieties as bury themselves in the mud (para. XLIV) during the dry months of the year, they must die, whether captured by man, killed by the lower animals, or destroyed by the sun as the water evaporates. *Lastly*, we have those tanks which are always unconnected with large pieces of running water, frequently due to their being situated upon an elevated portion of the country, and these are generally stocked with fish by the owners.

<small>Tanks useful as fisheries.</small>

XXIV. In large *jhils*, where the screw pine, *Pandanus odoratissimus*, or many weeds as the lotus or valisneria, cover their surfaces and extend themselves through their depths, or where grasses spring from their beds, or the roots

<small>Jhils: how naturally the fish in them may be protected from netting.</small>

(15)

of trees grow into them, fishing has usually to be carried on by means of traps, angling, or spearing.

The Fishes of the Fresh-waters.

XXV. *Fresh-water fishes.* The fishes which are chiefly useful as food in the fresh-waters of India belong to the order *Physostomi*, especially in its siluroid, cyprinoid and herring families, as well as those which are included in the order *Acanthopterygii*, sub-divided by some authors into two. The other orders which furnish examples to the fresh-waters are only employed as food by the very poorest classes, or even entirely rejected. (A list of the fresh-water fishes is appended, para. 430).

XXVI. *Migratory and non-migratory fishes. Breeding ones polygamous or monogamous. Seasons of breeding.* Another mode of dividing the fishes which frequent the fresh-waters of India is into the *migratory* and *non-migratory*. Some of the migratory forms (as *Barbus tor*) ascend the hill streams from the rivers of the plains for breeding purposes: or those which never leave the plains, although they belong to this division, may be marine (as *Clupea palasah*): or entirely fresh-water species (as several of the carps). Migrations in adult fish are effected for breeding or predaceous purposes, or to obtain some peculiarly desirable description of food. There are also, as already observed, the "non-migratory" fishes both in the waters of the hills, as some loaches and small siluroids, or in those of the plains, as the *Ambassis*, &c. Lastly, the breeding-fish will have to be considered, the majority of which appear to be polygamous, but some are monogamous: whilst the time of year at which they deposit their eggs varies with seasons and localities, the migratory forms almost invariably selecting the monsoon time.

XXVII. *Acanthopterygian or spiny-rayed order of fishes.* In the sub-class Teleostei, the spiny-rayed or Acanthopterygian orders of fishes, are not found in any great numbers in the inland fresh-waters of India, but are mostly confined to the plains, either within or but a short distance removed from tidal reach, or above the sea level. The larger the river, the greater the probability of these fishes extending their range up it. There are some genera which possess species that are able to exist some time after their removal from the water, and even to dive down and remain in the mud of tanks during the dry season, re-appearing with the returning rains. These hard-rayed fishes, which are taken in the fresh-waters, mostly belong to the following 18 genera, some of which are marine, others not so:—1, *Lates*; 2, *Ambassis*; 3, *Corvina*; 4, *Mugil*; 5, *Equula*; 6, *Gobius*; 7, *Euctenogobius*; 8, *Periophthalmus*; 9, *Eleotris*; 10, *Badis*; 11, *Nandus*; 12, *Catopra*; 13, *Anabas*; 14, *Polyacanthus*; 15, *Trichogaster*; 16, *Ophiocephalus*; 17, *Rhynchobdella*; 18, *Mastacemblus*.

XXVIII. The foregoing 18 genera are divisible into two distinct classes: *first*, those which entirely belong to the fresh-waters (although some of the species of the same genus may have marine representatives); *secondly*, those which are marine, and only ascend rivers for predaceous or breeding purposes. Of the true fresh-water ones (2, as *Ambassis Thomassi*; 4, as *Mugil cascacia*; 6, as *Gobius giuris*; 7, as *Euctenogobius striatus*; 8, as *Periophthalmus Schlosseri*; 9, as *Eleotris nigra*; 10, as *Badis dario*; 11, as *Nandus marginatus*; 12, as *Catopra nandioides*; 13, as *Anabas scandens*; 14, as *Polyacanthus cupanus*; 15, as *Trichogaster fasciatus*; 16, as *Ophiocephalus gachua*; 17, as *Rhynchobdella aculeata*; and 18, as *Mastacemblus armatus*)—some of these are monogamous, as Nos. 13, 14, 15 and 16, and probably also Nos. 6 and 7, all of which appear peculiarly adapted for tanks and *jhils*, as they live in the grass along their edges, where the larger varieties lie in wait for frogs or other animals on which they prey. Whilst the first four named genera being air-breathers (see para. XLIII) they have only to raise their mouths out of the water and take in their modicum of air. Others of these fresh-water genera are apparently *polygamous*, as Nos. 2, 10, 11, 12, 17 and 18. Of those genera which possess marine representatives, some of which breed in the sea, whilst others ascend rivers for this purpose, are Nos. 4, 5, 6, 7, 8 and 9. But some of these genera placed as polygamous, as the gobies, may eventually prove to be monogamous. Of the whole of these Acanthopterygians but few are generally distributed through the inland tanks far from the sea level or beds of large rivers; these exceptions are the little *Ambassis*; a goby, *Gobius giuris*; the small *Badis* and percoid *Nandus*; the walking fishes, *Ophiocephalus*, and the spined eels, namely, the *Rhynchobdella* and *Mastacemblus*. Of the second or marine division of this order of fishes, some (1, as *Lates calcarifer*; 3, as *Corvina coitor*; and 5, as *Equula*,) are marine, ascending rivers at certain seasons, as in the rains, in order to obtain food, sometimes going long distances up their course : thus, I have taken *Lates calcarifer* at Mandalay in Upper Burma, about 650 miles from the sea, evidently following the shoals of shad, *Clupea palasah*, for predaceous purposes.

XXIX. Fishes of the order PHYSOSTOMI, or those in which the air-vessel communicates with the pharynx by means of a pneumatic duct, contain the largest proportion of the Indian fresh-water fishes.

Physotomatous order of fishes, or those possessing a connecting duct between air-vessel and pharynx.

One of these families *(Siluridæ)* are destitute of scales, whilst they are present in the *Cyprinidæ*, which have no teeth in the jaws or palate, and also in the herrings *(Clupeidæ)*, the majority of which last have a trenchant or cutting abdomen (as the hilsa, *Clupea palasah*), or generally a few minute teeth in the jaws or palate. The *Notopteridæ*, which also belong to this order, furnish some species which are esteemed by the natives.

XXX. The siluroid family, *siluridæ*, are commonly known as cat-fishes, because they generally possess a number of long barbels, arranged around the mouth.

Siluridæ or scaleless fishes, often termed cat-fishes, as they generally have long feelers.

These fishes mostly prefer muddy to clear water, as such conceals their presence. The more developed and numerous these barbels, the better adapted these fish seem to be for an inland and muddy fresh-water residence; whilst on the contrary, those which are strictly marine do not appear to be so well furnished with these appendages. Siluroid fishes are also generally armed with strong spines in the fin of the back and pectoral fins, and which, as a rule, are serrated; with these severe wounds are often inflicted, which renders the handling of them dangerous. Tropical countries, which possess large and muddy rivers and tanks in their plains, such as Bengal and Burma, are more adapted for siluroids than such localities as Madras, where the rivers are smaller, and the waters clearer. Irrespective of being scaleless or unclothed (if we admit scales to be the clothing of fish), they would hardly appear to be suited for cold climates, and we find that they are much more numerous in tropical than in sub-tropical or temperate parts of the globe. The siluroid fishes which are captured in the fresh-waters mostly belong to the following 25 genera, excluding *Chaca*, some of which are marine, others not so :—1, *Akysis* ; 2, *Erethistes* ; 3, *Macrones* ; 4, *Rita* ; 5, *Arius* ; 6, *Pangasius* ; 7, *Pseudeutropius* ; 8, *Callichrous* ; 9, *Wallago* ; 10, *Olyra* ; 11, *Silurus* ; 12, *Clarias* ; 13, *Saccobranchus* ; 14, *Silundia* ; 15, *Ailia* ; 16,

Ailiichthys; 17, *Eutropiichthys*; 18, *Sisor*; 19, *Gagata*; 20, *Hemipimelodus*; 21, *Bagarius*; 22, *Pseudecheneis*; 23, *Glyptosternum*; 24, *Amblyceps*, and 25, *Exostoma*. Out of the foregoing 25 genera, some are residents in waters of the plains, also in rivers of the hills with or without Alpine sources. Amongst the 17 resident solely in waters of the plains, and not extending their range into hilly regions, we find that in eight, Nos. 2, 3, 4, 5, 6, 7, 8, 9, the air-vessel is free in the abdominal cavity and not enclosed in bone; whilst in ten, Nos. 12, 13, 14, 15, 16, 17, 18, 19, 20, 21, it is more or less so enclosed. Amongst those residing in rivers of the plains, and extending their range into those of the hills which have or are destitute of Alpine sources, we perceive four, Nos. 22, 23, 24, 25, which are found in the waters of the plains as well as in the hill rivers with Alpine sources; all have their air-vessels enclosed in bone, the two first have a thoracic adhesive apparatus, whilst the last three have representatives in the next division, and Nos 22 and 23 are furnished with a thoracic adhesive apparatus. The remaining three genera, Nos. 1, 10, 11, are found in rivers of the plains, and also in those of hills destitute of Alpine sources, whilst in none is the air-vessel enclosed in bone. From the foregoing it appears that the majority of the genera of the Indian fresh-water siluroids have their air-vessel enclosed in bone, whilst it is not so enclosed in any of the marine forms; that amongst the siluroids of hilly regions, those which ascend rivers having Alpine sources have the air-vessel enclosed in bone: whilst those which ascend rivers not snow-fed do not appear of necessity to have their air-vessel thus protected.

XXXI. The *fresh-water siluroids* may be divided into those of *the hills* and those of *the plains*; the *former*, or those of *the hills*, being small and often possessing a thoracic adhesive apparatus to enable them to adhere to rocks, and prevent their being carried away by descending torrents. The *siluroids of the plains* are very numerous, existing in almost every piece of fresh-water, whilst the larger rivers contain some, as the *Pangasius Buchanani*, *Wallago attu*, *Silundia Gangetica*, and *Bagarius Yarrellii*, which attain to several feet in length: in fact, up country, as in the upper portions of the Jumna and Ganges and in the irrigation canals, where they find abundance of food, and consequently grow to a very great size, they are erroneously termed "sharks." None of these siluroids possess any adhesive apparatus unless they are also

Siluroids of hills and plains.

common to the hills as the *Pseudecheneis* and *Glyptosternum*. In some species which are thus provided, as the *Glyptosternum striatum*, not only is this thoracic apparatus very distinct whilst residing in mountain streams, but even their pectoral and ventral rays are plaited inferiorly; but these additions are indistinct or completely absent in specimens of the same species when their size is larger, and they have been captured in the rivers of the plains.

XXXII. The respiration of these siluroid fishes is as varied as amongst those of other orders (see para. XLIII): thus, the *Clarias* and *Saccobranchus*, owing to the possession of accessory organs to their branchiæ, are compound-breathers, able to reside in the mud of tanks, and are much employed for stocking these places. Most of the siluroids are very long-lived whilst out of the water, even when accessory breathing organs appear to be absent, as in some of the *Macrones* and in species of the genus *Rita*, which are very slimy fish. As a rule, all which belong to this family are exceedingly foul feeders, more especially when there are but few small fish for them to prey upon; still for anglers who do not care whether the game affords play, these fishes give good sport when large, freely taking a frog or small fish. Some of the siluroids are migratory during the breeding season, and this is generally in the rains. They appear to prefer muddy-bottomed tanks and sluggish rivers, whilst pebbly streams, especially if the waters are clear, are rather avoided by them in the plains. Some even of the larger ones reside during the dry months in places where there would be no means of subsistence for them were it not for a sufficiency of small fish, which likewise retreat there, and afford them sustenance until the rains re-commence, and they can again move about.

Respiration of siluroid fishes.

XXXIII. In the family SCOMBRESOCIDÆ, the *Belone cancila* is found throughout the rivers and tanks, in which it breeds. Amongst the CYPRINODONTIDÆ are several small fresh-water species as *Cyprinodon Stolickanus* in Katch, and several species of *Haplochilus* in India and Burma, mostly in large rivers and near sea levels.

Family Scombresocidæ.

XXXIV. The carps or *Cyprinidæ*, as already observed, belong to the order Physostomi; this family are destitute of teeth in their jaws and palate, only possessing them on their inferior pharyngeal bones, whilst none of them have more than one fin

Family of Cyprinidæ or carps. First sub-family or loaches, with the air-vessel more or less enclosed in bone.

on the back. The family of carps is divided into three sub-families; the little loaches, *Cobitidinæ,* which extend throughout the length and breadth of the Indian and Burmese fresh-waters, from a sea level to many thousand feet above it, even breeding in places where the rivers are almost entirely replenished by melting snows. In all is the air-vessel more or less enclosed in bone. In those species found high up amongst the hills and in snow-fed rivers when ascending up to near their sources, as in *Nemacheilus,* it appears to be invariably so : whilst in the larger *Botia,* which mostly is taken in the plains or bases of hills, the posterior portion of the air-vessel is wholly or partially free in the abdominal cavity, only its anterior portion having an osseous capsule. It is remarkable that the single genus of this sub-family which is found high up in the hill ranges, *Nemacheilus,* is destitute of any offensive or perhaps defensive spine under the eye, but which is possessed by every genus in the plains, as *Apua, Acanthophthalmus, Acanthopsis, Cobitis, Lepido-cephalichthys, Botia* and *Jerdonia. Misgurnus* has been omitted as not found in India, but it has been taken in the hill ranges beyond Upper Burma ; it has no orbital spine. Loaches form excellent food for the larger fishes, and are also esteemed for this purpose by the natives of India.

XXXV. The second sub-family of the carps are the sand-grubbers, *Homalopterinæ* : they have no air-vessel, are insignificant in numbers and size, and reside under stones in streams along the bases of hills or at moderate elevations.

<small>Second sub-family of carps. Sand-grubbers, having no air-vessel.</small>

XXXVI. The third, largest and most important sub-family are the true carps, *Cyprininæ,* which are generally distributed and are most important as food : all have the air-vessel free in the abdominal cavity. Very few are merely vegetable feeders ; the barbels, *Barbus,* appear to be all carnivorous or omnivorous, and take the place in Indian rivers supplied by trout in the more northern climes. These carps are divisible into those of the hills and those of the plains. The *hill carps,* again, must be sub-divided into those which "permanently" reside there, and those which are occasional or periodical visitants that ascend for the purpose of breeding, or to obtain a change in their food. Strictly predaceous fishes do not appear to be found in hilly districts. The *non-migratory hill carps* furnish some of the most valuable articles of food

<small>Third sub-family of carps, air-vessel not enclosed in bone. The hill carps sub-divided into non-migratory and migratory forms.</small>

there for the resident population. Thus, the mountain barbel, *Oreinus*, often erroneously termed a "trout," because it is sometimes spotted with red, the *Oreinus sinuatus* is common in many of the Himalayan rivers; fishes of this genus possess a sucker on the lower jaw behind its broad mouth, by means of which it is able to adhere to rocks, and prevent its being swept away down stream; it is taken as high as Kulu, even to 5 or 6,000 feet elevation, and is common in the Ussun River, not above 4 or 5 miles from Simla. Also another small carp, *Discognathus*, exists in these elevated regions throughout the year (it is also found in the plains), and is furnished with a sucker in same situation as in *Oreinus*. As *migratory hill carps*, may be classed those which breed in the hills, but descend to the rivers of the plains, where they reside during the cold and drier months of the year, when the small hill streams would be unsuited for their residence, re-ascending to the base of the hills during the hot months, and, if possible, ascending up the rivers into the Sub-Himalayan range, or those of other hills, as of the Nilghiris or the Western Ghâts, with the first burst of the monsoon.

XXXVII. Amongst the *carps of the plains* are a very large and varied number of forms, some of which are migratory, others not so; these migrations are mostly effected for breeding purposes, and generally take place during the S. W. monsoon, but a few do so during the N. E.; but many of these latter are fish re-ascending towards their breeding-grounds to be ready for the S. W. monsoon of the succeeding year. The numbers and varieties of these carps of the plains show as great a difference as was remarked upon in the siluroids (para. XXX). Commencing with Southern India, there are innumerable small species of carps in the plains, but a paucity of large ones. This is not merely due to the universal slaughter which obtains there, but is also partly a consequence of smaller rivers and a hotter climate. As the Masulipatam District or the Kistna or Tambudra Rivers are reached, larger varieties of this sub-family come to notice; many large *Labeos* and the *Catla*, unrecorded as existing further south, as towards Madras, can now be taken. Whilst in the rivers skirting the base of the Nilghiris, as those along the Western or Malabar Coast, very large species of barbels, termed mahaseers, become apparent. The finest carps, as in the genera *Labeo*, *Cirrhina*, *Catla*, and the

Carps of the plains. Migratory or non-migratory species.

sub-genus *Barbodes* in *Barbus*, are mostly found in the larger rivers or pieces of water, whilst the latter are commonly perceived in those affluents of the Indus, Ganges and Brahmaputra, and other rivers that are near the bases of hills.

XXXVIII. The herring family, *Clupeidæ*, furnishes examples of both migratory and non-migratory forms to the fresh-waters of India, some being marine which ascend rivers solely for breeding purposes, whilst others are strictly fresh-water and non-migratory, generally breeding in tanks. The *migratory herrings* are those which ascend large rivers from the sea for the purpose of breeding in fresh-water, the most important of which is the shad, *Clupea palasah*, known also as the Hilsa or Ilisha, the Palasah of the Telingis, the Ulum of the Tamils, the Pulla of the Indus, the Nga-tha-louk of the Burmese, and the sable fish of the Europeans in Madras. There seem to be two classes of this fish which ascend the large rivers: those below one year of age, and which do not appear to breed, or if they do, it is at the very end of the year, or commencement of the succeeding one; secondly, there are those which breed at the commencement of, or during the monsoon. In the Cauveri and Coleroon these fish ascend with the first burst of the S. W. monsoon, and continue doing so the four succeeding months, but in diminished quantities, some evidently being later breeders or younger fish. In the Kistna, which has a great velocity, the freshes commence in June and continue until the end of October, after which the river subsides, but it does not become fordable until the middle or end of January. A few of these fishes arrive at the end of September, but it is not until the middle of October and the two following months that their main body appears to ascend, whilst they disappear by April. It is only when the rapidity with which the Kistna flows during the freshes commences to subside that they arrive in large numbers. In the neighbouring river, the Godaveri, which has a less rapid current than the Kistna, the fish ascend earlier, being most numerous from July to September, when the fishermen believe they migrate to the Kistna. In the Hoogli they continue ascending throughout the S. W. monsoon, and many are found to be still full of roe in September. Mr. Blanford has observed them at Mandalay in Upper Burma at the end of the year. In Sind, this fish ascends from the

<small>Herring family. Migratory and non-migratory forms.</small>

sea about February for the purpose of breeding in the river, from which it again descends to the salt-water about the end of September or commencement of October, after which none, even young, can be found. They are only taken in *dhánds*, stagnant pieces of water or canals, due to some accidental cause or unnatural obstruction having obliged them to turn aside from their natural breeding-grounds. The main body of these fish swarm up the large rivers of India and Burma generally as soon as the S. W. monsoon commences, but not always at the same period, such apparently at times being dependant upon the rapidity of the current and other causes. That it is not solely due to the presence of rain-water is shown by the Indus and Irrawadi; in the former, the floods are mainly caused by melted snows at this period (see para. VI), whilst in the Irrawadi these fish push on to Upper Burma, to which country the S. W. monsoon scarcely extends, and there the inundations are also due to melting snows. One reason why periods of flood are selected as those for breeding, appears to be due to their being practically acquainted with the fact, that at these times the shallows are covered with water, rendering ascent practicable, consequently they now come up to deposit their ova, which is always done in the rivers, never in tanks or canals. Amongst the *non-migratory herrings*, some species, as *Engraulis Chatoëssus* and the *Corica suborna*, appear to breed in rivers or even tanks.

XXXIX. There are also a few other fishes which, however, are not much esteemed as food, some of which belong to the order *Physostomi*. In the eel-like family, *Symbranchidæ*, but generally in fresh-waters or marshy places not far removed from the sea level, is found the curious *Amphipnous cuchia*. Amongst the true eels, *Murænidæ*, there are several species which are taken in fresh and brackish waters, but it is only *Anguilla Bengalensis* that appears to live at some distance inland.

Eels, &c.

XL. In the order LOPHOBRANCHII, a little pipe-fish is very commonly found in rivers, and in some places is termed the crocodile's tooth, from an idea that it is the vivified tooth of one; of these reptiles, in other districts it is called the crocodile's tooth-pick, from the use which it is said to be to those animals. It is the *Ichthyocampus carce*, and as food is useless.

Lophobranchiate order of fishes.

XLI. In the order PLECTOGNATHI, several of the family *Gymnodontes* are found ascending rivers for some distance, especially species of the genus *Tetrodon*, but they do not appear to be considered fit for food anywhere (except some sea species amongst the Andamanese). Still in Burma, a closely allied fish, *Xenopterus naritus*, is extensively taken in the lower provinces, and esteemed as food by the people of the country.

<small>Plectognathi.</small>

XLII. In the SUB-CLASS CHONDROPTERYGII, order PLAGIOSTOMATA, there are some species which ascend rivers for predaceous purposes, but are not esteemed as food. Amongst the family of sharks, the *Carcharias Gangeticus* ascends rivers, but not very often far beyond tidal influence; however, I have seen it at Cuttack, and in the Pegu river: whilst a species of saw-fish, *Pristis*, is likewise found to proceed as high; neither breed in the rivers. Amongst the *Trygonidæ*, the *T. uarnak* is also frequently found above tidal influence.

<small>Cartilaginous fishes.</small>

RESPIRATION OF INDIAN FISHES.

XLIII. Before commencing the subject of the sudden appearance of fishes in Indian tanks after falls of rain, and how they migrate during periods of floods, a few observations are necessary upon how they respire, as some remarkable variations from the usual manner are observable, evidently to enable certain tropical forms to resist causes which are not in existence in most extra-tropical regions. Three modes of respiration are perceptible: *first*, the usual one of oxygen obtained, except under peculiar circumstances, from air in solution in the water, and which is separated at the gills; these may be termed for description, not definition, "water-breathers," as the carps, *Cyprininæ*, or some of the siluroids, as *Macrones*, and they can live, as a rule, without rising to the surface. If any of these fishes are placed in a globe of water at a moderate temperature, with a diaphragm of net precluding their reaching the surface, their breathing remains unaffected. If, on the contrary, a bandage is stitched around the gill-opening, precluding their employing their gills, they rapidly become suffocated. This result in another form is perceived to occur in India, either artificially or naturally. Thus, when the water in which they reside becomes suddenly changed from clear to very muddy, their gills become choked, respiration is impeded, and death results.

<small>Respiration of fishes: water-breathers; compound-breathers.</small>

In the Haidarabad Assigned Districts, the Tehsildar of Buldana (para. 238) observes that "disturbing the water of a stream, so as to cause it to become muddy, is said sometimes to cause the fish to die." Also in Oudh, the Commissioner of Faizabad (para. 276) reports fish being taken in village ponds and *jhils*, in the months of Jeth and Baisakh, by hand, the water being first mudded by gangs of from 50 to 60 men. This sudden fouling with mud, causing death to water-breathing fishes, is likewise observed during the monsoon months, where a sudden descent of very muddy water suffocates this class of fishes. The Collector of Tanna (para. 101) remarks that, when the rivers become muddy at the commencement of the monsoon, fish die in large numbers, also when they become nearly dry at the close of the hot weather. Also (para. 187) in Sittimungalum, it is observed of the Bhowany River that fish die when the water is mixed with mud to a large extent, as during the monsoons; this has also been observed in Malabar. *Secondly*, some species, which, although they to a limited extent are "water-breathers," are more essentially "air-breathers," having a compound respiration, consequently muddy water hardly affects them. Thus, in carrying live specimens of *Ophiocephalus* from the plains to the Nilghiri hills, this was most successfully accomplished in water largely mixed with mud. They never obtain oxygen for any length of time from the air in solution in the surrounding water, but inspire it direct from the atmosphere, no matter how cool and charged with air the water may be; and if unable to inhale atmospheric air, become poisoned by the carbon remaining in their circulation. The compound-breathers expire in a longer or shorter interval if unable to reach the atmospheric air; amongst these are the climbing perch, *Anabas scandens*, and the species of the Acanthopterygian genera, *Polyacanthus*, *Trichogaster*, and *Ophiocephalus*, all of which possess a cavity above the gills for the purpose of the reception of air for respiratory requirements. The difference between the respiration of the "water-breathers" and the "compound-breathers," as defined, is very apparent when they are lying side by side at the bottom of an aquarium. Thus, the *Macrones carcio* has its gills in constant excited movement, whilst the *Ophiocephalidæ* scarcely move theirs, but at intervals rise to the surface, open their mouths, and take in air. This latter phenomenon of breathing the air pure, and not subsequent to its solution in the water, is especially visible in some species, as the *Polyacanthus cupanus*, which dart up suddenly to the surface, descending again as rapidly to the depths of the water. I instituted a considerable number of experiments (see Proc., Zoological Society of London, May 14th, 1868, p. 274) to investigate this question. Some live specimens of *Ophiocephalus gachua* were placed in a globe, which was filled two-thirds full of fresh water. A diaphragm of fine net was then stretched lightly across the inside of this globe, one inch below the surface of the water, thus effectually preventing them from ascending to the surface to obtain a direct supply of atmospheric air; death invariably ensued in a longer or shorter time, generally in accordance with whether they remained quiet or continued excited. A bandage stitched tightly around the gill openings, whilst it prevented their being used for respiratory purposes, did not appear to cause any inconvenience so long as they could inhale atmospheric air direct, and this although it was not removed for 24 hours. But it must not be considered that these fish are entirely prevented from decarbonising their blood if they are unable to obtain atmospheric air direct, as, although some died within the first 40 minutes, others lived 7 and one 17 hours whilst below the diaphragm. In wet grass, at the end of 3 hours, those placed there were found as lively as when first put there: one in a dry cloth lived for 3 hours and 25 minutes. The *Anabas scandens* are kept four or five days alive by the fishermen in Calcutta in earthen pots destitute of water, using daily what they require, the fish continuing as lively as when captured. In Burma the fishermen appear to be practically acquainted with the fact of some fish, especially *Ophiocephalidæ*, being air-breathers; thus, after nearly all the water has been removed from the tank to be fished, leaving only about five feet of slimy mud, through which their bamboo net *(gyan)* has been drawn, they are aware that many fine fish still remain. A large cloth is spread over the mud and left there two or three days, on removing which, the fish are seen stupefied and easily taken, their blood having become carbonised from a deficiency of oxygen, due to want of air for breathing. In short, my experiments, I think, proved that these fishes died when deprived of access to atmospheric air, not from any deleterious properties either in the water or apparatus employed, but due to being unable to decarbonise their blood solely from the water, ærial respiration being indispensable. Also that they can live out of water in moisture for lengthened periods, and for only a short and variable time in water, provided they are unable to obtain air direct: that the cavity above the gills does not contain water, but has a moist secreting surface in which the air is retained for the purposes of respiration, whilst it seems probable that the air, after having been employed for this purpose, is ejected through the mouth. Some of the venous blood appears in these fishes to be oxygenated at the gills, and the remainder in the superbranchial cavity by means of air; but if they are kept under the water without being able to obtain direct access to it, this cavity, which is surrounded by bony tissue, becomes filled with water, which cannot be discharged owing to its almost non-contractile powers. Thus, there being no means of emptying it, and the contained water probably becoming carbonised, the whole of the respiration is thrown upon the gills. This accounts for the fact that when the fish is in a quiescent state it lives longer than when excited, whilst the sluggishness sometimes evinced, may be due to poisoned or carbonised blood. An analogous instance may be seen in an eel, *Ophichthys boro*, in which the gills are contained in a large cavity in either side of the head, and which do not communicate with one another. The fish distends this receptacle with air taken in by the mouth. It appears to be able to respire either directly from the atmosphere, or by means of the air contained in the water. On its small gill-openings being kept closed, it takes in air by the mouth; should its mouth be held shut, it struggles until its head is released so as to be able to respire. If the gills are exposed by cutting away the outer gill-coverings, and it is then returned to the water, it begins to slowly move its branchiæ, and appears to feel little, if any, inconvenience in being unable to obtain air direct through its mouth. In some of the siluroids, there exists an accessory breathing apparatus; thus, the *Clarias* possesses a dendritic one on the convex side of the second and fourth branchiæ, which has much the appearance of a bunch of red stick-coral; this is received into a cavity posterior to that existing solely for the gills. In the *Saccobranchus* or scorpion-fish, a long air-vessel of a pulmonic character (in addition to the air-vessel proper which is enclosed in bone) extends throughout the length of the muscles of the back, and anteriorly opens into the gill-cavity. In the eel-like *Symbranchidæ*, the *Amphipnous cuchia* has a pulmonic sac for the reception of air connected with the gill-cavity. This mode of respiration appears to be a wise provision of Nature, to enable fish in tropical countries, during periodic dry seasons or in the rains, to migrate from pond to pond in search of water wherein their natural food exists. Also as they ascend small water-courses to breed during seasons of inundations, they are always liable to have the supply of water suddenly arrested, and then they regain rivers, &c., through muddy channels or moist pieces of grass. *Thirdly*, there are some fish which also appear to swallow air, and perhaps absorb oxygen through the skin, as the loaches, *Cobitidinæ*, and the spined eels, *Rhynchobdellidæ*, but no special air-breathing apparatus has as yet been detected.

ÆSTIVATION OF FISH.

XLIV. A curious phenomenon in Indian fresh-waters, and one which has never been satisfactorily explained, is the sudden appearance of healthy adult fish after a heavy fall of rain, and in localities which for months previously had been dry. When pieces of water inhabited by fish yearly dry up, what becomes of them? On 18th January 1869, when examining this question, I was taken to a tank, of perhaps an acre in extent, but which was then almost dry, having only about four inches of water in its centre, whilst its circumference was sufficiently dried to walk upon. The soil was a thick and consistent bluish clay, from which, and not nearer than 30 paces to the water, five live fish were extracted from at least two feet below the surface of the mud. They consisted of two of the *Ophiocephalus punctatus*, and three of the *Rhynchobdella aculeata*. All were very lively and not in the slightest degree torpid; they were covered over with a thick adherent slime. Amongst the specimens of fish in the Calcutta Museum is one of *Amphipnous cuchia*, which was dug up some feet below the surface of the mud, when sinking the foundation for a bridge. If when the water failed fish invariably died, the tanks would be depopulated the succeeding year, unless a fresh supply was obtained from some other source, whilst the distance from other pieces of water at which they re-appear excludes, in many instances, the possibility of migration, which must always to a certain extent be regulated by distance, time, and other local circumstances. Some species, especially "compound-breathers" (para. XLIII), are able to live in liquid mud, which they cannot employ for the purposes of aquatic respiration. The practical question is, whether, when food and water fails, some fish do not æstivate until the return of a more favourable season. Natives of India assert that they do thus become torpid in the mud. As the water in tanks becomes low, the fishes congregate together in holes and places in which some still remains, where they may be frequently seen in numbers, huddled together with only sufficient water to cover their dorsal fins. If disturbed, they dive down into the thick mud, so that a net is often found ineffectual to take them. The plan employed to capture them is for the fisherman to leave the net in the water, and to walk about in the surrounding thick mud; in time they come to the surface to breathe, and fall an easy prey. As the water gradually evaporates, the fishes become more and more sluggish, and finally, there is every reason to believe that some at least bury themselves in the soft mud, and in a state of torpidity await the return of the yearly rains. In Ceylon, Mr. Whiting, the Chief Officer of the western province, informed Sir Emerson Tennent that he had accidentally been twice present when the villagers had been engaged in digging up fish. The ground was firm and hard, and "as the men flung out lumps of it with a spade, they fell to pieces, disclosing fish from nine to twelve inches long, which were full-grown and healthy, and jumped on the bank when exposed to light." Many other animals which possess a higher vitality than fish æstivate during the hot months, as *Batrachians*, the *Emys*, the *Lepidosiren annectens*, and some of the *Crocodiles*. Molluscs and land-snails are commonly found in this state during the hot and dry seasons.

MIGRATIONS OF FISH.

XLV. The subject of the *migrations of fish* during the periods of rain is of great practical importance, it being mostly effected for the purpose of breeding, but in some few instances is due to predaceous fishes being in pursuit of their weaker neighbours. At the commencement of the rains fish become very excited and disturbed; apparently unsatisfied with the localities they inhabit, they restlessly seek a change to other pieces of water. This may be owing to the same instinct which causes the migration of marine fish to the fresh-water, or the necessity of obtaining a suitable place in which to deposit their ova. It is generally at this season that some have been observed travelling on land, and it has been imagined that places which are only occasionally covered by water become populated by fish after heavy showers of rain. The possession of the means necessary for locomotion on land, combined with those for direct aerial respiration, frequently leads to the almost sudden appearance of fish in unexpected places, and has given rise to numerous arguments and theories—amongst them, spontaneous generation, vivification of buried ova, migration, falling from the clouds, &c. Amongst persons testifying to having witnessed the migrations of fish is Mr. Morris, Government Agent at Trincomalee, who in 1857 stated,—" as the tanks dry up, the fish congregate in the little pools, till at last you find them by thousands in the moistest parts of the beds, rolling in the blue mud which is at that time about the consistence of thick gruel. As the moisture further evaporates, the surface fish are left uncovered, and they crawl away in search of fresh pools. In one place I saw hundreds diverging in every direction from the tank they had just abandoned to a distance of fifty or sixty yards, and still travelling onwards. In going this distance, however, they must have used muscular exertion sufficient to have taken them half a mile on level ground, for at these places all the cattle and wild animals of the neighbourhood had lately come to drink, so that the surface was everywhere indented with foot-marks, in addition to the cracks in the surrounding baked mud, into which the fish tumbled in their progress. In those holes which were deep, and the sides perpendicular, they remained to die, and were carried off by kites and crows. My impression is that this migration takes place at night or before sunrise, for it was only early in the morning that I have seen them progressing, and I found those I brought away with me in chatties appeared quiet by day, but managed to get out of the chatties at night. Some escaped altogether, others were trodden on and killed." The *Anabas scandens* is able to travel short distances on land, and has been seen by many Europeans whilst thus engaged. This migrating propensity of some of the fresh-water fishes of the East was no secret to the ancient Greeks, who frequently commented upon it, and although the truth of their statements were impugned by the Romans, the accuracy of their facts is above dispute. But the migrations of fishes during the rains is, perhaps, what is of most consequence in fisheries. In fields irrigated from rivers or tanks, breeding-fish swarm up all water-courses for the purpose of depositing their ova, and should be protected as much as possible. As regards the marine fish which ascend rivers, as the hilsa (para. XXXVIII), the weirs which span rivers bar their upward ascent, and thus cut them off from their breeding-grounds.

BREEDING OF FISHES IN FRESH-WATERS.

XLVI. Closely allied, in fact, inseparably connected with their migration, is the question of the *breeding of fishes** in the fresh-waters, which may be treated of in the following order:—non-migratory and migratory fish of the plains; non-migratory and migratory ones of the hills. Apparently, the migratory forms produce the largest number of eggs, probably as a compensation for the increased chances of their destruction. Thus, in a *migratory* herring, *Clupea palasah*, there were computed to be 1,023,645 eggs, and in a migratory barbel, 410,500 eggs, whilst carps in the hilly regions appear to have a larger proportion of ova than those in the plains. Amongst the *non-migratory* species, we likewise observe a difference: the *monogamous* not depositing so many as the *polygamous*, as a general rule, which is probably due to two causes,—*first*, in some localities the former appear to breed more frequently; and, *secondly*, they protect their offspring. Thus, a "monogamous" *Ophiocephalus* had only 4,700 eggs, whilst a "polygamous" non-migratory carp, *Cirrhina reba*, had 41,500, and a siluroid, *Callichrous canio*, 47,444. Amongst the shoals of hilsa which I have seen, more female fish were captured than males. The marine fish breeding in rivers usually deposit their ova in the sand: the non-migratory fish of the plains generally amongst the grass at the sides of rivers and at small watercourses, or the margins of tanks, occasionally in the sand. Some of these fish, as the hilsa, appear to deposit their eggs at one time: others, as some of the barbels, &c., to do so at intervals.

Breeding of fish in fresh-waters. Migratory and non-migratory ones of the plains.

XLVII. Of the *non-migratory hill fishes* (see para. XXVII) in the higher ranges, there are two situations in which they may breed:—the first is in water wholly or partially obtained from melted snows; the second is in tributaries or affluents of the main streams, as already adverted to (para. VII). It appears as if it were not merely the fact of elevation and difficulty of ascent which prevents more fish residing in the hill streams, but because some influence is exerted by the melted snow-water, deleterious at least to the ova, if not to the fry. In the upper ranges of

Breeding of migratory and non-migratory fish of the hills.

---

* Whether fish, full of spawn, æstivate, and consequently are ready to deposit their ova s soon as the rains commence, is a question not entered upon in this report. Unable to rove it by observed facts, I have considered it best to omit its consideration for the present

the Himalayas, personal enquiries lead me to believe that only the loaches, *Nemacheilus*, deposited and hatched their eggs in places where melted snow-water existed; however, no climate appears too hot or too cold for them. The mountain barbels, *Oreinus*, and all *non-migratory* fish (see para. XXXVIII), breed in small or large streams off the main snow-replenished ones, or even in rivers which contain snow-water in the winter months, as in those around Simla, but such is not present during the breeding season; whilst along with them were likewise many of the little loaches. The parent fishes appear to ascend these side streams with the first monsoon floods (see para. XXXVII), and having deposited their ova, to return to the main river as the amount of water diminishes, or their retreat to the rivers of the plains would be cut off. The eggs not hatching in sufficient time for the young to pass down in any quantities to the rivers, the later fry become detained in these side streams until the next floods. Thus, when examining these places just prior to the burst of the S. W. monsoon, thousands were seen in every small rivulet, whilst probably, due to food being scarce, they seem to grow slowly. Consequently for the first year they remain very small, until the monsoon rains enable them to descend to the larger rivers, when with the floods large quantities of food becomes washed down.

XLVIII. Of the *migratory hillfishes*, or those which ascend for breeding purposes (see para. VII), the various forms of large barbels, *Barbus*, termed mahaseers, furnish good examples. These fish do not breed in the main snow-fed rivers, but do so in the side streams of the Sub-Himalayan range. On the slopes of the Nilghiris I have observed the same occur, but with this difference, that they can deposit their ova in the main streams there, because they are small and not replenished by melted snows. The mahaseers after breeding return to the main rivers, but the young are not generally sufficiently grown to descend to the plains. The foregoing appears to be the rule, to which, however, there are numerous exceptions: thus, if the mahaseers are very large, they may have to deposit their ova in rivers near the base of the hills, due to their being unable to ascend higher; in these cases the young easily find their way into the main rivers of the plains. Mr. Thomas has observed in South Canara that almost the whole of the rain-fall occurs during the S W. monsoon, which commences with June and lasts about four months, and from September the rivers continue steadily to subside

Breeding of migratory hill fishes.

till the following June. When the rivers commence being in flood, grown fish are enabled to ascend to new feeding-grounds previously inaccessible to them, and ten-pound fish are to be seen half-way up the Mercara Ghât. In the high waters, the larger fish linger until the gradually subsiding streams warn them to drop gently downwards. The early spawners stay the longest to secure shallow water for spawning; this done, they keep dropping gently downwards with the continually decreasing waters, and before the spawn they have deposited is hatched, they are probably completely cut off from their fry, so that, till the commencement of the same monsoon in the following year, they cannot return to devour them. The fry thus not only have the heads of the rivers securely to themselves, but they have them also beautifully accommodated to their puny strength, the impassable torrent having become a mere driblet of an inch or so in depth. (*Report on Pisciculture in South Canara*, pp. 11, 12). These fine fish having deposited their ova in the hill streams, and returned to the rivers of the plains, descend down their course in search of food, and if the upper portions of these rivers are not of much depth, their range is extended very far down : thus, I have seen numbers of mahaseer netted in the Jumna below Delhi whilst returning up river towards their breeding-grounds. A drove of mahaseers also descending rivers with weirs and irrigation canals, naturally turn into the latter, and having descended over one of the vertical falls, become unable to return to their breeding-grounds (see para. XVIII).

XLIX. Of the *non-migratory fishes of the plains*, the *monogamous* and ubiquitous walking-fishes, OPHIOCEPHALIDÆ, are perhaps best known. As a rule, these fish do not deposit such a number of ova as the migratory forms, but they appear to breed oftener. Some of them reside in tanks, others prefer rivers, where they live in deserted holes they find in the banks. The tank varieties delight in lying in the grassy edges, where the water is only sufficiently deep to cover them, so that they have no difficulty in respiring atmospheric air direct (see para. XLIII on air-breathing fishes). In Mysor, Colonel Puckle observed that the striated walking-fish, *Ophiocephalus striatus* breeds twice a year, in June and December; the male constructing a nest with his tail amongst the vegetation, and biting off the ends of the weeds that grow in the water. Here the ova are deposited, the male keeping guard, but should he be killed or captured,

Marginal note: Non-migratory fish of the plains, some being monogamous, others polygamous.

the vacant post is filled by his partner. When the fry are hatched out, they are defended by their parents with great courage. They may generally be perceived swimming just below the surface of the water in one or two lines a little above their progenitors. As they increase in size they are usually driven away by their parents, or are said to be even eaten by them if they do not disperse and search for subsistence for themselves. In South Canara, the *Ophiocephalus striatus, O. diplogramme,* and *O. marulius,* are stated to breed in December and January; the last also to again do so in June and July, at which period the *O. gachua* is believed to lay its eggs. Mr. *Thomas* observes—the *Nandus marmoratus* and *N. marginatus* also build nests amongst the rushes at the margin of the water, deposit their eggs therein, and keep guard over them like sticklebacks. Some of the gobies, *Gobius,* are probably monogamous, as they construct regular nests for the reception of their young. The *polygamous* non-migratory fishes of the plains are very numerous, but by "non-migratory" must be understood that they do not migrate long distances for breeding purposes. The smaller carps are innumerable in places, as are also the siluroid magurs, *Clarias magur,* and the scorpion fishes, *Saccobranchus fossilis.* All these sorts during the rains pass up small water-courses or channels in order to deposit their eggs in irrigated fields, flooded plains, temporary formed tanks, or along the grassy sides of rivers.

L. Of the *migratory fresh-water fishes* of the plains, and which do not apparently, as a rule, ascend to the rivers of the hills to breed during the freshes, they are generally larger and stronger than the non-migratory. Amongst them there do not appear to be any of the spiny-rayed or *Acanthopterygian* order (see para. XXVII). Amongst the carps, *Cyprinidæ* (see para. XXXIV), a considerable number are affected by the monsoons, and at periods of inundation migrate for the purpose of breeding. A good illustration of this may be seen at the bridge over the Rohri canal near Sakkar, in Sind, and which is furnished with sluices, which can be kept open or closed in accordance with the amount of water which it is considered desirable should be permitted to enter. A little further on is a fall in the bed of the canal, which, however, becomes imperceptible when the water is high. As the yearly floods commence, many of the Dumra fish, *Labeo rohita,* go down the canal into the *dhánds* for breeding, but so soon as the waters begin to subside, as about September, and for one to one and half months, they attempt to return to the Indus, for which purpose they have to re-ascend the Rohri canal. Arriving near the bridge, the current is too strong, and they attempt to jump over the obstruction to their onward progress, and for 100 yards or more below the bridge they may be seen leaping out of the water. Unable to pass through the bridge, owing to the great force of water rushing through the under-sluices, they spring at the piers, and an apparatus resembling a native cot turned uspide down, or a cloth or a basket, or anything equally suitable, is hung over the sides of the piers, and into this they fall: thousands returning from breeding are thus captured.

LI. Of the *migratory sea fishes*, they are divisible into those which ascend rivers in order to find a locality suitable for depositing their eggs: and the predaceous sorts that also enter rivers, but solely to prey upon their weaker neighbours. Of those which ascend for breeding is a *Sciœna*, the *S. coitor*, some mullets, as *Mugil corsula*, and more especially the hilsa or shad, *Clupea palasah*, already remarked upon (para. XXXVIII) as ascending the larger Indian and Burmese rivers during monsoon months for the purpose of breeding. At these times there is too much water below such weirs as those spanning the rivers in Madras or Orissa for this purpose, whilst, should they deposit their ova in shallows below them, they will be left high and dry as the floods subside, and their fertility be destroyed: the same destruction to their fertility would follow their being deposited in the deep and rapid parts of the rivers. More than one official have questioned the accuracy of this, and given the opinion of native fishermen that the ova is deposited in the river water, and whilst being carried out to sea becomes vivified; therefore, weirs cannot injuriously affect the annual supply of the hilsa fishes in the rivers. The lower Coleroon weir, which was built in 1836, spans the river about $15\frac{1}{2}$ miles below the town of Combaconum; its perpendicular height 8·3 feet, and its width at its base 8 feet. It possesses narrow under-sluices, up which these fishes cannot ascend, whilst the rapidity of the current or other causes precludes them from passing over it. Formerly the shad extended as high as Trichinopoly in quantities, and were even taken miles above that town; the fishing, according to the Collector, prior

Migratory sea-fishes.

to the construction of this weir, extended over 80 or 100 miles of the river, instead of its being concentrated, as it were, on a single spot. The fishing decreased until a breach occurred, when it almost locally ceased, owing to the fish being able to obtain access to their breeding-grounds, and not being stopped by the weir, and they were taken even above Trichinopoly. It decreased, doubtless due to the fish being unable to breed: the year after this breach, when it had been repaired, a great increase was observed in the fish, evidently due to one season's breeding. Fruitless to deposit their eggs below these constructions, when between the sea and their spawning beds, and unable to pass them, extermination in such rivers will only be a question of time, should no remedial measures be adopted. This fish never breeds in tanks or canals. Amongst the *predaceous* sea fishes which are migratory, a large sea perch, *Lates calcarifer*, ascends sometimes hundreds of miles up large rivers as the Irrawadi, pursuing the shad. Sharks, *Carcharias Gangeticus*, and sawfishes, *Pristis*, also ascend high up rivers, and a favourite resort for them is below weirs, where they find ample means of subsistence in the shoals of fish detained by those structures.

THE FRY OF FRESH-WATER FISH.

LII. The immature or the *fry of fish*, where they are found, and their means of subsistence, and opportunities of growth, are questions which it is very material to offer a few remarks upon. I have already observed (para. XLVIII) how the fry of fishes are protected from their voracious parents in hill streams and rivers, by those localities being generally unequal to the supply of food for the mature or large fish, which migrate up these water-courses in order to deposit their ova: consequently, they drop down again into the rivers of the plains as the waters begin to subside, leaving the fry to descend with the next year's rains. These fry, however, appear to likewise continue their descent in a very quiet and gradual manner, but when they have an opportunity of going down-stream, they avail themselves of it. In the Himalayas numbers of these young fish descend into the *kools* or canals for turning mills (see para. XXII), where all are captured. Those which reach pools in these streams appear to often continue there throughout the dry months, unless destroyed, until the monsoon recommences. In the low country

Fry of fresh-water fishes. How, instead of being protected, they are destroyed.

it is in irrigated or flooded localities that the fry most abound, and generally with the monsoon rains every little stream and piece of water is resorted to by them to obtain food in. But by irrigated fields are not here included those irrigated by wells, but merely those in communication with running water and large tanks. In a large extent of irrigated country, the fields, which are divided off into embanked spaces in order to disseminate the water obtained from an irrigation canal, or embanked river or stream, the fry obtain an entrance along with the water which is kept at a depth which suits their puny size; whilst insect life abounds, excepting birds, they have but few natural enemies but man to contend with. If irrigation is carried on by dipping water out of canals at some depth, and this does not run off again into any other water-course, the fry of course must perish as the water dries up. But if the water is conducted from field to field, these localities should be excellent nurseries for young fish, but, as has been observed (para. XXI), they are now, as a rule, more useful in destruction than in propagation, as man is allowed to place traps at every outlet (and sometimes at inlets), and destroy all the young fish as they drop downwards towards the larger river. Fry also are found in abundance in sheltered spots at the edges of rivers and in shallow pieces of water, where there is no current to wash them away, and here an abundance of suitable food exists, but where, as will be shown, they do escape the search of the fisherman and man's destructive greed.

FISH IN AN ECONOMIC POINT OF VIEW.

LIII. Before enquiring into whether a wasteful destruc-
What proportion of people use fish as food. tion of fish takes place in India, it will be as well to observe upon *what proportion of people in India and Burma use fish as food, or rather can do so without infringing caste prejudices.* Amongst the various races inhabiting India and British Burma, this article, as food, is held in different degrees of estimation, and in proportion to such must be its economic importance. In the Panjáb, comparatively but few of the inhabitants are prohibited by their religion from consuming fish, but there are many Hindus who reject it, as well as the rural population of some districts. But of those residing in towns and in hilly ranges, it appears that, if the Brahmans are excepted, the consumption of fish is only limited by the paucity of the supply and the cost of the article. The price where fish

is sold is stated, respecting the better sorts, to bear the same proportion to that of the best mutton, as the inferior does to that of inferior mutton, and varies from one-third that of mutton to an equal price with it. In Sind, fish is generally eaten by the population of the province, whether Mussulman or Hindu, except the Brahmans. In the North-Western Provinces, containing about 28 millions of population (p. cxliv), out of 20 returns received from native officials, 17 give more than half of the people as not forbidden by religious scruples to eat fish. In Oudh, the majority of the people appear to eat fish, which seems to be more of a necessity than a luxury, whilst a larger number would consume it were the supply equal to the demand. In the Bombay Presidency, the returns appear to show conclusively that the majority of the inhabitants of the inland districts are consumers of fish when they can procure it. In the Assigned Districts of Haidarabad, fish, as food, is esteemed by a very large proportion of the residents. In Mysor and Coorg, that at least half the people are fish-eaters when they are able to obtain this species of food. In the Madras Presidency great numbers are fish-eaters, the largest exceptions being Brahmans, goldsmiths, high-caste Sudras, the followers of Siva, Jains, &c. The Collector of South Canara gives the proportion of fish-eaters at 89 per cent.; advancing southwards into Malabar, this proportion appears to decrease. In Tanjor and further towards Madras, exceptions to this strict carrying into effect of the rule of not consuming that which possessed animal life begins to be observed, but in many parts of the presidency salt-fish appears to be preferred to the fresh, more especially by the lower castes. In Orissa, all but the Brahmans and some religious fanatics seem to eat it, but not in its salted state. In Bengal Proper, from 90 to 95 per cent. (p. clxxix), and in Assam and Chittagong, almost the entire population (see Bengal Supplementary Report, p. ccxxvii). In Burma, the population, as Buddists, profess a religious horror at taking the lives of the lower animals; but being universally fond of a fish diet, they judiciously condemn the fishermen to eternal perdition, whilst they consume their fish in the form of *nga-pee*. Without entering more fully into this subject, it may be fairly advanced that fish is more suitable as a general food to the natives of the Indian Empire than the flesh of village sheep, pigs, and fowls, whilst the majority of the people eat it when they can procure it.

LIV. *How are the local markets supplied with fish?* In the Panjáb, out of 76 tehsils, in only 7 are they reported to be fully supplied, and in 48 insufficiently so throughout the year. Where fish are sold, the price of it bears a relative proportion to that of mutton. In Sind, markets near large *dhánds* on the River Indus are fairly supplied. In the North-Western Provinces, the markets are sufficiently supplied in 13 localities, insufficiently in 23, occasionally in 2, and doubtful in 2 more. In the Doon the size of the fish brought is yearly decreasing; whilst in Nynee Tal and Almorah a decrease is very noticeable (p. cxlv). In Oudh (p. cxxvii) three-fourths of the markets are stated to have a larger demand than supply. In the Bombay Presidency, every official who has answered this question, with the exception of one mamlutdar, asserts that the local markets are insufficiently supplied with fresh fish. In the Assigned Districts of Haidarabad, 7 native officials report that they are insufficiently so, and the remaining 1 that the "weekly markets" are well supplied, but that probably more could be sold, thus evidencing that the supply is unequal to the demand. In Mysor and Coorg, a generally insufficient supply of fresh fish is obtained in the markets. In Madras, when within easy reach of the sea, they would appear to be supplied: but out of 39 tehsildars who report from inland, 4 state the supply is sufficient, and 35 that it is insufficient, or absent. In Bengal Proper, there is a deficiency of native returns (p. clxxix). At Burdwan, the supply does not equal the demand. In Hooghly, the markets are said to be fairly supplied, but "the fishermen, however, try to keep up the market price by limiting the supply." In Assam, the reports are contradictory; in most places the amount sold is sufficient, but in some parts it is not. In Burma, only 18 returns from native officials have been received; 4 observe that the markets are fully supplied, 1 that they are fairly so, 2 that they are at times, 9 that they are insufficiently, and 2 that they are sold sometimes in sufficient quantities—sometimes more, sometimes less. Thus, out of 243 returns received from native officials giving definite answers, 180 observe that the markets are insufficiently supplied with fish, 7 that they are occasionally supplied, 3 that they are fairly so, but 1 of these remarks that they are marine fishes; 45 consider they are fully supplied, but 9 state that the supply is chiefly of sea species, often salted: the answers of 8 are doubtful.

[sidenote: Local markets insufficiently supplied with fish.]

Thus the bazars fully supplied are not one-fifth of the total, and one-fifth of those which are so, obtain such from the sea.

THE FRESH-WATER FISHERIES OF INDIA AND BURMA.

LV. Where no regulations exist as to the method in which fisheries should be worked, and should other circumstances be equal, that country or district which is most populated by man will be the most denuded of fish. Individuals would sooner live by fishing than by agriculture, as the trouble of capturing the finny tribes is less than tilling the soil, being simply catching without any idea of preservation. Naturally, fish have been endowed with certain means of increase, and protection, such as producing an enormous number of eggs or frequently breeding, or even by the action of periodic floods, when small-meshed nets cannot be used in rapid streams,* and by swamps covering a large extent of country, where shelter is afforded by grass, rushes, &c., rendering vain man's attempt to depopulate. But, as inhabitants augment, watery wastes become drained and cultivated, predaceous man increases his methods of destruction, and then a decrease of food becomes apparent. As the price of food rises, so that of fish increases, and if the fish-eating population yearly becomes larger, increased exertions are used to capture fish to meet their demands: the size of the mesh is decreased, weirs are augmented, and everything taken, no matter how small, as fishermen never appear to consider from whence the next year's supply is to come, but only the easiest method to take at the present time all they are able. Commencing in Burma, we observe in sparsely populated districts fish abound, and in quantities amply sufficient for the adjacent people; but where the population is larger and the means of disposing of the captures greater, increased modes of destruction are called into existence: streams are dammed and laded out, weirs of various forms are erected, and the use of small meshed nets, and the destruction of fry is carried on. In Sind, the Indus may be considered one large preserve where fish are reared, for owing to the constant change in its course, its banks (except at certain places) are not well adapted for the permanent residence of fishermen, the surrounding land being liable

How wasteful injuries to fisheries commence.

---

* This amount of protection does not extend to any great extent to the fry of fishes, as they would be washed away by a rapid current, consequently they seek the shallows.

to sudden and violent floods. The population near the river's banks are small, and sufficient large fish is obtainable for them without destroying the fry, and thus, during the yearly inundations, they are carried into the *dhánds* throughout the country.

LVI. Before entering upon the various modes of cap-
<small>Breeding-fish and fry wastefully destroyed.</small> ture, and omitting the questions of taking migratory breeding, and the poisoning of fish, I propose examining *whether fish are allowed to be wastefully destroyed either in the form of breeding ones or as fry*. Many fish, as already pointed out (para. XLVI, &c.), during the seasons of monsoons and inundations, pass up small channels into irrigated fields for the purpose of breeding; at these times they appear to have lost much of their natural timidity, and are only solicitous to reach a suitable locality to deposit their ova. No portion of this enquiry, as regards the non-migratory forms of fish, is more important than this, and the following are the answers received:—In the Panjáb, in a few tehsils the trapping of breeding-fish in the irrigated fields is recorded. In Sind, partly due to its almost absence of rain, this species of fishing can scarcely be carried on. In the North-Western Provinces, breeding-fish and the fry are destroyed in every division, in any way in which they can be procured (p. cxlvi); even if the simple destruction of fry is not waste, they are also shown to be killed, and in places left to rot (p. cxlix), as in damming hill streams; or at fishing weirs (p. clxi), where the large fish only are sold, the young left to perish and decay: or standing weirs are permitted to span whole rivers, and as the waters from above become unwholesome, fish attempt in vain to descend, but the owners of these weirs allow no passage, and as they die in myriads, cart them off as manure (p. clxii.) Out of 16 answers from native officials as to whether fish are trapped during rains in irrigated fields, 3 state they are not, and 13 that they are. In Oudh, some of the native officials assert that breeding-fish are not trapped during the rains, and 20 assert that they are in their districts. In the Bombay Presidency, every Collector who has answered this question (except Kaladghi) considers they are destroyed, and a native official in the Kaladghi Collectorate states they are in his district during the rains. In the Haidarabad Assigned Districts, but one opinion appears to prevail, namely, that they are taken in every possible way, but in some districts

trapping is not employed. In Mysor and Coorg, the native officials consider that fish, irrespective of time or condition, are captured in every conceivable manner. In Madras, trapping breeding-fish and young ones appears to be the rule. Fishing weirs are permitted to extend across whole rivers, not allowing even fry to pass; there is no close time whatever anywhere. Damming and lading out and poisoning waters are freely resorted to for fishing purposes. At Midnapur (p. clxxxii), breeding-fish are said to be destroyed to a great extent; in Burdwan (p. clxxxiii), they are largely taken for consumption; in fact, they are killed, it appears from the answers, throughout Bengal, whether in Orissa or in Assam. The parent fish being thus shown to be slaughtered whenever and wherever procurable, it is necessary to enquire whether the *fry* fare any better. In the Panjáb, prior to the introduction of the present rules regulating the minimum size of the mesh at $1\frac{1}{4}$ inches between each knot, large numbers of young fish were sold as *chilwas;* the destruction is considered to be now diminishing. In Oudh, it is asserted that in twenty districts fry are captured in large quantities, but that this does not take place in two; the reports from four native officials give 68,300 maunds of fry as yearly killed in their districts alone. If fry are calculated at one grain each, a destruction in four districts of upwards of 14,000,000,000 grains of young fish, which, in less than a year, would, taking an average of the sorts, weigh as many pounds—so the opinion that nothing need be done may be open to dispute. In Bombay, the fry of fish appear to be almost universally captured throughout the rains. In the Haidarabad Assigned Districts the same universal destruction is reported, as is it also in Mysor and Coorg. In the Madras Presidency, the fry are wastefully destroyed whenever and wherever they can be obtained; nets that will catch a "black-ant," or detain a mosquito, or even the eggs of fish are recorded, whilst the interspace of the substances forming traps is said to be less. In Bengal, fry are stated not to be wastefully destroyed, but only to be captured whenever they can be caught, either for eating or storing tanks with (p. clxxxi); as observes the Commissioner of Rajshahye (p. clxxxvi), bamboo contrivances for fish-catching are in use in every paddy-field; in Assam (p. ccxxix), "many of the river fish, some of which attain a large size, come annually up the smaller streams and deposit their spawn, and the young ones of these are during the rains dispersed over the surface of the country in rice-fields, swamps, drains and ditches. These endeavour subsequently to make their way to the large rivers, but the dangers which beset them on the road are more numerous than those which Bunyan's Pilgrim had to encounter. In the shallow waters in the rice-fields, women and children may be seen in crowds, fishing with baskets termed *jakai*, through the interstices of which a tadpole could not pass. Those that escape this danger, and, following the flow of the water, arrive at one of the innumerable little bunds separating the various paddy-fields, find their further progress barred by funnel-shaped bamboo traps, through which the water is made to pass, but whose outlets are so small that only the most minute fish can get through. Escaping to the smaller water-courses, their dangers seem to increase. The Assamese divide the channels into sections by erecting bunds, and from one of these they proceed to bale out all the water, capturing every fish, large and small: they then bund off another portion, and do likewise. The fish finally arrive at the smaller rivers, find their exit barred by weirs, which will let nothing pass, and not content with this, the Assamese will sometimes resort to poison." In Burma at Rangoon (p. ccxxii), it is observed that the right to catch breeding-fish only is rented out in some parts, separate from the fishery itself; so further remarks on how these fishes are treated in that province appear unnecessary.

LVII. Seeing that a fish diet is popular throughout India, that the markets are not sufficiently supplied, that the breeding-fishes are trapped ascending to their breeding-grounds, and the fry by every conceivable device, the question arises— *Is the supply of fish in the fresh-water increasing, decreasing, or stationary?* In the Panjáb, out of 78 answers from different talookas, an increase is reported in 13, a stationary state in 32, and a decrease in 33. In Sind, no alteration. In the North-Western Provinces, out of 17 answers (p. cxlv), 6 report a stationary state, 10 a decrease, but some think the fisheries are recovering. In Oudh, 21 tehsildars report an increase in 8, stationary in 10, a decrease in 2, and doubtful in 1. In Bombay, that the fish in rivers and tanks have generally decreased during late years. In the Haidarabad Assigned Districts, there is only one opinion, which is, that they have decreased. In Mysor and Coorg, the great majority of reporters give a decrease;

<small>The supply of fish in the fresh-water decreasing.</small>

the rest that they continue stationary. In Madras, out of 64 answers, 6 give an increase, 12 a stationary state, and 46 a large decrease or a decrease.

LVIII. *Whose are these fisheries?* Those which are Fisheries, whose property they are. leased out by Government of course are Government property; those in permanently-settled districts likewise would unquestionably belong to the owners of the soil. But these are not the chief ones in many places. In whole districts no rents have been collected for a longer or shorter number of years on philanthropic grounds,—a license which has been abused by the people, who have taken the advantage of slaughtering everything they possibly can. Can this license be considered equivalent to Government having given up their rights, or can they resume them? Paterson in his legal work. *The Fishery Laws of Great Britain*, observes respecting inhabitants of towns in claiming a right to fish, on the ground of ancient custom:—" In such cases the acts of such anglers are more likely to be referable to the license of the owner, who, if he pleases, may allow all the public or a portion of the public to angle there. But no length of time, during which such acts are capable of being explained on the ground of license, can prevent the owner putting an end to such license. He may resume his original rights at any moment and withdraw the license, for no man ought to have his rights abridged by acting liberally towards the public and his neighbour" (para. CV).

LIX. I now propose tracing out, from such records as Why British rules and regulations have had a disastrous effect on fisheries. are available, how it is that British rule appears to have had a most disastrous effect upon the fresh-water fisheries of the Indian Empire. I assume that it cannot now be denied (see para. LVII) that the amount of fish in the fresh-waters has decreased, and is yearly diminishing; but many of the reporters, erroneously as I believe, advance the opinion that fishing is carried on as it has been from time immemorial, consequently laws are not required for regulating the mode of capturing the finny tribes. I do not think that fishing is now what it was during native rule, but I believe it can be shown that great and most destructive innovations have been or are being permitted, and that the British, with the most philanthropic intentions, have given to the people license in fishing that has been greatly abused, and is now destroying the fisheries. The natives evidently perceive this themselves; thus, in the Central Provinces, the Tehsildar of Sironcha (para. 266) states that a decrease in the tank-produced fish is believed to have occurred since the district has formed a portion of the British territory : previously the people were prohibited from killing fish in tanks unless they paid some fees or share of fish to the local talukdar. If *nallas* are completely swept of fish, it is certain that the amount in the rivers will likewise fall off. The Tehsildar of Nursingpur (para. 264) remarks,—"it is to this wholesale destruction of small fish that the fish have decreased." In Madras, the Tehsildar of Bhimavaram (para. 173) observes, that it cannot be ascertained if the fish have increased or decreased, "as every one is allowed to fish as he likes since the abolition of the renting system." In the North-Western Provinces, three tehsildars in the Benares Division (p. clxxvii) consider that fish have decreased, "owing to the indiscriminate destruction of the young."

LX. *How were fisheries worked under native rule?*—

<small>Fisheries, how worked under native rule.</small> is a question that but few have thrown any light upon; but still it appears that it is possible to ascertain this,* and that fisheries formed royalties, mostly let out to contractors, who alone in the districts possessed the right to sell fish, and that they permitted the people on payment (para. 7) to capture fish for their own consumption. In fact, it was *a license on payment resumable at will*, as in the British law (see para. 88). Remains of this custom still exist at Lahore (para. 27), and the leasing of fisheries is even now pursued in many portions of the Indian Empire. Thus, if the following reports are looked through, it will be seen that the Deputy Commissioner of Kangra (para. 30), in suggesting what steps are advisable in future with reference to the fisheries in his district, observes, these measures must be practically a system of Government preserves, such as was always in force in the time of the Rajahs, partly by giving licenses to monopolists to supply the market, and partly by licenses for fishing with small nets for home consumption and not for sale. At Lahore, as already remarked, the system still exists, and none but the contractor may obtain fish for sale, and no one is permitted to sell this article unless it goes through his hands. Also Burma, where it appears pretty clear (p. cxciii) that in the time of native rule, this identical plan was carried on, there

---

<small>* A most useful enquiry would be—how were fisheries under native rule worked in your district? But the investigation would be troublesome, and probably trustworthy answers could not be obtained.</small>

were no free fisheries, but people were licensed to fish for home consumption on payment of a stipulated sum yearly to the contractor. In the Himalayas (p. clvii), it is observed that " the right of erecting weirs was not, I believe, carried on to the same extent in former days as now. They were not then so regularly or so generally made, and were not of the same impassible nature as those now erected." " The people living high up one of our rivers, an affluent of the Aleknunda, complained to me that, owing to the number of weirs, they found that very few fish can find their way up as far as their villages" (p. clvi). In Mysor and Coorg, I was informed that under native rule indiscriminate fishing was not permitted : contractors held the fisheries, and those not fishermen, who wished to capture fish for their own consumption but not for sale, had to pay for such license. It appears to me that, however beneficial our rule may have been in some respects, it is most disastrous to fisheries, and future generations will have even more reason to complain than those of the present time, if we do not revert to native precedent, modified by British law, not as proposed in India, but as existing in England. Lastly, I would draw attention to the fact, that even in places where Government permits an unlimited license, the native landowners do not, but raise an income from it. Thus, in Bombay (para. 97), it is stated in Wullubpur and Waree, which are on the banks of the Myhee, and are talookdaree villages, the Thakoos who are proprietors of them receive a third share of the fish caught within those limits. In the Central Provinces (para. 258), it is observed that in some portions of these provinces the land-owners claim the right to fishing in the rivers and streams running through their estates, and receive fees from fishermen resorting to them. It seems to be held by some officials that, as of late years license to fish has been permitted without the exaction of rent, therefore this license may have obtained the force of right defensible by a civil action by " the exercise of long practice having converted it into communal rights,"— an error in law, as it will be seen (para. 130) as no length of time can prevent an owner, in which position Government stands, from putting an end to such license. It will be perceived in the resolutions of the Madras Revenue Board that the fisheries may be thrown open to the public by their orders, and now the right of Government to interfere with this license is questioned, whereas, if it could have been legally permitted, why is it not legally resumable ?

LXI. *How are fisheries worked under British rule?*—
comes next for consideration. In permanently-settled estates, unless a stipulation exists, of course they go with the land. In some places the adjacent villagers or people are considered to possess certain communal rights with respect to them, in many cases, I suspect, through a misapprehension; thus, when proved that a land-owner has only received one-third or two-thirds of the proceeds, it appears to have been ruled that the remainder is the property of the neighbouring people, whereas in reality it only expressed the share of the fisherman in re-payment for his labour in taking the fish. It is the rule in India and Burma to remunerate by the proceeds obtained: sometimes the fisherman has to sell his share to the contractor or lessee at a given rate; more rarely the fish are sold, and he obtains a proportion of the money, or he may have it in kind. I do not propose entering upon how the fisheries have been or are being let, but regarding any regulations which exist in regard to the protection of the fish from wasteful destruction, and how license to capture the finny tribes has gradually crept in, until it has become a great abuse. In but few localities has it been stated that Government have never received some share of the fisheries, although such has been collected in different modes, either by selling direct, which is letting or leasing, or by a *moturfa* tax, which is clearly a license to net, either in the form of a capitation tax on the fisherman, or one on his implement of chase, identical with the tax now imposed in fishery districts in England, and has nothing whatever to do with letting the fishery. In fact, it is the same as a person who takes out a license to use a gun, but that license gives him no right to trespass on his neighbour's property to shoot his game. It may be generally asserted that Government have, until of late years, exercised their right as landlord in letting their fisheries, but they have not regulated in any way how those fisheries should have been worked, and at last, in many places, came to the decision to permit an unlimited license, perhaps partly due to the deterioration in their value. Thus, in Madras, the moturfa tax was abolished, and this doubtless in districts was equivalent to, amongst the fishermen, permitting them to capture fish without payment in any of the Government waters; and by the orders of the Revenue Board in 1849, it will be seen (para. 146) many leased fisheries were given up to the general public. This intended boon has

eventuated in their almost depopulation, now termed "a free industry," and with which it is proposed "no interference should be permitted," although their almost ruined state must be evident in many localities where such license has been allowed. The absolute giving-up of fresh-water fisheries to the people without any restrictions, experience, in every part of the globe, shows, always eventuates in their utter annihilation. These "free industries" would be more aptly termed "free poaching," or "wasteful destruction," and as such, I consider, strongly to be condemned, and for the following reasons :—That numerous individuals now fritter away their time on these fisheries instead of working at their legitimate occupations, and, whilst doing so, are being permitted to poach the breeding-fish and fry as freely as they please—a license which they are not slow in availing themselves of. I assert that this is one of the chief causes of the present decrease of this description of animal food (para. LVII), and that it is not only unfair to the fisheries, but also to the legitimate fishermen, whose occupation in many places is now a thing of the past. I believe this free fishing has been one, if not the principal, cause why they are in such an impoverished condition, and that doing good to the fisheries will not only tend to augment the food-supply to the general good, but also to improve the present condition of the fishermen. If it is still decided that these fisheries shall be continued open to all, and their comparative utter annihilation is not wished for, restrictions as to the use of fixed engines, poisoning of waters, and perhaps the size of the meshes of the nets employed, &c., will have to be laid down by authority, and to see them properly carried out, watchers or water-bailiffs would be necessary. It appears almost ludicrous, were it not lamentable, to observe many well-informed officials, who, in the following reports, have given their opinions, *very strongly*, that it will be hard on the people if Government issue any regulations to protect their own fisheries from a threatened destruction, and that the license now permitted and so grossly abused should be allowed to be continued in every species of poaching manner and without limitation. If rules are to be framed and carried out, who is to pay for them ?—if the general tax-payer, then the very existence of these fisheries would be a pecuniary burden. In Great Britain, this plan is not pursued,—there, local taxation (irrespective of rent) on the fishermen (a moturfa tax) is raised for this purpose. The Collector of Madras (para. 147) believes "the Secretary of State ruled that the right of fishing was not to be rented out, except where the practice had been previously in vogue;" but as this rule was promulgated in 1849, ten years prior to the appointment of a Secretary of State for India, I am inclined to think it was the Revenue Board's orders that were alluded to, as the despatch cannot be found. Lastly, Burma will be especially interesting as the country which has most recently come under British rule. The "Een Thoogyee" was the contractor, who alone might obtain fish for sale, and he permitted the public, on a stipulated payment (generally, I understood, one rupee yearly for every house), to take fish for their own consumption, but not for sale. At the present time (p. ccix), creeks not claimed by the fishery lessees fall to the share of the villagers, who forthwith choke them up in all directions with small dams. It appears, under the Burmese Government, dams were not allowed in any of the main streams. In the year 1861, the fishery laws in Burma were passed, and from this date I believe injuries to fisheries may be chiefly dated. From this period, I was informed, the practice of employing fixed engines in irrigated fields and water-courses, untaxed, commenced; weirs have largely augmented, any one being allowed to take fish any way he pleases, without payment, for home consumption, whilst no regulations were instituted for the protection of the fisheries from wasteful destruction. Irrespective of this, certain localities were set aside as free fisheries. The result is, that the fish are reported to be decreasing; for, if it is for one moment considered as to what such a course inevitably eventuates in, surely it must be admitted that unlimited license will cause unlimited waste. If persons may help themselves as they please, they will take those captured with the least trouble, and thus breeding-fish and fry are destroyed where they should be preserved. The people cannot be blamed for this; fishermen will do it, whether in Europe or in India, if so permitted.

LXII. The *fishermen* who carry on their occupations in the fresh-waters, or above where the tide ebbs and flows, are divisible into those who follow it out as a single means of livelihood, or merely as an occasional one, subsidiary to other employments. The first question, then, for consideration is—*Who are the fishermen?* Here, again, great innovations have crept in. Under native rule distinct crafts or castes followed this occupation, at least in the plains, and still remnants of fishing classes, transferred from one portion of India to another, can be traced. At Combaconum in Madras, "tradition asserts that this race of men were originally brought by some Hindu Rajah as bearers from Conjeveram." At Broach in Bombay (p. lvi), two sub-divisions of the fishing caste have "obtained their names from the villages whence they emigrated." Again, the moturfa tax in Madras affected all fishermen, being a species of capitation tax, or one on their trade or the implements with which it was being carried out, and the abrogation of this must have eventuated in many more persons following the occupation, especially as rents were also remitted in Madras. In the present day, "there is scarcely anywhere a numerous and distinct class dependant this pursuit for subsistence" (p. lxx). That such is the case, an example is furnished in the Panjáb, where taxes on fishing nets have been imposed, with the result that "the new regulations are admitted on all hands to have had a good effect in preserving the fish, whilst the fishermen have decreased." In Mysor, in the time of Hyder Ali, very stringent fishing laws existed, whereas now, we are informed, in the Nundidrug Division (p. cv), about two-thirds of the population fish occasionally, in addition to their other occupations. Nearly every ryot keeps a net, to be used as occasion or opportunity arises. In British Burma, fishermen must have increased since the period when every one has been authorised to catch fish, without payment, for home consumption, but not for sale, whereas formerly the contractor received payment for such. In short, in the time when districts were let, the contractors would not have been so short-sighted as to permit the general destruction now so freely carried on. At present every one encroaches on the fishermen's calling, who, seeing others slaughtering breeding-fish and fry, do the same: as remarked to me in Burma,—why should we save them if others kill them ?—or in the Panjáb, where they complained that their nets with $1\frac{1}{4}$-inch meshes could not take fry, whereas such were permitted to be sold in the bazar by people not fishermen. The result has been in most parts of India that the fisheries have become almost ruined, and amongst the arguments against action advanced in Madras exists this—that the fresh-water fishermen are amongst the most impoverished class of the community—a result to be anticipated, and a consequence of indiscriminate fishing. In fact, in some places they have had to give up their calling: in the Central Provinces (p. cxxiv), many have ceased to follow their original occupation owing to the demand for well-paid labour developed by the railway. In Madras (p. lxxxii), "fewer men are said to fish than formerly, but the rise of wages has more to do with it than the falling-off of fish." In Assam (p. ccxxviii), "fish has become of late years much dearer in Durrung; the fisheries are falling in value, and many of the Dome fishermen are, in consequence, I believe, taking to agricultural pursuits." The same is seen in Orissa. Fishermen who follow this calling as a supplement to other means of support have no interest in protecting fisheries, but only in procuring for themselves as much as they can, and whenever they can. Such are the fishermen of the Panjáb (p. iv), where they are stated to number 10,450 (p. viii): also of Bombay, in which presidency "few, if any, of the foregoing, numbering upwards of 50,000, are solely engaged in fishing, but they also follow other occupations" (p. xxxv). In Madras, the fishermen are, as a rule, agriculturists, palanquin bearers, small traders, coolies and others who carry on this pursuit when not engaged in their ordinary avocations, and as there are no restrictions, their only idea is to obtain what they can, when they can. Were all the fisheries ruined, it would not pecuniarily affect them, except in a secondary degree, as their living is not dependant upon fishing. The number of persons recorded as solely fishermen in the inland waters appears to be under 200 persons (p. lxiv). In Mysor and Coorg, the fishermen who pursue that trade seem to be few, but those who fish in addition to other avocations appear to be very numerous (p. ci): the same may be said of Haidarabad (p. cviii): the Central Provinces (p. cxv): Oudh (p. cxxvii) and the North-West Provinces (p. cxlv). In Bengal (p. clxxx), the fishermen, or people who fish, consist of three classes,—*first*, regular fishermen who are exclusively employed as such; *secondly*, the wives of the men of some castes who fish whilst their husbands pursue other occupations; *thirdly*, the general population. Thus, in Burdwan, out of 20,000 persons computed as capturers of fish, one-third are stated to be exclusively employed as such: in Hoogli, there are considered to be 3,000 fishermen by trade. It is as we approach the seaboard, and where large fish can ascend from the ocean, and man has not yet managed to largely ruin the fisheries, that we find the greatest proportion of people exclusively fishermen. In Burma (p. cxcvi), the people are of necessity boatmen and by choice fishermen. The present state of the fresh-water fishermen of India, as regards what would be the effect of legislation upon their calling, may be summed up in the words of the Officiating

Commissioner, West Berar, (p. cx), "that whatever restriction may be imposed, no class of people will be so affected as to interfere with their means of livelihood." If the fisheries are improved the fishing classes will be largely benefitted, and those localities possessing the best stocked waters (other things being equal) will have the most fishermen as a distinct class, because following this occupation is easier than agricultural pursuits, although the exposure is perhaps greater. Fishermen are an improvident class, and in India, whether Hindus or Mahomedans, are low in the social scale, whilst in British Burma, as Buddists, they are charitably doomed by the more righteous of the sect to eternal perdition in the next state of existence.

LXIII. The most economical way of working fisheries is

Fishermen, how they work fisheries.

by persons who make fishing a distinct occupation, provided there is a sufficiency of work. They may be divided into the *contractors* or *lessees*, who become tenants of rivers or portions of them, canals, tanks or *jhils*, often having sub-partners, who take shares in the fishery, and are remunerated by a proportion either of the captures, or else of the money received for such, after the payment of the rent and other expenses. Some have coolies or paid servants, who either receive a stipulated sum a day in money and fish, or else a certain or proportionate amount of the captured fish, which they dispose of: and these persons may be kept on regularly for merely the fishing season, or only occasionally as more hands are required. *Secondly*, there are those who, on payment of a license fee, are permitted to fish in the Government waters otherwise unlet. *Thirdly*, when the fisheries are declared free to all, and every one is allowed to capture the fish as suits his convenience best. *Lastly*, the general population may be given the right to take sufficient for home consumption where they like, and how they please, provided they neither sell nor preserve it. Contractors almost invariably give the workers a personal interest in the takes, and, whether sub-partners or coolies, they generally have to provide their own nets, and for this purpose the lessee or a banian advances money to purchase the raw material, and thus the coolie becomes irrevocably involved in debt. In some districts the fishing is free to every one without any restrictions. This may be due to several independent causes, such as the difficulty in making the fishing remunerative, owing to the rapidity of the current in rivers or canals: to the paucity of fish, as in some hill streams and depopulated rivers: the depth of tanks, or the presence of foreign substances as roots, trees, &c., or the poverty of the general population. In most of such districts, it is usually seen that fishing is not followed out as a distinct employment, whilst the mesh of the nets is as small as the rapidity of the current will allow to be used. Sometimes, even in districts where the fishing is, or was good, the general public have been permitted to act as fishermen, whether adults, throughout the year, or only during the rains, and even women and children assist, or a species of scramble occurs as to who shall get the most—a plan which soon eventuates in the poverty of fisheries, for only the conscience of the fisherman stands between them and their greed, the latter, as might be anticipated, rapidly gaining the mastery. With the deterioration of these fisheries the fishermen become poorer and poorer, unless they turn to other sources of earning money. At first, no doubt, pleased at not having to pay rent, and all restrictions being removed, they employ redoubled energy, and increase their profits; but soon the population find they may fish as well as the fishermen, and, taking advantage of this permission, the supply becomes temporarily augmented, the price slightly falling. At the end of one or two years, fish become much scarcer, and those who, for a time became fishermen, revert to their legitimate calling. As soon as the young fish are moving about, or shortly after the monsoons have set in, the wives of these men are sent out fishing, and they, with the aid of their children, obtain myriads of fry from every sheltered spot to where these small and immature fish retire for shelter and security, they not being able to face strong currents or live in deep waters. Every device that can be imagined is now called into action; nets, which will not permit a mosquito to pass, are employed; even the use of cloths is called into exercise. The sides of the rivers are denuded of fish, so far as human agency can contrive it. Neither are the agricultural population idle; they construct wicker-work traps, baskets, and nets; these traps do not permit anything to pass: a fish, once in, cannot return, as they resemble rat traps, having an easy entrance, but, once in, retreat becomes impossible. So soon as mature fish commence passing up the small water-courses at the sides of the rivers and streams, these traps come into play, and the breeding-fish are taken. The few which escape are not yet safe, for, as they return and the fry move about, these traps are reversed, so that every fish, down to those of the most minute size, attempting to pass down these water-courses towards the rivers or tanks, become entrapped. In irrigated fields, where it becomes necessary to throw water from a lower to the higher level, a basket is fixed to receive it and through which it passes, thus acting as a strainer; all the fish in it become a prey to the agriculturist. Nets of the most divers forms are likewise employed, some being fixed, others held in the hand, but all uniting in one character—that they allow nothing to escape. In short, by not letting or regulating fisheries, there is no headman or lessee whose interest it is to prevent injury to his property, by the slaughter of the breeding-fishes and the destruction of their young: self-interest does not exist, the only certain cause to prevent their annihilation. In British Burma, this trapping of fish in the breeding season was locally sanctioned, and in general use, without being taxed, it, as well as still more murderous forms, if possible, existed in 1869, and probably do so now. Even through the inundated paddy-fields, which are the known haunts of the fry of fish, the Burmese were being permitted to use an easy and very destructive apparatus. No distinct channels being present in which to place traps, while the ground was too rough for netting, besides the water being low, a large triangular-shaped basket was employed, and this, being harnessed to a pair of bullocks or buffaloes, was dragged through these muddy retreats of the fry. And how does this principle of throwing open the fisheries, without any restrictions, answer in practice? It results in decreasing the fish, and consequently diminishing the food of whole districts. Water should be as valuable as land for producing food, whilst indiscriminate farming is not permitted; were it, any farmer could easily foretell the result—how the strong would hold the richest lands, which, when exhausted, they would leave and move on somewhere else. There are districts, as British Burma, in which certain portions of the waters were set apart in every locality as free fisheries, where any one might fish, and these have been supplemented by a rule that any one may capture sufficient for home consumption, where they liked and how they pleased, provided they did not sell or preserve the spoil. Here we observe such fishers could have no interest in the welfare of the fishery, but would be merely intent on capturing, with the least possible trouble, sufficient for household wants. During the monsoon season they place traps in every likely run wherein breeding-fish may pass up narrow entrances, in order to reach suitable places wherein to deposit their eggs: they likewise slaughter the young fish by every simple contrivance when they begin to move about, and thus extensive damage to fisheries is occasioned. To all persons possessing fisheries, the protection of these young fish should be an object, so that in due season they may be able to recapture a remunerative number of adults: but seeing the fry generally destroyed, and aware that if they do not take when they can what they are able, as others are not so particular, they unfortunately often join in this suicidal occupation, thus assisting in the depopulation of fisheries, and, when too late, lament the state of affairs, but never admit that it is in a great measure owing to their greed, whilst the idea of their destruction they philosophically consider must affect the rising and not the present generation. Even when there are no restrictions, nor rent to be paid, fishermen after a time often discover the advantage of plying their occupation in concert, especially with other fishermen. It is by no means unfrequent for large bodies of villagers to proceed at certain seasons of the year to rivers which can be easily bunded, and there to kill every fish they are able. Amongst all the foregoing classes of fishermen, amongst every caste and creed, the invariable rule appears to obtain, to get everything they are able to-day, irrespective of the season, condition, or size of the fish, and entirely oblivious to the next year's supply. I do not, however, see that the natives, in acting thus, are more rapacious than fishermen have been or would be in England, were the fresh-water fisheries declared public property, and every one permitted to work them in any way he pleased, without any sort of restrictions being imposed. It becomes simply a scramble on the principle—" Should I not catch them, somebody else will." Neither do I think the fishermen, as described, are more greedy than persons following other occupations: thus, it is stated by *Colonel Campbell,* respecting the Orissa range of hills:—" Of the science of agriculture the people know absolutely nothing; they exhaust the soil with unintermitted crops until the land is barren, then they abandon their fields, and clear fresh jungle for future crops." The fishermen are not more far-seeing than the forester or the agriculturist, thinking of only to-day's wants, regardless of to-morrow's requirements; they only carry out, when able, in the rivers the same description of misapplied energy, until nothing but small fish remain, and the young have to be raised from ova deposited by parents of two or at the most three years of age, the more mature ones having been destroyed. And what is the result of this mode of treating fisheries, as regards the fisherman? Would prohibiting the wasteful destruction of breeding and young fish benefit or ruin their occupation? I am compelled to enter rather fully upon this question, as the well-worn epithet *experience* is so often advanced, and that without any arguments to back it, that the fisheries should be let alone, the fishermen being permitted to continue fishing as they always have done, such having been in operation for centuries, and still fish being present in the fresh-waters. It will, however, be apparent that such arguments entirely evade the points at issue, as they *assume* that the fishermen continue fishing as they have done from immemorial ages without any improvement in their means of capture: it also takes for granted that the captors of fish, the times employed in fishing, as well as the fish-eating population, have remained stationary ; and, lastly, that the fisheries are in an equally good condition under the sway of Europeans, who mostly do not notice the fresh-water fish, as they were in times gone-by, when natives ruled who esteemed this article of food, and doubtless gave protection to this legitimate source of revenue. The first assumption being improbable, the second, doubtless, incorrect, and the last in well-populated districts being directly opposed to the result of recent investigations. Even the exponents of the let-alone system have not attempted to demonstrate that these waters, where small fish are being so wastefully destroyed, are insufficient to support a very much larger number than they now contain. Every practical fisherman will assert they are, as a rule, insufficiently stocked, and if such is the case, as I have no doubt it is, and the fish were permitted fair play, a very much increased supply would be the result. And what, it may be enquired, would be the effect on the fisherman were restrictive rules sanctioned, as regards his prospects? Doubtless, many of the women and children, who now destroy myriads of fry and small fish, would have to cease such occupations, whilst agriculturists also would be unable to trap the breeding-fish and fry in the paddy or irrigated fields. These, however, would be temporary inconveniences, and would cease with the season. One of the important results would, however, be a vast increase in the non-migratory fishes, and a considerable augmentation in this article of food, more especially during the cold months. These rules being general would be equally fair to all, and complaints could not exist that the young fish, which were being protected in one part, were being destroyed in another. If the sale of the fry or fish under a certain size were illegal, much good might also be effected, especially in the breeding season; and this would not injuriously affect the regular fisherman, but quite the reverse. If fairly worked, the result must be an increase of the amount of fish in the fresh-waters, and with such at first the fisherman's gains will be much augmented, because the price will not fall so rapidly as the fisheries improve. Perhaps an increased supply would at first cause decreased price; but such can never occur to any great extent, where the price of fish in the bazar is regulated by the cost of mutton, which is unlikely to become cheaper; so the fisheries must improve in value in accordance with the care bestowed upon them. Should rent remain unraised, a great increase in prosperity ought to be in store for this, at present, poor class of persons, irrespective of the good which will be felt by the general community in having a considerable increase of wholesome animal food, and that obtained without any corresponding pecuniary outlay, but simply by making use of means now at hand, but at present left almost uncared for.

Fixed Engines.

LXIV. *Fixed engines* employed in the capture of fresh-water fish are thus defined in the fishery laws of England,—"stake-nets, bag-nets, putts, putchers and all fixed implements or engines for catching or facilitating the catching of fish," and "the section confers a power on any one of the public, whether interested or not, to destroy a fixed engine, and therefore he is not liable to an action for trespass for doing so." Fixed engines employed in India are mainly divisible into two varieties, (1) those manufactured of cotton, hemp, aloe fibre, coir or some such material; and (2) others constructed of split bamboo, rattan, reed, grass or some more or less inelastic substances.

<small>Fixed engines.</small>

LXV. Fixed engines manufactured of cotton or elastic materials would include all stake-nets, but when the meshes are of a fair size they may be considered as legitimate means when properly employed for the capture of fish, unless they are true fresh-water ones migrating for breeding purposes.

<small>Fixed engines of elastic materials.</small>

When these fixed nets have fairly-sized meshes their use does not call for notice, except so far as to deprecate their employment in weired rivers not far below those constructions. But in some of these fixed nets the size of the meshes is so minute that no fish can pass; there it stands immoveably fixed across a whole water-way capturing everything, as the water is literally strained through it. The meshes have been described as so minute that a big black-ant could not pass, or that they would arrest a tamarind or a mustard seed, and several Europeans observe on their being about the size of mosquito curtain net. Thus (p. xiii) an instance is adduced in the Panjáb of how a whole drove of mahaseer were captured by fixing a net across a river and dragging another down to it, which caused wholesale destruction, and as a consequence there was little or no rod-fishing that season. In fact, this mode of capturing all the fish in certain portions of rivers is common in India. In Amritsar, the moveable net is stated to be dragged as much as a mile to the fixed one (p. xxv): at Mettapolliam, in the Coimbatore district of Madras, an identical plan used to be pursued. In the Broach Collectorate of Bombay (p. xliv), nets are fixed across the stream shaped like a wall: some have a bag in the middle. In Ratnagiri (p. liv) the practice of throwing nets across creeks and rivers has done much to diminish the number of fish. In the Central Provinces at Jabalpur (p. cxxiv), two large nets are taken towards one central point, towards which the fish are driven by beating the water and noises of all sorts: or on a moonlight night a net is fixed across a stream and the fish driven into it (p. cxxiii). Even the greatest adherent of "communal" and prescriptive rights, or for permitting unlimited massacre of small fish, must admit that a net which will arrest the spawn of a frog, permanently fixed across a whole water-way, down which the fry must descend with the receding floods, before they can obtain access to a river, can hardly be conducive to the prosperity of a fishery. But as it may be suggested that surely such wholesale destruction cannot be going on unchecked in many places, I must here advert to where such practices are in vogue, and for this purpose, it will only be necessary to refer to a few of the appended reports. There is hardly a district in India (Sind, portions of Burma, and parts of the Panjáb excepted) where these fine-meshed nets are not employed as fixed engines. Likewise, as the floods subside, earthen banks are constructed across water-courses, each with an artificial opening cut for the current to pass; here a purse-net with minute meshes is firmly fixed, and all the descending fish are captured; this is employed in Bombay (p. xxxvii) : in Madras, in the Central Provinces (p. cxxiii-iv), and in fact in every place where such is possible, unless wicker traps are preferred. Or these fine-meshed nets may be fixed to the sluice of a tank (p. lxxix), so that the water that is let out for irrigation purposes passes through it, all the fish being arrested. Or at the yearly subsidence of the floods which extend miles across the country, the water being stocked with fry, bunds are raised, with an opening for the escape of the water : but here a purse-net prevents any exit for the young fish, consequently, as the waters will be entirely drained off leaving the fields dry, the fry has only to select whether it will be captured in the purse-net, or perish in the drying-up fields. These nets of various forms and many names are likewise fixed in the supply channels (p. xcvii) in irrigated fields, and nothing escapes them, especially as the water is not always flowing, so what is easier, when the channel is full, than to fix a fine net across its entire breadth, so that all the fish which have passed up for breeding or feeding purposes are unable to return as the water is being cut off? In the North-Western Provinces, "fish are killed, more or less, throughout the year, but the largest numbers are taken towards the end of the rainy season. As the waters fall, countless lakes or pools of all sizes are formed on the low lands by the rivers. These, which were, during the floods, mere extensions of the streams, now become lakes with one narrow exit to the river. Across this, nets are stretched, or a weir of grass constructed, and every fish that has wandered up becomes a certain prey" (p. clx).

LXVI. Fixed engines constructed of non-elastic substances are, however, still more destructive to fish than those made of net, and which are more liable to rents. The different forms are so numerous, whilst so many are fully described in the appendix, that a reference to them is all that is needed, their general design being only necessary to allude to, before commencing which, I may remark on the favour they are held in Europe. Fishing weirs, which prevent fish obtaining a free passage up a river, were pronounced by the Lord Chief Justice of England to be "illegal and a public nuisance." The size of the interstices between,

<small>Fishing weirs of non-elastic substances. How breeding-fish are destroyed.</small>

the substances of which weirs are composed, appears to be everywhere much the same, whether examined in the ghâts of Canara, the yomas of Pegu, the Himalayas or the plains of India and Burma, and that size is about sufficient to permit water to flow, obstructing every fish attempting to pass. *First*, are the weirs in the hilly districts or contiguous localities erected simply for fishing?—this is usually done as the violence of the monsoon floods subside, and the rush of the mountain torrent has decreased to that extent that these erections are not liable to be swept away. It is to the hills as already remarked (para. XXXVI) that some of the most valuable of the carps of India proceed to breed; in fact, such are the only localities well adapted for the reception of the eggs of a few species, and where their young should be reared in quietude. Where irrigation weirs exist *en route* to these hills as I have already observed (para. 12), they serve to impede or arrest this upward progress of the fish, some entirely so (para. 12), others to a lesser degree. Even at some of these irrigation weirs trapping these fish goes on, and in fact, in many places they experience the greatest difficulty in reaching their spawning grounds. But some overcome the difficulty of ascent, a few deposit their spawn, and now the force of the water lessens; it occasionally becomes a little clear, and one may as well follow the course of the parent fish trying to descend to the larger rivers of the plains. Here spearing, snagging, netting, angling, &c., are omitted, but only the existence of fixed engines will be investigated. Weirs are now raised every few miles, absolutely straining the whole of the water of these hill streams, whilst in every one are traps. The probabilities are that the great majority of mahaseer that reach the rivers of the plains are the last year's fry which have fortunately escaped destruction during the dry months, and with the first floods, when the standing weirs have been washed away, they have obtained a free highway. But the breeding-fish are unable to descend owing to the present poaching practices permitted, and due to fishing weirs being allowed, as the force of the floods abate, to extend across all the streams in order to arrest their downward passage. In the Himalayas (p. clvi), "weirs are erected as soon as the monsoon begins to cease, and they remain in existence till carried away by the first floods in the rains. They are placed usually at the tail of each pool, and there is almost always one at the junction of two rivers, thus entirely preventing fish running up till the weir is carried away by a flood." Another plan is to convert simple irrigation weirs into fishing ones as well (p. cliv), by placing at intervals from three to four feet, on such weirs, conical-shaped baskets, the point of the cone being below, and the open mouth of the cone on a level with the weir. This device is chiefly successful at night. The baskets are generally placed where the stream is strongest, and an unwary fish coming too close, finds himself hurled into a basket from which it is quite impossible to escape. But not only in the course of hill streams as they descend, but also after they have arrived in the low country, has the descending breeding-fish to run the gauntlet of fishing weirs that have no open time, whilst interstices between its component parts would arrest the most minute fry. The following is the plan of these constructions above South Canara (p. xci), annually adopted by the Coorgs to capture the fish returning from spawning. A line of strong stakes is driven in across the full breadth of a river, the highway of these fish; split bamboos are interlaced, making it like a hurdle, and the whole faced with bushes; no fish whatever can pass, the water is merely strained through. Gaps, however, are formed, every one of which is fitted with a basket-trap or cruive from one to twelve feet in length. These are made on the mouse-trap principle, allowing an entrance, but having springy bamboo spikes projecting inside, which prevent any exit. Wicker traps are likewise placed across convenient rapids, and so constructed that no fish can descend without passing into them, and these are examined twice daily. Or should there be no rapids, such are formed by laying stones in a V-shape across a stream, and at the apex of this is one of these traps. Or a mountain river is conducted down a slope into a large concave basket, so that descending fish are pitched into it, and speedily suffocated by the rushing water or other falling fish acting like a succession of blows, preventing their ever rising up again. In the Central Provinces (p. cxxi), it is reported from Jabalpur that breeding-fish are taken in weirs thrown across the large rivers, and in the narrows of them before the monsoons: nothing can pass, whilst traps are also set up in shallow places. The Magistrate of Goruckpur (p. clix) gives a description of one which he examined. "The dam resembles a screen made of common reed: the reeds are so close together that the smallest fry can hardly get through, and the dam is further plastered at its foot with mud, and strengthened with matting, so that no passage exists for anything. In mid-stream the screen opens into a long and narrow passage, walled and floored with the same materials, and this terminates in a basket, which is a hamper made of reeds, into which a small orifice in the side gives admittance to fish beneath the surface of the water, whilst the lid remains above the surface, and is opened from time to time for the removal of the spoil. As the water hardly finds its way through the interstices of the screen, it rushes in a strong current along the passage, carrying the fish with it, and a fall from the passage into the basket precludes all chance of escape."

LXVII. In addition to large weirs and traps, there are minor sorts most extensively used in the plains—some to capture breeding-fish ascending up minor water-ways during the rains to deposit their spawn: others to arrest them and their fry attempting to descend to the rivers, as the flood-waters recede, and there is not a place, except perhaps in Sind, where fields become flooded in the monsoon months, that this mode of capture is not carried on. This trapping breeding and young fish appears to be considered an inherent right of the land-owners or tenants. In the Panjáb it is considered in places as the zemindar's property (p. xii). In Bombay, some reporters suggest the license that has existed may now be be claimed as a right. In Madras, the Revenue Board appear to be of the same opinion, more than hinting that long custom may have converted it into communal rights, and without further quotations the same erroneous ideas have been advanced almost everywhere. If the English law is the rule, license gives no right, but is revocable at will (p. lxiv). And how has the British legislature treated this question in the British isles? In "The Salmon Fishery *(Ireland)* Act, 1863," it prohibited bag-nets "within a distance of less than three statute miles from the mouth of any river," and gave the owners of such the following time to remove them:—" within fourteen days after the passing of this Act," and, " for each day of so placing or allowing the same to be continued, incur a penalty of not less than five pounds, and not exceeding twenty pounds." Weirs without gaps might be removed at once, unless the owners undertook to erect a suitable fish-pass. Fixed engines were to be removed within fourteen days, unless a license had been paid, when they were permitted to the end of the year. Now, what do the reporters in the appendix

Fixed traps for capturing fish.

state of these small fixed engines in India—these devices so destructive that the British Parliament allowed fourteen days for their removal; these traps which were deemed a public nuisance that any one may destroy? Why, these contrivances are spoken of as communal and prescriptive rights, and their prohibition an interference with private property! I have already pointed out how universal is their use, and will now adduce a few examples of how they are used. In Bombay, fish in Nasik (p. xlvii) are "caught in shallows, small pools, and irrigating channels, by nets, baskets, or funnel-shaped wicker traps, placed where there is a current of water": in Puna (p. xlix), baskets are placed in openings constructed in artificial dams which are roughly thrown across streams." In Ratnagiri, that "banks are formed to make the fish pass through narrow channels: nets are employed, also baskets, and bag-like nets" (p. xliv). In Madras, the Revenue Board suggest (p. lxxii) that these traps should only be prohibited in rivers declared to be taken under Government conservancy. In Kurnal (p. lxxxiv), the minimum mesh of the nets is given at $\frac{3}{8}$th of an inch between each knot, but of the *oodulu*, or traps of wicker work, the interstices are of infinitely smaller dimensions, and these are placed in the smaller irrigation channels (p. xcvii). In Tinnevelli, baskets and traps are used, whereby large numbers of fish are taken in a most unfair and destructive manner, and (p. lxxxvi) that small fish are caught in baskets and screens at the rapids below waste weirs and sluices. In Coimbatore (p. lxxxvi), fry are caught in wicker-work traps. In Malabar, baskets are placed in small streams in such a way as to secure every fish in them. In South Canara (p. lxxxviii), there are bamboo labyrinth weirs to entrap fish going up stream, and bamboo labyrinth weirs to entrap them going down stream, and these are set in every tempting run, all other ways being stopped. At each drop from rice-field to rice-field the cultivator places a basket made of finely split bamboos, having a wide mouth, a narrow neck, and a wide bottom: it lets the water pass, but stops every single fry. In Mysor (p. cvi), the native officials of the Astragam Division report that during the rains large quantities of fish are taken in baskets prepared for this purpose, which are made with the fronds of the cocoanut palm: these have large open mouths, whilst their floor is covered by means of lattice-work of strings; they are placed against a current of water, which, rushing in, passes through the interstices, leaving the fish deposited in the basket. In the

Central Provinces, at Jabalpur (p. cxix), every little streamlet is dammed up, and woven bamboo weirs are placed in the dams. At Bilaspur (p. cxxii), breeding and young fish are wantonly and indiscriminately destroyed in all rivers, pools, streams and tanks throughout the district, also in rice-fields: in the latter they are caught at the outlets when the water at the close of the rains is subsiding: it is impossible for the smallest fish to get out of some of these traps. The Assistant Secretary to the Chief Commissioner of these Provinces observed that "in the Sagar and Mandla Districts, extensive destruction of fish occurs, more especially of the sor, and mahseer and paru. The occasion when this occurs is the beginning of the rains, which is the season for spawning; and it is said that in Mandla at that season the fish, while making their way to spawn in tanks and rice-fields (the entries into which are small and narrow), are carefully watched, and that large numbers of all sizes are killed by the villagers; while, again, on their return to the rivers, they are met at every outlet by nets, baskets, weirs and traps, so that few can get away altogether; some of them are so small as to be perfectly useless, and these are thrown away or left as food for dogs and crows." In Haidarabad (p. cxiii), fish are taken by means of *goomlas*, which somewhat resemble the straw envelopes for bottles; they are made of the reeds of the *nurgood* plant: these traps are placed in shallow streams in the rainy season; the fish enter, but it prevents their return. In Oudh, the same mode of using traps is adverted to. Small nets or baskets of various forms and shapes are hung over weirs just above the water; breeding-fish attempting to ascend the river find this barrier in their way, try to overcome it by jumping, and many are captured by falling into these fixed contrivances. The Commissioner of the Rajshahye Division in Bengal observes (p. clxxxvi) that bamboo contrivances for fish-catching are in use in every paddy-field. They are also employed throughout Orissa and the Midnapur Districts. Whilst in Assam, the Deputy Commissioner of Durrung reports (p. ccxxviii) that "everything, from a weir to a basket, is used, and the meshes of the nets are so small that no fry can escape." Also in Seebsagor (p. ccxxix) that "what with dams, traps, baskets and nets which the villagers use, very few fish escape to the larger streams." In Jorehat (p. ccxxx), the villagers, if left to themselves, are very fond of damming streams at the end of the rains, when fish, large and small, are running down: this they do in such a way that scarcely anything can escape the traps set in the dam." In British Burma, at Bassein (p. ccxxiii), "young fish are captured to a considerable extent by traps in the paddy-fields:" in fact, fishing weirs and traps are universally employed in this province, and of innumerable descriptions, whilst miniature ones were permitted in every small stream, irrigating channel or waterway to entrap fish ascending, and so finely constructed that even fry could not pass. I found agriculturists with as many as 60 or 80 traps in their possession, and working them daily in every water-way where ingress or egress for fish could occur (see p. cxlviii). In short, trapping breeding-fish and fry is universal, wherever permitted, and nowhere is it prohibited.

Moveable Fishing Implements.

LXVIII. Nets or moveable implements (in contradis-
<small>Moveable engines for taking fish.</small> tinction to those which are fixed), employed in capturing or facilitating the capture of fish, are composed of two varieties—(1) those manufactured of cotton, hemp, aloe fibre, coir, or of some such material, and (2) others constructed of split bamboo, rattan, reed, grass or other more or less inelastic subtances.

LXIX. Large drag-nets with fair-sized meshes are used
<small>Composed of elastic materials.</small> mostly during the dry months, and employed for the purpose of clearing out the fish from pools in rivers to which they have retired, awaiting the next year's floods. Thus, in the Godaveri (p. xlvii), they are remarked upon as 100 yards long: in the Kistna as 3 to 400 yards long (p. lxxvi), their length and depth being in accordance with the waters they are going to be employed in. But the moveable nets that do the most injury are those with small meshes, and which are employed for taking the fry of fish as they are first moving about. If one just refers to the appendix to this report, we cannot but observe how such are most wastefully destroyed all over the country; this is accomplished with cast-nets of fine meshes, small wall-nets dragged up little water-courses, purse-nets similarly used; even sheets are thus employed. It has been pointed out, however, that some fish never grow to any size, consequently they will escape if nets with small meshes are prohibited, and a very good idea has been propounded that if such is the case, let them be captured after the month of October, so that the majority of the fry have become more able to take care of themselves. In Madras, the Revenue

Board except casting-nets from their proposed regulations, overlooking the fact that if such are not open to supervision, a number may be joined together, and thus constitute a legal net. In Haidarabad several casting-nets are used joined together to stop up a stream, whilst others are employed above the obstacles (p. cxii). In the Central Provinces (p. cxxiv), *pandi,* or the smallest cast-net, is ordinarily about 15 feet long, weighted with iron : when it is considered desirable to net a considerable breadth of stream, several of these nets are used fastened together, making one very long net : in this almost every kind of fish is caught. Another plan of using casting-nets is, for several fishermen to surround a pool, each armed with one, and they throw them all together, so few fish have a chance of escape. A species of lave-net is also used and in various ways; their plan of construction is in a triangular frame. In Sind, the fishermen floats down the Indus on a gourd or hollow earthen pot, and this net is let down below him : as a hilsa fish, ascending up the muddy stream, strikes against the net, it is made to contract like a purse by means of a string the fisherman holds in his hand. These lave-nets are usually constructed of very minute meshes, and employed at the sides of rivers, ditches, irrigation channels or inundated spots where fry are feeding, and the current is not strong, and here the poor people destroy a few thousands for a single meal (pp. lviii, cxxiii, cxxiv).

LXX. Nets, or rather moveable contrivances of inelas-
Composed of inelastic materials. tic substances, are more freely employed in some districts than in others. In Orissa, a *saluwa* or *putti* consists of very fine split bamboos, bound together by means of grass, the interstices between each piece being equal to $\frac{1}{4}$th of an inch or less. This *putti* is about five feet high, and is in the shape of a regular wall-net. It is taken to a tank, and placed in the water in a V-form, whilst the fishermen on either side extend themselves outwards, and by beating the water drive the fish into the enclosure. The two ends are now brought together, and the fish penned into a small space. The sides are advanced nearer and nearer until they almost touch, and the fish are removed by a hand-net, or by the hand alone. Besides this, there are contrivances for a single person to use ; thus, a peculiar form is cone-shaped, open at both ends; this is thrust down in muddy water in places where fish resort to, and the enclosed fish removed from the upper opening. It is used in the Panjáb (pp. xxii, xxv), in the Central Provinces (p. cxxiii)—in fact, throughout India and

Burma. Sometimes a line of men work a shallow piece of water with them, and then they become rather destructive: however, eels and walking-fish (*Ophiocephalidæ*) are the sorts most commonly captured thus. The triangular lave-net adverted to in the last paragraph is often made of split bamboo: it is used extensively for the purpose of capturing breeding-fish passing into irrigated fields as observed upon in Kurnal (p. xcvii). In Burma, rattan or bamboo nets termed *gyan* (p. cxcix) have each piece fixed to its neighbour by grass or fibre in the place of string, the interstices being of various sizes from $\frac{1}{16}$th of an inch to 1 inch. *Yindoons* are a species of lave-net made of closely-woven split bamboos, and affixed to a long pole; it is employed to clear out all small watercourses of the fry of fish; it is pushed along them, and raised every now and then. In some places fixed weirs are placed in a piece of water, and one of the *gyans* is gradually dragged up to the standing weir.

LXXI. *What is the minimum size of the meshes of*
<small>The smallest size of the mesh of nets which is employed.</small> *nets* in general use in India and Burma (excluding Sind), where no regulations exist declaring what such should be? I here append the answers received from native officials; 91 refer to inches:—

	Size, in respect to inches, between knot and knot of meshes.										
	1 inch.	Below 1 inch.	$\frac{1}{2}$	$\frac{1}{3}$	$\frac{1}{4}$	$\frac{1}{5}$	$\frac{1}{6}$	$\frac{1}{8}$	$\frac{1}{10}$	$\frac{1}{12}$	$\frac{1}{16}$	$\frac{1}{32}$
91 Native Officials ...	5	5	18	5	24	1	5	18	4	2	3	1

Irrespective of the foregoing 91, answers have also been received from 70 more, and they compare the minimum size as follows:—

Size of finger or thumb 5
" $\frac{1}{2}$ ring finger 2
As big as a broomstick 1
Size of $\frac{1}{2}$ a rupee 1
" 4-anna bit 1
" $\frac{1}{4}$ of an anna 1
" 2-anna bit 5
" a pie 1
Size of a grain of wheat, mothi, mucca, gram, dholl, lamp-oil
  seed, barley, tamarind seed, or a small pea, pepper-
  corn, large needle, bodkin, quill, coarse muslin, ensnare an ant, or hardly anything can pass ... 53

The foregoing 161 reports from native officials give the minimum size of the meshes of nets employed in their districts, and if one just considers the sized fish such minute meshes will ensnare, it is impossible to avoid coming to the conclusion that an immensity of wee ones must be destroyed before they can attain a fair size. My own impression is that, were very exact returns sent in, the proportion of finer meshes would be even greater than is shown above. Although this question was not put to the European officials of these districts, some have observed upon the subject. My reasons for wishing rather to obtain this information from natives being, that it can hardly be expected civilians, who are worked all day in cutcherry, have time, even had they inclination, to examine paddy-fields and inundated portions of the country during the rains, and whilst the young fish are moving about, in order to ascertain the smallest size of the meshes of nets which are employed, whilst observations made in the cold season would not afford the desired information. In Bombay, out of 10 who reply, 1 says less than an inch, and 1 at $\frac{1}{10}$th, 1 at $\frac{1}{13}$th, 1 at $\frac{1}{7}$th, 1 at $\frac{1}{32}$nd, 1 at the size of a grain of wheat, and 2 at that of a large needle. But some even place it at a smaller size, as in Khandeish (p. xlv), where, when small-meshed nets are not available, the Bhils use their sheets, *saris* and *dhotars* for the purpose of taking fish. In Ahmednuggur, pieces of cloth are used as nets (p. xlviii). In Madras, 21 observe upon this subject as follows :—1 places it at $\frac{3}{4}$th of an inch between each knot of the meshes, 1 at $\frac{1}{2}$, 3 at $\frac{1}{4}$th of an inch, 1 at $\frac{3}{8}$th, 2 at $\frac{1}{8}$th, 1 at $\frac{1}{16}$th, 1 at $\frac{1}{20}$th, say the meshes are small, 7 that they are very small, of the size of a quill or red gram seed, and 2 that they resemble mosquito curtain net. In Mysor 8 European officials give the size of the mesh of the nets as follows :—1 at $\frac{1}{2}$ an inch between each knot, 2 at $\frac{1}{8}$th, 2 at $\frac{1}{12}$th, 2 as the size of mosquito curtain net, and 1 as small enough to take the spawn of fish. In Haidarabad 1 Deputy Collector returns the minimum size employed at $\frac{1}{3}$rd of an inch between each knot, 1 at $\frac{3}{8}$th, 1 at $\frac{1}{8}$th, 1 at $\frac{1}{11}$th, whilst in 2 they are stated to be too small to be measured. In the Central Provinces, out of 13 European reports, 3 give it at $\frac{1}{4}$th of an inch between each knot, 1 at $\frac{1}{6}$th, 5 at $\frac{1}{8}$th, 1 at $\frac{1}{10}$th, and 3 as the size of coarse muslin, a large needle, or very small. In Oudh, 9 European officials report thus :—1 that the minimum size of the mesh of nets employed is $\frac{3}{4}$th of an inch between each knot:

2, $\frac{1}{4}$th : 2, $\frac{1}{3}$rd : 2, $\frac{1}{6}$th, and 1 that it will arrest a grain of barley; thus, 67 European officials give the minimum size of the meshes of nets employed as follows:—from $\frac{1}{2}$ to 1 inch, 3 : from $\frac{1}{4}$th to $\frac{1}{2}$ an inch, 2 : from $\frac{1}{8}$th to $\frac{1}{4}$th of an inch, 10 : up to $\frac{1}{8}$th of an inch, 25 : small, 2 : very small, 8 : size of a grain of wheat or barley, 2 : of a large needle, 2 : of mosquito net or coarse muslin, 7 : too small to be measured, 4. In the N. W. Provinces, 16 European officials report as follows of the minimum size of the mesh of nets which are employed :— 1 at $\frac{1}{2}$ an inch, 1 at $\frac{1}{10}$th, 2 at $\frac{1}{3}$th, 3 at $\frac{1}{4}$th, 1 at $\frac{1}{5}$th, 6 at so minute that the smallest fish are stopped, 1 at the size of a grain of mucca, and 1 at that of a small pea. The Civil Surgeon of Azimgurh's statement of 4 inches between each knot is of course omitted from the foregoing. In Bengal (p. clxxxii), 7 European officials answer as follows :—1, that the meshes are minute : 1, $\frac{1}{20}$th of an inch : 1, $\frac{1}{8}$th : 1, $\frac{1}{4}$th, and 3 as large as a grain of mustard seed, rice, or mosquito net. Although the above gives the minimum size of the mesh, it must not be overlooked that, when formed of wicker-work, still smaller interstices, when possible, are employed. In Burma, 10 European officials report as follows :—2 give the smallest size at $\frac{1}{2}$ an inch, 1 at $\frac{2}{3}$rds, 1 at $\frac{1}{4}$th, 1 at $\frac{1}{6}$th, 1 at $\frac{1}{10}$th, and 4 as minute.

LXXII. A few observations are here necessary upon

<small>Seasons when different meshes are used.</small>

the meshes of the nets employed, and how it is that such different answers may be given by persons residing in the same locality, as to the minimum size which is used, whilst each merely reports on what he personally observes. The meshes of nets vary with the season of the year. Nets, whether used by one, two or more individuals during the rainy season, in inundated parts of the country, small water-courses, &c., have a very minute mesh; in fact, this is the period when those which will stop a grain of wheat ensnare an ant, not allow a large needle to pass, arrest the progress of a mosquito, or only permit water to go through, are called into play; now the fry are moving about, and seeking food and security in shallows and away from strong currents. As the muddy monsoon water subsides a little, and fishermen are able to wade up to their waists without the fear of being carried away by the current, the size of the mesh is increased, for the fry are becoming larger, roving further for their food, and the distance between knot and knot are found to have become as large as $\frac{1}{4}$th or $\frac{1}{3}$rd of an inch. As the river begins to clear, in places where large fish may still be taken in the plains, the distance between the knots often reaches one inch, whilst in the dry season even a greater mesh becomes employed. In localities as Burma, excluding the free fisheries, still larger meshes are used; likewise in Sind, where such would be considered an unwise procedure, but it will be found to be carried on elsewhere throughout the length and breadth of the plains, except where there is a lessee, whose interests would be affected thereby.

LXXIII. *Were the minimum size of the mesh of the net regulated, could such be a secondary cause of injury to fisheries?* Mr. Thomas, in his excellent report on the fisheries of South Canara, observes—the forbidding the use of a mesh of less than four inches in diameter would be unfortunate, as " the smaller sorts of fish, having an immunity from netting, must disproportionately increase on the larger netted sorts. Nature has arranged that the larger predatory fish shall balance the smaller, and thus maintain due proportions, but if one sort is netted by man and the other sort has immunity, the balance is disturbed, and the larger fish are no longer able to maintain their position." The Madras Revenue Board (Proc., July 13th, 1871), in their report on the foregoing, observe of the small fish :—" If a minimum of four inches be adopted, this quantity of fish will be, without any compensating advantage, entirely lost to the fish-eating population : further, the natural balance amongst the fishy tribes will be disturbed by killing only large fish, while the smaller kinds, which largely preponderate, are allowed by artificial protection to increase to an extent which must eventually cause certain kinds to disappear altogether." Now, I cannot coincide in this belief; I think it to be incorrect, and the proofs adduced, accurate as doubtless they are, may not be analogous to the state of affairs in India. I will, therefore, first examine this question theoretically, and secondly, give the result of actual experience in this country. It is a self-evident fact that amongst fish in the East, as in the other divisions of the animal kingdom, the forms which prey upon their neighbours are proportionately greater than in more temperate regions: Nature is on a vaster scale, but a few examples will make my meaning plainer. The wild-cat of Scotland is represented by the tiger and cheetah : the species of eagles and

[margin note: Effect of regulating the minimum size of the mesh of nets.]

hawks of England, by ten times the number and of far larger sizes; the lizards swell into crocodiles; the dog-fishes of European seas are seen in the form of many genera of sharks, some of enormous size; whilst, lastly, the herbivorous barbel assumes the proportion of the predaceous mahaseer fishes (for there are many species), all of which belong to the identical genus of their European relative. In fact, the waters of India are stocked with predaceous fish, and the question is, whether, if the small herbivorous forms, up to six inches in length, obtained immunity, they would destroy the larger predaceous varieties, either as eggs, fry, or by consuming all the food. It is here assumed that the fact is proved (which I give no opinion upon) that, due to immunity from netting, the smaller fish in the Thames are injuring the fisheries; also that minnows have starved out trout. It must be remembered that, due to indiscriminate netting, poaching, and the reception of filth in that river, salmon have disappeared and trout are now being artificially re-introduced; the state is abnormal. At Whitchurch, in Hampshire, I have seen the preservation of trout carried out so strictly that a sufficiency of food has not existed, and the fish have been starved. Likewise the destruction of hen-pheasants in preserves has been so energetically enforced, that the proportion between the males and females has been disarranged. But these are not analagous examples to what obtains in the East; the influence of over-protection is here unknown, whilst food for the fish is always abundant. Excluding marine forms, which are comparatively infinitesimal in South Canara rivers, we may divide the true fresh-water fishes as follows :—(1) large predaceous ; (2) large herbivorous ; (3) small predaceous ; and (4) small herbivorous kinds. Of the *large predaceous ones* we have two sub-divisions—those, as the mahaseer, which ascend to the hill streams to breed, leaving many of their young in the small pools there until the next year's monsoon permits them to descend to the plains; and secondly, those varieties, as the *Ophiocephalidæ*, which deposit their eggs in side channels in the plains. None of these could be included amongst the fish a four-inch, in circumference, mesh would not take. As they augmented, due to preservation of their fry, an increased supply of food would be desirable, and what could be superior to small fish which never attain any size ? As to the *large herbivorous ones*, protecting their fry could not injure fisheries. We now arrive at the small predaceous and small herbivorous kinds, which do not attain six inches in length, and whose existence in quantities might "eventually cause certain kinds to disappear altogether." Now, the most valuable species spawn on the hills, and which of the small predaceous fishes that do not attain six inches in length are found there? The solitary *Nandus marginatus*, Jerdon, usually rare and only seen in certain places. In the plains of Canara, are there more? Perhaps two, *Bagrus Malabaricus* and *Belone cancila*. I believe that, owing to the spines in the fins of this first, and the long-toothed snout of the second, they would be easily taken, when adults, in nets having meshes of the size proposed. I do not know another amongst these low-country predaceous fishes, able to destroy many young fish that would not reach six inches in length when adult. Lastly, we arrive at the *small herbivorous forms*. Certainly, there are several, some very numerous, but to accuse them of destroying the predaceous forms is like the old fable of the wolf and the lamb. I now come to the consideration of whether experience in India shows that such a result occurs where a like minimum size of mesh as proposed has been actually tried. I will only adduce two examples: others will be found in the appendix. First I would point to Sind, where nets with meshes below this size are not apparently in use (p. xxix, para. 47), but the due proportions are maintained, fish abounding; in fact, as the smaller herbivorous forms increase, so do the predaceous, which then appear to consume their neighbours instead of their own young. Likewise in the North-Western Provinces (pp. cxlix, cl), where, inadvertently having gone to a protected river, I reported how full it was stocked, a result due to destruction of small fish having been prohibited, a state of affairs differing from what was observed in contiguous pieces of water. Which, then, is most practical—to prohibit the destruction of small fish with the certainty of increasing the supply, or, fearing that if little fish were not taken, they might injurously affect or starve the larger ones, to permit their being freely captured? Or if such did occur, why not permit the capture of small fish during such months as fry are not moving about?

LXXIV. Damming waters may be done (1) for purposes of irrigation, (2) for irrigation conjointly with fishing, or (3) solely to obtain fish. Damming up waters for irrigation purposes has

<small>Damming waters for fishing purposes.</small>

already been discussed (pp. 7-14), as has likewise the conversion of simple irrigation weirs into traps for the taking of fish, and irrigation canals into vast slaughter-houses, besides unduly obstructing fish proceeding to their natural breeding-places, and by the use of fixed engines and traps in small water-courses, and at every drop from field, to field, forming a series of places for annihilation of fry. Here, therefore, the subject for consideration is damming waters for fishing purposes solely.

LXXV. Waters, as *rivers* or *streams*, may be dammed for fishing purposes with (1) or without (2) the assistance of weirs, or (3) hill streams may be dammed and diverted, or simply a a dam may be (4) employed to bund up, water, in order to facilitate the poisoning of fish. *Tanks* or standing pieces of water may be likewise dammed for fishing (5) as a common occurrence, or (6) else as the waters are drying up; (7) Holes may be dug at the sides of rivers with which a connecting channel is cut, the fish enticed in communication cut off, and the water baled out; or (8) small bunds be erected parallel to the rivers' course, fry driven or enticed in, and all destroyed. Hill streams may be dammed and diverted for fishing purposes—a plan which obtains in the Himalayas and elsewhere. The effects of damming up and diverting the minor streams into *kools* or channels for turning mills, and which is used as a fertile instrument of destroying small fish (pp. iv, xviii) has been already referred to. In the Panjáb, at Kangra (p. xvi), the zemindars do a great deal of mischief in the early part of the rains, by bringing the fish into side streams, and then draining off the water and leaving them on dry ground: young and old are caught in this way. In Bombay, at Satara (p. lix), fish are taken by diverting the natural course of a stream so as to make all the water pass through a large basket trap, or by throwing a bank of sand across a river or *nalla* and obtaining the fish in the usual way, *viz.*, by baling. In Haidarabad, it is observed (p. cxiii) that fish are taken by traps, which is done by erecting rough stone piles on both sides of a stream, then spreading a mat of the *nurgood* plant over the piles; the stream is then diverted so as to pour over the mat, on which, as the water falls, the fish are taken. *Hill streams* may be also diverted, and the modes employed are as follows:—In the Doon (p. cxlix) "from March to the beginning of the rains, streams are dammed and turned. In this district the mountain torrents,

<small>Damming and diverting rivers or streams, &c., for fishing.</small>

where they burst from the hills, have three or four different beds, all of which are full during the rains, but afterwards only one; one year the stream is in one of these beds, another year another, and so on. The poachers choose a spot where the stream and an old bed are in close proximity: both have good pools in them; they fix nets right across the stream, about a mile or more below this spot; first nets with large meshes, and then nets with smaller meshes. These nets are kept to the bottom with heavy stones. When the nets are all ready, they dam up the stream, and open a water-way into the old bed: the force of the water soon cuts a deep way for itself, and then the late bed of the stream is left dry, except in the deep holes: all fish that try to escape down are stopped by the nets." The large fish are taken away, the fry left to die as the pools dry up, and there they sometimes lie six or eight inches deep. The poachers do the same lower down, and after a month or so begin again at the top of the hill river as before. This is also carried on in Rohilcund (p. cliii). Or *low-country streams* may be dammed for poisoning purposes, as in Ratnagari (p. liv), in Belgaum (p. lii), or South Canara (p. lxxxviii): or for placing nets in artificial openings constructed in them, as in Puna (p. xlix): or to assist in baling them out, as in Nasik (p. lviii), Colaba (p. lix), and Dharwar (p. liii and lxii); also in Madras, as at Kurnal (p. lxxxiv), or in the Kistna Collectorate (p. xcv), as well as in Nellur (p. xcvi). In the Central Provinces, as at Jabalpur (p. cxix and cxxiv), and in Oudh, as at Sultanpur (p. cxxxviii). *Tanks* are drained at times solely for the purpose of obtaining the contained fish, as at Cuddalore in Madras; at Dharwar (p. liii): whilst at Tanjur it is said that it is only small tanks that are annually drained for the purpose of being filled with fresh-water from river channels, at which period advantage is taken to capture the fish in them (p. lxxix). In some cases as tanks are drying up (p. clxxxix) a bank is thrown across them—first one half is baled out, and then the other, and so all the fish taken; but this is said to be done to prevent them from dying in the mud (see para. LXVII). Holes are sometimes dug by the sides of rivers, as in the Panjáb (p. xxiv), or Burma (p. cxcviii); a connecting channel is cut; when fish have been enticed in, a bund is thrown across the connecting channel, the water in the hole baled out, and the fish captured; this is also done in Haidarabad (p. cxiii). In Orissa (p. clxxxix), damming is extensively practised; as the rivers commence drying up, earthen bunds are raised along its bed parallel with the course of the stream, but narrowing towards its lower end; fish are driven in, the ends are stopped, and every one is taken. This bunding and lading takes place everywhere in India and Burma for the purpose of capturing fish. In the latter province (p. ccviii) streams are bunded into tanks by an earthen dam being thrown across them, which of course causes the water to collect above : next smaller ones are erected parallel to the course of the stream, and cutting off a portion of it from the main channel. The water is laded out, the whole of the fish captured, and this is continued portion by portion till not a fish is left. In making the earthen dam, two rows of strong stakes, six feet apart, are driven in across the stream; the interval is filled in with grass and clayey mud.

LXXVI. Waters may be poisoned without such being done for fishing purposes, but the effects of which are injurious or even destructive on fisheries : such may be (1) accidental or natural, as by monsoon floods washing a large amount of mud suddenly into rivers and causing the fish to perish, as in Coimbatore (p. lxxxvii) and elsewhere; (2) with the muddy water some unwholesome agent may be conjoined, as decayed leaves of trees and shrubs, or other vegetable substances. It is observed in Satara (p. l) that when the rivers become muddy at the commencement of the monsoon, fish die in large numbers, also when they become nearly dry at the close of the hot weather; (3) such may also be due to the inherent poisonous nature of the fruit, leaves, or other component parts of trees or shrubs, which during the dry or cold season have fallen into contiguous streams, and there remaining, due to there being no current, have become an infusion of poison, which with the outburst of the rains is carried down to the main rivers. None of these causes appear susceptible of alleviation; but it is observed in the North-Western Provinces that in the Koana River (p. clxii), standing fishing weirs are permitted to block up the whole of the water-way: as the water becomes poisoned or otherwise unsuited for fish-life, all the fishes up-stream endeavor to descend to the purer portions of the river. But an impassable fishing weir quite stops the way; the owner allows no passage, so there they are allowed to miserably perish, and, useless as food, become carted away as manure. (4) In South Canara the refuse

Waters may be poisoned.

of the coffee pulpers is stated to be poisonous to the fishes of the rivers into which they are drained, but if no standing weirs exist below them, the injury thus occasioned cannot be compared to that done by fixed engines permitted to span streams. Coir is extensively manufactured in Malabar by decomposing the outer shell of cocoanuts in large pits dug by the sides of streams and backwaters. Here, covered over by mud, they are left to rot, and when these offensive pits are opened into the stream, the fluid decomposed vegetable substance which is washed out is a cause of destruction to fish-life. It is remarkable that putrid water does not invariably destroy fish residing in it: near Berhampur, I was shown a small tank in which the water was perfectly putrid, and the natives asserted that it had been so for months, but still fish resided there. The smell was most offensive, and its bed was deep in dark slimy mud. After much persuasion the fishermen were induced to net it, and the fish were as numerous as in other pieces of water in the vicinity; their colour was somewhat darker, but they were reported to be fit for food. However, the fishermen at last confessed that they did not intend personally to eat them, but proposed disposing of them in the bazar.

LXXVII. Water or fish may be poisoned for the purpose of obtaining the finny tribes. This is mostly done in one of the following ways :—The use of poisonous substances, or by rendering the water unfit to sustain their lives, or preventing the fish access to air necessary for respiration. (1.) As regards poisonous substances employed, these are numerous, and most are detailed in the Appendix—milk bush, tobacco leaves, *Cocculus Indicus,* many poisonous jungle fruits, &c. This is usually carried on during the dry months of the year, when the pools in rivers are still, and hardly any current exists. It is very easy to collect the poisons, to throw them into a deep still pool, and quietly await the fish floating up intoxicated to the surface. It is immaterial that thousands of immature fish and insects, &c., which form the food of adults, are thus slaughtered. The poacher is in no need of them; he obtains as much as he can bear away, totally unconcerned that his gains may be unwholesome, and the river water rendered poisonous to human beings, birds and cattle that imbibe it. He sells the proceeds of his nefarious work, and that without molestation, and, if spoken to, calmly terms such " a free industry" which is permitted by authority. In Oudh

(p. cxxxi), it is stated that fishing is carried on by channels of water being enclosed, and powders obtained from a poisonous wild fruit thrown in. An opening is cut to receive fresh-water, as the humane people think it wrong to kill all, and as the intoxicated fish float to the surface, they are beaten on the head with sticks or caught by the hands, and this wholesale destruction is done merely for sport, as those captured are not deemed good to eat. The same is reported from the Central Provinces (p. cxix), whilst the poison employed may render the water undrinkable for several seasons (p. lxxviii). Again, fish may be choked (2) by means of mud. As I have already explained (p. xl), some fish breathe by means of imbibing oxygen directly from the water; their blood goes to their gills; here the carbon formed by waste unites with the oxygen of the air in solution in the water, and the simple process of breathing is effected. Now, natives have discovered that if they stir up the mud, so as to thicken the water, and also frighten the fish they rush about, their increased movements require increased respiratory action, but the mud chokes their gills, and, half-suffocated, they become captured with ease. (3) Some fish are what I termed compound-breathers (see p. 24); they can imbibe air direct, and these are the tropical ophiocephalidæ (see p. 26), &c. The Burmese know that mud mixed with water will not affect them; they put their mouths above the surface and get what air they require. So here another plan has to be followed. As the water gets low and muddy, a large sail composed of cloth, split bamboo or anything of that sort is spread over the fluid mud where they are; this precludes their rising to respire, their carbon cannot unite with oxygen and be carried off; they become asphyxiated, and are thus captured.

LXXVIII. Besides the foregoing modes of taking fish, there are many other minor plans pursued. Sheets have already been remarked upon as used to take the fry of fishes which have gone up small water-courses, or got into shallow water. They are also used as dip-nets, being sunk in the water and simply hauled up again when fry have swam over their surface, as in the Panjáb (p. xx); or bushes may be placed over these cloths, especially in shallows; the fry seek shelter under them, and the whole are lifted up, as in Orissa; or those sheets as dip-nets may be baited with gram or bread, as in Bombay (p. lviii). Basket-work is also used by placing two rattans crossing one another in the middle; their ends

Minor modes of fishery.

are bent down, and the two arches thus formed are secured by strings in the shape of a square; here a net is attached, and this is jammed down upon fish, as in Panjáb (p. xxii), Orissa, and throughout the East. Fish may be simply frightened into permitting themselves to be captured: thus ropes, bones, as in Orissa, cocoanut leaves, as in Malabar, or other leaves, or the stalks of *kurbi* or *jowaree*, as in Bombay (p. xlvii), or pieces of pith (solah) or light wood, as in Bengal, or bundles of grass attached along their whole length, and by stretching such across a stream, and constantly jerking it, fish are driven into nets, or even take refuge under the rivers' banks where they are captured by the hand. When tanks are drying up, fish are taken in the mud by the hand, as observed upon in Bombay (p. liv.). Snares are universally employed, and these of most varied descriptions are (see pp. l, lix, xciii, xciv, xcv, cxiii, &c) used in rivers and *nallas* all the year round. Hooks for fishing are not employed in some parts, as inland in Orissa, or much in the hilly districts where poaching is preferred as easier and more killing: but there are many modes of using hooks as barbarous as they are destructive. One method is to fix a row of hooks on a line in a pass in a hill stream (p. cl) by which many fish ascending or descending become foully hooked; some are thus caught, more get away horribly injured. Besides this, snagging is employed in the Himalayan rivers; in fact, such appears to have been sold to the villagers in some places by the British revenue authorities (p. clvi). This "right or amusement" (p. cliv), which it is proposed should not be interfered with, consists of arming a cord with large iron hooks at intervals of two or three feet: by means of bits of wood they are retained with their points uppermost. This line is thrown across a stream and kept 18 inches or two feet below the surface: here it is held on either bank by a man, others drive the fish towards the spot, and, as one passes over this humane instrument of capture, the cord is jerked for a hook to transfix the game. Dexterity in the use of this line armed with hooks has resulted from constant practice, and many fish are thus captured. But if some are thus taken, very many more are merely wounded. The poachers endeavour to hook the fish by it under surface, but as may be anticipated, although some hooks enter sufficiently deep to obtain a firm hold of the abdominal walls, such is by no means invariably the case. The struggles of the wounded creature often causes it to break away, usually with a portion of its intestines trailing behind it. If its gill-covers have been injured, respiration may be wholly or entirely stopped: if its mouth is much torn, feeding may be prevented. Thus crippled, it wanders away to sicken, and, unless death soon puts an end to its miserable existence, it becomes emaciated, and, should it be so captured, it is useless for food except to the lower animals. Baited hooks are sometimes affixed to lines which are attached to bamboos fixed in the bed of a river, or to bushes at its edge, and these are so placed that when a fish is hooked, the line runs out. Or a line is placed across a suitable spot in a river, floated by gourds, so that the baited hooks which are attached to it by short lines do not touch the bottom: these are visited every few hours, and are found to be very killing. In the same way, two posts are fixed, one on either side of a stream or piece of water, a rope stretches from one to the other, and short lines with baited hooks are strung every yard or so along its entire extent. Night-lines baited with frogs are employed in places. Spearing fish is also extensively practised by torch light, as in the Panjáb (p. xx) or Bombay (p. lvii): or in the day-time, mostly during the cold months of of the year when they are not very active, two persons usually punt about as quietly as possible over places where fish lie, and the one standing on the prow of the canoe spears the game below him: this is done in Sind, the Panjáb (p. xxv), Madras, the Central Provinces (p. cxxiv), and elsewhere. Shooting fish with guns is reported as carried on in Oudh (p. cxxxviii), whilst the use of cross-bows for this purpose is not uncommon in Malabar. Breeding-fish are knocked on the head with sticks, as in Bombay (p. lxi); and in the Himalayas " breeding-fish are destroyed in the commencement of the rains in every conceivable manner: they at that time run up small streams, and are there killed with sticks, caught in nets, in baskets, in temporary cruives, by hooks fastened in great numbers on lines, and many other ways" (p. cxlviii); or as observed in Mysore (p. cii) by the amildars of the Nagar division, that fish are taken by nets, traps, hooks, cloths, and by hand, by baskets of different shapes, by damming and draining off the water, by shooting, by striking with clubs, with swords, or with choppers, by weirs and fixed engines; in short, by poaching practices of every kind, as well as by fishing with rods and lines, and by poisoning the pools of water. Even the eggs of fish do not escape this general hunt, to which the persecuted piscine tribes are subjected. In South Canara (p. xcii), men search in the rivers for hillocks wherein spawn has been left, gather the ova, and make it into cakes which are considered a delicacy. In the North-Western Provinces (p. clix) at Goruckpur, the Mallahs and Kewats dig up the spawn of fish, and after having prepared it, either sell or consume it.

VERMIN WHICH DESTROY FISH.

LXXIX. *What are the vermin which are inimical to fish?* A difficulty arises in commencing this subject, as to whether to begin with those which are most destructive to them in their ova state as fry, or when more mature. One Commissioner (p. clxvii) considers that my proposition of offering rewards for crocodiles appears to him *absurd*, and that "it would be equally or more advisable to proscribe frogs and paddy-birds which eat the spawn and young fry, and probably destroy far more fish than the crocodile." One step further, perhaps, might be suggested, that natives provided with microscopes should be entertained to examine all the spawning beds of fishes, in order to detect and eradicate the microscopic vermin which destroy the fertility of the fish-ova : or peons armed with nets be sent to arrest the water-beetles that make a meal of fish-eggs. Setting aside, however, such ultra views, I propose commencing with the crocodiles, of which there are two distinct genera in the waters of India. The Assistant Commissioner of Delhi suggested one rupee per running foot be paid for them : whilst the Madras Revenue Board proposed a somewhat smaller scale (p. lxxiv). Also in the Agra Division (p. clxxi), that "any effective measures for reducing the enormous number of crocodiles in our rivers would do much more, than any restriction on fishing, to increase the quantity of fish in them. The destruction of crocodiles' eggs could no doubt be extensively effected by the offer of an adequate reward. But any such scheme, to be of use, would have to be carried out, not only in these provinces, but all down the length of the rivers which traverse them : otherwise, so fast as the crocodiles were destroyed here, others would travel up and take their places from below." Likewise the Officiating Collector of Etawah observes (p. clxxi) that, "if Government will give a reward for crocodiles' eggs, there is no doubt that plenty would be brought in."

Crocodiles as vermin.

LXXX. The true fish-eating crocodile, *Gavialis Gange-*
The fish-eating crocodile. *ticus*, Gmelin, which attains upwards of 20 feet in length, is found throughout the Indus, Ganges, Jumna, Brahmaputra, Mahanuddi and their affluents, also in some of the intervening rivers, but I have not observed it in Burma or Madras. This species has a long and slender snout, is usually timid of man, excepting when the locality where its eggs are deposited in the sand is invaded. It does not appear to be a feeder on carrion, but fish, turtles and tortoises form its diet. In 1868 it was deemed one of the sights at Cuttack to watch these enormous reptiles feeding below the irrigation weir, which was impeding the upward ascent of breeding-fish. Their long brown snouts would be seen rising to the surface of the water, with a fish cross-wise in their jaws: they tossed their heads, the finny prey was thus flung up into the air, descending head foremost fell into their captors' comparatively small mouths. One could not resist thinking that the crocodiles were attempting to teach the Europeans and natives a lesson, by practically demonstrating to them the folly of permitting a wholesale waste of good animal food to nourish the carcasses of huge useless reptiles, and which might better be employed for the same purpose by man. To show their fecundity, I may mention that the overseer in charge of the Narraje weir, meeting with a brood, destroyed 69 in three hours by shooting. At this place I obtained a young one which had become entangled by its teeth in a fishing net, and on enquiring of the fishermen whether they ever killed them, they at once protested against such a course. Their argument was—"are not we both of the fish-destroying races, and how could we be so cruel as to slaughter them?" As to the destruction they occasioned, they merely remarked that they would do the same if they could, and I can personally testify to their catching all they were able. However, it must not be expected that fishermen will destroy those vermin when young, neither will they shoot them when old, as they do not employ guns. But will the native sportsman be likely to do this? Certainly not, as he has no inducement to do so, and he will never waste his ammunition on crocodiles, which would be of no advantage to him when killed. With fisheries that are deteriorating, the presence of these large fish-eating reptiles might be dispensed with, as they are not required to keep up the balance of Nature, neither are they useful as

scavengers, whilst their destruction can only be effected by the offering of rewards for them or their eggs.

LXXXI. The common crocodiles, *Crocodilus palustris*,

The common crocodile. Less., and *C. porosus*, Schn., are found in most parts of India. These reptiles, although usually termed man-eaters or snub-nosed crocodiles, also assist in depopulating the waters of fish, and it may be that it is only when unable to obtain a sufficiency of the finny tribes, or carrion, that they attack man and large mammals; but having once tasted blood, they appear to be eager to do so again. In some of the irrigation canals one or more of these creatures may usually be seen below the lochs where there are pools stocked with fish, and when the latter fails, they turn their attention to the cattle. To show how these monsters increase in suitable localities, I may mention that in December 1868 I saw four at Cuttack below the large weir; six weeks subsequently they had increased to nine, besides many little ones. As it must be admitted that 10 seers of large fish a day would be absolutely necessary for the sustenance of each of these nine adults, which measured from about ten to sixteen feet in length, or 90 seers in all, whilst the bazar price at this period was about four annas a seer, we see that good wholesome food to the value of Rs. 22-3 was being daily sacrificed at this one spot. My suggestion of a reward of Rs. 5 each was disregarded, although the amount would have amply sufficed. If, for argument's sake, we consider these nine have not increased, nor the young lived to grow up, and the daily amount consumed is computed to continue the same all the year round, what must be the result? As it is now upwards of $3\frac{1}{2}$ years since this saving, or rather non-expenditure of Rs. 45 was decided upon, and assuming the crocodiles' appetites have only induced them to limit their captures to fish, we might have a loss or waste of Rs. 28,732 worth of fish used for their support. I merely give this as an illustration of which plan is the most practical. Of course there are many disturbing elements, as they occasionally vary their diet by eating a human being, horse, or cow, which would reduce the amount of fish consumed; but the above figures are only intended to show the waste of food computed at the bazar rates as existing at the period I was at Cuttack. The Commissioner of Assam observes,—" at all events, I have little doubt but that the number of fishes destroyed by the crocodiles on the Brahmaputra is beyond all proportion greater than what is destroyed by man, and it would seem, therefore, that the first duty of a system of fish-conservancy for that river would be the killing of the crocodiles." The Collector of South Canara considers (Oct. 25th, 1872) that a most important subject is the destruction of crocodiles and their eggs, as well as otters. "Much of the preservation of fishes will be in vain if their natural enemies have liberty to feed and increase on them." Also in the North-West Provinces (p. clxiv), that "there is no doubt crocodiles destroy large quantities of fish, and might themselves be destroyed with very little trouble." Their destructiveness is also referred to at Jhansi (pp. clxvi, clxvii). Doubtless crocodiles have a redeeming quality, being the natural scavengers of rivers (p. clxxii), but against this may be placed the destruction of the lives of human beings and cattle yearly caused by them. If the fisheries become much further depopulated, from whence are these reptiles to obtain food? Human beings are no longer permitted to immolate themselves at the side of the Ganges, nor are relatives allowed, as a last filial duty, to fill their expiring parents' mouths with mud from its sacred bed, neither are corpses interred in that holy stream, so food must be diminishing. If fish likewise become insufficient, these reptiles will be compelled by the natural law of self-preservation to help themselves to cattle from the neighbouring country, or else feed on such human beings as unwarily approach too close to the waters they reside in. And this is no fancy sketch, but the simple fact. I will only adduce two instances. At Cullara, five miles below Kendraputna in the Nuna river, is a hole to which crocodiles resort in the dry season. Of course the fish in such pools are soon exhausted, and a short time before I was there in 1868 these monsters had carried off five adults. Near the Baropa weir two women and one horse were carried off in a single month by crocodiles in the Mundapur tank. However, taking all things into considerations, rewards for the destruction of crocodiles, usually termed man-eaters, might be fairly offered in certain localities for them or their eggs. Small rewards for the latter, it is observed (p. cli), would aid in the extermination of the reptiles, and this could be easily arranged for. Another result would be gained by demonstrating, and may be convincing, even those who are now averse to believe that destroying the eggs and the young, as well as killing the adults, may in time eventuate in a decrease of a breed of animals, even in India.

LXXXII. Otters do an immensity of injury in some rivers, especially in those of hilly districts; and when they have exhausted the fish, some turn their attention to frogs. Along the Himalayas they abound, but at Gurwal are reported not to destroy fish in the proportion man does, and offering sufficient rewards would be very expensive (p. clviii). In Jhansi they are included amongst the real enemies to fish (p. clxvi), and that they destroy the large ones in the deep pools of the rivers (p. clxvii). In Kumaon they are said to do some little injury (p. clv), also in Malabar and elsewhere; but until the more serious evil of standing fishing weirs and traps are dealt with, perhaps the otters might be left alone. An otter is not a fair eater: he prefers fish, but being an epicure, he limits himself to their most tasty portions, of which he takes a few mouthfuls, and, returning to the water, repeats the operation. Where fisheries are protected, and not wastefully fished, these animals would certainly form good objects for rewards: thus, amongst the excellent rules proposed by the Dehra Doon Association, exists one of rewards for otters. In Malabar otters form an article of food to some of the lower castes.

Otters as vermin.

LXXXIII. There are other vermin destructive to fish, but for which I do not propose any rewards should be offered; there are *birds* of many sorts too numerous to mention in this place. Likewise *snakes*, which luxuriate in irrigation canals, and revel at large weirs. At the Upper Coleroon weir, as the freshes began to subside, and only a little water was passing over the apron, I could plainly perceive them watching to capture the fish which were vainly endeavouring to ascend. I should imagine that I never saw less than twenty every evening on the down-stream face of this weir. I was present when the water was cut off from the Eastern Jumna Canal, and numbers of large snakes were then to be seen. *Tortoises* and *turtles* likewise are fish-consumers, whilst *predaceous fishes* prey on their weaker neighbours, amongst which freshwater sharks are frequently mentioned as at (pp. clv, clxvi). Near Ganjam an official informed me that he went out one night to see how murrul, *Ophiocephalus striatus*, Bloch., were captured. The native fisherman had provided himself with a long flexible bamboo as a rod, whilst his hook was

Minor vermin which kill fish.

baited with a live frog. Hardly had the frog splashed into the water, when a moderately sized murrul seized and swallowed it. Desirous of observing what would next ensue, the fish was left as a bait. Before long a large water-snake was perceived swimming towards it, and soon had the fish in its capacious jaws, thus the three were pulled out of the water at once, and the snake despatched. The porpoise, *Platanista Gangetica*, is stated likewise to be very destructive to fish (p. clxxi).

OBJECTIONS TO LEGAL ACTION BEING TAKEN.

LXXXIV. Objections have been advanced against any action being taken upon the present mode of working the fresh-water fisheries of India, and that by many officials. Some apparently judge from the district they are in; others from single localities, or the report of a subordinate, whose very observations demonstrate his ignorance. A wide and general enquiry appears necessary before giving any definite opinions, and those of others who have any knowledge upon the subject deserve most careful consideration. I, therefore, propose shortly adverting to the various reasons that have been adduced by those who advocate leaving matters alone, and such may be arranged under the following heads:—(1) Opposed to Divine laws. (2) General objections. (3) Legal objections. (4) As unnecessary. (5) On zoological grounds. (6) On political grounds. (7) For social reasons. (8) As interference with old customs. (9) Interference with trade.

<small>General objections to action being taken.</small>

LXXXV. First, prohibiting unrestricted capture of fry one official considered would be in opposition to Divine laws, but, as he does not advance such to be contrary to the "laws of Nature," one can only quote a recent writer's observation—"The laws of Nature are the voice of God." In Bombay at Kaira (p. lvii), the common superstitious belief is that the deities of the river have been displeased by the withholding of the offerings formerly made by travellers who crossed it in carts previously to the opening of the railway. As a consequence, Divine anger has shown itself in decreasing the fishes in the Mhye. Hindus think it better to take the life of one large fish than many small ones p. xiv), as observed in the Panjáb.

<small>Divine objections to prohibiting the capture and sale of fry.</small>

LXXXVI. Secondly, general objections. The Officiating Chief Commissioner of Oudh (p. cxxix) deprecates legislative

<small>General objections to legal action.</small>

interference with the capture and sale of fish, as it seems to him such can only be justifiable when it can be demonstrated that, unless the Legislature step in, the existence of that important article of diet will cease altogether. A contrary opinion to that advanced in 1868 by the Officiating Chief Commissioner, and it may perhaps be open to discussion whether waiting until fish have almost been exterminated is a wise and prudent course. In Oudh, three-fourths of the markets are said to have a larger demand than supply, and that fry are extensively destroyed. The Chief Commissioner of the Central Provinces (p. cxviii) considers that, should legislation be decided upon, a very wide discretion should be given to Local Governments in framing the rules, leaving such to be adapted to the case of each district and river. Whilst it has been proposed in the Panjáb that (p. xvi) every Deputy Collector should be left to his own devices to stop the destruction of fish, but it is here overlooked that they might have done this before now, but apparently have neglected the subject; consequently, if no rules are framed, what grounds exist for anticipating an improved state of affairs? It has been observed in Bombay that a general Act would be unworkable, therefore it would be better to have one which could be applied, when considered necessary, to particular rivers and localities favourable for fish-breeding (pp. xliii, xlviii), a subject which will have to be more fully considered. In the North-Western Provinces, that the irritation caused would be serious (p. cxlviii), although no such result has followed identical regulations in the Panjáb (p. cxlvii), whilst in the Doon, in the North-West, the zemindars (p. cxlix) have carried out the propositions to prohibit nets with meshes having less than $1\frac{1}{2}$ inches between each knot, and stopped the damming and turning of streams for fishing purposes. In Burma, the Chief Commissioner is satisfied "that any attempt to prohibit the capture of small fish would be as impolitic as it is unnecessary." Financial reasons have also been adduced that a loss of revenue would at first be a consequence of regulating the minimum size of the mesh of nets (p. xii), "although it is probable that it would recover itself as large fish increased in numbers, and the fishermen become accustomed to the system." That in Bombay additional police would be rendered necessary (pp. l, li), also in Madras (pp. lxxxii, lxxxvii), and Oudh (p. cxxi). However, in the Panjáb it is observed that for carrying out such a scheme

(p. ix), no separate establishment is proposed; and in Haidarabad (p. cxi) that no establishment would be necessary.

LXXXVII. Thirdly, legal objections. Here, however, such difficulties are advanced that they can scarcely be replied to. The principles of English law are entirely absent from some of the reporters' replies, and statements are advanced so utterly incorrect, that it has appeared better to reply to them where raised, and to give a short synopsis of what the British law really is: only drawing attention to the fact that license gives no right (p. lxiv), but is revocable at will. The Collector of Puna remarks—no private rights really exist, but that of prescription may be claimed (p. xlviii). Without reference to such being invalid by the law of Great Britain, I here give the observations of an officer in the North-Western Provinces (p. clv) on this subject:—"The prescriptive rights of the people will possibly require legislative action, but it is quite time that the common-sense principle was declared, once for all, that no people in the world, other than savages, who do whatever pleases them, have a prescriptive right to do anything which destroys or diminishes a spontaneous source of food. The same principle has been applied in the use of water and timber; why should it not be applied to so important an article as human food? * * Prescriptive right to do wrong things, or injudiciously exterminate a natural source of food-supply, has only existed until now, because there has not been a Government strong or civilized enough to control it. Thus 'suttee,' 'thuggee', 'human sacrifices' were all prescriptive rights in their way, and had, moreover, a certain amount of legal sanction, and yet, because they involved loss of human life, they were very rightly swept away, and so can this right of wanton destruction of human food be." Rights exist, according to the Madras Revenue Board (p. xc), for people to catch fish how they please in their own fields, a right not admitted by the British law, but highly punishable; even if such is legal, as observes the Collector of South Canara,—" I cannot but think that the time has arrived when intelligence should interfere between ignorance and waste." Communal rights are observed upon (p. lxxviii), as existing amongst village communities to fisheries within the limits of their own villages; whilst the Collector of Tanjur (p. lxxix) remarks that the right to the fishery of all tanks, as well as village

Legal objections.

channels in his district, belongs to the merassidars having been conceded to them in the orders of Government of 11th June 1857. The Commissioner of West Berar, on the other hand (p. cx), says fishing rights do not exist, for under a ryotwari settlement, all fisheries are common property, indeed, belong properly to Government. Finally, a curious legal objection to a law regulating the minimum size of the mesh of nets is propounded (p. lxxxiii) as follows:—"I do not believe any Magistrate would convict except under peculiar circumstances," and as this opinion comes from a gentleman, who, I believe is, invested with magisterial powers, it deserves attention, as it will hardly be of use framing rules if convictions under such are unobtainable.

LXXXVIII. Fourthly, that regulations are unnecessary. This plea is advanced under numerous heads. Thus, as remarked upon by the Collector of Kurnal (p. lxxxi)—"if anything could repress their destruction to any extent, it would be the forbidding to catch fish with roe; but this would be tantamount to depriving the people of a wholesome and pleasant diet, and interfere with the great traffic in fish-roes that now takes place." Whilst objections exist against prohibiting the sale of the fry of fish as they are more tasty (p. xiv), and that an esteemed delicacy are the fry of large fish (p. lxxv); that temporarily they form an important article of food for a number of the poor classes, and stopping such an enjoyment would be a hardship. It would be cruel (p. lxxxii) to stop the catching of little fish (p. lxix). That, of course, fishermen will protect them in leased fisheries, elsewhere their destruction is immaterial (p. ccxxii). That regulations are unnecessary, as the fish in districts are valueless, so it does not matter what becomes of them (p. xlvi); insignificant, so do not require protecting (p. lxxiv). That the supply of fish is said to be inexhaustible in Bellary (p. lxxix), and their capture requires encouragement, although the tehsildars consider a decrease already apparent, and the demand always greater than the supply (pp. xcvi). That in the Kistna in the Kurnal Collectorate (p. lxxxii), "let man use any appliances he can think of for taking fish, he will never be able to affect the supply in any appreciable way as regards this district;" whilst the Tehsildar of Ramalkota (p. xcvii) remarks of the same river in the same place, "that it is asserted by all the fishermen of whom I have enquired that the river stock has considerably decreased of late years." That in Rohilcund (p. cli), "the size and areas of water in the main streams of India are so great that the amount of fish taken out is nothing as compared with the stock remaining, and they need no protection." That it is locally unnecessary, as in portions of Sind, due to the paucity of population, the rapidity and dangerous character of the River Indus, and owing to the security the immature fish obtain during the inundation season. The same is also observed in Burma, where it is remarked that if the people may not kill the little fish, a large number of persons will stop fishing (p. ccxxii). Or that any such regulation would possibly deprive a poor man of his dinner (p. ccxxiv). Or that it is no use legislating for perennial pieces of water as they do not dry up, and fish may take care of themselves (pp. lxxxii and xlvi); whilst it would be equally useless legislating for those that are not perennial, because as the water dried up the contained fish would perish (pp. xi, xviii, xxxii, xli, lxxviii, lxxxi, lxxxv). In fact, it may be doubtful whether it is advisable or not to pass any rules as regards the minimum size of the mesh of the net which may be used in waters that yearly dry up, and after all communication has been naturally cut off from large contiguous tanks or running streams or rivers. No irrigated field is perennial whilst fish and their fry cannot be prevented from extending their range into such localities. A general destruction of fry is pointed out by some native officials as the cause of the present deterioration of the fresh-water fisheries (pp. cxxiv, cxxv, clxxv) of India. One European, however, observes upon the following strong reason for not regulating the minimum size of the mesh in future "that another class of poor people would be pestered with orders and regulations, which they and their neighbours would not understand" (p. cxix).

LXXXIX. Fifthly, zoological grounds are adduced why prohibiting the capture and sale of the fry of large fishes could not be enforced. The ignorance of the common policeman is adverted to as unable to discriminate between fry and adult fish (p. cxxxi); whilst in Bengal, Madras, and Burma the want of a work on the fishes of the Indian Empire is spoken of. Certainly, such a law, if passed, would be exceedingly difficult to work until a comprehensive and illustrated treatise is in the hands of executive officers. Thus, the term

Zoological reasons against action being taken.

mahaseer includes several of the large sorts of barbel, of which India possesses upwards of sixty species.

XC. Sixthly, on political grounds, regulations, it is surmised, might in the Panjáb (p. ix) give rise to irritation amongst a border population; or in Bombay, amongst the Bhils of Kandeish (p. xli), the forest rules having curtailed their privilege of cutting and selling timber from the jungles. That such might cause discontent, as regulating the minimum size of the mesh would be unpopular in Bombay (pp. xlvii, l), occasion great dissatisfaction in Madras (pp. lxxxvi, lxxxviii), or be fraught with annoyance and vexation to the fishing classes, or unpopular (p. lxxi) in the Central Provinces (p. cxviii). Or that regulations might set up alarm, due to "the natural dislike and prejudice of the rustic population against any innovation whatever in their implements for carrying on their craft (p. cxxxii), and that innovations would be opposed by prejudice (p. xli). That prohibiting catching fry would be interfering with a "free industry" (p. lxxi), and the prohibition of destroying fish-in-roe would interfere with the present traffic in fish-roe (p. lxxxi), whilst stopping the sale of the fry in the bazars would be a measure "obnoxious to sellers and consumers, and at present seems quite uncalled for." If fry are not permitted to be publicly disposed of, it is suggested that they will be privately sold or kept for home consumption (p. cxii). In the North-Western Provinces, that "the Tharoos who live in the Turai spend much of their time in the rains in catching small-fish (fry), and would be very discontented if their fishing were interfered with." So it is proposed to let them do it in any way (p. cliii).

<small>Political reasons against action being taken.</small>

XCI. Seventhly, regulations are disliked for social reasons :—thus, in Bombay at Ahmedabad, it is considered better that some fry be destroyed than that further opportunities should be afforded to the lower grades of Government servants, and to bigotted Hindus, to turn the intentions of Government to their own profit (p. xliii). In the Central Provinces (p. cxviii), that close and constant inspection would be necessary to keep the nets up to the standard, and the uses to which the opportunities thus given to petty officials would be put, can easily be imagined. In Madras at Kurnal (p. lxxxi), that the only way in which Government could interfere would be by means of an establishment of subordinates, who would avail

<small>Social objections.</small>

themselves of their authority to practise extortion and oppress the poor, and never really repress the destruction of fish. That the police would find in such a law the means of extortion in Oudh (p. cxxxi). That in the North-Western Provinces, their caste is so good that they could not be expected to interfere regarding fish, except to cause oppression (p. cli). In Mirzapur (p. clxiii), that to carry out rules, the police or revenue establishments who might have to see to it are so venal, that they would expect to obtain fish without payment. In Azimgurh, that any establishments " would be mere engines of oppression and extortion" (p. clxv). One official (p. clxx) considers the State has now enough to do " in carrying through public measures that are not supported by the opinion of the country;" therefore, regulating the fisheries should be postponed: another (p. clxx), that it is undesirable that the public mind should be disturbed " by gratuitous interference on the part of an alien administration, enforced by not very trustworthy agency." In short, several of the officials of this province consider the police, and subordinate natives under their supervision and control, are so very untrustworthy that regulations would eventuate in unlimited extortion! That it would be unkind to the very poor to prohibit the capture of fry, and enjoy the fish whilst obtainable without trouble; thus, in Madras, in the Coimbatore Collectorate (p. lxxxvii), "the Collectors, out of consideration for the poorer classes, have refrained from letting out tanks and streams," doubtless commendable in a philanthropic spirit, if to-day's requirements irrespective of to-morrow's wants is the only question, but, unfortunately, permitting unlimited license has ended in unlimited waste. The fishermen in Madras (p. lxxviii) are said to be an impoverished class, so they will consider that were renting re-imposed it would be a grievance: their position in the social scale is not high in the Central Provinces, so it is a question whether improving the fisheries will lead to their condition being bettered or the reverse.

XCII. Eighthly, that the fishermen ply their trade as they always have done, consequently,

Fishermen's objections.

as fish still remain in the waters, no interference is desirable (p. cxxx). This, however, is an assertion much similar to those answers which the Government received in 1868, that the supply of fish was hardly decreasing anywhere; in fact, that in some places it was augmenting,—general replies, in fact, which, unfortunately, more minute enquiries have shown to have been usually derived from erroneous impressions. This subject, therefore, has been more fully dwelt upon elsewhere.

XCIII. Ninthly, that doing anything would be an interference with trade (p. lxxxi, &c.) or "free industries" (p. lxxi) ; and doubtless if the present wasteful mode of fishing in some parts of India is regulated, it will be an interference perhaps with trade, certainly with poaching. It can hardly be denied that a certain comparison may be drawn between fish and grain employed as food. In the North-West Provinces (p. clxxv) the poorest classes eat small fish instead of meal or flour of any kind. It is observed in the Panjáb that the one is exchanged for the other (p. xxv) : thus, when grain is cheap, it obtains double its weight : when dear, an equal proportion. Also (p. xxvii) that fish are not sold, but whenever the zemindars feel inclined to eat it, they generally give the fishermen some grain in repayment for catching it. In Bombay at Kandeish (p. xiv), that in a bad season when grain is scarce and dear, fish forms a large proportion of the food of the Bhils. In Madras, the sub-engineer at the Dowlaishcram weir reported :—" The fish procured at the anicuts in great numbers formed a great part of the food to many poor classes of people in the late famine years" (before 1868). In Orissa, the Commissioner observed to the Famine Commissioners:—" While the condition of the residents of this place, where my camp is, is somewhat easier as living by their fisheries, they are not so affected by present circumstances." Now, if fish not only can be, but is, substituted in times of scarcity for grain as food, surely it is an important consideration whether a judicious interference which would augment this source of nutriment, would be a politic or an impolitic act. I cannot think that much would be believed of a farmer's sagacity, who, desiring fish, the cost of which was in accordance with the weight of grain, cut green corn in exchange : neither do I think he would be much more foolish than the fishermen who capture the fry or young, whose food costs nothing. The Burmese suggested that, if wrong, Government should stop it, and how could this class of people be expected to leave immature fish alone, when they would be liable to be taken in the next field or piece of water. If, then, killing the fry is folly, does such rest wholly with the fishermen ? In an English magazine (June 1st, 1867) occurs the following :—" Sometimes free trade in pearl-fishing has been advocated, but this would lead to an exhaustion of the banks by reckless fishing. The harvest of cinchona in South America, and that of teak timber in the Malabar forests, are known to have been injured by a greedy eagerness to bring as much to the market as possible, to kill the goose that lays the golden egg." It may be asked —is the use of fry as manure (p. cxxxvii) a free industry ? If the man who makes two grains of wheat grow where only one was previously raised is a benefactor to his race, in what position are we to place that individual in India, who, aware how fish can be substituted for grain, not only connives at but argues that its wasteful destruction should be freely permitted ? Surely waste, when it is not wilful, is as a rule the offspring of ignorance or prejudice, much as developing the resources of an Empire ought to be the natural consequence of matured investigations and conclusions based upon careful scientific enquiries.

XCIV. The result of fishing without regulations has generally been found to be destructive to fresh-water fisheries, so much so that in Great Britain and elsewhere most stringent rules are enforced for their protection, as liberty unrestrained eventuates in license, which last degenerates into destructive waste. *M. Soubeiran*, in an excellent paper on this subject, remarks that, although normally the fresh-waters of the *United States* contain a large number of excellent fish, they have for many years lost their old fertility, greatly due to the erection of weirs, mill-dams and other obstacles that have been constructed for the purpose of facilitating navigation or manufactures. The chief cause of depopulation he holds to be the very common employment of fixed engines, which but too well fulfil their purpose. The salmon have almost disappeared, and all-destructive man, in his greed, has succeeded but too surely in depopulating the waters. Now, the different States have officers whose duty it is to re-stock the rivers. In *Canada*, the same decrease is observed, due to the same cause. In *Nova Scotia*, Mr. Knight in 1867 observed of the river fisheries, that one can without exaggeration compare them to the mines of Golconda, so far that man has at his disposal an inexhaustible wealth, on the sole condition of following the laws of Nature. Instead of this, obstructions have been erected, destructive implements of capture brought into use, and the fisheries allowed no rest. Now, depopulation of those waters has

Result of fishing without regulations elsewhere.

begun, and the people demand conservative and not further destructive measures. Both the public and the fishermen complain and call for legislation for the purpose of restocking the waters, which they have been at such pains to depopulate.

SUGGESTIONS AS TO WHAT LEGAL ACTION SHOULD BE TAKEN.

XCV. Having now brought forward the various reasons that have been adduced for leaving the fresh-water fisheries alone, and permitting the present mode of working them to continue, on the general principle enunciated by one official (p. xlvi) that perhaps the next generation will be riper for protective legislation, it becomes requisite to examine the opinions of those who consider action is now necessary. The Secretary of State observed (p. lxviii) that the conservancy and control of the fisheries, and the measures suggested for the improvement of pisciculture throughout India, constitute subjects which certainly deserve attention. The Governor-General in Council (p. lxxii) remarked,—Is the present plan of non-interference likely to ensure to future generations the fullest possible supply of this food staple? Is it even such as to ensure their inheriting a supply equal to that which now exists? The Governor-General in Council apprehends that both these questions must be answered in the negative: and that not only is there no prospect, as matters now stand, of an increased supply hereafter, but that, owing to the absence of precautionary measures and reasonable restrictions, the existing supply is diminishing. His Excellency in Council believes, on the other hand, that it would be possible, by the adoption of such measures and restrictions, to increase the supply very largely in a few years. If this is so, it would clearly be the duty of the State to take the necessary measures. In Canara, the Acting Collector (p. lv) considers,—By the principles of the *Jus gentium*, large rivers belong to all the people of the country: in other words, are the property of Government which represents all the people of the country, so far as such rights are concerned. Where the fund of wealth is unlimited, it is better to leave the right of using it unlimited: but where this is not the case (and it is presumed all will admit it is not the case with river or tank fisheries), some restricting regulations are necessary. If the above statement be correct, the sooner the Legislature takes the fisheries of this district

Reasons for legal action being taken.

under its cognizance the better. As regards the present destructive modes of fishing, he continues, if these practices be continued, the rivers of the district will soon be swept clear of fish; a means of innocent sport for some, and of sustenance for many, will be stopped, and the chance of Government ever deriving any revenue from the fisheries, which, if they were protected, would be quite practicable and might be desirable, will be lost. The principle of protecting fish during the breeding season is too well known to need comment (p. xiv), and fish might be augmented, "adding to the food and comfort of the poorer classes, whose interests in this particular point have been hitherto neglected" (p. liii). Whilst in the North-West Provinces, the Commissioner of Meerut (p. cxlviii) considers "there is a fear that, unless the reckless system of wholesale destruction is stopped, the fish-supply may become scant." There are two main causes which lead to it: the facilities afforded by irrigation works, and the absence of any check in respect of rivers. The opinions will be collated in much the same way as those of the officials who hold contrary views, excepting that Divine laws have not been commenced with, although it might be observed that this article of food was probably intended for our use, not abuse, whilst destructive waste can hardly be brought forward as a Divine command.

XCVI. *First, general reasons for action being taken.*

General reasons for action being recommended.
In Bombay, the Officiating Revenue Officer of the Northern Division (p. xliii) observes that it is a question whether protective laws of moderate stringency would not be very advisable. More officials, however, hold that a general Act would be unworkable (p. xlviii), and would rather have one which could be applied, when considered necessary, to particular rivers and localities favourable for fish-breeding. That if such were commenced in selected localities, considerable light might be thrown on the question, and the advisability of extending such operations to other places, or not doing so, would be more clearly established (p. xliii). It is well observed that attempts should be made to remedy great rather than lesser evils (p. xv); but what are those greater evils? The remedy proposed is to make it criminal to use a net with a mesh below a certain size. In Assam (p. ccxxviii), it is remarked that, if the supply of fish is to be kept up, fishery laws are necessary. On other grounds

also local action is proposed; that only perennial lakes and second-class rivers should be subject to legal restrictions in Oudh (p. cxxx), but that large rivers should be left alone (p. cxxxii), but protection afforded in small streams to the spawning and young fish. In Madras, that certain rivers be taken under Government conservancy (p. lxxii), and officials be absolutely prohibited from interfering with minor channels, &c. In fact, amongst those who propose that legal action should be taken, most are in favour of an Act which might be modified to suit different localities, the same as in Great Britain, where certain principles are laid down which cannot be deviated from, but minor questions, which are subject to local variations due to local causes, may be dealt with by district boards. Some officials propose protecting the second-rate and smaller rivers, leaving the larger ones to take care of themselves; others would merely protect the larger ones, but not the smaller channels, &c.

XCVII. The regulations proposed are exceedingly varied, some being simply as applicable to hilly districts, whilst others refer to the whole country, and local modifications have been prominently adduced as desirable for certain places. "*Fence months*" have been proposed to be generally instituted, in order that fish might be allowed to breed in security, as in Bombay (pp. xliv, xlvii), but it is remarked that they would probably be evaded. A close season is likewise observed to be desirable in Ahmednuggur (p. xlviii) and the Central Provinces (p. xcvii). At Sambalpur, two months' cessation from fishing is also recommended (p. cxxii), provided it could be enforced, whilst at Seoni it is proposed that such should be from July to September inclusive (p. cxx). At Ratnaghiri, a close season of two months in the hilly districts is advised (p. liv); it is also proposed in Mysore (pp. civ, cv), in Haidarabad, at Buldana (p. cxi), and Akola (p. cxi), although in this last locality this is said to be the best fishing season in the district. In the Central Provinces, at Sagar and Jabalpur (p. cxx), a close season for the first two months of the monsoon, whilst in Berar, July and August are recommended as most suitable for this purpose. Again, *close seasons* have been proposed as locally desirable; thus, in the irrigation canals when the young of marine species, as the shad, are escaping down to the sea, it is thought that they had better have a free highway, so it is suggested that October to

Regulations proposed.

February are suitable (pp. lxxix, lxxiv) for then the floods have subsided, and the bulk of the fish are caught on their return to the sea: this period, however, is considered as too long by the Madras Revenue Board. Again, it has been suggested that in localities where the water becomes very low in the rivers during the dry season, certain pools should be protected, as the whole of the fish can be swept out of them with the greatest ease. This is especially recommended in hilly districts in the dry (not cold) months of the year in the Himalayas (pp. vii, xiv, xvi): also in Trichinopoly and Tinnivelli, in pools of rivers below irrigation weirs whenever a good stream does not exist (pp. lxxx, lxxxv): and in South Canara (p. xci). The measures stated to be necessary in the Kangra District of the Himalayas are, amongst others, "partially a system of Government preserves, such as was always in force in the time of the Rajas" (p. xvi). In some places, as the Himalayas, it has been proposed that the young of certain fish should be locally protected: also in Bombay (p. lii) and in Madras (pp. lxxii, xcii), but, as has been observed,—who is to decide what are the young?

XCVIII. Omitting weirs, fixed engines and bunding which have been separately dealt with, the next most prominent question is the necessity of regulating the minimum size of the mesh of the nets, on which subject very contradictory opinions have been advanced. Commencing with the Panjáb, in parts of which such have been tried, twenty-one answers from European officials have been received: seventeen (pp. x, xi, xii, xiii, xiv, xvii) consider that no objections exist, although one believes such to be unnecessary (p. x), and another (p. xvii) that it is unadvisable. Out of the four that object, one does so on account of a contiguous and evidently unruly border population (p. ix): a second, due to the want of a legal enactment, coupled with a direct loss of revenue which might accrue (p. xi): a third, that supervision would be impossible in the hills (p. xiv): and a fourth, that if the people might not eat the fry, what were they to obtain at that season? (p. xiv). In the Central Provinces it is observed that regulations must be legalised in order to be carried out (p. l).

On the necessity of regulating the minimum size of the mesh of nets.

Minimum mesh of net proposed.

XCIX. Of those who have proposed that a minimum size should be fixed by law, or that if such were so decided upon, what would be most desirable, the following answers have been received :—

Size proposed between knot and knot of meshes.	Panjáb.	Bombay.	Madras.	Mysor.	Haidarabad.	Central Provinces.	Oudh.	North-Western Provinces.	Bengal.	Burma.
2 inches	3	...	...	...	...	...	...	...	...	...
1¾ ,,	...	...	...	...	1	...	...	...	...	...
1½ ,,	3	...	...	...	...	1	...	4	...	...
1¼ ,,	4	...	1	...	...	1	...	3	...	...
1 ,,	3	3	1	1	4	5	3	1	...	4
⅞ ,,	...	...	1	...	...	...	...	1	...	...
¾ ,,	1	...	...	...	...	3	2	...	...	1
⅝ ,,	1	6	3	...	...	2	...	...	1	...
½ ,,	...	...	...	...	...	...	...	...	1	...
⅜ ,,	1	...	...	...	...	2	...	...	...	...
¼ ,,	...	...	...	...	1	...	...	...	...	...
2 grains of barley	...	...	...	...	...	1	...	...	...	...

One official (p. xv) observes that only large meshed nets ought to be permitted in the hills during the breeding season. Village officers, it is suggested (p. lxxviii), should be made responsible for the size of the meshes employed, or, if regulations are merely to affect leased fisheries, the size might be inserted in the contract (p. lxxix).

C. As to whether any difficulties exist as to prohi-
Prohibiting the sale of fry in bazars. biting the sale of the fry of fish in the bazars. Eighteen answers from Panjáb officials have been received. Seventeen see no difficulties (pp. viii, ix, xi, xii, xiii, xiv, xv, xvii), but one considers that persons might be permitted to sell small fish between April 15th and May 15th, also during the month of September (p. xiii). A second that, although such might be stopped within municipal limits, elsewhere a legal enactment would be necessary (p. xvii). One gentleman (p. xviii) considers such an interference with fishermen whose tempers might be irritated so much that they might relinquish their trade, and consequently the little fish would escape. In the Bombay Presidency, out of eight answers, six see no difficulty; one would rely upon regulating the size of the mesh of nets, and one denounces such an idea as an arbitrary interference with trade ! In Madras, such an order would cause consternation in the Vizagapatam Collectorate, whilst at Nagpúr, in the Central Provinces, the tehsildars are all unanimous in reporting that the sale of the fry of fish in the

bazars might be prohibited without causing any injury, and the prohibition would have the effect of causing larger fish to be brought to market. In Mysor, it is suggested (p. civ) that if they might not be disposed of, the people who caught them would eat them at home. In the Nerbadá Division two Collectors give their opinions: the first considers such a rule (p. cxxi) would be a beneficial one; the second, that it would reduce the sales by one-half, apparently overlooking the fact that if half the amount of fish sold are merely fry, what a wasteful destruction must be taking place; for, as observed in South Canara of fishes of this size captured for eating,—"I saw one day some thousands as fine as a straw within the compass of one earthen pot: they were to form the meal for one labouring man, whereas they might have sufficed to stock a lake or feed a town" (p. lxxxviii). Objections have been raised to prohibiting the use of a mesh under a certain size: one reason brought forward being, that some species of Indian fish are always of a small size, and you would thus prohibit their capture, to the great loss of this sort of food to the people of the country. Exclusive of the natural answer—that these are the young or the food of the larger sorts, so should be preserved—other propositions have been advanced. Thus *chilwas* and *moree* nets (p. li.), it has been suggested, should not be regulated, or all these fish will escape. The Chief Commissioner of the Panjáb observed—chilwa nets were not approved of, as such might be employed to take the young of larger fish (p. ii). Chilwas are said to be taken in Peshawur (p. ix). The Deputy Commissioner of Lahor (p. xi) observes that this fishing is carried on during July and August, the exact period when young fish are moving about, and it would be an extraordinary coincidence did these fish appear suddenly at this period, and were absent during the remainder of the year; the fact being that the vast majority of chilwas are in reality the fry of larger species of fish. The Extra Assistant Commissioner of Phillur suggests that chilwa fishing might be permitted in the early spring when fry are not moving about (p. xv); or in Kangra that taking chilwas might be allowed in those streams to which larger species of fish never resort (p. xvi). It has also been proposed that only during certain fixed periods may small fish be disposed of, whilst in Kangra (p. xvi), licensed fish-stalls, under a Government official, have been advocated. In short, that even were the proposition admitted, that small fish ought to be allowed to be taken, why not permit such during the first four or five months of the year during the time when the vast majority of the fry of the more valuable sorts are not moving about ? The destruction of the fry of fish, as already observed, some native officials appear to deem the root of the present evil (pp. cxxiv, cxxv), if a decrease of fish is one, as seems to be doubted by some reporters (p. xlvi); one native official volunteers the opinion in Madras (p. xcvii) that "nets and traps ought to have holes large enough for a 2-anna piece to go through" ($\frac{6}{10}$ths of an inch in diameter). In the Panjáb (p. xi), "Mian Mahbub Dhony, Magistrate, who is a great sportsman, thinks the mesh should not be less than nine inches all round."

CI. It has also been proposed that the use of nets within a certain distance of weirs, &c., spanning rivers and streams be prohibited. That measures be taken to prevent indiscriminate destruction of fish in irrigation canals as will be alluded to further on. That the use of loaded hooks be illegal, also the poisoning of waters (pp. lxxii, lxxiv, lxxv, lxxx, lxxxvi, cxvii, cxx), drainage of tanks (pp. lxxiv, lxxv); that the amount of captures be restricted (p. xvi), as well as the number of days in which fishing is permitted (p. xvi). That monopolists be allowed to rent fisheries and the sale of fish in districts (p. xvi), whilst the rulers of foreign States, whose territories are contiguous to those of the British, and through which the same rivers run, be requested to join in any plan adopted by the Legislature (p. xiv). That money obtained from fisheries, 'by leasing out those now permitted to run to waste and ruin, be applied for the protection and extension of their importance and usefulness (pp. lii, lxxii), and the destruction of vermin, &c. Thus, as observed by the Madras Revenue Board, that "with care a large prospective income may be relied on from this source," and to obtain such, *care* will be necessary, and waste must be stopped. Whilst as "in several districts the whole subject is inadequately attended to," a new *régime* must commence, not by introducing foreign fish and killing their fry as well as the old as soon as introduced, not by persecuting to destruction the indigenous races; not by artificially breeding fry to be indiscriminately destroyed as soon as turned into the water, refusing to kill vermin, and considering the poacher's interest as vested rights, but by applying the English law in a modified form to Indian

Further proposals.

waters, and considering the good of the fish-consuming millions as superior to that of the wasteful few.

FISHERY LAWS OF GREAT BRITAIN.

CII. In several of the following reports, such exceedingly incorrect assertions have been advanced respecting the *Fishery Laws of Great Britain* that I consider it advisable to give a few remarks on what really exists, unless lately altered, and that with but few comments on my part. Salmon and trout are not found in the fresh-waters of India, their place being supplied by carps and perhaps herrings. The reason why most of the laws in Great Britain appear to allude to salmon, appears to be as stated in the law of Scotland that "salmon fishing is a paramount right to which other fresh-water fishing must yield." Here, there being no salmon, protective laws should embrace all fresh-water fish. Whilst the fresh-water fisheries may be considered briefly as such which exist in fresh-waters which are not within tidal influence. There are four descriptions of fishery. A *common fishery* is that kind of right which all the public have alike to fish in the sea or a navigable river. A *several fishery* is the right of an individual to fish exclusively in a particular water, and it is not necessarily united with the right to the soil, though originally all owners of the bed of a river or water must have had a several fishery in such water as a constituent part of the right of property until they parted with it to another. A *free fishery* is the right of fishing along with other individuals in a water. A *common of fishery* is the right of a person to fish in waters of which the soil belongs to a different person.

CIII. "The next question is—Who is the person who has the legal right of fishing for trout [in India the word would be 'fish,' not 'trout,' for the reasons specified in the last paragraph] generally, *i. e.*, with nets and other competent means? The answer is, that all riparian owners have this right as an incident of ownership. Where the owner has, however, let the land to a tenant, the question may arise, whether the owner or the tenant is to enjoy the trout-fishing. If the lease expressly let the fishing to the tenant, there is an end of the question; but the difficulty arises whether, when the lease is silent,

Fishery Laws of Great Britain.

Right of fishing.

the right of fishing is in the tenant also." This point was decided *(Duke of Richmnod* v. *Dempster,* 14th January 1860, Just. c. 33, sc. Jur. 133.) The Court of Justiciary, consisting of five Judges, per Inglis, C. J., came to the following conclusion:—"We are of opinion that an agricultural tenant has not, as such, any right to fish in a stream running by or through his farm, with any net of any kind or description" *(Paterson)*—a decision said to be open to question.

CIV. "The nature of a right of fishery proper is an incorporal hereditament, and as such can be conveyed only by deed. A license of fishing is distinct from the right of fishery, and is at most only a justification for what would otherwise be a trespass. A license is revocable at will, and in order to be binding, even for an hour, must be granted by deed" *(Paterson, p. 57).* A "fishery may be let by verbal agreement; and even where no rent has been agreed upon, the landlord is entitled to sue the tenant for a reasonable rent under an *indebitatus* count for use and occupation" (p. 67.) "The purchasers of a fishery in the River Galway and Lough Corrib petitioned the Court of Chancery to be quieted in the possession and enjoyment of their several fishery. The defendants were represented by ten persons, who were paupers, who set up as a defence that the river was, except in a certain specified portion, open to the public, and had been so from time immemorial. Evidence was given on both sides, and the plaintiffs, who produced grants from the Crown, and evidence of user, contended that the evidence of user on the part of the defendants was evidence merely of a succession of trespasses. There had been a trial of an issue some years previously which settled the right to the fishery in the plaintiffs. The M. R. accordingly, without putting the plaintiffs to any further trial, granted the decree declaring the petitioners' rights and continuing the injunction (p. 117-8).

Nature of right of fishing.

CV. "Property is essentially an exclusive thing, and the incident of fishing is also so. All other persons, therefore, except the owner of the soil beneath, or the riparian owner, have no more right to fish in his water, than they have a right to seize any other perquisite of the soil. Whether a stranger fishes with a net or a rod can make no difference in point of law; it is the taking of the fish, not the manner of taking

Right of property in fishery.

it, that is important" (p. 120). "Sometimes an owner is careless of his rights, and tolerates strangers, who, knowing this lenience, invade his fields to angle or fish with nets, especially to angle. This, however, is a gratuitous concession on his part, and he can at any moment, without notice, resume his rights, and treat all such intruders as trespassers. Whether the land on which the trespasser goes is waste or cultivated, fenced or unfenced, it is equally a trespass for him to go there without the owner's permission. This has always been the law, and is still the law, as regards all rivers and streams whatever" (p. 120). "Sometimes the inhabitants of a village or town set up a claim to angle in a part of a river or water on the ground of of ancient custom. * * * In such cases the acts of such anglers are more likely to be referable to the license of the owner, who, if he pleases, may allow all the public, or a portion of the public, to angle there. But no length of time, during which such acts are capable of being explained on the ground of license, can prevent the owner putting an end to such license. He may resume his original rights at any moment, and withdraw the license, for no man ought to have his rights abridged, by acting liberally towards the public or his neighbours." "It may happen that after a number of years' use by the public promiscuously of the angling in a particular water or river, the public may begin to claim as a right what at first was merely a license, and litigation may arise as to whether the public have acquired the right or not. There seems, however, no trace of any such right being established in this way."

CVI. "The chief substantial interference with a common fishery is where a weir or similar contrivance exists. As already stated, such weirs are, *primâ facie*, a nuisance and illegal" (p. 103).

Fishing weirs only legal in England, provided they were so prior to Magna Charta. Declared a nuisance, and regulations affecting those which are legal.

" Lord Ellenborough, C.J., said:—the erection of weirs across rivers was reprobated in the earliest periods of our law, and they were considered as public nuisances. Magna Charta and subsequent Acts so treated them, and forbad the erection of new ones, and the enhancing, straitening, or enlargening of those which had aforetime existed" (p. 39). "No fishing mill-dam or fishing weir is legal, except it be ancient, and even ancient fishing weirs must have a free gap, and ancient fishing mill-dams must have a proper fish-pass, and no fishing is allowed at the head or tail of a mill, or within fifty yards below a dam, unless these have a fish-pass. As already stated, no weir or dam for fishing is legal unless its origin can be presumed to be older than Magna Charta" (p. 147). "A fishing weir is defined by the Act (section 4) a dam used for the exclusive purpose of catching, or facilitating the catching of fish. In all fishing weirs that are legal (i. e., which have had a legal origin before Magna Charta), and which at lowest water extend more than half-way across the stream, a free gap must be made of a size and form and situation prescribed by the statute, which can only be departed from by authority of the Home Office. The owners of such a weir were bound, within twelve months after 1st October 1861, to make such a gap under a penalty of £5 per day. The gap must also be maintained under a penalty of £1 per day; and any alteration or obstruction, or contrivance to deter the fish from entering the gap, is punishable by a penalty of £5 and upwards. The boxes and cribs used in fishing weirs or fishing mill-dams (i. e., dams used partly for fishing and partly for milling purposes) must be of a certain situation, and the bars or inscales of the heck or up-stream side shall not be nearer each other than two inches, under a penalty of £5 per day, and the same must be maintained under a penalty of £1 a day. Spur-walls, &c., more than 20 feet from the upper or lower side of the box or crib are always prohibited, under a penalty of £1 per day" (p. 159). "In all dams made in salmon waters after 1861, or raised or altered after that date, which obstruct salmon, a fish-pass of a form approved of by the Home Office must be made at the expense of the person making or altering the dam" (p. 158). In Scotland, respecting fixed engines, it is stated—"indeed the general rule has been repeatedly laid down that fishing by means of any fixed machinery, or apparatus whatever, or in any way except by net and coble, is illegal" (p. 179).

CVII. "It is an offence to use fixed engines of any description in any waters for the purpose of catching salmon. The engine is forfeited as well as the salmon caught, and a penalty of £10 a day is incurred besides. This section has nothing to do with fishing weirs and fishing mill-dams, which are dealt with in section 12. All possible waters which salmon frequent are comprehended in the phrase, inland or tidal waters. Fixed engines by the interpretation clause, section 4, include stake-nets, bag-nets, putts, putchers, and

<small>Fixed engines, irrespective of fishing weirs or fishing mill-dams: regulations in England.</small>

all fixed implements or engines for catching or facilitating the catching of fish. Where there is no several fishery, but the public generally are entitled to fish, they are prohibited by this section from using fixed engines, whether they have been accustomed to do so from time immemorial or not" (p. 146). "That both weirs and fixed nets and all other apparatus which prevent fish passing to and fro are illegal at common law, and form a good ground of action, seems to follow on principle. A fishery is merely one of the natural uses of the water to which all riparian owners are entitled" (p. 42). "Hence even independently of any statute, any fixed apparatus in a river or stream, which prevents the fish going up to the other riparian owners, is a good cause of action at common law, as it deprives him of one of the natural riparian rights" (p. 43).

CVIII. "No person, whether the owner of a fishery or a poacher, is entitled to fish salmon with a net less than two inches from knot to knot, otherwise he forfeits the nets, and incurs a penalty of £5. The offence consists either in taking or attempting to take salmon with illegal nets. The nets and tackle become forfeited, provided a conviction takes place" (p. 145).

<small>Size of mesh of nets in England.</small>

CIX. "Another illegal obstruction to fisheries was the practice of attaching nets to the posts on river banks, by day and night, across rivers, which destroyed the brood and fry of fish" (p. 41).

<small>Laws for the preservation of the fry in England, and prohibiting their passage being obstructed.</small>

"It is an offence to take, destroy, buy, sell or possess, obstruct or injure the young of salmon, or disturb a spawning bed. There is no definite age implied in the expression 'young of the salmon,' which is defined in section 4" (p. 150). "The third offence—'placing a device obstructing the passage'—is difficult of interpretation. It must mean a substantial obstruction, but the device need not extend to the whole width of the stream, nor is there any restriction as to where the device is to be put. The object in view was probably to render illegal all gratings put across the tributary streams of salmon rivers which would have the effect of obstructing the young salmon from going upwards. In order to convict of the third offence, it is not necessary to prove the actual obstruction, if in the ordinary course of things the device is calculated so to obstruct young of salmon coming there" (p. 150). Penalties for taking young salmon, or having them in possession,—to forfeit all the young of salmon found in his possession; all rods, lines, nets, devices and instruments used in committing any of the above offences: and shall for each offence pay a penalty not exceeding £5.

CX. "No person, whether the owner of a salmon fishery or a trespasser, is permitted to fish with lights, spears, gaffs, stroke-halls, snatches, or the like instruments, or even to have such things in his possession with the intent to catch salmon" (p. 143).

Other illegal mode of fishing.

CXI. "The section *primâ facie* subjects to a penalty all who knowingly put poisonous matter into waters containing salmon or any tributaries thereof. Therefore, the waters include the sea, mouths of rivers, and even tributaries where no salmon may usually be found. The test of poisoning is one of quantity, and of course the quantity of matter must be greater to poison fish in a large river than in a small stream. But it is not necessary that the fish be actually killed, if the quantity was reasonably calculated to kill fish which at the time might be there" (p. 136). "If any fish are killed, whether salmon or not, this is conclusive evidence of the killing power of the quantity put into the stream" (p. 137). "The tributary need not contain salmon in order to be protected" (p. 137). "The common law gives no right to any person to pour offensive matter into streams so as to prejudice the rights of those living nearer the sea" (p. 138). *Penalty*—first conviction, not above £5; second, not exceeding £10, and £2 for every day during which such offence is continued; on third or subsequent conviction, £20 per day during which such offence is continued, commencing from the date of the third conviction.

Poisoning waters.

CXII. "It is a criminal offence for any fisher, whether the owner of a fishery or a poacher, to use fish-roe for fishing, or to buy or to sell or have salmon roe in one's possession." "Scientific and other legitimate purposes are expressly excepted." "If a person were to buy some salmon roe, offer to sell some to A, then sell some to B, and keep the rest, it seems he may be guilty of four offences in one day" (p. 145).

Fish-roe.

CXIII. "During the open or fishing season, a space of nearly two days is given, *i. e.*, from 12 noon on Saturday to 6 A. M. on Monday, for fish to have a free run. Hence no fishermen are

Weekly close time in England.

allowed to fish for or catch fish during this weekly close time, by any means whatever, except rod and line. The penalty is a forfeiture of the net or moveable instrument used, and a penalty of £5 and £1 per fish taken" (p. 156). "The owners of putts or putchers are not obliged to draw them up during weekly close time, but they must let down a net or other device, so as to put them out of gear during those hours, and the owners of all fisheries where fixed engines are lawfully used shall leave all their cribs, boxes or cruives open during the weekly close time" under the above penalties.

CXIV. "The close time for salmon fishing is fixed by the statute, and it is illegal to fish salmon between the 1st day of September and the 1st of February following, inclusive, or for anglers to fish between 2nd of November and 1st of February following, both inclusive. The fish are forfeited, and the penalty increases with the number of fish caught." "All proprietors of fixed engines must remove their apparatus of boxes, cribs, &c., within 36 hours after the commencement of the close season, *i.e.*, of 1st September, so as to allow the fish free course, otherwise the engines are forfeited, and £10 per day is the penalty" (p. 155).

Close season in England. Fixed engines prohibited.

CXV. "No person, whether the owner of a fishery or or not, is allowed to take, buy or sell or possess unclean or unseasonable salmon, excepting accidents and scientific purposes." "'To take' does not imply manual possession of, or dominion over, the fish. The buying seems to be one offence, selling another, &c., even though in reference to one and the same individual fish, and the penalty attaches on each fish bought, &c.; thus cumulative offences may attach to one fish" (p. 149); penalty for each offence, £5.

Taking unclean fish.

CXVI. "The wilful disturbance or catching of salmon when spawning or near their spawning beds is punishable with a fine of £5; but catching salmon for scientific purposes is excepted" (p. 151).

Spawning salmon.

CXVII. From the foregoing extracts it will be seen "that the fishing that a subject hath in this or any private or public river or creek, fresh or salt, is subject to the laws for the conservation of fish and fry, which are many" *(Hale)*. *Paterson* observes respecting the fishery law—"the chief object of the

Fishing amenable to the laws.

statute is to prevent owners of fisheries from doing what they like with their own, that is, it prevents them from killing salmon at certain times and by certain kinds of means, in order to secure fair play to the fish and to the adjoining owners, and with a view to the public interest. It may be safely assumed that the law, as previously stated, applies equally to salmon as to other fish, except so far as varied by what follows in this statute" (p. 136).

CXVIII. "For the better protection of the proprietors of salmon fisheries, it is provided that the Justices in general or Quarter Sessions, may appoint conservators or overseers for the preservation of salmon and enforcing the provisions of the law within the jurisdiction of such Justices—24 & 25 Vic., c. 109, s. 33. They may apply to the Home Secretary and have a fishery district formed, and the committee is to elect the chairman and they appoint a Board of Conservators." Conservators, appointed under "The Salmon Fishery Act, 1865," have power within their district to appoint a sufficient number of water bailiffs; * * to issue licenses for fishing as provided in the schedule; * * for removing such weirs or other fixed engines as are illegal; and generally to do such acts as they may deem expedient for the improvement of the salmon fisheries ("*Baker*, p. 44.") In any fishery district, subject to the control of conservators, licenses are to be granted at fixed prices to all persons using rod and line for fishing for salmon, and in respect of all fishing weirs, fishing mill dams, putts, putchers, nets or other instruments or devices, except rods and lines, whereby salmon are caught: and the produce of such licenses is to be applied in defraying the expenses of carrying into effect in such districts " The Salmon Fishery Acts, 1861 and 1865" (28 & 29 Vic., c. 121, s. 33).

Boards of Conservators.

CXIX. From the foregoing it will be seen that in England fishing weirs are considered a nuisance, and, even if legal, must have a fish-pass in them or free gap: that other fixed engines are illegal: that the size of the mesh of nets and interstices between substances forming weirs is laid down: fry are protected, the very possession of them being a punishable offence: unfair modes of fishing are prohibited as well as poisoning of waters: a weekly close time is insisted upon to allow a free passage for the fish, whilst, during certain months of the year, all fishing with nets or at weirs is illegal, and

Weirs and fish-passes.

even the disturbing of spawning fish, or the possession of unseasonable ones. To carry this out, District Boards of Conservators are appointed, who levy a license tax on every one who fishes for salmon, whether with a rod and line, net, weir, or any other appliance whatever.

CXX. Having now enumerated the various opinions Respecting any remedies that may have been tried. of those who hold that the present mode of working the fresh-water fisheries of India is causing their deterioration, and of others who deny such, it appears desirable, prior to summing up the lessons which these reports seem to convey, to ask these questions:—*Have any remedies been attempted by those who advocate them? If so, what has been the result of such attempts?* Even did no wasteful destruction now take place, could it be clearly demonstrated that a great augmentation of animal food must be ensured by moderately and well-considered restrictive measures, the strongest advocates for the prescriptive right of the people to ruin fisheries, and thus diminish their neighbours' food, and the philanthropists who denounce fishery laws as engines of oppression and instruments of cruelty, surely must pause, and accord this enquiry that attentive consideration it so well deserves, but unfortunately does not always appear to obtain. It is not a subject in which assertions should convince, or statements unbacked by facts be allowed much weight. It is not merely in one quarter of the globe that the ruinous mode in which fresh-water fisheries have been worked, has escaped the observations of legislatures and even of their owners: in short, it is only of late years that mankind has commenced being aware that his mode of treating these fisheries may be, and probably is, based upon error. The license accorded by "man" is not invariably in accordance with the laws ordained by "nature;" and we have now to enquire whether any conservative measures have been attempted, and, if so, with what result.

CXXI. The measures for the protection of the fresh- Restrictive regulations have had a beneficial result locally in India. water fisheries of the Indian Empire may be divided into two. *First,* those which are natural ones, as described in Sind (pp. xxix—xxxii), and, consequently, do not call for further remarks. *Secondly,* those carried out by human agency. Fortunately, we are able to examine the reports from officials who have attempted such in two widely separated localities,—the one in South Canara in Madras, the other in the Doon in the North-Western Provinces.

Consequently two attempts have been made; if no destructive waste was occurring prior to these experiments, no augmentation of the fish in the fisheries would be apparent: if moderate restrictions had extensively beneficial results, such might lead to the enquiry whether it would not be possible to extend such elsewhere, and give to others benefits now confined to small localities, and due to the individual exertions of single officials. In South Canara, *Mr. H. S. Thomas* observes, that (p. lxxxix) it may be doubted whether poisoning rivers, or the wholesale destruction of fry, is most injurious to fisheries; whilst prohibiting the former, and also the closely woven bamboo cruives " has been that the most ignorant, and, therefore, the most obstinate opponents have been convinced by the testimony of their own senses, and have exclaimed to use their own words, ' truly the river is everywhere *bubbling* with fry;' and what is still more to the point, their practice has not belied their words, for they have taken to fishing on grounds that were before considered profitless. * * * Two years' discouragement of poisoning, and one year's discouragement of fine cruives, has worked such a change, that it has been demonstrated, beyond the cavil, even of the ignorant and of the most interestedly opposing, that marked advantages can be reaped from the adoption of these two simple measures alone." This is also interesting, because the Madras Revenue Board especially selected South Canara (p. lxxi) as one of the two Collectorates, wherein they urged Government to do nothing. In the Doon, *Mr. Ross*, with the consent of the landowners, has limited the size of the mesh of the nets employed to not less than $1\frac{1}{2}$ inches between each knot, and also prohibited the damming and turning of hill streams for the purpose of capturing fish. I went to the Song River in 1871, and was astonished at the amount of fry in it, reporting that " I never saw so many yearlings in the plains of India in such a small volume of running water." When I wrote this, I was in entire ignorance that any conservative measures were being carried out (p. cl). The foregoing showing that restrictive regulations tend largely to an increase in the fish supply, and are again arguments that some are generally necessary, if this description of animal food is deemed worth increasing, and its still further diminution undesirable.

CXXII. *What are the results of this enquiry?* Here I propose briefly bringing together what conclusions appear to me to be shown by personal investigations, or from the answers received from

Results of this enquiry.

the European and Native officials of the British Empire in India and Burma, several of whom have evidently taken considerable pains in obtaining the desired information. It appears that—(1) all the people of Sind, Assam and Burma, and the majority of those residing in other parts, are not precluded by their religion from eating fish (para. LIII); (2) that from the returns received (excepting Sind) more than half the markets are insufficiently supplied with fresh fish when away from the sea (para. LIV); (3) that breeding-fish and their fry are indiscriminately destroyed throughout the British possessions (para. LVI); (4) that the supply of fish in the waters (excepting Sind) is generally decreasing (para. LVII); (5) that the fisheries are mostly Government property (para. LVIII); (6) that non-regulating the fisheries under British rule has had a disastrous effect (para. LIX); (7) that the natives let out tracts of the country to contractors, who alone might dispose of fish, and certain conservative measures were likewise in existence (para. LX); (8) that the contractors under British rule have in many places been abolished, every one being permitted to promiscuously fish as he pleases, great innovations have crept in, and fixed engines are now universally employed, whereas they were not previously generally permitted (para. LXI); (9) that the fishermen, as a rule, unless in the vicinity of tidal rivers, are only thus engaged in addition to their other occupations, so are not dependant for their living on fishing (para. LXII); (10) that regular fishermen in places have been compelled to give up this trade, and turn to other means of gaining a livelihood (para. LXII); (11) that fishing weirs and fixed engines obstructing waterways, the high roads of fish, are everywhere employed, from entirely spanning rivers to every outlet in each irrigated field from whence water is flowing, whilst the mesh employed is so minute that the smallest fry cannot escape (paras. LXV, LXVI, LXVII); (12) that fishing nets with meshes of the most minute size are used for the purpose of letting nothing escape, and this in every district where the water will permit of it (paras. LXIX, LXX); (13) that, as a rule, more than half the minimun sized mesh of the nets is less than one-fourth of an inch between each knot, but even coarse cloths are employed to capture fry with (para. LXXI); (14) that rivers and streams are dammed and the water laded out for fishing purposes (para. LXXV); (15) that waters are poisoned almost everywhere to obtain the fish (para. LXXVI); (16) that the minor modes of fishing are most numerous (para. LXXVIII), destructive and wasteful; (17) that fish are in some places only killed to be thrown away, or carted off as manure, and that in localities where the supply does not equal the bazar demands (paras. LXXVI, LXXVII); (18) that irrigation weirs are largely destructive by impeding the ascent of fish to the waters where they breed, or the downward passage of those attempting to descend (paras. XII—XV); (19) that irrigation canals are exceedingly injurious, if they have vertical falls in them, up which fish are unable to ascend, for, as the old ones descend down stream to feeding grounds, they find a stone wall in their way, but a fine stream of water not so obstructed which leads them into one of these canals and once over a fall, they cannot re-ascend, but are destroyed there every time the water is cut off; (20) that the same destructive plan exists in nearly every irrigated field in India; (21) that there are certain vermin very inimical to fish, as crocodiles and otters, whose destruction would be most advantageous; (22) that in Great Britain and other civilized countries, the poaching of fish is forbidden (paras. XCVII, CXIX); (23) that where local restrictions on poaching fish have been tried in India, the result has been most beneficial (paras. CXX, CXXI).

PROPOSITION AS TO WHAT ACTION IS NECESSARY.

CXXIIII. The result of this enquiry has, unfortu-
Proposition that legal action nately, given but too good reasons
is now required. for believing that fish are wastefully destroyed as breeding ones or their fry, and the fisheries are almost everywhere deteriorating. The causes which have apparently led to this have been traced as closely as materials have permitted, and the remedies suggested have been as fully recorded. I now propose offering my single opinion on these points, premising that destructive waste seems to be proved, and a supply insufficient for the wants of the people to be brought for sale to the bazars. Respecting the carrying out of remedial measures, much will depend upon the cordial co-operation and tact of local officers: sudden and too stringent regulations would appear to be injudicious, as the folly of years cannot be entirely grappled with at once. In fact, in places it may be desirable at first to leave some breaches in regulations unnoticed, until the beneficial results of partial measures are clearly discernible. The natives, judging from the native officials' replies and personal

enquiries, appear more alive to the destructive waste in the fresh-water fisheries that is now being carried on than do the Europeans. Such might be anticipated; it comes more home to them, whilst a very little trouble would disarm their opposition.

A General Fishery Act.

CXXIV. It would seem then that, if any action is taken, a "Fishery Act" will be necessary. Here the question arises at the outset—should such be one adapted for all India? Should it be made applicable to certain places? Or should the general principles be laid down, leaving details to Local Administrations? In practice, it would probably be most efficient to follow the spirit of the British law, considering each "Local Administration" as a "board of conservators" who could enact bye-laws, and so modify general rules as to meet each different district.

A Fishery Act necessary.

CXXV. Should any such general skeleton Act be considered necessary, I would propose that its action should be simple, but still feel confident that if only a modicum of trouble is taken in carrying its provisions into effect, the results must be most beneficial. *First*, that poisoning of waters for fishing purposes, or permitting any poisonous substance entering into pieces of water so as to become deleterious to fish, be generally prohibited. *Secondly*, that all fixed engines be declared illegal. This probably will meet with some opposition, but fixed engines are at the root of the destructive waste which is proved to be going on in India. They are now used where previously they were never permitted (para. LX and LXI); whilst, due to there being no lessees or fishery contractors in large districts of country, the agriculturists are employing fixed traps in every irrigated and inundated field. Nothing is now spared. But whilst deciding that weirs and fixed traps are generally illegal, modifications or exceptions might be allowed by Local Governments with this proviso, that no fixed engines (excluding fishing weirs that are subject to rent in Government waters, or situated in permanently settled estates) may be employed between 1st June and 1st December, whilst, to be legal in the remaining six months of the year, a license must be obtained from the civil officer of the district, that, if destitute of a fish-pass, they should never entirely obstruct a water-way, and that 1 inch at least exists between the substances forming

Skeleton of General Act.

the traps fixed in fishing weirs, whilst a notice of all sanctioned should be yearly given in the district gazettes. *Thirdly*, that the bunding and turning of streams for fishing purposes, especially in hill-ranges, be entirely prohibited, which rule should also (subject to local exceptions) be applied to tanks in the low country, unless they yearly dry up, but it should only then be allowed after all communication with running water has naturally ceased. *Fourthly*, that every irrigation weir spanning a river have a practicable fish-pass in it ; and that all irrigation canals have either a grating or other contrivance at their entrance to prevent fish going down them, or fish-passes at every fall, and gratings at each distributary, whilst the killing of fish during such periods as the canals are closed be absolutely interdicted.

BYE-LAWS OR LOCAL ACTS.

CXXVI.—Local Acts or bye-laws will be most essential, in order to suit the requirements of districts, and here I propose adverting to what such seem to me to be necessary, and how some which are now approved of, I cannot think will work well when practically tried. In the appendix under the heads of the various Governments, I have observed upon such local regulations as appear to be desirable : so, here only general remarks are necessitated.

Local regulations.

CXXVII.—*Fence months, seasons, times, or in respect to species* of fish, whether in the hills or in the plains, appear to find many advocates, and may be briefly examined under the following heads. *First*, in the plains ; *secondly*, in the hilly *regions; thirdly*, in certain peculiar localities as at the tail of irrigation or other weirs ; *fourthly*, as the institution of stock-pools in rivers; and, *lastly*, as regards certain species of fish, of which it is proposed to declare it illegal to be possessed of their fry or young. Of course, the first local enquiry should be,—will the imposition of fence month act injuriously on the health of the people at large by depriving them at certain seasons of a necessary article of diet? Secondly, will the entire occupation of fishermen be cut off, leaving any number of them without any means of subsistence ? If we now examine the five enquiries which I have suggested, the first (1) is the policy or necessity of instituting fence months in the plains of India. I am unable to see how such could be practicably imposed, except at excessive cost, and if not

Fence months.

practicable, the use of issuing such a prohibition appears still more questionable. The period, were one imposed, would of course be that of the breeding season, from about June to November inclusive, but it is during this period that the shad ascends from the sea to breed, and it is only prior to such time that it is in good condition as food. That fixed engines with small meshes at this period ought to be abolished· no two opinions are possible, but, that all netting should cease, is, I think, open to a grave doubt, and would not propose such a course. Secondly (2), in the hilly regions, during the breeding season the mahaseer and other large carps which ascend to breed (irrespective of the dry season) most certainly need some protection : at any rate, weirs spanning streams to arrest breeding-fish going up, or capture them, or the most minute fry coming down, should be prohibited as destructive to the general fish-supply of the country at large. Whilst to protect the shad, one day a week might be kept free from fishing anywhere within $1\frac{1}{2}$ miles below an irrigation weir spanning a river up which they ascend to breed. Also, lines armed with hooks should not be allowed in passes in hill streams, as they not only capture some ascending breeding-fishes, but wound others that only escape to die a lingering death. Thirdly (3), there are certain localities in which netting, or fishermen engaged in the process, or servants employed by them, should be prohibited, as within a reasonable distance of irrigation weirs which span rivers. What this reasonable distance may be, must depend upon the character of the under-sluices, and the existence or the reverse of fish-passes. The same protection is also necessary in the canals. Fourthly (4), certain pools in rivers during the dry season of the year should be protected from being fished, except by anglers ; this would keep up a stock of breeding-fish in certain localities where now the larger fish obtain no immunity. Lastly (5), as regards rendering it penal to capture or possess the fry of certain kinds of fish. This is a subject which is most interesting, and one in which, could all informers and magistrates be quite clear about, I would urge should be the law as in Europe. But I fear that very great difficulties will arise in defining what fish are alluded to. Thus, it is easy to decide that a mahaseer under 1 or 2 ℔s weight should be an under-sized fish. But what is a mahaseer ? Of course, the reply is that it is a carp of the genus *Barbus*, but, unfortunately, several of the large species of this genus come under the generic name of mahaseers. Near Simla, in the Girri, the *Barbus hexastichus* is a mahaseer; in the neighbouring Ussun River, the *B. Himalayanus* is thus termed, whilst in the Hurriapore River, only a few miles off, the *B. tor* is so called. All of these are closely allied together; so, perhaps, it might be considered that such distinctions are immaterial. In answer to this is the reply that there are upwards of 60 species of this genus in India, some of which never exceed a few inches in length. This is not a solitary case; the genus *Ophiocephalus* offers equal difficulties (see page ccv). Seeing the obstacles in England where every fish that is protected has a very peculiar and distinct fin, which does not exist in any of the other sorts found there, I doubt if such rules could be carried out in India where no such distinct peculiarity demonstrates which fish it is that is to be preserved until it attains a certain age.

CXXVIII. Respecting the necessity, or the reverse, <small>Regulating the minimum size of the mesh of nets employed.</small> of regulating the minimum size of the meshes of nets, is another very important question that can be locally dealt with. Opinions vary so widely that, to disarm opposition, I think local Civil authorities might fix it, in doing which it should be remembered that it is in hilly districts during the breeding season that small-meshed nets are doing an immensity of injury to breeding-fish and their fry; also, that in the plains myriads of very minute fish are captured by this poaching practice. In the Panjáb, $1\frac{1}{4}$ inches between each knot of the meshes as the minimum size is found to work well, whereas amongst the propositions received from European Civil Officers (p. 98), we observe that in Oudh, meshes of the size of two grains of barley, in Mysore, $\frac{1}{8}$ of an inch, in the Central Provinces, $\frac{1}{4}$ of an inch are suggested. There can never be a necessity of having the distance between each knot less than $\frac{1}{4}$ of an inch; and even were such a minute minimum size decided upon, it would in certain districts do an immensity of good. A medium course is likewise open, instead of stopping all fishing during the breeding season to prohibit the use of fixed engines entirely spanning pieces of water, and regulating the minimum size of the mesh of nets from June 1st to November or December 1st only, so that the capture of fish which never attain any size be permitted during those months when the fry of the larger sorts have grown and are able to take care of themselves. Nothing will be gained in regulating the size of the mesh of nets in waters that yearly dry up, and after *all communication with running water has naturally ceased.* Neither should regulations extend to private ponds that never communicate with running water, and stand in the light of fish ponds in Europe. Moveable contrivances (para. LXX) made of inelastic substances, as fine split bamboos fastened together and forming a sort of net, are most destructive, and regulations regarding the interstices between each piece of the substance of which they are formed are desirable.

CXXIX.—There are other local means of destruction pursued (para. LXXVIII), several of which are most reprehensible, and may well be made penal by local bye-laws, especially fixing hooks or lines and snagging or snatching at fish. But many of the plans pursued which are considered poaching in Europe, I would suggest, should not be interfered with, at least at present. The greater evils had first better be grappled with, leaving the minor ones for future consideration.

Minor modes of fishing.

CXXX.—Vermin, as crocodiles, are most injurious (paras. LXXIX to LXXXII) and their destruction very desirable. If the fish are preserved, these great foes to them should not be permitted to live upon this species of food which is adapted for human beings; also otters are very ruinous to hill fisheries and those in their vicinity.

Vermin.

CXXXI.—Lastly, I would shortly draw attention to the following question that,—if anything is done to improve the fisheries, who is to pay for it? Are the fisheries to be improved for the good of the fishermen at the public expense, and are they to pocket the increased numbers of the finny tribes, but not pay towards such a result? In Great Britain, a tax (the moturfa) has been imposed for this purpose on all instruments used for taking fish, but in India angling may well be left free. There are three chief modes by which funds may be raised for this purpose,—(1) by again letting the fisheries, as of old, to contractors under certain specified stipulations, such as the size of the mesh of the nets to be employed, the protection of certain stock-pools, &c., and leaving them to protect the fisheries; this will save a great outlay, but to be effectually carried out, leases of from three to five years will be necessary; (2) nets may be licensed, as in the Panjáb,

Who is to pay for regulations, if any are to be carried out.

where the payment of the fee permits the fisherman to use his implement of capture in any Government waters, but the minimum size of the mesh of the nets is restricted to $1\frac{1}{4}$ inches. There is this objection that there are no overlookers as there are when contractors lease the waters; (3) Government may permit any one to fish, under certain conditions, keeping a staff of water bailiffs at the public expense to see their orders carried out—a plan which probably would fail in practice, and certainly be very expensive. But the modes in which free fisheries are worked deserve the most attentive consideration, as they are almost invariably carried on in a wasteful and destructive manner.

APPENDICES.

PANJAB.

Territory under the Panjab Government. Physical geography.

1. The territories under the Government of the Panjab and its Dependencies, excluding independent States, comprise the Cis and Trans-Sutlej Districts, placed under a Chief Commissioner in 1845; the Panjab Proper annexed in 1849, and the Delhi territories transferred in 1858, the whole lying between the 28th and 35th parallels of north latitude, and the 70th and 78th degrees of east longitude. It is computed at 102,001 square miles: bounded on the north and north-east by the Himalayan mountains; on the east by the river Jumna; on the south by the North-Western Provinces, Rajputana and the river Sutlej; on the west by the Sulimani hills and Afghanistan. The large rivers afford water communication for 2,902 miles, but the channels are shallow, sandy, and shifting, whilst during the rains the currents are very rapid. The river Jumna, as already observed, forms the eastern boundary of this province, as it emerges from the Sewalik range of hills, and between it and the Indus, on the extreme west of the Himalayan range, are five intermediate rivers, the Sutlej, Bias, Ravi, Chenab, and Jhilam, all of which eventually find their way into the Indus. These rivers are the drainage lines of the Himalayas, containing their least amount of water during the cold season, and subsequently increasing up to the monsoon time, owing to the increased heat augmenting the melting of the snows at their sources. "A remarkable feature in the topography of the province is the number of large rivers, which after pursuing their course for hundreds of miles in the valleys and glens of the mountain ranges to the north, debouch on to the plain country, dividing it into *Doabs*, and flow on in a direction generally southerly to the ocean. These rivers usually overflow their banks, sometimes to the extent of miles during the seasons of the heavy rains, and contract in the dry season till the slender stream is spanned by a bridge of a few boats, leaving dry beds of sand or mud on either side, which are brought under cultivation. Such being the character of the Panjab rivers, changes in their course, of greater or less extent, are not infrequent." Certain hollows or holes in the rivers, which are only united with the main stream during the inun-

dation season, are termed '*Boodhs*,' whilst '*Dhunds*' will be alluded to in Sinde. Besides these rivers and streams large irrigation works are being or have been constructed in the province.

2. Of the people of the Panjab, but few comparatively are absolutely prohibited by their religion from consuming fish; still there are many Hindus, particularly large zemindars, who have scruples on the subject, and these re-act upon the general rural population (always more superstitious than an urban one, and therefore more amenable to priestly craft), especially those dependant on and living around them. Thus the 'Deputy Commissioner of Delhi' observed (1870) of the people of the district, "none of the Hindu zemindars eat fish, whilst the Mahomedans are very much Hinduised in their habits. Hindu zemindars object on religious grounds to fish being caught in their village waters, and hotly contend with any Delhi fishermen caught poaching in their village ponds." But of those residing in towns and in the hilly districts, it appears as if, excluding the Brahmins, the consumption of fish is only limited by the paucity of the supply and the cost of the article.

Population of the Panjab; those in towns or in hills greater consumers of fish than those in rural districts.

3. In 1869-70 an enquiry was made into the fisheries of this province, as to whether a wasteful destruction of fish was taking place, and, if so, the best means to diminish any causes of injury for the future. The various reports gave the impression that a large amount of immature fish were yearly killed for food before they had been permitted to attain a fair size; and that this destruction was in many places being effected in Government waters, which had, or had not, been leased out for fishing purposes: consequently action was taken on the matter. In the Kangra valley the system of catching fish by means of dams, weirs, and stake-nets was prohibited, as being the chief cause of the destruction and diminution of the fish in the narrow hill streams, whilst throughout the Panjab a license for nets was ordered to be introduced gradually into localities where no revenue was derived from fisheries; the only description of net sanctioned being that which could be thrown from or held in the hand, the meshes of which were not less than 1¼ inches between knot and knot, or 5 inches all round. The license tax was proposed at Rs. 5 yearly for large nets, and Rs. 2 for small 'Chilwa' nets (see para. 13), but a discretion was left as to the amount with the local civil authorities. It was remarked that 'Chilwa' nets were not approved of, as such might be employed in taking the young of large fish. The license empowers the holder to fish generally, whether in Government waters or on private estates. For fishing in Government waters no further fee would be payable, but to enable him to fish on private estates, the holder would have to make his own arrangement with the landowner. By this plan, every person who professed to fish would require to hold a license. The license could only extend to fishing by net, and some officials insert in it the minimum size of the mesh that may be used; others have the nets brought to be inspected at the time the license is issued.

Enquiry in 1869-70 as to whether a wasteful destruction of fish existed. Prohibition of fixed engines, and the damming of hill streams. Introduction of a license system for nets. Chilwa nets.

4. With reference to the questions issued with my letter of September 17th, 1871, the following is a synopsis of the answers received. First, *as to the proportion of the general population who would eat fish could they obtain it?* Out of 41 native officials who have replied, the following are the figures given—

What is the proportion of the general population who consume fish?

5	per cent. eat fish in 1 Tehsil.						
12	,,	,,	,,	,,	,,	2	,,
20	,,	,,	,,	,,	,,	1	,,
25	,,	,,	,,	,,	,,	5	,,
33	,,	,,	,,	,,	,,	2	,,
44	,,	,,	,,	,,	,,	1	,,
50	,,	,,	,,	,,	,,	9	,,
66	,,	,,	,,	,,	,,	5	,,
75	,,	,,	,,	,,	,,	7	,,
80	,,	,,	,,	,,	,,	2	,,
90 to 95	,,	,,	,,	,,	,,	6	,,

Irrespective of these, in 10 'the majority of the people,' in 5 'a small proportion,' and in 1 'none' of population are said to eat fish, but in the last, the reason given is, 'because there are none to eat.' The Mahomedans, except the Sheeas at Jalandur, as a rule do so, unless prevented by local objections (see para. 2): most of the Hindus in towns or along the banks of large rivers, unless they are Brahmins, whilst the rural population is more averse to it.

5. *How are the local markets supplied with fish?* is a question answered by some Tehsildars directly; by others more indirectly. Seventy-six give definite answers, which may be thus divided: in 7 tehsils the markets are fully supplied; in 2 they are moderately so; in 10 sufficiently only during the cold season; in 1 only during the rains; in 48 insufficiently all the year round, and in 8 not at all. In Hushiarpur there are said to be no markets, the people only capturing fish for their own consumption; in 2 tehsils fish are exchanged for grain. Where fish are sold, the price of the better sorts bears the same proportion to that of the best mutton, as the price of inferior fish to that of inferior mutton, and varies from one-third that of mutton to an equal price with it. Salt-fish does not find much of a sale.

Local markets insufficiently supplied with fish.

6. *Have the fish increased, decreased, or remained stationary?* is replied to by 78 Tehsildars, an increase being reported by 13, a stationary state by 32, and a decrease by 33. A cause of decrease is stated at Delhi to be the Okla weir, which crosses the Jumna near that city, and does not possess any fish pass in it (see para. 43). In the Sialkot Division the wholesale destruction of Mahaseer by means of fixed nets is adverted to in the affluents of the Chenab. 'Colonel Macpherson' observes, that he "can testify to the fisheries in the Ganges and Jumna having deteriorated very greatly in the last eight years. * * One can hardly see fish moving now-a-day, whereas in the years I have mentioned (1861—63) we used to hear and see shoals of large mahaseer on the feed, three or four times a day."

Present state of the fisheries. Destruction of breeding fish in hilly districts.

7. *As to whose the fisheries are?* is, I conclude, a question which, though raised by some persons, scarcely admits of an argument. The residents, doubtless, have the same claims in respect to them as they have to the land, but no license gives a right. In the Panjab, under native rule, the fisheries are stated to have been annually let to a contractor, but whether he was bound to see the fisheries were not impoverished, there appear to be no records to show. 'The Deputy Commissioner of Kangra' observes, when proposing protective measures, that they must be partially a system of Government preserves, such as was always in force in the time of the Rajahs, partly by giving licenses to monopolists to supply the markets, and partly by licenses for fishing with small nets for home consumption, and not for sale.

<small>The fisheries the property of Government. How the Rajahs let them.</small>

8. *The fishermen* of this province do not appear to follow this occupation alone, but only as a supplement to other means of support, so none have an interest in protecting the fisheries, but only in procuring as much as they can, and whenever they can, for themselves. Consequently, regulations would not interfere with any sole means of subsistence affecting a class.

<small>Panjab fishermen not dependant upon this occupation as a sole means of subsistence.</small>

9. *Are breeding fish or fry destroyed?* is a most important enquiry. Previous to the introduction of the present rules into the Panjab, of regulating the minimum size of the mesh of the nets at $1\frac{1}{4}$ inches between each knot, large numbers of young fish were sold as 'Chilwas.' Since this time in many of the districts this destruction has been partially stopped; in others the regulations have not as yet been carried out. 'The Officiating Deputy Commissioner of Ambala' observes, that the restriction as to the size of the mesh of the net has only been held to apply to rivers, whilst in fields, tanks, and hollows, the smallest meshes are used; indeed, sheets are employed. In a few tehsils the trapping of fish in irrigated or inundated fields is recorded. The regulation as to the minimum size of the mesh at $1\frac{1}{4}$ inches between the knots appears a very good one, and does not entail much difficulty in being carried out.

<small>Are breeding fish or fry destroyed? Result of regulating the minimum size of the mesh of the nets.</small>

10. The *modes of fishing* pursued are exceedingly diversified, and the *wholesale* ones may be first adverted to. In Kangra the zemindars are stated to do a good deal of mischief, in the early part of the rains, by bringing the fish into side streams, then draining off the water and leaving them on dry ground; young and old are caught in this manner. Mr. Carleton observes, that the grain in the Himalayas is ground by hundreds of mills moved by water power, canals are constructed into which water is diverted to turn these mills, and into these, numerous small fishes, especially the young of the more valuable sorts, find their way. By shutting off the water from these 'kools' or canals, the fish become left on dry ground, and are thus captured. Personally I tried this mode of taking fish between Kutla and Kangra: by stopping the flow of water into this miniature canal, fish were seen struggling

<small>Mode of capturing fish wholesale in canals in the hills which are constructed for working mills. Impediment to their entrance should be imperative on the mill-owners.</small>

upwards to attain the head of this 'kool,' or else left in its dried-up bed: one native stands at the head of the channel, and by making a great splashing he frightens the fish from coming up to the stream, and thus, without using a net at all, numerous small fishes are taken, whilst these, or most of them, ought to be for the next year's supply. This mode of destruction must be very injurious to hill fisheries, but could be easily remedied, by compelling the owner of each canal to make a matted grating of boughs or bamboos or a similar obstruction at the head of each, which, without impeding the water, would prevent the entrance of the fish.

11. Analogous to the foregoing, is the diverting of hill streams and thus capturing all the fishes therein, also damming them up and lading them out, and the existence of weirs and impassable barriers, which are made instrumental in the capture of fish, and it was properly decided in the Kangra valley that "the system of catching fish by means of dams, weirs, and stake-nets was prohibited, as being the chief cause of the destruction and diminution of the fish in the narrow hill streams." Poisoning streams is not reputed to be carried on in the Panjab.

Diverting hill streams, damming them, the erection of weirs and barriers and poisoning the water.

12. Another mode of destroying large numbers of fish in the Panjab, is the existence of irrigation weirs without fish passes, across large rivers, and which permit valuable fishes, as the mahaseer, which breeds along the bases of the hills, to descend, but prevents any return to its breeding places as already described. Worse, if possible, probably, are the irrigation weirs which have impassable falls up which fish cannot ascend, but over which they may descend, and so become trapped. Thus the mahaseer go down these large channels, but cannot return. It has been suggested that they might continue their descent, and thus find an exit at the lower end, but this they will not do. As the canal becomes shallower towards its termination, the falls are lower, the holes formed below them less deep, and there is not so much food, consequently they will not be found there. This is not a theoretical opinion, but deduced from actual observation made when a canal was dried off. These canals are emptied at certain periods for repairs or other causes, and at this period many fish are left dry in the bed and are easily killed, but a large number retreat into the holes which exist and contain water. In some of these canals a custom obtains to permit the employees to kill all they are able, in any manner they can; in other places this is more or less prohibited; whilst in some the fishing is let out and every living fish destroyed, no matter how small; and as none can ascend out of the canals, the destruction is enormous and sufficient to ruin any fisheries. 'Dr. Allen,' of the 2nd Ghurkas, thus observed on these constructions:—" The fisheries are certainly decreasing as regards the number of fish, both in the Ganges and Jumna rivers. The chief cause of this, I believe, to be the drain on them caused by the canals. Mahaseer, rohoo, kalabeinse, &c., abound in all the canals both from the Jumna and Ganges. The mahaseer are very plentiful in the Jumna canal (Kurnal branch, which runs down to Hansi and Hissar) and in the Ganges canal. When these canals silt up, or the

Irrigation weirs and canals as at present existing, destructive to fisheries.

water is cut off from their head, for cleaning, repairing, or other purposes, hundreds of thousands of fish of all kinds and of all sizes are destroyed. When the water shallows sufficiently, men and boys go into it with sticks, and kill the fish in thousands, and this occurs every year. It must be very evident that so great a drain as this must decrease and injure the supply of fish in the main streams, as before the canals were cut, the whole of those now entering them remained in the Ganges and Jumna rivers and their tributary streams. The tributary streams may be netted and bunded, but such an amount of injury to the fishing from this cause would not happen in a series of years, as is produced in one year by the indiscriminate slaughter in the canals, when fish from a maund in weight downwards are destroyed through a hundred or more miles of country."

13. *Respecting the prohibiting the sale of the fry of fish in the bazars.*—This question opens up the enquiry—

<small>Suggestions respecting prohibiting the sale of the fry of fish in the bazars, or whether it should be only from June until November, so that chilwas might be taken during the cold season.</small>

what are chilwas? as these small fish are largely sold throughout the Panjab, and are asserted never to attain any size. That many such small fish do exist, is not open to doubt; in fact, chilwas may be defined, as any scaled fish not above a span in length, and which does not attain a larger size. I personally witnessed young mahaseer being taken as chilwas, and the young of other species of large and valuable fishes. There is a great difficulty doubtless in its being very clear to every one which are young fish and which adults of small sorts; and to obviate pressing rather unduly on all classes by prohibiting entirely the sale of small fish, one gentleman proposes that the fry of fish should not be allowed to be sold in the bazars from June to November, and this would certainly embrace the months when the young are moving about. At Ambala the fishermen complained that it was very hard that they might not capture small fish, whilst other persons who were not fishermen were allowed to sell such in the bazars. Twelve European officials would prohibit its sale entirely, one would not interfere. In several districts it is observed that such a regulation would be useless, as no fish is publicly sold. The possession of salmon fry is illegal in England.

14. *Respecting the applicability or the reverse of close months.*—

<small>Fence months; its advisability for two months during the rains in the hilly districts.</small>

They appear to be generally considered as desirable, more especially in the hilly ranges to which mahaseer and other valuable fish resort to breed, ascending rivers to the bases of the hills, in order to reach their breeding grounds with the filling of the mountain streams due to the commencement of the monsoon, generally in the first half of the month of June. Then ascending the larger streams, they turn aside into the tributaries, which are not replenished by melted snows, to deposit their ova, which are hatched out but do not generally descend to the plains until the next season. Now it seems desirable that these breeding fish should have free ingress and egress, and it is only by declaring a close season for these districts that such could be effected. The range wherein this should be carried out, and the time at which these two months should be insisted upon, about July and August, could be well left to the local civil authorities.

15. It has also been suggested, that certain deep pools in which fish take shelter during the dry (not cold) months of the year should be protected in the hills, as they are very easily netted there. Mr. Carleton proposes that certain streams should be considered preserves and kept for the breeding of the fish.

A few deep pools in hill streams, it is proposed, should be selected and preserved during the dry (not cold) months in the hill streams.

16. *Trapping fish* in irrigated fields ought to be most strictly prohibited, at least during the monsoon months, as an immense amount of injury must occur by destroying all, both young and old. If this mode of using fixed engines is to be permitted at all, the interstices between the materials of which such traps is composed should be at least 1¼ inches, or that laid down for the meshes of fishing nets, whilst they should be prohibited from April to November.

Trapping fish objected to, at least from April to November. Size of interstices should be the same as in nets.

17. It has, in addition to the foregoing, been suggested in the 'Sialkot district' (paragraph 28) that the Government of Cashmere be keenly urged to carry out whatever system of preservation is decided upon for India, as efforts in our territory to preserve this main staple of food must be considerably retarded without their support, because the affluents of the large rivers up which the fish ascend to breed are out of our districts. 'Mr. Carleton' also observes that the two States, Bilaspur and Sialkot, remain without a single restraint as regards fishing. Those States situated on the Sutlej occupy its finest fishing ground, and some of the best, if not the very best, streams for fish breeding, and no hill people are more addicted to fishing than those living within these two territories. He continues:—"I have lived three seasons along the head waters of the Ravi at Chumba, and five seasons along the head waters of the Bias at Kulu, and traversed over the Sutlej valley for ten years as far as Rampur, and nowhere have I seen such destruction of fish as in those two States, especially Sialkot. * * Many of the people have little close hand-nets, with which they regularly clean out the gorges of young fry."

Cashmere Government and those of Bilaspur and Sialkot to be requested to assist in protecting valuable fish ascending their hilly streams to breed.

18. Throughout the various portions of India which I have visited in investigating the fish and fisheries, in none have such excellent rules been framed as in this province, embracing as they do protection to the immature fish by prohibiting the use of nets having a mesh less than 1¼ inches between each knot, disallowing the use of dams, weirs, and stake-nets, and only permitting in the hill streams the employment of such nets as can be held by or thrown from the hand.

Present Panjab fishing regulations.

19. The further regulations which it is suggested by the 'Officiating Secretary to the Panjab Government,' are, prohibiting the sale of the fry of fishes in the bazars or mahaseer under 1℔. weight; a close season during July and August; the establishment of breeding tanks in connection with the irrigation canals, and by gratings or otherwise to prevent the fish going down these canals.

Further ones proposed.

20. In addition I would suggest to the foregoing (paragraphs 10 and 33), the owners of mills in hill streams should make obstructions, as matted gratings, at the commencement of their 'kools' or canals, which would prevent the entrance of young fish now so extensively destroyed therein. Fish-passes should be placed in all ascents in irrigation canals or at weirs, and the destruction of fish when the canals are closed should be strictly prohibited. Close seasons would probably only be required along the hilly ranges, and netting might be prohibited in a few deep pools in the hill streams during the dry months. Trapping fish, or having fixed engines for taking them, should be prohibited, at least between April and November, and even then the interstices in substances forming traps should be equal to the minimum size permitted between the knots of the meshes of nets.

Additional ones suggested.

21. The following are condensed from the opinions of the European and Native officials of the Panjab, received either in 1869-70, or else in answer to the questions circulated in September 1871.

Contents of the following synopsis of papers received from the Panjab.

22. The Officiating Secretary to the Government of the Panjab (July 16th, 1872) reports that there are 10,450 fishermen in the province, but in no district do they seem to follow fishing as their sole occupation. The fishermen castes are mostly Jewars, Machis, Kahars, and Kashmiris: those who also engage in fishing are Jats, Sunnias, Mains, Jhils, Singharis, Maithans, Pakhiwaras, Julahas, Jhabails, Sukkais, Mullahs, Dindars, Magus, Dhunniahs, Beluchis, Rahras, Pathans, Khokars, Bhattis, Manjris, Jhabals, Panwars, Patries, and Mahanas. Fish are largely eaten, the cost of the better sorts bearing the same proportion to that of the best mutton, as the price of inferior fish to that of inferior mutton, and varies from one-third that of mutton to an equal price with it. Under the present licensing system 1¼ inches square is the smallest size of mesh permissible to use; previous to its introduction large numbers of young fish were sold as "chilwas," and met with a ready sale. Even now in some districts very fine meshed nets are locally employed. The greatest destruction takes place after the rains, when the floods subside, leaving large quantities of small fish in the fields. It is generally considered that prohibiting the sale of fry in the bazar would entail no difficulty and but little hardship. The markets as a rule are well supplied (see para. 5), the new regulations are admitted, on all hands to have had a good effect in preserving the fish, whilst the fishermen have decreased. Probably due to the late hot seasons, no marked increase has yet been observed in the amount of fish. Several officers advise a close season during July and August. One and a quarter inches between knot and knot of the meshes of nets is generally considered the smallest that should be allowed. On the whole the reports show that the present system of licenses is working well, though the following additional measures might with advantage be taken for the preservation of the fisheries. To enjoin two close months, July and August; in districts where fish are very plentiful, to impose some limit on the amount of fish which may be caught under each license; to prohibit the sale of fry in the bazars, and that

Officiating Secretary to the Panjab Government. Summary of opinions received from the local officials of the province.

of 'mahaseer' of less than one pound in weight; to establish breeding tanks in connection with the canals; and by gratings or otherwise to prevent the fish from going down the irrigation canals.

The Commissioner of the Peshâwar Division observes, that he does not think fishermen do so much injury to the fish in his district as he has seen done in rivers down country; still he considers that it would be very right to give the fish a better chance of multiplying by insisting on the stoppage of all kinds of fishing during the close months, for carrying out which no separate establishment is advised. The size of the mesh of nets might be regulated to protect the fry, which, however, are not taken to any extent by the people of the country; but the Hindustani and Panjabi kahárs in the military stations make for themselves casting nets with which they catch 'chilwas.'

Peshâwar Division.—Opinions of the European officials of Peshâwar, Hazara and Kohát.

The Deputy Commissioner of Peshâwar states, that breeding fish and very young ones are destroyed in his district to a great extent, and at all seasons, by means of nets, fish-hooks and sheets, in the Indus, Cabul and Swat rivers, and in Lotaie and Baráh streams and the Boodnee canal, the smallest size of the mesh of the nets being $\frac{1}{4}$ of an inch between knot and knot. No difficulties would exist in regulating the minimum size to be employed, which he proposes should be $\frac{1}{4}$ of an inch for small fish, and 1 inch for large sorts. There would be no objection to prohibiting the sale of the fry of fish in the bazars. *The Deputy Commissioner of Hazara* gives the smallest size of the mesh of the nets employed at about $\frac{3}{4}$ of an inch square. If the minimum size were regulated, it would give rise to irritation amongst a border population, and require an establishment to see it carried out; but fishing might be prohibited for two months without much inconvenience. *The Deputy Commissioner of Kohát* considers that breeding fish and very young ones are not destroyed to any great extent in his district, and the smallest mesh employed is $\frac{1}{8}$ of an inch between knot and knot; that there would be no difficulty in regulating its minimum size, but has no opinion as to what that should be. As fry is never sold, its sale might be prohibited.

24. *The Commissioner of Ráwal Pindi* observed in 1870 that "fishing licenses are the only check we have upon the wholesale destruction of young fish, and I would on no account relax them." *The Deputy Commissioner of Ráwal Pindi* reports that breeding and young fish are not destroyed to any perceptible extent. The usual nets allowed have a mesh of $1\frac{1}{2}$ inches between knot and knot, but two licenses are given for 'chilwa' fishermen who use a much finer mesh for the purpose of taking small fish which never grow to any size. There are no difficulties in regulating the minimum size of the mesh, 1 inch between knot and knot is recommended. The people of these parts do not depend upon fish as their food; a very few touch it, therefore prohibiting the sale of the fry in the bazar would be a wholesome measure and strike at the root of the evil. There would be no objection to having a close season for two months in the hilly ranges. *The Deputy Commissioner of Jhilam* states that breeding and young fish are not destroyed to any great extent, as care is taken that the meshes of all nets have $1\frac{1}{4}$ inches between knot and knot. The

Ráwal Pindi Division.—Answers of the European officials of Ráwal Pindi, Jhilam, Shahpur, and Gujrát.

hill streams termed 'kus' dry up during the greater part of the year and are not fished, whilst there are no jhils or pools. In the river along the Pind Dadun Khan tehsil, 45 miles in length, no fishing is practised, due to there being no markets for the sale of fish, as the natives will not eat them. *The Officiating Deputy Commissioner of Sháhpur* reports, that neither breeding nor young fish are destroyed in his district; only one license was taken out, and that to supply fish to officers and Babus in the station. *The Deputy Commissioner of Gujrat* reports, that breeding and young fish are not destroyed in his district, whilst there are no breeding fish so low down the river. The minimum size of the mesh of nets employed is $\frac{1}{3}$ of an inch; no difficulties exist in regulating it, and $1\frac{1}{2}$ inches is proposed as suitable. Respecting what objections exist against prohibiting the sale of the fry of fish in the bazars? he remarks, "the fry of fish is not understood. Jheewurs, 'Hindus,' commonly sell fried fish in the bazars, and I hear of no objection to it." He considers that two months close time in the hilly districts might be introduced.

25. *The Officiating Commissioner of the Derajat Division* merely forwards papers received. *The Officiating Deputy Commissioner of Bánú* reports that breeding fish and very small ones are not destroyed to any extent in his district; that the smallest size of the mesh of nets is $\frac{1}{4}$ of an inch between knot and knot, whilst, as very few fish are caught, it is unnecessary to regulate the minimum size of the mesh employed. No fish are sold in the bazars. *The Deputy Commissioner of Dera Gázi Khán* observes, that very little fish are caught in the northern part of the district; the local market is well supplied, but by fishermen belonging to the Muzaffargarh side of the Indus. A certain quantity of fish is caught in Jámpur, but they are principally taken in the cold season in dhunds left by the subsidence of the Indus. A considerable amount of small fry is captured, and minute-meshed nets are in common use. There would be no difficulty in regulating the size of the mesh to be employed, but such restrictions are considered to be unnecessary. He continues that gulls take more small fish than fishermen! *The Officiating Deputy Commissioner of Dera Ismail Khán* observes, breeding fish and very young ones are not destroyed to a great extent. The smallest size mesh of the nets is $\frac{1}{2}$ an inch between knot and knot. There would be no difficulty in regulating it, and $\frac{1}{2}$ an inch between knot and knot is proposed as the minimum size. The fry of fish are said not to be sold in the bazars.

Derajat Division.—Answers of the European officials of Banu, Dera Gázi Khán, and Dera Ismáil Khan.

26. *The Officiating Deputy Commissioner, Jhang*, observes, that he thinks there is a tendency to destroy breeding and very young fish in the rainy season by the use of small meshed nets, but in his district the evil is not general, owing to the fishing population consisting of but few persons. The meshes of some of the nets are as small as about one-eighth of an inch square, and no difficulty stands in the way of the enforcement of any enactment on the subject of regulating the minimum size to be employed, which it is proposed should be one inch square. No objections

Multan Division.—Answers of the European officials of Jhang, Muzaffargarh, Montgomery, and Multan.

whatever exist against prohibiting the sale of the fry of fish in the bazars. *The Officiating Deputy Commissioner, Muzaffargarh,* reports that there does not appear to be any very extensive destruction of breeding and young fish, as fishing is chiefly carried on in pools formed by inundations, which soon dry up after the river subsides. Nets are not used with a mesh less than 1¼ inches between knot and knot, which might be increased by further regulations to 2 or even 3 inches. " Mian Mahbub Dhony, Magistrate, who is a great sportsman, thinks the mesh should not be less than 9 inches all round." There is no difficulty in regulating the minimum size of the meshes of nets; the sale of fry by fishermen should be prohibited, for, if they have been purchased by the retailers, it will be difficult to interfere with them. In 1870 the *Deputy Commissioner* of this place reported: "there is a great and wanton destruction of young fish by men with purse nets of small meshes," which he considered should be prohibited during June, July and August. *The Officiating Deputy Commissioner, Montgomery,* states that breeding fish and very young ones are destroyed to some extent in 'boodhs,' or hollow places in the rivers, which, during the rainy season, are united with the stream, but become detached as inundations cease. About ¼ of an inch between knot and knot of the nets appears to be the smallest size employed, and there seems no difficulty in regulating what it should be; 1½ inches is proposed for this purpose. No objections exist against prohibiting the sale of the fry of fish in the bazars. *The Officiating Deputy Commissioner of Multan* replies, that breeding fish and very young ones are destroyed to a considerable extent. Various kinds of traps and snares are employed in the district during the cold season in the 'dhunds'; a species of basket is commonly in use. The smallest size mesh of nets used is ½ an inch square, but these are rarely employed, they being generally from 1 to 2 inches. No difficulty is anticipated in regulating the minimum size to be sanctioned, which it is suggested should be 2 inches between knot and knot, and thus destruction of young fish, which is at present considerable, will be avoided. No objection exists against prohibiting the sale of the fry of fish in the bazars, which is considered to be desirable.

27. *The Deputy Commissioner of Lahor* reports, that breeding fish are not destroyed to a very great extent, as, owing to the period fish breed being in the rains, the current of the river is such, that netting is difficult. 'Chilwa' fishing is carried on in July and August, and small fish of all kinds are taken by hand-nets. " Breeding fish and their young are caught in July and August in the Deg, and in the chumbs and creeks connected with it; the former in ordinary nets, and the latter in small hand-nets with fine meshes. The zemindars catch the small fish in the chumbs in a variety of ways, with baskets or cloth bags, or fine nets, &c." The smallest size of the mesh of nets employed is about that of a pea. "The difficulties about regulating the size of the meshes of nets are mainly two: the legal difficulty in enforcing any rules on the subject; at present forfeiture of the license is the only penalty. Secondly, the financial difficulty: any attempt to introduce the license system or to regulating the size of the meshes would be attended with an immediate loss of revenue. It is probable, however, that the revenue would in time recover itself as large

Lahor Division.—Answers of the European officials of Lahor and Gujranwala.

fish increased in numbers, and the fishermen become accustomed to the system. As already stated, the attempt was made in this district, but had to be abandoned on financial grounds." [I must here point out that other local reasons exist at Lahor, the fishery at ·this place being let in a peculiar manner at Rs. 2,228 yearly, and the mode was thus described by the *Officiating Commissioner* in February 1870: "The lease is current for the financial year, and is put up annually to auction. It embraces the Deg nullah, the river Ravi, and the jhils and creeks connected with those rivers. Zemindars owning land on the rivers' bank may, without hindrance from the lessee, catch fish for their own consumption, but they are not allowed to sell any fish. Practically also, any one may fish with a hook, provided only he does not sell the fish which he catches. None but fishermen, authorised by the lessee, are allowed to catch fish with a net. The fishermen are well known; they congregate in a few villages near the river, and carry on their calling in gangs. Each fishing party is accompanied by a servant of the lessee, whose duty it is to see that all the fish caught are brought to the market which the lessee has established for the sale of fish at Data Gung Buksh, in the vicinity of Lahor, and that none are sold elsewhere by the fishermen. The fish, when brought to the market, are sold wholesale to dealers for what they will fetch. The sale proceeds of fish caught in the Deg are divided equally between the lessee and the fishermen; but as regards fish caught in the Ravi, the lessee's share of the proceeds is only 4 annas in the rupee, while the fisherman's is 12 annas. These rates were, however, altered thus in 1861; it was agreed that the following should be the lessee's share:—Fish from the Deg, $8\frac{1}{2}$ annas in the rupee; from the Ravi, $6\frac{1}{2}$ annas in the rupee; from other districts, $4\frac{1}{2}$ annas in the rupee. Fish are sometimes brought ·to Lahor from Montgomery by rail, and from other districts. In this case they are brought to market and sold through the lessee, who charges a commission of $1\frac{1}{2}$ annas a rupee on the sale proceeds. In the Lahor District, it is chiefly from the Deg that fish are caught; a considerable number are caught from jhils and chuppurs fed from the Deg. These jhils and chuppurs are regarded as the private property of the zemindars, with whom the lessee makes his own arrangement in regard to being allowed to fish in them. * * * Netting in the Ravi is a difficult operation, and is seldom attempted. The fish, which are taken nominally from the Ravi, are caught almost entirely in the nallas and pools left after the floods of the rainy season have subsided." Thus it can hardly be considered that it is simply the fisheries that are let, but fisheries and an octroi duty on fish that is disposed of.] One and a quarter of an inch is suggested as the proper minimum size at which the meshes of nets should be fixed, and there exists no objection to prohibiting the sale of the fry of fishes in the bazars. *The Deputy Commissioner of Gujranwalla* observes, that in the Chenab very young fish known as 'chahil' are largely caught; the smallest sized mesh employed is $\frac{1}{2}$ of an inch. There would be no difficulty in regulating the minimum size to be employed in future, " but the small meshed nets already in existence would continue to be used until worn out." No objections against prohibiting the sale of the fry of fish are known.

28. *The Officiating Deputy Commissioner, Amritsar*, does not consider that breeding fish are destroyed to any deleterious extent; a large number of young ones are killed during the rains in irrigated fields, the smallest mesh employed being 1 inch square. There are no objections to prohibiting the sale of the fry of fish in bazars; it could be easily carried out. Numbers of fish are said to be destroyed here in the irrigation canals, whenever they are dried off, irrespective of size, whilst all the holes are netted. The presence of a few tanks, it is suggested, connected with, but lower than the bed of, the canal, would not only enable many fish to escape the annual slaughter, but be valuable for fishing purposes throughout the year. *The Deputy Commissioner, Sialkot*, reports, that he does not think very young fish to any great extent are destroyed in the rivers and nallas of his district; but he holds the opinion that the fishermen net (as indeed do all native fishermen) indiscriminately and without consideration as to breeding time, and considers that it would be most necessary to enter a strict prohibition in the licenses against their fishing at all during breeding months, *viz.*, July and August. The meshes of the nets, since 1870, have not been used smaller than $1\frac{1}{4}$ inches between knot and knot, and no difficulties exist respecting regulating the minimum size, which he proposes should be $1\frac{1}{2}$ inches in future. He would advocate that as the bazar demand is great at times for the smaller or fry of fish (which are more of a luxury than an actual necessary staple of food) licenses be given for their sale between April 15th and May 15th; and again between September 1st and October 1st, but would prohibit their being sold in the markets or elsewhere during any other time. The following opinion of an officer of the district, who has much indulged in fishing, is enclosed: "First, if the proposal (of only permitting the employment of such nets as can be held by the hand) were carried into effect, nothing more need be done in these parts. In the Chenab, which encloses two sides of this district (north and east), the 'mahaseer' run in shoals, and are thick at one particular spot, and perhaps are not to be found for a distance of 10 miles. They abound chiefly where a tributary runs in, and where the water is usually warmer and there is good feeding. In the spring rains, they ascend these tributaries to breed, returning in the monsoons. If there is no depth of water where the tributary joins the Chenab, they probably drop in the winter into the deeper pools. I remember one instance in this district which was brought to my notice in 1869, and shortly after my arrival here. There was a large school of fish collected at the junction of the 'Tavia,' running from Rajowri (in the Cashmere Illakah) and the 'Chenab'. This could be easily netted, and the consequence was, a large net of about 40 to 60 yards in length was placed across the stream, and another dragged down the river for about 100 yards. Thus an innumerable number of fish were caught, and the result was, there was little or no rod fishing that season, which to a certain extent demonstrates the fact that the place had been denuded of fish. I have drawn the attention of the Cashmere authorities to the evil of this wholesale system of destruction in the tributaries of the Chenab within that territory, and I have also prohibited the practice as much as

Amritsar Division.—Answers of the European officials of Amritsar, Sialkot, and Gurdaspur.

possible in this district. There is no doubt that even now the mahaseer especially are a persecuted fish, particularly at that season of the year when the water is low (just before the rains), and especially in the hill streams (where they are spawning), when they are nearly all destroyed. I would strongly advocate, as regards this district, that the Government of Cashmere be keenly urged to carry out whatever system of preservation Government intends to enforce, as our efforts to preserve this main staple of food must be considerably retarded without their support." *The Deputy Commissioner of Gurdaspur* states, that since licenses have been issued the destruction of breeding and very young fish has diminished, but that the capture of fry during the rains is still carried on; they are taken with baskets, cloths, &c., in all shallow places in streams, after the rains have subsided. The minimum size of the authorized mesh is $1\frac{1}{4}$ inches. The impossibility of supervision is the chief difficulty in regulating the size of the mesh. This can only be met by finding out all men who make any part of their living by fishing and compelling them take out licenses. The recorded license-holders could be visited periodically, and their nets examined year by year, thus the fishing of the rivers could be brought more under control. The objection against prohibiting the sale of the fry of fish in the bazar, is, that they are more tasty; but on the other hand, Hindus think that it is better to take the life of one large fish than of many small ones. "The principle of protecting fish, and in fact all game, during the breeding season, is too well established to need comment. Should it entail any hardship on the population of the hills, it seems to me that they must bear it, as the fish are protected in the interests of the community at large."

29. *The Commissioner of Ambala* forwards the following from *the Officiating Deputy Commissioner:* that he

Ambala Division.—Answers of the European officials of Ambala and Ludhiana.

thinks breeding and immature fish are destroyed to a great extent; that the restriction as to the size of the mesh of the net has only been held to apply to rivers, whilst in fields, tanks, and hollows, the smallest meshes are used; indeed, sheets are employed. No difficulties exist against regulating the minimum size of the mesh of nets; but if the sale of fry is prohibited, it would simply deprive the public of a valued article of food. No objection obtains against prohibiting the capture of fish in hilly districts during the first two months of the monsoon season when they are breeding; in fact, he considers the suggestion expedient. *The Deputy Commissioner*, in 1870, stated, that "there are numbers of káhars and others, who at different seasons of the floods, when at leisure, catch great numbers of small fish, which appear principally to be washed down from the hills, and which if uncaught must perish in the drying up of the water. These fish form an important article of food temporarily for a number of the poor classes, and any attempt to prevent them from enjoying this article of food would be a hardship." *The Officiating Deputy Collector of Ludhiana* considers, that the breeding fish and very young are not destroyed to any great extent in the district, since the size of the mesh of the nets has been regulated. It is considered expedient to prohibit the sale of the fry of fish in the bazars.

30. *The Commissioner of Jalandar* observed in 1870—"I would remark that there is the most wanton destruction of fish in some of our jhils, which should I think be put a stop to." The *Deputy Commissioner*, the same year, stated—

Jalandar Division.—Answers of European officials of Jalandar, Phillur, Hushiarpur.

"I inspected some nets now in use: one was brought to me used for fishing in ponds, nine of whose meshes went to a square inch." *The Extra Assistant Commissioner, Phillur*, reports that breeding and very young fish are not destroyed 'wantonly' in this district to any extent; if they are at all, it must be in the rainy season, or a short time before, and then only by being caught in common with other fish ; 1¼ inches between knot and knot of the meshes is the smallest size employed, and there is no difficulty in regulating this or any other minimum size. When a chowkeydar sees a man fishing, he looks at his license and examines his net. Would propose that only large-meshed nets are permitted during the breeding season, but in the early spring when ' chilwa' fishing is carried on, would permit one inch between knot and knot. Respecting prohibiting the sale of the fry of fish in the bazar, he remarks— "Considered merely as an article of food, there is no objection to the fry of fish being sold in the bazar ; but I think it would tend to an increase of the supply of large fish in the markets if the fry were not allowed to be sold." *The Deputy Commissioner of Hushiarpur* observes that his replies must be accepted in a general way, and are not intended as touching upon the customs of his district alone, but the result of experience obtained in several. In the ponds and jhils left in the course of the Bizu river through the Jalandar district, and in similar places in other districts, there is a great destruction of young fish by netting with sheets, &c. Prior to the issue of the circular in 1870 regulating the minimum size of the mesh at 1¼ inches between knot and knot, great destruction with fine-meshed nets was personally witnessed. The only difficulties in regulating the size of the mesh of the nets are such as are general in preventing smuggling and poaching. The sale of the fry of fish is so small that it is hardly worth interfering with ; its capture is generally effected for home consumption ; what was sad to witness, was the huge numbers of very small fish dragged up with the weeds, &c., and left to perish as useless. In all out-lying villages fish are caught by men who require to eat them, not as a luxury, but as a necessary article of food; and if deprived of this, other means of subsistence should be provided for them, which would be no easy matter, if at all practicable. Attempts should be confined to the remedy of great evils rather than to an interference with small ones, which could be done by making it criminal to use nets with meshes smaller than prescribed. *The Deputy Commissioner of Kangra* reports, that he believes that young fish used to be caught and breeding checked until the new rules about licenses and limiting the size of the mesh were introduced. Doubtless, the Jeewun and Kahar castes catch fish by stealth all over the district, as there are no means of preventing this. The places in which they used to be most destroyed, were in those streams which become very shallow during the dry months, leaving, however, some deep pools in which the fish take shelter as the floods decline, and where they are easily netted. By way of testing the quantity and breeds of fish in one of these pools opposite Haripur in the river Ban-gunga, one was dragged. The fish were all driven into a corner, and there they swarmed; round hand-nets were used to catch them. Some four or five maunds were taken in a very short time; any number of nets were produced immediately they were asked for, but all, except hand-nets, had 1¼ inches between knot and knot of the meshes. Drag-nets are prohibited, but steps should be taken to preserve these pools. Would propose keeping a watchman at this place out of the license fees, which should be raised to Rs. 20 per annum, the number of fishing days to be restricted, as well as the amount captured on any one day. Each Deputy Commissioner should be left to his own devices to stop the destruction of fish. Arrangements should be made to bring the fish to market, which now is never done. By-and-bye we should find out what succeeded and what failed, and be able to frame some defined rules for the district. It is in the dry months that fish are destroyed, and in the early rains, rarely in the winter, when they take to the bottom and under the rocks, and are not easily disturbed. From March to July poaching goes on to the greatest extent. There are no difficulties in regulating the size of the mesh of nets. When licenses are granted the nets have to be produced; 1¼ inches is considered a very good size for the minimum: it certainly should not be less. Small 'chilwa' nets might be allowed in streams never frequented by the larger kinds of fish. So few fish are brought into the markets that no measures are necessary for prohibiting the sale of the fry. Would like to have a licensed fish stall under the supervision of Government officials at each chief market town, and take such steps from time to time as may be necessary for preventing the sale of fry. No objections exist to stopping fishing during the breeding season, except for special purposes under a special license. The zemindars do a great deal of mischief in the early part of the rains by bringing the fish into side streams and then draining off the water and leaving them on dry ground; young and old are caught in this way. The system of poaching fish and game wholesale should be made a penal offence, and district officers will soon find that other measures can be dispensed with. There are still abundance of fish in all the chief rivers, the Bias, Ravi, Chaki, Ban-gunga, Auvale, Niggul, and some others; but doubtless measures are necessary to prevent the population from reckless systems of netting them. These measures must be, partially, a system of Government preserves, such as was always in force in the time of the Rajahs, partly by giving licenses to monopolists to supply the market, and partly by licenses for fishing with small nets for home consumption and not for sale.

31. The *Officiating Commissioner of Hissár* (January 16th, 1872,) sug-

Hissár Division.—Answers of the Officiating Commissioner and Deputy Commissioner.

gests wire gratings at the top of the first fall in the canal to arrest the downward progress of large fish, if practicable in an engineering point of view; if not, that fish-ladders should be placed at the canal falls. He continues with reference to constructing fish-ladders at weirs spanning rivers: " I took up this suggestion some time ago when Deputy Commissioner of Delhi, and ascertained from the Superintending Engineer of the Agra Canal, that the construction of a fish-ladder would not cost more than Rs. 800 or Rs. 1,000. If it is found, when the weir in the Jumna at Okla is finished, that the bed is not dry below the weir at seasons during which fish ascend and descend the river, I think a fish-ladder should undoubtedly be made. The original cost of outlay and the extra loss of water entailed by fish-ladders are hardly to be set against the benefits to be derived from them. With reference to the construction of breeding tanks in connection with canals, I would remark that in this division there are tanks in direct communication with the canal, suitable for the breeding of fish at the following places (enumerated) which are sufficient for this division. Similar breeding tanks should be formed in connection with canals in other districts where they do not exist. At present the Engineers of the Western Jumna canal in this division prohibit fishing in the *canal* itself, but allow it (except during the breeding season) in the tanks, on payment of a fee of Re. 1 per net. I think this course should be reversed. I would permit fishing in the canal provided the meshes of the nets used are not smaller than $2\frac{1}{2}$ inches from knot to knot, but would prohibit fishing in the breeding tanks altogether. These tanks should not be disturbed, and fish should be allowed to freely escape into them when the water in the canal is turned off, and the tanks themselves should not be drained of water." The *Deputy Commissioner of Hissár* reports, that breeding fish and very young ones are not destroyed to a great extent; but, as a general rule, the fishermen pay no attention to the condition of the fish. The smallest size of the mesh of the nets employed here is $\frac{1}{8}$ of an inch between knot and knot of the meshes. No difficulty is apprehended in regulating the size of the mesh of nets, although there would naturally be a tendency on the part of the licensees to reduce the size to their own standard for catching small fry as well as large fish. From 2 to $2\frac{1}{2}$ inches between the knots of the meshes is proposed as the minimum size that should be permitted. Fish being so rarely bought and sold, owing to its scarcity and want of appreciation, save by a very small percentage of the population, no objections are anticipated against prohibiting the sale of fry in the bazars.

32. *The Commissioner of the Delhi Division* (March 14th, 1872)
Delhi Division.—Answers of the European officials of Delhi, Gurgáon, Sarsa and Kurnal. forwarded reports from the following officers, observing, that instructions have been issued this day, that for the future, no licenses to use nets of meshes below $1\frac{1}{4}$ inches between knot and knot shall be granted. The *Officiating Deputy Commissioner of Delhi* states, that many young fish are no doubt destroyed, but few breeding ones owing to the paucity of breeding grounds. The time at which the young fish are destroyed, is in the river from the first monsoon inundations until the month of November or later. No restriction exists as to the size of the meshes of nets employed, which is about $\frac{1}{4}$ of an inch between knot and knot. If the taking of small fish is to be prohibited, there would be no difficulty in regulating the size of the meshes by a clause in the license, and $\frac{3}{4}$ of an inch between knot and knot is recommended. No objections exist against prohibiting the sale of fry within municipal limits, elsewhere legal sanction would be necessary, where the sales, however, are insignificant: would prohibit the use of small-meshed nets from June to November, so that the taking of those sorts which are mature, when of small size, would not be prevented. The *Deputy Commissioner of Gurgáon* replies, that as the Jumna is the only river in his

district, people are not given to fishing as a rule, and no destruction to breeding fish takes place; neither are the fry destroyed. The smallest size of the mesh of the nets being $\frac{1}{4}$ of an inch between knot and knot, no difficulties exist against regulating it, but he does not consider interference advisable. Fry are not sold in the bazars. *The Officiating Deputy Commissioner of Sarsa* reports, that breeding fish and very young ones, are not destroyed to any great extent; $\frac{3}{10}$ of an inch between knot and knot of the meshes is the smallest size employed; and he considers, as to what difficulties there are against regulating its size, that it is as well that all the fish in pools which dry up should be caught, but that one inch between knot and knot is advisable for nets used in waters that do not dry up. The objection against prohibiting the sale of fry is, that they are chiefly taken in pools which dry up, and would die if left uncaught. No reasons exist against a close season of two months in the hilly districts. *The Extra Assistant Commissioner of Karnal* states, that breeding fish and very young ones are destroyed, but not to any great extent, the latter are taken in larger quantities than the former. In the Jumna, in tanks and jhils, very young ones are captured in the rainy season and floods, and large ones in all seasons when procurable. The smallest meshes employed in nets are from $\frac{1}{3}$ to $\frac{1}{2}$ an inch in circumference, and are used for taking prawns. The only difficulty against regulating the size of the mesh of nets is, that it would interfere with the fishermen, and, probably, many would give up their occupation if not permitted their own discretionary powers in keeping nets to their own liking. The size proposed is $1\frac{1}{4}$ inches between knot and knot of the meshes, leaving nets for taking prawns as they are. The fry of fish are said not to be generally used, as their sale would not be profitable. As to whether there are any objections against prohibiting the capture of fish in hilly districts for the first two months of the monsoon season when they are breeding, it is stated: "Capturing of breeding fish in hilly districts in the spawning time will, in a certain extent, decrease their generation."

33. *The Revd. W. Carleton,* of the American Mission, who has been ten or eleven years amongst the people of the Himalayas, and paid considerable attention to natural history, was good enough to favour me with his independent views respecting the fisheries of the hill streams at the Kangra valley and elsewhere. He observes that the laws or regulations that "have been introduced to preserve the Himalayan fish, do not meet the real difficulty in the way of making the products of the Himalayan rivers an abundant source of food." "I do not," he continued, "write in the interests of Government, so much as I do in behalf of the common people, who, fond of meat, get at present a scanty supply from the rivers; while, if a proper conservancy of the fish could be introduced, there would be a very good supply of food for the poor or common people. There are two or three species of fish of remarkable fecundity in the Himalayas, which, if they were properly cared for when young, would yield yearly a great supply of food. But there is one custom in many parts of the hills, which, more than any others, is 'ruinous' to the natural growth of these fish, and which the present laws about fishing do not in the slightest degree affect. The grain in the Himalayas is all ground in little mills

moved by water. These mills are all situated on the hundreds of small streams in the hill gorges. To get a good water power, the people construct small canals, or ducts, on a higher level than the streams, and by erecting a dam across the stream, most of the water is diverted into these canals, and carried along until a good head is attained, the fall of which carries or puts in motion these mills. Now the most valuable species of fish breed in these gorges, and the young do not enter, in any considerable numbers, the large rivers till after one or two years, and as these little canals are numerous in all the gorges, and at seasons take in nearly all the waters of the streams, the young of these several species of fish naturally find their way into these canals, and whether the men who own these canals have nets or not to catch fish, all they have to do when they want a meal of fish, is to shut off the water from their 'kools' or canals, and in twenty minutes it becomes dry, and they can go along and pick up the fish that were in it. A few years ago I wished to collect the species of fish in the Mandi river, a branch of the Bias, which enters the Bias at the city of Mandi. I had but two hours to stay at that place, and I called a fisherman, an old man, and told him to take a close net to a small stream and bring me any living thing he could obtain from it; in less than an hour he brought me a basket-full of life, the sight of which would have gladdened the heart of a naturalist, six species of fish, and several sorts of aquarium insects, shells, crabs, &c. I wondered how he alone got that basket-full. He told me he owned a mill, and all he had to do was to shut off the water from the 'kool' and pick up his basket-full from dry land." One species was *Oreinus sinuatus*, Heckel, "the most valuable for food to the common people on account of its wide limits of distribution and great fecundity. An intelligent native on the Bias river observed that it went up to the high hill gorges in the early summer to feed on rich food and returned in the cold season down the rivers very fat. * * * I have known females of 3lbs. in weight to ascend small streams 8 miles, in a few hours, after the first heavy shower of the rainy season." [As a corroboration of this I may mention, that on going across the Himalayas from Chumba to Choaree, I stopped at a little rill that formed small pools here and there, and in which were numerous immature fish. Having a net with me I procured a few, some were young loaches, *Nemacheilus rupecula*, McClelland, but the majority consisted of the fry of the mountain barbels, *Oreinus sinuatus*, Heckel, whilst none could be that year's fish. The locality was upwards of one hundred feet above the main stream, with a very steep ascent, and sufficient rain not having fallen so as to permit fish ascending so high, they must have been the fry of the preceding season; and from observations made in different places, it appeared to me most probable, that rapid growth does not commence until the presence of rain water in the rivers, which it is said, and probably correctly, brings down some peculiarly nourishing food.]

34. In the *Peshâwar* Division the *Tehsildar of Peshâwar* reports

Peshâwar Division.—Answers of native officials of Peshâwar, Haripur, Mausera, and Kohát.

there are 190 fishermen who also pursue other occupations; their castes are Jhewurs, Jhubal, Afghan and Meen. Local markets are not fully supplied with fish; more could be sold. About 10 per cent. of the people are fish-eaters. Fish have decreased of late years, very small ones are taken during the rains in nets made of thread, and occasionally with sheets; these last are spread out and sunk in the water and raised when filled with fish. The smallest mesh of the nets is ¼ of an inch between the knots. Fish are trapped in the irrigated fields along the banks of rivers, during the rains. *The Tehsildar of Haripur* observes, that zemindars and others fish when not otherwise occupied; the markets are not fully supplied, more fish could be sold. A small proportion of the people eat fish, the supply of which has slightly decreased. Immature ones are not caught in the rains, the smallest mesh being 1 inch between each knot of the meshes. Fish are not trapped in the irrigated fields; some are speared by torch-light. *The Tehsildar of Mausera* reports, that there are 160 fishermen, but they follow other occupations; the markets are not fully supplied; more fish could be sold; the majority of the people eat it, but more as a luxury than a staple of food. The supply has decreased of late years. During the rains quantities of the immature are taken, but breeding fish are not trapped in the irrigated fields. *The Tehsildar of Kohát* states, that only a few Kahars of the regiments in garrison occasionally net fish, and boatmen on the Indus capture some with hooks and lines. The consumption of fish is small, and confined to the city and cantonments, a very few of the general population being fish-eaters.

35. In the *Ráwal Pindi* district, *the five Tehsildars* report as follows:— In Ráwal Pindi there are 30 fishermen, in Attock 26, in Gujer Khan 0, in Fathi Jang 4, in Muni 1, all of whom follow other occupations. All the Kahars, the Machi, and Bhuttiara castes fish, and the Jhewurs and Mullas amongst the Mahomedans. The supply is insufficient or absent in four tehsils, and sufficient in one. In Ráwal Pindi 75 per cent. of the population eat fish, in Attock (being Mahomedans) nearly the whole, the same in Gujer Khán and Fathi Jang, but only 10 per cent. in Muni. In Ráwal Pindi and Muni the supply is stated to have decreased, in Attock to be stationary, and in the other two tehsils to have slightly increased. At Mouzah Gungal in Ráwal Pindi, fish are said to be trapped to a limited extent. In the *Jhilam* district *four Tehsildars* state, that in Jhilam there are 15 fishermen, but in the other three tehsils fishing is merely carried on in addition to other occupations. In Jhilam, only, are the markets fully supplied, and there about three-fourths of the population eat fish, the remaining 25 per cent., who are chiefly Brahmins, never do so; in Pind Dádan Khan $\frac{1}{10}$ (eight-tenth?, this being the proportion of Mahomedans to Hindus,) eat fish. Hindus have an aversion to it. In Chakwal it is not touched. In Talegang the people in the vicinity of the Soan river eat fish. In Jhilam fish are said to be increasing; in Pind Dádan Khán to have decreased, but to have remained stationary in the two other tehsils. Small ones are said to be taken in Jhilam during the rains. The minimum size of the meshes of nets vary from 1 inch between the knots in the larger nets, to from $\frac{1}{3}$ to $\frac{1}{2}$ an inch in the 'chilwa' nets. Fish are not trapped during the rains in the irrigated fields. In the *Gujrat* district, *the three Tehsildars* report as follows: in Gujrat there are 7 fishermen, in Khárim 2, and in Sáhem 1, all of whom follow other occupations. The local markets are not fully supplied, more fish could be sold. In Gujrat more than half the people eat fish, in Khárim

Ráwal Pindi Division.—Answers of Tehsildars of Ráwal Pindi, Attock, Gujer Khan, Fathi Jang, Muni, Jhilam, Pind Dádan Khán, Chakwal, Talegang, Gujrát, Khárim, and Sahem.

nine-tenths, Sáhem one-fourth. In two of the tehsils fish are said to have decreased of late years, and in one to have remained stationary. Small ones are caught during the rains, the minimum sized mesh employed being from ⅛ to ½ an inch between the knots. Fish are not trapped during the rains in two tehsils, but are in the remaining one.

36. In the *Derajat* division, *the four Tehsildars* of Bánú report as follows:—There are no regular fishermen, the zemindars occasionally catch fish, as do also the Mahomedans for their own eating: the markets are not supplied. The Tehsildar of Bánú reports that fish is very little eaten in his tehsil; in Isakhel that all the Mahomedans will when they can procure it; in Miamaoli that most classes will eat it when they happen to get it, but they do not take any trouble about it; and at Lakki that no one eats fish because there are none to eat. The supply appears to have remained stationary: very small ones are not taken in any quantity during the rains. The minimum size of the mesh employed is about ½ an inch between knot and knot. Fish are not trapped in the irrigated fields during the rains. *The four Teshildars* of *Dera Gázi Khán* state that in Dera Gázi Khán and Sangarh there are no fishermen, in Rájanpur there are 125, in Jampur 16, they follow other occupations. The markets in two tehsils are moderately supplied, but insufficiently so in the others, still in most more could be sold. In Dera Gázi Khán most of the city people are said to eat fish when it is in season; in Rájanpur three quarters of those who are within reach of the markets; in Jampur the majority. The supply has decreased in Dera Gázi Khán, but largely increased in Rájanpur and Jampur. Small fish are not taken during the rains, neither are breeding ones trapped in the irrigated fields. The minimum size of the meshes of nets employed is ½ an inch between the knots. In *Dera Ismail Khán the four Tehsildars* stated that there are 40 fishermen in the Dera tehsil, 10 or 12 in Liah, about the same number in Bhakkar, but only 4 or 5 in Koláchi. During the hot weather, as the river rises, all cultivate land: they are of the Jat caste, section Muchiarrah. The local markets are not fully supplied, and much more could be profitably sold. The proportion of people who eat fish is not large, even in the town of Dera Ismail Khán, and few depend on it in the district as a source of food. They have decreased this year owing to the heavy floods of last season. The smallest mesh employed in the nets is ½ an inch in size. Fish are rarely trapped during the freshes of the river.

Derajat Division.—Answers of the Tehsildars of Bánú, Isakhel, Miamaoli, Lakki, Dera Gázi Khán, Sangarh, Rájanpur, Jampur, Dera, Liah, Bhakkar, Koláchi.

37. In the *Multan Division* the Tehsildars report that there are 28 fishermen, all of whom are Mahomedans, and follow other occupations. Fish are never sold in the markets, although about 50 per cent. of the people eat them; the supply in the waters is more this year than last season. Fish are not taken during the rains, as it is a popular belief that if used as food at this period they occasion sickness. The smallest mesh employed is ⅛th of an inch square. Fish are not trapped in the irrigated fields. There

Multan Division.—Answers of the Tehsildars of Multan district; Ala dal Khan, Honorary Magistrate, Khángarh: Darogah Shere Shah (Hyatolla Khan); Minn Mahbab Garhmani; the Tehsildars of Muzaffargarh, Kot Adu, Montgomery, Gugaira, Pákpatan, Riaz Hossain, Multan, Shoojabad, Lodhran, Mailsi, Sernie Saidhu.

are three sorts of fishing : 1*st*, by means of baskets covered over by a piece of net termed ' kur'; 2*ndly*, by means of hooks ' kundee'; and *lastly*, by nets. In the *Muzaffargarh district, Ala Dal Khan,* Honorary Magistrate, *Khángarh,* replies that the fishermen caste are Jhabel ; the supply of fish is insufficient; the population as a rule eat it, but the Mahomedans more so than the Hindus. *Darogah Shere Shah* (Hyatolla Khan) reports that there are 128 fishermen on the Chenab, all of whom cultivate land. The markets are insufficiently supplied with fish, but it is generally eaten by the people. Fishing is not carried on during the rains ; the smallest mesh used is ½ an inch square. *Mian Mahbáb Garhmani* replies, that there are 60 fishermen in his ilaqa; they fish during the cold season, and cultivate in the hot weather ; their castes are Jhabel, Mahana, Sumeri and Manjri. The markets are insufficiently supplied, although most of the people eat fish, especially the Mahomedans. The supply remains stationary. Fish are not taken during the rains. The smallest mesh used is 1 inch square. *The Tehsildar of Muzaffargarh* states that there are 50 fishermen, who also employ themselves in cultivation. The markets are very insufficiently supplied, although two-thirds of the people eat fish, the supply of which has continued stationary. Fish are not taken in any quantity during the rains, nor trapped in the irrigated fields ; the smallest mesh employed is 1 inch between the knots. *The Tehsildar of Kot Adu* replies that there are 326 fishermen who have likewise other occupations. The local market is not sufficiently supplied. The population generally eat fish ; none are captured during the rains, or in the irrigated fields ; the smallest-sized mesh employed is 1½ inch between the knots. *In the Montgomery* district, the *Tehsildar of Montgomery* observes, that the fishermen are of the Jhumail caste, and they likewise cultivate land. The local market is fully supplied ; some fish are exported to Lahor ; the supply has remained stationary during the last few years : very small ones are taken in the rains ; the minimum size of the mesh of the nets is ¾ of an inch between the knots ; a few fish are trapped in the irrigated fields during the rains. *The Tehsildar of Gugaira* reports, that there are 125 fishermen who also follow other occupations. The local markets are not fully supplied, although two-thirds of the population eat fish. Very small ones are captured during the rains, with nets having minute meshes, and also by sheets ; the minimum size of the meshes is ½ an inch between the knots ; a few fish are trapped in the irrigated fields during the rains. *The Tehsildar of Pákpatan* replies, that there are 45 fishermen in his range, but they are also cultivators. The markets are insufficiently supplied with fish, although 90 per cent. of the people eat it. The amount in the waters has decreased until last year ; a few small ones are taken during the rains ; the minimun size of the mesh of the nets is 1 inch between the knots ; a few fish are trapped in the irrigated fields during the rains. The following are the modes of fishing : ' kanta' or 'koondi : ' koorli,' which is similar in shape to the ' khancha' or ' tapa' used for keeping fowls. Nets, 'jal,' of the following descriptions :—'ittar,' 'soomhi,' large net called ' kuchh' or ' leva,' and ' sathwan.' *The Tehsildar of Riaz Hoossain* reports 60 fishermen in his range; they follow other occupations, and all are Mussalmen. The local markets are not fully supplied with fish, although about $\frac{5}{8}$ths of the population eat it; the amount in the waters has decreased of late. Very few small fishes are taken during the rains, nor are large ones trapped in the irrigated fields; the minimum size of the mesh of the nets is 1 inch between each knot. *The five Tehsildars in the Multan district* report 95 fishermen, viz., 6 in Multan, 13 in Shoojabad, 35 in Lodhrán, 26 in Mailsi, and 15 in Seraie Saidhu; they also pursue other occupations. During the cold season the markets are fully supplied with fish, which are eaten by 90 per cent. of the Mahomedans and 14 per cent. of the Hindu population. The fish supply has remained stationary of late years; small ones are not taken during the rains, nor are any trapped in the irrigated fields; the minimum size of the mesh of the nets is ½ an inch between each knot. The local names of nets and traps employed for taking fish in this district are 'jals,' 'koor,' 'koondees:' the last is of three descriptions which are termed 'khatha,' 'nurra,' and 'satla.'

38. *In the Lahor District, the Tehsildar* of that place states there are 150 fishermen who also follow other call-

Lahor Division.—Answers of the Tehsildars of Lahor, Kásur, Chunia, Sharkpur, Gujranwalla, Wazirabad, Hafizabad.

ings. The markets are not fully supplied with fish, which species of food is eaten by five-sixths of the population. The amount in the waters has decreased of late years, due to a deficiency of rain; very small ones are taken during the rains with nets called 'satna,' the minimum size of its meshes about equal that of a grain of gram. Fish are not trapped in the irrigated fields during the rains. *The Tehsildar of Kásur* states, that in his range there are 50 fishermen of the 'Main' caste, who do not pursue any other occupation. The markets are not fully supplied. The amount in the waters is said to have decreased until this year, when an increase is reported. Very small fish are taken during the rains with a net termed 'sumbi;' the minimum size of the meshes employed is ½ an inch between each knot; none are trapped in the irrigated fields. *The Tehsildar of Chunia* reports 25 fishermen in his range, they also have other callings. The markets are insufficiently supplied; about half the population eat fish; the amount in the waters has decreased until the present year, when it has increased, due to the opening of the 'Kabora' canal. Very small fish are not taken during the rains, nor trapped in the irrigated fields; the minimum size of the mesh of nets employed is ½ an inch between each knot. *The Tehsildar of Sharkpur* states that there are 50 fishermen in his range, all of whom pursue other callings; the markets are insufficiently supplied; 95 per cent. of the population are fish consumers. The supply has decreased; small fish are not taken during the rains, but large ones are trapped at this season in the irrigated fields; the minimum size of the mesh of the nets is given at 1½ inches between each knot. *In the Gujranwalla* district, the three tehsildars give the number of fishermen at 105, viz., Gujranwalla 50, Wazirabad 25, Hafizabad 30, all of whom follow other occupations. None of the markets are sufficiently supplied. All the Mussulmen and generally two-thirds of the Hindus are fish-eaters, but the Brahmins and women usually reject it. In the first-named tehsil the fish are said to have decreased, but to have remained stationary in the other two; small ones are stated no longer to be taken during the rains; in one tehsil it is believed that they are unwholesome at this period. The minimum sized mesh of the nets employed is ⅓ of an inch between the knots at Wazirabad, and ½ at Hafizabad; in this last tehsil only are fish said to be trapped in the irrigated fields during the rains.

30. *In the Amritsar* district, the *tehsildars and two Extra Assistant Commissioners* report, that in the whole of the district which is bordered by two rivers, there are from 80 to 90 fisherman of several castes, viz., the 'Machees' and 'Jheenumrs,' who are also bakers and water-carriers; the 'Mullas' or boatmen; the 'Jhubhail,' who also trap birds, and the 'Summi,' who are mat-makers.

<small>Amritsar Division.—Answers of Tehsildars and Extra Assistant Commissioners of the Amritsar district; of the Tehsildars of Reyah, Pasrur, Zaffarwál, Sialkot, Shakergarh, Batala, and Pathankot.</small>

During the cold season the markets are generally well supplied, but Amritsar is insufficiently so. All the Mahomedans and half the Hindus eat fish, the supply of which is considered to have remained stationary. Fish are trapped in the irrigated fields during the rains, and numbers of small ones are also taken at this period; the minimum size of the mesh of the nets is given at 1 inch between each knot. The following modes are employed for taking fish:—Rods, nets, harpooning, digging holes in rivers' banks and allowing them to fill from the river, then cutting off communication with the stream, and lading out the water; also with baskets and ghurras and various sorts of nets. *In the Sialkot* district *the Tehsildar of Reyah* replies, that there are 70 fishermen in his range, all of whom follow other callings: they are Pukheewarahs, Machees and Kahars. The markets are insufficiently supplied with fish, which are eaten by two-thirds of the population. The amount in the waters has decreased of late years; many small ones are not taken during the rains; the minimum size of the meshes of nets are 1¼ inches between each knot. *The Tehsildar of Pasrur* reports, that there are 29 fishermen in his range, and that they all follow other occupations. The markets are very insufficiently supplied; some 11,000 Hindus out of 244,397 persons, or about 1 in 22, do not eat fish, the supply of which in the waters has decreased. The smallest, sized mesh of nets employed is 1¼ inches between each knot. *The Tehsildar of Zaffarwál* states, that there are 34 fishermen in his range, all of whom pursue other callings. The local markets are not sufficiently supplied with fish, which article of food is consumed by half the population. The minimum size of the mesh of nets employed is ⅜ of an inch between each knot. *The Tehsildar of Sialkot* reports, that there are 534 fishermen in his district, all of whom have other occupations. The markets are very badly supplied with fish, which are eaten by three-fourths of the population. Fish have decreased of late years; they are taken during the rains, but to no great extent, by the construction of dams across nalas, which are then netted; the minimum size of the mesh of the nets is one-third of an inch between the knots. Fish are not trapped in the irrigated fields during the rains to any extent. *In the Gurdaspur* district, *the Tehsildar* states, that there are 80 fishermen in his range, who have also other occupations. The bazars are insufficiently supplied with fish, which is used as food by all the people, except Bunias, Bhabras, and Hindustani Brahmins. The amount in the waters has greatly decreased during the last ten years, for, owing to the scantiness of rain, the chumbs and pools have not been replenished from inundations of the rivers, which is a great impediment to their spawning. During the rains small fish are caught to a great extent by hand-nets, the minimum size of the meshes being ¼ of an inch between the knots. Fish are also trapped in the irrigated fields during periods of inundation. The modes of fishing are, by large and small nets, baskets, traps, spears and rods. 'Mahajal' or drag-nets are worked by several persons, who drag it as much as a mile to where another net has been previously kept stretched across the river which is weighted below, and floated above by bundles of grass. 'Goodur jal' is fastened at the mouth of a pool or stream as a purse net. 'Veera jal,' or hand-net, is like a 'gughra' having iron rings all round the lower end, it is thrown by hand, and then gently pulled out of the water. 'Kooncha' or 'koorlee' is made of reed or bamboo in the shape of a cone with the two ends open, this is jammed down in shallow water, and the fish removed by the hand from the upper end. Spearing is pursued during the winter months when the fish are less active and the water still, the fisherman rows about in a small boat from which he uses his spear. 'Chip' is made in the shape of a chick, it is placed over the mouth of an outlet of a pool, the fish finding an obstruction there, fall back into a hole which had been previously dug on the side of the outlet, and are there taken by the hand. *The Tehsildar of Shakergarh* reports, that there are 104 fishermen who pursue other callings as well; the supply of fish in the towns is scanty, but they are generally sold in the villages to a large extent or rather exchanged for grain, when the latter article is cheap it obtains double weight, when dear equal proportions. Half the population eat fish, the supply of which has increased during the past year. Small ones are taken during the rains by nets and sheets: the minimum size of the mesh of the former is given at 1 inch between each knot. Fish are also trapped during the rains in the irrigated fields. *The Tehsildar of Batala* replies, that 23 licenses have been granted to fishermen (Jheewurs) during the year; besides these there are several persons who take fish as well as follow other occupations. The supply in the market is sufficient; one-third of the population eat it, but its amount has lately decreased owing to deficiency of rain, whilst the minimum size of the mesh of the nets is ¼ of an inch between each knot. *The Tehsildar of Pathankot* reports, that there are 130 fishermen in his range, they also work as laborers. The supply in the bazars is equal to the demand; three-fourths of the people eat fish, the amount of which has remained stationary during the past few years. Small ones are taken to a great extent during the rains, but none are trapped in the irrigated fields.

40. *In the Ambala Division the six Tehsildars* report as follows: that there are 357 fishermen divided thus: Ambala 30, Jagadri Irrigation Canal 75, Raossur 30, Kharar 28, Náráyangarh 94, Pipli 100, all of whom follow other occupations. In the first five tehsils the markets are not fully supplied; in the last they are said to be so. The following are the proportions of the population who eat fish: Ambala one-fifth; Jagadri two-thirds; Raossur one-fourth; Kharar two-thirds; Náráyangarh only the Mahomedans, and the Kutrees and Kyuts amongst the Hindus; whilst in Pipli very few do so. They have decreased in tehsils Nos. 1, 3, 4, increased in Nos. 2 and 6, but remained stationary in No. 5. Small fish and those in irrigated fields are not destroyed during the rains in Ambala and Raossur,

Ambala Division.—Answers of the Tehsildars of Ambala, Jagadri, Raossur, Kharar, Náráyangarh, Pipli.

but are in Jagadri; whilst young only are in Kharar, Náráyangarh and Pipli. The minimum size of the meshes of nets employed, is given at Ambala and Náráyangarh about sufficiently large to allow a grain of wheat to pass; at Pipli about ⅛ of an inch between the knots; at Jagadri ½ an inch, and Raossur 5 fingers.

41. *In the Jalandar* division, *Tehsildar Futteh Deen Khan of Jalandar* reports that there are five fishermen in the tehsil who also follow other occupations. The local markets are only well supplied during the rains. The whole of the population eat fish, except Brahmins, Bhabras, Banias, Vishnus and Mahomedan Sheeas. The amount in the waters has decreased: small ones are captured during the rains, and some are trapped in the irrigated fields. *The Tehsildar of Phillur* reports that there are four fishermen in his tehsil who hold licenses, and others who do not. The markets are not well supplied. Five per cent. of the people eat fish. The amount in the waters continued stationary for a few years, but latterly it has decreased. Small ones are netted during the rains, but none are trapped in the irrigated fields; the minimum size of the mesh of the nets is 1 inch between each knot. *The Tehsildar of Nawashahr* reports, 120 fishing licenses have been taken out, these fishermen likewise pursue other callings. The supply in the markets is not one-fifth of the demand; 33 per cent of the people eat fish, which has increased of late. During the rains fishes are taken in the fields. *The Tehsildar of Nacodar* states, that prior to the introduction of the license system, there were about 200 fishermen, now there are only 8 license-holders; they likewise engage in other work. The markets are not half supplied. Fifty per cent. of the population eat fish: the amount in the waters has much decreased of late, in fact scarcely any can be found. Small fish are not taken during the rains, but large ones are sometimes trapped in the fields. The minimum size of the mesh of the nets is 1 inch between each knot. *The Tehsildar of Hushiarpur* reports, that there are no regular fishermen in his range, there being no large river, but the Kahars and Bhatis generally net the small streams for the purpose of procuring fish for their own consumption, but their regular occupation is working mills. There are no local markets, but any quantity of fish offered is sure to find a ready sale, as three-fourths of the population are fish-eaters. The supply in the waters has remained stationary; small ones are not taken during the rains. The minimum size of the mesh of the nets is ⅛ of an inch between the knots. The modes of fishing pursued are as follow :—By 'maha jal,' which is employed for taking large fish, and is worked by five or six persons jointly; by a smaller net, which is used by a single man, and one rather larger used by two men. The local names of the nets in use are 'sittawan jal,' 'dundaiwala jal,' 'tup,' 'koondi,' 'moon,' 'douruh gulli,' 'chadur.' *The Tehsildar of Unah* replies, that there are about 37 licensed fishermen; the supply of fish is insufficient: about one-fourth of the population, mostly Mussalmen, eat it. The amount in the waters is stated to have increased; small ones are not captured during the rains. The minimum size of the meshes of the nets which are used is 1¼ inches between the knots. *The Tehsildar of Garhsankar* reports, that there are 7 fishermen

Jalandar Division.—Answers of the Tehsildars of Jalandar, Phillur, Nawashahr, Nacodar, Hushinpur, Unah, Garhsankar, and Dasuha.

xxvii

in his range; the supply of fish is insufficient for local requirements. It is eaten by 90 per cent. of the people. The amount during late years has been stationary. Some small fishes are trapped in irrigated fields during the rains. The minimum size of the mesh of the nets used is ¾ of an inch between each knot. *The Tehsildar of Dasuha* replies, that about 200 persons fish in addition to other occupations; the supply is insufficient for local requirements; 75 per cent. of the population are fish-eaters; the supply has decreased of late years owing to a diminution of rain. Small ones are not taken during the rains; no nets are used with a mesh less than 1 inch between the knots. Some fish are trapped in the irrigated fields during the rains: they also are taken by diverting a stream through a narrow opening in which a net is fixed, and by spearing.

42. In the Hissár division, *the Tehsildar* of that place states, there is only one fisherman in his range, and who also has other work. Out of a rural population of 107,442 persons, only one-third could eat fish, but not 2 in 1,000 are fond of it; at this rate there are not more than 70 individuals in the tehsil who care to eat it. The supply in the waters remains stationary. The only net has above 1 inch between each knot of the meshes. *The Tehsildar of Hánsi* replies, that there is only one fisherman in his range; 10 per cent. of the population eat fish, the supply of which has remained stationary. *The Tehsildar of Fathiabad* reports, that there are 13 fishermen in his range, all of whom have other occupations as well. Only the Mussalmen eat fish, but they are not very fond of it; about one-eighth, out of a population of about 32,047, consume it. The supply continues stationary; small ones are not taken during the rains; the minimum size of the mesh of the nets employed is ½ of an inch between each knot. *The Tehsildar of Bhawani* states, that there are no fishermen and no fish. *The Tehsildar of Barwála* replies, that there are 10 fishermen, all of whom follow other occupations. Fish are never sold, but whenever the zemindars feel inclined to eat it, they generally give the fishermen some grain in repayment for catching it. About one-eighth of the people may eat fish, the supply of which remains stationary.

Hissár Division.—Answers of the Tehsildars of Hissár, Hánsi, Fathiabad, Bhawani, and Barwála.

43. In the Delhi division, *the Tehsildar of Delhi* gives the number of fishermen at 4,810, only pursuing this occupation during the winter and summer months, whilst during the rains they are dooly-bearers. The castes are Sheikhs, Pathans, Mullas, and Kahars. The local markets are sufficiently supplied; the demand in the summer and during the rains decreases, and during the winter from 2 to 2½ maunds is consumed. The fish-eating portion of the population is given at 96,268 out of 608,450 [a proportion widely differing from that given in 1870 by the 'Deputy Commissioner,' who reported that 44 per cent. of the people were fish-eaters, when the price was sufficiently low to enable them to obtain it]. Fish are stated to be decreasing, due to the Okla weir across the Jumna. Immature fish are not taken in large quantities during the rains: the minimum size of the mesh of the nets employed is ¼ of an inch between the knots. The

Delhi Division.—Answers of the Tehsildars of Delhi, Larsauli, Ballabhgarh, Gurgáon, Rewari, Palwal, Nuh, Fázilka, Sarsa, Kurnal, Pánipat, and Kaithal.

zemindars do not permit fish to be taken in the irrigated fields. *The Tehsildar of Larsauli* states, that the Dheewur caste, to the extent of 1,061, catch fish, and otherwise subsist by labour. Out of 167,857 people the fish-eating community is 56,914. The supply is stationary; none are taken in the irrigated fields. *The Tehsildar of Ballabhgarh* replies, that the Dheewur or Kubar castes, of which some 520 inhabit the tehsil, during the summer catch fish for their own subsistence. The markets are insufficiently supplied; 50 per cent. of the people can eat fish; the population is 132,657. The amount in the waters has decreased. *In the Gurgáon* district *the four Tehsildars* report as follows :—In Gurgáon, Rewari, and Palwal no fishermen live, but there are 15 in Nuh. Fish are not sold. In the first-named tehsil 5 per cent., in the second no answer, in the third one-third or less, and in the fourth two-thirds of the population can eat fish; the amount in the waters has increased of late in the first two tehsils, decreased in the third, and apparently the fourth. The minimum size of the mesh of the nets mentioned is $\frac{1}{4}$ of an inch. *In the Sarsa District*, the *Tehsildar of Fazilka* reports 15 fishermen, who pursue other occupations. The local markets are not fully supplied with fish; all the people living along the river eat it, so do those in the towns, except the Brahmins and Mohajuns: it is not much eaten in rural districts away from the river, whilst Baguries reject it as food. The supply has decreased. A quantity of small ones are taken during the rains; $\frac{3}{10}$ of an inch is the minimum size between each knot of the meshes. A few fish are trapped during the inundations in the irrigated fields. *The Tehsildar of Sarsa* states there are 18 fishermen in his range, who also have other occupations; they are Mullas and Deendars. The supply of fish exceeds the demand; they are generally exchanged for grain. Less than 5 per cent. of the people eat fish, the amount of which in the waters, continues stationary. One inch between the knots is the smallest-sized mesh used. *In the Kurnal* district there are 42 fishermen, all of whom have other means of livelihood; in the Kurnal Tehsil there are 22, in Pánipat 10, in Kaithal 10; the castes are Mayo and Jheewur Mussalmen. The supply in the markets is enough in Kurnal and Kaithal, but insufficient in Pánipat, owing to a paucity of fishermen. In Kurnal half, in Pánipat one-fourth, and in Kaithal a little above one-fourth, of the population may eat fish. The amount in the waters is reported as stationary. Small fish are taken during the rains with nets having minute meshes, whilst the poorer classes use cloths: the minimum size of the meshes of nets is $\frac{1}{2}$ of an inch between the knots. Fish are not trapped in the irrigated fields.

SIND.

44. The fresh-water fisheries of this Province are mainly divisible into those which exist in the river Indus, or are formed by its yearly inundations, these last being principally in Upper and Central Sind. The portion of the river between the right bank of the Indus and the 'Phut' is slightly concave, owing to which circumstance, when the river overflows, the whole of this part of the country becomes more or less inundated. The 'Phut' is the tract of land along the base of the hills which divide Sind from Beluchistan, it averages about nine miles broad, and irrigated by water obtained from the hill streams, which is arrested by bunds and diverted into irrigation canals. The inundations on the left bank of the Indus do not appear to be so extensive as those on its right.

Fresh-water fisheries of Sind.

45. The river Indus is usually at its lowest in January or February: at the commencement of March the snow-floods begin, and its rise continues spasmodically until about August; whilst in September the subsidence is usually very rapid, and by November zero is attained. The floods, as a rule, may be expected to subside about the middle of September, when, or shortly subsequently, fishing commences.

River Indus.

46. The tanks or 'dhánds,' as they are locally termed, are chiefly of two sorts as regards their relationship to the Indus, viz., the 'isolated' and the 'connected.' In the former, weeds rapidly spring up forming a refuge for the fish. In the connected dhánds weeds are not so numerous, and the finny tribes appear to vary: if the water is very muddy, the siluroids abound, whilst the Dumra, *Labeo rohita*, a fine carp, although not so plentiful as in the dhánds where it is clear, still is rarely absent. In places where the water is clear, the largest amount of 'dumra' are to be seen: thus at Trigarti I found the connected dhánd in the river quite dark with them. Tanks useful for fishing extend in Upper Sind over a large extent of the country, and appear to be most valuable as affording animal food to the population inhabiting these malarious districts.

Tanks or dhánds, isolated or connected with Indus; their finny inhabitants.

47. As to canal fisheries, the capture of the finny tribes is here prohibited, to obviate the chance of the canals being injured; thus a most excellent opportunity was afforded of testing the correctness or the reverse of the opinion advanced by the Collector of South Canara, in his exhaustive report on the fisheries of that district, that were a minimum-sized mesh of four inches in circumference instituted, " the smaller sorts of fish, having an immunity from netting, must disproportionately increase on the larger netted sorts. Nature has arranged that the larger predatory fish shall balance the smaller, and thus maintain due proportions; but if one sort is netted by man, and the other sort has immunity, the balance is disturbed, and the larger fish are no longer able to maintain their position."

Canal fisheries. Proofs that if small-meshed nets are prohibited, the little fish do not disproportionately increase over the larger sorts.

Theoretically this may be very correct, but how is it practically? In Sind, nets for capturing fry do not exist, but still Nature maintains the due proportions, of which I will adduce one instance out of several that I have personally witnessed. At Muhu, the canal from the Indus joins the bed of the old Narrah, and fishing was prohibited. A deep hole existed at the confluence of these two pieces of water, and fish were most numerous. The muddy water of the Indus here joined the comparatively clear stream from the old Narrah, for, due to its more circuitous route, much of its mud and silt had become deposited. If a small fish appeared, it seemed to be at once disposed of by the large siluroids. At the first throw of a cast net, 10 of these fish weighing about 30 lbs. were captured: having crossed the old Narrah, in one more throw into the conjoined stream, 18 more were taken, weighing about 50 lbs. The same is seen in the thinly populated districts in Burma. Larger fish prey upon the smaller ones; thus I have taken a barbel out of a hard-rayed fish, *Nandus marmoratus*, that was one-third the length of its captor.

48. As to the fishing in the Indus itself, this chiefly consists in capturing the shoals of shad, which ascend from the sea for the purpose of breeding, about February, and return to the salt water about the end of September, for, " owing to the dangerous character of the river at all times, but especially during the inundations, there are strong contending currents," and other fishing is but little resorted to. Another reason that the river is but slightly fished, is, that the population in its vicinity is scanty, for, owing to the constant and occasionally sudden variations in its course, the neighbouring land is always liable to be ruined by the silt deposited upon it during inundations, and villages are in danger of being swept away.

Fishery in Indus, mostly of shad.

49. The fishes in the fresh waters of Sind are mainly of two descriptions—*first*, the river fish common to the Panjab, and the pulla, which ascends from the sea for breeding purposes, and it is this latter only that is much sought after by fishermen; *secondly*, the inundation fish, which are of two descriptions: (1) river fish, which have been carried by the overflowing of the Indus over the neighbouring country; (2) tank fish, which, from the same cause, have in like manner been distributed everywhere. No undue and preventible destruction of small fish appears to exist in Upper and Central Sind—*first* due to the paucity of population; *secondly*, because of the rapidity and dangerous character of the river Indus and the constant variations in its channel; and *thirdly*, owing to the security the immature fish obtain during the inundation season.

Fresh-water fishes consist of river and inundation sorts. No preventible destruction of the immature appears to obtain.

50. *As to the proportion of people who eat fish?*—Its use is almost universal, and here the Mahomedans do not object to the scaleless forms, under the belief that, if they have gill openings, it is a proof that they are allowed to the faithful, as the prophet cut their throats.

Fish universally eaten.

51. The markets seem to be sufficiently supplied during certain seasons of the year. The amount of fish appears to be stationary: breeding ones are not destroyed, as fishing has to be suspended

Fisheries peculiar. Wasteful destruction not observed.

during the inundation season; for like reason the fry escapes. Minute meshed nets are not employed, so far as I could ascertain, by the inhabitants of Upper and Central Sind, as it is found more profitable to permit the young fish to attain a fair size before capturing them. As the waters in the tanks subside and food begins to decrease, then netting is carried on. Owing to the peculiar character of the fisheries of this province and the smallness of the population, remedial measures do not appear at present called for (see Report on fisheries of Sind, March 18th, 1872).

52. *The Commissioner of Sind* (September 9th, 1868) reported, "the pulla [*Clupea palasah*, Cuv. & Val.] is the only description of fish caught in the river. Their appearance is restricted to a particular season, from March until September; they are not local, but come up from the sea to spawn, and are secured in nets capable of catching not more than one, two, or three at a time. Owing to the dangerous character of the river at all times, but especially during the inundations, when there are strong contending currents, fishing of any other description is never resorted to. In the 'dhánds' and hollows, considerable quantities of fish are caught in drag-nets; these are consumed by the inhabitants in adjacent towns and villages, and the residue is salted and sold in remote localities; but during the inundations these receptacles become very deep and extensive, when the use of nets is abandoned, and the supply of fish becomes renewed. Some loss of small fish is no doubt occasioned when the hollows dry up after the inundation has subsided; this, however, is unavoidable in consequence of the isolation of many places from their main feeder (the Indus), and cannot therefore be considered as a wanton destruction of fish."

Report by the Commissioner of Sind.

53. *The Acting Collector of Shikarpur* reported (1871), that the fisheries in the Collectorate are of two kinds, those on the Indus and those in the 'dhánds' or depressions which are supplied with water every year from the overflow of the Indus or the larger canals. All fisheries, with the exception of a few included in some jaghirs, and those in the territory of His Highness Meer Ali Morad, Chief of Khypur, are the property of Government, and the farm of Government fisheries is sold yearly to the highest bidder. The revenue from this source varies but little from year to year; in 1869 it was Rs. 32,023-7-6 for the whole Collectorate. In the Indus the fishing is restricted to that for the pulla, which annually ascends from the sea to breed, appearing about the end of February; it returns to the sea in September. The fishermen or Mahanas now resort to the dhánds to ply their occupation. Many of these dhánds dry up before the annual rise of the river replenishes the supply of water in them, others again are sufficiently deep to retain water all the year round. With the yearly inundations are brought a number of fish which are sufficient for the year's supply, so no system of preserving these fisheries seems necessary.

Shikarpur Collectorate; its fisheries.

54. *The Collector of Kurachi* observed (March 15th, 1872), that the rights of private parties in the fisheries have never been accurately defined, but that such rights exist by immemorial custom is well known. The Government right is to levy one-third of the fish

Kurachi Collectorate; its fisheries.

caught. It cannot, however, be said that even this has been accurately defined, but whenever a dispute has arisen between the Mahanas and the farmers, it has been ruled by the Revenue authorities that one-third of the fish was the limit of the latter's right. This third has never, so far as he is aware, been levied direct. The fishery revenue of the Kurachi Collectorate for a cycle of five years ending 1870-71 has averaged, for ordinary fish, *i. e.*, dhánd fishing, Rs. 13,593-6-0; for pulla fish, *i. e.*, river fishing in the Indus, Rs. 20,746-10-9 per annum.

55. *The Collector of Haidarabad* (May 27th, 1871) replied, that numbers of breeding fish, the pulla, are destroyed from February to August in the Indus.

<small>Haidarabad Collectorate; its fisheries.</small>

Capturing these herrings, however, will not decrease their numbers if there are no weirs in rivers, and they can ascend to their breeding grounds. The fry of other sorts of fish are, however, met with in the shallow lakes of water left in many places, and are consumed by the people; these form but a minute portion of what the great river must always contain; and, moreover, as all such lakes, termed 'dhánds,' dry up, these fish, if left, would die; consequently their consumption is not hurtful. It is not advisable to regulate the size of the mesh by law: *firstly*, because no necessity exists, *secondly*, because of the difficulty there would be in carrying out such rules, if made. For the same reasons the sale of the fry of fish should not be prohibited. The fisheries in this Collectorate consist, *firstly*, of the Indus itself; *secondly* of tanks or dhánds; and Government has a prescriptive right to a share of all these, ranging according to custom, from one-third to one-fifth. Private rights in these fisheries have also been long settled and prescribed by custom. The fishermen almost always belong to, and fish in, the limits of their own 'meances' or fisheries: and even on the river Indus, no fisherman is allowed to encroach on the limits of a fishery to which he does not belong. The farmers arrange with the fishermen as to the payments to them, representing the Government shares. As regards fisheries in jaghir lands, unless the sunnud contains a special grant, the produce of such is credited to local funds, and is not enjoyed by the jaghirdar.

56. In the *Haidarabad Collectorate* the *native officials* compute the fishermen at 3,230; they are also almost invariably cultivators of the soil and labourers.

<small>Opinions of native officials in the Haidarabad Collectorate.</small>

The common name of fishermen is 'Mahana,' but others who are not actual fishermen, as the 'Khebranees,' use the hand-nets in canals. The markets are well supplied with fish in the season of the pulla, and during the remaining five months, only those in the neighbourhood of the lakes or tanks obtain it. The whole population, Mussulmen and Hindu, except Brahmins, are eaters of fish, the supply of which is as abundant as ever, whilst Sind being in a rainless zone, young fish are not captured during the rainy season. The following are the usual modes of fishing:—"koondee," hook and line; "yar," a cast net; "matlee," a pulla pot; "sumbokee," a pulla net; "bhun," a cast net used from a boat; "korree," a basket net, besides fishing stakes and weirs.

BOMBAY.

57. The following are the Returns of the European and Native officials respecting the 'fresh-water' fisheries of the Bombay Presidency, those of Sind having been given separately (see ante). Thus limited, these fisheries may, for the sake of convenience, be sub-divided into two fishery districts. *First, the inland ones*, the rivers in which, north of the city of Bombay, have mostly a westerly direction; whilst those to the south, many of which are tributaries of the Kristna, take a more easterly course. *Secondly, the coast ones, viz.*, those bordering or near to the sea, which form a narrow strip from the Gulf of Cambay to Bombay itself, and are continued down the Concan and Canara, and might properly include those Madras districts which extend along the Malabar Coast to Cape Comorin.

Fresh-water fisheries of the Bombay Presidency, excluding Sind.

58. Some Returns have been excluded from the following analysis, as not being direct answers to questions; likewise those in which the official, although sending in a reply, appears not to have made full investigations, considering it "premature to harass the fishermen by enquiries into the size of the mesh now used in their nets."

Some few Returns omitted.

59. *The inland fisheries* of Bombay, as above limited, do not possess such fine rivers as Northern and Eastern India; still in many places, those which exist are evidently well adapted for the rearing of fish, and partially supplying the local markets with this wholesome article of food. Its numerous tanks are also well suited for the same purpose.

The rivers and inland tanks suitable for fisheries.

60. The first consideration which arises must be, *what proportion of the people eat fish?* In this enquiry, it is not the proportion that now do so, but what it would be could they obtain it. Unfortunately some answers specify the number of individuals in the talookas that do so, whilst the total of the population is omitted, and some replies are too vague to be of any service. It appears, however, that the proportion of fish-eaters to the remainder of the population is, in the Collectorate of Satara, from 25 to 96 per cent.; in Puna the majority; in Nasik, from 5 to 66, 75, or even 94 per cent.; whilst in one district, inhabited by Bhils and Kolis, all do so, except the Brahmins; in Ahmednugger 66 per cent.; in Khandeish 75 per cent.; in Sholapur 33 per cent.; in Kaladgi 25 per cent.; in Belgaum 20 per cent. In Darwar the numbers of fish-eaters are given in seven talookas at 205,000, whilst in an eighth talooka 20,000, or half the total of the population, consume fish. The foregoing figures appear to show conclusively that the majority of the inhabitants of the inland districts of the Bombay Presidency are consumers of fish, when they can procure it.

Proportion of people who eat fish.

61. *Are the local markets sufficiently supplied with fresh fish to meet the local demands?* is the next question for investigation. Every official who has answered this question, except one mamlutdar, asserts

Local inland markets insufficiently supplied with fish.

c

that the local markets are insufficiently supplied. In some, however, there is a fair supply of salted or dried fish from the coast, but this does not affect the general enquiry. In short, it is self-evident that the local markets are either entirely unsupplied, or inadequately so, with fresh fish, except occasionally, as during the rains, when young ones and those breeding can be destroyed by traps or any clumsy contrivance.

62. *As regards the market prices of large and small fish?* it is quite clear that the latter, weight for weight, are not nearly so valuable as the former. As a general rule, with the increase in the size of a fish, its value per pound largely augments; the smaller the fish, the less is its price per pound. Although the comparative price of mutton and fish appears in some districts to have a relative value, such does not seem to be the case in all.

Comparative prices of fish, large and small.

63. As it has been shown that the majority of the people would eat fish could they obtain it, but that the markets are insufficiently supplied to meet the local demands, the next enquiry that suggests itself is, *have the fresh-water fish in the rivers and tanks increased, decreased, or remained stationary of late years?* Twenty-two distinct answers to this question have been received from the native officials, comprising one who considers they have increased, fourteen who report they have decreased, and seven who assert they have remained stationary. In Ahmenabad one reports an increase, one a decrease, and two a stationary state of the fisheries; in Khandeish, Nasik, Ahmednuggur, Satara, and Sholapur, only a decrease is given; in Belgaum one asserts a decrease, another that the fisheries are stationary, which latter is also the report from Kaladgi: whilst in Darwar seven report a decrease, and three a stationary state of affairs. Thus in nine Collectorates we have the following results :—

The amount of fish have decreased.

Nine Collectorates.	Supply Increased.	Supply decreased.	Supply stationary.
In 5 Collectorates ...	......	5 *	......
,, 1 ,, ...	1 †	1 †	2 †
,, 1 ,, ...	......	1 †	1 †
,, 1 ,, ...	......	......	1 *
,, 1 ,, ...	......	7 †	3 †
Total 9	1	14	7

* Collectors' Reports.
† Mamlutdars' Reports.

From the foregoing it appears to be very evident that the supply of fish in the fisheries is generally decreasing; only one out of twenty-two reporters asserts an increase, whilst two-thirds of the remainder consider the supply to have decreased.

64. *Whose are these fisheries?* is a question for consideration. With some very immaterial exceptions, the whole of those in the inland waters of the Bombay Presidency appear to be the property of Government, which, however, for many years at least, has not disposed of the same, but permitted the adjacent villagers to capture the fish in any method which has best suited their convenience; so that every poaching practice known is freely carried on without check. In Nasik the people adjacent to fisheries consider them as their property, not to the exclusion of Government rights, but as against strangers netting these waters. Also in certain places there are religious objections raised against capturing fish, by the Brahmins, either on account of the sacred character of the locality or else of certain of the species of fish inhabiting a given piece of water, and which are fed in honour of a Hindu idol. The supply of fish from the rivers and tanks having thus been shown to have decreased in these Government fresh-water fisheries, the next question is, *how has this injury to the fisheries been occasioned?* This may be examined under the following heads:—*First*, who are the fishermen? *secondly*, are mature breeding fish destroyed, and if so, how? and *lastly*, are the fry killed to any great extent when they are first moving about in the shallow waters?

The fisheries mostly Government property.

65. *Who are the fishermen?* is the first enquiry, and is fishing confined to any distinct class of the people, or is it general? In answering this question, one official, in summing up the answers of the mamlutdars, includes " women and children" amongst the 1,000 " fishermen :" these numbers will consequently not find a place in the following analysis, but it seems to show that fishing in Sholapur is not confined to one class. In Ahmenabad the question is not answered. In Khandeish the number of fishermen is given at 23,600, Nasik 4,000, Ahmednuggur 2,000 to 3,000, Puna 800, Satara from 5 to 700 in each talooka, Kaladgi 400, Belgaum 435, Dharwar 17,393, exclusive of two talookas in which the numbers are omitted. Besides these, during the rains, many of the labouring population join in. Few, if any, of the foregoing, numbering upwards of 50,000, are solely engaged in fishing, but they also follow other occupations. In fact, there appear to be very few persons indeed who live solely by capturing fresh-water fish.

Fishermen, as a rule, follow other occupations as well.

66. *Are mature breeding fish destroyed, and, if so, how?* Every Collector who has answered this question (except of Kaladgi) considers they are destroyed; but as the native official of the Indi Talooka of the Kaladgi Collectorate reports that fish are trapped there during the rains, it becomes evident that breeding fish do not even obtain an immunity there. The principal and easiest mode of taking breeding fish, is by placing wicker traps during the rains in the small streams and irrigation channels up which they ascend for the purpose of depositing their eggs. Where 'well-irrigation' is employed, there would not be any opportunity for breeding fish to ascend into such irrigation channels, and in these districts of course this mode of taking fish is not employed,

Mature breeding fish are trapped and otherwise killed.

simply because it would not be of any avail. In the various Collectorates the following are the returns :—In Khandeish, Nasik, Sholapur, and Belgaum, fish are reported to be so trapped during the rains. In Ahmenabad they are in two talookas, not so in one. In Dharwar they are in five, not so in five others. In Ahmednuggur, Satara, and Puna, they are asserted not to be trapped, but the Assistant Collector of the last district reports the use of basket traps, so it may be considered doubtful whether they are not employed to take breeding fish should opportunities occur. The other modes in which these fish are destroyed in the inland waters of the Bombay Presidency will come under consideration with the implements employed in capturing fish.

67. *Are the fry killed to any great extent when they are first moving about in the shallow water?* The majority of Indian fresh-water fishes breed chiefly during the rains, at which time the adults deposit their eggs at the sides of rivers and tanks where the water is shallow, or in small channels or water-courses. The delicate fry can only inhabit such localities, due to two principal causes, the first is for the purpose of procuring food, and secondly, to prevent being carried away by a strong current. Now are these young fish thus situated protected or destroyed ? Every Collector who has answered this question (except of Kaladgi) reports that they are destroyed to a very great extent during the rains. If we examine the returns from the Kaladgi Collectorate, we find that nets are stated to be employed for fishing, having meshes the minimum size of which only equals that of a grain of wheat: it consequently follows that fry must also be destroyed in Kaladgi, because there is no mature Indian fresh-water fish that requires such a small mesh for the purpose of its capture.

The fry are destroyed to a great extent.

68. *What are the various modes resorted to for capturing fish?* is a question upon which very full answers have been received. They may be divided into netting, trapping, damming, poisoning, &c. As regards *nets*, the first subject that presents itself, is, not their size and form, but the minimum size of the mesh employed for the capture of fish. It is clearly manifest that if a very small one is freely used, very small fish must be extensively captured. The following returns have been given of the minimum size of the meshes of the nets employed, measured between knot and knot :—

Modes of capturing fish ; size of the meshes of nets.

Officials.	Size of a large needle or less.	Size of a grain of wheat or gram.	Size of mesh between knot and knot in inches.							Less than 1
			$\frac{1}{12}$	$\frac{1}{8}$	$\frac{1}{5}$	$\frac{1}{6}$	$\frac{1}{4}$	$\frac{1}{3}$	$\frac{1}{2}$	
European	2	1	1	1	1	1	...	...	...	1
Native	4	9	1	...	1	...	2	5	1	1

Thus, out of 32 returns, 16 reporters give the minimum size of the mesh of the nets to be that of a grain of gram or wheat or less, whilst 14 more state it to be one-third of an inch or less between knot and knot of the meshes, and two below one inch. But if the reports of those who assert that about an inch, or less than one, exists between knot and knot of the meshes are examined, one must be led to the conclusion that some error has occurred, as they state that very small fish are captured during the rains. In many places where the fish are so minute, that a net however small cannot capture them, a cloth is employed, and, as one official observed, this may be said to have no mesh at all. Consequently, if any fry do escape, it must not be attributed to the will of the fishermen, but rather to their inability to capture them.

69. *Trapping fish* is carried out in various ways, but the most common one appears to be by wicker cages resembling rat traps, into which a fish having entered cannot obtain exit from. These are made of such a fine texture, that the most minute cannot escape through the interstices of the various pieces of wicker work of which they are formed; even fry are taken in them. The course of streams is also sometimes diverted so that all the water has to pass through a wicker cage or over a wicker platform, by which means all the fish are captured. *Damming streams* or portions of tanks, emptying out the water and thus obtaining all the contained fish, is also carried on. On a dam being raised, an artificial opening is cut in it, and a wicker cage or an apparatus of bamboo and net is made use of, to take all the fish which are carried down in the current with the escaping water.

<small>Breeding and young fish trapped in various forms of cruives.</small>

70. *Poisoning fish* does not seem to be unknown in the Bombay Presidency. It is reported in Khandeish by means of hinganbet, yāthil, gīr, and thor; in Nasik by the "soopli," tobacco leaves, and the milk bush, as well as by the fruit of the "jel phul;" in Ahmednuggur and Dharwar by the milk bush; whilst in Nasik it is observed that this mode of taking fish used to be very common, but every attempt has been made to put down the objectionable custom. They are also reported to poison fish in the Puna and Belgaum Collectorates, but in the Gokah Talooka, in the latter, it is stated that the practice has to a certain extent been stopped, owing to the rules of the Forest Department, under which it is prohibited to cut the small twigs and leaves from which the stupefying drugs are made. This is a destructive method of obtaining all the fish in a nearly or quite stagnant pool or piece of water, which, irrespective of destroying old and young indiscriminately, cannot be supposed to obtain the proceeds in so wholesome a state, as if they had been taken by means of nets. The water itself is thus sometimes rendered deleterious to human beings and cattle that unwarily partake of it.

<small>Waters are poisoned to obtain fish in some of the Collectorates.</small>

71. There are other modes of fishing which are carried on by various means, as employing hooks and lines either suspended to poles in the water or used merely by anglers.

<small>Angling and line fishing.</small>

72. Before passing on to the second set of fisheries of Bombay, I think the following must be admitted :—

Resumé of conclusions respecting the inland fresh-water fisheries.

(1) that the majority of the inhabitants of the inland districts would eat fish could they obtain it; (2) that the markets are not sufficiently supplied to meet the local demands; (3) that the fish in the rivers and tanks have generally decreased of late years; (4) that the fisheries are Government property; (5) that every one fishes how he likes and where he pleases; (6) that breeding fish are extensively trapped; (7) that fry are killed whenever they can be obtained; (8) that nets with very minute meshes, and even cloths are used, wherewith to capture the immature fish; (9) that traps are also employed, made of wicker work of such fine texture that the most minute fish are killed; (10) that streams and tanks are dammed and every fish destroyed; (11) that poisoning whole pieces of water in order to obtain the fish is practised in many of these inland Collectorates. Whether it is or is not worth while to do anything to mitigate this evil, is a question I propose considering further on.

73. *The coast fisheries, viz.,* those bordering on or near to the sea,

Coast fresh-water fisheries of less consequence than the inland ones.

must not be considered as consisting entirely of sea-coast and marine or estuary fishes, as some of these Collectorates extend some distance inland; and it is in such localities that distinct fresh-water fisheries exist. But, as a rule, the value of such is not of much consequence, when there is a well-stocked and regularly fished sea-board within easy distance. These fresh-water fisheries on the coast may be briefly examined in the same manner as the inland ones have been.

74. *As to the proportion of persons who consume fish to the general population?*

Majority of people eat fish.

It is set down in Broach at from one-third to one-fourth; in Kaira at one-sixth; whilst in four talookas in Colaba it is given thus, in one at seven-eighths, in two at three-fourths, and in one at one-half. As a rule, in the other Collectorates the questions were not circulated to the native officials, or at least the answers have not been received; consequently some details are not so full as they might have been. The Acting Collector of Kaira, for instance, observes, "the majority of the population being vegetarians," &c., but does not furnish the mamlutdars' answers. However, it would seem from the reports that fish are not consumed so largely by the population on the sea-coast as they are along the inland districts of this Presidency. Some of the local markets appear to be fully supplied with salted and dried sea-fish, in others the supply is less than the demand, whilst from the majority of the talookas the returns are a blank.

75. Whether the fresh-water fish have increased, decreased, or re-

State of the fisheries.

mained stationary, there are only eight answers, which report a stationary state in six, and a decrease in two.

76. All these fisheries, with but very few exceptions, appear to be

These fisheries Government property.

Government property, but no right has been exercised over them for a long period, owing to their being of little or no pecuniary value.

xxxix

From this, however, must be excluded the fresh-water fisheries along the sea-coast south of Bombay, some of which appear to be valuable; and the Collector of North Canara reports that they are Government property, except in those tanks formed by private persons at their own expense.

Number of fishermen. 77. As to the number of fishermen, the answers again become vague, except in Broach, where they are computed at 390.

Fish trapped during the rains. 78. The mature fish are said to be trapped in the irrigated fields during the rains, except where only 'well-irrigation' is employed.

Fry destroyed to a great extent. 79. The fry also are reported to be destroyed to a large extent during or after the rains, in most of those talookas from which answers have been received.

Smallest size of the mesh of nets that are employed. 80. The following returns have been given of the minimum size of the mesh of nets employed:—

Officials.	Size of a large needle or mosquito net.	Size of mesh between knot and knot in inches.		
		¼	⅓	½
European	2	1	1	0
Native	1	1	3	1

Thus out of 10 returns, three reporters give the minimum size of the mesh of the nets to be about that of mosquito nets, and all the rest at or less than one-third of an inch between knot and knot.

Modes of fishing. 81. The modes of fishing in the fresh waters of these sea-coast districts hardly vary from those more inland. Nets of all forms and sizes are employed, some being fixed, others not so. Dams are erected and openings made, where nets or basket traps are placed, so as to capture every fish. In the Colaba, Ratnaghari, and North Canara Collectorates fish are also said to be killed by poison, whilst in Kaira torch-fishing by night appears to be carried on.

Resumé of conclusions respecting the coast fresh-water fisheries. 82. It would appear from the foregoing that in the fresh-water fisheries of the coast districts (1) the proportion of people who eat fish is less than in the inland districts; (2) that the markets which are sufficiently supplied with fish obtain them from the sea; (3) that the fresh-water fish appear to be stationary or decreasing; (4) that the fisheries are Government property; (5) that there are no restrictions as to the modes of fishing; (6) that breeding fish are trapped; (7) that fry are killed wherever obtainable; (8) that nets with minute meshes are employed to destroy small fish; (9) that wicker traps are in use; (10) that streams are dammed; (11) that waters are poisoned, and (12) that torch-light fishing is pursued, at least in one Collectorate.

83. Having thus briefly analysed the opinions given in the ensuing returns, they all more or less clearly show the great use to which the fresh-water fisheries might be turned; their present impoverished state and inefficiency to meet the demands of the local markets, owing to which thousands of persons who would eat fish, could they obtain it, are now entirely deprived of this wholesome article of food. That this appears to have been produced by the permission of reckless and indiscriminate fishing in fisheries the property of Government, and how the slaughter of the breeding fish and the destruction of the fry by every conceivable means, even to nets with such fine meshes, and wicker traps the interstices of which will not permit even the passage of a fish's egg, down to damming streams and standing pieces of water, trapping the breeding fish and the fry, and even poisoning the fisheries by which everything is obtained to the most minute, the latter of which being sometimes killed only to be thrown away. Lastly, that the fishing classes, as a rule, do not solely pursue this occupation for a living, but only as an addition to their ordinary means of livelihood, so that the passing of any measures which might even temporarily put a check to this pursuit could not bear hardly upon any class.

Conclusions.

84. Having thus briefly adverted to the present state of affairs, the consideration arises, would it be better to leave matters alone and trust to chance, or might it be advisable to put a stop to the present wasteful manner in which these fisheries are being worked, and by some simple, but effective, measures permit the adult fish to breed in peace, and the young to grow out of their babyhood before being caught, and thus to afford a very largely increased amount of animal food to the poorer classes?

Is it advisable to let matters continue as they are, or do anything to mitigate evils which exist?

85. It will be well first to examine the views of those *who would leave these deteriorating fisheries alone*, the principal reasons which are adduced for such a course being as follows:—The Assistant Collector of Khandeish denies that inland fisheries in small rivers have ever proved of any economic or commercial advantage, unless protected as private property, &c., therefore it is no matter what becomes of them in Khandeish and the Deccan, whilst in the larger rivers the fish may take care of themselves; and with such views, would give out the fishery tenures as far as possible to those who now employ themselves in these fisheries, and thus at one stroke render them private property, &c. Thus, without placing any limitation on the minimum size of the mesh of the nets made use of, he would give the monopoly of these fisheries, without any restrictions, to some of the very people who are now impoverishing them by every means which their ingenuity can suggest. In Ahmenabad it is considered "better that some fry be destroyed than that further opportunities should be afforded to the lower grade of Government servants and bigotted Hindus to turn the intentions of Government to their own profit." In Kaira it is considered that restrictions, if imposed, would be of little or no benefit. In Nasik that such would be unpopular and difficult of enforcement in outlying districts. In Tanna no restrictions are recommended, whilst any would render additional police necessary.

General and local objections to interfere.

In Dharwar it is thought that it would be extremely difficult and unpopular to regulate the minimum size of the meshes of nets employed in those small tanks which dry up every hot season, because, as the water subsides, the fish are taken in the mud even with the hands. In Khandeish it would be impossible to curtail the present privileges of the Bhils by regulating how the fisheries should be worked, because the forest rules have deprived them of one source of livelihood, *viz.*, the sale of timber cut in the forest; but that prohibiting the poisoning of water-courses for fishing purposes should be the only first step taken. Thus the *general objections* appear to be that the fisheries are of little, if any, economic value at present, and no benefit would accrue from trying to improve them, whilst any regulations respecting the nets would be difficult to carry out. The *local objections* against regulations are, that it would be impolitic as in Khandeish; in Dharwar that such should not extend to tanks that yearly dry up; whilst in Ahmenabad that they would be used as a means of extortion by the lower grades of Government servants.

86. On the other hand, the following opinions have been advanced; by *those who would do something to improve these fisheries and render them more economically useful.*

<small>Proposals to interfere and increase the importance of the fisheries.</small>

The Acting Collector of North Canara observes that the fish are the public property, the public being represented by Government. Were these fisheries an unlimited fund of wealth or inexhaustible, it would be better to leave the right of using them unlimited; but as they are not inexhaustible, but are deteriorating, restrictions have become necessary. The Acting First Assistant Collector of Ahmednuggur considers that legislation will be the only effectual stop to the present mode of depopulating the fisheries, but that a general Act would be unworkable, therefore it would be better to have one which could be applied when considered necessary to particular rivers and localities favourable for fish breeding. The Second Assistant observes that a prohibitive measure regulating the size of the mesh of the nets would not be unpopular. In Satara that no difficulties exist against regulating the size of the meshes of the nets, except the want of some legal provision by which offenders might be punished. In Broach that there would be no objection in regulating the minimum size of the meshes of the nets to be henceforth used, beyond the prejudices of the fishermen. The Collector of Ahmednuggur considers that, if an Act were passed, one or two years' notice would be necessary, as the nets with smaller meshes would become useless. In Kaladgi and Rutnaghari the only objections appear to be the difficulty of detecting infringements of any regulations that may be decided upon. In Belgaum that there would be no trouble, but prawn and 'moree' nets should be exempted; the Assistant Collector likewise sees no difficulty in regulating the size of the meshes of the nets to be used at different seasons. The Acting Collector of Dharwar considers that there would be difficulties, but in no degree insuperable ones, to regulating the minimum size of the meshes of nets used in the rivers and in the large tanks that do not dry up. Thus some legislative interference to stop the present mode of depopulating the fisheries appears to be considered necessary by the majority of the European civil officials who have given their opinions, and regulating the minimum size of the meshes of the nets to be employed, appears to be looked upon as the most effectual measure. It is said that such will be difficult to be carried out in some districts, and it is suggested that a general Act applicable to the whole of India would be unworkable, and it would be better to have one which may be applied (with modifications) to particular rivers and localities.

87. Should any regulation be enacted defining the minimum size of the mesh of the nets to be hereafter used in any fresh-water fishery, the following are the opinions of the various European officials as to what that size should be. Eight answers are given : one proposes from half an inch to one inch ; a second, half an inch for bag-nets, and one inch for drag-nets ; three others suggest half an inch, and the remaining three 1 inch. Such propositions would of themselves be sufficient to show to how small a size the mesh of the nets in this Presidency has dwindled down. One inch between knot and knot, however, appears to be the most generally approved size.

Opinions as to what the minimum size of the mesh of nets should be.

88. Along with the size of the mesh of the nets, must be considered the question as to whether it is advisable to prohibit the sale of the fry of fishes in the bazars, or those which could not be taken in the legal nets, and so must have been obtained by unfair means. *The Assistant Collector of Surat* denounces the idea as " an arbitrary interference with trade, such as could not be enforced save by a penal statute of an obnoxious character." "No such restrictions are enforced anywhere in Europe that I am aware of." ["No person is allowed wilfully to take or destroy the young of salmon, to buy, sell, or expose for sale, or have in his possession the young of salmon, to place any device for obstructing their passage, to wilfully injure them, or to disturb any spawning bed, or any bank or shallow on which the spawn of salmon may be ; and any person acting in contravention of these provisions is liable to forfeit all the young of salmon found in his possession, as well as all rods, lines, nets, devices, and instruments used in committing any of such offences, and to incur a penalty not exceeding five pounds for each offence." (*Laws relating to Salmon Fisheries of Great Britain*, J. Baker, 1868.)] *The Collector of Puna* also objects, but on the grounds, that instead he would rely on regulating the size of the meshes of the nets. The Collectors of Broach, Nasik, Ahmednuggur, Satara, and Belgaum, as well as the Assistant Collector in the latter district, see no objections to this prohibition.

Opinions as to prohibiting the sale of the fry of fish.

89. As regards fence-months, more especially in the hilly districts, in the rivers of which localities the larger sorts of fish, as the Mahaseers, resort for breeding during the first few months of the monsoon. In Kaira it is observed a fence season would be no hardship. In Nasik and Rutnaghari that no objections exist against prohibiting the capture of fish for the first two months of monsoons in the hilly regions where they are breeding, except the difficulty of carrying out such a regulation. The Collector of Ahmednuggur considers a close season desirable. As regards poisoning waters to obtain the fish, this is universally condemned where practised, but

Opinions respecting the necessity or the reverse of fence-months, and poisoning of waters for fishing purposes.

more stringent laws appear to be necessary before it can be put a stop to.

90. The *Chief Secretary to the Government of Bombay*, in forward-

Opinion of the Bombay Government. ing the returns from which the following were compiled, observes that very little is known regarding the fresh-water fisheries of this Presidency, or the practicability of increasing and developing this source of food supply; whilst it is clear that a great deal of wasteful destruction takes place.

91. The *Officiating Revenue Commissioner, Northern Division* (Oc-

Opinions of the Revenue Commissioners. tober 1st, 1868) stated :—"I believe a large destruction, both of fish and of small game, is caused more or less throughout India by netting during the spawning and breeding season, and it is a question whether protective laws of moderate stringency would not be very advisable. * *· The subject is not without importance, and I think it would be advisable to prohibit netting, both fish and game, during the spawning and breeding season." The *Acting Revenue Commissioner, Southern Division* (October 9th, 1868) observed :—"I consider that it would be almost impracticable to enforce laws for the preservation of fish throughout India; but that if certain localities were selected for preserves, and guarded under a legal enactment for the purpose, considerable light might be thrown upon the question, and the advisability of extending such operations to other places, or not doing so, would be more clearly established than at present."

92. The *Acting Collector of Ahmedabad* reported (June 10th, 1871)

Opinions of European officials in the Ahmedabad Collectorate. that fish exist in the Saburmuttee, the Meshwa, and the Kharee rivers, also in the Bokh and in all the larger tanks. In the rivers and in the Bokh they are often of a large size, but in the tanks their average weight is half a pound, although large fish are also caught there. There are no private rights in the fishing. The *Acting Collector* (February 20th, 1872) merely observed that there are no fisheries proper in his district, and that he deprecates any attempt to regulate, as suggested, the capture of fish, considering that it is better that some fry be destroyed than that further opportunities should be afforded to the lower grades of Government servants, and to bigotted Hindus, to turn the intentions of Government to their own profit.

93. The *Acting Collector of Broach* reported (May 26th, 1871)

Opinions of European officials in the Broach Collectorate. that there are fresh-water fisheries in the Nerbudda, the Mhye, and the Dhadur, but no special rights are enjoyed by any class of people or the Government, the fisheries being open to all persons wishing to make use of them. The *Acting Collector* (March 8th, 1872) observed that as the fisheries of the district are open to all persons wishing to make use of them, and every sort of net is used, there is reason to believe that breeding and very young fish are destroyed to a considerable extent. This destruction occurs chiefly in the Nerbudda during the rains, and within about five or six miles of Broach both up and down stream; it also takes place at Hansote on the same river. The smallest size of the mesh of the nets used is one-sixth of an inch in diameter, but there would be no difficulty in regulating its size for the future, beyond the prejudices of the fishing communities, who have never been subjected to any restrictions in the exercise of their calling. There would be no objection to prohibit the sale of the fry of fish in the bazars. The *First Assistant Collector* reported that at Ahmode there are different ways of catching fish :—(1)—By a net termed nādi by the Bhoees, and bhandar by the Wágris ; it is fixed across the stream, shaped like a wall, and strengthened at intervals by stakes ; these stakes are not stuck into the ground, but tightened by a couple of ropes at either end ; it is sometimes dragged by these ropes along the river. Another very similar one has a bag in the middle ; it is termed sooprá-jhal by the Bhoees and beheri by the Wágris. The ordinary cast-net is called hāth-jhal by both castes.

94. The *Acting Collector of Kaira* (February 7th, 1872) reported that the rivers in which fresh-water fisheries exist, are the Mhye, Watruck, Sheree, and Meshwa. The majority of the population being vegetarians, the principal fish trade is with Baroda, and mostly confined to marine fish which are taken in the tidal waters. The *Assistant Collector* observed, a certain quantity of fry are destroyed, but the supply exceeds the demand. The fishermen claim no exclusive right to the fisheries, and would easily submit to any restrictions imposed by Government in the way of a " fence season," &c., and such would be no hardship to them. He continued that he is disposed to think that such restrictions would prove of little or no benefit to any one, and are therefore not desirable. Moreover, he is of opinion "that until the *general principles* of interference in the fisheries of this country are settled, it would be premature to harass the fishermen by enquiries into the size of the mesh now used in their nets." " My own opinion is, that we know too little as yet of the habits of the fresh-water fishes of India to devise any scheme of interference which would be practically operative,   *   * it is necessary to ascertain *in what* months the fish of particular districts spawn," and this, he continued, he is unable to ascertain, so is opposed to fence-months.

Opinions of the European officials in the Kaira Collectorate.

95. The *Collector of Surat* reported (May 25th, 1871) that there are no regular fresh-water fisheries in his zilla, fish being captured in most of the rivers running through the talookas, and also in some of the larger tanks. The amount of fish taken is stated to be inconsiderable, Dooblas and other Kallipuruf people of the low aboriginal castes being the chief fishers ; but they do not confine their operations to any particular part of the river, nor do they fish for trade purposes. " Machees" (fishermen by caste) fish generally for retail sale. Government derive no rent or revenue, as also there are no private rights. Subsequently (March 12th, 1872), whilst forwarding the opinions of the Assistant Collectors, he observed that they contained all the information which he had on the subject owing to want of local experience. The *Secretary to the Surat Municipality* stated that between Variov and the camp there is so little fishing carried on that he is unable to say whether breeding fish or fry are destroyed, but judging from those brought to the markets, he considers they are not. The size of the mesh of the prawn nets

Opinions of the European officials in the Surat Collectorate.

is one quarter of an inch. The *First Assistant Collector* reported that all fish are taken indiscriminately in nets, but owing to the proximity to the sea, fresh-water fish are not much sought after; those captured in the rivers and tanks are mostly taken during the monsoon and autumn months. The minimum size of the mesh of the nets is one-fourth of an inch in diameter; it would be difficult to regulate such, owing to the close supervision of the fishing classes which would be entailed, but one inch between knot and knot of the meshes is considered to be a fair size. Prohibiting the sale of the fry of fish in the bazars " would be an arbitrary interference with trade, such as could not be enforced save by a penal statute of an obnoxious character; no such restrictions are enforced anywhere in Europe that I am aware of" (see para. 88). The *Assistant Collector* observed that in these districts there seems to be a very small trade in fish except at Mandvi; the fishermen generally using all they catch for home consumption. The chief places for fishing in Bardoli are upon the Mindhola, which runs past Kamalchool and Bardoli Kasba. In Walod fish are caught at Buhari, Walod, and Banjipura or Kamalchool; in Mandvi only in the Tapti. In Bardoli the fry appear in July, but are let alone until the end of September or beginning of October, and are then taken. In Walod there are more fishermen than in Bardoli, and the destruction of young fry is very great. The nets used are extremely fine-meshed, some containing four meshes within the space of three quarters of an inch. The people chiefly eat all they capture, but send any large ones to Gundevi. However, they say they cannot catch mature ones, so they get the fry. In Mandvi and Bodhon they catch fish down to the smallest fry, and therefore use the very finest meshes. There must be large fish in the Tapti, but the people say they cannot get hold of them, and therefore destroy the fry. The latter come up in May and September, and are caught indiscriminately. These people live entirely by fishing, and could not be willingly induced to allow the fish a chance of stocking the waters before they are killed.

96. The *Collector of Khandeish* reported (April 22nd, 1871) that there are no fresh-water fisheries in the district; but that fish exist in all the rivers, and are caught by the Bhils and low castes, forming an important article in their food, but that they are not of sufficient importance to be called fisheries, and Government has never exercised any control over them. On April 22nd, 1872, he reported that breeding and very young fish are destroyed wherever they can be obtained, in the few rivers and streams that yield fish, by means of nets, baskets, weirs, traps, cloths, poison, and in fact anyhow. As regards what is the minimum size of the mesh of nets, this question may perhaps best be answered by stating that when small-meshed nets are not available, the Bhils use their sheets, saris, and dhotars for the purpose of taking fish. This may be said to be no mesh at all. Respecting what difficulty exists against regulating the size of the meshes of nets, the Collector forwards the following opinion of *Major Probyn*, in which he fully concurs:—" The objection to interference at present is, that the fish caught by the Bhils, in all but the large rivers, forms a great portion of their food, especially in a bad season when grain is scarce and dear, and it is the more necessary to avoid curtailing their privileges in this matter, because our forest

rules have deprived them of one source of livelihood, *viz.*, the sale of timber cut in the forest. The catching of fish by poisoning the watercourses, causing the most wholesale destruction of spawn and everything else that should be spared, if put a stop to, will be a first and great step towards the preservation of fish, without causing alarm to the Bhils, which would probably follow any more pointed measure of fish conservancy." The *Assistant Collector* observes :—" In no country have inland fisheries in small rivers ever proved of any economic or commercial importance, except when such fisheries were protected by rights of private property, special legislation, and special police, besides possessing the advantages of markets, transport, available capital, and means of preservation. Not a single one of these advantages is possessed by the fisheries of Khandeish and the Deccan, and consequently it is very little matter what becomes of them." [Without giving any opinion on this statement, I would point out that the native officials report that three-fourths of the people eat fish, that there are 23,600 fishermen in the district, and the markets are not fully supplied.] The *Assistant Collector* continues, "in the case of large rivers like the Tapti and Nerbadda, the fish will take care of themselves against any onslaught likely to be made by the miserable Bhils (professional fishermen) of this generation, and perhaps the next will be riper for protective legislation. If, however, Government are bent on protecting the fish, two courses are open to them; either to apply the Survey Act to water as well as to land, giving out the tenures as far as possible to those now employed in the fisheries, and thus at one stroke rendering all fisheries in the country private property, and applying the most powerful stimulus to improvement known to economists; or else to give the District Officers power to call the fishermen together, and frame rules for the fisheries separately after the practice obtaining in Ireland, and I believe in Scotland and England." [This is all a mistake.] " Disobedience to rules so framed might be made punishable by fine and forfeiture of the instruments and fish."

97. The *Acting Extra First Assistant Collector* in charge of the Punch Mahals reported, on May 6th, 1871,

Opinions of European officials in the Punch Mahals.

that no fisheries exist in the district, as there are no large rivers except the Myhee, which runs on the western frontier, and only touches two or three villages. In these there are no fishermen who earn a living by catching fish, and the few who reside there generally catch them more for home consumption than for sale. The tank at Godra contains fish of small size. Government in connection with fishing has never exercised any restriction, because, owing to the demand being limited, they are only taken to a small extent, and not for trade. In the villages of Wullubpur and Waree, which are on the banks of the Myhee, and are talookdaree villages, the Thakoos who are proprietors of them, receive a third share of the fish caught within those limits. The *Extra First Assistant* observed (March 11th, 1872) that the district produces few fish or fishermen. There is no fish market whatever, and the very small number of mud-flavoured, worthless fish caught in the tanks and half-dry rivers of the country are really not worth being reported on.

98. The *Collector of Nasik* reported (June 14th, 1871) that there are no organized fisheries in the Collectorate, though almost every river is more or less fished by the villagers residing on its banks. The principal fishermen are the Bhils and Kolis, and also the Bhoees, and they fish principally for the purpose of providing food for home consumption, but not for sale. In the Godaveri, there are in some of the pools vast numbers of fish. Although there are no defined rights as regards fisheries, the people of villages look upon the fishing places adjoining their domiciles as belonging to them, not to the exclusion of fishing on behalf of Government, but as against any other villagers with large nets fishing within their boundaries. Indeed in some places they object to even a small net being thrown by any stranger. In a later report (April 10th, 1872) the Collector observed that breeding and very young ones are destroyed to a great extent. Fish are caught all the year round, and little or no regard is paid to breeding seasons, nor are any, however small, ever returned to the water. They are destroyed in the pools in rivers and in tanks by means of large drag-nets. He observes that he has seen a net of nearly one hundred yards long, used for the purpose of dragging a large pool in the river Godaveri; after it had been stretched across this river, one end was gradually taken round, thus enclosing a considerable space. While the dragging was going on, many fish commenced jumping over the net, when men with smaller nets placed behind the larger one, caught them as they jumped. Cart-loads were taken in this trial, and of many kinds. Smaller nets are more numerous than drag ones, especially cast, purse and other varieties. Fish are also caught in shallows, small pools, and irrigating channels, by nets, baskets, or funnel-shaped wicker traps placed where there is a current of water. Poisoning used to be very common, but every attempt has been made to put down this objectionable custom. But there are many other ways of catching fish. Bhils fish in the following manner:—At every six or eight feet of a long rope, a piece of the stalk of kurbi or jowaree is tied. The rope is then stretched across the river, the men holding it going up stream, and three or four others coming after the rope beating the water. The fish take refuge under the river's banks, whilst other Bhils catch them with their hands. These fish are generally under two inches in length. Dams are also used in shallow waters, and the places so enclosed are dragged with cloths or baled out, and all the fish taken. The meshes of some of the nets are very small, as any are permitted, Government never having attempted to frame any rules or to interfere in any way. There would be considerable difficulties in regulating the size of the mesh of nets: *first*, it would be unpopular with a large class who gain their livelihood by catching small fish, and no one would interfere to prevent breaches of the law; *secondly*, there are so many out-of-the-way places that it would be difficult to enforce any order if issued. The sale of fry might be prohibited, and this would be effective as regards bazars in large towns, but not in the majority of the villages. No objection exists to prohibiting the capture of fish in the hilly districts during the first two months of the monsoon, when they ascend there for breeding purposes, execept that such an order could not be enforced. The Bhils and others would endeavour to evade it, and there would be no way in the hills to compel obedience.

Opinions of European officials in the Nasik Collectorate.

99. The *Collector of Ahmednugger* reported (July 8th, 1871) that the rivers Bheema, Seena, Godaveri, Goor, Proura, and Moolla, which pass through or border the district, contain considerable quantities of fish, which, however, are mostly of an inferior description, and have little market value. The "Dohs" or holes where the fish congregate are fished by all persons without restriction. No rights in the fisheries, in opposition to those of Government, are known or acknowledged, and it is not likely that the right of Government to sell or restrict fishing would anywhere be disputed. The Collector subsequently (February 22nd, 1872) observed, that the rivers in the Collectorate are dragged and fished by all persons without restriction as to season, and there is no doubt that destruction of small fishes is the consequence. The *Acting First Assistant Collector* reported as follows :—
"As far as my own knowledge goes, I am sure that in places where fishing is carried on to any extent, there is a great and indiscriminate destruction of spawning and under-sized fish. I do not see that there is any way of preventing this except by legislation, and even then considerable difficulties would arise, for any general Act would be unworkable, and must in most parts of the country remain a dead letter. It would, I think, be better to have an Act which could be applied, when considered necessary, to particular rivers and localities favourable for fish breeding." The *Acting Second Assistant Collector* remarked as follows :—" From conversation with fishermen here, I have ascertained that they are quite aware that the quantity of fish in the rivers is less than it was, and that a prohibitive measure regulating the size of the nets would not be unpopular, and I do not think any great hardship would be caused by closing the fisheries during breeding time, as the greater number of the fishermen are then employed in agriculture or other pursuits. I think some measure for the conservation of the fish is necessary." The *Collector* likewise observed :—" No doubt very young fish are destroyed in nallas, shallows, &c., by persons who are not regular fishermen, and at all seasons with nets, pieces of cloth used as nets, &c. The smallest mesh of the nets is less than an inch; it has never been attempted to regulate their size, but such might be done; still one or two years' notice should be given beforehand, as the nets with smaller meshes would become useless; the minimum size might be from half an inch to one inch between knot and knot. The sale of fry might be prohibited, and a close season is desirable."

100. The *Collector of Puna* reported (June 30th, 1871) that in the district there are two large rivers, *viz.*, the Bheema and the Neera; the former has seven large affluents, *viz.*, the Pooshpawuttee, Kookree, Meena, Goar, Bhama, Indrayunee, and Moola Moota; the latter has one, *viz.*, the Kurra: each of these has its large and small feeders. Most of these streams retain large pools during the hottest season; in some the water flows perennially. The fisheries are generally appropriated by the villages within which they are situated. Government have hitherto never claimed rent. No private rights really exist, but that of prescription may be claimed. [License, however long enjoyed, gives no right according to the British law.] The *Assistant Collector* at the same time observed that the natives of the Deccan refuse to eat crabs, turtles and tortoises for reli-

gious reasons, whilst the Kolis eat both. The turtles or tortoises are put into wells where they eat up any rubbish that may fall in, and keep down the crabs, who are great enemies of all masonry work. Although only Government rights in respect to the fisheries exist, there is half an exception in the case of so-called sacred fish at Wozre Talooka, Indapoor. A similar case is at Wozer in the Joonere Talooka, a village belonging in Dewusthan Inam to a temple of Gunputi. The inhabitants objected to any persons catching fish in their pool of the Kookree river, and first brought false accusations against the Joonere fishermen of poisoning the water. Afterwards they said that the Joonere Mussulmen who came to fish insulted the women drawing water. On a personal investigation, it came out that "these fish are fed in honour of our god, and we do not like their being killed." At Chinchwad, where the village on one side belongs to the god who does not even pay joodee, and the other shore is his inam garden, the Karbharee stated the god claimed no proprietary right in the fish fed from the temple steps. The existence, however, of a few sanctuaries is probably useful to the fisheries. The *First Assistant Collector of Puna* (April 10th, 1872) remarked that there is a strong Brahmin element in the district, which is sufficient to deter fishermen from plying their trade in many places. When, however, they are not interfered with, they catch fish in all seasons by every means in their power, chiefly by netting, sometimes by poison, and less frequently by baited hooks. In the large rivers fishing cannot be carried on during heavy floods, and throughout the year the priestly influence, above noted, greatly protects the fish. Breeding and very young ones are caught to some extent, whilst, on the subsidence of the floods, bag nets and baskets are placed in openings constructed in artificial dams which are roughly thrown across streams. During the rainless season, the large deep pools, which abound in the rivers, are netted. These rivers cannot be said to be perennial, so far as the fish are concerned, for in many places the stream that flows during the hot weather is so slender as to be useless for them, and occasionally merely oozes through the gravelly bed of the river. No size of the mesh of nets is disallowed; the minimum size obtained is $\frac{1}{10}$th of an inch between knot and knot (sample enclosed). As regards the appropriate regulation-size for the mesh of nets, it should not be less than half an inch between knot and knot for bag nets, and one inch for drag nets. He objects to prohibiting the sale of the fry of fish in the bazar at first, but would rely upon regulating the size of the mesh of the nets.

101. The *Collector of Tanna* reported (August 12th, 1871) that no large fresh-water rivers exist in his district, all of that description being large streams formed as natural outlets for the rainfall flowing from the Ghâts and high lands. During the monsoon months these rivers are full, the body of water flowing down these outlets towards the sea with great force. During the dry weather the beds of these rivers are dry, excepting where large and deep reaches exist. Here fish are found, and fishing is resorted to by the various villagers dwelling in the vicinity; in hardly any instance, however, have they any right in such fisheries, other than that of a prescriptive one. At Callian there is a place into which fresh water pours during the rains. The right of fishing is held

Opinion of the Collector of Tanna.

d

by a Parsee, who pays five rupees a year, and has done so since the time of the Peshwas. The rights in all instances, except in that at Callian, appear to be of custom, and in respect to which the parties can claim none under documentary title. Government has never exercised its right, simply because the fisheries are of little, if any, value; to now do so would no way benefit the State, and would merely lead to discontent. Subsequently (January 6th, 1872) the Collector observed, that his being a sea-coast district the fresh-water fisheries are but small, the only waters being in the rivers Bheema and Seena. No distinction is made between breeding fish and others, whilst the young are also caught. There is no restriction whatever, none is recommended, whilst any restrictive law would render additional police necessary to prevent its infringement.

102. The *Collector of Colaba* (March 23rd, 1872) observed, that, owing to the flatness of the country, the tides run so far up the different creeks that the fresh-water fisheries are very restricted and of little value. A Statement appended shows the rights of Government and private parties with respect to the fresh-water fisheries in the Collectorate. Sheets of water, more or less deep, formed in a hollow in the bed of a river, are termed "Doho's." All these fisheries belong to Government, but any one is allowed to fish in them without payment, with the exception of two small ones in the talooka of Peun which are the property of the Inamdar of the village. Breeding and very young fish are destroyed to a great extent by snares both in rivers and nallas during all seasons of the year. The smallest size of the mesh is one which will just admit a large needle. One inch between knot and knot should be the minimum size, but the fishermen would not obey any such regulation unless it were legalised.

Opinion of the Collector of Colaba.

103. The *Acting Collector of Satara* reported (June 22nd, 1871) that fish of about fifty kinds are caught in the larger streams in the district, *viz.*, the Kristna, Yeana, Cormooree, Tarla, Koina, Warna, Yerla, Maun, Neera, and Bheema. They are chiefly taken in the long deep reaches of the larger streams in which there is always water. No rights over particular spots are legally reserved either to Government or to the villagers, but the inhabitants of each village fish in the contiguous waters. In certain places on the Kristna, near temples, the Brahmins, on religious grounds, prevent any fish being caught. The *Collector* observed (March 16th, 1872) that breeding and very young fish are destroyed to a considerable extent by means of nets in pools both in great rivers and in nallas. When the rivers become muddy at the commencement of the monsoon, fish die in large numbers, also when they become nearly dry at the close of the hot weather. The smallest size of the mesh of the nets varies from three-quarters to one-eighth of an inch in circumference ($\frac{3}{16}$ths to $\frac{1}{32}$nd of an inch between knot and knot of the meshes). No difficulties exist against regulating the size of these meshes, except some legal provision in order to punish offenders. Half an inch between each knot is proposed. There are no objections of any weight, against prohibiting the sale of the fry of fish in the bazars.

Opinions of European officials in the Satara Collectorate.

104. The *Collector of Kaladgi* reported (March 1st, 1872) that it is believed breeding fish and very young ones are not destroyed to any great extent in his district, but the smallest size of the mesh of the nets is about equal to a grain of wheat. There are no persons who are strictly fishermen, nor are there any considerable fisheries, and, were the size of the mesh of the nets regulated in future, it would probably be difficult to detect any infringement, as it would not be easy to discover in which part of the river the people were netting. Beyond this, there is no reason why the size of the meshes of the nets should not be regulated, and half an inch between each knot is proposed as the minimum size. Fry of fish are said not to be sold in the bazars.

Opinion of the Collector of Kaladgi.

105. The *Acting Collector of Sholapur* reported (May 24th, 1871) that there are two rivers in the district, the Bheema and the Seena. The right to net fish in these rivers or in other places is not sold by auction, because of their not containing fish enough to render it worth while for people to become purchasers. Subsequently (February 7th, 1872) he reported that fishermen take every sort and size of fish without distinction, that no restriction exists as to the size of the mesh of the nets employed, and he does not recommend any for the future, as additional police would be necessary, and the necessity for such a prohibition is not apparent to him.

Opinion of the Collector of Sholapur.

106. The *Collector of Belgaum* reported (May 25th, 1871) that fish in abundance, but for the most part small and of inconsiderable value, are caught in the Mulpurbha, Tambraparni, Gataprabha, and Markundya rivers. As regards fisheries, the respective rights of Government and of private parties have never been determined. Neither Government nor private individuals reserve rights, and the inhabitants of any of the villages on the banks of the rivers are in the habit of catching the fish for their own consumption. The Collector subsequently (March 19th, 1872) submitted a report compiled from information furnished by the First Assistant, the Assistant Collector, and Deputy Collector, who are severally in charge of districts. He observed that there would appear from the various reports to be no difficulty in regulating the size of the meshes of the nets used, ruling that none smaller should be employed except for prawns and "morce" fishing. Moreover, by doing this, there would be no inconvenience caused to fishermen. There exists no objection against prohibiting the sale of the fry of fish in the bazars. The *First Assistant Collector* observes that breeding and young fish are not systematically destroyed, although fishermen have no compunction in slaughtering them when they come to hand. In consequence, however, of the Mulpurbha, the only river of any size in the district, being flooded during the rainy season, fishing is suspended at this time, which is the breeding period for fish: consequently they become spared to a certain extent. Breeding fish and young ones are caught in nets, and no fisherman ever thinks of throwing them back on account of their condition or puny size; the fishermen in the villages on the banks of the rivers throughout the district being equally glad to catch them at any time in hauling their nets. Bottom-fishing

Opinions of European officials in the Belgaum Collectorate.

is carried on by persons from the banks throughout the year, and a number of breeding fish must be victimised in this way. However, the mischievous practices of poisoning the waters and trapping the fish appear to be unknown. The smallest distance between the knots of the meshes of the nets, it is considered, should be half an inch; the public sale of the fry does not appear to be known, they being consumed by their takers, or, should there be a surplus, being privately disposed of. The *Assistant Collector* remarked of his district, that in addition to fishing by means of nets and trapping, nallas, rivers, and tanks are in the hot weather dammed up with bunds, and poisonous drugs are thrown into the water, so that the fish either die, or, becoming stupefied, float on the surface, and are easily caught. Angling is occasionally resorted to, but only, as a rule, where the water is too deep to admit of a bund being erected. The practice of poisoning fish has, to a certain extent, been stopped in the Gokah Talooka, owing to the rules of the Forest Department, under which is prohibited the cutting the small twigs and leaves from which the stupefying drugs are made. The size of the mesh of the nets does not seem to vary very much in the different talookas, the smallest being from one-sixth to one quarter of an inch between the knots. In Belgaum, however, and the neighbourhood, a net with even smaller meshes is used for the purpose of catching prawns and a small fish called "moree." Nets with minute meshes are used, as a rule, during the rains, and with larger meshes during the cold season and hot weather, but this is not strictly observed. No difficulty is considered to exist, in organising a scheme to prevent the present wholesale destruction of fish, by regulating the size of the smallest mesh of the nets that will be permitted, by determining at what seasons nets with different sized meshes may be employed, by prohibiting the sale of the fry of fishes in the bazars, and forbidding the capture of fish at any rate during the first two months of the breeding season.

107. The *Acting Collector of Dharwar* (March 29th, 1870) proposed selling the fisheries by auction, either yearly, or for a period of three or four years at a time, in order to give the lessee time to improve them. He observed that a former Collector on several occasions had done so at Seerburdghee in Bankipur Talooka; selling that in one tank for 200 rupees, for others as much as 80 to 100 rupees have been given. There are, taking the district all round, upwards of two hundred tanks in which the right to net fish might be sold. There should be strict rules as to the size of certain fish that should not be allowed to be removed, but beyond fixing a minimum of mesh, and protecting the young of certain descriptions, other restrictions are not advocated. The money collected from this source would, in this Collectorate, probably yield about 16,000 rupees per annum, and should be credited to local funds, to be expended on the tanks which afford fishing. In many cases, steps might be taken to provide an inner and deeper tank into which the fish might be driven on the water becoming very low. Thus, not only the tanks would be improved, but the amount of fish might be augmented, adding to the food and comfort of the poorer classes, whose interests in this particular point have been hitherto neglected. Subsequently (November 29th, 1871), the

Opinions of the European officials of the Dharwar Collectorate.

Acting Collector reported that the fresh-water fisheries existing in the eleven talookas in his district are as follows :—In Nowlgoond and Roan fish are caught in the Mulprabha river, which skirts the northern boundary of these talookas. In Dharwah fish are taken in some of the large tanks which retain water all the year round ; in a few they are large and plentiful, chiefly the " murrell" and "parah." In Hooblee there are no streams from which fish are to be had, but they are found in large tanks which do not dry. In Dumhull they are obtained from the Toongbhudra river which skirts its southern boundary, and also in the larger tanks that do not dry up. In Kulghutghee they are found in one or two small streams, also in the larger tanks which do not become dry, *viz.*, Devikope, Budneeguttee, and Tumboor; these always contain a large supply of fish. In Bunkapur there are numerous tanks containing fish, but those of the largest size and the most numerous are found in those which retain water all the year round. In Kurujghee numerous fish are obtained in the rivers Wardah and Toongbhudra, as also in a few of the tanks. In Hangul the river Wardah and numerous tanks and ponds that are perennial contain them, likewise in similar ponds and tanks in Kode and Raneebednore; in the former talooka is also the Toongbhudra skirting its southern boundary, and in the latter the same river forms its eastern limits. The only private right of fishing is in the Bunkapur Talooka at Nagpoor, which the Collector in 1832 declared belonged exclusively to the Wuttundar Patel of Husan Aga. In Kurujghee formerly, the fisheries in some of the tanks and in the Toongbhudra river used to be sold by Government by auction, but this has not been done of late years. In a third Report (March 28th, 1872) it is observed that fishing in the talookas is carried on all the year round in the rivers and large and small tanks. Fish are caught wherever they can be found; whatever is brought ashore by the net is kept. The minimum size of the mesh is very small; in some samples appended, it varied from one-tenth to one-thirteenth of an inch between the knots; even the very smallest fry cannot escape. In the larger rivers, the Wardah and Toongbhudra, fishing is continued throughout the year, except when they are in flood. In the smaller rivers which soon dry up, it is carried on during the rains. It is also continued all the year round in the large tanks that do not become dry; such, however, are rare in the black soil districts of Dharwar, Nowlgoond, Roan, and Dumbul. Fish appear to exist in larger quantities in tanks situated in red soil. Besides the long nets dragged by a number of men, cast-nets with very fine meshes are used in the rivers. In the tanks, besides nets, night lines are employed, and people daily visit them to secure the captures. In some cases the tanks are drained, or nearly so, and then everything that can be caught is taken ; thousands, not one and a half inches in length, being captured by various sorts of nets by the hand, and by fishermen throwing a large sort of basket-net over them. There is no limit either by law or custom as to the size of the meshes of the nets, fishing not being interfered with. Were it proposed to regulate the size of the meshes of the nets, there would be difficulties, but in no degree insuperable ones, the chief being in the supervision that would be required. The Acting Collector observed, that he concurs in the *Assistant Collector's* views on this subject, namely, that it would be extremely difficult and unpopular to fix the size of the meshes of nets to be employed in catching fish in the small tanks which dry up at every hot season, and it would be of little use, because the fish are caught by the hand even in the mud as the water subsides, and the quantity captured by man is small in comparison to the enormous numbers destroyed by the large flocks of birds that prey upon fish. The *Collector* continues, that in large tanks that do not dry up and in the rivers the mesh might be regulated by law, but in tanks and rivers that dry up during the hot season it is proposed that nets should not be interfered with. For the former localities the minimum size of the mesh proposed is one inch between knot and knot. To attempt to make a larger limit would be very unpopular, because there are so many descriptions of fish that are eaten, and which never grow to any great size.

108. The *Acting Collector of Ratnaghari*, with his report of June 16th, 1871, enclosed one from the *Deputy Conservator*, who stated that he had obtained good fresh-water fishing in the Jog river near Dapoolee. No private parties exercise any exclusive rights in regard to such fisheries. One reason probably why the fish are so few in number, is that they are caught in vast numbers when they have only just spawned, as is thus described by the *Assistant Collector*. The people in this part of the country are not in the habit of catching fish either by means of lines or nets. In some places they raise dams across streams, which do not allow the water to run off, and into the pools thus formed they throw the juice of the hoora plant, which blinds the fish, after which they are easily taken. The usual method, however, is by placing baskets in convenient situations in the current. Such a system of capturing fish newly spawned, and the practice of throwing nets across creeks and rivers, has done much to diminish the number of the fish in this country. The *Acting Collector* subsequently (March 20th, 1872) observed that there are no fresh-water fisheries, properly so called, in his zilla. The chief fisheries, exclusive of the sea ones, are those up the numerous creeks or arms of the sea, which penetrate inland for several miles along the whole length of this coast district. Far inland, in depths too shallow for navigation, at low tides and during the monsoon, some parts of these creeks contain fresh water, and in regard to them, both breeding and very young fish are destroyed to a great extent. The rivers are swept with close nets at all seasons of the year from their source, and principally by Bhoees, but also by the villagers generally. Banks are formed to make the fish pass through narrow channels; nets are employed, also baskets and bag-like nets. Fish of a very small description are caught all the year round, but the principal time for this pursuit is during July and August. There is no doubt that breeding fish and very young ones are not spared. Any sized mesh is used which the fishermen choose, and the difficulty in regulating the minimum to be employed in future is the want of supervision in remote villages. Half an inch between the knots of meshes is proposed as the smallest legal size. Fry do not appear to be sold in the bazars, but used for home consumption. Prohibiting the capture of fish in hilly districts for the first two months of the monsoon season, when they are breeding, would be of great advantage to the country, but rules would be difficult of enforcement.

Opinions of the European officials of the Ratnaghari Collectorate.

109. The *Acting Collector of Canara* observed (January 13th, 1872), the fisheries may be roughly divided into tanks and running streams. The former exist in considerable numbers and size above the Ghâts; below the Ghâts they are neither so large nor so numerous. The principal rivers in the district are the Kalanuddee, Gungawutty, Yuddry, and Sirawutty; it is the last named which forms the Geirsoppa falls. There are other small streams where fish are to be found, but not in such numbers as in the rivers above mentioned. The Kalanuddee and Sirawutty in particular, with their deep pools and large rocks, afford a shelter for fish not to be found in smaller streams. There is a general agreement amongst those who have given their opinions on the subject, that the rivers and nallas, and the greater number of the tanks, are the undoubted property of Government. Tanks have been constructed by individuals at their own expense; some are attached to temples and other religious edifices; the right of private parties to the fish therein contained would, I apprehend, be admitted. But the fish in tanks constructed by Government, at the public expense, are morally and legally Government property. As a further proof, it is stated that Major Peyton has known in Canara, when the tanks became low and likely to dry up, the tehsildars and mamlutdars selling on account of Government the right of catching fish. By the principles of the *Jus gentium*, large rivers belong to all the people of the country; in other words, are the property of Government which represents all the people of the country, so far as such rights are concerned. Where the fund of wealth is unlimited, it is better to leave the right of using it unlimited; but where this is not the case (and it is to be presumed all will admit it is not the case with river or tank fisheries), some restricting regulations are necessary. If the above statement be correct, the sooner the Legislature takes the fisheries of this district under its cognizance, the better; not only do the fishing class of natives use nets fitted to catch everything, from a quarter of an inch upwards, but they continually kill by poison the whole of the fish in a pool. The bark of certain trees, such as the Châpal karu, Garooda, Koorada, &c., is pounded and thrown into the water; the fish come to the surface floating on their backs, and are carried off. If this practice be continued, the rivers of the district will soon be swept clear of fish; a means of innocent sport for some, and of sustenance for many, will be stopped, and the chance of Government ever deriving any revenue from the fisheries, which, if they were protected, would be quite practicable and might be desirable, will be lost.

Opinion of the Collector of Canara.

110. In the *Ahmedabad Collectorate* eight native officials have sent in returns, and those who have answered the first question have apparently considered the "number of fishermen" as the "number of castes of fishermen;" consequently it does not appear how many persons following this employment would be affected by any new rules. However, it is evident they must be few. The *Mamlutdar of Duskroee* reports the Mahomedans, Purdessees, Bhoees, and Boochas as the fishermen which are in his district, amongst whom the Bhoees are also employed as palanquin-bearers and the Boochas as grass-cutters. The local fish markets are not fully supplied; more could be sold. As regards the pro-

Opinions of native officials in the Ahmedabad Collectorate.

portion of people who eat fish? it is remarked that Brahmins and high-caste Hindus do not, but the rest, who are allowed by their religion, do. The fish are said to have increased, and that very small ones are not captured during the rains, but the minimum size of the mesh of the nets will only let a needle go through, whilst fish are trapped in the irrigated fields during the rains. The *Mamlutdar of Gogo* observes that Kharwas and Bhugwagurees take fish; the former do not engage in other occupations; the latter do, being sailors. The markets are sufficiently supplied with fish. A list of several castes is given, as the proportion of people who eat fish, the supply of which article of food is said to have decreased. Very small ones are taken during the rains by means of hand nets; the minimum size of the meshes will allow "half the last finger" to go through. Fish are said not to be trapped in the irrigated fields during the rains. The *Mamlutdar of Purantey* says, the fishermen are Kolees and Bhoees, who also pursue other occupations. The markets are not fully supplied with fish. The proportion of the population who eat fish is not given, but a few castes are, terminating with "and such others eat fish." The supply of late years has been stationary. Very small ones are captured by children during the rains. A finger can go through the minimum sized mesh of the nets. Breeding fish are trapped by children in the irrigated fields during the rains in a cage called "Jako." The *Mamlutdar of Sanund* reports an absence of fishermen, a market insufficiently supplied with fish, the quantity of which in late years has remained stationary; notwithstanding, he continues, very small fish are captured with cloths during the rains, whilst the smallest sized mesh of nets that are employed is almost of the size of a toour seed. The *Mamlutdar of Dhundooka* observes that there are neither fish nor fishermen. The *Mamlutdars of Dholka, Veerumgam and Morassa* give such vague returns that an analysis of them is of no practical use.

111. In the *Broach Collectorate*, the *Mamlutdars* report that there are about 110 fishermen in *Broach*, 100 in *Jumboosur*, 40 in *Ahmode*, and 150 in *Hansote*; besides fishing they all twist coir ropes, build and repair houses, and work as day-labourers. The following are the castes of fishermen in *Broach*; Dheemar máchee, Maktomporiá máchee, Hansoteea máchee, the last two having obtained their names from the villages whence they have emigrated. In *Hansote* the fishermen are by caste Talabda coolies, or Jumboosur máchee, &c., and in *Ahmode* Wagris and Bhoees. The markets in Jumboosur, Broach, and Hansote are fully supplied with fish, and large quantities, both salt and dried, are exported: in Ahmode and Anklesur the supply is less than the demand; between one-third and a quarter of the population of the Broach District would appear to consume it. The supply at Broach and Ahmode has decreased of late years, whilst that in Jumboosur and Hansote has remained stationary. Little fish during the rains are captured with small nets at Broach and Hansote, but not elsewhere at that season. The smallest size of mesh employed in Jumboosur at the seaward end of the net is one inch, landwards half an inch: at Ahmode one quarter of an inch, and in Broach one-sixth of an inch. Breeding fishes are not trapped in the irrigated fields, during the rains, as a rule. In Broach and Hansote nets are fixed across the stream where the water is shallow. Cast-nets are likewise

Opinions of native officials in the Broach Collectorate.

used in deeper water. Large nets supported at intervals by light hollow gourds are stretched out in the river, one end being attached to a boat.

112. The *Mamlutdars of the Kaira Collectorate* report that it is difficult to give the exact number of fisher-men, as they are, as a rule, agriculturists likewise, and often employ themselves during the monsoon in plying ferry-boats on the larger rivers. On the banks of the Mhye there are probably about 500 persons employed in supplying the Baroda market with fish, both fresh and salt. The only fisherman caste is the "Máchee," but many coolies and Mussulmen engage in fishing as well. There is stated to be little or no demand for fresh fish in the local markets. Possibly about one-sixth of the population have no religious scruples about eating it, but few comparatively use this food from choice. It is supposed that the supply of fish in the Mhye has decreased of late years. The common superstitious belief is, that the deities of the river have been displeased by the withholding of the offerings formerly made by travellers who crossed it in carts, previously to the opening of the railway. Fishing is common during the rains; all sorts are captured; the nets allow none to escape; the minimum size of the mesh is about one quarter of an inch in diameter. Fish are not trapped in irrigated fields during the rains, as irrigation is chiefly derived from wells. The following are the principal implements employed in fishing: rod and line "gul"; torch-fishing by night, "Ook"; hand nets, "hath jhal"; or cast-nets, ("fulolu"); and large nets, "maha jhal."

Opinions of native officials in the Kaira Collectorate.

113. The *Mamlutdars in the Khandeish Collectorate* report that there are 23,600 fishermen in the whole of the district, but they do not depend upon fishing alone as a means of livelihood, as they also pursue different occupations. The names of the fishermen castes are Koli, Pardi, Kokné, Wanjāri, Bhui, Mahār, Barādi, Bhil, Diwar, Kotil, Mussulmān, Mawaché, and Thudwi. The local markets are insufficiently supplied with fish, that captured being principally for home consumption. Three-fourths of the people eat fish, the amount of which in the district has decreased of late. During the rains many small ones are captured in every possible way. The smallest mesh employed is down to one quarter of an inch, after which a cloth is used, or no mesh at all. Fish are trapped in the irrigated fields during the rains. The different means used for capturing fish are jali, nets; basket traps; gul, a hook used only in the rains, cloth, poison of sorts as follows, hinganbet, yāthil, gīr and thor.

Opinions of native officials in the Khandeish Collectorate.

114. The *Mamlutdars of the Nasik Collectorate* report that there are about 4,000 fishermen in the district, but some only are at times solely thus employed, as they are also agriculturists and day-labourers. The fishermen castes are Maratha, Bhoee, Kahar, Koli, Bhil, Taroo, Taral, Kokné, Warli. Many Mussulmen and Koonbees also fish. None of the markets are sufficiently supplied. With respect to the proportion of persons who eat fish, the reports vary, in some talookas only one in twenty-two of the population are stated to do so, in others two-thirds or three-fourths, or even fifteen-sixteenths do. In the Penit State,

Opinions of native officials in the Nasik Collectorate.

chiefly inhabited by Bhils or Kolis, all but Brahmins are said to eat fish, Of late years the amount in the waters has decreased; small ones are taken in greater or less quantities everywhere during the rains, by means of small nets, baskets placed under water with bread and gram in them, basket traps fixed in currents, and by hooks. The smallest mesh of the nets employed is of the size of a grain of gram. Breeding fish are trapped in the irrigated fields during the rains in some of the talookas. The modes of taking fish are given as follows; nets of sorts, as drag-nets for the pools in the rivers, cast-nets of various sizes, also others somewhat similar to shrimp nets, termed " Chabha" and " Pelne," namely, those fixed to a triangular frame of wood, with a handle for fishing; these are used in the shallow streams. Basket traps, " Malai," are of the usual kind, or the rat-trap principle, so that no fish once in can get out. Large cloths, " Jholes," are often used as a substitute for nets. Poison is frequently had resort to in order to kill or stupefy fish. The leaves of a plant called " Soopli," *Clitorea turnatea*, are much used for this purpose, also tobacco leaves and the milk bush, as well as the " Gel Phul" or fruit of the *Vangneria spinosa*, which is powdered and thrown into the water. Dams are also constructed in small streams; the water laded out and the fish captured, or else after the completion of the dam they are driven into traps or nets of different kinds.

115. The *Mamlutdars in the Ahmednuggur Collectorate* report that there are from 2 to 3,000 fishermen in the district, but they follow other occupations besides that of fishing, such as cultivation, day-labourers; &c.; their castes are Bhoee, Koli, Kahar. The markets are said to be insufficiently supplied. On an average two-thirds of the population will eat fish, but it does not, unless they are fishermen, form a portion of their regular diet. The number of fish are said to have decreased of late years owing to the deficiency of rain. The minimum size of the mesh of the nets is stated to be equal to that of a grain of gram. Fish are said not to be trapped in the irrigated fields during the rains. Besides the use of nets and hooks, waters are poisoned with the milk bush.

Opinions of native officials in the Ahmednuggur Collectorate.

116. The *native officials in the Puna Collectorate* state that there are about 800 fishermen, but they do not confine themselves to fishing for a livelihood; their castes are Murathu Bhoee, Kolis, Kongadee Bhoee, Kar Bhoee (Purdesee), Wuradee Bhoee. The markets are insufficiently supplied. There is nothing to prevent the majority of the people eating fish. Many small ones are captured during the rains, but they are not trapped in the irrigated fields, as there are but few of such. The implements employed are a large casting net, " Pagur;" a small drag-net with poles attached resembling a cricket net, " Zilla;" small nets termed " Bhoosū" and " Waoree;" large drag-nets " Pundee" and " Luhowkaree;" " Tivree," which resembles the Bhoosū, but has a larger mesh; " Patee" and " Challum," made of bamboo and net, and placed at the opening in a dam constructed across a stream; " Ganjwa" is a sort of drag-net, and " Surkee," a small net; " Basgul," " Chhudigul," and " Lumdore" are reels containing different lengths of line with baited hooks attached.

Opinions of native officials of the Puna Collectorate.

117. The *native officials in the Colaba Collectorate* report as follows:—The *Mamlutdar of Alibag* gives the fishermen at 2,000, the majority pursuing other occupations; their castes are Koli and Bhoee, both Marathas. Fresh-water fish are not brought for sale; one-half the population eat fish, whilst the supply has remained stationary. Very small ones are taken by snares, by "Bhokshee," a round cane basket with a hole at the top; Koin, Bugadee, and Buggala, whilst the smallest mesh of the nets is only sufficient to admit a large needle. Fish are trapped in the irrigated fields during the rains. The various modes of fishing employed are, killing with sticks, damming up and lading out water, snaring, poisoning, and netting. The *Mamlutdar of Penn* states, the fishermen are 4,000, most of whom pursue other callings as well; their caste is Koli. The local markets are fully supplied with sea-fish; seven-eighths of the people are fish-eaters, the supply of which has remained stationary of late. Very small ones are captured to a great extent during the rains by snares and basket traps. The smallest mesh of the nets is given at one-quarter of an inch. Fish are trapped in the irrigated fields during the rains. Damming is reported to be carried on in this talooka. The *Mamlutdar of Roha* observes that there are 200 fishermen, who mostly pursue other occupations in his talooka; their castes are Koli and Bhoee, both Marathas. Fresh-water fish are not brought to market; one-half of the population eat fish, the supply of which has remained stationary. The smallest sized mesh of the nets is one-third of an inch, and fish are trapped in the irrigated fields during the rains. The *Mamlutdar of Mangam* computes the fishermen at 500, most of whom have also other employments; they are Koli and Bhoee, both Marathas. Fresh-water fish are not brought to market; three-fourths of the people eat fish, the supply of which has remained stationary of late. Very small ones are captured during the rains in cane baskets, whilst the minimum mesh of the nets is one-quarter of an inch. Fish are trapped in the irrigated fields during the rains. The *Mamlutdar of Mhar* gives the fishermen at 100, of the Bhoee caste. The local markets are fully supplied with marine fish; three-quarters of the people are fish-eaters; the supply of late years has remained stationary. Very small and other fish are trapped and caught during the rains; the smallest sized mesh is given at one inch (in circumference?)

Opinions of native officials in the Colaba Collectorate.

118. The *Mamlutdars of Satara* report that the number of fishermen in the several talookas of the district varies from 5 to 700, most of whom follow other occupations as coolies and agricultural labourers, and their castes are Bhoees and Kolis. Sometimes Mahomedans and Conbus also take fish for their own use. The local markets are not fully supplied with fish, and the proportion of people who consume it varies in the different talookas from 25 to 96 per cent. The amount of late years has decreased; small ones are taken in large quantities during the rains by netting, hooks, &c., whilst the minimum mesh of the nets is one-eighth of an inch in circumference (one thirty-second part of an inch between knot and knot). Fish are not trapped in irrigated fields during the rains. Fishing is carried on by various descriptions of nets, by angling, and by diverting the natural course of a stream so as to

Opinions of native officials in the Satara Collectorate.

make all the water pass through an open receptacle resembling a large basket, also by erecting a bank of sand across a river or nalla and obtaining the fish in the usual way.

119. The *native officials in the Kaladgi Collectorate* report that there are about 400 persons who follow fishing in conjunction with other occupations, but there are likewise distinct fishing castes. Fish are but rarely sold in the bazars; about one-quarter of the people are fish-eaters; the supply of late years is considered to have remained stationary. Very small ones are not taken in any quantity during the rains, whilst the minimum mesh employed is about the size of a grain of wheat. In the Indee Talooka fish are trapped during the rains in the irrigated fields.

Opinions of native officials in the Kaladgi Collectorate.

120. The *native officials at Sholapur* give the number of fishermen in the district at 1,000, including women and children! The Bhoees are the fishermen caste; they are also palkee-bearers. The markets are insufficiently supplied with fish; one-third of the population eat it when obtainable; the supply is said to have decreased of late; very small ones are captured with nets and baskets, the latter of which are of such a fine texture that nothing can escape through the interstices.

Opinions of native officials in Sholapur.

121. The *Mamlutdars of Belgaum* report through the Assistant Collector as follows:—*Mr. Stewart* states that in his district there are only about 250 fishermen, who also engage in other occupations; they are chiefly of the Bhoee, Koli, and Takur castes, but a few Mussulmen likewise carry on this pursuit in a small measure, mostly for home consumption. The markets are glutted with salt-fish imported from Goa and the sea-coast, there being but a slight demand for fresh fish; but if the opportunity were given to the natives to purchase fresh fish cheap and good, there could be no doubt that the use of this wholesome article of consumption would be more wide-spread. The relative price of fish and mutton is much the same in the different talookas, but the cost of the former is considerably more than that of the latter. About 20 per cent. of the population eat fish, the supply of which has remained stationary of late years, but very young ones are not destroyed during the rains to any great extent. *Mr. Fleet* states that in his district there are about 60 fishermen of the Bhoee, Madrassi Holler, Koli, and Takur castes in Belgaum and its neighbourhood, whilst there are from 25 to 30 in the Gokak Talooka of the Kabalgé, Mussulmen, and Rajput castes; most of them are likewise palkee-bearers or Hamals. The Belgaum market is insufficiently supplied with fish, but in the Gokak Talooka the supply equals the demand; the same may be said of the other two talookas. The supply in the rivers has seriously diminished of late years, due to increased demand and decreased rainfall. Many very small ones are captured during the rainy months; fish are very generally caught with nets, or trapped in the fields that are permanently irrigated. *Mr. Luxmon Jagoonoth* reports that there are fifteen villages in his district on the banks of the rivers, and which contain about 125 fishermen, chiefly of the Maratha, Mussulmen, Kidbodee, Bagace, and Bhoee castes. A large number of very small fishes are captured during the rains with nets having minute meshes.

Opinions of the native officials of the Belgaum Collectorate.

122. In the *Dharwar Collectorate* the native officials report as follows:—In the *Dharwar Talooka* there are 600 fishermen, who likewise pursue other occupations; their castes are Surdur Bhoee, Village Bhoees, Maratha, Bedur, Wudurs, Mussulmen, Maratha Dhobies, Gungi Makalu, Kuber, and Amiger. The local markets are fully supplied with dried sea-fish imported from Goa, but very insufficiently with fresh fish. About 50,000 persons eat it, the supply of which has decreased of late years owing to diminished rainfall. Very small ones are taken during the rains, the minimum size of the mesh of nets employed being about equal to that of a grain of gram; fish are also trapped in the irrigated fields during the rains. The modes of taking are "Gana," hook and bait; "Bis-buli," casting net; "Tatabuli," and "Khandelbuli," drag-nets; "Kooni," wicker baskets; also by hands. The Wudurs make use of dams. In the *Petta Moogud Talooka* there are about 32 fishermen, who also pursue other occupations; most are of the Bhoee caste, but the Rajputs and Mussulmen catch fish occasionally. The local market is not fully supplied; half the population (which is about 20,000) are fish-eaters. Small ones are taken during the rains; the minimum size of the mesh of the nets employed is equal to that of a grain of gram; fish are not trapped in the irrigated fields: the means for catching them are by "Toputti," a triangular casting net with minute meshes, and which is extensively employed; "Bis-buli," a casting net with larger meshes; "Khandelbuli," and "Gana," this last being of two kinds: "Want gana" is a pole to which a line having a hook and bait is suspended; "Dawani gana" consists of two poles which are fixed in the ground in the water at some distance apart; a string connects the two, and from this, lines with hooks and baits are suspended and descend into the water. In the *Hooblee Talooka* there are three professional fishermen, but 50 other persons occasionally join in; the castes are Bhoee, Mussulmen, &c. The local market is insufficiently supplied; the fish have decreased of late years; the minimum size of the meshes of the nets is equal to that of a grain of gram; fish are not trapped in the irrigated fields; they are taken by nets and baits. In the *Nowlgoond Talooka* there are 150 fishermen, but they also follow other occupations; the castes are Bhoee and Mussulmen. The fish supply has remained stationary of late; very small ones are taken during the rains, the minimum size of the meshes of the nets being about equal to a grain of gram; fish are not trapped in the irrigated fields. In the *Dumbul Talooka* there are about 50 fishermen, who also pursue other occupations; their castes are Bhoee, Mussulmen, Ambiger, Killikyat, and Boodboorki. The local market is not fully supplied with fresh fish, but salt fish is imported from the Bellary District. About 10,000 persons in this talooka are said to eat fish, the local supply of which is decreasing. Small ones are taken during the rains, but are not trapped in the irrigated fields. In the tanks and nallas in the Doni hills the Lumbanees poison the waters with the milk bush. In the *Bunkapur Talooka* there are about 6,000 fishermen, who also pursue other occupations; their castes are Bhoee, Aree, Wudur, Killikyat, Dombaru, Bedur, Gungimakalu, Mussulmen, Boodboodkeroo, Jateegaroo, Korwaroo, &c. The local market is not fully supplied with fish, whilst about 50,000 persons eat it; the supply of late has remained

Opinions of native officials of the Dharwar Collectorate.

stationary; very small ones are netted during the rains, the minimum size of the mesh being equal to one-fourth of an inch between knot and knot; fish are also trapped in the irrigated fields. In the *Hangul Talooka* there are 9,000 fishermen, who also pursue other occupations; the castes are Areroo, Golaroo, Telaga sunajageroo, Yeeleegerroo, Lumbani, Mucheejar, Hulépaki, Rungari, Oopar, Rajput, Mussulmen, Hunamarroo, Kamatti, Kuber, Wudur, Mahars, Dhors, Koorbus, Chetreroo, Dasroo, Byadroo, Jataroo, Korwaroo, Telgaroo, Kotagar, and Erguntti. The local fish market is fairly supplied, especially with marine sorts. About 30,000 persons eat fish, the supply of which has decreased of late; very small ones are taken during the rains, the minimum size of the mesh of the nets being equal to that of a grain of gram; fish are also trapped in the irrigated fields and poisoned with the milk bush and powder of Mungari-kai. In the *Ranebedume Talooka* there are several castes that fish, Mussulmen, Koorbur, Tulwar, Ambiger, Telgaroo, Sabroo, Madgeroo, Areroo, Rungareroo, Neikaroo, Bhoee, and Wudur. The local markets are not fully supplied with fresh fish, but during the hot months salt-fish comes from Coompta. Three-sevenths of the population (of 70,000) eat fish, the supply of which has decreased of late years; very small ones are taken in quantities during the rains, the minimum size of the mesh of the nets being only equal to that of a grain of gram; none are trapped in the irrigated fields. In the *Kurujghee Talooka* there are 1,000 fishermen, but they also follow other occupations. The local market is fully supplied with salted marine fish from Coompta; about 15,000 persons are stated to be fish-eaters, the supply of fresh-water ones has decreased of late; very small ones are captured during the rains, the minimum size of the mesh of the nets equalling that of a grain of gram; fish are not trapped in the irrigated fields. In the *Rutghutghee Talooka* there are about 150 fishermen, who also pursue other occupations; the castes are Gungimakaloo, Gowreemakaloo, Wudur, Maratha, Mussulmen, Hubsi, Chundi, Mydar, Korwarroo, Holeroo, Lumbani, Kuber, and Byad. The local market is fully supplied with salted marine fish which are brought from Coompta, whilst the supply of fresh-water sorts has remained stationary of late. About 25,000 persons are said to be fish-consumers; very small ones are captured during the rains; the minimum size of the mesh of the nets is given at one inch in circumference; none are trapped in the irrigated fields. Wicker traps are employed for taking fish; they are likewise poisoned by the milk bush and the powdered fruit of the Mungari. Dams are also erected, and water laded out in order to obtain all the fish. In the *Kode Talooka* there are about 500 fishermen, who also have other occupations; the castes are Mussulmen, Kuber, Wudur, Bedur, Killikyat, Holer, Chulwadi, Arer, Lumbani, and Korwar. The markets are insufficiently supplied with fish, whilst there are about 25,000 persons who eat it; the supply is decreasing; very small ones are captured during the rains; the minimum size of the meshes of the nets are said to be equal to a two-anna silver piece, and even less; fish are trapped in the irrigated fields.

MADRAS.

123. The following reports from the European and native officials of the Madras Presidency are mostly the result of enquiries made in the years 1867, 68, 69, the questions circulated in 1871 having only been replied to by two Collectors. As, however, the two series were rather similar, this summary has not been further delayed awaiting them. In some of the Collectorates full answers, in others only a few, from the native officials have been received, whilst in some they have been entirely omitted.

Origin of the present answers concerning the fisheries of Madras.

124. The fresh-water fisheries of this Presidency may be divided into those of *rivers* and *tanks* in all their various forms and sub-divisions; some of which are perennial, others not so, a most important consideration with respect to the following draft instructions for the guidance of Collectors, issued by the *Revenue Board* (December 18th, 1869) :—" Collectors will understand that these orders apply only to tidal estuaries of considerable extent, and to inland tanks and streams, which, as a rule, retain water throughout the year."

The fresh-water fisheries being of rivers and tanks.

125. The rivers of Madras are not of that large size observed in the west of India, as the Indus: or to the east, as the Ganges, Brahmaputra, Irrawaddi, and Salween in Burma, and few retain a perennial supply of water. These rivers are chiefly the Godaveri, the Toongbhudra, Kristna, Cauvery, and those of Malabar, most of the remainder being more or less dry during the hot months. As the Board of Revenue objects to making any order applicable to the rivers that are not perennial, so the Collectors, as of Kurnal and Malabar, object to anything being done for those which are so, considering they should be left alone.

Madras rivers, few perennial; objections to instituting rules respecting the fisheries.

126. Respecting tank fisheries, those existing in inundated districts and in irrigated fields, the above-quoted instructions (para. 123) direct that "it is not intended to interfere with the usual practice of catching fish in small tanks which do not retain water throughout the year, nor with any rivers excepting those possessing a perennial supply of water," and even here large exceptions appear to be admitted.

Rules framed not to affect any but perennial rivers and tanks that do not dry up.

127. The first consideration is, *what proportion of the people eat fish?* or perhaps, may do so without infringing caste prejudices, could they obtain it? It will be seen from the following answers of both European and native officials, that the great majority of the population can eat fish, the largest exceptions being Brahmins, goldsmiths, high-caste Sudras, the followers of Siva, the Jains, &c.; that fresh fish is usually chosen in preference to the salted article, except in some few talookas, whilst low-caste people and Mahomedans in some districts

Majority of people fish-eaters.

prefer salt-fish to fresh. Even at Bellary there appears to be a good demand for salt-fish, but in a few of the inland talookas it cannot be sold. This seems to have reference in some places to the proportion and caste of the Hindus.

128. *Are the markets well supplied?* Along the coasts and in places within easy reach of the sea they would seem to be so, but not inland. Out of 39 Tehsildars of Collectorates not, or only slightly, bordering on the sea, the following are the replies, that the markets are sufficiently supplied in 4 : insufficiently or hardly, if at all, in 35.

The inland markets insufficiently supplied.

129. *Have the fish in the fresh waters increased, decreased, or remained stationary?* Omitting vague answers, 64 Tehsildars' replies have been received; they are as follows :—6 report an increase in the amount in their talookas ; 46 either a large decrease or a decrease ; and 12 that the supply remains stationary, or else that no decrease is perceived this year.

Fish supply in the waters has generally decreased.

130. *Whose are the fisheries?* is a question adverted to by some of the reporters, and it appears to be almost universally considered that those existing in inland waters, with a few exceptions, are Government property, but doubts are entertained by the Revenue Board whether the " sanction of a legal enactment may not be necessary to enable the Government to interfere with the exercise of practices which long custom may have converted into communal rights." [Paterson, ' Fishery Laws of Great Britain,' observes of persons who claim right of fishing due to long custom— " no length of time during which such acts are capable of being explained on the ground of license, can prevent the owner putting an end to such license. He may resume his original rights at any moment and withdraw the license, for no man ought to have his rights abridged by acting liberally towards the public or his neighbours."] How and when numbers of the fishery rents ceased to be collected is adverted to in para. 146.

Fisheries Government property.

131. The *fishermen,* as a rule, are the agriculturists, palanquin-bearers, small traders, coolies, and others, who carry on this pursuit when not engaged in their ordinary avocations, and as there are no restrictions, their only idea is to obtain what they can, when they can. Were all the fisheries ruined, it would not pecuniarily affect them, except to a secondary degree, as their living is not dependant upon fishing. In some districts, as Rajahmundry, Chingleput, Combaconum, and a portion of Coimbatore, some few persons exist, who appear to be entirely dependant on this occupation.

The fishermen, with but few exceptions, only, follow this occupation in addition to their usual work.

132. *Are breeding fish destroyed, and, if so, how?* In every district this can be said to be carried on, principally in one of the four following manners :—*First,* irrigation weirs which detain breeding fish ascending or descending, and their being allowed to be netted at those places; this seems to be considered unavoidable, due to the want of fish passes. Irrigation canals, where there are deep

Breeding fish are destroyed by irrigation weirs arresting their progress, being trapped whilst ascending to breed or returning to the rivers, by weirs and other fixed engines, and by poison.

falls, without passes, likewise exercise the same deleterious effects; also drying off irrigation canals. *Secondly*, fish during the monsoon time frequently migrate for breeding purposes, and often into ponds that are not perennial; it consequently occurs that should the floods cease before they can regain the rivers, their retreat is cut off, and with the evaporation of the waters they are captured. *Thirdly*, and much more effectually, by the use of fixed engines as cruives or traps made of wicker work, and placed in every run where fish are likely to ascend to breed or to return after having done so. Or in the form of fishing weirs across whole streams and minor rivers in which not a single means of passing is left, the only gaps being where a cruive or trap is fixed. *Fourthly*, by poisoning the water both in rivers and ponds.

133. *Are the fry killed to any extent when just moving about?*

<small>Fry destroyed in large quantities; modes enumerated.</small>

Evidently they are, and in every district, by the second, third and fourth means by which the breeding fish (para. 132) have been stated to be destroyed. Besides this, nets of minute meshes are employed, and what should be the succeeding year's supply is cut off. In some irrigated fields, if there were not fixed traps in every opening and fall, these fry might return to the rivers in the waste water, provided open channels were left permitting them to do so (see para. 169); in other places the water is entirely expended on the field, and if the fry once get access, they must be destroyed as evaporation takes place.

134. *As to the various methods resorted to for capturing fish*, they are almost innumerable. Without describing the

<small>Minimum size of the mesh of nets employed and interspaces in cruives.</small>

different forms of nets, an important question is, what is the minimum size of the meshes of those employed in the fresh waters? As far as can be calculated from the answers received from 48 Tehsildars or subordinate officials, either the minimum size of the meshes in use or the usual size may be thus tabulated:—the size of a finger or thumb 4: of a pie 1; of one-fourth of an anna 1; of a two-anna bit 1; of one-fourth of a rupee 1; of half a rupee 1; of one inch 3; of half an inch 6; of one-fourth of an inch 8; of one-eighth of an inch 8; of one-tenth of an inch 1; of one-sixteenth of an inch 1; of the size of a grain of dholl, gram, a pepper corn or tamarind seed, 11; such as would ensnare an ant 1. In most of the portions of the Madras Presidency I have visited, the meshes of the nets used for capturing fry during the monsoons would be almost or quite sufficiently minute to be employed as mosquito curtains. The cruives or traps may be defined as sufficient to only permit water being strained through. Weirs have but little wider interstices between the substances of which they are constructed. Simply the prohibition of poisoning the rivers in South Canara for two years and forbidding the employment therein of cruives the interstices of which would not permit a finger ($\frac{3}{4}$ths of an inch) to pass, resulted in a vast extension of the fish and fisheries (see para. 169).

135. Trapping breeding fishes and young ones appears to be the rule; fishing weirs exist in many places,

<small>Weirs, fixed engines, damming and lading out pieces of water, and the use of poison.</small>

especially across those streams which are in the vicinity of or upon hills, because many species of fish resort there to deposit their eggs

e

and return again to the larger rivers of the plains before the advent of the dry season would impede their descent. Damming and lading out pieces of water for capturing fish occurs in several parts. Whilst poisoning is reported as existing in the Collectorates of Nellur, Trichinopoly, Kurnal, Chingleput, Salem, Tinnevelli, Coimbatore, South Canara and Malabar.

136. The following reports will, I conceive, render it conclusive, that (1) the great proportion of the inhabitants of the Madras Presidency are fish-eaters, generally preferring it fresh; (2) that the markets, as a rule, are insufficiently supplied; (3) that the amount of fish in the fresh waters has generally decreased; (4) that the fisheries are Government property; (5) that the fishermen, as a rule, do not follow this occupation as a sole means of support, but rather in addition to their regular occupations; (6) that breeding fish are trapped and otherwise netted (as at irrigation weirs) when migrating for breeding purposes; (7) that the fry are wastefully destroyed whenever and wherever they can be obtained; (8) that nets with the most minute meshes are employed; (9) that fixed engines, as cruives and weirs, are unfairly and largely made use of; (10) that damming up and lading out waters, is in existence, in order to procure fish; (11) that poisoning is also resorted to for this purpose.

Conclusions based upon the following reports.

137. And now the consideration arises, as to what measures of amelioration have been proposed on these points by the various officials of the Madras Presidency. All admit that whenever Nos. 10 and 11 exist they should be prohibited, leaving only for enquiry how the unfair destruction of breeding fish should be lessened, the general massacre of young fry diminished, as well as the best method of treating the question of nets and fixed implements. At the onset, it may be observed that the Revenue Board would leave matters as they are, as they "cannot but view with reluctance the necessity of State interference, with what are at present free industries."

Measures of amelioration which have been proposed in Madras.

138. I proposed (December 1st, 1868), after having examined many of the fisheries, that 'free fishing,' if I may so describe it, should be abolished on economic grounds, my reasons being that the effect of giving up the fisheries to the public free of cost had resulted in their being almost destroyed; that letting them out would cause the lessee to look after them; that no lessee could oppress the fishermen, for if they refused to work, he would be powerless to obtain the fish. I suggested yearly auctions (which, however, have been objected to by various officials), which would, after five years or so, show the value of the fisheries, and subsequently they might be leased out for five years at a time. (I never contemplated yearly auctions to be continued, as appears to be supposed); that the minimum size of the meshes of nets should be four inches in circumference; of course, this would include the interstices between the substances employed in cruives, weirs, and all fixed implements; the destruction of vermin, as crocodiles and otters; the slaughter of snakes at irrigation weirs, and the construction of fish passes at these places.

Personal propositions in 1868.

139. *The Madras Government* (30th April 1869) directed that all pieces of inland waters should be leased out in order to give a distinct interest to some person in preventing indiscriminate fishing, that provision should be made in the contracts, for the protection of fish in regard to the size of the mesh used, *viz.*, four inches in circumference, the periods and localities for fishing, the draining off water in tanks and the poisoning of rivers; that fish passes should be constructed at anicuts, and rewards given for the destruction of vermin that destroy fish, and the prohibition of fishing during certain months, October to February inclusive, in the irrigation channels through which the young fish pass down to the sea; and that such should come in force on July 1st, 1869. These orders also included the prohibition of the use of nets within 100 yards of anicuts and such like masonry works extending across streams. *The Revenue Board* (May 28th, 1869) considered that headmen of villages should hold the fisheries at a small royalty, or that protective rules should be embodied in a brief Fishery Act. They neither approved of an inch between the meshes of nets, nor prohibiting the taking of breeding fish detained near irrigation weirs. *The Madras Government* (June 25th, 1869) saw no reason why protective measures should be deferred, but would not object to the details being modified as regards letting the fisheries, and the minimum size of the mesh of the nets. *The Board of Revenue* (August 27th, 1869) again objected, stating that 13 Collectors agreed in reporting that no wanton destruction of fish takes place, and that no protective measures are needed. *The Madras Government* decided "no orders are necessary on these papers." The instructions to district officers were called for. *The Board of Revenue* (October 23rd, 1869) stated that no detailed orders on the subject were issued. *The Madras Government* (November 19th, 1869) observe, "that they saw no reason why the protective measures suggested should be deferred, but permitted some of the details to be partially modified as proposed by the Board. On the receipt of this last communication, it was clearly the duty of the Board to have immediately issued the necessary orders to Collectors, but this it appears has not been done. The Board will, accordingly, now be instructed to give effect to the orders which should have been brought into operation on the 1st of July last." On December 18th, the Board issued their instructions (para. 148), modifying the minimum size of the mesh of nets to three inches (instead of four) all round, and offering certain rewards for vermin killed within one mile of irrigation weirs. Fish were to be passed over weirs (see para. 152), whilst the subsidiary orders partially nullify the original propositions. *The Acting Secretary to the Madras Government* (October 5th, 1869) reported to the Secretary to the Government of India that "the Government have already decided on adopting the protective measures advocated by Dr. Day for fresh-water fisheries." Finally (July 12th, 1872), on being asked for "information showing the results from letting the fresh-water fisheries from July last year" (1871), *the Acting Sub-Secretary to the Board* replied, "the Board are not aware that any special measures have been adopted in the matter of leasing fisheries during the past revenue year;" from which it would almost appear doubtful if the foregoing instructions have yet been brought into oper-

ation. *The Secretary of State for India* (June 17th, 1869) observed, "that the conservancy and control of the fisheries, and the measures suggested for the improvement of pisciculture throughout India, constitute subjects which certainly deserve attention from your Government, (that of India) and I fully approve of the arrangements that have been made. * * In carrying out your views, much will depend on the interest that is taken by local officers."

140. I may here mention that prior to the commencement of this enquiry, I observed in the 'Madras Medical Journal'—"Amongst the animal productions of India, fish meet with the least sympathy, and the greatest persecution, especially as regards the fresh-water tribes, which have to struggle for bare existence in rivers that periodically diminish to little streams, and often dry up during the hot months; or in tanks from which the water totally disappears. Besides these and many other disadvantages, they have their natural enemies in the ova state, in youth, and maturity; but amongst these foes mankind is perhaps the greatest. A fish diet is much esteemed and procurable at a comparatively cheap rate, because these unfortunate creatures are captured by every one who gets the chance: the larger species are killed irrespective of time and season; the young are destroyed for curries; water-courses are poisoned for the purpose of obtaining them in large quantities for salting and transmission to distant markets; whilst they meet with no protection even from inferior foes. Now that every article of consumption is increasing in value, the propagation of fish must become a subject worthy of great consideration, especially as they live in places which are otherwise unserviceable to man in the production of food, excepting in a secondary manner; whilst no grain is required for their support, but little trouble for their protection, and they thrive in places which but for them would be deserted wastes. Were it not for the vast number of eggs which fish deposit, the probabilities are that, long ere this, they must have been exterminated in India, excepting in thinly populated or uninhabited districts, for man allows them no law, and were they noxious reptiles, could not more anxiously compass their destruction * *. But now the piscine tribes seem to have fallen on evil days, being only protected in or near Hindu temples, for in fact elsewhere they appear to exist solely because man has been unable to destroy them."

Fresh-water fisheries in Madras, prior to the commencement of this investigation.

141. Since the foregoing was written, I have visited several of the districts of the Madras Presidency to investigate the present state and future prospects of its fresh-water fisheries, and extract the following from my reports. Across the Kistna river is the Bezwada irrigation weir, which on its first construction by preventing the ascent of breeding fish, caused them to be detained below it, where they were netted in numbers. Since these first two years there has been a gradual diminution of the shad, as well as of all other kinds of fish, whether strictly fresh-water or partially marine; whilst the fishermen complain that they cannot now (1868) supply half the local demand. Abusing the anicut as the cause of this, they will not perceive that they are doing quite as much mischief by destroying the fry of the fresh-water species. I saw little

Personal observations in districts in Madras.

boys sent out to fish whose duty it was to bring home a daily supply for their families, the size being no object, and a sufficient amount the only criterion. Hundreds of small fry are thus daily destroyed by the nets of these little urchins, whilst the adult fishermen also assist in this work of destruction. At Rajahmundry, above the weir, the price of fish in the bazar was reputed to have risen 100 per cent. in seven years, and a great decrease of fish. Here the fry and immature fish were being captured in myriads. At Combaconum I sent out some fishermen for two days to see what specimens they could collect for me, and during that time they brought me upwards of 5,000 young fish, these being, as they stated, the quality they were capturing in and near the station. That the destruction of fry is carried on to an excessive extent must be patent to the most casual observer who travels during the monsoon months. It appeared to me that the principal reason for the decrease of fish, was that the fry were captured in excessive numbers owing to the minuteness of the size of the meshes in nets; that irrigation weirs and falls in canals arrested the ascent of breeding fish, which were also trapped in irrigated fields and water-courses; and lastly, that indiscriminate fishing was disastrous.

142. One official (para. 158) having remarked upon my propositions,—"I believe any law regulating the size of the mesh would be inoperative in this country; it would be cruel to the poor people who for the most part live on small fish," I am unable to see the *cruelty* in attempting to augment the food supply of the poorer classes. I have examined magnificent pieces of fresh-water in the Madras Presidency not containing sufficient fish for the few inhabitants along their banks. In large districts any one may fish in whatever way best suits his individual views, and ignorant natives, who never look beyond to-day's wants, take what they are able irrespective of size, and fish where they please no matter how. As the large fish are cleared off, smaller meshed nets are employed, until at last the fry, as a rule, become the sized fish which are taken. A staff of water bailiffs would be expensive, but if fisheries are let, the lessee becomes their keeper: his people the watchers. Self-interest would never allow his permitting every little boy to have and use a net wherewith he is destroying the fry. It is sometimes asserted that it would be hard on the poorer classes not to permit them to capture these little wee fish: it seems to be thought that fish come of themselves, are not worth protecting when young, but should at all times be game in every manner to the whole of the population. But how have these pseudo-philanthropic views answered in practice? By decreasing the fish and consequently diminishing the supply of food in whole districts. Thus, when famine years come round the waters will be found depopulated, the little fish have been eaten by the poorer classes, and consequently larger ones will be sought for in vain. I deny the philanthropy of such proceedings, but on the contrary hold that practically, although unintentionally, when carried out, they will be found amongst the most *cruel* in their effects of any that could be devised. At first permitting any one and every one to fish as they please, temporarily increases the quantity captured, but at a permanent injury to the fishery, by decreasing future years' supply, and, if continued, almost annihilating them. Water should be as valuable as

Observation on an opinion that prohibiting the destruction of fry by regulating the minimum size of the meshes of nets would be cruel to the poor.

land for producing food, and indiscriminate farming is not permitted: forests have been ruined in this country by the same 'free forestry' having been allowed as is now destroying the fresh-water fisheries, and much the same objections were raised against preventing the *poor people* cutting fuel when, where, and how they pleased; the result is too well known to comment upon.

143. Lastly, my propositions, in addition to those in paragraph 138, are to interfere as little as possible with the natives, excepting to prevent unfair fishing. Whether the fisheries are let for this purpose or a net tax is instituted, does not appear so material, as that a certain minimum distance be declared shall always exist between each knot of the meshes of nets, or in the interstices of substances forming weirs, traps or cruives, or in any fixed trap or traps used in the capture of fish. This distance, I would suggest, should be one inch, but this is a detail that might be modified to suit different districts. No fixed fishing weirs should be permitted to exist entirely barring a stream; a free passage should be imperative. Cruives or wicker traps, or those formed of wire or any other substances used as fixed traps, should only be permitted on a written authority, and the month in which they are permitted to be employed should be stated. In Great Britain they are absolutely prohibited in fresh waters. Either immature fish should be prevented from entering irrigated fields, or a free passage permitted as proposed by the Collector of South Canara. Fence-months in hilly regions I consider highly desirable, during such periods as large fish are ascending to breed or returning to the rivers in the plains. This might be fixed at a period, not exceeding two months, to be selected by the local authorities.

Further personal propositions.

144. The Madras Revenue Board suggest the appointment of two Inspectors of Fisheries with establishments, but prior to this being carried out, it would appear desirable to decide, whether any measures are going to be taken to preserve the fresh-water fisheries of that Presidency, and, secondly, what are those measures to be, if any are adopted?

Proposal of Revenue Board to appoint two Inspectors of Fisheries.

145. In the Proceedings of the *Board of Revenue of Madras* (May 28th, 1869), with reference to fisheries in waters above tidal reach, it is observed that there is scarcely anywhere a numerous and distinct class dependant on this pursuit for subsistence, though the Godaveri river may furnish an exception. As regards prohibiting the use of nets below a certain size, it appears to the Board impossible to forbid the use of a mesh of less than four inches in circumference (or one inch between each knot of the meshes), for they believe that whiting [*Sillago sihama*, a marine fish at Madras, is so termed, and here is an objection made which is capable of being proved or disproved. This fish is as wide as high, and its height is one-sixth of its length; now it is well known no whiting under 10 or 12 inches is fit for the table; such would only just escape a net with 2 *inches* between each knot of the meshes] of the average size, and all the smaller mullet [also a sea-fish] could pass through meshes of that size, to say nothing of prawns, immense numbers of which are consumed in Madras and elsewhere, and which

Proceedings of the Board of Revenue; their draft rules for fresh-water fisheries.

are taken in fine-meshed casting nets. The total prohibition of fishing near the anicuts (weirs) does not appear necessary to the Board, although it might be well that a sufficient time should be allowed to enable the fish to ascend the ladders (where such are provided) unmolested, after which the fishing could be unrestricted. It is very desirable that unfair and wholesale destruction of breeding fish at the anicuts and elsewhere should be prevented, and that a stop should be put to the poisoning of water and drainage of tanks for the purpose of catching fish. In a further report of proceedings (dated December 18th, 1869), " the Board cannot admit the correctness of Dr. Day's assertion, [My assertion was based on an extensive enquiry amongst the fresh-water fishermen; also the *Collectors* of the *Godaveri District* and of *Coimbatore* say six months: the *Collector* of the *Kistna* and the *Head Assistant Collector* of *Kurnal* observe one year's notice will be sufficient: the *Collectors* of *Nellur*, of *South Arcot* and *Madura* likewise suggest one year's notice: the *Collector* of *Bellary* that no notice is absolutely necessary, but merely a stipulation in the contract: and these include the whole of the answers to the question, "How long notice do you consider it would be necessary to give, provided it were deemed advisable to prohibit fishing with very small-meshed nets in waters which are let?" and it is to be presumed, that before replying, an enquiry was made,—how long do nets last?] in para. 40 that fishing nets only last a year. At least the Board would recommend the proposal be so far modified as to substitute three inches for four as the limit for the size of the net's mesh, and to exempt casting nets and prawn nets altogether from the restriction. The Board entertain some doubts whether the sanction of a legal enactment may not be necessary to empower the Government to issue orders which greatly interfere with the exercise of practices which long custom may have converted into communal rights, (see para. 130) maintainable by a civil action. The Board would also draw the attention of the Government to the letter from the Collector of Malabar [This appears to be a mistake; it was the *Officiating Collector* who raised these objections, November 5th, 1859, being unable to see the injuries going on in the fisheries which had been adverted to by the *Acting Collector*, February 12th of the same year, preferring the opinion of a *Sub-Collector* whose acquaintance with fish and fisheries does not appear to be very extensive, judging from his letters], who deprecates the introduction of orders into his district as unnecessary and likely to be highly unpopular, and would beg to suggest that the application of these rules either to Malabar (see para. 167) or South Canara (see para. 168) should be suspended. In further proceedings (dated July 13th, 1871) the Board observe upon Mr. Thomas' report, on the result of one year's experimental trial of protecting fish in South Canara, my reports on the Madras fresh-water fisheries, their own former proceedings, and the orders of the Madras Government, and continue, " the Board cannot but view with reluctance the necessity for State interference with what are at present free industries, and deprecate the conversion of measures attended alike in the interests of the people and the Government, for the conservancy of an important article of food, into a means of raising revenues for the general purposes of the State." [The Government of India observed, October 2nd, 1871, " The real point for consideration is this :—Fishes, if properly preserved, are susceptible of becoming an important, because abundant, cheap, and wholesome article of food. Is the present plan of non-interference likely to ensure to future generations the fullest possible supply of this food staple? Is it even such as to ensure their inheriting a supply equal to that which now exists? The Governor General in Council apprehends that both these questions must be answered in the negative: and that not only is there no prospect, as matters now stand, of an increased supply hereafter, but that, owing to the absence of precautionary measures and reasonable restrictions, the existing supply is diminishing. His Excellency in Council believes, on the other hand, that it would be possible, by the adoption of such measures and restrictions, to increase the supply very largely in a few years. If this be so, it would clearly be the duty of the State to take the necessary measures."]

146. The *Revenue Board* continue—" they think that they cannot now but recommend Government to prepare a draft Act, drawn in accordance with the spirit and provision of the Land Acquisition Act, X of 1870, to enable them to undertake the conservancy of all waters to which its provisions may be extended, with due provision for inviting and deciding counter-claims and rights by the Collector or Courts, and for compensating the owners of such rights or easements where such rights are interfered with or resumed." The Board proposed the Act should contain provision that tanks and streams not perennial be free [a provision *strongly to be deprecated*, as most of the Madras rivers are so, more especially as the Board suggest only prohibiting traps in rivers declared to be taken under Government conservancy, but permitting every species of poaching (except damming and poisoning) in fields, minor channels, and ponds.] That in rivers and tidal estuaries it shall be declared lawful for Government to levy a tax on fisheries in such waters, either in the form of rent, or of fees on implements of fishery; the collection of such fees to be kept directly under the management of Government or farmed out. That poisoning of waters for the purpose of catching fish, and the pollution of waters by the refuse of coffee-pulpers and other deleterious works be interdicted under heavy penalties. That the minimum size of the mesh of nets be defined by law at two inches in circumference in fresh waters, and that immature fish, the description and size of which are to be determined and notified by Government, captured are to be returned to the water under penalty. That the interruption by dams and traps of the entire waterway of public rivers, and the use of cruives and the like devices be prohibited in rivers declared to be taken under Government conservancy. That no interference is intended or to be permitted with the existing rights of the people to catching and retaining fish in their own fields, minor channels, and ponds, but that it shall be lawful for the officers entrusted by law with the conservancy of fisheries, to insert gratings in the head of any channels leading to such fields. That rod and line-angling be untaxed. That a separate fishery department be constituted under the Board, who suggest that all rents derived from fisheries should for the present constitute a fund for the protection and improvement of this industry. These now amount, on the average of five years, to Rs. 80,000, with a steady upward tendency. It must be borne in mind that, practically, nothing is credited under this head in the

Proposal for draft fishery Act.

statements for the districts of Vizagapatam, Godaveri, Nellur, Cuddapah, Kurnal, Canara, and Malabar, and in several districts the whole subject is inadequately attended to. The Board think, that with care, a large prospective income may be relied on from this source, while the taxes and licenses may be kept so low as to be anything but oppressive.

147. With regard to the districts from which no fishery rents are received, it will be necessary to refer, as a reason, to the *Circular Orders of the Board of Revenue*. On November 27th, 1848, Collectors were requested " to take measures to introduce, in future, the system of disposing of village, tank, and channel fisheries on rent, should such a course not have been hitherto adopted." But to the ' Collector of North Arcot, on receiving his letters of December 8th and January 29th, 1849, the Board observed, they " will not press the extension of the renting system in respect to the tank fisheries of North Arcot, but will leave it to the discretion of the Acting Collector to continue the management of that branch of revenue in the manner which appears to him best suited to the circumstances of his district." In reply to a letter from the Collector of Guntur, dated January 29th, 1849, the Board did " not consider it advisable to revise the practice of renting the tank and channel fisheries in Guntur." The Agent in Kurnal was directed " not to take any measures for renting the fisheries of his district," whilst the Collector of Bellary was " not to make any demand on this head upon fisheries that have not heretofore been subject to tax." Again, in 1862, the following was circulated to all Collectors :— " The Board are decidedly opposed to any extension of the fishery rents, and more especially so where involving in any form the re-imposition of the burden from which the abolition of the moturpha tax relieved the poorer classes." [The *Collector of Madras*, June 14th, 1869, observed, " it appears that some years ago it was ruled by the Secretary of State, that the right of fishing was not to be rented out, except where the practice had been previously in vogue. I have not the Secretary of State's despatch to refer to, but I suspect that it was really intended to apply only to inland fisheries, such as village tanks, jungle streams, and channels, and was done probably in recognition of the prescriptive rights of the inhabitants to enjoy the fish within their limits without any tax."]

<small>Circular Orders of Revenue Board in 1848, as to what fisheries were to be let, and what free.</small>

148. As already observed, the *Board* objected to a 4-inch mesh being introduced; so they were allowed to modify the order, and they considered a 3-inched mesh sufficiently small as a minimum, and on December 18th the following instructions were issued to Collectors with reference to fresh-water fisheries :—" Notice should be given that, from the 1st July 1870, the right of fishing in all Government tanks, rivers, and streams having a perennial supply of water will be let by public auction for a period of three years. Renters will be called to enter into agreements to abide by the general rules for the regulation of fisheries that may be passed by the Board, and to any orders issued by Collectors in reference to special localities. The use of all nets having meshes less than three inches in circumference (casting nets and prawn nets excepted) should be prohi-

<small>Instructions from Revenue Board to Collectors respecting the fresh-water fisheries.</small>

bited; this prohibition to take effect from the 1st July 1871, and to be in force in all waters, both salt and fresh, classed as Government fisheries. The draining of all tanks, the property of Government, for the purpose of catching fish, and the poisoning of water for the purpose of catching fish in all tanks, rivers, and streams, should be strictly prohibited. Notices should be issued that persons detected in the last-named practice will be proceeded against criminally. All fishing with nets or loaded-hooks within 200 yards of any anicut or other masonry work extending across a Government stream should be prohibited. All fishing in irrigation channels, the property of Government, which communicate with the sea, from October to February, both inclusive, should be prohibited. The following scale of rewards for the destruction of vermin should be offered if killed within one mile of an anicut or masonry dam :—each alligator [*crocodile* was the animal for whose destruction I suggested rewards should be offered, and the Madras Government agreed to. I hardly think it would be of use giving them for *alligators*, as those reptiles are peculiar to the American continent] 6 feet long and upwards, Rs. 5; from 2 to 6 feet, Rs. 2; under 2 feet, Re. 1; every egg, 2 annas; each otter, Re. 1. Collectors should submit a list of the localities in their respective districts where they would recommend that rewards should be given. Collectors of Godaveri, Kistna, and Tanjur will take measures for passing a certain number of fish over the anicuts by netting them in the manner proposed by Lieutenant Vibart, R. E. Collectors will understand that these orders apply only to tidal estuaries of considerable extent, and to inland tanks and streams which, as a rule, retain water throughout the year in sufficient quantity to keep up a constant supply of fish, and are the property of Government. A list of all such estuaries and fresh-water reservoirs and streams as Collectors consider should be classed as Government fisheries, should be submitted without delay. It is not intended to interfere with the usual practice of catching fish in small tanks which do not retain water throughout the year, nor with any rivers but those possessing a perennial supply of water. Channels, however, such as those under the Godaveri and Kistna anicuts, which, although dry for certain seasons, communicate with rivers and backwaters having a perpetual supply of water, may be included.

149. The *Acting Collector of Ganjam* (June 14th, 1870) observed that no protective measure in respect to fisheries appear to be necessary in his district, as the rivers have little or no water in them save when the freshes come down; most of the tanks are also in the same condition for some months in the year. The water is never poisoned or drained for the purpose of catching the fish. The practice of renting out the right to fish in rivers, tanks, 'tamparas' (large lakes), backwaters, &c , for a term of years already obtains in the district.

Opinion of the Collector of Ganjam.

150. The *Collector of Vizagapatam* (July 17th, 1869) remarked, that the fresh-water fisheries of the district are utterly insignificant; the rivers are mere hill streams, dry for the greater part of the year, and there are few tanks of a sufficient size to make fishing in them of any consequence. Until the abolition of the moturpha, a tax was levied upon fishermen which might perhaps be called a rent for the right of

Opinion of the Collector of Vizagapatam.

fishing, but which was in fact a capitation tax on the castes that exercised the fisherman's calling. At the permanent settlement, the amount of this tax was set down at Rs. 3,463-2-9, but this sum included the tax on sea fishermen, from whom by far the greater portion of it was collected, as appears from the incidence of the tax falling almost entirely on the estates on the coast. "With reference to Dr. Day's proposition to prohibit the use of nets with meshes under four inches in circumference, I believe the result of such an attempt would be to put a stop to freshwater fishing altogether. The fish that form the favorite food of the fish-eating community are small, and not larger than white bait. I do not profess any knowledge on this subject, but have heard it stated that the above delicacy are the fry of large fish; and yet I have never heard of any proposition to prevent their capture in order to increase the general fish-supply. Such an attempt could not create greater consternation at Blackwall, than Dr. Day's measures for preventing the capture of small fish would throughout the Presidency." [These conclusions appear to be based on the proposition, that preventing the massacre of the fry of fish will not augment the fish-supply; as regards Blackwall, it is difficult to understand how views entertained at any locality in Europe within tidal influence can have any bearing upon what measures would be most efficacious in India to prevent the extermination of fishes in freshwaters above the influence of the tides.] "The practice of poisoning water to obtain the fish is not employed in these parts; but that and draining tanks for the purpose of securing all the fish in them might be properly prohibited."

151. The *Collector of the Godaveri District* (October 28th, 1869)

Opinion of the Collector of the Godaveri districts.

observed, that the fisheries in his Collectorate formerly realised from 3 to 10,000 rupees yearly, but for the last few years rents have not been taken. To re-open the renting system would oppress the fisher class, *i. e.*, those who live by fishing alone. If the returns proved good, the leases would be taken by outsiders, and sub-let by them at a higher rate to the fishermen; and if small, a class who make but at most a sufficient livelihood now, would be heavily taxed. The introduction of a Fishery Act would certainly entail the necessity of an establishment to see its provisions carried out, for the closest supervision would be needed. Draining or poisoning tanks for fishing purposes is not practised in the district. Renting out the fisheries "will certainly result in the re-imposition on the fishing class of the abolished moturpha, though in another shape, and be in my opinion a backward step in our legislation." [If *renting waters* for fishing is a backward step, it is difficult to see how the *renting* of *land* can be justified, or charging for the use of water for the purpose of irrigation, thus, as remarked by the 'Chief Commissioner of British Burma' in 1853, "they who gain their livelihood from working the waters, may with equal justice pay tax, as those who obtain it from the lands, and fishing may be looked on as the most profitable employment of the two." If the money raised by these rents is to be used for the purpose of improving the fisheries, as is that received from taxes on fishing nets and angling in Great Britain, and so to largely augment the food of the public and consequently lower its price, the objection to collecting the Government rents appears to vanish, excepting that at the first the price of fish will be raised to pay the rent, but as fish augment, it must fall.] The Collector also reported that there are a few zemindary estates over which Government do not possess the right of fishing. There would be an objection to leasing out fisheries in tanks and channels employed for irrigation and drinking purposes, as they would be spoilt by using nets in them, as it would continually stir up the mud and foul the water. If fisheries are let, they should be for at least three years at a time. There is one irrigation weir at Dowlaishweram across the Godaveri river. At first after its construction the take of fish below it was enormously increased, and diminished above; this effect continues to the almost total destruction of the fisheries above the weir; below it the large takes continue as the ascent of fish is arrested. [There is apparently some error in this answer, as the same official observed on September 11th, 1867.—" The fishermen say that they do not catch the sable in such abundance now as they used to do, immediately after the anicut was built," and the result of personal investigations was the same. The *Revd. Dr. Murphy* wrote, in 1868, that the fish had decidedly decreased since 1861, and one of the causes was, " the universal and unrestricted capture of the fry in the rivers and irrigation channels."] That young fish are largely destroyed, the size of the mesh of the nets being very small; but there would be considerable difficulty in regulating its minimum size in fisheries which are rented out, but were such done, fishermen should have six months' notice. There is no reason against prohibiting all fishing, except with hooks and lines, within 100 yards of all anicuts, weirs, dams, locks, or masonry works extending across streams or canals of fresh water.

152. The *Acting Head Assistant Collector of the Kistna District*

Opinion of the Collector of the Kistna District.

observed (October 21st, 1867) that fish ascend the Kistna river, after the freshes are over, as clear water flows, or about November. Prior to the construction of the Bezwada weir which spans it, they ascended in large number to 50 miles higher up where they spawned; now the shoals are arrested. The local fishermen employ small nets, but those from Dowlaishweram bring some 3 or 400 yards long, and 12 to 14 feet deep, and the largest quantities are taken in the deep pools below the weir, the net being first fastened or fixed at one end, then taken round a wide sweep, and gradually drawn in. The sable is locally termed ' yekkudi chakka' from its perseverance in attempting to surmount the weir and ascend the river, from the Telugu word ' yekku' to climb. Unable to pass, the whole shoal is taken at the weir, either by nets or hanging baskets near the edge of the water, so that those which jump fall into them. The fishermen unanimously assert that these fish do not spawn between the weir and the sea. " I do not think it would be possible to contrive any means to enable the fish to ascend, without interfering with the damming up of the river water, which in November and December is necessary to ensure the rice crop." The *Executive Engineer* (November 5th, 1867) observed, " the shoals of Palasa come up from October to April, while the river is low. * * * The fish could easily pass through the under-sluices, [this is a mistake; they are unable to pass through, even if they were open], but when the river is low, it is of importance that these should be kept closed during the irrigation season. Doubtless, temporary ladders might be formed to allow the fish to pass over the anicut; but during the months of November, December, and January a stone bund is placed across the anicut, and water, as far as possible, prevented from flowing over the anicut. It has been suggested to me that Government should institute an establishment to catch the fish below the anicut and place them in the river above." The *Acting Collector* (November 12th, 1867) continues, "should Government approve of the proposals for conservancy of Messrs. Stuart and Vibart, I have the honor to request that sanction for a sum of not more than Rs. 200 may be given for the purpose." The *Madras Revenue Board* (January 28th, 1868) observe, "the Board are inclined, however, rather to favor the plan proposed by Mr. Stuart * *, namely, the entertainment of an establishment of fishermen, for catching the fish below the anicut and putting them in again above." The *Collector of the Godaveri District* (February 7th, 1868) continues, " I do not think the idea of employing fishermen to catch spawning fish below the anicut and put them into the river above it a good one. I think that the fish will very probably be injured in so doing." The *Madras Government* (May 27th, 1868) observe, "the proposal to employ an establishment of fishermen to transfer fish from below to above the anicut does not commend itself to the judgment of Government." I reported (December 1st, 1868) on those herrings, which die almost as soon as they are removed from the water: "at the Kistna is no bridge across the anicut, and fishing must be carried on for at least 250 yards below that structure; therefore, the fish would have to be captured, landed, and carried up above the anicut. Doubtless, some would survive the process if a sufficient number were taken, but the ova would be injured, and probably almost irretrievably so. For anything to succeed it must be a natural pass." The *Revenue Board* (December 18th, 1869) direct that "Collectors of Godaveri, Kistna, and Tanjur will take measures for passing a certain number of fish over the anicuts by netting them in the manner proposed by Lieutenant Vibart." The *Officiating Collector of the Kistna District* (November 10th, 1868) observes, that the introduction of the system of renting out the fisheries should be gradual, so as to avoid causing hardship to those who have hitherto enjoyed the rights of fishing without restriction. The meshes of the nets in use are from one to two inches in circumference, and the fishermen assert that larger meshes will not take most of the fresh-water fish. [This is an error, as the great majority of the fish in the Kistna river attain to a large size, although seeing those as now captured, one would be led to suppose they could never grow large. There are not above two sorts of all the siluroids or scaleless fish, which at six or eight months of age would go through a mesh of four inches in circumference, and some of those whose fry I witnessed being taken in the Kistna attain several feet in length. The same remark applies to most of the carps. A list of 38 species which I collected in that district exists in Proceedings, Madras Government, February 4th, 1869. The *Head Assistant* in June 1869 reported, "no doubt here, as in other districts, there is much destruction of young fish by the use of nets with small meshes."] He continues that in the district all channels and tanks dry up in the hot weather; consequently even those larger kinds of fish can only grow for a short time, and if they are not caught before the water is exhausted they must perish, unless they bury themselves. It is consequently proposed that two inches should be the minimum size of the mesh of the nets. The village officers should be made responsible for carrying this rule into force, under the general supervision of the Police and Talooka officials, and punishment in cases of breach of the rule brought to notice would ensure its being generally observed in a short time. Fishing in tanks of drinking-water should be forbidden. The destruction of small fish and fry is more likely to be carried on if the fisheries are let by the year, than if they were for a longer term: in the latter case they will not be destroyed every year, as the contractor knows that the benefits to be reaped from preserving them would be his; but in the former case he would never feel sure of getting the fishery next year, and would therefore do his best to get all the fish he could, whilst he had the opportunity. Besides, contractors prefer renting for more than one year, as it is more difficult to settle with sub-renters or fishermen every year in good time. The Bezwada weir on the Kistna has proved itself to be a great bar to the sea-fish going up the river for breeding, and those above this construction have decreased. Besides small-meshed nets, baskets are used which have the smallest interstices. Fish, when very young, are undoubtedly destroyed to a great extent. There would be no difficulty in regulating the minimum size of the mesh of nets in all fisheries that are rented out, but it should be done gradually, and one year's notice will be sufficient; two inches in circumference is proposed; no objection exists to prohibiting netting within 100 yards of weirs. On April 20th, 1871, a list of the fisheries which it was proposed to let out was sent to the *Revenue Board*, who direct "that special provision may be made for ensuring that villagers shall, as far as possible, be allowed to retain the fishery rights of all waters within the limits of their villages."

153. The *Acting Collector of Nellur* (October 26th, 1869) reported that the right of Government to let the fisheries in this district has not been fully exercised as yet, and has not been called in question in the few cases in which it has; some fishermen will consider having to pay rents a grievance, while the revenue would be insignificant, and press hardly on an already impoverished class. There is an irrigation weir on the Pennair in Nellur, and it is supposed that fish have decreased in consequence; they have also diminished above the anicut, and their ascent is arrested by it. No particular care is taken not to destroy the fry. There would be great difficulty in regulating the size of the mesh of nets; a year's notice should be given. *Major Clay*, Assistant Engineer (October 17th, 1867) mentions a case in which "a small gunta was poisoned by some Mussulmen with a view of taking the fish. No fish have been seen in the pool since, and the effect of the poison on the water seems, in the opinion of the natives, to be such, as still to prevent them using the water;" and this was two years subsequently.

Opinions of European officials in the Nellur Collectorate.

154. The *Collector of Bellary* (July 17th, 1869) states, he is not of opinion that the introduction of any measures, such as those proposed, is either necessary or advisable. The only localities

Opinions of European officials in the Bellary Collectorate.

in which fish are obtainable in numbers are the river Toongbhudra, which bounds the district on the west and north, and some eight or ten of the large tanks scattered through the collectorate. The single tank for fishing is at Darogee, situated within 19 miles of Bellary. The only mode resorted to for catching fish, is that of placing a net across the mouth of the sluice, and thus capturing all those that are forced through by the pressure of the water. The size of the mesh of the net thus used is of no consequence, as all fish escaping this net must of necessity die within a short time afterwards by the drying up of the channels. In the river the want of large markets along its banks will probably prevent fishing in it from being a profitable speculation for some time to come. The fishery here may be regarded as practically inexhaustible, and it does not appear necessary to place any restrictions on it. It would rather seem to need encouragement. It is not considered that the right of Government to let any fisheries in the district would be disputed. No rule exists why they should not be let, except that it is not probable that any persons would be found to bid for them; letting by a term of years is preferable to annual auctions, so that the contractor has an opportunity for recovering in a good year what he may have lost in a bad. Fish, when very young, are not destroyed to any great extent. The nets used in fishing are usually of a small mesh, but they are, as a rule, cast nets, and merely catch those small fish that lie in shallow water [this is exactly the place where the fry are to be found.] The nets used in the Toongbhudra are generally of a large mesh. If it were deemed advisable to prohibit the use of small-meshed nets, it would merely be required to insert it as a stipulation in the contract; no notice is absolutely necessary. The *Acting Collector* (June 4th, 1870) propose to let out the fishing of seven tanks, but he considered it impossible to give out that of the river on lease, and reported that no protective measures were necessary.

155. The *Collector of Tanjur* (November 15th, 1867) observes that previous to the construction of the lower Coleroon anicut in 1836, the sable fish, *Clupea palasah*, was caught in the neighbourhood of Trichinopoly, but since that year it has, according to general report, disappeared. It comes up stream from June to the middle of August. On July 26th, 1870, the same official reported, that the right to the fishery of all tanks as well as village channels in this district belongs to the Merassidars, having been conceded to them in the orders of Government of June 11th, 1857, No. 576, paragraph 29; and if, therefore, it is intended to prohibit the draining of the tanks for catching fish, he thinks it must be done by legislative enactment. In a previous letter dated August 17th, 1869, the Collector observed that all rivers in his district are let by auction, and that this does not appear to entail any hardship on the fishermen classes; it is only small tanks that are annually drained, for the purpose of being filled with fresh-water from river channels, at which period advantage is taken to capture the fish in them. Waters are not poisoned in Tanjur. Fishing near anicuts is forbidden on engineering considerations; a close month in irrigation canals from October to February is approved of, because it is after October, when the floods have subsided, that the bulk of the fish are caught on their return to the sea.

Opinion of the Collector of Tanjur.

156. The *Collector of Trichinopoly* (October 12th, 1869) observed that in Trichinopoly the supply of fish is altogether unequal to the demand; "thus I remember last year catching with a live bait a Killatay, *Macrones aor*, of about four pounds, and a Deloyet at once exclaimed 'that would fetch a high price in the fort;' in fact any amount of good fish could be sold in the town, or indeed elsewhere, at remunerative rates. In order to have a firm hold on the fishermen and their actions, we should certainly rent out fisheries under prescribed conditions, and it might even be necessary to have a legal enactment. No doubt the size of the mesh should be regulated; five inches in circumference would be a proper minimum. One only difficulty arises; there are daily brought to market basketsful of exceedingly tasteless, small fishes called 'Vellichay,' *Chela clupeoides*, and they never grow bigger than three or four inches, and are largely purchased by the poorer classes to eat with their rice. By limiting the size of the mesh, we virtually prohibit the capture of these little creatures, and thus cut off an article of food. But then arises the natural question, is it worth while losing the salmon for sake of the gudgeons? Poisoning should certainly be prevented; it is a barbarous kind of usage. Tanks are not often drained for mere fish; the water is too valuable:" would allow fishing in the pools near irrigation weirs only to a limited extent, as when all of them are connected by a good stream; because at certain seasons, especially when the waters are very low, fish are congregated in them, and can all be captured with the greatest ease. The *Acting Collector of Trichinopoly* (July 30th, 1870) reported, that with the exception of the Cauvery, its branch the Coleroon, and the Vellyaur, which form the northern boundary of the district, there are no running streams of such permanence as would come under the category of rivers; the Iyaur and others being mere jungle water-courses which are filled only after local rains, and subside as rapidly as they fill. The supply of fish within the limits of the district, as an article of local consumption, is therefore very limited; and, such being the case, he does not consider that any very extensive measures for the conservancy thereof are either necessary or called for. [That the supply of fish in the Coleroon and Cauvery is insignificant, is the very reason why some remedial measures appear to be called for. About 10 miles from Trichinopoly, where the Cauvery divides, it is 1,466 yards broad, and becomes separated by the island of Serungum into two parts, the most southern or smaller being 666 yards wide, retaining the name of the Cauvery; the largest is 800 yards wide, and is termed the Coleroon. As a weir exists here 750 yards broad, divided by a small island 216 yards wide into two portions, bunding up the river to from five to seven feet in height, it can hardly be conceded that such a stream should be almost destitute of fish, especially as much of the district is freely irrigated.] "According to Dr. Day's proposition, fishing should not be allowed during the time the rivers are in communication with the sea, and this time he fixes between October and February; here, however, this could not apply, and I have, therefore, fixed the season during which fish are not to be taken, between the 15th June and the 15th September. [It is evident my views have been misunderstood in this report, my wish being to allow the young and spent

breeding fish to escape to the sea, as so fully understood by the Collector of Tanjur in the last para. Stopping fishing during the periods specified would appear to show most conclusively that the sable fish now no longer comes into this Collectorate during the freshes, as it did prior to the construction of the lower Coleroon weir.] The Acting Collector continues, "I agree with the Board in thinking, at present, no restrictions as to the size of the meshes are necessary or desirable." [As the supply of fish in this, for the south of India, well-watered district, is said to be "very limited," whereas it was formerly abundant, it is to be regretted that the period at which restrictions are proposed to be commenced has not been recorded.]

157. The *Collector of Cuddapah* (July 24th, 1869) reported that

Opinion of the Collector of Cuddapah.

as the average rainfall of the district is only 17 inches, and the rivers and tanks annually dry up, there are next to no fish. Consequently it does not appear necessary to record any other reply to Dr. Day's string of questions. No revenue has ever been attempted to be raised here from fish, nor is Cuddapah once mentioned in his reports. [The question is not one of revenue, but of food supply. The reason the district is not mentioned by me, is due to not having as yet had the opportunity of personally examining it; but it is to be regretted the Collector has not given his personal experience by replying to the questions on its fish and fisheries.] On November 1st, 1869, the same officer observed that there are no fisheries to speak of in the district; so he has taken no measures on the Government orders respecting letting them; and on March 7th, 1872, that there are no perennial streams in his collectorate, and with but few exceptions no water in any tank all the year round; consequently there are few fish and no means of improving the breed. Legislation is uncalled for; and therefore he had considered it unnecessary to collect the information which has been called for.

158. The *Collector of Kurnal* (February 25th, 1869) reported that

Opinions of European officials in the Kurnal Collectorate.

the chief rivers in his district are a part of the Kistna, a part of the Toongbhudra, the Hindry, and five others which, with the exception of the two first, dry up more or less during the hot season. There is a long extent of the Kistna which has no villages on its banks, and which is never fished in. This reach may be looked on as a large breeding place, which is seldom approached by man, and where the fish are undisturbed. "I would deprecate in the strongest terms, any measures being taken by Government to interfere with the fish-supply of the inhabitants of this district. The only way in which Government could interfere, would be by means of an establishment of subordinates who would avail themselves of their authority to practise extortion and oppress the poor, who are generally the only people who fish, and never really repress the destruction of fish. If anything could repress their destruction to any extent, it would be the forbidding to catch fish with roe. But this would be tantamount to depriving the people of a wholesome and pleasant diet, and interfere with the great traffic in fish roes which now takes place. Some fish, too, are only good for eating when heavy with roe, such as the sable, caught extensively by means of baskets hung over the water as it falls over the Toongbhudra weir. I would strongly recommend leaving

f

the natives alone regarding the fish and its means of capture, and I think I may safely say that, considering the extraordinary re-productiveness of fish and the fine reaches of the Kistna, let man use any appliances he can think of for taking fish, he will never be able to affect the supply in any appreciable way as regards this district. [The *Tehsildar of Ramalkota* (see para. 180) observes on the decrease, and that it is "asserted by all the fishermen of whom I have enquired, that the river stock has considerably decreased of late years," and that this is due to the weir across the Kistna.] The same officer (November 6th, 1869) observed that no fisheries are let in his district. The rivers Kistna and Toongbhudra divide it from the Nizam's territories; consequently, it may be doubtful in such localities as to the proportion of the fishery which belongs to the British: in all other waters they belong exclusively to Government. "If fisheries are let, there would be a greater inducement to destroy fish, than allowing things to be as they are. The renters would naturally use their utmost endeavours to catch as many fish as possible to make their rents profitable. They would in a few years do more damage than the present occasional fishermen do in a century. I do not advocate their being let at all. The effect of the anicut is not appreciable [see Tehsildar's answer, para. 180.] Fewer men are said to fish than formerly, but the rise of wages has more to do with it than the falling off of fish." [The Collector here appears to chiefly examine this question respecting whether renting out fisheries, hitherto unlet, will exercise a good or prejudicial influence on the fish. I would point out that it is the preservation of the fry and stoppage of the use of very minute meshed nets that is one of the chief alterations that appears desirable, and letting out fisheries would give the lessee an interest in protecting such immature fish. When I was stationed at Kurnal a few years since, I had two large mahaseer brought to me one day; the first weighed 38lbs, the second 14lbs. On the same evening I saw the fry of these fish being caught in a minute meshed net, whilst the adult was stated to attain 50 to 60lbs weight; and at this period a great scarcity of fish was being complained of, whilst they were said to be diminishing. I suspect this was so; for, as wages have risen in the district, the price of fish would have increased also; as more people could afford to purchase it.] Is unable to say if fish have decreased above the weir, but they are stopped by it. Men are seen catching them in a sort of landing net as they try to leap over the anicut, which is impossible, because the weir at Sunkesula (a few miles above Kurnal) is vertical and has no curtain; many fish are caught below the weir. Young fish are destroyed to a great extent, but more perish from the drying up of rivers and tanks than from any other means. Nets are employed whose meshes do not exceed the size of open mosquito curtain material. There would, however, be no difficulty in regulating the minimum size to be employed, except that carrying out such a regulation would require a water police establishment, the cost of which would probably exceed the rents. The *Assistant Collector* (July 26th, 1869) reports that very young fish are destroyed to a very great extent with nets, the meshes of which are not larger than those of mosquito curtains. "I believe any law regulating the size of the mesh would be inoperative in this country; it would be cruel to the poor people, who, for the most part, live on small fish. I do not believe any Magistrate would convict except under peculiar circumstances. This is the case at home." [The enquiry appears to be misunderstood. Here is a district in which the fry of fish are caught to a great extent, and how preventing such destruction and so increasing food would be '*cruel*,' it is difficult to see. As to Magistrates refusing, except under peculiar circumstances, to administer the law if one existed, is a question I need not enter upon: but Mr. Turner is mistaken as regards fishery districts at home, as may be perceived by turning over the files of any newspapers devoted to practical natural history, sport, and law.] The *Acting Head Assistant Collector* (March 16th, 1869) reported, " the rivers within my division are inconsiderable in size; but from what I can learn, I believe that both in them and also in tanks when the water is low, the people catch, by means of nets and buskets, fishes of various sizes indiscriminately: the mischief of this practice being, that fish are caught whilst still very young and before they have attained their full growth." He continued that he had frequently seen taken "just whatever they could get, some of the fish caught being only an inch or two, and some a foot and upwards in length." That the fish were poisoned, and " it seems very advisable that some measures should be taken for the protection of the fish against such destruction." He subsequently (September 1st, 1869) observed that it seems highly desirable that the measures proposed for the prevention of unfair and wanton destruction of fish should be adopted. " The letting to certain individuals the exclusive right of fishing in all large pieces of water and rivers not navigated by sea-going vessels, seems to be the most effectual means of preventing the wanton destruction of fish. It might be as well not to limit in all cases the period of renting to one Fusly (year), but the fisheries might sometimes be let for lengthened periods, such as for two or three or even for five years at a time, though at first, I suppose, it would be advisable to let them for more limited periods. I do not think the headmen of villages ought to have any priority of right above others. I do not think the letting by auction would have the effect of giving the fisheries into the hands of outsiders, as I believe the competition would generally be limited to the inhabitants of the villages where the fisheries are situated, or of adjacent villages. It is doubtful whether the profits would be sufficiently large to attract persons from any distance." Four inches as the minimum size of the mesh of nets is considered too large. Irrigation weirs must have decreased the fish above them, as no ladders exist; fish descending over them are now unable to re-ascend. Fry are destroyed to a great extent by poisoning the waters generally by a substance called 'mallum,' the bark of the ' Billu' tree, and also by small-meshed nets. There would be some difficulty at first in regulating the minimum size of the meshes, but it would cease after some time; a notice of six months, or a year at most, would be sufficient. The *Acting Head Assistant* observed January 15th, 1872) that breeding fish and very young ones are not killed to any great extent, but that in the hot season fish of all sorts are destroyed. A very small mesh is used, and it would be impracticable to regulate it. The fry of fish are not sold, but only captured for individual consumption. The *Deputy Collector of 'eapally* remarks that the fish in tanks are indiscriminately destroyed, whether they are breeding or young ones. The smallest-sized mesh of the nets is one-fourth of an inch. As the fish are small, regulating the minimum size would prove a failure to the pursuits of the fishermen, but half an inch between the knots of the meshes is considered an advisable restriction, and as it is desirable to prevent the destruction of very small fish, the sale of the fry in the bazars may be prohibited. The *Deputy Collector of Kurnal* reports (April 16th, 1872) that breeding fish and very young ones are destroyed to a great extent, principally between April and June, as the water in the larger tanks fails. Nets of various sizes and traps of wicker work are used during December and January; weirs are set up across the streams and the fish captured. Sometimes earthen dams are raised across streams, and the water baled out to catch fish. The smallest sized mesh employed is three-eighths of an inch between each knot: of the 'Oodulu' or traps of wicker work, the interstices are of infinitely smaller dimensions; five-eighths of an inch between the knot of each mesh is proposed as a fair size; as the fishes from the hilly districts are mostly small, it is suggested that prohibiting the sale of fry might cause the poorer classes to suffer.

159. The *Acting Collector of Madras* (June 23rd, 1870) observes that the fresh-water rivers in his district are dry, except during seasons of inundation.

Opinion of the Collector of Madras.

The fisheries in the smaller tanks are enjoyed by the village communities, subject to the payment of a nominal rent; whilst those in the larger tanks, or tanks irrigating several villages, are put up to public auction, whenever the right of fishing in them is considered worth being let. The smallest meshes employed are three-fourths of an inch in circumference or even less; there is no objection prescribing in each lease the size to be employed, of which one year's notice would be sufficient, and two inches in circumference as a minimum size would be a good limit.

160. The *Acting Collector of Chingleput* (April 18th, 1872) reports that all tanks and rivers in the district are usually dry in the hot weather, with the exception of the larger tanks, and these occasionally dry up. Fishes of all sizes and in every state, if good for food, are caught whenever possible. In the hot months, as the water becomes low, all the fish are caught, the district being dependant yearly on those brought down in the annual floods or on ova or other vitality remaining dormant in the mud of tanks. No restriction as to size of mesh of nets is necessary. Fence months in hilly districts would be advisable where useful fish exist.

Opinion of the Collector of Chingleput.

161. The *Collector of Salem* (November 5th, 1869) considers leasing fisheries for five years and upwards, as preferable to annual auctions, and would let as such all tanks that have an ayacut of not less than 25 acres. "I agree with the suggestion of my Sub-Collector that in such tanks as yield the chief supply of water for drinking purposes to large towns or villages, the fishing should be prohibited, as tending to preserve the purity of the water." Objects to a 4-inched mesh being the minimum size, as too large.

Opinion of the Collector of Salem.

162. The *Collector of North Arcot* (October 26th, 1869) observes that there are no perennial rivers in his district, and the tanks, even the largest, are either dry or so low at intervals of two and three years that every fish in them, great and small, is caught. He continues, "I have collected materials with a view of submitting my views on the whole subject at an early date" [not forwarded.] The *Acting Collector* (June 6th, 1872) reports, "that there are no perennial rivers in this district, and that the tanks are either dry or so low at intervals that nearly every fish in them, great and small, is caught. It has, however, been ascertained that there is no wanton destruction of fish in this district."

Opinions of the Collectors of North Arcot.

163. The *Collector of South Arcot* (January 6th, 1870) replies that as the streams for the greater part of the year are almost entirely dry, he does not see any actual need for establishing fishing monopolies. In this district tanks are leased permanently at a fixed annual rent, and the villages, where such leases exist, enjoy a common fishery puttah in recognition of this right. There are seven irrigation weirs in the district, but is not aware whether, as a rule, fish have or have not decreased above them. Fish are caught and disposed of indiscriminately, and those of small size are never let go. Doubtless, the proportion of small fish caught to large ones is great by comparison. The average size of the meshes of nets employed is about one inch square, and it would be practicable to make the size of the mesh of the net a condition in all leased fisheries; one year's clear notice should be given. There would be no difficulty in prohibiting fishing within 100 yards of all weirs, and no doubt it would prevent the wholesale destruction of fish where such now takes place periodically. The *Sub-Collector* (November 16th, 1867) observes that the only sea-fish which ascend the Coleroon in any numbers are the shad and the mullet, termed *madavai*, the former arriving from May until August, and, being arrested by the lower weir, are captured there; the *madavai* (mullets) spawn from October to December, and ascend the Coleroon from September to April.

Opinions of the Collectors of South Arcot.

164. The *Acting Collector of Tinnevelli* (February 22nd, 1870) replied that, as far as protection of fish in tanks, rivers, and estuaries is required, he would institute a close season, to vary in different districts, of two months in each year, during which all fishing should be prohibited; and in his Collectorate June and July are proposed for rivers and back-waters, and from the 15th of October to the 15th of December for tanks. The indiscriminate and unfair way of taking fish at the various irrigation weirs when the water becomes low, it is proposed, should be entirely prohibited, and no net fishing be permitted within 200 yards of them, whilst fish ladders should be constructed. The meshes of the nets employed varies from two to four inches in circumference. If close months were adopted, regulating the minimum size of the mesh of the casting nets, it is considered, would be unnecessary. "What I *would put down* entirely is the use of baskets and traps, whereby large numbers of fish are taken in a most unfair and destructive

Opinion of European official in the Tinnevelli Collectorate.

manner." Considers that the shad do not get up the river as they used to do before the irrigation weirs spanned them, since which period fish have decreased in the rivers above these constructions. When fish can neither ascend on account of the weirs, or return to the sea on account of the shallowness of the river, they are generally caught in the pools. It is all fish that comes to the fisherman's net. He would consider it a most unwise proceeding to return the small fry on which he makes a good and immediate profit. The size of the mesh employed is very small, but regulating it would cause great dissatisfaction. The *Collector* (March 27th, 1872) reported, " small fish are caught in baskets and screens at the rapids below waste weirs and sluices, and larger fish are caught with the hook. In the small rivers, channels, and tanks, the water left in the pools in the dry season is baled out and the fish caught."

165. The *Collector of Madura* (dated December 18th, 1869) observes that the tanks and rivers are dry for the greater part of the year. Fish are taken without regard to age; nets with meshes of all sizes are used. Were the minimum size regulated, one year's notice would be necessary. The *Acting Collector* (May 17th, 1872) reports that breeding fish and very young ones are destroyed to a great extent; all are caught that can be caught, in nets with meshes of all sizes and by placing baskets in streams. No regard is had to season or age. The ordinary mesh is rarely below half an inch in circumference, but baskets and other arrangements for capturing the smallest fry are freely employed. In fisheries rented out, the size of mesh of the nets might be fixed; in other places legislation would be necessary, but in tanks and channels that are dry during the greater part of the year the destruction of the fish could not be prevented. Proposes the size of the mesh to be one inch between knot and knot. *Mr. Nelson* observes " that the repair of tanks, or, at all events, the more important ones, seem to have been executed by Government, and to have been paid for out of the proceeds of the fishery of the tanks when drying up. A letter dated 1713 states that the fishing of a single tank produced occasionally 2,000 crowns, and that sums so realised were invariably applied to the execution of repairs."

Opinions of officials in the Madura Collectorate.

166. The *Acting Collector of Coimbatore* (May 7th, 1869) stated a considerable destruction of small fry, chiefly of the Gendai, *Barbus*, takes place; poisoning the water is carried on; fry are caught in wicker-work traps, and by the erection of dams across shallow waters. Owing to the constant netting, fish are driven from their natural feeding grounds to seek shelter in deep holes to obtain protection from the ravages of the net. " The erection of dams and poisoning of the streams should be peremptorily forbidden, the size of the meshes should be regulated, and an annual close time allowed." Subsequently, the *Acting Collector* (December 20th, 1870) reported that the fish have increased since the construction of irrigation weirs across the rivers, which are believed by the fishermen to have multiplied the fish [this is evidently a misapprehension; doubtless the fish are checked in ascending and descending, so that at such places, owing to the existence of an obstruc-

Opinions of European officials in the Coimbatore Collectorate.

tion, more are congregated than was formerly the case], which, when young, are destroyed to a great extent, the smallest mesh used being one-fourth of an inch in circumference. There would be a difficulty in regulating the size of the meshes of nets to be used, as a preventive service would be necessary; but were they regulated, a six months' notice should be given. One inch in diameter is quite large enough, 6″ circumference=1·91 [one inch in diameter or between knot and knot multiplied by the four sides=4 inches in circumference.] Considers it would be a great hardship to prohibit fishing near irrigation weirs, &c. On February 4th, 1871, he observed, " that the Collectors, out of consideration for the poorer classes, have refrained from renting out tanks and streams, except in such places where the right of fishing has always been leased out. * * I would add that I do not think Dr. Day has succeeded in showing that there has been any sensible diminution of the fish-supply in fresh waters." [See para. 128, anté'.] *The Collector* (July 9th, 1872) replied, fish of all sizes of and ages are caught and eaten when and wherever they can be; the smallest mesh used is one-eighth of an inch. *Mr. Grant,* a former *Collector,* about 1864, intimated to the Government the necessity of protecting the fish in the waters of this Collectorate from the indiscriminate destruction to which he considered they were subjected. *The Collector* (May 7th, 1869), observed, " the means of destruction consist of nets, casting and seine, and poisoning. Small fry are caught in wicker-work baskets, very much like an eel trap cut in two; and are also destroyed by the erection of dams across shallow water."

167. *The Acting Collector of Malabar* (February 12th, 1869) stated, " many of the nets used are so small in the mesh as to spare none, however small. Baskets are placed in small streams in such a way as to secure every fish in them. In these ways, no doubt, myriads of fish are uselessly destroyed, that is, destroyed in the form of ova, and before they have attained to anything like maturity." The rivers are occasionally poisoned, and on these occasions, no doubt, large numbers of fish and possibly vast quantities of ova are destroyed. " I conclude the poisoning of rivers may be dealt with under the Penal Code, but I do not see how we can interfere with baskets and small meshes without special legislation." *The Officiating Collector* (November 5th, 1869), observed, "before it is decided to lease the fisheries, the expediency of the step must be shown. In districts where the practice has obtained from time immemorial, there can be no possible objection to its continuance. In this district the right has never been exercised since our acquisition of the country, we have derived no revenue from fisheries, and I have not been able to find from the records any precedent for the introduction of the system. A moturpha tax was formerly levied from fishermen, both by our Government and by that of the native rulers of the country, but this tax is far different in its nature to the measure now proposed" of renting the fisheries. [" Renting them (fisheries) out will certainly result in the re-imposition on the fishing classes of the abolished moturpha, though in another shape." *Collector of the Godaveri Districts,* para. 151.—" Fisheries have always formed one of the items of moturpha revenue." *Deputy Collector of Nundial.*] Under a moturpha, every fisher-

Opinions of European officials in Malabar.

man paid a tax on his profession, and could exercise it without hindrance." " As regards the necessity for the measure, the opinion of the District Officers does not coincide with that of Dr. Day," and this Sub-Collector (for only one opinion is forwarded) is averse to the fisheries being let. No further legislation is necessary respecting poisoning waters. He doubts if leasing fisheries would tend to their conservation, and, if carried out, will be most unpopular and give rise to great discontent.

168. The *Acting Collector of South Canara* (March 5th, 1869), observed, " every contrivance that the ingenuity of man can suggest is so actively employed against the fishes of the district, that one is driven to the unavoidable conclusion that the poorer classes are eagerly aiming, with one accord, to accomplish at an early date the extermination of the species. * * * The large still pools in the rivers are annually poisoned with a mash made of croton oil seeds, soap nut, cocculus Indicus, chillies, fowl's dung, and other deleterious substances, which destroy not only the larger fish preserved for food, but also a multitude of small fry, only killed to be thrown away. * * * The pools in which, when the rivers are at their lowest, the fish are chiefly congregated, are thus thoroughly depopulated, and the stream is tainted for some way down, and thus rendered unwholesome, not only to fishes and insects, but also to men, beasts, and birds that unwarily drink of it. A regular time is fixed, and the villagers unite to dam the stream, collect poisons, and gather the fish. Then there are wall-nets, and cast-nets, and stake-nets, and Chinese-nets, and purse-nets, and trawl-nets, and drum-nets, and shrimp-nets, nets with large meshes, and nets with very small meshes. There are bamboo labyrinth weirs to entrap fishes going up stream, and bamboo labyrinth weirs to entrap them going down stream, and these are set in every tempting run, all other ways being stopped. Their name is legion. Smooth paths are made for little fish to glide into pleasant places, which end in a purse-net, or are dammed up and baled out. The myriads of small fry that are thus destroyed is beyond all computation. I saw one day some thousands as fine as a straw, within the compass of one earthen-pot; they were to form one meal for a labouring man, whereas they might have sufficed to stock a lake and feed a town. I have also seen basket-loads of fish about the size of a man's thumb,—fish of a sort which I know grow to the size of a man's thigh. Small fry of many sorts is sold by the seer. * * * Even the crocodile, with its cruel eye, is wiser, less suicidal, and less wantonly destructive than man ; it is not so short-sighted as to commit wholesale massacre of the small fry. * * * I cannot but think that the time has arrived when intelligence should interfere between ignorance and waste. It is so obvious that the beneficent arrangements of Nature have been ordered, with the express view of the intelligent interference of the Lords of Creation, that it really seems nothing but indolence of thought, or indolence of action, that prevents us from reaping the intended advantage, more especially as the almost incredible reproductive powers of fish place it in our power to redeem in the course of four or five years the folly of a century."

Opinion of the Collector of South Canara.

169. On November 28th, 1868, the Madras Government sanctioned Rs. 3,000 (2,000 was only expended) towards carrying out a year's experimental trial of pisciculture in the rivers of South Canara, concerning which the *Collector* (August 7th, 1870) reported in full. Many of the rivers descend from the Ghâts of Mysore and Coorg, and their origins and portions of their course are in foreign territory. The poisoning of fish is popular, and has been lessened with great difficulty, more especially as it is freely resorted to in Mysore and Coorg, and thus, irrespective of the immediate injury they cause, the rivers become tainted for miles below. During the season of the coffee crops the pulpers are always at work, and their refuse runs into the head of the Puiswani river, defiling it for miles and apparently killing the fish, which is said not to be a necessity. It may be doubted whether poisoning rivers or the wholesale destruction of fry is most injurious to fisheries; and although it was found impossible to obtain exactly accurate information upon the number of small-meshed cruives employed in the districts, sufficient data existed for concluding that there were at least 1,050 on the Netràvaty river and its affluents, and calculating that every one of the cruives captures on an average 3,000 fish in a day, then there are as many as 94,500,000 tiny fry destroyed for no adequate purpose, in a single month, in one river alone. These closely-woven bamboo cruives were forbidden and vigorously hunted out of the rivers, and the result of these two steps alone, of prohibiting poisoning and the use of these small cruives in the rivers, " has been, that the most ignorant, and therefore, the most obstinate opponents have been convinced by the testimony of their own senses, and have exclaimed, to use their own words, " truly the river is everywhere *bubbling* with fry," and what is still more to the point, their practice has not belied their words, for they have taken to fishing on grounds that were before considered profitless. * * * Two years' discouragement of poisoning, and one year's discouragement of fine cruives, has worked such a change, that it has been demonstrated beyond the cavil even of the ignorant and of the interestedly opposing, that marked advantages can be reaped from the adoption of these two simple measures alone. * * * While the south-west monsoon prevails, the ample rainfall on this coast supplies abundant water for irrigation purposes, and the rivers are the while too turbulent to be diverted. But as the dry season commences, and water is wanted for the irrigation of the second crop of rice, the rivers have settled down to more manageable proportions, and near their sources, it becomes an easy matter for the farmers to collect the boulders in the stream, lay them in a line across it, and after filling in the interstices with shingle from the bed, to stop the whole with clay and bushes from the banks. A temporary and inexpensive, yet effective dam, is thus run up annually by every farmer that has ground conveniently situated for irrigation, though it is completely swept away by the first flood of the next south-west monsoon, it lasts throughout the hot weather, throughout the life-time of the fry, and the river or rivulet being thus completely cut off, is diverted entirely into an irrigation channel." The fry gliding down the stream pass with the water into the irrigation channel and so into the rice " fields that have been carefully levelled by man, and partitioned with narrow and

<small>Experimental trial of pisciculture in South Canara.</small>

shallow embankments, so as to economise the water and spread it over the largest possible area. From a piscicultural point of view, the whole stretch of rice-fields has the appearance of a vast and admirably constructed nursery. A whole river or rivulet has been turned on, a river, too, that has been stocked with ova, the water has been economised to the utmost, the depth regulated to exactly suit the fry, large predatory fish thoroughly excluded, the whole manured, ploughed, and planted so as to provide the maximum of insect life, with the desired modicum of varying shade under the growing rice, and the area of the nursery is measured, not by the inch and foot, but by the acre or square mile. In this extensive nursery therefore, which costs the pisciculturist nothing, the fry thrive admirably, and still following their instinct, go feeding, dawdling downwards with the stream. This takes them leisurely from rice-field to rice-field, and in the direction of the waste water, which of itself not unfrequently runs into the river again, or might almost always be contrived so to run. But at each drop from rice-field to rice-field, the cultivator places a basket, made of finely split bamboos, having a wide mouth, a narrow neck, and a wide bottom. It lets the water pass, but stops every single fry, and what was an admirable nursery, becomes one vast trap for destroying the majority of the fry in the river. So highly are these juicy morsels appreciated, that no peasant fails to place a basket at every outlet." [The *Madras Revenue Board* consider that a fishery Act should contain, amongst other things, provisions to the following effect :— "(6). That no interference is intended, or is to be permitted, with the existing rights of the people in regard to catching and retaining fish in their own fields, minor channels and ponds, but that it shall be lawful for the officers entrusted by law with the conservancy of fisheries to insert gratings in the head of any channels leading to such fields." Thus the vast traps now existing for fry, and so ably described by Mr. Thomas, should continue unchanged. The Burmese were wiser than this, taxing highly the use of bamboo traps and such like contrivances for capturing fish.] The Collector continues, " This is not unavoidable or accidental destruction, but is wilful, reckless, and preventible. Some of these fry, it will be remembered, are capable of becoming fish of 10 or 20 pounds in weight." [If this destruction is forbidden, the Revenue Board appear to consider that such would be a *grievance to the proprietors of fields*, and would allow such to continue as *vested rights* : but would not that ignore the great loss to the public at large in the fearful waste of animal food.] But " it would seem that they have very little, if any more right to complain than has the English miller. They are like each other in diverting the rivers for their own benefit, and of each of them the request made of them would be the same, namely, that they should do it without injury to the fisheries. The Indian farmer may, like the English miller, claim that he has a prescriptive right to the water, and that it is no part of his business to protect the fry. It has, nevertheless, been decided against the English millers equally with the companies or persons in charge of artificial channels for navigation, or for supplying towns with water, and that they shall put gratings so as to prevent the passage of salmon fry to their destruction, and that failing to do so, " they shall incur a penalty not exceeding five pounds for every day" of delay, and " a penalty not exceeding one pound for every day" during which they may fail to maintain them when erected. If, as already described, the Indian farmer diverts the whole stream in places, "the option might be given him, 'either you must leave a fair passage in the river for the fry, and put a grating before your own artificial channel, or if you must needs have every drop of water in the river run through your own fields, then you must leave that passage unobstructed to the fry,' so that eventually, if possible, they may rejoin the river by means of the waste water." Some fish spawn below these dams, other young fish remain in the pools above, consequently all are not destroyed, and stock pools, it is proposed, should be conserved in all these rivers. The fixed engines, in use in South Canara, are closely-woven cruives termed 'Kuri,' which is a basket made on the same principle as the mouse-trap, with narrowing entrances, and springy bamboo spikes projecting inwards, preventing any exit, and from one to twelve feet in length; the smaller ones are placed in irrigated fields, the larger ones in main runs. The 'Voddu' or 'Woddu,' or fishing weir, is like a large hurdle the full breadth of the river, a line of stakes being driven in across a river, split bamboos are interlaced, and the whole faced with bushes, so that the stream passes, although all fish are stopped. Gaps exist, and here cruives or 'kuris' of 10 or 12 feet in length are fixed. The Coorgs annually place these Woddus at the heads of the Canara rivers to intercept all the fish returning from spawning. The 'Kàndàri' is just like a large kuri with the addition of an upper lip extended forwards and upwards at an anglé of 45 degrees. It is placed in a natural run in the river, between boulders of rock, filling up the whole passage, minor ways having been blocked up. The long protruding lip ascends above, and prevents fish passing over the trap; thus every descending fish is captured, and twice daily it is examined. Where there are no convenient rapids, they are artificially constructed in the shallows, by placing long lines of stones in a V shape across the river, the apex being fitted with a 'kàndàri.' The 'yépu' and 'báikuri' are on the same principle, but better adapted to falls. The first is a platform made of bamboo, somewhat bellied so as to hold the stream, and propped up so as to lead ladder-wise from the top to the bottom of the waterfall at an angle of 45°. The fall is thus broken, and conducted with a rush into the báikuri, or wide-mouthed kuri, the construction of the báikuri being very similar to that of an ordinary kuri, and the rush and concentration of the water being heavy, fish once down cannot re-ascend, but are quickly beaten to the bottom and smothered by other fish. The yépu is a less elaborate adaptation of this last contrivance to smaller falls. The 'kunjol' also is a rude sort of kuri. If a few stock pools are reserved, and poisoning and the use of fixed engines prohibited, a close time may be dispensed with. The size of the mesh employed is from three-fourths of an inch in circumference and upwards. Prohibiting the use of nets with meshes of less than four inches in circumference is deprecated, on the ground that the smaller fish having immunity from netting must disproportionately increase on the larger netted sorts. [To show that this is not the case, I would refer to the Sind fisheries, para. 47; and to those of the sparsely populated districts in British Burma. The Thames fisheries are not analogous to those of India, as in this last country the majority of the finny tribes, even the most of the carps, are greedily carnivorous, but this is not the case in the

Thames.] A minimum of two inches is proposed, and that all of the following fish, when less than nine inches in length, should be returned to the water:—*Labeo calbasu,* 'karta' [which attains 3 feet in length]; *Labeo nigrescens,* which is said to attain 18 inches in length; *Barbus pulchellus,* 'katladi,' attains upwards of 17 inches; *Barbus Carnaticus,* 'Té-min,' growing in Canara to 18 inches; *Barbus Mysorensis,* 'Púrli,' taken to 18 inches; *B. mosal* and *B. tor,* 'meruvál,' both said to grow to 36 inches in Canara. [They attain to even above 90lbs. in weight where they are allowed to grow, and are the famous mahaseer]; *Ophiocephalus striatus,* 'virál,' growing to 24 inches [it may be taken in places to three feet or even more]; *Ophiocephalus diplogramme,* 'kuch-chi,' attaining 20 inches; *Ophiocephalus marulius,* 'birál,' growing to 24 inches, and the spined and common eels. Otters and both the crocodiles and their eggs, it is proposed, should be destroyed. "Men search in the rivers for hillocks wherein spawn has been left, gather the ova, and make it into cakes, which are considered a delicacy. The eggs of the 'kari,' *Labeo calbasu,* and 'kalmuri,' *Discognathus lamta,* are highly prized." Fixed engines should be prohibited, and certain river pools protected from netting; these should be selected, not only with a view to their being convenient to the fish and fry, but also with some reference to their being easy to protect; consequently those in the neighbourhood of the land or house of the head of the village would be preferable. He also observes, with reference to the construction of reservoirs, that instead of making them, as at present, to drain out the very last drop of water, it might be wiser in all fresh constructions, and when possible in repairs, to follow the example of Hyder, who so placed the sluice that after all the water available for irrigation purposes had been drawn off, there was still left in the reservoir some six or ten feet of water at the embankment, and this water served in the dry season, and more especially in times of drought, the purposes of feeding wells, and thus supplying drinking water to men and cattle, as well as keeping alive a nucleus of fish wherewith to re-stock it on the return of the rains. [This, it has been proposed, should be done in the Bombay Presidency from fishery rents (see para. 107); of course no fishing should be permitted so soon as the level of the upper edge of the reservoir were attained.]

170. The reports of the *Native and subordinate officials* of the Madras Presidency are nearly all compiled from the answers which were circulated in 1868, which, it will be observed, are not complete, as from some districts no answers have been forwarded.

Reports of Native officials in the Madras Presidency.

171. In the *Ganjam Collectorate,* the *Tehsildar of Chicacole* reports that some of the fishermen have cultivation as well, and others work for daily hire as labourers. The Meela, Pully, Khaudra, Jalary, and Neyala castes fish in the fresh and back-waters. There is generally, but not always, a sufficient supply in the local markets: the fresh (not salted) are most approved of; 250,000 persons consume it; the amount in the waters appears to be stationary. The *Tehsildar of Gumsur* states that persons of the Nolia, Tiyaro, and Kevuti castes fish in the fresh waters. The local market is insufficiently supplied; about 130,000 persons in this talooka, of all castes except Telugu Brahmins

Opinions of Native officials in the Ganjam Collectorate.

and Gavara Comoties or Banians, eat fish, either fresh or salted. The amount in the waters remains stationary. The usual size of the mesh of nets will allow the little finger to be introduced. The *Tehsildar of Berhampore* observes that some of the fishermen are engaged in cultivation; some work at ferries, others are also labourers. The castes that fish in the fresh waters are the Tero, Kevuti, Kandra, and Mila. The local markets are fully supplied, but more are not captured than could be sold. About 200,000 persons of all castes, except Telugu Brahmins and Comoties, a few of the Oriya Brahmins and Ranguni and Pattusali (a set among weavers) eat fish, but they prefer it fresh. The usual size of the mesh of the nets is as large as a two, four, or eight-anna piece.

Vizagapatam Collectorate, no answers.

172. In the *Vizagapatam Collectorate* no returns from subordinate Native officials.

173. In the *Godaveri Collectorate*, the *Tehsildar of Ramachendrapur* reports that fishermen are likewise employed as boatmen, servants, and coolies. The Pallevallu and Bestavallu fish in back and fresh waters. The local markets are insufficiently supplied. The number of the fish-eating population cannot be correctly ascertained, but all castes do so, except Brahmins, Banians, and some of the goldsmiths; both salt and fresh are equally appreciated. The supply in the waters has not increased of late years. The *Tehsildar of Amalapuram* states that the fishermen employ most of their time at fishing, while a few are engaged in cutting firewood, making and selling nets, or as boatmen. Fish are only sold at the weekly fairs. About 141,927 persons of all castes, except Brahmins, Banians, Goldsmiths, and a few others, eat fish, preferring it fresh. The amount in the waters has decreased of late years. The size of the mesh of the nets is from half a rupee to one rupee in circumference. Basket traps are used for fishing. The *Tehsildar of Narsapuram* reports that the fishermen known as Pallevallu and Bestavallu, also the Vaddi caste in certain villages, fish in rivers and back-waters, but besides fishing they employ themselves as boatmen for hire. The fish-eating population is 53,846. The markets appear to be well supplied; fresh and salt are indiscriminately eaten. The supply of fish in the waters has decreased of late years. The usual size of the mesh of the nets varies from one-fourth of an inch to 12 inches in circumference. The *Tehsildar of Rajahmundry* observes that the fishermen do not otherwise employ themselves. All except Brahmins, Banians, and some of the goldsmiths, eat fish, about 70,000 in number; the local markets are insufficiently supplied except at certain seasons [when the shad ascend the Godaveri and are stopped at the Dowlaishweram weir.] Fish have decreased of late years. The size of the mesh of the nets is from one-fourth to three inches in circumference. The *Tehsildar of Bhimavaram* states that the fishermen are also employed as cultivators. About 70,000 persons of all castes, except Brahmins, Banians, and a few goldsmiths, eat fish, preferring it fresh. It cannot be ascertained if the fish have increased or decreased, "as every one is allowed to fish as he likes since the abolition of the renting system." The size of the mesh of the nets varies from one-fourth of a rupee to a rupee. Basket and other snares are used in fishing. The *Tehsildar of Tanuku* replies

Opinions of Native officials in the Godaveri Collectorate.

that the Vaddi are the fisherman caste, but Sudras catch fish for their own eating. The fishermen are also cultivators. About 120,000 persons of all castes, except Brahmins, Banians, goldsmiths, and oilmen, eat fish, preferring it salted; the local markets are insufficiently supplied, and the amount in the waters has decreased. The usual size of the mesh of the nets varies from half to two inches in circumference. Basket snares are used for fishing. The *Tehsildar of Peddapuram* answers that the fishermen are also boatmen and coolies. Seven-eighths of the people eat fish, preferring it fresh; the markets are insufficiently supplied, and the amount in the waters has decreased. The minimum size of the mesh of nets employed "will be the size of a red gram" seed. Baskets and snares are used for fishing. The *Tehsildar of Ellur* observes that the fishermen are also palanquin-bearers. About 89,029 persons of all castes, except Brahmins, Banians, oilmen, goldsmiths, and a few Bindilos or Rajputs, eat fish; the markets are not well supplied; salt-fish is preferred to fresh, and of late years the amount of fish in the waters has largely decreased. The size of the mesh of the net is about that of a grain of Bengal or cow gram. Baskets and basket snares are employed in taking fish; some are caught in irrigated fields. The *Tehsildar of Coconada* states the fishermen also act as boatmen. About 50,000 persons eat fish, preferring it fresh; for half the year the markets are well supplied, not so in the other half; the amount in the waters has decreased during the last four years; the circumference of the mesh of the nets equals one-fourth of an anna. Basket or wicker-work snares are employed for fishing. The *Tehsildar of Tuni* replies that the fishermen are also employed as coolies. The local markets are supplied; 39,370 persons of all castes, except Brahmins, Banians, some of the goldsmiths, and the Jungum sect, eat fish, whether fresh or salted. The size of the mesh of the nets equals a pie. The *Tehsildar of Pittapur* answers that the fishermen are also coolies; 69,000 persons eat fish, the Sudras preferring it fresh, whilst the Pariahs, &c., like it salted. The amount in the waters has decreased of late years. Baskets are used for fishing. The *Tehsildar of Yernagudem* observes that the fishermen are also agriculturists and collect lotus leaves (? seeds) from tanks and sell them. About 90,000 persons of all castes, except Brahmins and Banians, eat fish, preferring the salted article. The weekly markets are supplied; the amount in the waters appear to "have increased in former years." The meshes of the nets are half an inch in circumference. Netting, baskets and basket snares are employed. The *Tehsildar of Coringa* states that some of the fishermen have also other trades. About 18,000 persons of all castes, except Brahmins, Banians, and goldsmiths, eat fish, generally preferring it fresh; the local markets are fully supplied, and the amount in the waters has increased of late years. Of the mesh of the nets, the smallest in use would ensnare an ant. Baskets are used in fishing.

174. In the *Kistna Collectorate*, the *Tehsildar of Narsarowpeta* replies that fishermen are also agriculturists;

Opinions of Native officials in the Kistna Collectorate.

very few people eat fish, and they do not care whether it is fresh or salt; the local market is not supplied; the amount in the waters decreased until this year when, owing to large falls of rain, they are again abundant. The *Tehsildar of Bapatla* answers vaguely to the first few questions, continuing that fish have decreased of late years. Nets used for tank-fishing "have meshes of one inch or half inch." Fish baskets, fish snares, and fishing stakes are employed in taking fish. The *Tehsildar of Bunder* observes that the fishermen are also agriculturists and coolies. About 2,000 persons eat fish; the markets are not sufficiently supplied, but generally are so when there is a fair. The amount in the waters are not increasing. The minimum size of the mesh of the nets is one-fourth of an inch. The *Tehsildar of Repalli* replies that the Palla, Mutrachulu, and Besta are fishermen; they also engage in other work. About 600 people eat fish; in fact all castes, except Brahmins, Vysyas, goldsmiths, and carpenters, preferring it, however, fresh. The local markets are never supplied; 10 or 12 baskets of small fish are brought for sale once a week. The minimum size of the mesh of nets is that of the ring finger. The *Tehsildar of Gudewada* observes that fishing baskets, fishing stakes, and snares are employed; water also is dammed up and baled out. The *Tehsildar of Sattenapally* answers that the fishermen only are engaged in this work for a portion of the year; during the remainder they employ themseves in other trades. About 20,000 persons of all castes, except Brahmins, Komaties, and Kamsalies or goldsmiths, eat fish, preferring the salted article. Fish are only brought to market to a small extent; the amount in the waters has decreased of late years; the smallest sized mesh employed is one-tenth of an inch, the largest one inch. A basket snare termed 'Ota,' and a snare called 'Mavu,' are used for fishing. The *Tehsildar of Palnad* observes that the fishermen are likewise agriculturists and coolies; none earn their living by fishing. All castes eat fish, except Brahmins, Komaties, goldsmiths, and Linga Balijalu. The local markets are not sufficiently supplied; the amount in the waters has continued stationary; the usual size of the mesh of the nets is from one pie to a 4-anna piece. Fishing baskets and other wicker snares are employed. The *Tehsildar of Bezwada* replies that the Waddies and Jalars catch fish in the rivers. Persons of all castes, excepting Brahmins, Komaties, Linga Balijis and Kamsalies, eat fish, with which the markets are insufficiently supplied; the fresh is preferred to the salted. The amount in the waters has decreased. The minimum size of the mesh of the nets will admit one finger. [This is incorrect; I have seen nets used there which would not permit a fly to go through.] Basket and wicker-work snares are employed. The *Tehsildar of Guntur* answers that the fishermen are also agriculturists; all castes, with the exceptions previously noted, eat fish, preferring it salted. The markets are very insufficiently supplied, and the amount in the waters has decreased. The smallest mesh of the nets employed is one-fourth of an inch. Baskets are used in fishing. The *Tehsildar of Vinukonda* observes that there are no regular fishing castes, but that agriculturists and others capture fish. About 200 persons of all castes, with the exceptions previously noted, eat fish, preferring it fresh; the markets are not sufficiently supplied; the amount in the waters continues to be stationary. Fishing baskets are employed in this talooka.

175. In the *Nellur Collectorate*, nine *Tehsildars* report that the fishing population employ their time at this occupation when fish are to be had, and at other times act as agriculturists, labourers, palanquin-bearers, coolies, &c., and only a very few live exclusively by

Opinions of Native officials in the Nellur Collectorate.

fishing. The chief time for catching fish is when the water in the tanks is very low, and the labourers have been allowed to capture them in compensation for their performing kudimaramut; whilst by fishing, the water in the tanks becomes filthy and unfit for use. With the exception of Brahmins and Komaties all castes are said to eat fish. In the talookas of Nellur, Ongole, Kandukur, Atmakur, Udayagiri, and Gudur, fresh fish is preferred to the salted; both are indiscriminately used in Kanigiri Rapuru, and Kavali. In all the inland markets the bazars are insufficiently supplied, the amount of which in the fresh waters is said to have considerably decreased. The minimum size of the mesh of nets given is one-fourth of an inch. Fish are generally captured by means of nets, fish-hooks, wire or baskets called 'Kodama,' fishing baskets termed 'Uta,' and sometimes by breaking a fruit called 'Mangakaya', which thrown into the water poisons them. Spearing is also resorted to. In three talookas tanks are reported to be sometimes emptied to obtain the fish.

176. In the *Bellary Collectorate*, the *tehsildars* reply, generally that the Boya are the fishing caste, but they have also other trades. The great majority, of the people, with the exception of the Brahmins and Komaties, eat fish, the demand for which in the markets is always greater than the supply. Traps are reported as used.

Opinions of Native officials in the Bellary Collectorate.

177. From the *Tanjur Collectorate* no answers to the questions for Tehsildars have been forwarded.

Tanjur Collectorate no answers.

178. In the *Trichinopoly Collectorate* five *Tehsildars* answer, the Mavilliars, Valayers, Abulkars, and Lubbays, besides being fishermen, more especially when the water in the reservoirs are low, are also employed as agriculturists and palanquin-bearers. The Sembaders, about 30 in number, in one talookas are stated to be exclusively fishermen. All the people, except Brahmins and the followers of Siva, eat fish; the number in four talookas who do so is estimated at 557,682, and the fifth, 15-16ths of the population. In two, fish is indiscriminately eaten, whether fresh or salted; in two, the fresh is preferred; in the remaining one the salted article. In three the markets are stated to be insufficiently supplied. The amount in the fresh waters has decreased in four districts, and increased in one. The minimum size of the mesh of the nets employed is given as a grain of dholl in one, half an inch in another talooka. Basket traps are used for taking fish, also baited pots. Poisoning the water by means of the milk hedge is reported as obtaining in three of the talookas, but is not resorted to in the other two.

Opinions of Native officials in the Trichinopoly Collectorate.

179. From the *Cuddapah Collectorate* no answers to the questions for Tehsildars have been forwarded.

Cuddapah Collectorate, no answers.

180. In the *Kurnal Collectorate* seven *Tehsildars* report that Bestas, Boyas, Telugus, most of the low caste Hindus and Mussulmen fish, but they also have other occupations, as agricultural labourers, palanquin-bearers, &c. All the people, except Brahmins, Visyas, Komaties, Linga Balijas, blacksmiths, carpenters, and a few others, are

Opinions of Native officials in the Kurnal Collectorate.

said to eat fish, the number of whom in six talookas is estimated at 390,389 persons; in six fresh fish are preferred, in one the salted article. The local markets, except that of the town of Kurnal, are said, by those who have answered this question, to be insufficiently supplied, whilst the amount in the waters is reported as stationary by three, and decreased by four. The *Tehsildar of Ramalkota* observes that " after the construction of the anicut (weir) at Sunkesula, and the opening of the irrigation canal, wages have so greatly risen at and near Kurnal, and the fishes in the river have so perceptibly diminished, that fishing has become, more or less, a secondary occupation. Bearing palanquins and working on the irrigation canal for hire form their chief occupation. The fish have undoubtedly decreased since the construction of the anicut in 1861. Their ascent during the spawning season is barred by the anicut, and they are captured in roe, just below it, at Kontalapad and the villages of the Nizam situated on the opposite bank. It is therefore asserted by all the fishermen of whom I have enquired that the river stock has considerably decreased of late years, except, of course, at Kontalapad, where the fishes are now caught in comparatively greater numbers than before, in the Madugus (deep holes) in the river to which they return after repeated attempts to get over the anicut, and also at the sluices. The Curnum of Kontalapad assures me that in the best fishing season there are not more than eight or ten men who go out fishing." The usual size of the mesh of the nets is variously given from that of a grain of dholl, or Bengal gram, or tamarind seed, or pepper corn, or one-eighth of an inch to the size of the thumb or larger. Fishing baskets and wicker traps are stated to be employed. He subsequently suggested that nets and traps ought to have holes large enough for a 2-anna piece to go through (six-tenths of an inch in diameter). The *Tehsildar of Markapur* observes that small fish are caught during the rainy season, in the supply channels, and in the calingulahs when the water runs a span deep, a conical shaped net, ' Kodimay,' is kept against the current, constructed with small split bamboos, having holes large enough for a big black ant to pass through. Its mouth is covered in a similar manner with fine split bamboos inwardly woven, leaving a space to allow the fish enter; once in, they cannot return. It becomes filled with small fish if kept for about three hours in the water. The size of the smallest mesh of nets is equal to that of a grain of Bengal gram. The ' Udu' or conical basket is employed for capturing breeding fish as they are seen ascending into irrigated fields.

181. In the *Chingleput Collectorate* six *Tehsildars* report that in some places the fishermen do not follow any other occupation, but, as a rule, they are also agriculturists, palanquin-bearers, boatmen, coolies, and petty traders and artizans. All the people, excepting Brahmins, Komaties, Jains, Sivites, and a few others, eat fish, the numbers being computed at 694,147 persons; salt or fresh are indiscriminately taken in three, but fresh are preferred in two. The markets in the vicinity of the sea are stated to be well supplied, whilst the amount in the fresh-waters is asserted to have decreased in all the talookas. [Since this was written, the *Acting Collector* (April 18th, 1872) has reported that the Native officials assert that the supply of fish remains stationary, but

Opinions of Native officials in the Chingleput Collectorate.

that it should be noted that all tanks and rivers are dry during the hot season.] The minimum size of the mesh of the nets employed is given by one Tehsildar as equal to a grain of gram, another as one-sixteenth of an inch, and by two at one-eighth of an inch. Baskets or basket traps are spoken of as existing in four talookas, poisoning of the waters to obtain fish in three, and doubtful in a fourth.

182. In the *Salem Collectorate* the three *Sub-Magistrates* or *Tehsildars* observe that all persons who engage in fishing have other occupations as well.

Opinions of Native officials in the Salem Collectorate.

All the people, excepting Brahmins, Komaties, and a few others, eat fish, the numbers in two talookas being estimated at 250,000, and in the third at four-fifths of the population. The fresh is preferred to the salted. The markets are sufficiently supplied in one, small quantities are sold in another, whilst in the remaining talooka sufficient is not obtainable. The amount in the waters is stationary in one district, whilst it has decreased in the other two. The minimum size of the meshes employed are from one-fourth to half an inch. Baskets are reported as employed for taking fish, and poisoning of the waters for this purpose as resorted too at Oossoor.

183. From the *North Arcot Collectorate* no answers to the questions for Tehsildars have been forwarded.

North Arcot Collectorate, no answers.

184. In the *South Arcot Collectorate* the replies appear to be from one *Tehsildar*, who has also answered the queries put to Collectors. He observes that there is a tax annually which includes fish, grass, and the other productions of tanks which is charged to the village in a lump sum, and paid by the village community in certain specified shares. Fish are caught as soon as bred, and not allowed to remain for any length of time; large and small are indiscriminately taken; the mesh of the nets being as small as one-eighth of an inch in diameter. How much soever fresh fish is brought to the markets meets a ready sale, but it does not keep long in this country, but putrefies within a few hours of its capture, more especially the smaller kinds. The fishermen are Pullies, who are known as Shemdavars; they are agriculturists, and fishing is a subsidiary occupation. About 90 per cent. of the people eat fish, the Brahmins, Sivites, and Jains excepted; the fresh is most esteemed; the supply is quite inadequate to the demand; the amount in the waters has decreased.

South Arcot opinions of Native officials.

185. In the *Tinnevelli Collectorate* eight *Tehsildars* report as follows:—The chief castes that fish in the fresh waters are Savalakarars, Paravars, and Lubbays, but they all have other occupations, as agriculturists, coolies, arrack-distillers, musicians, &c. The majority of the people, excepting Brahmins and high-caste Sudras, eat fish, the amount being computed in seven talookas at 800,685 persons, and in the remaining talookas at three-fourths of the population. Fish is preferred to fresh; in six talookas the markets are insufficiently supplied; in two sufficiently; a decrease of the amount in the waters is reported in four talookas, an increase in three; no distinct answer in the remaining one. The minimum size of the mesh of the nets varies from the size of a grain

Opinions of Native officials in the Tinnevelli Collectorate.

of dholl to one-eighth, one-fourth, half an inch up to one inch. Wickerwork traps and bamboo labyrinth weirs appear to be generally employed, and the poisoning of water by tobacco and other substances for the purpose of obtaining fish is reported by two Tehsildars.

186. In the *Madura Collectorate* the answers from the Tehsildars are given as follows (May 17th, 1872).

<small>Opinions of Native officials in the Madura Collectorate.</small>

There are very few professional fishermen in the district, except in the town of Madura, but all have other occupations. The local markets in large towns are not fully supplied with fish, and at certain seasons they are very scarce. During the season the supply in many villages is sufficient, but more could always be sold in the larger towns; 80 per cent. of the people eat fish. The amount in the waters has continued stationary of late years. Very small ones are caught in considerable quantities, chiefly in baskets. The minimum size of the meshes of nets is about half an inch in circumference. Fish are not generally trapped in irrigated fields during the rains. They are caught in baskets of two kinds. In shallow water, when tanks are drying, they are baled out in various ways.

187. In the *Coimbatore Collectorate*, the replies from ten *Tehsildars* are as follows:—The fishermen, as a rule,

<small>Opinions of Native officials in the Coimbatore Collectorate.</small>

have other occupations, the exceptions being that 40 families in the Dharapuram talooka, 100 in the Perindoray talooka, only employ themselves in fishing, whilst in Coimbatore 156 fishermen also act as palanquin-bearers. The majority of the people, excepting Brahmins, Komaties, Sivachars, and high-caste Sudras, eat fish, the amount being estimated at 11,37,924 persons; it is preferred fresh in seven talookas, it is immaterial in two; whilst in one it is stated the Hindus prefer it fresh, the Mahomedans salted. [*The Acting Collector* (February 4th, 1871) observed, "another point which I think has been lost sight of, is, that the consumption of fresh fish by the people of the country, as compared with that of salt-fish, is exceedingly small." But that such is *a fact* does not appear to be coincided with by the native officials. That it is more largely consumed may be at times due to the absence of fresh-water fishes owing to the wasteful destruction which now appears to be existing, apparently due to an absence of proper precautionary measures.] In one talooka the local market is stated to be sufficiently supplied, in the remaining nine that they are not so, or else that more could be disposed of if brought. The amount of fish in the waters is said to have decreased in six talookas, remained stationary in two, increased in one, and no definite answer is given from the remaining Tehsildar. The meshes of the nets employed appear to vary from one-eighth of an inch upwards; basket traps are reported as in use for fishing, and poisoning of the water in order to obtain the fish as noted by seven out of the ten Tehsildars. In Suttimungalum it is observed of the Bhowany river that the fish die when the water is mixed with the mud to a large extent as during the monsoons, and due to this cause large fish are scarce. This was also reported upon by Mr. P. Grant, a former Collector; it also occurs in Malabar, and the mixing of mud with water is stated to be employed in order to facilitate the capture of fish.

188. In the *Malabar Collectorate* the reply of a *Sub-Collector*, apparently who has not seen the questions circulated, has been received. He observes, "so far am I from thinking that any steps should be taken to prevent the destruction of fish in these rivers, that I am of opinion it would greatly benefit the country if Government took steps to procure superior engines for their capture, and instruct the people in the use of them." [From personal observations I can endorse the former Acting Collector's views that the most minute fry are destroyed by every poaching practice in Malabar. Perhaps it is intended to mean that the supply is very deficient, the markets being insufficiently supplied, surely such would be a reason for some remedial measures being employed.] Poisoning of the waters occurs in Malabar.

<small>Answer of a Sub-Collector in Malabar.</small>

189. From the *South Canara Collectorate* no answers from the Native officials have been received, but Mr. Thomas' reports are so full as to leave but little to be desired on that head.

<small>South Canara, no answers.</small>

MYSORE AND COORG.

190. In the elevated table-land of Mysore and the hilly district of Coorg exist some fairly-sized rivers, and many more which in comparison may be termed streams. Besides these in Mysore there are a considerable number of lakes and large tanks that rarely dry up, and many of a smaller size, estimated at 20,000, which, either during the hot months or on the occasion of any considerable drought, become entirely or nearly dry.

Fresh-water fisheries in Mysore and Coorg.

191. *Respecting the numbers of the population who eat fish?* they are reported to be as follows :—In the Nundidrug division two-thirds, Astragam half; in Hassam district 95 per cent., Chituldrug 55, Shimoga 65, Kadoor 50; whilst in Coorg they are computed at three-fourths of the population. In short, it may be fairly assumed that at least half the people of Mysore and Coorg are fish-eaters, when they are able to secure this species of food.

At least half the people of Mysore and Coorg are fish-eaters.

192. *As to whether the markets are sufficiently or insufficiently supplied with fish?* the following are the reports in the Nundidrug division : local markets near large reservoirs are fairly supplied so long as the water lasts. In the Astragam division six markets are stated to be insufficiently supplied, and four others to be well supplied. In Hassam the markets in six of the talookas are insufficiently supplied, and in one only is it sufficient. There is an insufficient supply of fresh fish in all the markets in the Nagar and Coorg districts, but in the latter salt-fish are imported from the coast. In short, a generally insufficient supply of fresh fish obtains in the markets of Mysore and Coorg.

Markets generally are insufficiently supplied with fish.

193. *Respecting whether the amount of fish in the rivers and tanks have increased, decreased, or remained stationary?* In two of the Mysore divisions they are reported by all the amildars to have decreased of late years owing to the drought, whilst in the third division the majority of the native officials give a similar report, and the remainder assert that they have remained stationary. This question appears to have been overlooked in Coorg. It appears, however, that in all but a few talookas, wherein the supply is stationary, the amount of fish in the rivers and tanks is reported to have decreased.

Fish are decreasing.

194. *The fishermen* who only pursue that trade seem to be few, but those who fish in addition to other avocations appear to be very numerous. In Nundidrug these are computed at two-thirds of the population, nearly every ryot keeping a net to be employed as occasion or opportunity arises. In the Astragam division, Hassam, and Nagar they are given at 171,359, but

Fishermen also follow other occupations.

they also engage in other occupations; whilst in Coorg all the ryots are said to fish more or less, but none are strictly fishermen.

195. *Respecting whether mature breeding fish or immature fry are destroyed to any great extent?* If one looks at the reports of the whole of the officials, one cannot help observing that fish are taken in every possible mode without regard to breeding season or the size of the immature fish, even down to the fry when they are just moving about. Nets with very small meshes appear to be universally employed. In the Nundidrug and Astragam divisions the size between knot and knot of the meshes is given at one-sixteenth of an inch; in Nagar that its minimum size will not permit the smallest fish to escape; in Coorg that the meshes are so small as to allow only the water to pass through; whilst weirs, spanning streams and rivers, as well as poisoning waters, is freely resorted to. (See Report of Collector of South Canara, para. 169.)

Breeding fish and fry are extensively destroyed.

196. The modes of fishing employed may be summed up as reported by the amildars of the Nagar division, by nets, traps, hooks, cloths, and by hand; by baskets of different shapes, by damming and draining off the water, by shooting, by striking with clubs, with swords or with choppers, by weirs and fixed engines; in short, by poaching practices of every kind, as well as by fishing with rods and lines, and by poisoining the pools of water.

Every poaching mode of fishing pursued.

197. Considering that at least half the population of this district eat fish when they can obtain it, that the markets are insufficiently supplied, and the fish are decreasing; taking also into consideration that the fishermen only pursue this avocation, as a rule, in addition to their ordinary occupations, that in Coorg the whole of the ryots are said to be fishermen, and in Nundidrug that nearly every ryot keeps a net to be used as occasion or opportunity arises, whilst breeding fish and fry are indiscriminately slaughtered by nets or traps with the smallest meshes or interstices, the next consideration is whether it is worth while to do anything.

Conclusions from the reports.

198. There appear to be two classes of localities where fishing is carried on: *firstly*, those tanks which dry up at certain seasons of the year, and in which the fish would only die if not captured; *secondly*, rivers, running streams, and such of the large tanks as retain a supply of water throughout the year.

Localities where fishing is carried on.

199. *Firstly*, tanks that dry up. It seems to be assumed that, under the above circumstances, no regulations should be applicable to the small tanks that yearly dry up, as the fish in them must die, or be eaten by lower animals, if not captured by man. A little difficulty appears to have escaped notice, that if nets, with the most minute meshes, are permitted in these places, the excuse for their possession would always be that they were only kept for tank-fishing; in fact, such could hardly be interdicted. So long also as these tanks possess water communications with rivers, streams, or large tanks, the small fish can obtain an exit to where they could grow. Practically speaking, it is of course but little use prohibiting fishing in any way people choose in tanks

Fisheries which have no perennial supply of water.

that yearly dry up, and *after all water communications between them and the second class of waters* (now to be referred to) *has naturally ceased*, provided such would not create a difficulty as regards regulating the size of the mesh of nets throughout the country (by allowing the existence of those of minute size,) supposing it is considered advisable to do so.

200. *Secondly*, with respect to regulating the modes employed in fishing in rivers, running streams, and such of the large tanks as retain a supply of water throughout the year.

Fisheries in which a perennial supply of water exists.

The Chief Commissioner observes that the right of fishing in a few of the large tanks has been already brought under regulation with satisfactory results. As regards this second description of pieces of water, no objections are raised by any one against regulating the size of the meshes of nets, etc., and the prohibition against standing weirs and poisoning the water. Likewise of the five who answer the question as to whether any objections exist against prohibiting the sale of the fry of fish in the bazar, they appear to see no difficulty in it. Respecting fence-months during the commencement of the monsoon in the hilly districts in order to prevent the destruction of breeding fish, this also appears to be called for, especially in Coorg and the hill ranges.

201. The "Officiating Secretary" to the *Chief Commissioner of Mysore and Coorg* observes that the Chief Commissioner is disposed to think that the suggestion made to revive the practice of farming out the right of fishing is not undeserving of consideration, as regards rivers and running streams, and such of the large tanks as retain a supply of water throughout the year, and that the erection or use of barriers to prevent fish passing up and down the running streams should be altogether interdicted. But with regard to the larger number of tanks in Mysore that dry up at certain seasons of the year, estimated at upwards of 20,000, Colonel Mead is of opinion that the case is different, and does not require consideration in connection with the question at issue, and that these tanks might be left without any rules being framed for the regulation of their fisheries. It may be added that the right of fishing in a few of the larger tanks has been already brought under regulation with satisfactory results.

Opinion of the Chief Commissioner of Mysore.

202. The *Superintendent of the Nundidrug Division* observes that, as tanks and channels become dry, small fish in large quantities are taken in baskets and nets, the smallest mesh of which is one-twelfth of an inch; that as only a few tanks retain water during the dry weather, it is of no use regulating the size of the meshes to be employed. There would be no difficulty in prohibiting the sale of fry in bazars if such a measure is thought proper.

Opinion of the Superintendent of Nundidrug.

203 The *Deputy Superintendent of the Bangalur District* considers that very small fish and breeding ones are not destroyed to any large extent, but that, when tanks discharge during the rains, young fish are caught by means of baskets and closely-meshed nets. They are also taken during the irrigation season in the channels for water. The mesh of the nets is stated to be about the size of coarse

Opinion of the Deputy Superintendent of Bangalur.

mosquito curtains; there would be no difficulty in regulating it; but he considers it would not be of much use, as the little fish would get into the fields and die, or be eaten by birds, but the smallest size he proposes for tank-fishing is half an inch. If selling the fry of fish is prohibited, it is surmised the catchers would eat them themselves, to the loss of the fish-eating community of towns, whilst accustomed means of livelihood and food-supply should not be lightly interfered with.

204. *Colonel Puckle*, in a report to the Chief Commissioner (July 17th, 1869), observed, respecting the fish market at Bangalur, that large-sized fish are often bought by the European community at a dearer rate per pound than butcher's meat, and that the natives buy large numbers of small carps for the merest trifle, amongst which are always a considerable quantity of the immature fish of a large kind. That netting goes on all the year round. Drag, wall, cast, and purse-nets of every size of mesh are used, and in some of them it is so small as to resemble a coarse mosquito curtain; whilst, owing to their indiscriminate use and other poaching practices, the food-supply is out of all proportion to the natural fecundity of the fish.

<small>Opinion of Colonel Puckle.</small>

205. In the *Nagar Division*, the *Deputy Superintendent of the Shimoga District* reports that breeding fish and very young ones are not destroyed to any great extent. The minimum size of the mesh of nets is so small that even spawn of fish is taken. There are no objections against prohibiting the sale of the fry of fish in the bazars. The *Deputy Superintendent of the Chituldrug District* observes that there are not many tanks or reservoirs wherein large numbers of fish are to be found, but of the few that are to be found, the fishermen as well as other classes catch indiscriminately fish of all sizes, both for home consumption and for sale. Most fish are taken during the hot season, when the tanks and pools are becoming dry: damming and draining off the water is employed for this purpose. The smallest size of the mesh of the nets employed is one-eighth of an inch in diameter. No difficulties exist in regulating the minimum legal size of the meshes to be employed, but does not anticipate any benefit following such a course; neither are there any objections against prohibiting the sale of the fry of fish in the bazars. The *Deputy Superintendent of the Kadoor District* considers that breeding fish and very young ones are destroyed to a great extent. Dams are constructed across rivers and channels where the water collects, and also in natural pools in the rivers. Fishing is carried on at all times during the hot weather; also in irrigated fields fine wicker baskets are placed at the outlets, so as to take the smallest fish. The nets generally employed have a mesh of half an inch. There appears to be no difficulty in regulating the minimum size of the mesh of nets to be employed in future, and one inch between the knots is proposed for this purpose. No objection seems to exist against prohibiting the sale of the fry of fishes in the bazars, or forbidding the destruction of breeding fishes during the first two months of the monsoon in the hilly ranges.

<small>Opinions of European officials in the Nagar Division.</small>

206. The *Deputy Superintendent of the Tumkur District* says, a great number of fish are destroyed, but the quantity of breeding fish and young ones amongst these cannot be ascertained. When

<small>Opinion of the Deputy Superintendent of Tumkur.</small>

the tanks are low, fishermen employ a particular kind of basket, as well as nets, the smallest size of the mesh of which is one-eighth of an inch square. There would be no difficulty in regulating the size of the mesh, and he proposes one-eighth of an inch for small fish, one inch for the second kind, and from an inch and a half to two inches for the largest size. As regards prohibiting the sale of the fry of fish scarcely any objections exist, but some of the poorer classes will suffer by being prohibited from selling it.

207. The *Deputy Superintendent of the Kolar District* observes that breeding and young fish are destroyed to a great extent, except in private wells, where they are taken care of by the owners. The principal times when young fish become destroyed are when tanks overflow in the rains or dry up during the hot months. The smallest size of the mesh of nets used is about one-twelfth of an inch. As the tanks are shallow and periodically dry up, regulating the size of the mesh of the nets is considered to be unnecessary. As regards prohibiting for the first two months of the monsoon the capture of breeding fish in the hilly regions, he sees no objection to it "if arrangements can be made to provide means of livelihood to those living upon fishing solely."

Opinion of the Deputy Superintendent of Kolar.

208. In the *Nundidrug Division* the reports of the *Amildars* are condensed. About two-thirds of the population are stated to fish occasionally in addition to their other occupations. Nearly every ryot keeps a net to be used as occasion or opportunity arises. The professional fishermen are few in number, and all pursue other occupations, except near Bangalur, where their time is well occupied in supplying the large local demand. The Besturs, Palligars, Voklagars, and Tighurs are the regular fishing castes. The local markets in proximity to large reservoirs are fairly supplied, but the supply fails as reservoirs dry up; and except for large towns like Bangalur, or where there are the headquarters of a district, the people principally fish for their own consumption. Nearly all classes eat fish when they can procure it, or when it happens to be cheap. The amount of fish depends upon the quantity of water, as when the latter is plentiful, the fish multiply extremely rapidly. The smallest size of the mesh of the nets is given at one-sixteenth of an inch. During the rains the practice of trapping fish is almost universal. Every form of net, snare, and basket are used, but poisoning the water is never resorted to.

Opinions of the Native officials of the Nundidrug Division.

209. In the *Astragam Division* the *Amildars* report that the amount of fishermen in the various talookas is 36,448, but fishing is not the only occupation of the number of people above enumerated, as they also engage in agriculture, commerce, etc. The fishermen castes consist of Besturs, Thorayer and Oopaligur, as well as Mussulmen. The markets of the talookas of Mysore, Chamrajnugger, Astragam, Pariapatna, Heggadadevenkote, and Nanjengode are not fully supplied, whilst those of Mallavelly, Gundlupete, Yedatori, and Muddur are well supplied. The proportion of the fish-eating population is given at above half (444,011 out of 756,041). In some places the fish have

Opinions of Native officials in the Astragam Division.

decreased owing to the droughts, whilst in others they have remained stationary. All the Amildars report that a great quantity of small fish are caught during the rainy season by means of different kinds of nets, rods and lines, and baskets prepared for this purpose which are made with the fronds of the cocoanut palm; these have large open mouths, whilst their floor is covered by means of a lattice work of strings; they are placed against a current of water which, rushing in, passes through the interstices, leaving the fish deposited in the basket. They all likewise give the smallest mesh of the nets at one-sixteenth of an inch. The different modes of fishing are rods and lines and baskets. The following are the native names of every form of net in use: Beesoobalay, Yelabalay, Thadalabalay, Seegadibalay, Bidubalay, Thadubalay, Gooroobalay, Urjoonabalay, Hayabalay, Kybalay, Elappanabalay.

210. In the *Hassan District* the *Amildars* report that the fishermen are generally known as Bestharoo; they trade and cultivate besides, whilst their numbers are recorded as 128,239, exclusive of Manjarabad, where it could not be ascertained. The names of the fisherman castes given are Bestharoo, Byadaru, Vakaligaru, Wooparroo, Koramaru, Telugaru, Agasaru (Dhoby), Mussulmen, Myadam, Madigaru, Holiaru, Koorabara, Waddaru, Voolitigalaru, Edigara, Dasrees, Lumbanee, Swalparu, Jabataru, Jengalarm, Landroo, Ganigaru (Oilmongers), Karachooneha, Koombarroo, Kalikarroo, Goller Bylakisalaru, Native Christians, Teliga Hajamer (Barbers), Jettiroo, Devarroo Tigalaru, and Koracharu—Devangadavaru Gijjegaru, Jelagaroo. The Amildars of Harukalli, Magamangala, Maharajendurga, Narsipura, Bailuru, and Arhalagudu, state the bazars are insufficiently supplied with fish, but in Hassan only is the supply sufficient. Salt-fish is also imported from Mangalore, but not in large enough quantities for the demand. The population of fish-eaters is given at about 95 per cent. (404,807 out of 422,539). The Amildars universally say fish are decreasing owing to drought. Breeding fish are trapped in the irrigation channels during the rains, and also in some localities in the paddy-fields as well. They are likewise poisoned by earagooli, date-thorn, eachel moolloo, and gorway. They are also taken by the Sigadi net (for small fish), Harajana net, Beesa net, Aga net, Balla net, Bida net, Gorkooli, Barjakooli, Grankooli, Sumrakooli gana, Kolu Kolli, Karay Kayee, Balu Goomkay leaves, cooked leaves of Sawe, Kodamay net, Gana dadee net, Kadala net, small Kooli, Baju bees net, Katoo net, Serpent net, Golaga net, and hooks.

Opinions of Native officials in the Hassan District.

211. The *Amildars in the Nagar District* report that the numbers of fishermen aggregate 6,672, but they carry on other trades, as manufacturers of chunam, whilst there are also boatmen and bearers amongst them. The fishermen castes are 'Bestur,' and likewise others are termed Gungemakalso, Koboligaroo, Haloy Bhoees, and Kabbaru. The markets are insufficiently supplied with fish, partly due to a want of rain and partly to a want of rest for the fisheries. The proportion of the fish-eating population is about 55 per cent. in the Chituldrug District, 65 per cent. in Shimoga, and 50 per cent. in Kadoor. Fish are decreasing owing to the absence of rain, and are captured by means of hooks, different forms of traps, and by placing funnel-shaped

Opinions of the Native officials in the Nagar District.

bamboo baskets in streams and waste weirs of tanks; small purse-shaped nets are also employed. The minimum size of the mesh of the nets used will not permit the smallest ones to escape. Fish are trapped in the irrigated fields during the rains. The modes of fishing are as follows; by nets, traps, hooks, cloths, and by hand; by baskets of different shapes; by damming and draining off the water; by shooting, striking with clubs, with swords or choppers; in short, by poaching practices of every kind, as well as by fishing with rods and lines, and by poisoning the pools until the fish float to the surface of the water.

212. The *Amildars of Coorg* report that nearly all the ryots fish more or less, none are strictly fishermen, but these last are known as Boyees or Besturs (bearers). The bazars are insufficiently supplied with fresh fish, but fully with dried ones from the coast. The price of a seer (weighing $27\frac{1}{2}$ rupees) of large fish is two annas, of small ones half an anna, of a seer of first sort of mutton (weighing 80 rupees) 6 annas, for second sort 5 annas. Three-fourths of the people eat fish. During September, October, and November, large quantities of small fish are captured, whilst the meshes of some of the nets are so small as to allow only the water to pass through. During the rains breeding fish are trapped in the irrigated fields. One mode of fishing pursued is by throwing a jungle fruit about the size and shape of a green walnut into the rivers and streams. The effect of this is to stupefy the fish, and they come up to the surface and turn on their backs, when they are easily caught. This practice has been strictly prohibited, and is not now openly carried on. The nets are called Cunneebale, Beesoobale, Jadibale, and Goribale, whilst the traps are termed " Coolies" and " Podas."

Opinions of the Native officials in Coorg.

HAIDARABAD.

213. In the Assigned Districts the rivers are not of any large size, whilst the constant droughts of the last few years are considered to have done much to impoverish such fisheries as exist in these smaller rivers and tanks.

Fisheries in the Haidarabad Assigned Districts.

214. *The proportion of people who eat fish if they can obtain it* is thus given by the various Tehsildars:—in Buldana nine-tenths, in Bassim two-thirds, in Akola one-third, in Amraote and Mortizapur one-quarter, and in Woon at seven per cent; these figures clearly showing that fish as food is esteemed by a very large proportion of the residents.

Fish esteemed by a large proportion of the population.

215. *As to how the markets are supplied with fish?* Seven native officials assert that they are insufficiently so; and only the Tehsildar of Bassim that the "weekly markets" are well supplied, but that probably more could be sold, conclusively demonstrating that the market supplies do not equal the demands.

Markets insufficiently supplied.

216. *Whether the fish have increased, decreased, or remained stationary?* There is only one opinion, which is that they have decreased.

Amount in the water decreasing.

217. *As regards whose these fisheries are?* In West Berar, it is stated that fishing rights do not exist, for under a ryotwari settlement all fisheries are common property, indeed belong to Government, and there do not appear to be any village tanks where the right of reserved fishing could be claimed.

Fisheries Government property.

218. *The fishermen,* or the class who mostly indulge in it, are the Bhoees and sub-divisions of that caste, numbering in the eight Tehsildarships 8,289 persons, most of whom, however, pursue other occupations.

Fishermen have, as a rule, other occupations.

219. *Respecting whether breeding fish and fry are destroyed* but one opinion appears to prevail, namely, that they are, in every possible way, although in some districts trapping is reported not to exist, and fry only to be taken in small quantities; but as from the same districts it is stated that stopping the sale of fry would be a little unpopular amongst fishermen and fish-eaters, it seems very evident that the amount captured cannot be very small.

Breeding fish and fry destroyed to a great extent.

220. If we examine the various minimum sizes of the meshes of the nets employed, we find the six Deputy Commissioners report as follows:—In two they are too small to be measured, in one one-eleventh of an inch, in one three-eighths, in one one-eighth, in one one-third of an inch between knot and knot of the meshes.

Smallest meshes of nets used.

221. Trapping fish is reported by two Tehsildars; one observes that this does not take place in his district, but on this point the others are silent. Snares appear, however, to be universally in use. Damming and lading out, or poisoning pieces of water in order to obtain the contained fish, is almost universal.

Trapping and snaring, damming up and lading out waters, as well as poisoning them, is reported.

222. *As regards prohibiting the sale of fry in the bazars,* the Deputy Commissioner of Akola considers it would be difficult to discriminate which were the fry; on that head alone he would rather regulate the mesh of the nets. In Buldana it is considered that at first it would be unpopular, but the advantages of this restriction would soon make themselves apparent to all; in the other districts that no difficulties exist, except that it would temporarily decrease the gains of persons who make a livelihood by catching fry during the rains.

But little difficulty would exist in prohibiting the sale of fry in the bazars.

223. The following opinions have been advanced respecting whether there is or is not a necessity for a measure of protection to be afforded to the fish. The Officiating Commissioner, West Berar, considers there is nothing to prevent the imposition of rules for the preservation of the immature and breeding fish, and that some of a general kind are called for. In Akola it is doubted whether it would be worth while to legislate on these points, as fish are so scarce; but there would be no difficulty in regulating the size of the meshes of the nets. The other five Deputy Commissioners observe that there would be no difficulty in such regulations.

Opinion as to whether protective measures are required.

224. As rules of a general kind appear to be desired, the next question is, *how would such affect the fishermen classes?* The Commissioner of West Berar observes, "whatever restrictions may be imposed, no class of people will be so affected as to interfere with their means of livelihood, nor does any portion of the community depend on fish as an article of food; therefore remedial measures found necessary will not even be hard or distressing to any class of people." This opinion, however, varies from some of the Deputy Commissioners who consider that if fence-months were introduced, some of the fishermen would be put to great hardships.

How would rules affect the fishing classes.

225. As regards the minimum size of the mesh of the nets that should in future be permitted, four of the officials consider that it should not be less than one inch between the knot and knot of the meshes, and one that the minimum size should be 1¼ inches.

Proposals regarding the minimum size of meshes of nets that should be allowed.

226. These reports appear to show, (1) that a considerable proportion of the people would eat fish could they obtain it; (2) that the markets are insufficiently supplied; (3) that the amount of fish in the rivers and tanks is decreasing; (4) that the fisheries are Government property; (5) that the fishermen, as a class, have other avocations as

Conclusions from the following reports.

well; (6) that mature breeding fish and the immature ones are destroyed at all seasons of the year and in every possible way; (7) that nets with very minute meshes are employed; (8) that fish are trapped in some districts and snared in all; (9) that waters are dammed, laded out, and even poisoned in order to take the fish; (10) that there would be no difficulty in prohibiting the sale of the fry of fish in the bazars; (11) that some protection to the fish is called for; (12) that such would not affect the fishermen to any appreciable extent unless fence-months were instituted; (13) but that these appear to be necessary in the hilly districts during the first two months of the monsoon; (14) that the minimum size of the meshes of the nets should be one inch between knot and knot; (15) that the poisoning of waters to obtain fish should be prohibited.

227. The necessity of fence-months in the rivers of the hilly districts during the commencement of the monsoons when large fish ascend for breeding purposes appears to be apparent. "This is," one Deputy Commissioner observes, " the best fishing season," the breeding fish in fact at this period easily falling victims to the most clumsy contrivances.

Fence-months.

228. Poisoning waters to obtain the fish is universally condemned.

Poisoning waters condemned.

229. The *Second Assistant Resident,* Haidarabad, remarks that the class chiefly devoted to fishing in this part of India are the Bhoees, who do not, however, confine themselves to this occupation only, but seek their living also as domestic servants, and monopolize what remains in this part of India of the work of palkee-bearing. Throughout the Assigned Districts fishing is pursued free from any restrictions, and all sorts of fish are indiscriminately captured in all possible ways.

Opinion of the Second Assistant Resident.

230. The *Officiating Commissioner,* West Berar, reports that as fishing is quite unrestricted, every sort of fish is captured in every possible manner, and those too small for use are thrown away. The class chiefly concerned in fishing are the Bhoees, but the trade is inconsiderable, and they pursue other occupations. Moreover, other classes also engage in it when the fish are sufficiently plentiful to attract them. It follows, that whatever restrictions may be imposed, no class of people will be so affected as to interfere with their means of livelihood, nor does any portion of the community depend on fish as an article of food, therefore any remedial measures found necessary will not even be hard or distressing to any class of people. Further, fishing rights do not exist, for under a ryotwari settlement all fisheries are common property, indeed belong properly to Government, and there does not appear to be any village tanks where the right of reserved fishing could be claimed. Hence there is nothing to prevent the imposition of rules for the preservation of the immature or breeding fish, and some of a general kind are called for under the state of things exhibited in these reports. The rules proposed are, (1) the prohibition of fishing during July and August, and if need be also September; (2) the interdiction of the use of nets with the knots of the meshes nearer together than one inch; (3) declaring it illegal to poison the water with the object of killing the fish.

Opinion of the Officiating Commissioner, West Berar.

231. The *Deputy Commissioner of the Akola District* observes, the evils alluded to by Dr. Day exist in this district equally with other parts of India. There being, however, no large lakes or rivers, the amount of harm done is proportionately less. Breeding fish and very young ones are destroyed so far as it can be made to repay the trouble expended, but not being plentiful, what is not worth catching elsewhere is worth something here; thus being a luxury, and not a staple article of food, it fetches a high price. They are destroyed in every way, at all places and in all seasons, and considering the great drought of the last and those of preceding years, which must have had a direct effect in diminishing the quantity of fish in these rivers and streams, and the numbers yearly caught by snares, nets, poisoning, &c., the only wonder is how any fish have survived. There are no orders respecting the size of the mesh of nets, and they are used as small as one-eleventh of an inch, but there could be no difficulty in regulating their size. As it would be difficult to discriminate fry of fish, he would rather its sale were not prohibited, but that the size of the mesh of nets were regulated. Poisoning fish he proposes should be unlawful, and fishing should be stopped in certain months. "To carry out these two methods no establishment would be necessary; but it remains an open question whether it is worth the trouble to introduce legislation on these points in a country like Berar where fish is so scarce." As regards the question whether there are any objections against prohibiting the capture of fish in the hilly districts for the first two months of the monsoon season when they are breeding, he replies, "Not that I know of, except that this is the best fishing season in this district."

Opinion of the Deputy Commissioner of Akola.

232. The *Deputy Commissioner of the Buldana District* reports that breeding and young fish are not destroyed to any great extent. The smallest size of the mesh of the nets employed is one-third of an inch; there are no difficulties against regulating it authoritatively, and there ought to be 1½ inches between knot and knot. As regards prohibiting the sale of the fry of fish in the bazars, he continues that such might be a little unpopular amongst fishermen and fish-eaters, but the advantages of this restriction would soon make themselves apparent to all. Also as to taking breeding fish in hilly districts during the first two months of the monsoon, he remarks it would cause the temporary loss of employment to those who fish at this season, but they would soon learn to regard the restriction as a wise one and become reconciled to it.

Opinion of the Deputy Commissioner of Buldana.

233. The *Assistant Commissioner in charge of the Bassim District* observes that owing to the great want of rain, all the tanks of the district have dried up; many of them were full of large fish, all of which have been entirely destroyed. Such a drought has not been known in the memory of man. Cart-loads of fish have been carried away, and it will take years to re-stock the tanks. These remarks also apply more or less to the rivers. Most of the tanks are but small, but there are the remains of very large ones in the district which might be repaired and restored at a small expense, affording irrigation to a considerbale quantity of land, and consequently would be very remunerative if

Opinion of the Assistant Commissioner, Bassim.

Government would sanction the repairs. They might easily be stocked with fish. Both breeding fish and small fry are caught without any regard to size and in great numbers at all seasons, and until some laws are passed nothing will prevent it. Hooks are used, also netting, poisoning, and damming of streams and small pools where the water is sluggish or stagnant. The nets vary in size; casting ones are generally used, and sometimes several are joined together to stop up a stream, whilst other casting nets are employed above the obstacle. The meshes may be said to be as small as can possibly be produced; no objections exist to regulating the size of these meshes, which is most desirable. One inch from knot to knot would not be too small. Objections do not exist to prohibiting the sale of the fry of fish in the bazars, laws for which must be framed and breaches of them punished.

234. The *Deputy Commissioner of Amraotee District* remarks that breeding fish and young ones are destroyed to a considerable extent; that the smallest size of the mesh of the nets is from one-eighth to half an inch; that no difficulties exist against regulating it, except that he believes people who gain a precarious livelihood thereby will partially starve; that meshes of nets should not be below an inch; that no objections exist to prohibiting the salt of the fry of fish in bazars, but if the fishermen might not bring the fry of fish for sale, they would retain them for home consumption, and it would be very difficult to enforce any prohibitory order.

Opinion of the Deputy Commissioner, Amraotee.

235. The *Officiating Deputy Commissioner, Ellichpoor District,* says that it is believed breeding fish and very young ones are destroyed to a great extent by means of fine nets, poisoning the waters, and by basket weirs used at all seasons except the height of the monsoon. The great majority of the smallest sized nets are one-third of an inch in mesh, but there are even smaller, whilst there are no difficulties against regulating the size, and the only objection against prohibiting the sale of the fry of fish in the bazars would be lessening the livelihood of the fishermen.

Opinion of the Deputy Commissioner, Ellichpoor.

236. The *Deputy Commissioner of the Woon District* reports that breeding fish and very young ones are not destroyed to any great extent, because there is not much fishing carried on, but nets with small meshes are used in rivers and tanks during the monsoon. The smallest size of the mesh used is three-eighths of an inch, and there would be no difficulty in issuing orders regulating it, except in seeing them obeyed. The meshes should have one inch between knot and knot. As regards prohibiting the sale of the fry of fish, orders should be issued, and precautions taken against catching them; therefore the prohibition of sale would as a matter of course result.

Opinion of the Deputy Commissoner, Woon.

237. The *Tehsildar of Akola* places the number of fishermen within his range at 1,480; they belong to the Bhoee and sub-divisions of that caste. The local markets are not fully supplied with fish; it is a luxury, and a large amount could be sold. Its cost is very uncertain owing to the limited supply. It is difficult to say what is the

Opinion of Native official at Akola.

proportion of people who eat fish, but probably one-third if they could get it. The supply has decreased owing to their having been more sought after and the late droughts. Large quantities of very small fish are taken in nets during the rains, the smallest size of the meshes being one-eleventh of an inch. Breeding fish are not trapped in the fields during the rains. The various sorts of fishing carried on are netting, trapping, snaring, and poisoning. The nets are common to those employed elsewhere in India; their local names are as follows:—Pelue, Suwale bhuwar, Pagájáll, Furukjáll, Máhájáll, Mullputty, Helku, Khuwara, Nahootree.

238. The *Tehsildar of Buldana* states that there are about 3,000 fishermen in the district, amongst whom a very small number restrict themselves to fishing: their castes are Mulharkollee, Bebekollee, Bhoee, Bhamtee. The local markets are not fully supplied with fish; there is a demand for more. The cost of fish is for large sorts four, and for small eight seers for a rupee; for mutton first sort four, second sort six seers a rupee. Nine-tenths of the population are fish-eaters. The supply has decreased of late years owing to the droughts. Very minute ones are taken in small quantities during the rains by means of nets and cloths. The minimum size of the mesh of nets employed is one-third of an inch. Fish are not trapped during the rains. The various sorts of fishing are as follows: first by means of nets termed "jalla;" secondly by hooks called "gull;" thirdly by traps, "Essara," which is done by erecting rough stone piles on both sides of a stream, then spreading a mat of the "Nurgood" plant over the piles; the stream is then diverted, so as to pour over the mat, on which as the stream falls the fish are taken. This mode is resorted to when the water is as deep as the knee. Fish are also taken by means of "Goomlas," which somewhat resemble the straw envelopes for bottles; they are made of reeds of the "Nurgood" plant; these traps are placed in shallow streams in the rainy season into which the fish enter, but it prevents their return. Another plan is to make a pit in the bed of a river, then to cut a channel into it from the stream; as the water goes in the fish enter with it. Disturbing the water of a stream so as to cause it to become muddy is said sometimes to cause the fish to die.

Opinion of Native official at Buldana.

239. The *Tehsildar of Bassim* states there are 500 fishermen known as Bhoees in the district, but they all have other occupations; fishing, however, is not restricted to a particular class, for excluding the Brahmins, men of all other castes at times join in it. The weekly markets are well supplied with fish, but probably more could be sold, two-thirds of the people being fish-eaters. Fish are indiscriminately caught in all seasons without regard to size. The smallest size of the mesh of the nets may be described as so very minute as not to admit the escape of any but the very smallest fry. Fish are taken by hook, "gull;" nets, "jhalur;" damming streams, and by means of poison, "jher," but no other traps or snares are in general use.

Opinion of the Native official of Bassim.

240. The *Tehsildar of Amraotee* gives 80 fishermen, "Bhoees," all of whom follow other occupations. The markets are insufficiently supplied. The cost of fish is, for large, 8 annas, and for small, 4

Opinion of Native official of Amraotee.

p

annas a seer: of mutton first sort 4 annas, second sort 3 annas a seer. One-fourth of the population eat fish, the supply of which has decreased. Very small fish are captured by nets in large quantities during the rains.

241. The *Tehsildar of Mortizapúr* gives 175 fishermen, "Bhoees" and Mahomedans. The markets are insufficiently supplied; large fish obtains 6 annas, and small 3 annas a seer; first sort mutton 4 annas, second sort 3 annas a seer. One-fourth of the population eat fish; the supply has decreased; very small ones are taken during the rains in large quantities.

Opinion of Native official of Mortizapúr.

242. The *Tehsildar of Chandore* gives 546 fishermen, consisting of Bhoees, in his district. The markets are insufficiently supplied with fish; the cost of which is, for large sorts 6 annas, small sorts 3 annas a seer; whilst first sort mutton realises 4 annas, and second sort 3 annas a seer.

Opinion of Native official of Chandore.

243. The *Tehsildar of Morsee* gives 648 Bhoees and Mahomedan fishermen in his district. The markets are not fully supplied with fish; the larger sorts cost 4 annas, and the smaller 3 annas a seer; whilst the first sort of mutton also obtains 4 annas, and the second sort 3 annas a seer.

Opinion of Native official of Morsee.

244. The *Native official of the Woon District* observes that there are 1,560 fishermen of the Bhoee and Deemur castes in the district, but they also pursue other avocations. The local markets are insufficiently supplied with fish, the larger sorts selling at 5, and the smaller at 6 seers the rupee: whilst the first sort of mutton costs 4 seers, and the second 5 seers the Rupee; but this latter article of diet is but little consumed in the district. About 15 per cent. of the people are said to occasionally eat fish, but these creatures have decreased of late years. Small ones are taken during the rains, but not in large quantities, the minimum mesh of the nets being about three-eighths of an inch. Fish to a small extent are trapped during the rains in the irrigated fields. The names of the nets, &c., used are Bhowt jall, Julee, Burdee, Maah Jall, Thickuttake, Maleuse thagnee, and Murwuth.

Opinion of Native official of Woon.

CENTRAL PROVINCES.

245. It appears from the following reports, that in the 19 tehsils from which answers have been received, in four 50 per cent. of the people *eat fish*, in eight from 50 to 75 per cent., in three from 80 to 90 per cent., and in four upwards of 90 per cent.

The majority of the people in the Central Provinces may eat fish.

246. *Whether the markets are sufficiently supplied?* is thus answered by 20 tehsildars, as sufficiently so in 8, insufficiently in 12.

Markets how supplied.

247. *Respecting whether the amount of fish in the waters has increased, decreased, or remained stationary?* seven consider it to be stationary, in two it appears doubtful, whilst nine report a decrease.

Whether the fish in the waters have increased or decreased.

248. *Respecting the number of fishermen?* they are given at 80,928, but the women and children belonging to their families are included by some of the tehsildars; one evidently adds in those who used to be fishermen, as he remarks that "many have ceased to follow their original occupation, owing to the demand for well-paid labor developed by the railway." Out of these persons, all are said to follow other occupations, with the exception of 200 persons in the Upper Godaveri district.

Fishermen, as a rule, have other occupations.

249. The opinion appears to be unanimous, that breeding fish are destroyed to a large extent by fixed nets, by weirs spanning whole rivers, arresting them whilst they are ascending to breed, especially at a little prior to the commencement of the monsoon, and likewise stopping their downward progress as they return to the larger rivers; by traps in irrigated fields, capturing them as they try to reach good spawning grounds; by netting in every possible way the pools in the rivers in the dry season, and by poisoning the waters. Various forms of traps, nets, &c., are also employed.

Breeding fish how destroyed.

250. Fry appear to be destroyed to a great extent when just moving about, and in every possible way. One tehsildar computes the destruction in his district alone at 25,000 maunds (2 millions of pounds), and the tehsildar of Nursingpur says, that "it is to this wholesale destruction of the small fish that the fish have decreased." Traps of fine split bamboos appear to be placed at every outlet in irrigated fields, and netting is carried on universally, as well as the use of dams, weirs, and poison.

Fry destroyed wholesale.

cxvi

The smallest size of the mesh of nets.

251. *The smallest size of the mesh of the nets employed* is thus recorded by the European and Native officials:—

REPORTERS.	OF AN INCH IN DIAMETER.						Size of coarse muslin, a grain of wheat or barley, a large needle or very small.
	½	¼	⅛	⅙	⅛	1/10	
13 Europeans ...	...	...	3	...	1	5	1	3
18 Natives ...	...	1	6	1	1	5	1	3

When the above are not considered sufficiently minute, a cloth is employed.

252. The other modes of taking fish are adverted in the reports of the various Native officials. Weirs exist permitting nothing but water to go through, detaining all the fish; fixed traps are placed in every run where young or old are likely to pass, even at each opening through which the waste water in the rice fields flows from a higher to a lower level; streams are dammed and laded; poisoning is freely resorted to. Every form of net appears to be employed, from large-meshed to small-meshed ones, fixed or moveable, whilst rivers are swept by a number of cast-nets being connected together and dragged their whole width; night lines and day lines; baits fixed to bamboos inserted into the beds of rivers; torch-light netting and spearing; in short, every mode of poaching is said to be freely employed.

Other modes of fishing.

253. *As to remedial measures which have been proposed*, the Chief Commissioner suggests that poisoning waters should be prohibited, and no great opposition would be encountered in attempting a close season, but deprecates any action as to regulating the minimum size of the mesh of the nets to be employed; still if Government legislates, he urges a very wide discretion be given to local Governments in the framing of the rules. Personally I would also wish to see the local Administrations deal with the evils which exist, and provided they will do so, that regulations respecting the minimum size of the mesh of nets be left to their decision, only recommending that it never be permitted to be less than half an inch between each knot of the meshes. In fact this would be in the spirit of the British law, considering each local Administration in the place of a 'District Fishery Board' at home, and only subject to certain regulations, which I have already proposed. Forbidding any fixed engines as weirs or cruives, at least during breeding months, and the poisoning of waters, and the protection during the dry season of a few pools, would, I am convinced, at once show how easily remedial measures improve the condition of fisheries and augment the food-supply of the people.

Remedial measures proposed.

254. *Respecting regulating the smallest size of the mesh which may be employed*, one European official suggests that it would not be easy to do so in tanks and ponds, but that he sees no difficulty in rivers and nallas; four others consider

Respecting regulating the minimum size of the mesh of nets, and what such ought to be.

it inexpedient, mostly because a large preventive establishment would be required, one "that another class of poor people would be pestered with orders and regulations, which they and their neighbours would not understand," and ten do not see any objections. The following are the minimum sizes proposed; ¼th of an inch between the knots of the meshes by 2; ½ an inch by 3; ¾ths of an inch by 2; 1 inch by 5, 1¼ inches by 1; 1½ inches in rivers and nallas by 1.

255. *Should the sale of the fry of fish be prohibited?* is answered by ten; seven are in favor of it, three see objections. They consider such might lead to oppression, and small fish, which are not fry, might be considered as such. This rule might be modified thus, that no small fish are to be sold during the breeding months, to be decided in each district; if the young are thus destroyed, the supply during the rest of the year can hardly be expected to materially increase.

<small>Ought the sale of the fry of fish to be prohibited?</small>

256. Respecting fence seasons in the hilly districts during two months of the monsoon, when fish are ascending to breed or returning to the rivers of the plains, they appear to be generally approved of where they can be carried out. All weirs and fixed engines of every description should be prohibited at these periods if any are now permitted.

<small>Fence-months.</small>

257. The *Assistant Secretary to the Chief Commissioner, Central Provinces* (August 22nd, 1872) observes of the replies received from his districts to the questions which were circulated:—"The following facts are very clearly brought into view:—(1) that in these Provinces there are more than 80,000 persons who gain a livelihood, either in whole or in part, from fishing; (2) that from 60 to 75 per cent. of the population consume fish as an article of diet; (3) that no restrictions whatever exist, either as to the time or mode of fishing, or to the size or age of the fish caught, and that much indiscriminate and wanton destruction of fish takes place, not only by netting and trapping, but also by the very reprehensible practice of drugging and poisoning pools; (4) that notwithstanding all this, the markets are generally not fully supplied; (5) that every where the price of fish per seer is very much below the price of second class bazar mutton. In some districts it is alleged that there has been a decrease in the number of fish, but of this there is no very satisfactory proof. In the districts of Jabalpur and Seoni it is said fish decreased very perceptibly owing to the drought of 1868-69, but that they are now again on the increase. The facts elicited by the present enquiries, seem to the Chief Commissioner to indicate very clearly the necessity for some regulation of the fisheries in these provinces, and I am now to confine myself to an expression of the Chief Commissioner's opinion as to the restrictions which should be imposed. The practice of poisoning and drugging pools should certainly be put a stop to, and it is probable that no very great opposition would be encountered in attempting to appoint a "close season" during which the fish might breed in security. The object of a restriction of this nature would be obvious to all, and such a restriction could also be enforced with comparatively small difficulty. Theoretically, a regulation of the size of

<small>Opinion of the Chief Commissioner of the Central Provinces.</small>

meshes of nets is desirable, but any introduction
would be so fraught with annoyance and vexation t
that Mr. Morris would deprecate any action in
measures necessitating minute interference, it woul
of petty oppression and annoyance, independentl
to the trade. Close and constant inspection would
the nets up to the standard, and the uses to wh
thus given to petty officials would be put can
Moreover, it does not appear that, as yet, there i
number of fish, and it may be that a very consid
small fish caught are not young fry, but full
species evidently possessing a remarkable power
case, then, the Government of India deems th
matter of fisheries is called for, the Chief Comn
strongly urge that very wide discretion be given t
in framing of rules. No attempt, he thinks, shoul
such rules in the Act. The amount of hardsh
restrictive measures is only known when the meas
and if local Administrations are left unfettered, the
to the case of each district or river. In some portio
the land-owners claim the right to fishing in th
running through their estates, and receive fees fron
to them. No enquiry has been made as to the n
or to the period since which they have been ex
necessary to do so if the Government should de
regulation of the fisheries.

258. The *Collector of Nagpur* believes that bi
young ones are destroyer
Opinion of the Collector of
the Nagpur Division. pecially during the rains
The smallest-sized mesh
fourth of an inch in circumference, he considers that
if any difficulty in regulating the minimum size the
and would recommend that it should not be less tha
inch between knot and knot, but it would be more
inch as the fixed standard. "The Tehsildars are all u
that the sale of the fry of fish in bazars might be pr
ing any injury, and the prohibition would have the e
fish to be brought to the market. In this I conci
Bhandara observes, that breeding and very young
great extent in tanks, nallas, and rivers, especially in
the months of April and May, and for the first six
The smallest mesh employed is one-sixth of an inch.
culty in regulating the minimum size of the mesh
in tank fishing, but not so much in rivers and nallas
latter places might be laid down at 1½ inches.
objection to prohibiting the capture of fish in ri
the first two months of the monsoon, at which peric
to the markets for sale. The *Collector of Chanda*
and very young fish are destroyed to a great e:
and smaller streams, in the tanks, jhils, and temp
damming up rice-fields and nallas in the rainy se

caught in the rains chiefly by nets, hooks, jhinkars, and bamboo derias. The nets which have meshes of a very small size are dragged across the water. Dhimars do not usually use hooks, but in the larger rivers during the monsoons they not unfrequently place a rope across the stream, the rope having hooks with different kinds of baits at a distance of about a cubit apart attached to it, and resting upon pumpkins, they examine it every few hours. Weirs are stretched across water-courses. The Goonds are reputed to poison fish; in fact they are destroyed indiscriminately at all times of the year, including the breeding season. The smallest sized mesh in use takes five meshes within one inch, but there would be considerable difficulty in regulating it, unless the police force were augmented: however, were it regulated, would propose three-fourths of an inch between each knot. No valid objections exist against prohibiting the sale of fry in the bazars, the supply being above the demand. *The Collector of Wardha* answers, that breeding fish and young ones are destroyed to the same extent as in the rest of India, being captured most readily during the breeding season. The breeding fish often linger in the pools before the rains commence, and there fall easy victims to all sorts of people. The smallest size of the mesh used is between one-fourth and one-tenth of an inch square, but even cloths are extensively employed; the only difficulty in regulating the minimum size in future is "that another class of poor people would be pestered with orders and regulations, which they and their neighbours would not understand." "If any regulation is considered necessary, it should be a simple prohibition to use cloths or nets of a smaller mesh than three-fourths or one inch square for the capture of fish." Prohibiting the sale of fry would be useless; "if the mesh of nets is regulated, and the rules really enforced, there would be no necessity for it; if nets are not interfered with, the fry will be caught and disposed of privately, as the greater portion is now." *The Collector of Balaghat* replies, that breeding fish and young ones are destroyed to a great extent, mostly in the rains, by means of nets with very small meshes, in the rivers, smaller streams, rice-fields, and tanks. Fine bamboo-matting is also used, as well as sticks and cloths. The smallest meshes of nets are less than one-fourth of an inch; regulating their size would be useless, no orders could be carried out, and would not recommend prohibiting the sale of the fry in the bazars.

259. *The Deputy Commissioners'* answers of *the Jabalpúr Division* are amalgamated. In Jubalpúr fish are said to be taken all the year round regardless of season. Breeding and immature ones are destroyed to a great extent in Mandla and Seoni, but not so in the Sagar District. In Damoh it is considered that breeding fish are not destroyed wholesale during the hot season. Spawning fish appear to be generally taken whilst migrating up stream in June or July for breeding purposes, and the fry in September or October whilst attempting to pass from the shallows where they are bred to the deeper water. The modes are thus described in the Seoni District. "Every little streamlet is dammed up, and the fish are baled out in thousands, by people standing in the water. Those escaping this attack are caught in the woven bamboo weirs of the dam. In some of the wilder parts of the district, the poisoning of stagnant pools, and of temporarily dammed water, is resorted to in the hot weather. Not only are all the fish in the pool

Opinions of the Deputy Commissioners of the Jubalpúr Division.

killed, but when there is an overflow, the stream below is often infected for some distance, and many of the fish killed. Cattle coming to drink, and human beings also, are liable to suffer. The fish thus killed are said to be unpleasant to the palate and unwholesome." In Damoh, after the monsoon is over, nets of all sorts, with meshes to one-fourth of an inch or less in width, are employed; drag-nets are used, and split bamboo weirs are constructed across favourite runs. As the streams begin to dry, the pools are drugged with a fruit called 'Aka' pounded and mixed with flour. Rivers and tanks abound with turtles, tortoises, and crocodiles, which destroy large quantities of fish. The smallest size mesh of nets is given at one-eighth of an inch in Mandla and Seoni, one-fourth in Jabalpúr and Damoh, and so small that no fish can pass in Sagar. All the Deputy Commissioners consider there would be but little difficulty in regulating the minimum size of the mesh of nets, but the one of Damoh considers discontent would be caused, not only amongst the fishermen, but the consumers, as little fish are in great demand, and meet with a ready sale. The Deputy Commissioners would adopt the following as the minimum size: Seoni and Damoh half an inch between the knots, Mandla one inch at the base, and two inches or more higher up, Sagar one-fourth of an inch in diameter for general fishing [a pencil would almost be arrested in such a mesh], Jabalpúr one inch. The general impression is, that the only valid objection to prohibiting the sale of fry in the bazar, is the loss of income to the fishermen, and irritation amongst native fish-eaters, who ordinarily belong to the lowest and least intelligent class of the population. As regards fence-months, the Deputy Commissioner of Seoni would have them from July to September inclusive, in the districts of the Satpura Range, as then the greatest destruction takes place. The Deputy Commissioners of Sagar and Jabalpúr would condemn the capture of fish during the two first months of the monsoon. The Deputy Commissioners of Damoh and Mandla give no definite opinions, owing to not having had any experience of the kind in hilly districts, to which the question solely referred.

260. In the *Narbada Division*, the *Collector of Betul* observes, that there is no check to the destruction of breeding fish and fry, which, it is said, are destroyed in large numbers by nets, baskets, and poisoning the water. The smallest size mesh of nets employed is about one-eighth of an inch square; does not apprehend any difficulty in regulating the minimum size or prohibiting the sale of fry in the bazars. *The Collector of Chhindwara* answers, that what fish are caught are captured irrespective of whether breeding ones or fry; the smallest mesh in use is about one-fourth of an inch; there would be no difficulty in regulating the minimum size provided there were a law, which he would propose at one inch; there would be no objection to prohibiting the sale of fry. *The Collector of Hoshangabad* reports, that breeding and very young fish are destroyed to a great extent by means of nets, funnel-shaped baskets, and poisoning pools. Fry are caught in small streams and in the shallows of large rivers, especially during June and July, by narrow-meshed nets and baskets, and in stagnant water by poisoning the whole pool. The smallest meshes of nets are one-eighth of an inch in diameter; there would be no difficulty in regulating them except in the distant wild parts of the district,

Narbada Division. Opinions of the Collectors.

and one inch in diameter would be advisable. There is no objection to prohibiting the sale of the fry of fish in the bazars, or fixing a close time in the hilly districts. *The Collector of Narsinghpur* observes, that breeding and young fish are destroyed in considerable numbers. The breeding fish are taken by weirs thrown across the large rivers, and in the narrows of them, before the monsoons, nothing can pass, whilst traps are also set up in shallow places. Waters are poisoned in the smaller streams during the two first months of the monsoon, whilst the fish are spawning. Not only are the fry taken in every conceivable way for food, but they are also wantonly and uselessly destroyed by village children. These causes have impoverished the fisheries, and decreased the supply. The smallest mesh of nets in use is one-eighth of an inch; there would be but little difficulty in regulating the minimum size, which it is suggested should be $1\frac{1}{4}$ inches between each knot. Close months in hilly districts, it is suggested, could not be enforced, instead " regulating the size of the mesh of nets to protect the fry, and prohibiting the snaring of fish altogether in the breeding season, or the prohibition of weirs and traps on any river or stream during the breeding season, unless sufficient openings were given to enable a proportion of the breeding fish to reach suitable places to deposit their eggs, would be sufficient to improve the fisheries, rendering them more valuable to the fishermen, and more productive of food;" would prohibit the sale of fry in the bazars as " beneficial to all districts; fish eaten at such seasons are the reputed originators of disease, with what truth I am unable to say." The *Collector of Nimar* replies, no distinction is ever made as to whether the fish is breeding or young; they are destroyed in pools, tanks, streams, and rivers; in fact in every place where they can be got and in all seasons, except during very heavy rains, when fishing is unprofitable; the smallest mesh employed is one-eighth of an inch. No difficulties exist in regulating the size of the mesh of nets, except that such might reduce the supply, whilst the only objection against prohibiting the sale of fry is, that such would reduce the sales one-half. A fence season of two months in hilly districts could be easily carried out, whilst the people would understand the reason.

261. *Chhattisgarh Division.—The Collector of Raipur* reports, that breeding and young fish are indiscriminately taken, the latter to a greater extent than the former. The capture takes place a month or two previous, also during the rains, in nallas, tanks, and small pools, by nets, traps, cross-bow bolts, fouling the water of pools, and angling. The smallest-sized mesh of the nets employed is one-fourth of an inch; the difficulty in regulating the minimum size would be in its evasion, as the majority of the people would sympathise with the fishermen, rendering a large protective establishment necessary : but the minimum size should not be less than one inch. Prohibiting the sale of the fry would " deprive the poorer classes of the enjoyment of this kind of animal food, which has hitherto been procurable with ease by fishermen, and is cheaply placed within the reach of the buyer's means: but the case would be different when the large fish alone are to be caught." *The Collector of Sambalpur* considers that breeding fish and very young ones are not destroyed to any great extent, as during the rains the rivers cannot be

Chhattisgarh Division. Opinions of Collectors.

netted, whilst the country contiguous to them is covered with dense jungle, and but sparsely populated. Numbers of small fish are captured during the monsoon months in the rice-fields, and sometimes in creeks filled by the back-waters of the rivers in flood; in the rice-fields wicker baskets are placed at the drainage openings of the fields, and those in the creeks and estuaries are taken by a net which is lowered into the water and raised after an interval of a few seconds by means of a long bamboo pole. The smallest-sized mesh of the nets is one-eighth of an inch; regulating it would require "an immense and expensive establishment, which would probably prove a greater evil than that which it is intended to provide against." If a minimum were fixed, it should be one inch between knot and knot. It would be impossible to prevent the sale of fry, as "they are chiefly hawked about by the boatmen from house to house, or purchased by the people at the river side, as the boats pass up." No objections exist to a fence season in hilly regions during the first two months of the monsoon, provided such could be enforced, which appears to be impossible. The *Collector of Bilaspur* states, that breeding and young fish are wantonly and indiscriminately destroyed, in all rivers, pools, streams, and tanks, throughout the district, also in rice-fields; in the latter, they are caught at the outlets when the water is no longer required in the fields. Wholesale destruction takes place at the close of the rains when the waters are subsiding. In shallow streams, traps of various devices—baskets, bamboo weirs, and funnel-shaped nets whose meshes are as close as those of coarse muslin—are used. It is impossible for the smallest fish to get out of some of the traps. Waters are also poisoned. The smallest-meshed nets in use would just admit of a fly crawling through. No difficulties exist in regulating the minimum size of the mesh of nets, which he would place at one-fourth of an inch. Objections might arise in prohibiting the sale of fry, as advantage could be taken of such an order for the purpose of oppression.

262. In the *Nagpúr Division*, the five *Tehsildars* report 35,377 fishermen, but in two tehsils the families are included; all of them likewise carry on other occupations. The fishermen castes are Palwar, Kahar if Pardasis, Bendura, Bhanara, Mashide, Telang, Kevat, Dhimar or Bhogis, Binjawars. Respecting the supply of fish in the markets, the Tehsildar of Nagpúr reports that it is sufficient in two markets, and insufficient in two others. In Bhandara, Chanda, and Balaghat, that it is sufficient; and in Wardha, that it is not so during the hot season. The comparative cost of mutton and fish cannot be ascertained from the replies received. As to the proportion of the population who eat fish, it is given in Nagpúr and Chanda at 75 per cent., in Bhandara at 92 per cent., in Wardha at 86 per cent., and in Balaghat at 80 per cent. The amount of fish in the waters is said to have remained stationary in two tehsils, and to have decreased in three. Large quantities of fish are said not to be taken in one tehsil during the rains, but to be so in the remaining four. The smallest-meshed nets are given by three at one-fourth of an inch, by one at one-fifth, and the remainder at one-sixth. In four tehsils fish are said to be trapped during the rains, in the fifth not to be so. The following are stated to be the modes of fishing employed: nets termed 'Jale' or 'Bhoi Jale,'

Nagpúr Division. Opinion of Native officials.

small fish hooks, 'gal;' by 'tatti' or 'pinjra,' which is generally placed against a running stream of a nalla, the water passes through, but the fish that are carried away by the current of the water are driven into the crevices of the tatti, and are thus entrapped; by 'phanta,' when a screen is placed against the current in a shallow river or a nalla, on one side it has a sheet of cloth attached to it, whilst on the other a net is spread, as the current is arrested by the screen, the fish, in attempting to pass, leap over it, and fall into the nets spread on the other side; 'Pailni' is a triangular-shaped net (lave-net) on a pole used for catching fish in shallow water; 'Bhovasent,' a circular net about 18 feet in diameter; 'Tagoi,' a net from 90 to 175 feet in length; the 'Jhorti' is very similar, but with a larger mesh; the 'Topari' is another species of net; 'Bhewar jal' or cast-net; the 'Kothla' is a bag-shaped bamboo trap, and is generally used in irrigated fields; snares termed 'Phas;' poisoning water by 'milk bush,' 'hinganbet' or 'meni.' In Balaghat the following plans are likewise reported:—'Dupka,' a conical bamboo coop; 'Lamdora,' a night line baited with a frog; 'Kunkur,' a spear; 'Dawan,' night-lines with several hooks on one string; 'Tepon,' another form used during the day-time; 'Surki,' fine bamboo chicks, as are also 'Chunga' and 'Maindhar.' 'Dhaer,' or a piece of large hollow bamboo three or four feet in length, open at both ends, is left in running water: its weight sinks it: it is suddenly lifted, the two ends being closed by the two hands. 'Chapa,' by lights at night, when the fish jump on to a piece of bamboo matting. 'Ooran,' a large net, which is stretched across a stream in a moon-light night, and the water is beaten towards it by men in canoes.

263. In the *Jabalpúr Division, five Tehsildars* reply, that there are 10,923 fishermen, who almost invariably pursue other occupations; the names of the castes are Dhimars and Khevats. The local markets are fully supplied in three tehsils, but not so in two. Respecting the amount of the population who eat fish, it is given as follows:—Seoni three-fourths, Mandla all but Brahmins and Banias, Sagar and Jabalpúr half; Damoh two-thirds. As regards the amount of fish in the waters, in Seoni and Jabalpúr it is stated that they were abundant previous to the drought of 1868-69 when numbers died, now again they are increasing; in Damoh they are stationary: in Mandla and Sagar they have decreased. In Sagar small fish are not taken in any quantity during the rains, but they are in the four other districts, at the end of the rains, by damming and lading, by taking those left by receding waters in hollows and rice-fields, and by fine nets; in fact, at Mandla about half of the young fry may be said to be so caught. The smallest-sized meshes are thus given in four districts; one at half an inch, two at quarter of an inch [in one it is subsequently observed of the Pilna net, that it has "fine meshes through which a needle for sewing gunny can with difficulty be passed], and one at the size of a grain of wheat. Young and old fish are taken during seasons of irrigation, in the fields, by means of traps set at the outlet of every enclosure in three of the districts, but in the remaining two no fields are irrigated at this period, but wherever there is any overflow, the people destroy the fry how they can.

Jabalpúr Division. Answers of the Native officials.

The following are the modes of fishing recorded :—'Pilni,' or smallest net of all, chiefly employed for taking prawns; it is a hand (lave) net fastened to a triangular bamboo frame. 'Pandi,' the smallest casting net, this is ordinarily about 15 feet long, weighted with iron; when it is desired to net a considerable breadth of stream, several of these nets are used, fastened together, making one very long net, in this almost every kind of fish is caught; the substance of which it is composed is three or four threads of cotton which forms a very fine cord; it is a heavy net, requiring three or four men to drag it. The 'Mahajal,' or great fishing net, is resorted to in large streams, &c., generally used out of boats: two are taken from different directions towards one central point, the fish being driven by beating the water and noises of all sorts, to the point where they are caught, between the two Mahajals. The 'Kamni' or 'Kawria' is a net fixed opposite the opening in a bund or dam, into which all the fish are swept by the stream : in some localities the dam is of stone, and a net stops the openings; in other places the dam is a bamboo screen, and the orifices are lined with tatties, leading the fish into a bamboo-grating enclosure (cruive) which allows the water to pass, but retains the fish. In the 'Kurar' fishing, a funnel or cone-shaped bamboo net is put down, extinguisher fashion, from a boat passing over a shoal of fish. 'Ulechna' means 'to bale out;' in this mode of fishing a channel of the river is dammed up with stones, which permits the water to flow through, but detains the fish; as the water gets low, the fish are baled out in flat bamboo baskets. 'Pahao' is a trap made of wood and bamboo cuttings, it is placed in narrow and shallow streams, the water flows through it, but the egress of the smallest fish is prevented. 'Dauni' is a baited night or day line. 'Kankur' is fish spearing. Most of the other plans have been already referred to in the last paragraph.

264. *In the Nerbada Division, the five Tehsildars* reply as follows :

Nerbada Division. Opinions of Native officials.

there are 5,659 fishermen, all of whom have other occupations; in one tehsil it is remarked that "many have ceased to follow their original occupation, owing to the demand for well-paid labor developed by the railway." They are mostly Dhimars, a term applicable to boatmen and sellers of parched gram; Kahar, Bhoee, applicable to palki-bearers, Singhrora or sellers of the Singhara nuts, and Mussulmen. The local markets are stated to be sufficiently supplied in one district, but insufficiently so in the remaining four. In two districts about 50 per cent. of the people eat fish, in one from 50 to 75 per cent., in one 75 per cent., and in the remainder upwards of 85 per cent. In two districts, the amount of fish in the waters has continued to be stationary of late years, whilst it has decreased in the remaining three. In all the tehsils, a great destruction of fry is recorded as occurring during the rains. The Tehsildar of Narsingpur observes, "it is to this wholesale destruction of the small fish, that the fish have decreased." The minimum mesh of the nets in use is given in all five districts at one-eighth of an inch; in four of the districts fish, large and small, are trapped in the irrigated fields. The modes of fishing are similar to those described in the two last paragraphs, in addition to which the poisoning of the water is reported in Chhindwara, Hoshangabad, and Minar : also a lighted torch is taken in a canoe over deep water; the fish collect near the light and are netted.

265. In the *Chhattisgarh Division*, three *Tehsildars* report as follows :—that there are 24,728 fishermen, all of whom have other occupations, they are of the same castes as in the other divisions; the markets in all of the three districts are insufficiently supplied, except during the rainy season, when a considerable amount of fry is taken and disposed of. In two tehsils 75 per cent., and in one 95 per cent., are said to be fish-eaters; the amount in the waters is stated to be stationary in two districts; no answer from the third. Large quantities of fry are reported to be captured during the rains, computed in one tehsil at nearly 25,000 maunds (2,000,000 ℔s, reckoning the maund at 80 ℔s.) In two tehsils the smallest mesh of the nets employed is given at quarter of an inch; in the remaining one at the size of a grain of barley. Fish are extensively trapped in the rice-fields in all the three districts. The modes already alluded to in the other divisions are in existence in this, and poisoning of the water is stated to occur in two of the tehsils.

<small>Chhattisgarh Division. Opinions of Native officials.</small>

266. In the *Upper Godaveri District*, the *Tehsildar of Sironcha* reports 4,241 fishermen, but few indeed of this number, perhaps 200, are solely dependant on the taking of fish for a livelihood; their castes are Dhimar, Gollawal, Orawal, Bestwal, and Benarwal. Fish are only bartered; 97 per cent. of the people would eat it could they procure it. A decrease in the number of the tank-produced fish is believed to have occurred since the district has formed a portion of the British territory. Previously, the people were prevented from killing fish in tanks, unless they paid some fees or share of fish to the local Talukdar. The quantity in the rivers is not known to have decreased, but if the nallas are completely swept of them, it is most certain that the amount in the rivers will likewise fall off,' and therefore it is thought that there must be a decrease. Large quantities of fry are destroyed in the rains; the meshes of the nets are about a quarter of an inch in width. There are no irrigated fields, except from wells, in this district, but fish are trapped.

<small>Upper Godaveri District. Opinion of the Tehsildar.</small>

RAJPUTANA.

267. The Secretary to the *Governor General's Agent in Rajputana* forwarded two letters, with enclosures, from the *Commissioner of Ajmir*, who observes that there are no perennial streams in his district, but four perennial tanks or lakes, *viz.*, Anasagur Lake, in which the supply of fish is most inadequate, and some of the better descriptions, as the Rohoo, *Cirrhina rohita*, are not found; the Pushkar, a holy lake, where neither the lives of fish or crocodiles can be taken, though probably there would be no objection to the eggs of the latter being destroyed; the Ramsur, where the fish supply is good, provided water exists, but this was so deficient last year that it only contained a cupfull; lastly, the Nearan, which, when full, has a fair amount of fish; however, it was quite dry in 1871. Sometimes there is a fifth at Bhir. The rivers Bunas and Khari are perennial streams, which, whilst passing through the British territory, contain no fish.

Rajputana. Opinion of the Commissioner of Ajmir.

268. The *Deputy Commissioner of Ajmir* reports that water only exists in the streams in his district for a few days during the rainy season, and that they do not contain edible fish. "The Khari Nuddi, and Bunas on our borders, are the only streams in which fish could be bred and preserved, but the localities are not in our district, but in (I believe) the Jaipur State." The fishing in the Ramsur and Nearan tanks are generally leased out, as water is usually present all the year round, and a fair supply of fish is afforded to the cantonment of Nusirabad. "This year the lease has been taken up by a banker of Ajmir with the avowed purpose of preventing the catching of fish." This preservative process, it is suggested, will bring up the supply again after the loss sustained by the late drought, whereby the Nearan tank became quite dry, and that at Ramsur had only about a cupfull of water left in it. He observes that "were we to be provided with reservoirs holding water all the year round, it would be a great boon to have them stocked with good edible fish, and they could be readily preserved. Till such time as we have reservoirs of this kind, it will be useless to attempt to preserve fish in the district." Crocodiles are only found in the Anasagur tank (except the sacred Pushkur one), and their destruction he considers perfectly feasible at a small expense; if sanctioned, they could be killed by Shikaris, and rewards offered for their eggs.

Opinion of Deputy Commissioner of Ajmir.

OUDH.

269. In *Oudh* the Officiating Chief Commissioner gives his opinion, that fish have neither increased nor decreased in the province; that legislative interference is unnecessary, and in fact can only be justifiable when it is demonstrated that, unless the Legislature steps in, the existence of that important article of diet will cease altogether,—an entirely contrary opinion to that of the Chief Commissioner in 1868. But it is likewise observed that there would be no difficulties in regulating the size of the meshes of the fishing nets, if desirable, or prohibiting the sale of little fish in the bazar, but the last, it is stated, would be obnoxious to both buyers and sellers, besides being uncalled for.

Opinions of Officiating Chief Commissioner.

270. Amongst the replies forwarded from this province are those of 25 Tehsildars and Native officials, &c.; all but the one at Sitapur answering the question as to "*what proportion of the people eat fish?*" Whilst the numbers at Unas and Suffipur are computed at 85,000 in either place, the amount of the general population is not recorded. At Kantha, Bangermore, Putti, and Pratabgarh, the fish-eaters are given as half the people; at Purwah, Mohan, Faizabad, Baraich, Gondah, Hurdui, and Rai Bareili at two-thirds; at Sundeela and Sultanpur at three-fourths; at Bilgram, Shahabad, and Behar at from 80 to 97½ per cent., and at Lucknow all; whilst at Nawabgunge, Fathipur, Sanalughat, and Hyderghur, it is asserted a large proportion of the people eat fish, and more would do so could they obtain them. The foregoing shows that a fish-diet is most important to, and is in fact not a luxury, but a necessity, amongst the people of Oudh, and that more would be fish-eaters were the supply equal to the demand.

Large proportion of people are fish-eaters.

271. The next consideration is, *whether the supply is really unequal to the demand?* Whether the fish inhabiting the waters have increased, decreased, or remained stationary, appears to be a disputed point, but it ought to be easily demonstrable whether the supplies in the bazars are equal to the demands of purchasers. Rather contradictory accounts are given from four. In one the bazar is said to be fairly supplied; in one well supplied, but only during the rains; in two to be fully supplied, and in eighteen to be insufficiently so. Thus, three-fourths of the markets are stated to have a larger demand than supply, apparently demonstrating that, were the quantity of fish brought to market more considerable, it would be to the advantage of the people at large.

Supply in markets unequal to demand.

272. As the fish-eating population is very considerable, and the bazars are not fully supplied, we arrive at the question as to *whether very small fishes are taken in any quantities during the rains?* In twenty localities it is asserted that very small fish are so captured in large

Fry killed largely during the rains.

quantities, and in two it is stated that this does not occur. It, of course, is difficult to prove without a personal visit, whether the small fish sold in the bazar are the fry of larger sorts, but as all fish breed in the rainy months, when little fish appear to be most largely sold in the bazars or used as manure in the fields, it must be conceded that a strong presumption is raised, that immature fishes are very largely destroyed in Oudh. · In Baraich alone 8,000 maunds; in Unas 10,000 maunds; in Suffipur 300 maunds; in Purwah some hundreds of maunds; in Putti 40,000 maunds, are reported as being killed during the rains, and only in the Tehsil of Fathipur and Sanalughat are they stated not to be so captured. Thus nearly 75 millions of ounces weight of small fish are stated in 4 Tehsils alone to be taken during the rains, and it is very evident that the destruction of small fish, when the fry are about, is the rule, not the exception.

273. *What is the smallest size of the mesh of the nets employed?* is

<small>The smallest size mesh in use, and that proposed.</small>
a very important question, because it can hardly be asserted to be judicious to massacre the young of any species of fish, much less of those of the largest sorts. We have two classes of reporters; first those who assert that the size of the smallest mesh employed is from a quarter of an inch to an inch square. In these localities but very little interference could be asserted to be occasioned by prohibiting the minimum size being less than one inch between knot and knot. At Hurdui and Shahbad, however, it is observed that a grain of gram will be stopped; at Sultanpur that hardly anything will pass; and at Putti that a grain of mothi cannot go through. If all the immature fish are to be destroyed in this manner, it seems impossible that the markets could be fully supplied. As regards regulating the size of the mesh of the nets for the future, an objection is raised that it will be unpopular, because of the natural dislike and prejudice of the rustic population against any innovation whatever in the implements, for carrying on their craft. But no innovation is proposed, only prohibiting the use of very minute meshes in their implements; and the general opinion of the Oudh officials is, that one inch between knot and knot should be the smallest legal size.

274. *Are fish trapped in the irrigated fields during the rains?* is

<small>Fish trapped in irrigated fields when breeding.</small>
another very necessary enquiry, for it is at these periods that many breeding ones ascend to deposit their eggs. Some of the native officials say they are not destroyed, but 20 assert that they are; and if young ones are so ruthlessly massacred as in Oudh, it does not appear very probable that the adult would meet with mercy. Besides this, what do the officials report? At Faizabad, that all breeding fish are indiscriminately netted; at Hurdui that breeding and young fish are destroyed without discrimination and to a great extent. That, as at Deogaon, waters are poisoned, and the large fish, when intoxicated, are beaten on the head with sticks and thus destroyed, whilst they are not considered good to eat. That in Sitapur, waters are dammed to obtain the fish; at Hurdui, that traps are used to collect fish of the smallest size. At Rai Bareli the destruction of all sorts of fish is considerable: and at Sultanpur and Pratabgarh breeding fish and young ones are destroyed,

Further extracts are not required to demonstrate how breeding fish and their fry are ruthlessly destroyed in Oudh; and it may be questionable, whether wantonly poisoning fish, and destroying them in a manner that renders them uneatable, or else dangerous to health if employed as food, or whether indiscriminate destruction, as damming waters in order to kill all the fish in them, are not proceedings that should be prohibited, when it is shown that the fish supply is not sufficient for the wants of the people. The same also applies to weirs and trapping breeding fish in irrigated fields.

275. In answer to the enquiry *about prohibiting the sale of the fry of fish in the bazar*, the objections are that the Police would interfere, and make such a means of extortion, especially as they could not discriminate between mature small fish, and the immature of the larger sorts. This may be obviated by prohibiting the sale of fish that will not easily pass through the meshes of the net of a regulated size, leaving it to local committees to pass bye-laws for the preservation of the more valuable kinds.

Should the sale of the fry of fish be prohibited?

276. The *Commissioner* and *Deputy Commissioner of Faizabad* consider that any interference should be confined to the control of perennial lakes and second class rivers and streams, as it would not be of any use to legislate for jhils and pools which dry up, or such large rivers as the Ganges and Ghogra, as they may take care of themselves.

Faizabad Division. Opinions of the European officials.

277. The *Officiating Secretary* to the "Officiating Chief Commissioner" *in Oudh* (May 14th, 1872) observes, "the general tendency of the answers, however, go to show that if the fish in this province have not increased, neither have they decreased; and as far, therefore, as Oudh is concerned, the Officiating Chief Commissioner would deprecate any legislative interference with the capture and sale of fish. Such interference, it seems to Sir C. Cowper, can only be justifiable when it can be demonstrated that, unless the the Legislature step in, the existence of that important article of diet will cease altogether." As regards whether objections exist to prohibiting the sale of immature and small fish in the bazars? it is observed "that such a measure would be obnoxious to sellers and consumers, and at present seems quite uncalled for." "There are no difficulties to the introduction of the measure" of regulating the size of the mesh of nets "if it be thought desirable." "Nothing can be more easy than to increase the size of the meshes, and to prohibit the sale of fish below a certain specific size in the bazar, though it would not be so easy to distinguish between full-grown little fish and the fry of larger fish." The *Financial Commissioner* (September 18th, 1868), in answer to the enquiry whether any wanton destruction of fish takes place in Oudh, and if any protective measures are necessary? replied by giving the opinions of several of the civil officers that such does take place, and concludes thus :—" my own opinion is, that such measures, though not positively necessary, are at least very desirable." The *Secretary to the Chief Commissioner* (September 22nd, 1868) was directed

Opinions of the Officiating Chief Commissioner and Financial Commissioner, &c.

to state "that the Chief Commissioner concurs in the opinion expressed by the Commissioner of Sitapur that there is great destruction from ignorance, not from wantonness, and that the measures of protection required are, the publication of the breeding seasons for the various kinds of river and tank fish, the institution of close seasons, and the prohibition of fishing during those seasons."

278. The *Commissioner of the Faizabad Division*, in forwarding the replies from the Deputy Commissioners of Faizabad, Baraich, and Gondah in letter No. 1202 of April 1872, considers there is no reason to anticipate a rapid increase either in the number of fishermen or of the fish-consuming population, that the fishermen carry on their occupations as they have done from time immemorial, and that their operations have not led to a sensible decrease in the supply; consequently no special legislation appears to be called for at present, and that such would be unpopular; but he thinks "that the question is a very important one, and that it should not be lost sight of, but that periodical enquiries should be made, with the view of ascertaining beyond a doubt whether the fish supply is increasing, decreasing, or stationary." He observes that "if we are to have legislative interference, I concur in the opinion of the Deputy Commissioner of Faizabad, that it should be confined to the control of perennial lakes and second class rivers and streams, as it is not worth while to legislate for jhils and pools which dry up, and in such rivers as the Ganges and the Ghogra the capture of fish cannot perceptibly affect the supply." The remedies he points out as "likely to be most efficacious and feasible in this province are the regulation of the size of the mesh of nets for use in minor streams and perennial lakes, and the prohibition of capture of fish during the breeding months and of the sale of fry in the bazars."

Faizabad Division. Answers of European officials.

279. Colonel Reid, the *Commissioner of Faizabad*, also observes that the replies of the *Collectors* are of a general nature. All breeding fish or fry are indiscriminately netted; there is no restriction in the size of the mesh employed, which is about one-third of an inch. It is considered difficulties would arise in regulating the mesh of nets owing to difference in the size of the various mature fish inhabiting the same localities; that it would not answer to prescribe different sizes of meshes for netting small, middle-sized, and large fish, but at the same time the present minimum is smaller than is required to catch the most minute fish, and that it might be increased to half or three-fourths of an inch at least. It is observed that prohibiting the sale of the fry of fish in the bazars might occasion loss to the owners of waters which would reduce the fishermen's gains, and prevent the present purchasers of fry obtaining their accustomed food, as full-grown fish are considerably dearer. On the other hand, it is observed these objections might be only temporary, and an augmentation of food and decrease of price be the result after two or three years. "Very small fishes are caught during the rains, principally by nets; in Gondah it is estimated that the weight of small fishes so caught annually is about 8,000 maunds, of which 500 maunds are dried and sold to the Nepalese after the rains." "Fish are trapped in the fields when streams and tanks overflow, and the water from them

Faizabad. Opinion of Commissioners and Collectors.

pours into the fields, but not (I believe) in merely irrigated fields." "The smallest size of the mesh of the nets employed is about one-third of an inch between knot and knot." "Fishing is carried on *in rivers* from boats by casting and dragging nets, spears, lines, rods, and hooks; in *village ponds and jhils*, in the months of Jeth and Baisakh, by hands, the water being first mudded by gangs of from 50 to 60 men. Large fish are sometimes killed by lathis. The Talukdar of Deogam states that drains full of water are sometimes enclosed on both sides, and powders obtained from a poisonous wild fruit named "Bisteud or Kuhar" thrown in. A channel is then cut to receive fresh-water in the enclosed drain, so as to save the fish from wholesale destruction. The large fish get disturbed (intoxicated or poisoned) and float, when people beat them on the head with lathis or catch them with their hands." But, he adds, the fish taken in this manner are not good to eat. The principal implements of fishing are detailed as follows: 1, Khancha (a sort of basket net); 2, Tap; 3, Mahi; 4, Pukhai (for small fish); 5, Chatbri; 6, Chilwar; 7, Laga; 8, Tappura; 9, Dudhi; 10, Kurail; 11, Chutur; 12, Ganj; 13, Bhukha; 14, Palni; 15, Chitta (for large fish); 16, Unghi; 17, Jhagri; 18, Lukia.

280. The *Collector of Lucknow* reports, "the tanks and rivers are netted without restriction throughout the year, and necessarily fish, breeding or not breeding, big or small, are taken as they come to the net. The greatest destruction takes place just before the end of the cold season when the tanks are drying up. There is no restriction as to the size of the mesh of the nets; the smallest size employed is about a quarter of an inch, but regulating it in any locality would be objectionable until there existed a well ascertained want for the passing of such a measure, as all unnecessary interference with the people is to be deprecated." Still, he continues, one-inch regulation between knot and knot of the meshes of the nets seems to be really necessary. The objections advanced against prohibiting the sale of the fry of fish in the bazar are ignorance of the ordinary Policemen, who, being allowed to interfere with the fish-hawkers, would find in such a law a means of extortion, besides being unable to discriminate between fry and adult fish.

Lucknow. Opinion of the Collector.

281. The *Collector of Unas* reports, very small fishes are destroyed during the rains, and cultivators use them as manure. The smallest size of the mesh of nets is one-sixth of an inch; no difficulty existing regulating such, and one inch between knot and knot he considers advisable. If the sale of the fry of fish in the bazar is prohibited, both owners and fishermen, it is considered, will suffer.

Unas. Opinion of the Collector.

282. The *Collector of Bara Banki* considers that breeding and young fish are not killed to any great extent; any which are destroyed are those got in tanks. Three-quarters of an inch is the smallest mesh of nets employed; no difficulty exists in regulating such, and he proposes three-quarters of an inch as the legal size. No fish are brought for sale in the bazars.

Opinion of Collector of Bara Banki.

283. The *Collector of Sitapar* says, young fish are caught, but not to any great extent; they are taken by damming in the smaller streams during the dry weather, and in irrigated fields during the rainy season. The minimum size of the mesh of nets employed is about a quarter of an inch; no difficulty exists in regulating its size, which might be fixed at one inch. He opposes altogether prohibiting the sale of the fry of fishes, observing—" no real harm is done by catching young fish in tanks, jhils, or irrigated fields, for these fish, if left alone, would never find their way back to the river." *Captain Thompson*, in 1868, reported from this place—" fishing goes on at all seasons of the year, and there can be no doubt that in the small rivers and tanks the supply would be materially increased by a short 'close time.' Still I hardly think that the protection is necessary in the large rivers. But the narrow and shallow streams of this district can be well nigh cleared of fish with the net, and the supply is scanty in consequence. In such rivers the protection of the spawning fish would, no doubt, have a very good effect."

Opinion of the Collector of Sitapur.

284. The *Collector of Hardui* reports, breeding and very young fish are destroyed without discrimination and to a great extent. They are caught in nets and baskets in jhils, tanks, and rivers at all seasons, but in greater quantity during the rainy season, and especially at its close. The smallest size of the mesh of nets employed is one-sixth of an inch. Traps are also used to collect fish of the smallest size, and are made of reeds. Were it politic, there would be no difficulty in regulating the size of the mesh of nets, but as he does not consider such a time has arrived, he refrains from suggesting what size of meshes he should consider advisable in his district. When fish are scarce in "hilly districts, and as well elsewhere, there appears to be no objection against prohibiting their capture for a limited period when they are breeding." The *Settlement Officer of Hardui* in 1868 complained that there "is no close season for fish here; they are caught every day of the year. Further, the meshes of the nets are made of any size, and occasionally fish are intoxicated or half-poisoned by a jungle fruit termed *mainphul*, but this can only be done in still water, ponds, and the like. Some land-owners preserve fish and guard them, but the bulk of the proprietary bodies certainly do destroy fish wantonly. They take every fish they can catch at all seasons, whether the females are breeding or not, and whether the males are what is called 'spent fish' or are in full condition."

Hardui. Opinion of Collector.

285. The *Collector of Rai Bareli* considers the destruction of all sorts of fish as considerable, the principal season for fishing being in the hot weather and during the rains. In the former the big fish are mostly trapped; during the latter the smaller fish are more extensively caught than at other seasons of the year. The smallest size of the mesh of nets employed is from a quarter to one-third of an inch. The difficulties in regulating the size of the mesh of the nets consists in the natural dislike and prejudice of the rustic population against any innovation whatever in the implements for carrying on their craft, so he deprecates such, and gives no opinion as to what size he considers advisable. The fry of fish, he observes, are not sold separately from the fish in

Opinion of Collector of Rai Bareli.

this district, and therefore the prohibition of the sale of the fry would be superfluous.

Sultanpur. Opinion of the Collector.

286. The *Collector of Sultanpur* observes that breeding fish and young ones are destroyed, but not to any great extent. Those taken are from tanks and marshes fed by the rain, or filled by the overflow of rivers such as the Goomti. The meshes of the nets are small enough when so required to catch fish about the size of a gudgeon. Interference is not considered desirable, because there would be a difficulty at first in the novelty of making regulations laying down the size of the mesh of nets, and he refrains from answering what size he considers advisable. As a rule, the fry of fish are reported not to be sold in the bazar, and he would avoid all novel regulations suitable for European countries, interfering with property and old customs. He considers no objection exists to a close season for breeding fish in hilly districts.

Opinion of the Collector of Pratabgarh.

287. The *Collector of Pratabgarh* reports that breeding fish and very young ones are destroyed indiscriminately, and to a very great extent, from April to the end of June and from September to October, wherever they can be captured in rivers, jhils, tanks, and nallas, by means of nets, traps, or by hand. The minimum size of the mesh of nets will admit of a corn of barley passing through it, and nothing larger. There is no difficulty in regulating the size of the mesh of nets except the unwillingness of the people to let even the smallest fish escape them, and he proposes at first, as an experiment, to double the size now in use. There can be no objection to prohibiting the sale of the fry of fish in the bazars, or any other reasonable measures being adopted to arrest the senseless destruction of breeding fish and of the very young ones now going on. Some restriction also should be put on the capturing of fish in the breeding season.

Faizabad reports from Native officials.

288. The *Tehsildar of Faizabad* reports through the Commissioner that there are about 700 fishermen, 42 of whom only have no other occupation; whilst 1,500 are given as at *Baraich* and 2,830 at *Gondah,* all of whom follow other occupations; in the last locality the boatmen and palkee-bearers are included, which augments the total. In the periodical fishings of village tanks, many persons not included as fishermen join in. The names of the fishermen castes are given as follows: Gooriyas, Mullahs Chakees, Khowicks, Kuhars, Coniyas, Gharooks, Jhabjhaliyás, &c. Fish are said to be only sold in the large bazars; some of the Faizabad markets are fully supplied, others are not, as in Baraich, where the supply is not equal to the demand, whilst in Gondah contradictory accounts are given. The relative prices of fish and mutton are as follows:—

	Faizabad.			Baraich.			Gondah.		
	Rs.	A.	P.	Rs.	A.	P.	Rs.	A.	P.
Fish, large, per seer ...	0	1	0	0	1	3	0	1	3
„ small „ „ ...	0	0	9	0	0	9	0	0	9
Mutton, 1st class ...	0	2	0	0	1	6	0	2	0
„ 2nd „ ...	0	1	9	0	1	6	0	1	9

The price of fish is not regulated by the price of mutton, which is mostly consumed by Europeans; some kinds of the former are said to obtain considerably higher prices than the above. Generally about two-thirds of the population are fish-eaters, but occasionally the proportion is lower. As regards the increase or decrease in the numbers of fish, reports differ materially. In Faizabad, a slight increase is given as compared with the preceding year. In Baraich and Gondah generally they are said to have doubled. In some places the increase is reported to be confined to the small fish, the number of large fish remaining stationary. In one Tehsil in Baraich, a decrease is reported; in another an increase; both said to be due to heavy rains. One Teshildar in Gondah givet an increase owing to floods during the rains, whilst two Tehsildars repors that from the same cause many fish have been carried off to the larger rivers.

289. The *Tehsildar of Lucknow* can give no approximate number of the fishermen, for this occupation is not pursued by many as their sole business, but principally by boatmen, Passis, Mussulmen, labourers out of employ, and Kahars in their spare time. The fishermen castes are Kahars, Mullahs, Koris, Kanjars, Jhabihalias, and Pathans. The supply of fish equals the demand; large ones realize two annas a seer, and small fish one anna; bazar mutton two annas a seer. The small fish are eaten by all classes, the supply of which by all accounts, has remained stationary. Large numbers of very small fish are taken by children in shallow pools and lesser streams. The smallest nets have about a half-inch mesh. Fish are not trapped in the irrigated fields during the rains. Fishing is carried on by rod and line, casting-nets, drag and hand-nets. The local names are Sukhaui, Pailni chinta, Pandi, Khara, Jhunsti, and Halka, the various names referring to the same nets only differing in size one from another.

Opinion of Tehsildar of Lucknow.

290. The *Tehsildar of Unas* considers the fishing population at about 1,000, but they also follow other occupations. They consist of Kahars, Lodhas, and Passis. The market is fully supplied with fish, the cost of the larger sorts being from one anna to one and a half annas a seer; of the smaller, from 9 pie to one anna and a half. The first sort of mutton is two annas a seer, the second one and a half annas. About 85,000 people in this Tehsil are reported fish-eaters. The fish are stated to have increased. About 10,000 maunds of very small ones are said to be taken during the rains. The smallest size of mesh of nets used is given at half an inch, and fish are trapped in the irrigated fields during the rains. The native names of the traps and nets used are Pandi, Chhata, Lokari, Chowruhi, Bisari or Ulgi, Kanta (hook), and Tapa made of reeds and rushes, Kurwar and Halka.

Opinion of Tehsildar of Unas.

291. The *Tehsildar of Suffeepur* calculates the fishermen at about 300, but they also pursue other occupations. They are Kahars, Lodhas, Dhanhus, Passis, Chamars, Kurhers. The markets are not fully supplied. The price of large fish is from one-half anna to one anna a seer; of small fish, from one pie and a half to three pie; whilst the first sort of mutton is two annas, and the second one anna and a half per seer.

Opinion of Tehsildar of Suffeepur.

The number of the fish-eating population is set down as the same (85,000) as in the Unas Tehsil. The fish are also reported to have increased, and about 300 maunds of very small ones are stated to be caught during the rains. The smallest mesh is given at half an inch, and fish are said to be trapped during the rains, but not to any great extent. The implements enumerated as used in fishing are the same as in Unas, to which has to be added a small net termed Dhebeea.

292. The *Tehsildar of Purwah* considers that about 2,000 fishermen reside in his Tehsil, but they follow other occupations as well, and are of all castes. The local markets are not fully supplied. The price of large fish is from one-half to one anna a seer; of small ones, from three to nine pies. Two-thirds of the population are considered to be consumers of fish. The supply has increased during the last year. Some hundreds of maunds of small fish are taken during the rains. The minimum size of the mesh of nets used is given at three-quarters of an inch, and fish are said to be trapped in irrigated fields during the rains. The descriptions of nets given are Pandi, Pailni, Khadar, Chhata, Halka, Kurwar, Tap, Tapa, Dugun, and Shist.

Purwah. Opinion of Tehsildar.

293. The *Tehsildar of Mohan* reports about 300 fishermen in his Tehsil, all of whom likewise follow other occupations; they are Kahars, Passis, Koris, Lodhas, &c. The bazars are not fully supplied. The cost of large fish is six pie, and small ones three pie a seer. About half the population eat fish, whilst the supply has remained stationary. Some hundreds of maunds of small fish are taken during the rains, whilst the mesh of the nets is stated to be one inch. Fish are trapped in irrigated fields during the rains. The nets employed are Dokari, Chhinmari, Pandi, Bilni, Kurwar, Shist, Tapa, and Halka.

Mohan. Tehsildar's opinion.

294. *Rungit Singh, Talukdar of Kantha*, observes that cultivators and others catch fish, but are generally people of the following castes, Kahars, Passis, Koris, Lodhas, &c. The market is not fully supplied. The price of large fish is half an anna, and of small ones a quarter of an anna a seer. About half the population are fish-consumers. The supply has remained stationary. Small fish are taken, but not to any great extent. The mesh of the smallest nets employed is half an inch. Fish are trapped in the irrigated fields during the rains. The following are the nets and traps used:—Haluka, Kuruar, Tap, Kuttra, Jal, Koena, Khowra, Phutka or Supa, Garie ulurna, Kagurna, Lokarel, Sahjurya, Ghughuroah.

Kantha. Talukdar's opinion.

295. *Ganga Sahib*, the Manager of the Mara Wan Estate, reports 199 persons as fishermen, but they also follow other occupations. They are Kahars and Passis. The bazar is not fully supplied with fish; the cost of the large ones is from one to one and a half annas, and of small ones, from a quarter to half an anna a seer; 14 out of 15 of the population eat it. The supply has remained stationary. About 150 maunds of very small fish are taken yearly, whilst fish are trapped during the rains in the inundated fields. The traps and nets employed are Haluka, Bansi, Khuroar, Jal, Tapsa, Phutka, Jhutjhal, Juduria, Kuruar, Kutia.

Mara Wan Estate. Opinion of the Manager.

cxxxvi

296. *Chowdry GopalSingh,* Talukdar of Bangermoro, gives about the same proportion of fishermen as the foregoing; they are Kahars, Kadhairs. The bazar is not fully supplied. Large fish sell at from six to nine pies, and small ones at two and three pies a seer. The supply has remained stationary; very small fish are taken in quantities during the rains. The minimum mesh of the nets is given at three-quarters of an inch. Fish are said to be trapped in the irrigated fields during the rains. The following are the nets and traps used Jal, Pindi, Pansa, Bissiari, Lokuri, Khuwur, Kanta.

Bangermoro. Opinion of the Talukdar.

297. *Barabanki, Tehsildar of Nawabgunj,* reports there being 200 or 300 persons who fish, but all pursue other occupations. The fishermen castes are Gurias and Kahars. Very few fish, and only in the cold season, are sold in the weekly markets, the larger sorts at one anna, and the smaller at a quarter of an anna a seer; whilst first class mutton fetches three annas, and second class two annas a seer. A larger proportion of the population, it is observed, would eat fish if they could obtain them. The supply has not increased. The smallest mesh of nets is given at half an inch square. Fish are trapped during the rains in the irrigated fields. Nets and implements for taking fish are Katia, Balbi, Shist, and Tappa.

Nawabgunj. Opinion of the Tehsildar.

298. The *Tehsildar of Futtehpur* states that no persons give themselves up to fishing as a sole pursuit, but the castes that fish are Guryas and Kahars. The weekly market is stated to be sufficiently well supplied, the cost of large fish being one anna, and small fish half an anna a seer. A larger proportion of the people, it is asserted, would be consumers of fish could they obtain it. The supply has not increased, and the size of the smallest mesh of the nets is given at one inch or thereabouts. Fish are trapped in the irrigated fields during the rains. The implements used in fishing are Jal, Tappa, Halka, Paihra, Dagganshist, Barbat, Choundhi, Chan, Dor pauri, Khowri.

Futtehpur. Opinion of the Tehsildar.

299. In the *Tehsil of Samahi ghat,* it is stated that there are about 200 Guryas and Kahars who catch fish, but that they also pursue other occupations; that a sufficient amount is brought to the bazars "to give the vendors means of subsistence." Rohoos obtain two annas a seer, other large fish one anna, and small sorts three pie. A larger proportion of the people would eat fish if they could get it. The supply has not increased. Young fish are said not to be captured at all, nor fish trapped in irrigated fields during the rains. The size of the smallest mesh of the nets is given at about three-quarters of an inch square. The nets and implements employed are Pakla, Chunda, Barour, Pandi, Chilband, Nadhni, Kuttya shist.

Samahi ghat. Opinion of the Tehsildar.

300. In the *Tehsil of Hydergurh* there are about 200 Kahars who fish as well as pursue other occupations; the markets are scarcely supplied at all with fish; more could be sold. The small ones realize nine pies a seer. A larger portion of the population would eat it could they obtain it. Very small fishes are taken with nets, the mesh of which

Hydergurh. Opinion of Tehsildar.

is three-quarters of an inch. Fish are also trapped in the irrigated fields during the rains.

301. At *Sitapur* the Native official observes that the Kahars and Guryas take fish at certain times, but their regular occupation is agriculture. The local markets are not fully supplied. Large fish obtain two annas, small ones one anna a seer; mutton two annas a seer. He is unable to give the proportion of fish-eaters. The general opinion is that fish have increased, due to several consecutive years of floods. The smallest size of the mesh of nets is given at a quarter of an inch. Fish are trapped during the rains in the irrigated fields. The native names of the nets and traps in use are Pundi, Jal, Locari Jal, Maha Jal, Kharia Jal, Patia Jal, Pailna Jal, Tapa Jal.

Sitapur. Opinion of Native official.

302. The *Tehsildar of Hardui* gives the fishermen at 2,000, all of whom are said to also follow other occupations, their castes are Kahars and Bourias, especially the latter. The local markets are insufficiently supplied with fish; more, it is observed, could be sold. The large sorts realize from one to one and a half annas a seer, the small from six to nine pies a seer, and mutton two annas for the same quantity. Two-thirds of the population are stated to be fish-consumers. The supply is asserted to have increased; very small ones are taken in large numbers in nets and baskets of various sorts, whilst the minimum size of the mesh of the nets will not allow a grain of gram to pass. Fish are also trapped in inundated fields during the rains. The nets employed are Tapa, Dhundhi, Katia, and Khanchas.

Hurdui. Opinion of Tehsildar.

303. The *Tehsildar of Shahbad* computes the Kahar fishermen at 2,126, all following other occupations. The markets are insufficiently supplied, whilst about 90 per cent. of the population eat fish. The supply in the waters has remained stationary. Very small fish are taken in large numbers, whilst a grain of gram will not pass through some of the nets. Fish are also trapped in inundated fields during the rains.

Shahbad. Opinion of Tehsildar.

304. The *Tehsildar of Sundeela* gives the fishermen at 250, consisting of Kahars, Passis, and Arakhs. The market is insufficiently supplied. Large fish obtain from six to eight pies a seer, and small ones from three to six. Three-fourths of the population are reputed to be fish-eaters. The supply in the waters has remained stationary. Large numbers of very small fish are captured, whilst the mesh of the nets will arrest a grain of gram. Fish are also trapped during the rains in inundated fields.

Sundeela. Opinion of the Tehsildar.

305. The *Tehsildar of Bilgram* states there are 200 Kahars, Araths, and Bouriah fishermen. The markets are insufficiently supplied with fish, the larger ones of which obtain nine pie, and the smaller six pie a seer; 80 per cent. of the population eat fish. The supply has decreased. "More fish are caught in this Tehsil than in any other. They are exceedingly plentiful in Sandi, where small fish are often used as manure, and fry are sold in quantities for little or nothing; the smallest mesh of the nets will not pass a grain of barley." Fish

Bilgram. Opinion of the Tehsildar.

are rarely trapped during the rains. The nets employed are, besides those enumerated, Pandi Kahar, Ghunghia, Kaut, Bahana, Chaunghi, Phatka.

306. The *Tehsildar of Rai Bareli* says there are about 1,825 fishermen, but who also have other occupations; they are Kahars, Passis, Lodhas, Mullahs, Kunjrahs, Khatiks. The markets are generally well supplied, but more could be disposed of during such seasons as grain is scarce. Large fish realize from three-quarters to one anna, and small ones from a quarter to half an anna a seer; first sort of mutton two annas, and second sort an anna and a half a seer. About two-thirds of the population eat fish. Many very little ones are yearly netted, the smallest mesh of the nets being from one-sixth to one-fourth of an inch, but very few fish are trapped in inundated fields during the rains. The nets and traps are Surkuta, Tapka, Supa (for small fish), Chutta, Chowndhi, Phikwa or Chappa, Pailni, Lowkari or Murhar.

Rai Bareli. Opinion of the Tehsildar.

307. At *Sultanpur*, the Native official estimates the fishermen at from 900 to 1,000, all of whom have also other occupations; they are Mullahs, Kahars, Kewats, and Guryas. The markets are said to be fairly supplied with fish, the larger sorts obtaining from an anna and a quarter to two annas a seer, and the smaller from three-quarters to one anna and a quarter a seer; whilst the bazar mutton obtains from one and a quarter to two annas a seer. Three-fourths of the population are said to eat fish. The amount in the Goomti are said to have decreased of late years. Very small ones are netted and taken by a trap called 'Puhra.' The mesh of the nets "is so small, hardly anything can pass." Fish, but not to any great extent, are trapped in the inundated fields during the rains. Streams are dammed and fish thus taken; various sorts of nets, traps, and hooks are also employed.

Sultanpur. Opinion of Native official.

308. In the *Putti Tehsil* it is observed fishing is not confined to one class, but Kahars, Lunias, Kewats, Passis, Kurmis, and Kori, all follow it, as well as other occupations. The markets are not fully supplied with fish; the larger sorts obtain two annas, the smaller one anna and a half a seer, and mutton two annas; about half the population are stated to be fish-eaters. The amount in the waters is said to have increased this year. About 40,000 maunds of very small fish are annually netted, the mesh of some of the nets being " so small that a grain of mothi cannot pass through it." Boys generally trap fish in fields during the rains. "Fish are destroyed by Akhsah; the names of nets and traps are Jal, Kuryar, Halka, Chahtur, Khore, Choundhi, Pahrah, Tap, Harya, Punchkhi, Pailni, Bissari, Gunj, Tameri, Kantiya."

Putti Tehsil. Opinion of Native official.

309. The *Tehsildar of Pratabgarh* observes that fishermen are generally Kahars, but some are Lunias. The markets are not fully supplied with fish; the price of the larger sorts is seven pie, smaller sorts four pie, and mutton two annas a seer. About half the population are stated to eat fish. The supply in the waters this year has increased. Very small ones are taken by means of nets. "Fish are shot with guns, and caught by means of Tap, Tengali, and Pahra, and by hand when the water dries up in the month of Jeth."

Pratabgarh. Opinion of Tehsildar.

310. The *Tehsildar of Behar* observes, Kahars and others follow the occupation of fishing in addition to their regular work; besides these, there are Kewats, Kunjrahs, and Passis. The bazars are not sufficiently supplied with fish; the larger sort fetch one anna, the smaller three-quarters of an anna a seer; whilst the first sort of mutton realises two annas, and the second one anna and a half a seer. Upwards of 97 per cent. (97·78) of the population, it is asserted, are consumers of fish, the supply of which has increased this year. Very small ones are taken in large quantities by means of nets with very minute meshes, the size of which is equal to a grain of barley. Fish are not trapped during the rains in the inundated fields. The following are the nets used: Patli, Pahrah, Packkhi, Tilheri Jal.

Behar. Opinion of Tehsildar.

NORTH-WESTERN PROVINCES.

Area and Population of the North-West Provinces.

311. The North-West Provinces, according to the census and statistical account taken in 1865, contains an area of 25,375,327 acres, out of which 22,293,819 are cultivated, and 3,081,508 are unassessed. Some changes in the province have occurred of late years, as in 1858 a greater portion of the Delhi district, including 2,195,180 persons, was transferred to the Panjáb, the Pergunnah of Lonee, on the left bank of the Jumna, alone being retained, and it was merged into Meerut. In Mr. Probyn's report, it was observed that the North-West Provinces have an area of 216,152 square kilometres, with an average population of 139·30 to the kilometre, the density being thus amongst the highest on record. Of the 30,110,615 persons who were present in 1865, the agricultural class numbered 21,342,403, or two-thirds of the whole amount. "The extremes of density (1865) in the sub-divisions, into which the districts of the North-West are divided, vary from 6,773 to the square mile in Dehat Amanut of Benares (which contains the city of that name), to 37 to the square mile in Agoree, Robertsgunge, in the Mirzapur district. * * The Agra division is the most thickly populated, containing 474 to the square mile; next in order is Gouchpur, with 465 to the square mile. Benares stands next with 447 to the square mile; then Rohilcund with 440; last in order are Meerut 415, Jansie 198, Ajmere 160, and Kumaon 58 to the mile." Nearly 26 millions are Hindus, and 4½ millions Mahomedans, the latter being most numerous in Meerut and Rohilcund, where they comprise one-fifth of the population, whilst more than half of these reside in the northern districts. There are 560 castes or sub-castes of Hindus, irrespective of Christians, Mahomedans, Parsees, Bengalees, Madrassees, Thibetans, and Chinese, raising the number to 574. The Brahmins number 3,541,692, and have 70 sub-divisions; the Kshatryas 2,827,768 with 175; the Vaisyas 1,091,250 with 65; the Sudras 18,304,309 with 230; those unnoticed 12,336; Sikhs 1,425; Jains 49,983; other sects 195,977; Christians 37; Mahomedans unclassed 2,207,576; Sheiks 1,140,108; Pathans 515,526; Syuds 170,248; Moguls 41,748; Parsees 76; Bengalees 1,148; Madrassees 26; Thibetans 67, and Chinese 37.

Rivers and Canals in the North-West Provinces; also the rainfall.

312. The most important rivers in the British territory are the Ganges and Jumna, which, arising in the Himalayas, pass down through the Sub-Himalayan Sewaliks, and joining at Allahabad are continued into the Lower Provinces. These rivers, near their sources and first parts of their course, receive numerous hill affluents, many of which are not snow-fed, and these warm streams are the natural breeding-grounds of most of the important species of fish, especially the mahaseer; irrespective of this, however, very many of the sorts which, though despised by Europeans, are consumed by natives, find here the natural locality in which to deposit their spawn. All, or nearly

all, the affluents, coming from the east to the Ganges, likewise take their origin in the Himalayas, and they are equally the breeding-places of fish. The Ganges and Jumna do not appear to normally extend, during the monsoon time, in a lateral direction, over the contiguous country, to the same wide extent as do rivers in some portions of India, as the Indus in Sind; the low lands or "khadirs" being generally bounded by higher ground, termed "bangur," beyond which floods rarely pass. Both the Ganges and Jumna rivers, near the places where they emerge from the Sewaliks, have irrigation weirs across them, diverting water into the Ganges canal at Hurdwar, and the Eastern and Western Jumna canals near Karrah; lower down below Delhi exists the Okla weir across the Jumna, diverting water into the Agra canal. The rainfall in five years ending 1869-70 is stated to have averaged 33·4 inches.

313. The Ganges and Jumna rivers are replenished from two prominent causes, exclusive of springs; during the hot months the supply is derived from the ice and snow at their sources which, having accumulated during the winter, now becomes melted by the action of the sun; and in the Ganges at Hurdwar, a daily rise of about $1\frac{1}{2}$ inch and a corresponding fall are distinctly apparent. During the monsoon season, the supply comes directly from the rains, flooding all the small affluents, or indirectly due to their action on the snows; the rivers consequently at these periods are filled in rather a spasmodic manner. During the cold months, unreplenished by rains or melting snows, and much of their water being required for irrigation canals, the volume flowing down them is in places very small.

Ganges and Jumna rivers how replenished.

314. The fishes of the North-West Provinces are divisible into those of the hills and those of the plains, some of each of which classes are migratory, whilst others are not so. Upon the non-migratory hill-fishes no remarks are here needed. Amongst the fishes of the plains calling for observation are the migratory ones, especially such carps, as the mahaseer, which reside in the low country rivers during the cold months when the hill-streams are too small and too cold to afford them sustenance; but when the rains re-commence, they migrate to the hills, and ascending some distance up the cold waters of the larger rivers, turn aside for breeding purposes into their warm side-streams. Thus, these side-streams, unreplenished by snow water, are the natural breeding-places of most of the more valuable fish of the carp family residing near such places, and anything preventing their access to these spots, or destructive of the fry raised there, must necessarily injure the fisheries. A large majority of the young remain in the hill-streams until the next year's rains (see para. 168). There are likewise migratory marine fishes, as the hilsa, ascending for breeding purposes, and barriers across rivers must impede their progress; but in this province these fish, in an economic point of view, are of much less consequence than the mahaseer. The local non-migratory fishes pass up small water-courses and channels, depositing their eggs in irrigated fields, flooded plains, temporary formed tanks, or the grassy sides of rivers or lakes.

Fishes of the North-West Provinces.

315. Having thus briefly enumerated the rivers and waters used as breeding-places, and the fishes inhabiting them, the consideration arises—do any causes exist which impede their carrying out in a satisfactory manner these natural instincts? First, we have irrigation weirs across the two large rivers, which, unfurnished with fish passes, entirely preclude the re-ascent of fish having once passed over them, or happening to be below them. This must arrest every marine migratory fish ascending to breed, so they are rendered practically useless for increasing their species. Next, all the migratory carps that have passed over them during the cold months in their pursuit of food cannot re-ascend—they also become *hors de combat*. And, lastly, of the irrigation works, there are the canals which act in precisely the same way. Perhaps it will be well to give facts as witnessed by others. *The Collector of Muttra* (para. 334) observes,—"I have watched the first rush of water let in, and have been astonished at the shoals of fish brought down by it. * * In the Meerut district I saw hundreds of mahaseer come down; they were all carried over the fall as they had been over a dozen higher up between that point and Hurdwar, not one of which could by any possibility have got back again up the canal." (See para. 12 on irrigation weirs and their effects.) These canals thus form traps on a large scale wherein fish are destroyed wholesale whenever the water is cut off, and that this is not seldom, I adduce the following figures to prove. In the Eastern Jumna canal the number of times and days it has been without a supply of water are as follows :—

Marginal note: Impediments to fish breeding in the North-West Provinces.

4 years ending December 31st, 1840. No. of times closed, 58   No. of days closed, 203
5   „   „   „   1845.   „   „   53   „   „   356
5   „   „   „   1850.   „   „   48   „   „   194
5   „   „   „   1855.   „   „   47   „   „   265
5   „   „   „   1860.   „   „   36   „   „   267
5   „   „   „   1865.   „   „   31   „   „   240
5   „   „   „   1870.   „   „   14   „   „   216

If we now examine as to the comparative number of days on which the canals have been closed, we find the longest period from 29th October 1845 to December 15th, 1845, or 47 days, and the shortest a single day, thus—

During the first 4 years closures averaged $3\frac{1}{2}$ days each.
„   next 5   „   „ $6\frac{1}{2}$ „
„   „   5   „   „   4   „
„   „   5   „   „ $5\frac{1}{2}$ „
„   „   5   „   „ $7\frac{1}{2}$ „
„   „   5   „   „   8   „
„   „   5   „   „   15   „

The frequent closure of canals must be destructive to fish, unless they are able to retire into deep holes or contiguous tanks, where they may remain quiet until the canal is refilled; but of course should the canal be left dry for very long periods, as over eight or ten days, the probabilities are that the water will have become so foul that the fish will die. Out of 287 times this canal was closed between January 1837 and December

1870, we find as follows regarding the times closures occurred, with reference to the number of days—

```
From  0 to 10 days, 238 times.
 „   10 to 20  „   31   „
 „   20 to 30  „   12   „
 „   30 to 40  „    3   „
 „   40 to 50  „    3   „
```

In the Ganges canal slaughtering all the fish, whenever it was closed, was carried on when I was there, the numbers of times and the days such has occurred during the last 15 years being as follows :—

```
5 years ending December 31st, 1860.  No. of times closed, 3.  Days  27
5       „           „        1865        „           „   10    „   156
5       „           „        1870        „           „    7    „   160
```

Thus, in round numbers, this canal during the last five years has had six times more days without water than in the first five years under review; whilst the period of time it has been kept dry have risen as follows :—

```
1st 5 years—No. of days dry at each closure,  9
2nd 5   „          „         „       „       15
3rd 5   „          „         „       „       23
```

316. We now come to the fixed engines permitted to exist in these provinces, as shown by the local civil officers. First, fishing-weirs spanning hill-streams, up which large carps are attempting to ascend to breed. In those of Kumaon (see para. 330) "practically it requires a very clever fish to go up for breeding purposes, and return to the point started from uninjured! for it has to cross and re-cross several of these weirs, both on its journey up and down streams." Again in Gurwal, "the rivers are so dammed up by weirs made on purpose to catch fish, that they cannot always ascend to their spawning grounds, and fall an easy prey to the people who are on the watch for them." "Weirs are erected as soon as the monsoon begins to cease, and they remain in existence till carried away in the first flood in the rains. They are placed usually at the tail of each pool, and there is almost always one at the junction of two rivers, thus entirely preventing fish running up till the weir is carried away by a flood." Then in the plains, as the yearly floods begin to subside, when the fish which have bred, and the young which have been raised, try to obtain an exit to the rivers with the falling waters—what is it that is done? Weirs are constructed across the little streams which are the natural drains into the rivers down which they are striving to go; thus, it is stated at Bustee (para. 331) that "fish are killed more or less throughout the year, but the largest numbers are taken towards the end of the rainy season. As the waters fall, countless lakes or pools of all sizes are formed on the low lands by the rivers. Those which were during the floods mere extensions of the stream, now become lakes with one narrow exit to the river. Across this, nets are stretched or a weir of grass constructed, and every fish that has wandered up becomes a certain prey, being either caught at the weir, or left exposed as the waters fall. The same process takes places on a smaller scale in every field that is under

Fixed engines for capturing or destroying fish, as well as damming streams, &c.

water; the exit is closed, and countless small fishes are taken." In fact, fixed engines are everywhere employed, even across some of the rivers as in Goruckpur and Bustee, capturing everything. But this is not all: some fish are taken, as at Bustee, only to be wasted; and likewise the following is reported in the Koana river—"there is a trap under every bridge that spans it, where fish are caught and slaughtered in numbers;" the water having become poisoned from some natural cause, "the fish sickened and died in thousands; on the up-stream face of each of these bridges and traps, you would see millions of fish eager to get down past the obstruction, and escape from the poisoned water. In a hundred yards or so the river was a mass of living heads. The fish sickened and died in a day or two, and birds of prey came from all parts to devour them. I saw this myself, and heard that it was not of infrequent occurrence, and that the dead fish were so numerous on these occasions that they were carted off as manure." Then another amusement of the hill-people, or of fishermen who resort there to ply their poaching trade, is thus detailed :— "The poachers choose a spot where the stream and an old bed are in close proximity; both have good pools in them; they fix nets right across the stream about a mile or more below this spot. First, nets with large meshes, and then nets with smaller meshes, and these nets are kept down to the bottom with heavy stones. When the nets are all ready, they dam up the stream and open a water-way into the old bed; the force of the water soon cuts a deep way for itself, and then the late bed of the stream is left dry, except in the deep holes; all fish that try to escape down-stream are stopped by the nets. The poachers then take away all the fish they want, and leave the rest to perish gradually as the pools dry up. I have sometimes seen the small fry lying dead, six and eight inches deep, in these holes. The poachers in a day or two do the same thing somewhere else lower down, and after a month or so, when the fish have become accustomed to the new bed, they commence at the top again, and return the stream into its late bed," &c. These extracts will suffice to show the causes of the asserted decrease of fine fish in this part of India; of course, with such wholesale poaching not only connived at but approved of by some of the senior local authorities, other modes, as small meshed nets, snatching, fixing ropes covered with hooks across streams, &c., find few legal opponents. Thus the Commissioner of Kumaon observes on prohibiting breeding-fish being unfairly captured during the spawning season by the institution of close-months in the hills—" I do not perceive how the hill-people would be benefited by allowing them to go, as they would only come up to the hills during the close season ;" and as all are eaten, he considers no waste occurs, whilst the rights and amusements of these tribes should not be interfered with.

317. *What is the proportion of the general population who would eat fish could they obtain it?* Owing to only a few of the answers to the questions sent to the Tehsildars having been received, the figures are not so complete as they might have been. In the Meerut division, the Tehsildars of Bulundshuhur compute them at 60 per cent.; of Allyghur at 50 per cent.; in Bijnour 50 to 60 per cent.; in Bareilly and Rohilcund 75 per cent.; and all but high caste Hindus in Shahjehanpur; in Kumaon apparently all the hill-people, and in the Turai

Majority of Population may eat fish.

most of the inhabitants. In the Benares division, the Tehsildars of Mirzapur compute the numbers at 60 per cent.; those of Goruckpur and Benares at 75 per cent.; of Bustee at from 75 to 90 per cent.; of Azimgurh at 80 per cent.; whilst those of Ghazeepur give them as follows:—one at 50 per cent., four at 75 per cent., and one at 80 per cent. In the Jhansi division, there are no replies from the native officials to this question, but the Europeans state it is not a staple article of food with the people at large. In the Allahabad division, the Tehsildars of Banda give them at 50 per cent.; of Futtehpur at 60 per cent; of Hurripur at all but Brahmins, Banias, and some Thakoors. In the Agra division, the Tehsildars of Etawah compute them at 75 per cent., whilst in Muttra the greater proportion of people are forbidden to do so by their religion. If we consider districts in which all the Tehsildars' replies are given in a single figure as 1, we arrive at the following results:—

In 3 Tehsildarships	50	per cent. of the people.
,, 1	,,	50 to 60 ,, ,, ,, ,,
,, 3	,,	60 ,, ,, ,, ,,
,, 8	,,	75 ,, ,, ,, ,,
,, 1	,,	75 to 90 ,, ,, ,, ,,
,, 2	,,	80 ,, ,, ,, ,,
,, 2	,,	all but high caste Hindus. ,,

Thus, out of 20 returns, 17 give more than half the people of the North-West Provinces as not forbidden by their religion to eat fish.

Markets insufficiently supplied with fish.

318. *How are the local markets supplied with fish?*—Is thus replied to by the native officials—

Sufficiently	in	13
Insufficiently	,,	23
Occasionally	,,	2
Doubtful	,,	2

Whilst in the Doon, it is observed that the markets are fairly supplied, but the size of the fish brought is yearly decreasing. Those districts where fish are not to be obtained have been omitted. Amongst the European officials, in the Nynee Tal and Almorah markets a decrease, as compared with former years, is said to be very noticeable.

319. *Have the fish in the waters increased, decreased, or remained stationary?* Out of 17 answers, 6 report a stationary state, and 10 a decrease, but some of these latter consider that, owing to late heavy rains, the fisheries are recovering themselves. I should mention that heavy rains wash away fixed engines, which is the cause why fisheries in the years succeeding floods are always found better than in previous seasons. Three Tehsildars give, as a reason for a diminished amount, that it is "owing to the indiscriminate destruction of young fry." In the Etawah Collectorate, the fish in the Jumna are said to be decreasing, due to the irrigation weir near Delhi. In the hilly districts, a very general decrease is reported by the local European officials.

Fish in waters decreasing.

320. The *fishermen* of this province appear but rarely to follow this occupation as a sole means of subsistence, but merely as subsidiary to other occupations.

Fishermen, as a rule, also pursue other occupations.

k

321. *Are breeding-fish and fry destroyed?*—They are evidently, and in every division, taken in any way they can be procured.

<small>Breeding-fish and fry destroyed.</small>

322. The *modes of fishing* are very diversified; at para. 315, I have enumerated some of those which are pursued;—weirs across streams which are, or ought to be, the highways for breeding-fish and their fry, both in the hills and in the plains; screens, fixed nets, and traps capturing breeding-fish and their fry attempting to find an exit to rivers as the yearly floods subside; the damming of whole rivers in the hills diverting their courses, and taking out the large fish, leaving the fry to perish. The placing of strings armed with hooks across the usual run of fish so as to capture some, but injure many; the use of lines thus armed for the purpose of snagging breeding-fish by which some are taken, but far more, barbarously wounded, wander away to die; by knocking breeding-fish on the head with sticks, or capturing them by any poaching practice as they go up small streams in order to deposit their eggs. In short, by the taking of fish from breeding to the most minute in every possible way,—a plan which is said not to be waste, because they are eaten.

<small>Modes of fishing employed.</small>

323. The foregoing appear to show—(1) that more than half the people of the North-West Provinces might eat fish could they obtain it; (2) that the markets are not sufficiently supplied; (3) that the fish in the waters, especially of the hills and in the Jumna, are decreasing; (4) that there are no restrictions against the most destructive and barbarous modes of poaching; (5) that breeding-fish are trapped everywhere; (6) that fry are killed, often wantonly, wherever obtainable; (7) that fixed and unfixed nets with most minute meshes are used to destroy immature fish; (8) that weirs and wicker traps with very fine interstices are employed wherever they can be fixed, without any close time; (9) that waters are dammed to obtain the fish, and (10) that they are sometimes poisoned.

<small>Conclusions.</small>

324. We now arrive at the reasons that have been advanced for permitting matters to continue as they are, and which would probably come under one of the following heads:—(1) that fish are not employed to any extent as food, consequently are not worth legislative interference. This proposition is disposed of in paragraph 317, which would show that above half the population, which in 1865 comprised nearly 28 millions of people, might eat fish could they obtain it. (2) That no wasteful destruction of fish occurs, so remedial measures are uncalled for. This likewise cannot be maintained, as even were the destruction of fry not waste, they are shown to be killed, but left to rot in places, as in damming streams in hills, in weirs as in Goruckpur, and by keeping up standing weirs, as in the Koana River, preventing the fish escaping from poisoned waters, and which, when so captured, could only be used as manure. However, some officials admit waste, but (3) consider such as a prescriptive right attained by long usage. To this, omitting the legal question which comes under the next head, I will only answer by quoting the opinion of one of the local officers:—"Prescriptive right to do wrong

<small>Reasons for masterly inactivity.</small>

usly exterminate a natural source of food-supply, has
, until now, there has not been a Government strong
to control it. Thus 'suttee,' 'thuggee,' 'human
rescriptive rights' in their way, and had, moreover, a
legal sanction, and yet, because they involved loss of
re very rightly swept away, and so can this right of
of human food be." (4) It is assumed that the
truction of fish is a legal right obtained by license.
lds good, license gives no title, but is revocable at will
5) That anyhow, it had better be left alone for political
sons do not exist in the Panjáb, it is remarkable that
orth-West Provinces, more especially as the Superin-
reports that the native land-owners are carrying out
with great success. (6) That the remedies are
being a matter of opinion, I do not propose advanc-
osition to some of those which have been adduced.
are such high-caste people, and the subordinate
have to be employed, are so untrustworthy, they
nited extortion. This, being a matter of fact, must
local officers, who have the supervision and control

w enter upon what measures would doubtless prove
most effectual, and I would suggest might be
carried out in the North-West Provinces.
or nets should be prohibited: in fishing-nets the
be less than 1 inch between each knot; damming
purposes, whether hill-streams or flooded fields,
ed; fish passes to be placed in all irrigation weirs,
f fish in all canals prevented whilst the water is
ng or poisoning of waters be likewise interdicted,
all hill and minor rivers to be kept solely for
allowed within 200 yards of all weirs across
destroyed. As regards close months, if they are
ins, the first two or three months of the monsoon
ost appropriate, but, with the abolition of fixed
ght be dispensed with, at least for the present. In
, and from July 1st to October 1st are considered
months.

officials oppose these steps, I would suggest, as an
intermediate plan for the present, what
rary might modify the evils which exist. No weirs
or fixed engines of any description to be used in
1st to November 1st inclusive, but when permitted to
in writing as a license, and that they never have
een the knots of the meshes of nets, or the interstices
which they are composed: irrigation works, as in the
ning, lading, diverting streams, or poisoning waters
o be prohibited: close months from net fishing to be
tricts for three consecutive months of which one
selected by the local civil authorities; snagging to

327. The Secretary to the Government of the *North-West Provinces** observed :—" The wanton destruction of fish does no doubt exist to some extent, but, in the *Lieutenant-Governor's* opinion, it would be quite impossible to check it without introducing much greater evils, such as, the opportunities of extortion, and their interference with the habits of the people; and the irritation that would be the result of any attempt to do so would be serious. At the same time the annual recurrence of the rainy season forms a sort of close season for the protection of the fish: the supply of fish is not proved to be decreasing to any material extent, and altogether His Honor considers that there is no sufficient ground for any special action on the part of the legislature."

Opinion of Government of N. W. Provinces.

328. The *Commissioner of the Meerut Division* remarked:—"I think it may safely be concluded that the proportion of the population, who live by fishing as a trade, is not large; the proportion of persons who have no other occupation than fishing as a means of livelihood is small, but it is increased by others who resort to fishing at odd times, probably in times when they have nothing better to do; so far then as the fishermen class is concerned, I do not think there is much to fear of their efforts making any appreciable impression on the fish-supply. But there is a fear that, unless the reckless system of wholesale destruction is stopped, the fish-supply may become scant. There seem to be two main causes which lead to this wanton destruction of fish; the first is by reason of the facilities afforded for doing so in the canals and rajbahars (irrigation works), and the second is the absence of any check in respect of rivers." He continues that nets or gratings at the head of canals will be liable to be carried away in heavy floods, so proposes fish-ladders at each fall. " The main points for consideration would be(1) to prevent damming streams for the purpose of catching fish; (2) a limit to the size of the mesh in nets; (3) a close season, say * * from 1st July to 1st October, seems to be essentially necessary, and catching fish within these dates should be prohibited. The close season need not apply to every kind of fish, but to those more generally used for food; * * the limit to the size of the mesh of nets would only stop the fry being caught, but the prohibition to damming or diverting streams would also prevent the wholesale destruction which now takes place." The *Commissioner of Meerut* reported (October 29th, 1868) that there is no doubt that the most wanton destruction of fish does take place, and that fish are disappearing from the sub-streams of the Ganges and Jumna. Where 20 or 30 years ago fish of 10 or 15 ℔s could be caught, none are now to be seen except fry, and such fry the native fishermen net and snare in every way at all seasons. The *Superintendent of Dehra Doon* stated (January 29th, 1872) that " breeding-fish are destroyed in great numbers, and small fry were, until lately, also largely captured. The breeding-fish are destroyed in the commencement of the rains in every conceivable manner; they at that time run up small streams, and are there killed with sticks, caught in nets, in baskets, in temporary cruives, by hooks fastened in great numbers on to lines, and many other ways. Small fry are taken at

Opinions of European Officials in the Meerut Division.

---

* These reports were received October 10th, 1872.

the end of the rains in baskets placed in fields at the outlets for irrigation water; in the cold weather small fry are caught in nets of all kinds having very small meshes. Streams are turned, the large fish taken out, and the small fry left to perish. Waters are poisoned by which fish of all sizes and kinds are destroyed. Formerly nets with every size of mesh were used, but now, with consent of the land-owners, it has been limited to one and-a-half inches between each knot. I have found no difficulty in regulating the size of the mesh. In all streams or lakes, where there are large sorts of fish, no net with a mesh, less than that given above, should be allowed. In places where there are only small kinds, smaller meshes may be permitted, but very guardedly. No objection exists to prohibiting the sale of small fry in the bazars; it is quite easily carried out; neither are there objections to preventing the catching of fish in the hills for the first two months of the monsoon. This, however, would be difficult in the Himalayas as the streams are all in Native States. The Chiefs would, however, readily co-operate." The same officer reported (December 11th, 1871) that "wasteful destruction of fish is carried on to a fearful extent; the following are the chief modes:—from March to the beginning of the rains, streams are dammed and turned. In this district the mountain torrents, when they burst from the hills, have three or four different beds, all of which are full during the rains, but afterwards only one; one year the stream is in one of these beds, another year another, and so on. The poachers choose a spot where the stream and an old bed are in close proximity; both have good pools in them; they fix nets right across the stream about a mile, or more, below this spot. First, nets with large meshes, and then nets with smaller meshes. These nets are kept down to the bottom with heavy stones. When the nets are all ready they dam up the stream, and open a water-way into the old bed; the force of the water soon cuts a deep way for itself, and then the late bed of the stream is left dry, except in the deep holes; all fish that try to escape down are stopped by the nets. The poachers then take away all the fish they want, and leave the rest to perish gradually as the pools dry up. I have sometimes seen small fry lying dead, six and eight inches deep, in these holes. The poachers, in a day or two, do the same thing somewhere else lower down, and after a month or so, when the fish have become accustomed to the new bed, they commence at the top again, and return the stream into its late bed, catching all the fish in the new bed, &c. This used to be one of the most deadly modes of poaching; besides this, during the above period, they were in the habit of using nets of very small meshes, with which they caught the young fry of the big kinds of fish. In conjunction with the zemindars, I have put a stop to these two ways of poaching, and hence the number of small fry seen by Dr. Day; if he had seen the Song in 1868, he would not have seen the quantities of small fry he alludes to, and if, when he did see them, he had had the river netted, he would have found a total absence of fish four or five years old." [My report was in 1871, and as follows:—" The Song River, one of the tributaries of the Ganges (not replenished from melted snow, or ice water), joins the main river a few miles above Hurdwar, and when examined (February) contained but little water, except every here and there, where deep pools existed. Owing to the clearness of the stream,

I was enabled to distinctly distinguish its fish, and I may safely assert that *I never saw so many yearlings in the plains of India in such a small volume of running water.* In one pool I counted upwards of 20 mahaseer (last season's) about 6 or 8 inches in length, and these were irrespective of numerous other species of the genera *Labeo, Barbus, Rasbora, Barilius,* and *Belone.* This was not merely in one spot, but all along the course of the stream, which I followed for upwards of 2½ hours." The foregoing enquiry and report were written by myself in entire ignorance of Mr. Ross's most interesting endeavours to stop poaching on that stream; the papers furnished me at Allahabad clearly deemed poaching fish one of the vested rights of the people which ought not to be interfered with, and, whilst at the Song River, I expressed my surprise at its being so well stocked, and the reason given me there was, "that the fish were rarely molested, owing to the neighbouring rural population not eating them, and the small sale there was for fish in the sacred town of Hurdwar." It is now clear that the reason is not due to the abstinence of the fishermen, but the rules of Mr. Ross and the zemindars.] This most interesting and instructive report continues :—"The mahaseers commence to run up about the end of March or beginning of April. Like salmon and some other kinds of fish, they push their way up as high as they can get; the consequence is, that in June and July, you will see ten and fifteen pound fish in little streams not more than a yard wide ; these are all heavy with spawn, and fall easy victims to poachers. In the hills in places where the streams run between narrow rocks, the natives fasten a series of strings with sharp strong barbed hooks every three inches; a vast number of fish are destroyed in this way. The hill-men also frequently poison the rivers. In the plains, at the commencement of the rains, fish run up little streams and are easily caught. When the fish have run up and spawned, the young fry are caught in myriads at the outlet for irrigation water in ricefields and elsewhere. All the above kinds of poaching can easily be checked; only four orders are necessary : (1) damming, turning, or poisoning streams never to be allowed; (2) weirs and fixed engines to be prohibited; (3) no fish to be caught between 1st July and 1st October; (4) no nets to be used with a mesh less than 1½ inches from knot to knot. To these might be added (5) no fry of fish to be sold, and no mahaseer under 3℔ in weight. These rules are quite sufficient to prevent the destruction of fish by men, and can be easily enforced; in fact, all the land-holders, through whose estates the streams run, would combine with Government in enforcing these rules. The penal clause need not, at any rate for the present, be heavy. Rs. 50 or one week's imprisonment might be fixed as the maximum punishment. I do not suppose it is within my province to animadvert on the wholesale destruction of fish caused by canals, and Dr. Day has pointed that out quite clearly." The *Collector of Seharunpore* "has no remarks to offer on the subject." The *Collector of Meerut* (February 22nd, 1872) observed that "there is no question that considerable damage is done to the young fish, by the indiscriminate use of nets with extremely small meshes without any regard to the spawning season, and in the smaller streams by the practice, freely resorted to by the fishermen and others, of bunding up the streams, drying off the portion below, and then taking out the larger fish, while the smaller are left to perish. I do not think the establishment of a close season would meet with any opposition. At the spawning season fish are considered impure and scarcely fit for food, and it is only the very poorest part of the population that makes use of fish at that season. There would be little difficulty in the introduction of a fixed close season, and this would greatly protect the fishing interests.* * I think a close season from 15th June to 1st November would give a fair time for spawning, and the growth of the young fry. The mesh I would recommend should be one inch and a half from knot to knot, or perhaps even two inches. * * Small rewards for crocodiles' eggs would aid in the extermination of those reptiles, and this could be easily arranged for." The *Assistant Collector of Meerut* reported that " as little fishing is carried on in the rains, the destruction of breeding-fish and fry is not very great. No doubt, there is considerable destruction, for all fish, breeding or not, are, when caught, killed without distinction." Difficulties would exist in regulating the minimum size of the mesh of nets, and is "opposed to Government doing anything, especially as regards fry, because the subordinate native officers and the police being high-caste men amongst the Hindu population, it would rest with persons, quite unacquainted with distinctions in classes of fish, to decide as to what is fry and what was not, while we may be sure that considerable oppression would be exercised." The *Collector of Mozuffurnuggur* (March 29th, 1872) reported—(1) that there is no limit to the size of mesh employed, but that nets having very small meshes are used mainly for fishing jhils and ponds, and nets with larger meshes for river-fishing; (2) that nature practically provides a close season for fish during the monsoon; (3) that the consumption of fish in the district is not excessive, and consequently, the destruction of small fry does not appear to take place systematically. " Except occasionally, when fields are flooded in the rains, there does not seem anywhere, or at any time, to be any wholesale destruction of small fry;" sees no practical difficulty in regulating the minimum size of the meshes of nets, or prescribing a close season, but does not consider such necessary in his district.

329. The *Officiating Commissioner of Rohilcund* observes,—" I regret it is a subject to which I have never turned my attention, and that my own views would be worth perhaps but little, but I must state that whatever small degree of evil there may be existing from the present mode of catching fish, it is infinitesimal as compared with the greater evil of instituting at present any remedial measures. Any legal enactments prohibiting fishing at certain seasons, or the use of nets with meshes under a certain size, and the measures and means by which the law would have to be enforced, would be most annoying, irritating, and dangerous. The size and areas of water in the main streams of India are so great, that the amount of fish taken out is nothing as compared with the stock remaining, and they need no protection. The inland streams and nallas, drainage lines, and tanks are generally liable to be dried up in the hot season; and unless we believe in the popular idea, that during such seasons the fish hide themselves deep in the mud, the catching and eating of the small fish, or 'fry,' as it is called, is only bringing to use an article of food otherwise to be

Opinions of European Officials in Rohilcund.

lost. As stated before, for political reasons, I think the time has not arrived for interference, nor do I think any decrease of food-supply has been proved, which should call for repressive measures." The *Collector of Budaon* (February 23rd, 1872) reported,—" There is no doubt that fish of every age, and in any condition, are captured in this district in every season. I am not aware that there is any season especially selected for this purpose. They are taken with drag-nets and casting-nets, in baskets, and by damming up the shallow beds of rivers, leaving a passage through which the fish must pass, when they are without difficulty caught. I have seen nets with meshes of 3-10ths of an inch between the knots, and I have no doubt smaller ones are used. I have seen baskets where the interval between the straws is not more than the thickness of cardboard. * * Very small fish are taken in the rains, and also at other seasons. Whenever water drains off the land or out of streams, the water-holes are emptied of all the fish they contain. Nets with meshes 3-10ths of an inch and baskets are used for fishing, and very small fishes are thus captured." " The classes who fish for profit are chiefly Kahars and Bhatiaras." The markets are stated to be fairly supplied with fish, which is eaten by all except the higher castes of Hindus. The supply in the waters " is said to have decreased within the last few years" " It appears to me that although complete protection to fish could not be afforded in the breeding season, yet that sufficient protection might be afforded to ensure a future supply." A close season is considered possible in the larger rivers, as fish ascend to deposit their spawn, and " the size of the mesh might be restricted to 6-10ths or 8-10ths of an inch." But these measures, it is considered, would necessitate the keeping up of an establishment for the purpose. The *Officiating Collector of Shahjehanpur* (February 24th, 1872) observed,—" I have seen very small fry caught during and after the rains, by placing strips of sirkee or other similar matting across water-courses, and at outlets of jhils. All fish of whatever size caught in the nets are used for food. The supply is less in the winter than other months." " If May, June, and July were made close months, the supply of fish would be likely to increase. Zemindars could usually put a stop to fishing in their villages, if they exerted themselves, but it would require a special law to enforce their duties." The Collector, in 1868, stated " he is of opinion that an imposition of duty on fish would be the best course to protect them, and prevent any wanton destruction." [Levying a duty or license on nets has apparently commenced to have this effect in the Panjáb.] The *Collector of Bijnour* (1869) reported that a wanton destruction of fish is carried on to a certain extent in the Rivers Ramgunga and Khoh, by means of stake-nets, stretching from bank to bank. He recommended licensing nets, and regulating the minimum mesh at $1\frac{1}{2}$ inches between each knot. The Collector, in answer to the questions circulated (March 2nd, 1872), answered, as to whether breeding-fish and very young ones are destroyed to any great extent,—" I cannot speak from my own experience, but from the reports furnished by the Tehsildars in answer to the questions put to them, I think there can be no doubt that fishing is carried on all the year round, and that all fish that are caught are used; neither breeding-fish nor any young ones can escape." The mesh of nets is so small no fish can pass; does " not see how it would be possible to regulate the size of the meshes, unless fishing without a license were forbidden; in that case nets might be examined and stamped before the license was granted." Considers Government employés and the natives of India so ignorant as to the difference between fry and adult small fish, that the prohibition against selling fry in the bazars could not be enforced. The *Collector of Moradabad* (February 29th, 1872) reported,—fish of every sort are caught indiscriminately, especially in the rainy season. The smallest mesh of nets used is one quarter of an inch. " If meshes of less than one inch from knot to knot are prohibited, other means will be sure to be adopted for capturing the very small sorts of fish." One inch from knot to knot might be adopted as the smallest measure experimentally ; but it is anticipated such would give great dissatisfaction, and not remedy the real evil much. Respecting what objections exist against prohibiting the sale of fry in the bazar,—" Practically impossible, except with a large establishment, to pick out the 'fry' of the better sorts of fish, and when caught, the fry may just as well be eaten as be thrown away." The former Collector (1868) observed that wanton destruction of fish takes place in this district when fishermen go up in gangs to the rivers where they come out of the hills. And that damming a river, and diverting it from its bed, with a view of catching all the fish at one time for several hundred yards of the stream, should, without express permission, be forbidden. The *Officiating Collector of Bareilly* (March 2nd, 1872) stated that breeding-fish, and also fry, are largely destroyed on the waters subsiding after the rains, in streams, small rivers and water-courses by nets and traps, the meshes " not being large enough to admit a grain of mucca to pass through." He continues, " I do not believe any restriction is necessary. I do not believe in the alleged destruction of fish to an extent which requires interference." " As far as my experience goes, and I have fished a good deal in the Himalayas, the hill-streams are too powerful to admit of the capture of fish in the two first months of the monsoon. Fish are slaughtered wholesale in the dry months."

330. The *Commissioner of Kumaon* (1869) replied that in the smaller rivers all the fish that can be caught by any means are killed by the villagers during the cold weather and summer. The Commissioner (February 27th, 1872) observed that "the Tharoos who live in the Turai spend much of their time in the rains in catching small fish, and would be very discontented if their fishing were interfered with. I consider that it would be unwise and unnecessary to stop the inhabitants of the Turai fishing in any way." He continues—large rivers are too extensive to suffer from any system of fishing. That up the small streams, spawning-fish ascend and are killed by the villagers, all of whom try to get what fish they can. That fish can only ascend during the rains, and that for the last thirty years, he has seen that any fish, large or small, that could be caught, has been caught, and that as the rains return, more fish ascend from the plains. "If the fish that come up to the hills are allowed to go down again, as I understand from Dr. Day's report, they would do, I do not perceive how the hill people would be benefitted by allowing them to go, as they would only come up to the hills during the close season. I feel certain that every fish, large or small, however caught, is eaten—not one is wasted. And the villagers having from time

Opinions of European Officials in Kumaon.

immemorial supplied themselves with fish in any way they could, I would not recommend that this right [is it a *right* or a *license*, see paragraph 129; and is it abused or not so?] and amusement be interfered with." To carry out any rules, he considers that he should require a large police establishment, the subordinates of which would be beyond all control and of no use whatever. But that poisoning streams which is only done in very little ones should be prohibited, and could be easily carried out. The *Officiating Senior Assistant Commissioner of Kumaon, Major Fisher*, remarked (January 29th, 1872), that "both breeding-fish and very young ones are destroyed in this district to a very great extent, so much so that the absence of them as an article of diet in the Almorah and Nynee Tal markets, as compared with former years, is very noticeable, and it is a comparatively rare thing now to see good fish for breakfast, even at a European table. The destruction of fish and their absence now from some of our large rivers, such as the Surjoo in the Eastern, and the Ramgunga in Western Kumaon, is equally noticeable. In parts of these rivers, where a good angler could take his six or eight fish of a day, averaging from 6 to 12 lbs. each, the same man would not now take 2, although the angler of to-day has many devices in the way of artificial baits, which the sportsman of former days had not." There are three or four ways of destroying young and large fish: (1) by a heavily leaded cast-net, the fisherman wading waist-deep into the stream to employ it. (2) "By the use of a stout cord, thrown right across a stream; to one end is attached a short stick for a man to hold, whilst the other end of the cord is held slackly by a man on the opposite bank. Then two men generally stand on commanding rocks, overlooking some deep pool where the current is not rapid. The cord itself is armed with large iron hooks at intervals of two or three feet, being each of them about the size of one used in a patent weighing machine. The cord, thus armed, is kept about 18 inches or two feet, sometimes deeper, below the surface of the stream. Some men now go down below the pool, and with bamboos or poles stir up the fish from below, whilst, at the same time, the water from this process becomes muddy. The half-blinded and frightened fish make for the deep water of the pool above, and as they pass over the cord, the man holding the stick, jerks the cord with great skill and strength, and many a fine fish is hooked by the gills, or the tail, or through the lower portion of the stomach: as to the Kumaon it is immaterial how, so long as the fish is landed. This process not only destroys large numbers of fish, but wounds and injures very many others which go away only to die. (3) By placing at intervals from three to four feet, on a weir used for irrigation purposes, conical-shaped baskets, the point of the cone being below, and the open mouth of the cone on a level with the weir. This device is chiefly successful at night. The baskets are generally placed in portions of the weir where the stream is strongest, and an unwary fish coming too close to the weir finds himself hurled into a basket from which it is* quite impossible to escape. It is needless to point out how injurious this process of destruction is to the ascent of fish before the breeding season, and their descent when breeding is over; practically, it requires a very clever fish to go up for breeding purposes, and return to the point started from uninjured, for it has to cross and re-cross several of these weirs both on its journey up and down stream. (4) A way of destroying fry, chiefly resorted to by boys, of damming up small streams, but not worth any detailed notice." Otters, and a large siluroid fish, are also mentioned as doing some little injury. "The seasons in which most fish are destroyed are during summer when the water is very clear and the river low, and again in the winter, after the monsoon has subsided, and the rivers are reduced to their ordinary level. The smallest-sized mesh of the nets employed in Kumaon are from half to three-fourths of an inch between knot and knot. They are chiefly used to catch the small fry which swarm on both banks of a river during the hot months, and also to take fry which have been left in ravines running down to a river, or in stagnant pools when the river has subsided to its natural bed after the monsoon." No difficulties are anticipated in prohibiting the sale of "fry in the bazars of Kumaon, because I do not believe there is any class of the community in towns, dependent solely on this description of food, and, if I remember rightly, the practice is already prohibited in some municipalities without causing public inconvenience. The advantage is that sales of fry being prohibited, the supply, and with it the destruction of fry, will at once cease in all streams within marketable distance of bazars." Fence months, it is suggested, should extend from 1st April to 1st July. The question of *prescriptive rights* is thus alluded to : " the prescriptive rights of the people will possibly require legislative action, but it is quite time the 'common-sense principle' was declared once for all, that no people in the world, other than savages who do whatever pleases them, have a prescriptive right to do anything which destroys or diminishes a spontaneous source of food. The same principle has been applied in the use of water and timber : why should it not be applied to so important an article as human food ? If compensation must be given, then let it be; it only shows what the State is obliged to be responsible for, by too strict a respect for these so-called ' prescriptive rights;' the people themselves will be the eventual gainers, and on these grounds alone the legislature should take the matter in hand at once. Prescriptive right to do wrong things, or injudiciously exterminate a natural source of food-supply, has only existed, because, until now, there has not been a Government strong or civilized enough to control it. Thus 'suttee,' 'thuggee,' 'human sacrifices' were all prescriptive rights in their way, and had, moreover, a certain amount of legal sanction, and yet, because they involved loss of human life, they were very rightly swept away, and so can this right of wanton destruction of human food be." He proposes (1) a close season from 1st April to 31st July, in each year, for all fishing other than rods; (2) the minimum size of the mesh of nets to be $1\frac{1}{4}$ inches between knot and knot, and the prohibition of the sale of fry in the bazars; (3) that the forest patrols or special police enforce a close season ; (4) that fixed traps at weirs, and cords with hooks attached, as above described, be prohibited ; (5) that a system of licenses be established to pay for a conservancy establishment. The *Officiating Senior Assistant Commissioner, Gurhwal* (December 23rd, 1871), reported that almost all classes use fish as food when procurable. "The wholesale destruction of fish and their fry commences in these hills. The rivers and streams here are the breeding-grounds of the mahaseer, kalonee or kala-banj, and other fish which ascend them in the rains to spawn. Not only are large fish destroyed on their upward and downward route, but the fry are caught wherever they are to be seen. Moreover, the rivers are so dammed up by weirs made on purpose to catch fish, that they cannot always ascend to their spawning-grounds, and fall an easy prey to the people, who are on the watch for them. There are several modes of catching fish; the principal are netting; by weirs with one exit, at which a wicker basket or trawl is fixed; and by snagging, or as it is called the 'raksha;' fishing with rod and line is rarely practised. Netting is carried on at all times of the year, but chiefly during floods, when the water is dirty, and the fish come to the edge to feed, or when the water is very low indeed. Weirs are erected as soon as the monsoon begins to cease, and they remain in existence till carried away by the first floods in the rains. They are placed usually at the tail of each pool, and there is almost always one at the junction of two rivers, thus entirely preventing fish running up till the weir is carried away by a flood. Snagging is, in my opinion, by far the most uselessly destructive method. It is carried on as follows:—Two men, one on either bank of the stream, hold a long and strong line between them. To this are attached several large hooks, between each of which are fastened flat pieces of stick, so placed as to keep the hooks with the point upwards. The hooks are allowed to sink to the bottom, and when a fish, working his way up stream, comes over the hooks, the man on the higher bank jerks the line, and very frequently transfixes the fish. Of course, many fish must get away maimed; but 1 have seen numbers, amongst them mahaseer of 15 to 20 lbs. weight, caught in one pool in this manner. All villagers living along the larger rivers pursue this method during the cold season when the water is clear, and very few large fish can escape them. Were it not for the damage done by maiming fish, it would not be so objectionable, as what are caught are eaten; but as it is, I think it a pernicious plan, and one which almost completely clears the fish out of the deep pools where they rest during the cold season." Some villages have purchased the right to catch fish thus, but they must be few. Large quantities of fry and small fish are said to be destroyed in the numerous small streams, and interference might create dissatisfaction. "That the number of fish is decreasing is well known and acknowledged, so much so, that the people living high up one of our rivers, an affluent of the Aleknunda, complained to me that owing to the number of weirs, they found that very few fish can find their way up as far as their villages. Being a fisherman myself, I too can testify that in some rivers where there used to be first-rate rod-fishing, it has greatly deteriorated in the last few years, while the size of the fish has also decreased." The following are Captain Garstin's propositions: "(1) that no weirs be allowed at the junctions of rivers; (2) that every weir should have in the deep stream an escape, which should never be blocked up by nets or wicker baskets; (3) that no weirs should be allowed where the people have not a distinct recorded right permitting them to erect one; (4) that there shall be a close season from netting, during the months of July, August and September; (5) that snagging be prevented wherever the people have no recorded right allowing of it; (6) that a certain number of pools in every river shall be held public property, in which no means of catching fish, save by rod and line, should be practised. It may be urged that the first three points infringe on the rights of the people; but, on the other hand, such rights must militate against the welfare of the majority, and not only prevent the proper increase of fish, but also damage the rights of others living along the same stream, but higher up, by preventing fish reaching them. ["But a fishery is, in its nature, enjoyable wherever the fish have a free passage. The right of a riparian owner may be injured by the acts of other riparian owners, both above and below him, but more frequently by those beneath him, seeing that fish are in some way connected with, and come from the sea." In India, the large rivers to which mahaseer resort during the dry season would stand in the place of the sea in England, and their migrating up those hill-streams to breed is necessary to their due propagation. "If, therefore, one riparian owner fix a net or erect a weir which entirely obstructs the fish, he necessarily deprives the upper riparian owners from deriving from the water one of the uses to which they are entitled. Though one riparian owner may by fishing by net or rod at all hours, and, by means of servants and assistants, almost use up the fish as effectually as by keeping fixed nets, this kind of user could not properly be a cause of action, just as one owner, who has a large number of cattle, would not be liable to an action at the suit of another who has no cattle, and so takes no use of the water. But it is otherwise where a total obstruction occurs. Hence, even independently of any statute, any fixed apparatus in a river or stream, which prevents the fish going up to the other riparian owners, is a good cause of action at common law, as it deprives him of one of the natural riparian rights." Paterson, *Fishery Laws of the United Kingdom*, p. 43; also Lord Ellenborough gave the following judgment:—" Though twenty years' acquiescence may bind parties whose private rights only are affected, yet the public have an interest in the suppression of public nuisances though of longer standing;" and such he ruled weirs to be. Likewise, although the public have indulged in license from time immemorial, it gives no right in fishing. "A license of fishing is distinct from the right of fishery, and is at most only a justification for what would otherwise be a trespass. A license is revocable at will, and in order to be binding, even for an hour, must be granted by deed," Paterson l. c. p. 57.] The right of erecting weirs was not, I believe, carried on to the same extent in former days as now. They were not then so regularly or so generally made, and were not of the same impassable nature as those now erected. For I have seen some which none of the fish inhabiting these rivers could possibly pass. Besides, where a matter becomes one of public importance, as the preservation of fish is, surely the rights of private parties, especially when in the minority, ought to give way. In the hills, too, a fishing right does not bring in much pecuniary advantage, as fish are not sold to any great extent; and by somewhat curtailing it, the only hardship inflicted would be, that the possessors would not be able to destroy fish to the extent they now do, and yet would always be able to get sufficient for their wants, while an equal supply would be available through the whole course of the several rivers." Considers it would be very difficult to regulate the size of the mesh of nets, so would prohibit netting from July to September inclusive. Respecting the 6th proposition, "it is one that might be easily carried out, as there are numbers of pools on all rivers which belong to no one, but which are netted and weired. Any such might be declared public property, and all fishing, except by rod and line, prohibited." Levying licenses, it is considered, would not answer, as such would require a large establishment to see it carried out. Otters do not destroy fish in the proportion man does, and offering sufficient rewards would be very expensive. "If rules for the preservation of fish are introduced, there must be punitive measures also, as without these no amount of rules will have any effect on the natives. The punishments, to be of any avail, should be heavy, as the difficulty in bringing home offences is so great that light punishments would have no effect." "The rivers in which rules are to be enforced should be publicly proclaimed, as some, such as the Alcknunda, Pindur, and other snow rivers, are of such a nature that fish cannot easily be destroyed. It is the warmer and shallow streams which are the spawning-beds, and where the greatest mischief is done. A small establishment might be necessary for patrolling, but these could be paid out of the fines. Even if Government had to pay them, considering the benefit that must eventually arise from the preservation of fish, the money would be well spent. In conclusion, I would add that I have not, owing to the nature of the district, been able to give statistics in support of my arguments; but having taken a considerable interest in the matter, and knowing the amount of unnecessary destruction that is caused to fish, I feel sure that unless some measures are taken for their preservation in our hill-streams, the better kinds, which have already decreased in quantity, must soon become very scarce; and my opinion is not only based on personal observation, but on what I have been told by the people themselves." The *Superintendent, Turai District* (January 20th, 1872), observed—that the pergunnahs forming this district stretch along the foot of the Himalayas, having nowhere a greater width than 14 miles. They are traversed by streams which debouch from the hills; whilst, in the pergunnahs themselves, rise numerous springs, which, increasing in volume, finally, as nallas, fall (some in the Turai itself, and some in the country to the south) into these hill-streams. The streams from the hills are dry during the hot weather, and the discharge from the other rivulets is but small. The greater number of these smaller streams are used for irrigation, and for the cultivation of rice. This was formerly done by the erection of large earthen dams, which, backing up the waters for some distance, formed places favourable for fish. An escape permitting a free passage for fish generally existed. On sanitary grounds these bunds have been removed, and only dug-out channels are now permitted. The whole community, except a few prohibited by caste, are consumers of fish, which are generally caught by the Deemur caste, but others, when at leisure, also employ themselves in this pursuit. Amongst the Bhoksas and Tharoors, the whole inhabitants of villages will go together at a time hunting for fish. With the exception of the "roh," "sol," and "kerril," the fish spawn in Asarh, but these do so in Chait. The mahaseer are so few they are not worth taking into account. The three fish mentioned are the only ones fit to eat according to European taste. All these fish are said, during latter years, to have become scarce, but it is attributed to the removal of the dams. [It is a very remarkable circumstance that a reason is always found · to account for a decrease of fish, and that reason is rarely put down as man; it is too little or too much rain; but fishing-weirs totally impeding any passage to spawning-grounds, capturing breeding-fish, or destroying the fry are omitted from the category.] During the rains numerous small fish are caught in the fields and *gools*. " I do not think it would be advisable as regards the Turai to impose any restrictions, and for the following reasons. The tract is excessively narrow (14 miles), and the fish found in it of little value, the result of any conservancy would be trifling; [if 14 miles length of rivers existing between the hill where fish ascend to breed, and the plains to which they descend in the cold season, ought to be permitted to be poached by fixed weirs, it is difficult to understand why fish should be protected anywhere. Here is their road,—is such to be open or closed?—should all narrow highways be blocked?] the waters are insignificant; the removal of the earthen dams has, I believe, enabled the fish to pass to and fro, and any fishing in the Turai rivulets can have little effect on them." He continues that small fish are the chief object of the fisherman's labour, and were catching them prohibited, perhaps the agriculturists would migrate.

331. The *Commissioner of Benares*—Replied (in 1869) "that fish are taken at all times of the year, irrespective of the spawning season, which must seriously affect their increase." In answer to the questions now circulated, the Commissioner (May 20th, 1872) reported the supply of fish may be said to be unlimited throughout large portions of the district, owing to extensive *jhils*; considers the rainy season as practically a close one, whilst regulating the minimum size of the mesh of the nets, to be effectually carried out, would lead to the obvious evils of interference by untrustworthy subordinates, but the sale of the fry of fish might be stopped by municipalities in the bazars. The *Magistrate of Goruckpur* (February 28th) observed on the destruction and waste of fish,—" It is sufficient to remark that the natives catch fish all the year round, at all times, and in all places, without any regard to the spawning season and the mixture of the fry, to show that great destruction must be committed. Their greediness also in sparing nothing, however small, which can contribute towards a meal, is an equally strong evidence of waste. It is even said that the *mallahs* and *kewats* dig the spawn of fish out of the banks of rivers (see paragraph 166, p. xcii), and after preparing it in a certain manner, either consume it themselves, or offer it for sale. Small auxiliary waters are the chief scene of this destruction, and the chief agent is a dam, called *chilwan*, which is stretched across a stream, and catches all the fish, however small, which may descend, while at the same time it entirely interrupts their ascent. I have inspected two of these dams constructed in the *Rohan Nuddi* at Domingarh, and have carefully examined their construction and operation. The dam *chilwan* resembles a screen made of common reed called *surput*; the reeds are so close together that the smallest fry can hardly get through, and the dam is further plastered at its foot with mud and strengthened with matting, *chatuie*,

Opinions of European Officials in the Benares Division.

so that no passage exists for anything. In midstream the screen opens into a long and narrow passage walled and floored with the same materials; and this terminates in a basket, named *kotera*, which is a hamper made of reeds, into which a small orifice in the side gives admittance to fish beneath the surface of the water, whilst the lid remains above the surface, and is opened from time to time for the removal of the spoil. As the water hardly finds its way through the interstices of the screen, it rushes in a strong current along the passage, carrying the fish with it, and a fall from the passage into the basket precludes all chance of escape. The months during which the greatest destruction of fry and small fish takes place are Sawan, Bhadon and Kunwár. A considerable quantity is taken all over the surface of the inundated country, both by means of traps, and nets, called *jheenguree*, a casting-net, and *eenliyáree*, one which is spread over the irrigated fields, and dragged along the ground. It is called *eenliyáree* because it has small pieces of bone and brick attached to it, in order to attract the notice of the fish. The small size of the ordinary mesh in nets is another important feature in the progress of destruction. Being only a quarter of an inch or less between the knots, it suffers very few fry to escape. The tehsildar of the sudr tehsil remarks that there has been a continuous decrease in the supply of fish in this district for the last twenty years." It is proposed— (1) to regulate the minimum size of the mesh of nets; (2) that a close season be instituted extending over the breeding period, and whilst young fry are moving about; (3) that the sale of fry be, as far as possible, prohibited; (4) that the construction of fishing dams be checked or regulated; if permitted, they should not be used during the breeding season, and never constructed of such close materials as at present; (5) that nets and dams be licensed; (6) that rewards be given to informers; (7) that the destruction of spawn should be penal; (8) that a small force of peons be entertained to see the regulations carried out. The *Collector of Bustee* (January 13th, 1872) reported,—" I believe, no doubt, here as well as in every other part of India, the fisheries are not used to the best advantage, and that if well-considered restrictive measures were introduced, the supply of fish might be immensely increased." " Fish are killed, more or less, throughout the year, but the largest numbers are taken towards the end of the rainy season. As the waters fall, countless lakes or pools of all sizes are formed on the low land by the rivers. These, which were, during the floods, mere extensions of the streams, now become lakes with one narrow exit to the river. Across this nets are stretched, or a weir of grass constructed, and every fish that has wandered up becomes a certain prey, being either caught at the weir, or left exposed as the waters fall. The same process takes place on a smaller scale in every field that is under water. The exit is closed, and countless small fish are taken. The smaller streams, too, are dammed up, through their length, for irrigation purposes; and when no more water is required, a small opening is cut in the dam: a basket, or most frequently a grass screen, is put in the opening, which prevents the very smallest fish passing, and thus every one is killed. But it is useless to detail what may be seen in almost every district. During the rains it appears to be an instinct with every fish to ascend the stream, even when there is barely sufficient water to cover them, and having thus got into danger by resorting to the shallowest waters, they are assailed in every possible way by nets of all kinds and of the very smallest mesh, and by fixed engines of the most deadly nature, which, when once set up, remain permanently, without even the weekly open time so strongly insisted on in England, and with the water-way often closed, not merely by a net, but by a screen of reeds placed so closely together that none but the very smallest fish could get through. In this district which is low, and very swampy, the numbers can be renewed every rain from the rivers, but I have often wondered how any fish of the smallest kind could remain in *jhils* such as I have seen in Oudh. There are numbers there, often miles from a river, which I have seen dragged with the smallest meshed nets, so as to take apparently every fish two inches long; then emptied of their water in February for irrigation, and yet after the bed has lain dry from February to June, there are again next year apparently as many fish as ever. Poisoning of the water is said to be another means of destruction, but I have never known it done intentionally. I remember hearing in the Humeerpur District that it occurs naturally every year. The Bela Tal at Jeitpur is formed by an embankment across a low valley, and the course of a small hill-stream lies through it. During the hot weather this stream becomes almost dry, only retaining water in holes in the midst of the jungle. These holes become full of dead leaves, and with the first burst of the rains, the putrid contents are swept down into the lake. The consequence, I was told on the spot, is, that numbers of fish are perfectly stupefied and float on the top of the water, an easy prey to any one who will take them." [This is a very interesting instance of destruction of fish which at these seasons may be occasioned by one of the three following causes—(1) mud in waters, (2) the action of infusions of dead leaves or fruit, due apparently either to simple putrescence, (3) or else to the leaves or fruit having an inherent poisonous character.] "There can be no doubt that the supply is said, in many places, to be falling off, though this is not the case here as yet, and that if a proper remedy can be found, it might be largely increased." As to close seasons they should vary in different localities; it would do great good, and during April and May fishing should be prohibited. There would be great difficulty in regulating the size of the mesh of nets, or to decide upon what are fry, were their sale prohibited. Mr. Hobart reported of this district (see para. 334)—" In Bustee, and I believe in Goruckpur, manorial rights exist in fisheries, in the innumerable tanks, *jhils* and rivers there are very valuable, while cases of dispute about them are of daily occurrence. There, there is undoubtedly a most wanton destruction of fish. I remember the Koana used to overflow its banks yearly, and millions of fish used to come into the quiet waters of the lagoons lying near the stream. There was a system of staking the mouths of those lagoons, when the water fell in the river at the end of the rains, as the fish tried to get away. Except the very large fish, which leaped the artificial barrier (and it was more than four feet above the water), the rest of the fish were slaughtered in tens of thousands, and an incalculable waste occurred. Had the fish been gradually killed and sold, the plan has its advantages; as it is, it requires restriction very badly. Again, in that same river, especially in the remote parts, there is a trap under every bridge that spans it, where fish are caught and

l

slaughtered in numbers. I have never heard of poisoning being used as a means to capture fish there, but I remember seeing the stream poisoned naturally. At the end of the cold season some rain had fallen, and had washed the forest leaves into the water, which turned from this, or other cause, to a dull red colour. The fish sickened and died in thousands. On the up-stream side of each of the bridges and traps I have mentioned, you could see millions of fish eager to get down past the obstruction, and escape from the poisoned water. In a hundred yards or so, the river was a mass of living heads. The fish sickened and died in a day or two, and birds of prey came from all parts to devour them. I saw this myself and heard that it was not of unfrequent occurrence, and that the dead fish were so numerous on these occasions that they were carted off as manure. This is certainly a crying evil and demands a remedy. * * Legislation is called for in Bustee." The *Officiating Collector of Bustee* (April 4th, 1872) remarked :— "It is during and immediately after the rains that a very large number of small fish are taken. The whole country becomes a swamp during the rains, and when the waters subside, every field that has been flooded becomes the scene of slaughter. Most of the fields here are surrounded with a high bank, to keep up the water, if necessary, for the rice, and the cut at the lower corner of this is obstructed by a basket or grass screen; this effectually prevents the escape of any fish, and as the water runs off, they are left exposed." " There can be no doubt that the mesh used is as small as can conveniently be made. There is hardly a method of fishing which is not practised, except, indeed, fixed engines in river-beds. These could not be permanently employed to any great extent, for the yearly floods would sweep them away." Nets of all sizes and shapes are used in the rivers, but the greater part of the fishing is carried on in the lakes and shallows formed by the overflow of the rivers. Where the waters are shallow and drying up, bunds are erected and fixed traps placed, as in the outlets to rice-fields; nets and all kinds of devices are employed, and finally the remains of the water are baled out; thus nothing escapes. In smaller pools water is baled out into a channel; a screen is placed there; the most minute fish are unable to get away. Should lakes communicate with large rivers, the channels are embanked, and as the water subsides every fish is taken. "The only method, not practised to any extent, is poisoning the water, and this indeed could hardly be carried out effectively here, for it requires a running stream to spread the poison through the pools, and shallows below, where the fish may be picked up." Considers too great difficulties exist to regulate the size of the mesh of nets, and would give rise to extortion; the same difficulty would be in the way of prohibiting the sale of the fry of fish in bazars. The *Collector of Mirzapur* (February 12th, 1872) observed:—" My own opinion is, that if the Government resolve on interfering with the present practice of fishing, that interference should be very limited in its extent, and confined to such large rivers as the Ganges, Jumna, &c., which pass through civilised and rich countries, the inhabitants of which will be better able to appreciate the motives of Government. It will be unfortunate if any further measures of an unpopular character are introduced this year on the top of the income and acreage taxes, the commutation of jaghirs, and the census, and I am quite sure that however limited the restriction on fishing may be, it will be looked on with disfavour and dissatisfaction, and the machinery which will have to be used to restrain fishermen will not be the least burdensome feature of the measure. Supervisors and a host of chuprassies will have to be let loose about the country, who by their rapacity and oppressiveness will cause a measure of usefulness and ultimate profit to be hateful to the fishermen, and indirectly to the consumers of fish. If it is objected that the measure can be carried out by the existing Police force and Tehsil establishments, as probably it can be, then every fisherman in the district will be under the eye and dependent on the favour of the Police or Revenue establishments. And the result is plain to see—not a fisherman would be in favour with these officials, unless the tables of the latter were freely supplied with fish, &c. The fact is, in this part of the country, there is enough fish for all who want it, and to spare, and there is no need whatever for any change of practice, and I strongly deprecate any interference whatever" [With such strong opinions of reprobating action in a question which he admits may "cause a measure of usefulness and ultimate profit," it is to be regretted more reasons are not adduced to show if any regulations are needed, and if so, what such ought to be. The following notes, however, are forwarded, which do not seem to prove that the fisheries are well cared for in this district.] The *Assistant Collector*, whilst repeating the above objections, observes:—"In this district breeding-fish and very young ones are undoubtedly destroyed indiscriminately to a very great extent. In the Ganges and other rivers, in tanks, ponds, flooded lands, &c., principally during and after the rainy season, by nets of all sorts, by rods, by traps, by draining off water, and so stranding them, or lading them out, and in some places even by poison. The meshes of some of the nets used are no larger than a small pea." If the minimum size of the mesh of nets is regulated, such should only be in force for the two or three months following the breeding season, but "the people concerned will look upon legislation on this subject as a new interference with, and an unfair restriction of, their rights." That no objections exist against prohibiting the sale of fry in the bazars, which would be easily put in force, at least in the principal bazars. The *Officiating Collector of Benares* (January 11th, 1872) observed:—"Although it is doubtless true that both breeding-fish and very small fry are extensively caught, the result of enquiries instituted by me does not prove that there has been any observable diminution in the supply of fish in the city of Benares during the last few years." Hindus, except Baishnus and Jains, use fish as food, as do also the Mahomedans, with this reservation that the Shias reject the scaleless forms. A belief appears to exist that during the hot weather and rains fish are not so wholesome as during the cold months. "Amongst the Brahmins, I am informed that about 25 per cent. eat fish, while amongst the rest of the population, 75 per cent. may safely be put down as fish-eating." The larger kinds of fish are sun-dried and salted at certain seasons, and are almost wholly sold to Bengalis. About 50 maunds of fish per diem are consumed in the district, except in April and May, when the supply is largest. "(1) Breeding-fish are extensively destroyed in this district, also very young ones, but the latter only in the rivers and streams. (2) From the months of March to June, breeding-fish full of roe are extensively caught by means of the nets in ordinary use. From July to September, young fry are caught, but they are not specially fished for in this district; indeed, in *talabs* belonging to private parties, I am informed that special care is taken not to destroy the fry at this season, but that frequently these *talabs* are replenished with young fry caught in the rivers. (3) The smallest size of mesh used is so small as to arrest the most diminutive fry." If the minimum size of the mesh employed is fixed, complaints are anticipated, but no objections are known against prohibiting the sale of fry in the bazars. The *Collector of Ghazeepur* (February 9th, 1872), being only new to the district, considered it better to forward a memorandum submitted by *Mr. Joseph Smith*, Deputy Collector, who reported as regarding whether there is any great destruction of breeding-fish and fry? "I believe this question must be answered in the affirmative. I cannot say that the destruction is greater or less than in any other district, but I have seen very young fish destroyed in very large numbers. I have seen baskets-full of fry carried past the Gará Bazar on many occasions, containing very small fish, an inch or $1\frac{1}{2}$ inches long, and have little doubt a good proportion of these would be absolutely wasted from the want of purchasers or consumers. What were left would be thrown out as refuse; it is stated that fish are recommended as a manure for vines. As for breeding-fish, I do not think the slightest attention is paid to the season in which they are caught. A native fisherman would not hesitate to catch fish in whatever condition it was, provided he could sell it or eat it." They are taken "in every manner, wherever possible, and at all times. I have seen hundreds caught with a small hand-net on the banks of the Ganges in front of my own house. Many basket-nets are used in irrigation channels and the outlets of *jhils*, &c." Difficulties are considered to exist in regulating the minimum size of the mesh of nets, due to the "prying it would entail into the houses of those who kept nets, and the untrustworthy character of the subordinate native agency through which it would have to be done. It would open another door to bribery, which it would be impossible altogether to prevent, and hard to detect and check. I would have no net less than $1\frac{1}{2}$ inches between knot and knot. Prohibiting the sale of fry in bazars would be an interference with trade, as there must be a demand to cause a supply; but this objection loses its weight in this case, where a valuable source of good wholesome food is being destroyed wantonly, or at least becoming scarce. Close seasons, it is considered, could not be effectually carried out." "There is no doubt crocodiles destroy large quantities of fish, and might themselves be destroyed with very little trouble. A small reward would cause the production of numbers of eggs, and a larger one would result in the destruction of many of the mature reptiles." As regards who eat fish? "With two exceptions I can hear of no class or race of the inhabitants of this district that does not use fish as food. Brahmins, Rajputs, and all classes are allowed to eat it, that is, they may if they like, and would not be turned out of caste for so doing. The two exceptions are (1) Bhaguts, and similar persons who are under a vow; and (2) Agurwala Baniahs. I was surprised to hear that these latter are prohibited from eating fish, and must confess I never heard it before, and I cannot discover any satisfactory reason for this prohibition; the only one given is, that it has been the custom from all time. I am assured, however, that an Agurwala Baniah would be turned out of caste for eating fish, while a Brahmin would not be. "The *Collector of Azimgurh* (May 13th, 1872) observed that at his "request Dr. Wood, Civil Surgeon of Azimgurh, has drawn up a very full and interesting memo. on the subject which I enclose." (I omit transcriptions from it, as it will be referred to.) "Much of the water-supply is diverted for irrigation, or otherwise dries up by evaporation, and it is then that the principal destruction of fish and fry ensues. But it appears to me that this destruction is unavoidable from the nature of the case, and that unless we are prepared to prohibit irrigation from these streams and ponds when the water is low, a proposition which could not be seriously entertained;" &c. [neither has it ever been proposed, that I am aware of, any more than the existence of fixed engines for the destruction of the fry of fish, at every outlet in flooded fields, has been advanced as necessary for purposes of irrigation.] He considers it would neither be just nor expedient for Government to interfere with present customs, whilst rewards for crocodiles would only result in the expenditure of a considerable sum of money. Is "totally averse from all interference in other parts of the district." Any measure would necessitate establishments which, "it is to be feared, would be mere engines of oppression and extortion. Further, the adoption of protective or prohibitive measures would everywhere give rise to general misconception and misapprehension of the views of Government, and foster those feelings of discontent which the taxation of recent years has undoubtedly engendered." The memo., drawn up at the request of the Collector by the *Civil Surgeon of Azimgurh*, is very discursive, but the following are a synopsis of his replies. As to whether breeding-fish or very young ones are destroyed to any great extent? Of "those fish spawned and matured in the district, that is, those found in *jhils* and their offshoots, * * when the rains cease, the temporary streams gradually lessen and dry, and then it is the destruction of fry takes place. Then the fishermen most exert themselves, and by the employment of nets, and they often of a most minute mesh, catch wholesale fairly grown fish and fry alike. There is no doubt that by such practice much waste is caused." He goes on to define this waste that if the fish were permitted to grow, more food would be available; still he does not think this waste, because they are actually consumed. "Damming is said to be the favourite method of fish, or rather perhaps fry, killing. Very common and very fatal is the construction of small dams and embankments into which the water is first led, and then drained off, leaving the fish;   *   *   these are generally fry, high and dry, an easy prey to the village children, in these cases very frequently the depredators. These fish, however, are also used as food, and seen never to glut the market." In large rivers during the rains, netting is stated to be impracticable; that subsequently the mesh is "4 inches from knot to knot." "When these rivers overflow their banks, and that is no rare occurrence, then considerable loss of fry and fish life results, as the water, retreating, leaves them stranded on the higher ground; but even these are not actually lost or wasted, as the lower caste people collect and consume this, thus so easily obtainable, staple of food." " With respect to the fishing in the Gogra, special conservative customs prevail. From May to September is regarded as a close season, and all fishing by nets is abandoned, it may be because impracticable." [If this gentleman's statements were thus tested, I fear that he would soon ascertain some error must have occurred, *viz.*, fishing in the Gogra to be prohibited from May to September, and when such is permitted, all nets to have a mesh of 4 inches between each knot. He holds, if fry are eaten, capturing them is not waste, although "the fry and fish by any and every way obtained are all consumed, and are not in excess of the need of the people;" if so, it must be "waste" to destroy so much young life. What would be considered of such an argument as this—"a nation of savages, who possess large herds of cattle and live on animal food, find it becoming scarce, yet they eat all their young lambs and infantile calves." Would common sense not think such waste? The only analogy I can see to such arguments as are adduced, would be what an Andamanese might bring forward, as they cut down trees to obtain the fruit, regardless of next year's supply. Are we to take them as our model?]

332. The *Commissioner of Jhansi* (May 3rd, 1872) observed—that the district of Jalom possesses no lakes, and the only river is the Jumna. In the Lullutpur district the only streams which contain fish of any size are the Betwa, Sujad, Sujnam and Jumnee, and their beds are, as a rule, too rocky to admit of the use of large nets; indeed, these rivers appear to be but little fished—the Dheemurs and very lowest classes alone living on the produce. There is little, if any, wasteful destruction; the real enemies of the fish are the crocodiles, otters, and fresh-water sharks which abound in the largest and deepest pools. At present no rules for the preservation of fish are necessary: the population is scanty and scattered. Great numbers of fish are undoubtedly killed during the spawning season in the small streams and feeders to the lakes when they should not be disturbed. It might prove advantageous elsewhere to prohibit river-fishing from June to October as suggested by Mr. Sturt, but it is not necessary in Bundlecund where fish cannot be said to form the staple food of any class of the people, save the Dheemurs, and they are not a numerous body. The *Deputy Commissioner of Jalom* (May 7th, 1872) reported:—"Breeding-fish and very young ones are indiscriminately caught, and very young ones destroyed to a great extent. This destruction goes on at all seasons by netting, weirs, &c. Meshes of different sizes are used, but the usual mesh is about a quarter of an inch." The difficulty in regulating the minimum size is that such "would revolutionise all ideas of native fishermen on the subject, and meet, therefore, with much opposition." The *Deputy Commissioner of Lullutpur* (December 27th, 1871) remarked,— "All the information I have been able to collect tends to show that fish is not an article of diet sought for or used at all generally by the inhabitants of the district; that where it is so used, it is amongst the lowest classes, such as Chumars, Dheemurs, &c." "The river Betwa and its tributaries, *viz.*, the Jumnee, Sujnam and Sujad are our fish-containing rivers. In all but the last, there are large quantities of mahaseer of all sizes, but these, I may say, are literally never caught, unless it be a dozen or so yearly by European officers with rod and line,

Opinions of European Officials in the Jhansi Division.

and perhaps an equal number shot by the thakoors." In the dry season, as the rivers become low, fish in the pools sustain injury from crocodiles, otters, &c. The *Assistant Commissioner* observed in a memorandum: " The river-fish enjoy comparative safety from the Dheemurs (fishermen) whilst they are in the deep pools of the big rivers, but are a prey to crocodiles, otters, &c. During the rains they run up the tributaries to spawn, and a great number meet with destruction on their return down to their permanent haunts, not only by nets, but other contrivances by which they are shut up in small pools of the tributaries, and subsequently destroyed wholesale by the drying up of the pools, netting, or even poisoning them. The lakes in this district have not been allowed hitherto to run dry, and the only destruction committed on fish is in the rainy season, when they run up the feeders of the lakes, and go down the escape-weirs, when of course none of these can escape destruction one way or the other. Tons of the smaller description of fish are killed during the rains when they try to escape out of the lake, but their preservation, I think, is not of much consequence." For the river-fish, a close season, from June 15th to October 1st, is proposed, when net-fishing should be prohibited; also in the rocky pools of the smaller rivers to which they resort for breeding purposes. During the rest of the year, the minimum size of the mesh of nets might be limited to 1¼ inches between each knot. The following is a list of the principal fish found in the rivers and lakes of Bundlecund: " Mahaseer" (*Barbus tor*), " Kursowur" (*Labeo calbasu*), "Bissar" (*Cirrhina mrigala*), " Rahoo" (*Cirrhina rohita*), " Bawus" (*Catla Buchanani*), " Koorsa" or " Khoorsee" (*Labeo curchius*), " Sinia" or " Phubs" (*Surpoothee*, Beng.) The above not living on their kind. " Sour" or " Gujal" in Bengal, " Sourlee" (*Ophiocephalus*), " Pareen" (*Wallago attu*,) commonly known as the river shark, " Tengra" a siluroid (probably (*Macrones aor*, but " Tengra" is a common term for a siluroid); " Lambur" (*Rita*), " Galur" or " Golalee" (*Barilius*), " Papta" (*Callichrous*), " Butala" (a carp), " Buchooa" (*Pseudeutropius*.) The foregoing are said to live on their kind.

333. The *Officiating Commissioner of Allahabad* (August 7th, 1872) reported :—" All castes eat fish except Brahmins, Banias, and a few of the Thakoors. Shiahs reject scaleless fish, as prohibited in the Koran, but it is not a popular food, and appears to be sought for chiefly by the poor, as it is cheaper than any other kind of animal food. There are none who practice fishing exclusively as a calling." " The supply is fairly equal to the demand." " There is no close time, and no size or condition of fish is spared; the spawning-fish and the smallest fry are alike caught; there are nets used with meshes small enough to retain the smallest." " Every imaginable kind of net, trap, and snare is used. Waging war against such fish-destroying animals as crocodiles appears to me absurd. It would be equally, or more advisable, to proscribe frogs and paddy-birds which eat the spawn and young fry, and probably destroy far more fish than the crocodile; and further, I have no doubt at all but that a general destruction of crocodiles would directly frustrate the end hoped for by their destruction. Their very presence in numbers, it being given that they live on fish,

Opinions of the European Officers in the Allahabad Division.

shows that the supply of fish is abundant, which is all that any one requires, and Nature in these matters, if left alone, keeps the balance even, and resents interference. [Are irrigation weirs and canals which destroy fish wholesale, as at present constructed, to be deemed natural causes? If not, why is inactivity recommended?] It is presumed the crocodiles consume alike the rapacious kinds of fish, and those that are not rapacious; if, then, they are destroyed, the rapacious fish lose a great enemy, and their increase being unchecked, they must prevail against those kinds that are not rapacious, and this latter class happens to include mahaseer, ruhoo, mullet, and the choicest kinds of the river produce. The crocodiles had better be left alone." [The remark that it appears *absurd* to kill crocodiles requires attention. Some reporters are opposed to it, because of their usefulness as river scavengers, or the cost which would be entailed by offering rewards for their being killed, but this is the first time that their destruction has been deprecated on the ground that they assist in the conservation of fish, *because* they kill the rapacious as well as the non-rapacious sorts, and that if they did not do so, the former would rapidly preponderate. One little fact is here overlooked, *viz.*, that both classes of fish are equally used as food, and no reason exists why man should not equally capture either, and thus employ as food what now goes to nourish crocodiles. Also, surely if it would be absurd to kill crocodiles that destroy mature fish, it would be equally so to wage war with frogs and paddy-birds, as it cannot be supposed that they discriminate the spawn, whilst they are said to probably destroy far more fish than the crocodiles—thus the absurdity would be increased. Really, here poor *Nature* also is rather unfairly treated, if she resents interference in killing noxious animals, why are not tigers left alone to keep the balance between man, cattle, and the soil from which they derive their food? Why do human beings object to poisonous snakes assisting in such laudable undertakings? In fact, epidemic diseases are natural causes or effects, and as yet it has not been generally ruled that they should be permitted to hold their sway, to keep the balance even. Lastly, the assertion, that the mahaseer is not a rapacious fish, does not coincide with the views of fishermen, as live bait are generally most killing in the hands of the sportsman.] Interference "is not required; it would not be understood; it would be costly and meddlesome, do harm, and no good at all." "I think his (the Collector of Allahabad) inference has escaped the observation of those officials who have suggested inquiries into these subjects, that if you enlarge the mesh of the nets, so as to allow small fry to escape, the young of the rapacious kinds and their victims both escape to live on each other, so they may as well be caught young." [Really to carry such an argument to extreme limits, it might equally be urged to poison all the waters; then all the rapacious fish will be destroyed; of course the destruction of the others would be overlooked by such advisers.] "If any legislation is required anywhere, it can only be near the sources of our rivers, where weirs are constructed, but even there a weir can do but little harm, and in no river have we more than one large weir, or are likely to have." [First, the facts here stated are erroneous; secondly, the argument founded thereon do not appear more correct than the facts. Weirs are of two kinds, irrigation and fishing ones;

taking the Jumna as an instance, and I could adduce more, it possesses the Okla one below Delhi, and the Karra one higher up for the Eastern Jumna canal, and a third for the Western. If fishing ones are alluded to, I would refer to the reports of officers in the hill ranges, and fishing-weirs are more numerous in many rivers than here stated. That these weirs can do but little harm, I also refer to the reports from local officers who have watched their effects. My personal opinion is in accordance with that of the British law, that fishing-weirs are a public nuisance.] The *Collector of Jompur* (20th March 1872) observed :—"This district is traversed by the Goomtee and Sair, and it is from these rivers chiefly that the supply of fish is drawn." "The supply of fish rarely exceeds the demand, and often, especially in the dry season, falls far short of it." "Fishermen assert that of late years the supply of fish has decreased." "The cost of fish has undoubtedly increased." The breeding season is that "when most fish are taken; both breeding and very young ones are captured without limit or reserve in the streams, and during the rains in the open fields." Tanks are stocked with fry obtained at this period. A close season might be imposed, and the months of Jeth and Asarh would be the most appropriate. The *Officiating Collector of Futtehpur* (March 22nd, 1872) reported that breeding-fish and very small ones are caught to a great extent, by nets and hooks, in *jhils*, tanks and rivers during the rains; the smallest size mesh of the nets being almost $\frac{1}{4}$ of an inch; no regular fishing class exists. The *Collector of Allahabad* (April 8th, 1872) remarked that " there is no doubt that destruction of fish of all sizes and at all seasons of the year takes place, especially in the Ganges and Jumna, not only by fishermen, but any persons who can get hold of a hand-net. This is particularly practised after a flood, when it is by no means uncommon to see small fry being captured by traps, hand-nets, &c., in the small rivulets from which they are trying to escape into the river on abatement of the floods." The smallest mesh employed is said to be $\frac{1}{8}$ of an inch, and that there would be no difficulty in regulating it at $1\frac{1}{4}$ inches. The chief destructors of small fry are crocodiles and fish of prey. [When I was at this town at the commencement of February 1870, a deficiency of fish was complained of, and as I went daily to the markets, I think I may personally agree that the complaint was well founded. The fishermen asserted that the supply had decreased of late years and the demand increased, whilst the same views seemed to be held by the vendors in the market. At the height of the monsoon, or the end of July and the commencement of August, I was likewise at the place, and found a varying amount of fish being brought to market, spent fish were being sold, also young fry as fine as a straw, of species which attain a hundred or more pounds in weight. Thousands of young fish were being daily captured, whilst the poverty of the river, as giving a sufficient supply, was being complained of. The cause was obvious, and the remedy is as clear.] The *Officiating Collector of Hunipur* (February 6th, 1872) replied that "breeding-fish and very young ones are not destroyed to any great extent in this district. What fish are taken are caught in the Jumna and Betwa Rivers, and in tanks. The smallest size of mesh employed is so small that a grain of gram cannot pass through it. There would be little difficulty in regulating its minimum size, as there are none who make a living solely by fishing, consequently there would be little objection raised." "The destruction of crocodiles' eggs might be secured by the offer of a suitable reward." " Whatever regulations it may be found necessary to introduce in other districts could, of course, be introduced here; but there is not in this district such a wanton desecration (? destruction) of fish as to diminish the annual supply, or endanger a natural source of cheap food for posterity." The *Collector of Banda* (August 2nd, 1872) observed that " fish abound in the district: the fish market in the town of Banda itself is overstocked with fish of all kinds during the rains, but the supply is deficient during the other seasons of the year; * * the breeding-fish and the young fish are destroyed in large quantities in the *nallas*, streams and rivers; the extent is variously estimated, and may be said to vary from $\frac{1}{3}$rd to $\frac{1}{2}$ in the rivers and perennial streams, and from $\frac{1}{2}$ to $\frac{3}{4}$rd in the other streams and *nallas*." The smallest mesh used is $\frac{1}{4}$th of an inch from knot to knot. Would not recommend any action in future, either as regards the mesh of nets, the sale of fry in the bazars, or the destruction of fish during the breeding season. The *Officiating Collector of Cawnpore* (April 25th, 1872) replied: " I have the honour to observe that, as far as my knowledge goes, I am unable to corroborate the impression that the fish of the rivers in the parts of India I am acquainted with, are decreasing in quantity. The arguments for the probability of such being the case, derived from the analogy of a decrease in certain kinds of fish in English rivers, are not generally applicable to the condition of things in India. In the ordinary consumption of fish as food, only an inappreciable part of the myriads which come to maturity every year is destroyed. * * The State has on its hands as much as it can well undertake, in carrying through public measures which are not supported by the public opinion of the country. I would suggest that any proceeding so unpopular, as the prevention of fishing, might with advantage be postponed, until the minds of the people are in a more settled condition than is the case now."

334. The *Commissioner of the Agra Division* (in 1869) says that he attributes the opinions expressed by the district officers rather to their imperfect knowledge of the subject than to any ascertained data, and observes upon the great destruction of fry which takes place in the vicinity of large towns. In answer to the questions circulated, the Commissioner (February 23rd, 1872) replied that there is " no reason to apprehend that any wholesale destruction of fish goes on in these parts. A close time might no doubt be introduced by law for the protection of fish during the breeding season, but it does not appear to me that it would be easy to carry out such a measure, or that there is any compensating object to be gained. * * For the rest, it is a useful maxim—*de minimis non curat lex*—minute legislation is unbefitting our position in this country, and more likely to expose our Government to ridicule than to lead to any results of important benefits to the people; * * it is in the highest degree undesirable that the public mind should be disturbed by gratuitous interference on the part of an alien administration, enforced by not very trustworthy agency." The *Collector of Furruckabad* reported (February 13th, 1872) that " the principal season for catching fish is

Opinions of the European Officials in the Agra Division.

from the end of the rains to February or March. They are caught also in the hot weather in favourable places, and in the rains when practicable, but the water is mostly too heavy then for any serious damage to breeding-fishes. Their fry are largely caught as the waters subside after the rains. It is a common thing to see men and boys scooping up the muddy water from the drying pools in the hollows of their hands, and letting it run through again, whilst the fry remain in their palms. The fry and small fish are also caught with small meshed nets, and with coop-shaped basket or *khanchas.*" The supply is considered to remain the same. Fish-ladders to irrigation weirs and tanks, into which they could retire as the canals are dried, are considered the most necessary measures proposed for preserving fish. " Any effective measures for reducing the enormous numbers of crocodiles in our rivers would do much more, than any restriction on fishing, to increase the quantity of fish in them. The destruction of crocodiles' eggs could no doubt be extensively effected by the offer of an adequate reward. But any such scheme, to be of use, would have to be carried out not only in these provinces, but all down the lengths of the rivers which traverse them; otherwise, so fast as the crocodiles were destroyed here, others would travel up and take their places from below." Close seasons and regulating the minimum size of the mesh of nets are considered impracticable, as they could not be effectually enforced. The *Officiating Collector of Etawah* (February 16th, 1872) observed, that "no doubt breeding-fish and very young ones are destroyed to a large extent in all places where there is water and they can be got at. Nets are largely employed, but they are also killed with sticks in the shallow water, and even caught with the hand: some kinds are shot. The smallest sized mesh of the nets used here is ⅓rd of an inch square. Great difficulties, it is considered, would militate against regulating the minimum size of the meshes of nets, or prohibiting the sale of the fry of fish in the bazars." Were close seasons decided upon, from June to August are suggested as the most appropriate. " The only preventive measure that could be enforced without much difficulty is, I think, the prohibition of all weirs in the smaller rivers and streams." " If Government will give a reward for crocodiles' eggs, there is no doubt that plenty of eggs would be brought in: but otters are quite as formidable to fish as crocodiles, and there is also an animal called 'sús' or 'súsmar' (porpoise) which preys on fish, and these seem to require as much attention as crocodiles." The *Collector of Agra* (February 13th, 1872) replied, that he had no personal knowledge on the subject, and therefore expressed no opinion. *Mr. Adams* (in 1869) reported, respecting Agra, that in his "opinion a wanton destruction of fish does take place. In the cool of the early morning, when the fry swim about the banks of the river, a class of boys are in the habit of dredging for prawns and shrimps, and then great quantities of fry are thrown into baskets." The *Assistant Collector's* memo. on the subject was enclosed. He observed that the Agra market, he believes, is supplied with fish all the year round. The *Collector of Muttra* (February 13th, 1872) reported:— " I cannot but think that the destruction of fish, through capture of breeding-fish or fry, bears a very small proportion to the injury caused in this part of India by canals. I have seen much of the Ganges and Jumna canals that run through Meerut, and

I know that in both, quantities of fish are annually destroyed when the canals are allowed to run off. I have watched the first rush of water let in, and have been astonished at the shoals of fish brought down by it. One instance I recollect. I was at the Mussoorie fall on the Ganges canal in the Meerut district, when I saw hundreds of mahaseer come down; they were all carried over the fall, as they had been over a dozen higher up between that point and Hurdwar, not one of which could by any possibility have got back again up the canal. Such a constantly recurring drain on the supply of fish in the head-waters has naturally produced a great diminution in the numbers of the species of fish, and as it is the one most generally taken by the Europeans, the loss is more apparent. But I have little doubt that this injury to other descriptions of fish is equally great. There are only two ways to prevent this injury: the first and best would be by opposing some obstacle at the head of the several canals to prevent the ingress of fish, or if this is impossible, then to construct ladders at the different falls to enable the fish to re-ascend the canals." [I would here point out that this alone will not be sufficient. All destruction of fish should be totally prohibited during the time the canals are closed, because fish only migrate upwards at certain periods, and these may not coincide with the closure of the canals; as the water becomes lower, the ladders will be useless as no water will pass over them, and the fish be retained in the deep holes, consequently they will need protection at that time. The fish-ladders will be eminently useful to permit fish migrating for breeding purposes, and so continue their species. Mr. Watson's most interesting report distinctly shows how fish are now carried over impossible ascents; fixed engines in small water-courses act in the same way when breeding-fishes are seeking shallow spots wherein to deposit their spawn, and for this purpose push their way into irrigated fields, &c.] He continues—
" If either of these plans were adopted, I have no doubt that the fish-supply, so far as it is injured by the canals, would soon regain its former condition. I have never seen the system of poisoning waters carried out, but there can be no doubt that it is a most pernicious one, and ought to be declared illegal." The destruction of crocodiles is not approved of, first, because they are the scavengers of the rivers, [crocodiles of the genus *Crocodilus*, doubtless, are also scavengers besides destroying fish, but the true fish-eating crocodile, *Gavialis Gangeticus*, and which is found in the Indus and all its affluents, the Ganges and Jumna and their feeders, also in the Brahmaputra and Mahanuddi, &c., entirely lives on fish, and is never a scavenger;] secondly, because of the difficulty. " In fine, I would advocate fence months, a regulated size of mesh according to license, with removal of all fixed engines, and prohibition of poisoning." The *Deputy Collector of Etah* (February 6th, 1872) replied, that there is little or no fishing carried on in this district, but he gives a very interesting account of Bustee (see para. 331).

335. The answers from the *Native Officials*, as a rule, are vague,

Answer from Native Officials not complete.

incomplete, or not sent: most of those received have been collated, in doing which more pains would have improved them. As a sample, I give the following. In answer to the question—are the markets fully supplied with fish, or could more be sold?—one Collector condenses the replies of the Tehsildars into "yes." Thus, much will have to be omitted.

336. In the *Meerut Division*, the answers of the *Tehsildars in the Doon* are thus given:—There are no people who subsist on fishing as a sole occupation, but Kahars and Myras engage in it when not otherwise employed. The markets are fairly supplied, but the size of the fish brought is yearly decreasing. The average price of fish is 1½, and of mutton 2½ annas a seer. All classes eat fish occasionally, but none depend upon it as food: a great decrease has occurred within the last 6 or 8 years. Nets with minute meshes were used, but for the last two years 1½ inches between the knots has only been allowed. Fish are trapped in irrigated rice-fields by cultivators for their own consumption. The *Deputy Collector of Bulundshulun* condenses the native reports, and adds the information he has personally collected. Breeding-fish and their young are destroyed here as elsewhere, only inasmuch as they are not discriminated from other fish. Waters are not poisoned, neither is much fry destroyed, because the consumption of fish is but limited, as few depend upon it as a principal source of food. "The spontaneous fish which appears in the tanks and pools is caught and eaten by the poorer classes, but apparently with no great eagerness." The rainy season is the most prolific of fish in the pools, and the smallest mesh of the nets used is ¼ of an inch between the knots. The natives generally recommend that the minimum size of the mesh of nets should be equal to a rupee. He gives the replies of Tehsildars as follows:—There are not above 12 or 15 families who subsist on fishing, but about 2,000 Kahars, Mullahs, Aberias, who also pursue other avocations, likewise do so. More than two-thirds of the population, or three lacs of persons, have no religious scruples to eating fish, the supply of which in the waters has remained stationary of late years. "The smallest size of the mesh of nets is somewhat less than 1¼ inches from knot to knot." [Just previously, from personal observation, he stated the size to be ¼ of an inch between the knots.] The amount of fish consumed yearly in the district is computed at more than 2,000 maunds. The *Tehsildars of Allygurh* report that there are 39 Malhaia caste fishermen in the district who do not follow other occupations, whilst there are many others who do. The local markets are not fully supplied with fish, the price of the larger sorts averaging 1½, and of small 1 anna the seer. First-sort mutton fetches 2, and second sort 1-9 a seer. A little over half the population, or 488,000, belong to castes who do not object to fish as diet, the supply of which in the waters is considered to have remained stationary. Small ones are not taken in any quantity; the smallest size of the mesh of the nets being ⅓rd of an inch. Fish are not trapped during the rains in irrigated fields. The *Tehsildars of Meerut* observe that in Baghput there are no exclusive fishermen; in Haupur 20; in Meerut about 100, but 40 of these have other occupations, and only fish during the cold season; in Gazeeabad 20, but some of these are not solely fishermen; in Mowana none; in Sirdhana about 50, who occasionally fish. Their castes are (1) Mussulmen, particularly of the Belooch division; (2) Kahars, who are constantly dabbling with water in getting *boriyas* (matting materials), planting *singharas*, &c.; (3) Kolis; (4) Kathicks. The supply of fish is equal to the

demand, large ones obtaining 2 or 1¼, and small ones 1 anna a seer. Bazar mutton of the first sort fetches 2, and second sort 1½ or 1 anna a seer. The proportion of fish-eaters is not clearly defined. The amount of fish in the waters has continued stationary except in the Ganges, where a slight decrease is reported, and considered due to the irrigation canal. During the rains fish are usually considered unwholesome. The smallest mesh of the nets is given at ⅛th of an inch between the knots. Fish are taken in irrigated fields during the rains. One mode of capturing fish is erecting a bund or embankment across a stream or pond, leaving only a single small opening where a net is placed. The fishermen with sticks beat the water; the frightened fish make for the opening, where they are captured.

337. In the *Rohilcund Division*, from *Budaon*, no replies have been received to the questions for the Tehsildars. In the *Moradabad* Collectorate, 6 Tehsildars have sent in replies which have been condensed. The number of persons who are strictly fishermen by trade are about 5,000; these men also work as bearers, &c. Besides these, there are hundreds of other men, women, and children, who in the rains either employ or amuse themselves in catching fish. The fishermen are mostly Hindus, but there are a few Mahomedans. The supply of fish in the markets has fallen off since 1857, but during the last two years has slightly risen a little, due to better rainy seasons. During the rains fish costs about half that of the flesh of sheep and goats, whilst in the cold and hot season the price of the two is much the same. It is estimated that about ¾ of the people eat fish, nearly all the Mahomedans, and all the lower castes of Hindus. Amongst the Brahmins, Kunojias only eat fish generally. Baniahs say they do not, but they do at times. The amount of fish in the waters is said to be much less during the last 12 or 14 years than formerly; very small ones are taken in quantities during the rains. ⅛ of an inch between the knots of the meshes is given as the minimum size employed. Fish are not trapped in the irrigated fields. The local fishermen do not ply their trade in the Ganges, but drag the back streams and pools left by the rain floods. In the *Bareilly* Collectorate, the Tehsildars compute the fishermen at about 12,109; they have other occupations likewise; they are Kahars, Buttiaras, Cheereemar, Kulbooteea, Gooreea, and Pasee. About 48,050 maunds of fish are believed to be consumed during the year. The amount in the waters is stated to be stationary; very small ones are captured during the rains with cane-nets having minute meshes, and by other contrivances. The meshes are not sufficiently large to permit a grain of *mucca* to pass through. Fish are trapped in the irrigated fields during the rains. Fish in the villages are commonly bartered for grain in certain proportions. In the *Shahjehanpur* Collectorate, the Tehsildars report that Kahars amongst the Hindus, and Buttiaras amongst the Mahomedans, are the fishing castes, and live a good deal on their fishing. All other classes except Khutrees, Agurwala Banias, Brahmins with the exception of Kunojias, habitually eat fish with other food, the annual consumption of which is set down at between 30 and 40,000 maunds. The largest amount of fish are taken from August to December, in less numbers during April and May, and occasionally during the remainder of the

year. The kinds of nets generally used are as follows:—*ghoonowa*, a common cast-net, with a mesh one-third of an inch, made of cotton thread; *bhukkowa*, a larger kind, with a mesh of one-half inch, and constructed of hemp string; *pundi*, a drag-net for small fish, made of cotton thread, with a mesh to one-third of an inch; *ghaseeta*, a larger sort, of hemp, and meshes of one inch; *juleea*, a net, with meshes of one-third of an inch, is stretched between two bamboos, and dragged along by two men; *julka*, a large drag-net, with equally small meshes, made partly of cotton, and partly of hemp; *kurhera*, a still larger one, with meshes of one inch; *binhore*, used in *nallas*; it is made of cotton thread, and has meshes one-third of an inch and less; *tuppar*, is a net fixed at the bottom of a bamboo cane frame, which the fisherman uses in shallow water, its mesh is one-third of an inch; *koorcha*, a conical basket open at both ends. In the *Bijnour* Collectorate, the *Tehsildars* report that there are about 12 or 1,300 fishermen, all of whom pursue other occupations as well. There are (1) Mussulman Kahars, also (2) Hindu Kahars, (3) Buttiaras, (4) Joolahas, (5) Mullahs, (6) Sirkhooles, a wandering gipsy tribe. The supply in the local markets is insufficient, more fish could be sold: it is eaten from between 50 to 60 per cent. of the people, *viz.*, all Mussulmen, and all Hindus except Brahmins, Banias, Sonars, carpenters, black-smiths, Bishnoees, and Goojurs. About 2,700 maunds of fish are computed to be yearly consumed; the amount in the waters has decreased of late years: small ones are taken during the rains by nets, damming streams, and letting the water carefully off so as not to permit the escape of any, or should an opening be left for the passage of the water, a net is fixed across it; lastly, by digging holes close to the edge of a stream, and filling them with rotten *singharas*, the smell of which attracts the fish, and they jump in. The minimum-sized mesh employed equals that of the holes in an *attah* (flour) sieve. Fish are trapped in the irrigated fields during the rains.

338. In the *Benares Division*, the *Tehsildars of Goruckpur* report that three-fourths of the population eat fish, and some of the castes make it the chief item of their diet; none avoid it entirely except the Agurwallas and Khutrees, and the class of persons called Bhagats or " abstainers," who entirely abstain from animal food. The sect of Vaishnavars are all " abstainers," and so are several castes belonging to the Shivas. The poorest classes eat small fish instead of meal or flour of any kind. It is calculated that 118,096 maunds of fish are yearly consumed in this district. Scarcely any class of people are solely fishermen, and even they are also boatmen or agriculturists, but a large number of castes employ themselves in it more or less. One Tehsildar reports the supply in the markets as equalling the demand, but five others state deficiency to exist. The *Tehsildars of Bustee* observe the fishermen follow other occupations as well. Men in almost every village catch fish, more or less, according to their opportunities. They also cultivate land near the waters which become exposed as the floods subside, or else take a lease of the water produce. Where, as at Bukhra, the lake is of very large extent, some members of the family will be entirely occupied in fishing, or in gathering the reeds, whilst others devote themselves to the fields on the shore. In other cases, cultivation may be the primary,

Answers of Native Officials in the Benares Division.

and fishing only the subsidiary, occupation. Two Tehsildars estimate the fishermen at 4,500; the others give no answers. All the fish brought to market are sold, so " it may fairly be presumed that more could be." The percentage of fish-eaters is given at from 75 to 90 per cent. of the population. The minimum size of the mesh is stated at "about the size into which a finger could pass." One Tehsildar, however, limits this to " the little finger of a child ten years old." Damming is extensively employed (see para. 331), as is also the use of every form of fixed engine. " Where the bottom is too weedy to be netted with effect, and there is no clear spot where a net can be drawn, but the depth is not great, and the water clear, 'spearing' is much practised. The weapon is an ordinary bamboo *lathie*, split into fifteen or twenty pieces, each of which is tipped with iron. These are bound together again, and the centre one being thickened by string wound round it, the others stand out and form a bundle of spears, having a radius of eight or ten inches or more. The men are expert enough with these to be almost certain of hitting a fair-sized fish at 12 or 15 feet off, and if hit, it can hardly escape, so that numbers are killed by this means, the waters being regularly beaten by a line of five or six canoes, each with one man paddling or poling, and another standing in front with his spear." In the *Benares* Collectorate, the *Tehsildars* report about 450 fishermen, who live almost, if not solely, on their earnings as such; the number of Mullahs is about 8,000; but the majority have other occupations. Mullahs and Kahars are the fishing caste; many Mahomedans and Rajputs, however, engage in fishing, though seldom as the sole means of earning a living. "The supply in the city of Benares is, and has been for some time back, quite equal to the demand;" [when I was at Benares, the supply was unequal to the demand, and very small fish were being exposed for sale]; large fish obtaining from two to four, and small from one to one-and-half annas a seer; about 75 per cent. of the people are given as fish-eaters; very small fish are extensively caught during the rainy season in nets and traps, the mesh being as small as that in a purse. They are also taken in the paddy-fields during the rains by means of a grating made of thatching-grass stalks, termed *pahra*; and also towards the close of the rains by damming up the outlets for the water, they are caught with the hand by the people wading in the fields. The *bisari* is a fine meshed lave-net. The *khawai* is a long conical bag used in small streams at the commencement and end of the rains while there is still a current; the mouth of the net is kept open by stakes, and the space between the banks blocked up with bamboo tatties; the force of the current drives the fish into the bag, and on account of its long nose and the pressure of the water they cannot get back. The *pasha* is a grating made of the stalks of thatching-grass, in the shape of a sloping plane. It is placed at an opening in the side of a tank or in a dam, or thrown across a *nalla*; all the water is made to flow through this opening by stopping up every other outlet. The fish coming down with the flow of water are carried on to the grating and left there dry, as the water passes through to underneath." The *chop* is a conical basket open at both ends, and is much used by fishermen in shallow *jhils* and tanks. In the *Ghazeepur* Collectorate the *six Tehsildars* give the following replies. Four return about 19,660 fishermen, but they have other occupations as well; the markets are well supplied in four, insufficiently in one, whilst in the last it is said to be sufficiently so in October and March until June, but in the other months not so. In four tehsils 75 per cent. of the people eat fish, in one 50 per cent., and in one 80 per cent. Three of the Tehsildars assert fish have decreased "owing to the indiscriminate destruction of young fish;" one that they are stationary, and two that an increase is apparent " owing to the copious rains of last year:" all report very small fish to be captured, and the minimum size of the mesh is given at ½ an inch. Every Tehsildar states fish are trapped in the irrigated fields during the rains. In the *Mirzapur* Collectorate, the *Tehsildars'* replies have been collated. There are said to be over 100 fishermen in the district, who have no other occupation. Two Tehsildars consider the markets well supplied with fish, one that the demand is much greater than the supply; two-thirds of the people eat fish. All the Tehsildars consider the quantity has been much below the average for the last few years, but that, owing to the abundant rain-fall in 1871, it is recovering again. Very small fish are trapped in quantities during the rains: they are also poisoned. In the *Azimgurh* Collectorate, six *Tehsildars* report as follows:—there are about 4,295 fishermen, all of whom appear to have other occupations also. In four of the tehsils the supply of fish in the markets is said to be sufficient, in the other two not to be so; 80 per cent. of the population may eat fish, but only from five to ten per cent. do so. The amount in the waters is given as stationary by three, and "increased last year" by floods in three; previous to which the Tehsildar of Nizamabad states " the number had somewhat diminished." Very small fish are taken in numbers during the rains, by weirs and other fixed engines; nets with very minute meshes are reported to be employed. Five who have answered state that the fish are trapped in irrigated fields during the rains. The same sorts of nets and traps are employed as adverted to in other districts, the names, however, of some being different.

339. In the *Jhansi Division*, in the *Jalom* Collectorate, the replies to the answers from *Tehsildars* are thus given:

Answers of Tehsildars in Jhansi.

The fishermen likewise follow other occupations; the Calpee market alone is sufficiently supplied with fish, which is not in much demand, except amongst the lower orders; "impossible to say if fish have increased, decreased, or remained stationary of late years: there are no statistics on the subject." Very small fish are taken during the rains in irrigated fields and elsewhere.

340. In the *Allahabad Division*, and *Banda* Collectorate, " the information gleaned from the *Tehsildars* and others is as follows: there are about 2,000 fishermen in the district, but they, almost without exception, pursue other occupations. The fishing castes are Kahars, Kewuts, Passies and Ghags." Two bazars are plentifully supplied during the rainy season; more might be sold at other seasons if obtainable. About 50 per cent. of the people of the district have no objection to eating fish when they can procure it. Some report a decrease in the amount in the waters—none an increase: large quantities of little ones are taken during the rains; the smallest mesh employed is ¼th of an inch between the knots, but even cloths are used. Weirs, and stake-nets

Replies of Native Officials in the Allahabad Division.

spanning streams exist; netting and spearing are also employed. In the *Futterpur* Collectorate, the *Tehsildars* report that there are no regular fishermen, but labourers, when at leisure, employ themselves at it; the markets are not fully supplied with fish : about two-thirds of the population eat it. During the last two years, and due to heavy rains, the fish have increased; large quantities of small ones are taken in the monsoon months, the minimum size of the mesh of nets being ⅓rd of an inch. In the *Hurripur* Collectorate, the *Tehsildars* reply that there are no persons who make fishing their sole trade; the local markets are seldom supplied with fish ; more could undoubtedly be sold; the proportion of people who eat it " is small on account of deficient supply, but with the exception of Brahmins, Banias and some Thakoors, all others are not prohibited by caste from eating fish." The amount in the waters has continued stationary of late years; small ones are taken in any quantity during the rains, but are not trapped in irrigated fields.

341. In the *Agra Division*, and the *Etawah* Collectorate, the *Tehsildars* report that there may be 10,000 persons who more or less regularly catch fish when they have an opportunity : they are Mullahs, Kahars and Lodhees. Sometimes the markets are well supplied with fish ; at other times they are not so : three-fourths of the people eat it. A decrease of fish is reported in the Jumna, due to the irrigation works near Delhi. Very small ones are captured during the rains by hands, in cloths, with sticks, and by nets; they are also taken in the fields during the rains. In the *Agra* Collectorate, the *Tehsildars* observe that there is no class who exclusively follow the ocupation of fishermen ; there is no market for fish except in Agra city; people eat what they capture. In the *Muttra* Collectorate, the *Tehsildars* report that there are 141 fishermen in the district, termed " Machooa" or " Mulliah :" the first restricting themselves to this calling, the latter having other occupations as well. The supply is deficient in the cold season, but equals the demand in the hot weather, especially just after the rains. It is eaten by but few of the people " who, in this district, are, as a general rule, bigotted Hindus; the greater portion are either forbidden to eat fish, or, though permitted by their caste rules to do so, refrain from such diet through regard to the prejudices of the majority of their neighbours. In Brindabun, where very large numbers of Bengalees congregate, who are notoriously fish-eaters, they to such an extent give up the diet that, as far as I can discover, no fish is sold there, openly at all events. Out of the whole population of the district, perhaps one-fifth are permitted to eat fish; the rest are prohibited." The supply in the waters is said to remain stationary. Small fish are taken during the rains, the smallest mesh of the nets being given as " about the length of a barleycorn."

BENGAL.

342. The districts under this Government are of an exceedingly wide extent and diversified character; portions being densely, others sparsely, populated. A large tract lies in the Delta of the Ganges; some others are hilly, with ranges of a more or less wild character. Excepting Orissa and a few isolated portions, I have not as yet had an opportunity of personally examining the fisheries, and this is the more to be regretted, as the returns are amongst the most incomplete that have been received.

Province of Bengal.

343. The main rivers are the Brahmaputra to the east, taking its course through Assam, receiving many affluents from the Himalayas, and finally falling into the Ganges, which last river, in its numerous sub-divisions, descends through the centre of the province. On the extreme west is Orissa, a district about 200 miles long, and situated between the ghâts and the sea; it is intersected by a large number of streams crossing it on their passage from the hilly country to the Bay of Bengal. These are generally large water-courses, torrents during the rains, but nearly dry, sandy beds in the dry season. The most westerly of the larger of the rivers is the Mahanuddi.

Main rivers of Bengal.

344. *What proportion of the general population would eat fish could they obtain it?* In Burdwan the amount is set down at about 95 per cent., in Hooghly 90 per cent., and these are all the answers to this question circulated to the native officials of the extensive province of Bengal. The Commissioner of Rajshahye, however, reports that in his division fish are largely consumed by all classes of people. From Assam and Orissa no replies at all have been received, but in the latter province, from personal investigations made in 1869, I was given to understand that, with the exception of religious mendicants, and those who have taken a vow that neither themselves nor their descendants shall eat fish, all classes join in its consumption. However, there may be, and probably are, some other exceptions, still the average given in the Hooghly and Burdwan of from 90 to 95 per cent. being permitted to eat it, also probably obtains in Orissa. In Assam I see it is stated that most of the people will eat it. Thus it may fairly be concluded that at the very least three-fourths of the population may be set down as not prohibited by religious scruples from consuming fish.

Fish largely eaten in the province.

345. *How are the local markets supplied with fish?* Again, there is the same want of native returns, which are much more likely to be correct than such from Europeans, who rarely visit the native bazars. In Burdwan Division, the native report is that the supply is not equal to the demand, and if more were brought to the market, they would find a ready sale. In Hooghly, the markets are stated " to be fairly supplied; the fishermen, however, try to keep up the market price by

Local markets insufficiently supplied.

limiting the supply." This answer is composed of two distinct statements:—(1) the latter part of which gives the supply as limited, and as a cause, fishermen combining to do so to keep up the market price. Here the fact of limited supply may be accepted but not "the cause," for how would it be possible in a single division, possessing 3,000 fishermen, for all these people to combine together, doubtless the supply is unequal to the demand, due to deficiency of fish; (2) that to the markets being "fairly supplied" may be added "occasionally." Certainly throughout Orissa, except at such seasons as sea-fish are obtainable, whether from the coast or due to their migrating up rivers, the supply in localities I visited was stated to be unequal to the demand. The only observation from Assam (see para. 360) gives a scarcity of fish as existing. It may be concluded that the fish-supply in the markets of Bengal, except at certain seasons, is unequal to the demand, and when equal, is due to the extensive capture of breeding and young fish.

346. *Have fish increased, decreased, or remained stationary?* The Commissioner of the Rajshahye Division considers the amount has fallen off to what it was 20 years ago. In Orissa, this was the general complaint when I visited it. In the Burdwan Division, a diversity of opinion exists amongst the native officials, some considering it to be stationary, others that it has decreased; it is also said to be stationary in Hooghly. In Assam, a decrease appears to exist. The returns are manifestly most imperfect, but no one speaks of an increase, several of a decrease—a complaint which I have found universal in localities I have visited; consequently I believe that such is general.

<small>Fish have decreased.</small>

347. The *fishermen*, or people who fish, consist of three classes;— (1) regular fishermen who are exclusively employed as such; (2) the wives of the men of some castes who fish whilst their husbands pursue other occupations; (3) the general population. Thus in Burdwan, out of 20,000 people computed as capturers of fish, one-third are stated to be pretty exclusively employed as such; in Hooghly, there are considered to be 3,000 fishermen by trade.

<small>The fishermen.</small>

348. *Are breeding-fish destroyed?* In Midnapur, they are to a great extent; in Burdwan, they are largely taken, but not wastefully destroyed, the distinction drawn being because they are eaten; in Hooghly, to a considerable extent in paddy-fields, &c. in Darjeeling, to a great extent; in Julpigoree, not to such an extent as to endanger supply; in Goalpara, that there is a wanton and ruthless destruction of them, whilst certainly this occurs all through Orissa. In short, every one who has answered this question agrees that breeding-fish are destroyed to a greater or lesser extent.

<small>Breeding-fish destroyed.</small>

349. *Are the fry of fish destroyed?* They are in Midnapur; only taken in Burdwan; captured to a considerable extent in Hooghly; the same at Darjeeling, Goalpara, and through the Rajshahye Division; not to such an amount as to endanger supply at Julpigoree, whilst in Orissa such is most ruthless. The native officials of Burdwan state that during the rains small fish are taken by traps and

<small>Fry wastefully destroyed.</small>

nets with minute meshes, and the same is also reported from Hooghly. The observation of the Commissioner of the Rajshahye Division is doubtless applicable to the whole province,—" there can be no doubt that the destruction of small fry must be enormous, not only in rivers, but in every paddy-field of Bengal."

350. Fry are not wastefully destroyed, state two of the reporters,—(1) because they are eaten; (2) because they are only taken to stock ponds with, and not as food. *First*, whether killing fry of fish as an article of consumption is waste, or a beneficent arrangement of nature to limit a superabundance of food in localities where the supply does not equal the demand?—is such a matter of opinion that arguments seem uncalled for. *Secondly*, as regards young fish in the Burdwan District not being captured for food, the modes employed contradict this, as well as the numerous fishermen engaged in the trade, even did the native officials not distinctly observe that a considerable amount of small fish are trapped in the irrigated fields, * * and this species of fish is consumed. Next, it is urged that only those which die in transit to ponds, whither they are being taken, are sold or used as food, is so utterly opposed to the habits of the natives that it cannot be seriously entertained. Lastly, as regards stocking ponds with the fry of valuable sorts of fish during the monsoon months. This is extensively practised in Orissa, Bengal, and the North-Western Provinces, and without detailing each local plan, I may as well here give a brief summary of the modes employed. Tanks which are yearly stocked with fish belong either to private parties who purchase the young fish wherewith to stock them, or else to fishermen who rent these pieces of water, and themselves stock them with fish. The species taken for this purpose are the more valuable sorts of carps, as the *Catla*, various *Labeos* and *Cirrhinas*, all of which are asserted not to breed there, so it is simply done for a supply of food, and never for breeding purposes. Some of these tanks are perennial, others yearly dry up, whilst those which do not communicate with rivers are best suited for this purpose. Sometimes heavy freshes or rains occur after ponds have been stocked, and as the surplus water flows off, these young fish are carried with it, and this may occasion the necessity of re-stocking two or three times in one year. At Cuttack the fishermen having collected the fish, sort out the desired species, and the rate at which they were disposed of for stocking purposes was one rupee an earthen pot or *handi*-full, and this was computed to hold from two to four hundred small fishes. At Balasur some of the owners of private tanks permitted me to net them in order to examine their contents, the fish being subsequently returned to the water; here the cost of the young fish was the same as at Cuttack, but each *handi* was computed to hold only 200 fry, and less trouble was taken in selecting the species. Near Allahabad the young fish I found were sometimes kept a week or so before being sold; thus those which had been injured or were sickly died off. Small fry of some of the carps judiciously placed in ponds about June attain about ten inches in length by the succeeding January, and it is at this period that netting the stock-ponds usually commences; some owners do it every two or three months, others only once a year. In ponds that yearly dry up, as they begin to get very shallow, they have a dam thrown across the middle,

Stocking ponds with fry.

and the water is laded out, so that all the contained fish are taken. The amount of fry used as stock-fish for ponds is utterly insignificant to the quantity taken; because, if too many are placed in a tank, unable to obtain sufficient nourishment, they become lean and useless as food. One would naturally wish to agree with the Collector of Burdwan that " the fry of large fish are not sold in the markets as an article of food; self-interest teaches the parties not to do so," but, unfortunately, facts are opposed to this being correct as applied to the natives of India, except where some contractor holds the fishing of a district, and prevents such destructive waste.

351. The *modes of fishing* pursued are various, as netting, trapping, damming, poisoning, &c. First, as regards *nets*, some are fixed, as in rivers or tanks; others are not so, whilst every possible device is employed; therefore, it will be simply necessary to advert to the smallest size of the mesh of the nets which are used. To this seven answers from Europeans are given—one says they are minute; one, $\frac{1}{20}$th of an inch; one, $\frac{1}{8}$th of an inch; one, $\frac{1}{4}$th; one, the size of a grain of mustard seed; one, as a grain of rice, and one, as mosquito curtain net. Of the two native replies—one gives it as the size of a grain of mustard seed, the other as a small pea. These meshes alone entirely disprove the comfortable theory that the fry are only being used to stock ponds with, for what would be the value of fish whose bodies were the size of a mosquito curtain net or a grain of mustard seed for this purpose? Next, are nets made of split bamboo (see page clxxxix); such are very destructive, having the interstices between each piece of wood of which it is formed $\frac{1}{8}$th of an inch or less. Then there are fixed engines, as weirs which cross small streams and hill-water-courses having a trap at the only opening and which takes every fish. Also fixed traps are placed in every outlet of all irrigated fields through which the water is strained, capturing breeding-fish and their fry. Damming has been adverted to. Poisoning is likewise carried on certainly through the Orissa hills, at Goalpara, and in Assam. Other plans are recorded by the various reporting officers.

Modes of fishing. Minimum size of mesh of nets. Fixed traps. Damming and poisoning waters.

352. I think the following must be conceded :—(1) that the majority of the people are not prohibited by religious scruples from eating fish; (2) that the supply in the local markets is unequal to the demand; (3) that the amount in the waters has decreased; (4) that breeding-fish are universally captured; (5) and their fry destroyed wholesale; (6) that nets with minute meshes are used; (7) that weirs of a most destructive character are employed; (8) that trapping fish in irrigated fields is universal; and (9) poisoning waters locally carried on.

Conclusions.

353. The consideration now arises—what are the remedies proposed? These may generally be summed up under the plan of do-nothing till things become worse, and leave to others to remedy to-morrow the want of forethought which is permitting such waste to-day.

Remedies proposed.

354. In the *Burdwan Division,* the *Collector of Midnapur* reports that breeding-fish and very young ones are destroyed to a great extent, especially during the rains, as every rill from paddy-fields is

Burdwan Division. Report of European Officials.

made to pass over or through fine reeds or strong nets, the smallest size of the latter which is used being ⅛th of an inch in diameter. No difficulties exist in regulating the size of the mesh of nets, but there will be in enforcing the regulation. No objections militate against prohibiting the sale of the fry of fish in the bazars; the local manager should be made personally responsible. The *Collector of Burdwan* observes that breeding-fish are largely captured for consumption, but do not seem to be wastefully destroyed. " Very young ones of important sorts are taken during the rainy season in the shoals of rivers, and are thrown into tanks for preservation. They are seldom, if ever, used as an article of food. This fishing gives ample occupation to a great number of fishermen in the River Bhagiruttee, the Damuda, Delkissar, and in the internal rivers and channels within the district, and sometimes becomes the subject of cross-rights and disputes. Breeding-fish are captured in the months of April, May, and June, and the fry of important species, such as ruhu (*labeo*), mirgah, catla, calbeinse, &c., are taken during the rains with a view to their transfer to tanks, where they are reared. It is generally believed that large fish cannot spawn in tanks." The smallest size mesh of the nets would only permit a grain of mustard seed to pass through, and that with difficulty, but attempting to regulate such will create much discontent. " Admitting, however, they are wastefully destroyed, it is obvious that these young fry are produced in such multitudes as to outlive these perils in a sufficient number to arrive at maturity, and by depositing their ova in time to prevent the species from perishing. It is, therefore, clear that the continual waste is far less than the continual re-production. [I question this, and hold a contrary opinion, believing that the previous facts have not been proved, especially as, were the observations here made literally correct, fish should increase, whereas reports go to show that the reverse is occurring]. I would allow the existing system to remain undisturbed. In the event, however, of the restriction to the sizes of the meshes of nets being determined upon, I would fix the smallest size at ⅓rd of an inch. As a rule, the fry of large fish are not sold in the markets as an article of food. Self-interest teaches the parties not to do so, inasmuch as the fry sold for rearing generally fetch 20 times as much value as when sold for food. It is only when the young ones die, on being taken from one place to another for transportation, that they are brought to market for sale as food. The sale of fry as stock-fish cannot be well prohibited on any account. [The Collector has apparently been imposed upon by some interested individual in regard to the materials from which this report has been drawn up. The following are his data;—(1) breeding-fish are destroyed; (2) fry are merely caught for stocking ponds, and (3) never sold as food unless they die during transportation; (4) whilst numerous persons find occupation during the rains in capturing fry; (1) must be conceded, but that it is not wasteful may be questioned; (2) is shown not to be the case by the reply he forwards from his native subordinate, who asserts that "during the rains a considerable amount of small fish are trapped in the irrigated fields. * * This species of fish is consumed by the middle and lower classes of people, and is sold much cheaper than the large fish." Fish captured in traps are rarely adapted for stocking ponds with; for this purpose they are taken in nets as I have alluded to (para. 350). If numerous fishermen find employment in capturing small fish, it stands to reason that it cannot be only for the purpose of stocking ponds with, but must be for sale as food, in fact, a wasteful destruction of fry]. The *Collector of Hooghly* replies that breeding-fish and very young ones are destroyed in his district to a considerable extent in paddy-fields and swamps in the rainy season by means of *ghoonee* or wicker traps, *ara*, one of a different shape, *barr*, a weir for closing openings in the low tanks round paddy-fields, in front of these traps are placed: *koora-jalee*, a sort of small net, as well as by ordinary nets and angling. They are also sometimes baled out of the water in pots, caught in ordinary sheets—*dhootees* worn by the people—in fact, anyhow; the fry are very numerous, and the people very skilful; the smallest size mesh of nets employed is about $\frac{1}{20}$th of an inch square, but it would be impossible to regulate such, but if it were, would suggest half an inch. " Fry are sold at the beginning of the rains for supplying tanks. Many tanks quite or nearly dry up in February. The fish not previously caught by ordinary casting-nets or the rod are taken by the hand, 60 or 70 people going into the water together. In June fresh fry is purchased and thrown in. It would be bad, therefore, to prohibit the sale altogether. No organization can prevent the consumption of fry in the rains when the whole country is covered with water, and the water is swarming with fish."

355. The *Officiating Commissioner of the Cooch Behar Division*

Cooch Behar Division. Opinion of European Officials.

observes—" considering that the subject of pisciculture is a new one, on which information has for the first time been called for, I think the reports of district officers contain all the information that could be reasonably expected to be obtained; if enquiries are prosecuted and district officers' attention directed to the subject, more valuable information may hereafter be gained from them." The *Deputy Commissioner of Darjeeling* reports that " breeding and very young fish are destroyed to a great extent in this district. Fish with eggs in India as in England is considered a delicacy. They are caught between Choitro and Bhadro in the Terai, and from March to May in the hills, by means of nets, bamboo cages, and by turning off water." The smallest sized mesh used is not much larger than that of mosquito curtains; in the Terai it is said to be the size of a grain of rice; in the hills it is larger; interference would occasion much dissatisfaction. " It would entail a great deal of enquiry, with its attendant corruption and extortion. Natives consulted deprecate any interference. What is required is to conserve the fish in particular places, and to teach the people that it is for their own interest to allow the young fish to escape." [How would it be possible to adequately preserve fish in certain pools in rivers, when standing weirs are permitted to exist above and below these spots? weirs also that have neither close times nor gaps, and in which the interstices are so minute as even to prohibit the passage of fry. It would end in failure, and the lesson to be taught to the native would be the folly of permitting certain individuals to obstruct the rivers for their own greed, and to the general decrease of the supply of food]. The same objection exists against prohibiting the sale of the fry of fish in the bazars. The *Deputy Commissioner of Julpigoree* replies that breeding-fish and very young ones are not destroyed to such an extent as to endanger supply; the smallest sized mesh used "being of the size of a minnow net, and interference would be as unpopular as it is unnecessary." The sale of the fry of fish in the bazar is but small, and he "does not advocate any prohibition which would be unpopular with the people." [If utility should be subservient to popularity, then certainly measures of economic moment as regards fish might probably have to give way to wasteful destruction, see para. 349]. He likewise observes that, were "a glossary published, giving the native, as well as the scientific, and, where there is any, the common English name of the fish of India, it would greatly facilitate enquiries which district officers may make." The *Deputy Commissioner of Goalpara* replies that "there is a wanton and ruthless destruction of breeding-fish and young ones. They are not so much destroyed at the weirs as in pools, streams, and in fields. The country being adjacent to the hills, during the rains it is overflowed. At this time the non-migratory fish resort to paddy-fields and small streams for breeding, and the people use all sorts of contrivances for catching them and the fry. The most common method is by nets, baskets, harpoons; traps being also used; many weirs do not exist, but the nets are so skilfully made of small meshes that few escape, and they never let any fish, however young, loose again. Poison is sometimes used, which destroys fish in large numbers. Angling, sifting water through a cloth, and baling the water from pools are also resorted to. The destruction commences in the rains, and continues till the water dries up." The smallest size mesh of nets employed is about $\frac{1}{8}$th of an inch; if regulated, the trade of small fish will be interfered with. Thinks "some penal provision should be made to prevent the capture and sale of the fry of large fish." Does not anticipate any objection will be raised in prohibiting the capture of fish in the hilly part of his district during the early part of the monsoon. The *Deputy Commissioner of the Garo Hills* states,—"I cannot, I am sorry to say, give you much information regarding the fish in these rivers, though in some of them fish of many kinds are abundant. I have never made the fish a subject of my study, and I really do not know the names of the various descriptions."

356. The *Commissioner of the Rajshahye Division* reports—"there are no sea-fish, unless the Gangetic porpoise and hilsa are considered to come under that head." [The hilsa certainly is a migratory sea-fish, ascending the rivers to breed, but not so the porpoise, which does not belong to the order of fishes, but is a mammal appertaining to the whales. The sea-fish which ascend above tidal influence will be alluded to amongst the list of fishes frequenting the fresh waters, and which is appended]. "Fish is largely consumed by the inhabitants of this division, both Hindu and Mahomedan, high and low, rich and poor; in fact, with a large part of the population it is the principal animal food consumed. Hindu widows of higher classes and Jains who have emigrated from the North-West, however, abstain from fish on account of religious scruples, but the number of both of these is very small in this division. Fish is hardly ever salted in this division for home consumption, nor is it salted to any great extent for export, except in Pubna,

Opinion of the Commissioner of Rajshahye Division.

where hilsa fish is said to be salted for export to Calcutta. The practice of drying or preserving fish is not resorted to, to any great extent, either for home consumption or for trade, though some of the lower classes dry it in the sun in small quantities for home consumption. Some salted and dried fish is imported to the division, especially to Rungpur and Dinagepur, from Dacca and Mymensing. Except in Pubna, where there is a large trade in hilsa fish, there is no extensive fish trade to distant places in any districts in the division. The fish caught is almost wholly locally consumed, though it is not unfrequently the case that, in the cold season, the fish is carried to distant *hauts* and markets for sale at some distance from the rivers. The supply of fish has fallen off to what it was some twenty years ago. This is attributed to the destruction of the fry and the young fish, and to the silting up of small rivers and *bheels*. The supply having fallen off, and the demand being great, owing to increase of population, its price has also, as a matter of course, nearly doubled to what it was before. People possessing tanks are generally in the habit of rearing up fish, but not for sale as a trade; the fish thus reared are either consumed, or given away to those who ask for them. There can be no doubt that the destruction of small fry must be enormous, not only in rivers, but in every paddy-field in Bengal; but I cannot say that I see any way to any feasible suggestions for the prevention of fish-catching in the rainy season all over Bengal." It is suggested, close seasons might be applied to rivers for certain species of fish, and something might be done "in the way of prohibiting the use of nets of less than a certain width of mesh in rivers; but how the bamboo contrivances for fish-catching, which are in use in every paddy-field, are to be put a stop to, I do not see, nor do I think it would be a wise measure to attempt to do so."

357. The *Commissioner of Orissa* (June 20th, 1872) replied,—"I don't believe the weirs affect the fish; there are no migratory fish to my knowledge,

Orissa. Opinions of Europeans.

except the hilsa, requiring to pass the weirs, and hilsa arrive after the freshes, when there is plenty of water, and the weirs can be passed without difficulty. Ordinary river-fish remain in the deep pools during the dry season; there is never sufficient water in the rivers to permit fish to migrate, except during freshes, and then the weirs offer little or no obstruction. Hilsa do not remain throughout the year in the rivers, at any rate not in fresh water; they arrive in July, or in end of June, with the first flood, and come up from the sea. In the dry season there are no hilsa in the river, and in the floods I have no doubt they get over the weirs. I have seen hilsa caught nearly 100 miles above the weirs, and this proves that they can, and do, get over." The above reply, it is observed, "made regarding the weirs is considered by the Lieutenant-Governor to be satisfactory." It was not accompanied by answers from any of the district officers; however, as they replied in 1868-1869, I fill up the gap from those reports. The *Officiating Collector* enquired about the fisheries, "and the fishermen neither knew nor cared anything about the habits of these creatures, which afford food to so large a proportion of the population of Orissa, and no satisfactory statement could be compiled from their accounts." He came to the conclusion that there was no immediate necessity for taking active steps; at the same time he admitted injury must eventually ensue. The *Officiating Collector, Mr. Armstrong*, however, continues,—" I venture, with much diffidence, to dissent from Mr. McPherson's opinion, and would earnestly urge the necessity of immediate action in this matter. I think that if effectual measures of remedy be not now taken, every one interested in the prosperity of this district will regret it afterwards. I am certain a wholesale destruction of fine fish of full growth is day by day going on at the Mahanuddi weirs, and what is worse than this, the young fry perish in numbers beyond calculation." He also remarked upon the great destruction so easily carried on by the clumsiest contrivances below the weirs. *Mr. Levinge, the Chief Engineer* of these irrigation works, observing upon the obstruction caused by these same weirs, says,— " the real injury to the fisheries is probably caused by the wholesale slaughter of fish by the natives whilst thus temporarily stopped, and I think it would be quite proper if an Act were passed, rendering it illegal to haul a net or otherwise destroy fish within a distance of half a mile below a weir during the season at which fish migrate." *Mr. Fouracres*, in charge of the Naraje weir, observed,—" the fish are certainly stopped for about eight months of the year." *Mr. McMillan*, Executive Engineer in charge of the Jobra or great Mahanuddi weir, reported,—" to a certain extent the weirs have enabled the fishermen to catch more fish than they did before during the dry weather. * * Below the weir the fish are taken, as it were, wholesale, and great destruction takes place." I will here mention that the weirs on the Mahanuddi and its branches are the following, proceeding down-stream from Naraje, which is 67½ miles from the sea, where the river divides into two portions: the one termed the Kajuri, passing Cuttack on one side, descends to the sea; the other division, under the name of the Mahanuddi, runs past the other side of the town *en route* to the ocean. It having been found that too large an amount of water was running to waste down the Kajuri, besides causing extensive injuries, due to the river flooding the country, a bund or weir was thrown across it a little below its head, so as to direct more water into the Mahanuddi branch of the main stream: this of course decreased the supply in the Kajuri to the same amount as it increased it in the Mahanuddi branch. A mile below Cuttack another weir termed the Jobra, 60 miles from the sea and 6,400 feet long and 12½ feet high, was constructed across the Mahanuddi, thus deepening the river on that side of the town and for some distance up-stream, whilst near this second weir the river gives off a third or the Baropa branch, which also has a weir across its head. From personal investigation I most unhesitatingly deny that breeding-fish ever pass up the narrow under-sluices of these weirs, but those in the centre of the Jobra and Midnapur weirs, from 45 to 50 feet wide when open, can cause but little impediment to the ascent of fish; it is a wide open gap than which nothing can be better. But it is whilst the fish are waiting for them to be opened, and at such times as they are obstructed at these weirs, that their slaughter goes on; likewise in the dry months, when the spent ones and their fry are endeavouring to return to the sea, and all the waterway is closed against them, that injury is caused. The destruction of large fish when in season would of course be useful as food, but unfortunately everything is taken from fry ⅛th of an inch in length. Crocodiles congregate in large numbers at this place, where abundance of food is obtainable without trouble. Sharks, saw-fishes, begtis, tortoises, and turtles revel in these pools below the weirs, and as soon as the water shallows sufficiently, nets and every device that man can command are brought to bear on the finny tribes. Whilst the Commissioner observed—"*I don't believe the weirs affect the fish,*"—what say the fishermen? They asserted, when I was there, that fish of all sorts were decreasing, and that those detained in the pool below the Jobra weir were being slaughtered in numbers. One zemindar observed that he had two small pieces of water, the first in the Kajuri river three miles below Cuttack, but owing to the irrigation works having diminished the supply of water, his fishery has been ruined. A fisherman of the Kajuri also complained of the decrease of fish in that river, but observed as some compensation that their price has largely increased. I examined the main stream of the Mahanuddi river above the weirs and higher up than where it first divides, and the following were some of the results arrived at. At Davacota, about one mile above the sub-division of the river at Naraje, were seven fishermen; they complained that since the construction of the weirs the fish had much decreased, large ones being then almost entirely absent from the river. At Daspore, still higher up, in ten hauls of a large drag-net nothing was obtained, and the fishermen stated their intention of leaving this part of the country and migrating to below the weirs, where they believed fish to be more abundant. At Kundapur, the fishermen complained of a great decrease of fish; at Ustia and Subunnapur were the same reports, and it was observed that the diminution had commenced since the erection of the weirs. At Banki, the highest point I examined, the Tehsildar remarked that it was very evident that since the construction of the weirs, fish had become much scarcer; in fact, that a few years since two pice a seer was about the cost of what was then charged six pice for, whilst the fishermen observed on the great decrease of sea-fish which used to ascend thus far. But it is useless continuing extracts from my report of 1869; but I will now turn to another great plan of destroying the fish in Orissa, and here again I shall give independent testimony when available. *Mr. Levinge* observed,— "the objectionable practice of the natives catching large basketsful of the small fish or fry is doubtless more destructive than anything else; * * fish when very young are destroyed in incalculable numbers, not so much at the weirs as in all the small pools, streams, and paddy-fields throughout the country: were it not for this wholesale destruction of the young fry on their migration to the main rivers in October and November, I believe the numbers of the fish in the rivers of this part of India would be much greater. They are caught when the waters are let out of tanks and *jhils* and paddy-fields in small baskets and in nets of very small meshes." *Mr. Fouracres* also remarked,—" I think that the fish are destroyed to a great extent when young, for the reason that the nets employed are almost in every case with very small meshes." Without continuing extracts of opinions, which are nearly all similar, I may mention that the most serious injury was, and no doubt is still, being effected in this district by the use of fixed engines for capturing breeding-fish and their fry. Drag-nets and cast-nets of different sizes, also purse-nets and lave-nets, are employed, and nearly all the other forms mentioned as existing in the former reports, consequently they do not call for recapitulation here. Drag-nets for the rainy season have a mesh of $\frac{1}{5}$th of an inch and even less between the knots: as the floods subside and the fishermen are able to wade up to their waists, the force of the current now becoming less and the fry a little larger, $\frac{3}{10}$ths of an inch is the usual distance; as the river begins to clear, $\frac{7}{10}$ths of an inch is the average size; and when the waters are clean, $1\frac{1}{10}$th inches between each knot comes into play. The reason of this is obvious: the young fry move about with the first freshes, and then the minute meshed nets can kill them; but it is not until the cold season that the water is clear, the fry have grown, and very fine meshes are generally inapplicable. I say "generally inapplicable," for it is the rule that fish breed during the rains, but some do so likewise at other periods of the year. But these are not the finest nets used: a purse-net fixed to a wooden hoop, having meshes $\frac{1}{2}$ an inch in circumference or $\frac{1}{8}$th of an inch between each knot, is employed to capture the fry up every little channel, and a lave-net with as minute meshes is likewise used for the same purpose. Even these, however, are not the most destructive practices in vogue in Orissa; rattan or basket-work is brought into play; one form is termed a *salwua* or *putti;* it consists of very fine split bamboos bound together by means of grass; the interstices between each piece being equal to $\frac{1}{8}$th of an inch or less. This *putti* is about five feet high, and is in the shape of a regular wall-net. It is taken to a tank and placed in the water in a V form, whilst fishermen on either side extend themselves outwards, and, by beating the water, drive the fish into the enclosure: the two ends are now brought together, and the fish penned into a small space: the sides are advanced nearer and nearer until they almost touch, and the fish are removed by a hand-net, or the hand alone. Weirs are used in the larger streams, and traps in every irrigated field; one of these last is of a horn shape; it is constructed of basket-work, with the interstices, between the substances of which it is made so fine that even the smallest fry are captured. This is placed at most outlets or in small channels during the floods; and, as all the water must go through it, every fish is taken. When not of a sufficient size to entirely fill a channel, it is supplemented by bamboo walls, extended laterally on either side. Another is shaped like a shoe, but the principle is identical. Damming is extensively practised; as the rivers commence drying up, earthen bunds are raised along its bed, parallel with the course of the stream, but narrowing towards its lower end. Fish are driven in, the ends are stopped, and every one is taken. In the same way, when tanks begin to dry up, one portion is bunded off from the rest, the water laded out over the bund, and all contained fish destroyed. *Lieutenant Kittoe,* in his account of a journey through the forests of Orissa, describes the weirs employed in the hill-streams there, and which resemble those described by H. S. Thomas, Esq., in Canara. What are the effects of these "free industries?"—and in giving the results of what I saw, it should be mentioned that the following refers not only to the Orissa, but part of the Midnapur District. *Mr. Toynbee* at *Bhudruk* reported,—" all that come to the nets are destroyed, whether young or old, great or small. The nets are made with the express object of letting none escape." The *Assistant Magistrate at Balasur* also remarked,—"all that come to the net are consumed." In the Brahmini River no irrigation weir exists. I commenced my enquiries on it twelve miles from Denkkenal, the Rajah of which place kindly giving me assistance, as did also Mr. Faulkner of the Irrigation Department. The paucity of fish was very apparent: this, I was informed, had been going on for the last seven or ten years, and had occasioned a great falling-off of the productiveness of the fisheries, whilst the size of the mesh of the nets had visibly decreased during this period. About 30 miles below this portion of the Brahmini I again examined the river. I obtained the assistance of 25 fishermen, who employed long nets; the flank one had a mesh of two inches in circumference; the centre ones of 4 inches; their depth was about six feet. In the first haul three siluroid fishes (*Rita*) were captured, of an average weight of $1\frac{1}{2}$ ounces; subsequently nothing could be taken. Asking the reason which had caused this paucity of fish, the fishermen observed that there had been a gradual decrease of true fresh-water fishes for some years, so much so that for the last three seasons this portion of the river had not been fished at all. This decrease was attributed to the destruction of the fry of the fish in the rainy season, which they accused the Gokar caste of effecting, they being Keots. I next turned my attention to the Gokar fishermen, and obtained the services of eight. They brought a *putti* with them made of fine split bamboos as already described. I saw 500 fish taken at the first haul at a tank, amongst them were the young of the ruhu, barkur, mrigala, and other species, the largest of which they considered about four months old. They replied that, by means of fixed engines or nets, they captured large quantities of fish during the rainy season. They also remarked that the quantity of fish of all sizes have much decreased during the last ten years, but asserted their present mode of capturing them had existed from time immemorial. The Byturni River was low, and its fisheries were said to be but slightly better than those of the Brahmini and its branches. In the Salundi the amount of fish was but trifling, and were said to have much decreased of late years. At Balasur, the Borabolung is tidal, and no decrease of fish was reported; but there were not many tanks or *jhils* in its vicinity; consequently the destruction of small fish during the monsoon months was not so great as on the edges of the Mahanuddi and Brahmini Rivers. In taking a survey of the fisheries of the foregoing district, I cannot help drawing attention to the great richness in the number of species, as I collected 114 distinct sorts: notwithstanding this, there was a general poverty of the rivers in furnishing food to the population at large. Whether rivers, with or without weirs, were examined, a general absence of large fisheries was very apparent, except during the monsoon months, when fish ascend from the sea to deposit their eggs or prey upon their neighbours. Doubtless weirs act deleteriously by impeding the ascent of fish and so assisting in their destruction, as well as by preventing the descent of the young to the sea; but a yearly and general slaughter, carried on by every conceivable means and throughout the whole country during the rainy or breeding season, is probably the chief cause of the injury.

358. The replies of the native officials of Bengal have mostly been omitted, whilst those sent are unfortunately more in the gross than in detail; however, I give them as received.

Replies of Native Officials very bare.

359. The *Tehsildars of Burdwan* reply that the number of fishermen is about 20,000, one-third of whom are pretty exclusively employed as such; the others follow different occupations as well. The fishermen castes are— 1, Koibarta, 2, Keot, 3, Malo, 4, Tiyur, 5, Jelia, 6, Bagdi, 7, Dulia, and 8, Bauri. Nos. 1 to 5 live chiefly on fishing; 6 to 8 ply the double occupation of fishermen and palki-bearers, the males following the latter, the females the former pursuit: most of them also till the land. Some men of superior caste angle as a means of recreation. The supply of fish is not equal to the demand; if more were brought to the market, they would find a ready sale; the quality is decidedly bad. The amount from the Damuda and other rivers towards the centre of the district is decidedly limited. The chief supply may be taken from tanks, the water in which has of late years become bad and poisonous, so much so as to kill the fish. The average price of large fish is 3 annas, of small fish (*chuna*) from 1½ to 2 annas per seer of 60 tolas. First class bazar mutton realizes 5 annas, and second sort 3 annas, a seer of the same weight. All classes of people, excepting widows of high-caste Brahmins, Boidus and Kaits, join in the consumption of fish; probably 95 per cent. are fish-eaters. As to whether the fish in the waters have increased, decreased, or remained stationary of late years, a great diversity of opinion exists, some alleging that the fresh-water fish have decreased, others that the supply has remained stationary. During the rains small fish are taken by means of *ghoonee* and by small nets of fine texture: communications are now opened between the rivers and *bheels* (swamps), and the small fish are introduced into the latter. At this season the fry of large fish are also caught in large quantities, by nets called *bisal* and *khina*, in the shoals of the Damuda and the Bhagirutti, with a view to their being transferred and reared in tanks. The smallest meshes employed will not permit a mustard seed to pass. During the rains, a considerable amount of small fish, *chuna*, are trapped in the irrigated fields by means of *ghoonee*, *barh*, *ara*, and hand-nets termed *chaukni*. This species of fish is consumed by the middle and lower classes of people, and is sold much cheaper than the large fish. The forms of fishing reported are, by nets both large and small; *birties*, a trap made of split bamboos and placed against a current; *palues*, made of split bamboos and resembling a conical shaped basket; angling and harpooning; *hoary* and *shikti:* the first is made of branches of trees and thorns tied together and placed in the river where the current is not strong, small fish take shelter therein, and are taken by means of *shikti* or *chaukni* nets. The names of the other nets, &c., are—*bar* or *maha-jal*, a large drag-net. *Binti-jal*, a net fixed to posts in the middle of a river where the water is deep; *dara-jal* resembles *bar*, but is used only in tanks; *khapla*, a cast-net. For taking small fish there are the following:—*Shinti-jal*, resembling *khapla*, but with smaller meshes; *ganti-jal*, stretched across a tank, and the little fish become entangled by their heads; *feta-jal*, a lave-net; *chakni-jal*, a

Opinions of Native Officials.

purse-net attached to a circular frame; *chabi-jal*, a net attached to a pyramidal frame-work of two bamboos, which, crossing one another at the summit at right angles, are bent down into a pyramidal form at the base of which the net is affixed. The traps are as follows:—*ghoonee*, very common; *ara, aishta, polu*, and *barh* are also bamboo traps. In the *Hooghly Collectorate*, the *Tehsildars* report perhaps 3,000 fishermen by profession, but all classes catch small fish: the castes are Mannah, Patoo, Mullik, Bang, Koormee, Teor, Jellya, Mulla, Pode, Noda, Barrik, Santra, Khora, Mal, &c., but the Jellya are the true fishing caste. The markets are fairly supplied; the fishermen, however, try to keep up the market price by limiting the supply. Nine-tenths of the population eat fish, the amount of which in the waters is stationary. Very small fish are taken during the rains both for eating and stocking ponds; the smallest sized mesh of nets employed is such as peas can go through. Fish are trapped in the irrigated fields during the rains. The following traps are used:—*ghoonee, ara*, and *aishta*; also eleven forms of weirs.

360. From *Assam* no returns have been received; the following appeared in the columns of the *Englishman* of July 5th, 1871, respecting this division:—
"There is a system of wholesale poisoning and trapping fish, which aims at the destruction and extermination of the species." The writer goes on to describe how some pools are poisoned, others dammed, and the fish harpooned; how streams are embanked, and wicker traps employed, with a scarcity as the result.

Observations from Assam.

BRITISH BURMA.

The provinces of which British Burma is composed.

361. The provinces of British Burma, which have been acquired in the first and second Burmese campaigns, were first placed under a Chief Commissioner in 1860-61, by amalgamating Arracan to the north, Pegu in the centre, and Tenasserim to the south, which territory extends nearly a thousand miles along the eastern side of the Bay of Bengal, and reaching to where, zoologically speaking, Wallace defines the Malay Archipelago to commence, from its northern boundary the Naf estuary at 20° 50' north latitude, to the Pakchan stream in the south at about the 10° of north latitude. The whole aggregates about 90,070 square miles, with a population of about 26 to the square mile.

The mode of disposing of fresh-water fisheries under native rule.

362. The fresh-water fisheries in British Burma are of considerable value, as will be seen by the revenue returns, as upwards of 540,000 rupees a year are received from the licensing the use of nets and farming out the tank and smaller river fisheries. Major Sladen having obtained for me from Mandalay a statement of how the fisheries under the King of Burma are managed, I insert it in this place. It has been the practice in Upper Burma to annually collect revenue from the fisheries of lakes and ponds, the amount in each case being assessed by the local officials; but should the Revenue Minister mistrust the statement, he sends a Deputy to examine and decide. In villages where there are "amhoodans" or hereditary slaves of the Government, whose necks and hands are tattooed, they and the headman of the village only, and to the exclusion of everybody else, are entitled to become the lessee of any fisheries which may exist. In the absence of "amhoodans," the headman becomes the renter: should there be both, they have the fisheries on alternate years. The sub-lessee works from October to April, and fisheries are formally made over in the presence of a witness, care being taken that the rent is duly paid. Sub-lessees often allow other fishermen to net their waters, the original owner receiving two-thirds of the captures. The former sovereigns used to permit the queens, concubines, princes, princesses, ministers, and members of the Royal Dancing Company to enjoy the revenue from the fisheries, but the present king has appropriated them and pays the foregoing persons monthly salaries instead. Some sub-lessees pay direct to the Royal Collectors, others through the heads of villages and townships. In case no lessee comes forward, the inhabitants round a lake or tank have to provide the annual revenue, for which the headman is responsible. If fishermen wish to carry on their employment in the river, leave has to be obtained, and a defined tract is let out to each, others being prohibited from interfering. Lately, at the instigation of the Buddist priests or Poongees, an order has been issued, prohibiting, under pain of imprisonment and other penalties, any one fishing within the limits of the Royal City of Mandalay; also in some lakes, ponds, and even a portion of the Irrawaddi River, which are deemed to be

under holy keeping. In some districts, as Pegu, it was stated that some of the fisheries prior to British rule were in the possession of certain persons or hereditary Een Thoogyees, who paid a fixed annual rent, and kept their overseers and employed coolies, but no one could fish without their permission, for which a small annual sum was charged. Irrespective of the direct revenue, large indirect sums had to be given as gratuities. It appears to me that the statements in Pegu are in reality good proof that the plan which now exists in Upper Burma was also the rule there prior to 1852, when the country was annexed. The Een Gaygyee Lake fishery appears to have possessed a far-famed celebrity for a long period of time, traders coming from great distances in the month of June to invest in fresh, salted, dried, or smoked fish for disposal in distant markets. According to O'Riley, "owing to the profits realized on this trade, the competition for the purchase of the fish at the lake became so great, that it was not unusual to make advances several seasons previous to the completion of the contract. So valuable a source of revenue to the Burmese Government as this fishing appeared was not allowed to escape easily; accordingly the sum of 60 viss of silver, or about 6,000 ticals, each equal to Rs. 1-6, or Rs. 8,237-8 annually, was exacted as a Royal tax from the hereditary Chief of the lake."

363. There are two principal descriptions of fisheries, namely,
Rivers and tank fisheries. those in the rivers, and those in tanks or "eengs," which are due to the inundated state of the country during the rains, either augmenting the size of those existing, or turning large tracts of country into enormous expanses of water. In Arracan the amount of fresh-water is insignificant in comparison with what exists in the other two Commissionerships, and which call for a more detailed notice.

364. The principal rivers of British Burma are the Irrawaddi
Principal rivers in British Burma, some with Alpine sources. and Salween, which have Alpine sources, and the Pegu, an affluent of the first, which is destitute of such an origin, as it takes its rise in the Pegu hills or "Yomas," as they are termed, and which divide the Pegu District from the Tenasserim, wherein is the Sittoung or Poungloung River. The Irrawaddi has various affluents, and in its course divides and sub-divides into many branches, becoming comparatively shallow during the dry season of the year, but an impetuous torrent in the rains, flooding the surrounding country, turning plains into lakes, and uncultivated tracts into vast fishing districts. The most northern portion of the Irrawaddi, where I commenced my investigations, was at Mandalay, the present capital of Native or Upper Burma. In this State the river, as a rule, did not appear to have any large amount of contiguous tanks suitable for fish-breeding, which would be filled as the river overflows; consequently most of it is carried on in the stream and small creeks along its course. As the Irrawaddi commences to pass the frontier, the natural tanks and sub-divisions of the river increase, and the fisheries become augmented; in fact, below Prome the country of Pegu may be looked upon as one large delta formed by this river, and entirely distinct from the comparatively dry condition of Upper Burma, which the south-west monsoon very slightly affects, and where the river possesses high banks. In, or prior to, the June or south-west

monsoon, this river commences to rise, owing to its Alpine origin, and due to the melting of the snow in the mountains, from which it takes its source. Thus, although the yearly rain-fall in Rangoon is probably about 110 inches or more, the amount decreases as the north is approached—at Meanoung being above 50, at Prome below 50, at Thyetmyo, our frontier station, only 20, whilst at Pachan, in Upper Burma, I was informed that it was only about 2 inches. Thus, the south-west monsoon does not fill this river in Upper Burma, which would be a serious drawback to fish-breeding, especially for the shad which ascend from the sea for this purpose; but fortunately this period is concomitant with that of the greatest heat at its snowy source, which keeps the river in full flood above where the south-west monsoon reaches, and thus renders it suitable for the ascent and spawning of marine and other fishes in its higher reaches. The Sittoung or Poungloung River rises in the hills 25 miles north of Yemethen and about 130 from Tounghoo. It mostly flows in a southerly direction through the middle of the district, but its tortuous course has been not inaptly compared to the writhings of a wounded snake; it frequently deviates to almost every point of the compass within a distance of a few miles. The Salween arises somewhere in the Province of Yunam in China; receiving many affluents as it passes through the Shan States, it passes in a southerly direction towards Moulmein; it is divided from the last-named river by a range of hills, and receives near its termination the Gynne, from a north-easterly or easterly direction. This river is connected by creeks with the Sittoung, and that again with the Pegu River, which is an affluent of the Irrawaddi through its Hleing or Maimakhat branch, which is given off near Prome, and runs direct through that district to the town of Rangoon and so on to the sea. It does not again join the main stream directly, with which, however, it has several connecting creeks and channels.

365. The tanks or "eengs" are principally due to the yearly inunda-

Tanks or "eengs." tions of these rivers, which increase the size of those existing, or form vast expanses of water in large tracts of the country, and these, or small water-courses and tanks or channels in paddy-fields, are great places for fish to breed in, (see para. 46—*dhunds* in Sind). These watery tracts are mainly of two sorts, those which are perennial, and those which yearly dry up; the latter, provided free ingress to, and egress from, them is permitted to breeding and young fish, will scarcely require any measures being adopted for their care after all communication with the running water is naturally cut off, as I shall subsequently allude to. More especially in the Pegu District are many plains, which become vast sheets of water in the rainy season, but which it is unnecessary to enumerate. At Rangoon are the so-called Royal Lakes, originally a marsh, deepened and bunded by a native governor some 40 years since. There are many marshes useful for fishing stations during the rains. Certain lakes termed "Bayme" are deemed to possess a sacred character, so are not fished; also, as a rule, all waters within the enclosure of a "Kyoung," or Buddist monastery.

366. The races of British Burma may be referred, according

Races of Burma fish-eaters. to the late Chief Commissioner, to four great families—the Talaing or Mon, the Burman, the Karen, and the Shan or Tais. As Buddists they profess a horror of taking the lives of the lower animals, but being exceedingly partial to a fish diet, they console their consciences, whilst indulging in it, with the idea that the deaths of these creatures will be laid in a future state to the fault of the fishermen by whom they were captured. Even their " Poongees " or priests who eat fish, adorn the approaches to their temples with illustrations, showing what will be the award to fishermen in eternity. In some of these interesting representations are large fires being stirred up by devils, whilst other demons or " Beloos " are dragging one or more fishermen in a net towards these roaring furnaces, helping each on by means of striking fish-spears into them from behind, and hauling them forwards by hooks and lines towards the place of punishment.

367. In districts where large rivers exist, the Burmese are from necessity boatmen and of choice fishermen.

Burmese generally boatmen and fishermen.

This has an important bearing upon the fisheries, as the capture of the finny tribes is not in the hands of a certain limited class of people.

368. *As to the proportion of the general population who eat fish*, it may be concluded that all do so, as the exceptions are too trivial to be worth noticing.

Burmans are a fish-eating race.

369. *How are the local markets supplied with fish?* It is unfortunate that the answers sent in in 1869, or replies to the question circulated last year, have, in the majority of instances, not been forwarded, so only general replies are available for examination. It would appear that, as a rule, they are well supplied, but in the Amherst District, they are stated to be insufficiently so. Out of ten returns, three assert the markets to be fully supplied, one fairly so, and in six insufficiently so, but some of these localities are near the sea-coast, and the supply partly depends on the tides.

Local markets generally supplied with fish.

370. *Have the fish increased, decreased, or remained stationary?* This question is responded to by only ten native officials, five of whom assert that the amount in the waters remains stationary, whilst the other five report a decrease. When in Burma, the impression prevailed at Prome that fish were decreasing. At Henzada, the fishermen held the same opinion, and considered the decrease due to the small meshed nets which were being used. Around Pegu they were also asserted to be diminishing; the same is now reported from Shwégyen and Amherst.

Amount of fish in the waters decreasing.

371. *As to whose the fisheries are?* As a rule, they appear to have always been Royalties in Lower Burma, as they still are in the Native State, and may be considered Government property, although certain private or communal rights may co-exist. Rules were framed by a former Chief Commissioner, in order that the renting system might cause the least possible amount of hardship to the people, so the general public were permitted to take whatever fish they pleased anywhere for home consumption, but not for sale; only the lessee could sell fish. Besides this, certain localities were set aside as free fisheries, and, so far as I could ascertain, any one might now use fixed traps (except in certain leased localities) free of tax. This I believe to be the origin of the

Fisheries Government property.

present assumed deterioration of these fisheries; the rules are not regularly carried out: thus, amongst the untaxed nets at Thyetmyo are recorded sorts 400 cubits long, &c., which it is impossible can be employed simply to take fish for home consumption. Again, below Prome I examined a boat in which two men had been fishing for home consumption, who had as many fry of fish in it as they could carry, perhaps 150lbs. weight. In fact, the philanthropic plans allowed are most grossly abused, and these free fisheries and unlimited fishing ought to be subject to regulations.

372. *Are breeding-fish or fry destroyed?* I cannot see how two opinions can exist upon this subject; every reporter (except General Fytche) agrees that they are, and my own observation (see paragraph 374) led to the same result. Fixed traps and engines, weirs completely barring streams, damming up and lading out waters, nets with meshes so fine that scarcely more than water can pass, and the interstices of traps still more minute, are freely used: even poisoning the waters is carried on, as will be detailed.

<small>Breeding-fish and fry generally destroyed.</small>

373. The *Secretary to the Chief Commissioner of British Burma*, General Fytche, reported (August 3rd, 1868)— " I have the honor, by direction of the Chief Commissioner, to acknowledge the receipt of yours No. 3006, dated July 16th, and in reply to state that there is a tax upon nets and fisheries in British Burma, that fish are carefully preserved, and that no wanton destruction takes place within the province."

<small>Opinion of the Chief Commissioner that fish are carefully preserved throughout British Burma.</small>

374. Having been directed, in 1869, to proceed to Burma and investigate into the state of its fisheries, the following are some of the conclusions I came to, deduced from personal observation, as to whether a "wasteful" destruction of fish occurs in the province, and I considered that it did, and to a great extent. This was being effected by two ways—fixed engines and small meshed nets. *Fixed engines* were of two main descriptions: (1) large weirs, "Tsays," or bunds crossing whole rivers, and with the interstices between the pieces of bamboo of which they were formed, or of those in the cruives or other moveable traps, so fine that only water could pass through. Some of these, viz., bunding, I shall allude to further on (paragraph 384). No regulation whatever existed; streams were simply let out, and the native fishermen permitted to capture everything they were able, in any way they pleased. Weirs had been left standing for years, not only taking every fish ascending or descending, but impeding navigation, &c. Every villager who liked might fix a weir where he wished, and at each creek within high-water mark, these weirs were placed so that fish passed over these bamboo fences to their best feeding-grounds as the flood-tide made, but as it ebbed they were left floundering in the mud due to this weir standing as an insuperable obstacle to their returning to the river. The same process was permitted where large tracts of lands were yearly inundated from the river; fish passed into these places, but weirs were fixed to prevent even the smallest fry ever obtaining an exit into the river, the bamboo weir being too fine in its texture

<small>Personal opinion that a wasteful destruction of fish occurs throughout British Burma.</small>

even to permit them to pass. (2) Secondly, traps of innumerable descriptions and miniature weirs were permitted in every small stream, irrigation channel or water-way to entrap breeding-fish ascending or descending, and so finely constructed that even the fry could not pass. This destructive mode of fishing was said to have been the subject of a tax by the native Government, but made free about 1863. If ever there was a mode of fishing employed calculated to ruin fisheries, it is this *kadone*, so properly prohibited in Great Britain. I found agriculturists with as many as 60 and 80 traps in their possession, and working them daily at every small water-way where ingress or egress for fish could occur. These traps were termed *kya*, whether in the shape of a horn or a shoe, and were extensively employed in paddy-fields. Weirs in streams sometimes had a platform, *khonsin*, thus constructed: a bamboo fence was fixed entirely across a stream or water-way, reaching some feet above its surface, except in one spot, where it was cut down either to the level of the water or three or four inches above it. Thus, a fence entirely bars the stream, except where the free gap exists. Now a platform is constructed of fine bamboo, having raised bamboo walls on three sides, and this platform just fits the gap already described. In the dry season, as October, when the fish, which have bred, and their fry are descending, this platform is fixed below the opening; in the rainy season, as they are ascending, it is fixed above it. This platform touches the water, or nearly so, at the gap, and here its wall is absent, so that fish reaching a weir which has only a gap in its middle jump at that spot, but only to fall on the platform. In some places weirs are not permitted to go quite across rivers, because such impedes navigation, and this open spot, as far as the river's bank, is studded with reeds, which makes a noise as the water passes through them, thus frightening the fish to the opposite side where the weir with a gap exists; they jump at the lowest part, and are safe on the *khonsin*. Occasionally a *tsanda* is constructed: a number of stakes are driven into the bed of a river in a V shape, the apex of which is a rattan net that is raised every few minutes by means of ropes running over drums and worked on a stage erected for the purpose. Another very common mode of capturing fish by the aid of a tank is as follows: should one exist near a paddy-field, or some water-course well stocked with fish, or up which they proceed to deposit their spawn, it is just what is desired, and the time of year for working it is the rainy season. A shallow channel is cut from the tank, leading into an enlarged space about three feet deep—a stew, in short; from this the channel is continued into the paddy-field or place where the breeding-fish are known to be. In this outer channel, or just external to the stew, is a small weir permitting fish to go up, but preventing their return. Water from the tank is made to flow down the new channel through the stew, and so on to the fishes' haunts. Breeding-fish finding this nice stream press up it, pass the weir, but become prisoners in the stew, from whence they are removed next morning by a hand-net. Traps in the form of long conical baskets or cages were also used in rivers, and other contrivances were everywhere employed to take both breeding-fishes and fry; and observing this being carried on with impunity, founded one of my reasons for believing the Chief Commissioner had been mistaken or misinformed when stating that fish were carefully preserved in the province.

375. Secondly, *moveable engines*. These, again, are of two sorts: (1) those constructed of bamboo, rattan, reed, or some such substances; (2) those in the form of nets. Rattan or bamboo nets, *gyan*, have each piece fixed to its neighbour by grass or fibre in the place of string, the interstices being of various sizes, from $\frac{1}{16}$th of an inch to 1 inch. *Yindoons*, or a species of lave-net, of an elongated triangular shape, made of closely woven bamboos and affixed to a long pole, is employed to clean out all small water-courses of the fry of fish; it is pushed along them and raised every now and then, as it usually is as wide as these channels; fry are easily captured thus. Another and larger form is dragged by bullocks or pushed by men through the haunts of the fry; it lets none escape; for, as it goes through the muddy water, the weeds, &c., choke up all the interstices, so not the smallest fish can pass. There are other descriptions, but the principle is identical not to allow anything, except water, to pass. (2) Those in the form of nets are also variously constructed, but it is in the free fisheries more especially, that I witnessed the most minutely meshed nets employed. *Mek-kwoon* or *limbet* is a form of net which has very small meshes; it is about 12 feet long, having a bamboo along either end, whilst one side is attached to a boat, so that it can be lifted like a board affixed by a hinge. The boat is moored broadside on, in an appropriate situation, the fish, mostly fry, are frightened to above where it is placed, and all the fisherman has to do is to raise the net, when the fish fall into the boat. Purse-nets are used, fixed or moveable, in the small water-courses. I went the whole length of that portion of the Irrawaddi which is in British territory, either in steamer or country boat, up the Pegu River to the town of that name, across by boat to Sittoung, and down again to Moulmein. Wherever I went I found small meshed nets being employed by the villagers to obtain fish for their own consumption, and as they had no interest in the leased fisheries, whilst fry are most easily captured, these they were destroying wherever they had the chance. Near Rangoon, nets, 30 feet long, were being dragged along the sides of the Irrawaddi in the haunts of the fry, the mesh of which was $\frac{8}{10}$ths of an inch in circumference. I counted 15 such in use at one time and on one bank of the river between Rangoon and the sea. Nothing escapes them, nothing is returned to the river, and thus excessive injury must be caused. At Prome I saw two women fishing with a short drag-net, the meshes of which were $\frac{8}{10}$ths of an inch in circumference. I took some 20 of the young of the "Nga-hoothans," *Labeo calbasu*, out and weighed them; they just turned the scale at $\frac{1}{2}$ an ounce, whilst in a few months more each individual fish should weigh, if alive and well, $\frac{1}{2}$ a pound. The same long drag-nets as observed at Rangoon were being used all along the British portion of the Irrawaddi; also numerous other forms of fine meshed nets and minutely woven baskets. But not only here were the fry being destroyed wholesale by those who were permitted to fish without payment, but also in every other portion of Burma which I visited; and this is a second reason why I consider that, even if the Chief Commissioner was correct in stating that no wanton destruction takes place in the province, he must have admitted a wasteful one, had he time to investigate the subject.

376. But it may be pointed out what is the reason that some of the Burmese fisheries are still pretty fully stocked, even if some decrease is reported, especially as throughout that province the same rules obtain. I am unable to give the European authorities credit for anything that has been done. I could not ascertain that young fish, except in some leased fisheries, or religious tanks, were preserved at all. I saw those good-natured thoughtless Burmans only regarding to-day's wants, and in fact, preservation was due to a sparse population, large swamps and vast inundated tracts of country, as well as the impetuosity of the current in the main rivers. Assuming the census returns to be correct, the demands for fish must have been yearly becoming greater, for, with an augmented fish-eating population, an increased supply must be a self-evident necessity. This has probably been met by additional methods of capture. Weirs, not permitted by the Burmese, seem to have been allowed by the British, until every outlet is now choked by them, and the fish fry are captured by the whole population. Now, the increased supply must have been derived from fisheries previously insufficiently worked, or else due to their being now overworked, leaving future years to suffer from diminished supply, consequent upon the immature fish being taken to meet present demands. In most places it was said that the supply was decreasing; anyhow, the fisheries were being fully worked, and in an economic point of view, I proposed the following measures as deserving of consideration.

Reasons fisheries are not more depopulated.

377. I do not intend making any remarks upon the mode of letting Burmese fisheries, except a proposition "that fish should be considered the property of the people, and Government should remit all rents on fisheries." The absolute giving up of fisheries to the people—I think the reports from Bombay, Madras, Mysore, and elsewhere distinctly show—eventuates in their annihilation, unless rules for the preservation of the fish from unnecessary and wasteful destruction are passed and strictly carried out. Where everybody observes that all his neighbours are permitted to capture fish as they like, it is very improbable that he will be exceedingly particular not to kill the young, as a Burmese fisherman, who fully admitted that were the destruction of fry prohibited, such in time must work good, but he remarked he was a yearly tenant and got all he could, whilst if harm is really being done, he supposed Government would have interfered. Thus, restrictions would be necessary, and water-bailiffs an indispensable portion of the scheme; whereas, if all waters, except reserved ones, were let, the lessees would have an interest in preserving the immature fish. Likewise a prevalent belief seems to obtain to let the fisheries "as cheaply as possible," and for the good " of the consumer." Nothing can be a greater fallacy; the lessee does not sell his spoil below market rate because he obtains his fishery cheaply, any more than the farmer will take less than the market rate for his rice because he lives on an untaxed farm. The difference goes into the pocket of the lessee, not into that of the consumer. To benefit the consumer, the fish should be protected, so that the largest possible amount is obtained from the water, and that is the only true way in which

Letting fisheries cheaply not of any use to fish-consumers.

the general public will be benefitted, for, as the supply augments, prices will fall. However, as the native official at Akyab pithily remarks, " more could be sold, but if more were brought to market, the price would fall, and then perhaps it would not pay the fisherman." Looking at both sides of the question, one naturally considers—are the fish simply for the good or gain of the fisherman, or to be employed in the most advantageous manner for the benefit of the people at large?

378. As a temporary measure, and solely in order to meet strong local objections, I would not propose to carry out at once measures that are certainly very desirable, but to work by degrees. In this way I feel sure that eventually the local officers will see the necessity or advantage of conservancy being fully established everywhere, except in tanks which yearly dry up, and after all watery communication with flowing streams has been naturally cut off. I would, therefore, propose as a commencement that (1) no fixed engines of any description be permitted either in rivers, streams, tanks, irrigated fields, or water-courses, unless such are leased fisheries, whilst it would be very advisable to insist upon 1 inch between the interstices of all substances forming such. These would have to be dealt with at a future date, as the fish commence to increase; (2) that a mesh of 1 inch between knot and knot be the minimum size permitted in any nets employed in free fisheries or along the banks of any river; (3) nets and weirs for the capture of prawns might be exempted, provided the latter did not extend above 30 feet in length, such distance not being more than one quarter of the breadth of the river, at low water, at the place where they are being used; (4) that poisoning of waters to obtain fish be strictly prohibited.

Present propositions as temporary measure to obviate local objections.

379. The answers to the questions on Burmese fisheries, circulated at my request by General Fytche in 1869, have not as yet been received (September 1872), which is to be regretted.

Answers to questions circulated in 1869 not yet received.

380. The *Chief Commissioner of British Burma* (Mr. Eden) proposed (April 4th, 1872) that in future, when leasing fisheries, " no lessee of a lake fishery, nor any person licensed to use nets and traps in rivers, shall use a net having a mesh of less than 4 inches in circumference, that is, 1 inch from knot to knot, nor any weir having less than 1 inch between the bamboos, rattan, reed, or other substance of which such weir is composed. Provided that this shall not apply to the use of weirs of not more than 30 feet in length, or $\frac{1}{4}$ the breadth of the stream or river in which they are placed, whichever may be the shorter, where such weirs are used solely for the purpose of catching prawns." Dams to be prohibited. Subsequently (July 19th, 1872) the *Officiating Secretary to the Chief Commissioner* observed,—" the report of the Committee of experienced officers to the effect that the prohibition contained in sections 18 and 19 (above) of the provisional rules would necessitate the entertainment of an expensive establishment of inspectors, and that a considerable loss of revenue would be occasioned thereby, seemed to the Chief Commissioner sufficient grounds for modifying these sections." The *Committee* observed, first, as regards the minimum

Proposals of Chief Commissioner.

size of the mesh of nets and the distances between the substances forming weirs:—" There are in inland lakes and rivers upwards of a dozen kinds of fish (these are generally the most numerous and plentiful) that would pass through nets and weirs of that size, and would be lost to the fishermen. These small fish are used in the manufacture of ngapee." If not taken by man, it is suggested they will be by water-fowl, and a great loss of fish and revenue must result. They proposed as follows:—" The use of weirs across all streams and channels not included in fisheries is strictly prohibited, provided that this shall not apply to weirs of not more than 30 feet in length, or ¼ of the breadth of the stream or river in which they are placed, whichever may be the shorter, when such weirs are used solely for the purpose of catching prawns." * * " Several fisheries in the province, if the use of dams is prohibited, cannot be worked. The Committee are quite aware that the use of dams is often injurious to paddy crops, in so far that at present streams get gradually filled up by them, and in consequence crops are inundated." They proposed that, in exceptional cases, they should be allowed, but not to be erected prior to January 1st, and to be removed by April 15th in each year. The *Government of India* (August 6th, 1872) decided with reference to a mesh of 4 inches in circumference:—" His Excellency the Governor General in Council is disposed to doubt whether this is not too small, and whether a mesh of 1¼ inches from knot to knot, or 5 inches in circumference, would not be preferable." The *Officiating Secretary to the Chief Commissioner* (August 29th, 1872) observed:— "The Chief Commissioner agrees in the views expressed by the Commissioner of the Tenasserim Division, who has given the subject great attention, and has personally discussed the question of the size of the mesh frequently with Mr. Eden. There is, I am to say, no occasion in the present condition of the population to take any such measures for the preservation of fish as will involve serious interference with the people. It is impossible to have establishments to prevent the people taking fish fry in the creeks and paddy-fields, and if they were not caught, they would be eaten by birds, or die as the waters recede. The supply of fish throughout the country is ample, and indeed in the Tenasserim Division this year, fish is so cheap as to make the fisheries unremunerative. The great article of consumption in Burma is ngapee, which is made from young fish mixed with other fish. The Chief Commissioner had this year ordered that the meshes of nets should be not less than 1 inch, and the consequence was such unwillingness to buy the fisheries that the rule had to be altered."

381. The *Commissioner of Arakan*, Colonel J. F. J. Stevenson, (July 22nd, 1872,) remarks, that in the report from the Deputy Commissioner of Akyab, he has revised the original text in three or four passages and also given marginal notes. The *Deputy Commissioner of Akyab* observes that "breeding-fish are destroyed to some extent. Very young ones are also caught for consumption. Shrimps are taken from October to May, the greater portion of which is used in making ngapee." ["It will be borne in mind that we have no 'eeng' (tank) fisheries in Arakan; no leased fisheries whatever, only a tax on nets." J. F. J. S.]

<small>Arakan. Opinion of European Officials.</small>

The above fish are caught by nets and traps in the sea, rivers, creeks, streams, *jhils*, ponds, and tanks throughout the year. In the rainy season, during the months of June and July, small fish are caught in the fields. The smallest mesh employed is about $\frac{1}{2}$ an inch square, but the net by which shrimps are taken is roughly woven like cloth, the holes of which are about $\frac{1}{10}$th of an inch in size. The meshes of nets might be regulated without difficulty, according to the description of fish it is desired to take. The ordinary size is from $\frac{1}{2}$ to 8 inches from knot to knot. Prawn nets are not adapted to catch large fish. Screens made of split bamboo, fastened close together, are also used along the banks. ["I believe, as said above, that alterations can easily be introduced. I am not aware that there is any economic necessity for it in Arakan, though on general principles it may undoubtedly be desirable."—J. F. J. S]. As to whether any objections exist against prohibiting the sale of the fry of fishes in the bazars, he continues:—"Prohibition seems to be absolutely necessary. But the fry of fish is of course sold in considerable quantities in the bazars, and is eaten cooked and made into ngapee." ["It is, of course, as I have above remarked, probable that unnecessary destruction results."—J. F. J. S.]. There are no objections against prohibiting the capture of fish in hilly regions during the first two months of the monsoon when they are breeding. ["I cannot say; not so, I think, as to Arakan."—J. F. J. S.]. The *Deputy Commissioner in Ramree* (July 17th, 1872) observes that the fresh-water fisheries in the district are very insignificant. There are no lakes or ponds, and but four small rivers, in which fresh-water fish are found. Breeding-fish and very young ones are not destroyed to any great extent, as the fishing is limited, but to a considerable extent when compared with the amount of such fishing; the breeding ones in November and December by nets, the young ones by making dams and baling out the water; by bamboo scoops, placing bushes in the stream, and when the small fish have got among them, surrounding them with cloths or very fine nets, at all times of the year. The smallest mesh employed is $\frac{1}{2}$ an inch from knot to knot, but coarse cloth is often used for the smallest nets. No practical difficulty exists in regulating the minimum size; one inch between the knots is proposed. No objections against prohibiting the sale of fry in the bazars, or forbidding fishing for two months in the hilly regions, when the fish go there for breeding purposes. The *Officiating Deputy Commissioner of Sandoway* (July 11th, 1872) reports that breeding-fish and very young ones are destroyed in his district by the use of small meshed nets. The young fry are usually taken during August and September in the paddy-fields and small creeks with traps made of bamboo. They are not caught in large quantities, and in this district are rarely sold. The smallest meshed nets upon which a tax is paid are $2\frac{1}{2}$ inches square, but the nets which are free of tax, and generally used by the people to supply their own wants, have a mesh which is $\frac{1}{8}$th of an inch square. There is no objection whatever to regulating the minimum size, which it is proposed should be $\frac{3}{4}$th of an inch between each knot, whilst fry might be prohibited being sold in the bazars.

382. The *Deputy Commissioner of Thyetmyo* (July 29th, 1872) observed that he fully replied to the questions circulated in 1869 [the answers to which the Chief Commissioner never forwarded], and that he believes that report contained the whole of the information now applied for with regard to the entire Prome District, of which Thyetmyo then formed a part. No great destruction of breeding-fish, except the shad, occurs, judging from the fish in the bazars. " Very young fish, I fear, are destroyed in great numbers during the rainy season. At this period of the year they leave the river, and ascend any little stream or backwater they can find, and here they fall an easy prey to men, women, and children, who pursue them with all sorts of contrivances, which, though generally very simple, are very killing. Two women, for instance, holding a sheet between them, will in half an hour or so collect a few pounds of small fry. The smallest mesh of the nets in use is ½ an inch each side. The greatest objection to regulating the size of the mesh would be, that if the size of mesh is decreased (?) there would be a diminution of the Government revenue." For the fisheries one inch between each knot is recommended. If fry are allowed to be caught, they may as well be eaten; therefore there would be no use prohibiting their sale.

Opinion of Deputy Commissioner of Thyetmyo.

383. The *Commissioner of the Tenasserim Division*, (July 15th, 1872) reported that breeding-fish and very young ones are destroyed in his district to a great extent by nets, weirs, hooks, basket-traps, *dameng*, traps in streams and rivers, and in other different ways in rented fisheries. They are caught at all seasons of the year, and in inland fisheries from January to April. There is no restriction as to the size of the mesh of nets employed, and there would be many difficulties in regulating such, the chief of which is, that fish, both large and small, are mixed up to form the compost called ngapee. Without the small fish the bulk of the large fish caught would be small, and the value of the fisheries very much reduced. Deprecates any rule fixing the minimum size of meshes, but would leave the people to use nets as they found them best suited for their work. Fry not sold in the bazars would be turned into ngapee, so any prohibitory order against its sale would be of little use. " In my opinion, generally in this province, the rivers and creeks are so large and numerous, and the space of country covered by inundation every year so vast, that there is yet ample breeding-ground for fish without imposing any strict rules as to preservation of fish and their fry. As population, however, increases, and as embankments are raised to confine the present spill-water of the rivers within narrower bounds, then it may be necessary to assist Nature by causing less destruction of the fry; but I am sure that, as yet, generally the supply is enormous, the breeding-grounds are extensive, and there is no need of any great interference to preserve the stock. To give the large breeding-fish and their fry free ingress and egress to the inundated plains from the rivers, the use of *tsays* or bamboo traps across streams not rented as fisheries has been prohibited. This is all that is required at present. As time goes on, other restrictions can be made as they were found to be necessary." [If prohibiting " the use of bamboo traps

Opinion of European Officials of the Tenasserim Division.

across the streams not rented as fisheries" is necessary, it is difficult to see why permitting their entirely blocking rented streams can be anything but injurious, especially as they only allow water to pass, stopping every fish. Likewise at present fixed traps, nets, &c., prevent migrating breeding-fish from freely obtaining ingress to, or egress from, the inundated plains, and the mesh is so small that the most minute fry are entrapped; surely these ought to be prohibited or subject to some regulation as to the size of the mesh which is employed. This mode of fishing is entirely illegal in Great Britain.] The *Deputy Commissioner, Amherst District* (July 11th, 1872) replies that the answers of four of his most experienced native officials (*myo-okes*) are unanimous in saying that the supply of fish brought to the bazars is not equal to the demand. Breeding-fish and fry are destroyed to a very great extent in the district, most so "at the commencement of the rains, when breeding-fishes migrate to spawn : in this condition the fish are said by the Burmans to be utterly reckless as regards capture, and passively allow themselves to be taken in very great numbers. Those fish which escape this critical period spawn in shallow water, from which, generally speaking, the small fry have little chance of returning to the larger streams. Another cause of wholesale destruction is the practice of unrestricted fishing, that is to say, the indiscriminate use of traps, nets, and dams, by which fish of every kind are caught, with regard only to present wants rather than the probability of future scarcity." The smallest mesh of nets used is $\frac{1}{2}$ an inch between each knot; the difficulty in regulating it would depend upon the nature of the regulations themselves. Any sudden restriction upon the present means of supply would cause great inconvenience, and temporary misery, perhaps, to the poorer classes, because the staple food of a whole people would for a time be sensibly diminished, and the revenues would temporarily deteriorate; the smaller kinds of fish in tanks, *jhils*, and paddy-fields would become a prey to birds instead of food for man. [This, of course, only refers to those pieces of water which are not perennial, in which, after all communication between them and the rivers has ceased, they gradually dry up, and the fish, unless taken by man, would die or be eaten by the lower animals]. The supply in the bazars now is unequal to the demand; regulations would decrease the present supply, although they would eventually increase it. If possible, would prohibit the capture of the fry of those species which grow to a large size, especially of the "Nga-yans" [*Ophiocephalus striatus*]; and if their possession or sale under a certain weight and size were declared penal, some stop might be put to its indiscriminate capture, and the result would be a great increase in the present food-supply." [This course I do not think could be carried out; it is true that this is a most valuable fish and attains 3 feet or more in length, whilst the young are killed in numbers as small fry, but the practical difficulty would be as follows :— There are several species of *Ophiocephalus*, termed thus, with one or two words added to show which is meant. Generally "Nga-yan" was the large *Ophiocephalus striatus*, but near Henzada it was termed "Nga-yan-pa-nan." The *Ophiocephalus punctatus*, which closely resembles the last species, excepting that, though very broad, it rarely, if ever, exceeds a foot in length, at this place was termed " Nga-yan-thin-ohn," whilst the perhaps

lesser *Ophiocephalus gachua* was known as "Nga-yan-goun-doh," and the possessor of one of these smaller species might be considered as having obtained the young of the larger sort. It appears to be a more practical plan to forbid fixed traps and nets, and poisoning water at first, and then, as fish augment, to see if any regulation, affecting the minimum size of the mesh of the nets which might be employed, would not be feasible. Perhaps, at first, passing regulations on those used in the free fisheries might be tried, prior to doing so in the rented fish farms.] Major Sladen appends the names in Burmese of the following fish with remarks:—" Fish which become large, but are not captured when young, owing, it is said, to their keeping to the deeper portions of the rivers:— 'Nga-bat' [*Wallago attu*]; 'Nga-gyin' [*Cirrhina mrigala*]; 'Nga-tan' [*Gagata typus*]; 'Kah-thamyin' [*Pseudeutropius taakree*]; 'Kah-thaboung' [*Eutropüchthys vacha*]; 'Kah-kooran:' 'Nga-ywe' [*Saccobranchus fossilis*]; 'Nga-young' [*Arius Burmanicus*]. The following fish are caught indiscriminately, large and small, but they never attain to over 5lbs. :—'Ngahpannua' [*Equula ruconius*]; 'Nga-pyêma' [*Anabas scandens*]; 'Kah-kadit:' 'Nga-khoomma' [*Barbus stigma*]; 'Nga-khoo' [*Clarias magur*]; 'Ngakyay' [*Datnioides polota*]; 'Nga-nuthan' [*Callichrous macrophthalmus*]; 'Nga Tsin-bya' [? *Pellona Sladoni*]; 'Nga Tsin-yeing' [*Perilampus atpar*].*
The *Deputy Commissioner of the Tavoy District* reports that breeding-fish and very young ones are destroyed to a considerable extent, the former being captured in the beginning of the rains, about May or June, when they ascend the tidal streams to deposit their spawn; they are caught by damming up the stream with bamboo screens (weirs), leaving a passage in the middle of the stream, where basket traps with enclosures (cruives) are laid to catch them. Some also use casting-nets called *koon* at the mouth of the streams. Large fish as well as young ones are caught in a similar way during the three months, commencing in September, about the close of the rainy season, but on a much larger scale by an arrangement called *tshai* when all fish, large and small, descending the stream, are captured. [These are the fish which have completed their spawning, and the young which are attempting to pass to the deeper parts of the rivers.] The smallest mesh used is ⅜th of an inch; there may be some difficulty in regulating it, as it may affect the capture of prawns and shrimps employed for the manufacture of ngapee; still, if the present small mesh be permitted, immature fish will be taken. "The only way to get over the difficulty will be by appointing fishery inspectors, whose duty it will be to see that rules decided on are not evaded. These rules should prescribe what nets, screens (weirs), and traps (cruives), are legal, and in what month and in what places they may be used. To issue orders without informing them will be useless: every one, from the 'Thoogyee' (fishery lessee) downwards, is too much interested in obtaining the fish to care about the way in which they are caught." Would permit the meshes to be, as at present in use, under proper restrictions. "The capture of fish in streams should be prohibited during May and June, when the fish ascend the streams for spawning, and again during three months from September, when they descend to the river with the fry;

---

* The scientific names have been added by myself from information I obtained in Burma, but I have not received specimens of the above, so some errors may exist.

and, further, the taking of fish by baling out pools and ponds should be prohibited. The use of *lamoos* should also be prohibited: these are screens (weirs), the rods of which are placed very close, and when the tide is high and the fish are feeding amongst the bushes and grass on the side of the tidal creek, those screens are so placed as to enclose a large tract. When the tide falls, all the fish left are naturally caught. The large are taken by the fishermen, but the small are left to die. The space between the rods of *lamoos* allowed should never be less than 1 inch. Here also an inspector would be required to see the order is not evaded." The *Deputy Commissioner of Shwégyen* (July 13th, 1872) remarked that "breeding-fish get out of the deep rivers and ponds at the very commencement of the rains, and force themselves up the runs of water flowing towards the freshly covered plains. Many are caught in screen traps made of split bamboo or reeds stretched across the small creeks and runs. The young fish (four months old) are caught by the same contrivance on their way back to the deep water in October." The smallest mesh used is about $\frac{1}{2}$ an inch. In reeds or bamboo screens (weirs), the interstices are frequently under a $\frac{1}{4}$ of an inch. "The only difficulty against regulating the size of the mesh is a pecuniary one as regards rents. There would be a little more trouble in making the lessees of fisheries use screens of a certain space between the rods, but only at first, and public and religious feeling amongst the Buddist population would certainly be in favor of letting small fish escape, but there would necessarily be some loss of revenue." Does not know of any objection against prohibiting the sale of fry in the bazar. "It appears to me that there is not much known upon the subject of the fresh-water fishes of Burma and their habits. As books of reference are not available, I would suggest that the head-quarters of each district be supplied with some comprehensive work on Indian fishes." [None exists; the late Dr. Jerdon's manuals did not extend to this class of animals, and without native names and illustrations, works simply giving descriptions would be of little, if any, use.] "Officers will then be able to turn their attention to the subject. The breeding times and the habits of different species might be learnt by enquiring of the fishermen, that is, as far as they themselves know. A few of the smaller kinds which are supposed at present to be distinct species, but which may be only the fry, should be transferred to an enclosed piece of water to see what they would come to. "There are many fish supposed to be adults, as 'Nga-khoo' [*Clarias magur*]; one species of 'Nga-yan' [*Ophiocephalus gachua* or *punctatus*]—see my observations near the commencement of this paragraph under the head of the Amherst District]; 'Nga-gyee' [*Saccobranchus fossilis*]; 'Nga-hpan-ma' [*Mola Atkinsonii*]; 'Khoan-ma' [*Barbus stigma*], &c., which would pass through in bamboo screens, the interstices of which are an inch apart, and before absolutely prohibiting their use, closer enquiries and more knowledge of the subject is necessary to show at what seasons such may be used, and at what times they should be prohibited." [With the exception of the 'Khoan-ma,' *Barbus stigma*, adult of all the other fish would be stopped by a one-inched mesh between the knots, calculating that the fullest stretch would be $1\frac{1}{4}$ inches, some due to their width, others to their depth or their spines. Even large ones of the last species would be unable to pass.] "Generally the closing of water-courses to fish ascending in the month of May should be prohibited, and the use of close screens until after November." The *Deputy Commissioner of Mergui* (August 3rd, 1872) reported "that the fishing in his district is all sea-fishing, and it is not known where the fish breed, &c." [This will stand over for the report on the marine fish and fisheries.] The *Deputy Commissioner of Tounghoo* (June 24th, 1872) observed "that all fish caught are killed, both breeding and young ones." Fish breed in June and July, in which latter month the country becomes inundated, and the fry enter the small creeks, and thence find their way to the paddy-fields, and are caught by the cultivators. The 'Nga-yan' [*Ophiocephalus striatus*] is, I believe, the only large fish which, when very young, leaves the rivers and is found in the paddy-fields. The people use 'yethai,' a bamboo frame-work, with a mat bottom, dragged sometimes by buffaloes and sometimes pushed by a man; no fish, let the size be ever so small, can escape. These instruments are used in the paddy-fields and swampy ground during the monsoon generally." Sees no reason for altering the mesh of nets or fence months in hilly districts.

384. The *Commissioner of Pegu* (March 27th, 1872) reported upon

Opinions on bunding streams for fishing purposes.

"the damming up of certain creeks in the Pegu township with bunds, by the fishermen renting the same, to the impeding of their free navigation and the flooding of the neighbouring lands. The Principal Revenue Settlement Officer, in the course of his season's work, observed the same evil which has been brought to notice by the Assistant Engineer in charge of the Pegu and Iwantay roads." [Respecting this bunding of streams by fishermen, I observed on my report on the fisheries of that province in October 2nd, 1869, "but the other form of bunding tanks, or rather bunding streams into tanks, is most destructive, for it must be remembered that in Burma there is no necessity to conserve water as in India; on the contrary, they have generally too much. An earthen dam or bund is thrown across a stream, which, of course, causes the water to collect above it: next, smaller ones are erected parallel with the course of the stream, or cutting off a portion of it from the main channel. The water is laded out, the whole of the fish captured, and this is continued portion by portion, till not a fish is left. The injury is not prospective, it is now going on, and thus in one fishery alone the rents have sunk, owing to decrease of fish, as follows: Rs. 700 to 500, and this year to Rs. 200. It is a lazy, destructive, and iniquitous mode of fishing, doing injury to the river, for its bed silts up behind this bund, and thus the neighbouring paddy-fields suffer in times of floods, as well as positively destroying the fisheries; all this bunding of streams should be absolutely prohibited; the renters can employ bamboo weirs;" para. 16. "In making an earthen bund, two rows of strong stakes, 6 feet apart, are driven in across the stream, the interval is filled in with grass and clayey mud. When all the fish have been destroyed above this by lading out the water, they leave it and raise another bund lower down the stream. The old stakes and banks are never removed, but remain to be an obstruction to navigation, and floating trees, which often permanently remain; sometimes the bunds give way, a great volume of water suddenly rushes down, and fortunate for any bridges in its course, if they are not injured or carried away," para. 57. "That bunding rivers for fishing purposes be absolutely prohibited," para. 60.] The *Deputy Commissioner of Rangoon* (March 22nd, 1872) stated,—" I have reason to believe that the damming up of the water does inundate the country round Pegu, and I fear a similar result is felt in other parts of the district. There is much land in the Syriam township kept uncultivated for the personal benefit of a few fishermen." The *Senior Revenue Settlement Officer* (March 21st, 1872) reported that in the Rangoon District, in some tidal streams, certain large fishery dams exist, which appear to be productive of great evils. "The dams are permanent structures. The fishery-holders also put up, within the limits of their fisheries, numerous small dams termed baling-out dams, while creeks not claimed by the fishery lessees fall to the share of the villagers, who forthwith choke them up in all directions with small dams. These, it is true, are broken down in the rains, but stakes and *débris* remain, which contribute more or less to impede the flow of the water. The principal dams have been in existence some years; one, indeed, is said to have been erected in the time of the Burmese rule, but more probably was about the time of the last war, when the affairs of the country were in some confusion, for from enquiries made, it appears that under the Burmese Government dams were not allowed in any of the main streams; they cause the channels to silt up, hinder the passage of boats, and land is rendered difficult of access. Owing to the above causes, it has to be assessed at a much lower rate than it would be under other conditions. Crops are frequently destroyed by floods owing to the obstructions to the flow of water, and revenue is lost through this conversion of extensive tracts of land into swampy wastes, which, prior to the construction of the dams, were well cultivated. The loss of revenue, which the removal of the dams might at first sight seem to threaten, may be provided against if the neighbouring pond fisheries, and all places suitable for the formation of such fisheries, be assessed for terms of years, as the opening of the main streams will enhance their value, and low spots unfitted for cultivation, and now unremunerative, may be readily turned to a very profitable account, as fisheries, and even in the first year of the removal of the dams, no loss of revenue need be incurred." [The Deputy Commissioner of the District was directed to see to their removal before the rains, and prior to the new settlement.]

385. The following are the native reports, including the modes of fishing in the fresh waters, showing which nets are taxed and which untaxed.

<small>Observations upon the native official reports.</small>

386. In the *Akyab District*, the *native official* reports that out of a population of 268,000 persons, 1,982 took out licenses for fishing in the district this year; some work as fishermen entirely, others also follow other occupations. They are composed of Mussulmen termed "Judiahs," Madrassees, and natives of Chittagong, Arakan, and Burma. The markets are fairly supplied with fish: during spring-tides the most are taken from the sea, and the least during the neaps. "More could be sold, but if more were brought to market, the price would fall, and then perhaps it would not pay the fishermen. The whole population eat fish, the supply of which is stationary. Very small fish are taken in the

<small>Opinion of native official of Akyab.</small>

o

fields, lakes, ponds, or *jhils*, and everywhere by nets and traps, and by emptying water from the hollows during the rains. This practice might be stopped with advantage." The following are the *taxed nets* used in the fresh and back waters of this district:—(1) *Hmyaw-paik*, each piece 60 feet long and 18 deep, with a mesh from 1 to 4 inches square; these are drift-nets; (2) *Kyee-doung*, very similar to the last; (3) *Laigwenpaik*, 60 feet long, 15 deep, with meshes of 3 or 4 inches square, and are fixed in shallow parts of rivers and across streams; (4) *Nga-tha-louk-paik*—these are cast-nets employed from a boat, and used for the purpose of taking the shad as they ascend the rivers for breeding purposes; (5) *Ngin-paik*, 60 ×18 feet, 2 to 3 inches square in the mesh, and used from boats; (6) *Paik-gyee*, 75 to 120 feet long, and about 38 feet deep at the mouth, with meshes from ½ an inch to 6 inches square; these are fixed in the shallow parts of the bay and in rivers; (7) *Paik-tsoon-kyoo*, from 30 to 36 feet long, and about the same depth at the mouth, with a mesh from ½ an inch to 4 inches square; sometimes they are used as fixtures, at other times dragged in the streams and creeks; (8) *Tsein-paik*, in one set of six traps (cruives), 37½ feet long and 9 to 12 wide at the opening, and composed of split bamboo fastened close together; these bamboo traps are fastened to posts fixed in the rivers and creeks; (9) *Tshway-paik-gyee* or *Paik-htouk-gyee*, from 1,200 to 2,400 feet long, 18 deep, and meshes of 2 or 3 inches square; they are drag-nets; (10) *Tshway-paik-galay* are also drag-nets, 120 × 6 feet, with meshes 1 or 2 inches square; (11) *Yim-dwin-paik*, stationary nets in the rivers, about 30 feet square bagnets, and ½ to 4 inches square in the meshes. Irrespective of the foregoing taxed nets, the *untaxed* contrivances for capturing fish are rods and lines, traps and small nets in fields, and also in shallow streams by means of bamboo weirs.

387. In the *Ramree District*, the *native official* reports that there are about 50 fishermen, including those who use bamboo scoops; the greater portion of the cultivators likewise use these scoops during the rains. The markets are fully supplied, but the amount of fish in the water has slightly decreased. Very small fish are taken in considerable quantities, in comparison with the extent of the fresh waters, by making dams, with bamboo traps and scoops; the minimum mesh employed is ½ an inch, but a coarse cloth is used for small nets. Bushes are also placed in side streams, and when fish have taken refuge in them, they are surrounded by nets.

Opinion of native official of Ramree.

388. In the *Sandoway District*, the three *native officials* reply that very few of the fishermen make fishing their sole occupation, there being no local markets; fishing is only carried on to supply personal requirements; however, the price of fish is given at from 8 to 24 lbs. weight the rupee. The whole population eat fish, the amount of which is believed to have remained stationary. Very small fish are taken, as the river rises during the rains, by men and women along the banks of the streams; one-sixth of an inch square is the smallest size of the mesh of the nets that is employed. Fish are also trapped to a small extent in irrigated fields during the rains. Nets, traps, and weirs are used for inland fishing.

Opinion of native officials of Sandoway.

389. In the *Thyetmyo District,* one *native official* answers as follows :—That there are 137 resident fishermen, but many others come down temporarily from Upper Burma; as a rule, the fishermen do not follow any other occupation. The local markets are generally fully supplied: now and then the fishermen take a holiday, and then no fish at all is to be had. The supply of fish has always been equal to the demand. Fish are trapped in the irrigated fields to a small extent. The *taxed nets* in use are as follows :—(1) *Hmaw,* 240 × 8 cubits, and an 8-inched mesh [several of the sizes of meshes given, being erroneous, are omitted], it is floated down a river; (2) *Let-matan-paik,* 250 × 8 cubits, with a mesh of 1 inch, one end is affixed to a sand-bank, and the other is carried out into the stream and brought round to the sand-bank; (3) *Paik-woon-boo,* 800 × 35 cubits, with a mesh of 1 inch, drifted down the river by the aid of two boats and hauled on to the bank; (4) *Kwoon-gee-paik* or *Mek-kwoon-paik* are casting nets; (5) *Paik-lot,* or *Hna-loon-queng* is similar to No. 2, but is only made in Upper Burma; (6) *Hmyaw-aing-dan,* 25 × 10 cubits, used in backwaters close to the river's bank, one end is fastened to the shore at the head of the backwater, and the other end anchored out in the stream; (7) *Ret-gweng,* 25 × 25 cubits, and a mesh of ¼ an inch, this is like the Chinese dip-net, and said to be very destructive to the young shad. The *untaxed nets* are given as follows :—(1) *Nga-tsein-paik,* 50 × 1 cubit, with a mesh of 1 inch, it is pulled along in shallow waters during the dry season near the shore; (2) *Oo-tsein-paik,* 60 × 4 cubits, with a mesh of an inch used as the foregoing; (3) *Roung-ma,* a casting net; (4) *Paik-byon,* 80 × 8 cubits, having a mesh of 3 inches, worked like No. 1 of the taxed nets; (5) *Let-pyit-kwon,* 7 × 7 cubits, with a mesh of three-fourths of an inch, pulled along in shallow water; (6) *Khyee-kwon,* 400 × 7 cubits, and a mesh of 2 inches, these nets are worked like the last, and are now and then brought down from Upper Burma; (7) *Kwon-neng,* 6 × 7 cubits, with a mesh of 4 inches between each knot [?], a casting-net; (8) *Daing-won,* a prawn-net; (9) *Gaw,* a net let down to the bottom of the stream and baited; (10) *Doo-khyoon,* a float-net used in large rivers to capture ascending fish during the dry season.

Opinion of native official of Thyetmyo.

390. From the *Amherst District,* the answer of four *Myo-okes* have been received: they report that the great majority of the fishermen are cultivators, and very few solely employed in this occupation. The markets are stated not to be fully supplied in any of the districts: the whole of the population eat fish. The amount in the waters is considered to have remained stationary in two, and to be decreasing yearly in the remaining two. Small fish are caught in the fields and creeks during the rains by means of dams, *tamans,* and traps, *yeen* and *yethai,* and other contrivances. The smallest mesh employed is ¼ an inch in the hand nets. Fish are trapped in the fields during the rains, and caught by means of *hmyone, yeen, koondoung,* and *yethai,* &c. The names only of the implements employed in fishing is given. [Poisoning of waters is also resorted to during the dry season in this district, as will be observed from the following report furnished by *Mr. J. W. Inglis, Executive Engineer of the Amherst Division,* in 1869 :—

Opinion of native officials of Amherst.

" In the Amherst District, about six or eight miles from the sea, it has been frequently brought to my notice, and I have also observed, the practice prevails extensively of poisoning the water of the streams for the purpose of obtaining the fish. The process adopted is as follows :— Pools formed in the streams by some natural obstructions are chosen for carrying out this iniquitous mode of capturing fish. Different methods are pursued. In one the bark of the Bunboay tree is floated on the surface of the water for a short space of time, when the fish come to the surface intoxicated, and are easily removed by the hand. The reason for removing the bark so quickly from the water is, that the fish might not become unwholesome, because too much of this substance causes the flesh of the fish to act deleteriously on the health of the person who eats it. The other modes are similar. The bark of the Kyee, or the leaves and root of the Hong, or the fruit of the Bongalong, are used. I have seen considerable quantities of fish obtained in the above manner. They would measure 2 feet down to the minutest size. In fact, these substances appear to intoxicate every fish which may be in the pools at the time they are used; the time of the year this is adopted is the dry season, when I have large numbers of workmen employed in the construction of the Yeh road, many of whom are rendered sick, due to the state of the water, as well as eating fish which has been procured in the manner described."]

391. In the *Tavoy District*, answers have been received from one native *official*, who observes that four-fifths of the fishermen are likewise engaged in other occupations. The local markets are only sufficiently supplied with fish at certain seasons, which is eaten without exception by every one in the district. The amount in the water has decreased during the last five or six years; the fry are captured in large quantities during the latter end of the rains in the months of September, October, and November; they are taken in *tshais*, a building constructed in the middle of the streams with bamboo screens or weirs placed across the stream, leaving the part, where the building is, open, in which a sloping tray, about 20 yards long, is placed, one end touching the ground, and the other above water, with wall-like screens on each side of the tray: over this is placed another moveable tray or lift, which, when the fish are driven in by the current, is tilted up, and they are caught, or baled out and put into baskets kept in the water. The smallest sized mesh of nets is ⅜ths of an inch. Fish are trapped in the irrigated fields during the rains in a few places, by laying screens and bamboo basket traps in the water-courses when the water recedes from the fields: this is generally done by lads for home consumption only. The following are the fishing implements employed :—

Opinion of native official of Tavoy.

    1.—*Tshway-paik-gyee* (see Akyab, No. 6); mesh ⅜ths of an inch.
    2.—*Tshway-paik-galay* (see Akyab, No. 10); mesh ⅜ths of an inch.
    3.—*Hmyaw-paik-galay*, a river net floated; mesh 2½ inches.
    4.—*Tsanda-gyee*, a place built in the river or at its mouth, where fish are caught on a large scale, worked by eight men: there is ½ an inch between the bamboos of which the screens are made.

5.—*Tsanda-glay*, similar, but smaller, and built in the narrow part of the river, worked by four men : ¼ of an inch between the bamboos.

6.—*Umyoon* and *Khaya*. The first is a cylindrical bamboo basket, from 3 to 6 feet in length, and from 1 to 2 feet in diameter, with a trap-door at both ends, in which fish are caught; it is used in the streams. The latter is a long cone-shaped basket, held under water in a strong tide; the fish gets in and is jammed at the sharp ends ; when the tide recedes the basket is pulled up by means of a rope : ⅜ths of an inch between each piece of bamboo.

7.—*Htsay* is the same as *tsanda*, but constructed in tidal streams.

8.—*Kwoon*, a casting-net.

9.—*Tsoung*, a conical basket, open at both ends ; the lower one is put down over fish in shallow water, and the fisherman removes the game from above : ¼ of an inch between the bamboos.

392. From the *Shwégyen District*, one *native official* reports that most of the fishermen engage in other occupations : the local markets are fully supplied ; the price has not risen, " but there seems to be a general impression that fish are decreasing. This is what the fishermen say ; there is no means of testing it." Numbers of small bright silvery fish, termed " Shoay-hmong," or gold-dust fish, are found, after the first week's rains, ascending some of the rivers in prodigious shoals. They swim close to the banks, avoiding the deep water and current, and are caught in great quantities by women and children with pieces of mosquito netting or cloth. These have all the characters, to the casual observer, of fish-fry, but the Burmese say they grow no larger. The smallest sized mesh of nets is ½ an inch and a ¼ of an inch between bamboos, or even less. Fish are taken in the inundated fields. The names of fishing implements are given.

Opinion of native official of Shwégyen.

393. Replies from the *Mergui District* have been given by four *Thoogyees* and *Myo-okes*, but as their answers refer to the sea fisheries, they will be included in that report.

Replies from Mergui.

MADRAS.

(Supplementary Report).

394. The *Acting Collector of Bellary* (7th September 1872) observes—breeding-fish and fry are destroyed in the tanks, but if not taken, they would only die when the water dries up. The smallest size of mesh in use appears to be one through which a quill can just be passed : it could only be regulated in leased waters, a proceeding he does not consider necessary, and as regulations are not recommended, "fry will still be caught, and when caught, it must be sold." The *Collector* (see page lxxix) stated, as regards letting the fisheries of this Collectorate, that it is not probable that any persons will be found to bid for them. They have been put up to auction this year and realized 672 rupees. The *Sub-Collector* contradicts all the others who assert breeding-fish and young ones are destroyed, but gives the minimum size of the mesh of nets at $\frac{1}{10}$th or $\frac{1}{20}$th of an inch; replies as to what difficulties there are against regulating it—"none much. The Police would be always able to get fish for nothing, by the threat of charging fishermen with fishing with an improper net." Prohibiting the sale of fry in the bazars would be useless, as they would be sold just as much, though more privately; whilst were a close season declared for two months during the monsoon in hilly districts, such might "cause the wild tribes to starve during the breeding season." The *Head Assistant Collector* replies—all fish are caught irrespective of their size and condition: by nets and basket-traps chiefly, and in the tanks when the waters are low. The minimum mesh in use is given at probably $\frac{1}{8}$ an inch in diameter, and as to regulating such, "it will be as easy a matter as the prohibition of illicit arrack-stills, and I do not think that much hardship would ensue:" one inch between the knots of each mesh is proposed.

Opinions of European Officials in the Bellary Collectorate.

395. The *Acting Collector of Trichinopoly* reports (10th August 1872) that fishermen spare no fish, however small; a tremendous destruction takes place below the irrigation weirs where their ascent is arrested, and in the pools of the river as they subside, also in tanks that are rented out. One-eighth of an inch is given as the smallest size mesh employed, which ought to be regulated as tending to increase the fish population, and thus secure a good supply to the market; five inches in circumference is proposed.

Opinion of the Acting Collector of Trichinopoly.

396. The *Acting Collector of the Kistna* (29th August 1872) observes that fish are caught wherever found, and in every possible way; hence breeding ones and fry can hardly escape. The smallest mesh will hardly permit a grain of red gram to pass, but great difficulties would exist in regulating it, or prohibiting the sale of the fry

Opinion of European Officials in the Kistna District.

of fish. Is not satisfied that a diminution of fish has been proved, or that if it exists, such can have been caused by destroying the breeding ones and their fry; therefore sees no necessity for legislation, but if decided that something is to be done, a short close season would be the least objectionable and unpopular form it would take. The *Head Assistant Collector* replies that it has been shown that " fish of all ages and sizes, clean or otherwise, are taken at all seasons,"· whilst as to regulating the minimum size of the mesh of nets he sees "no difficulty. The fishermen are all known; and their nets can be inspected when being used or being dried." He ventures, "however, to express an opinion that a case for the legislature interfering with the capture and sale of fish has not been made out. Salmon decreased in British rivers from two main causes—(1) the pollution by manufactories, (2) from the increased demand. [This opinion is correct, yet incorrect, except that (1) the pollution of rivers was one of the causes of decrease of fish, but (2) the increased demand can hardly be given as the only other, unless that such led, due to the baneful absence of proper regulations, to every poaching practice being resorted to; each owner of a fishery "sought to do what he liked with his own part of the river, and often selfishly resorted to weirs, dams and fixed engines, with the view of driving every living inhabitant of the waters into his own net, regardless of the impoverishment of his neighbour." "The decay of the fisheries having then become conspicuous, it was necessary for the legislature to intervene on the ground of public policy, and with an eye to the benefit of all parties, to restrain the suicidal policy of the riparian owners, making it no longer possible for each to do what seemed good in his own eyes." Fixed engines were considered the chief cause of this injury in many places.] The *Acting Sub-Collector* (24th April 1872) reported that breeding-fish and very young ones are destroyed to a great extent. The fishermen catch them at all times and in any way they can, but most of all in the hot season, when the Kistna is fordable in many places. "In riding through fishing villages on the coast, I have often seen numerous large heaps of fish of the very smallest size. I have no doubt but that the villagers mainly live on them in some seasons, and sell their larger fish. If small fish are caught in such quantity on the coast, I see no reason to doubt but that the same thing goes on in the fresh waters." In Guntur the salesmen considered the markets fully supplied. [The Tehsildar, p. xcv, reported the markets as very insufficiently supplied, and re-states it now: also that the amount in the waters had decreased.] No wasteful destruction of fish occurs, except the use of the young as food. "It is not used at all as manure, or only to a very small extent."

397. The *Collector of South Canara* (September 9th, 1872) replied that the first six questions have been answered (see paragraphs 167 and 168.) Fortunately the use of nets is practically prevented during the first two months of the monsoon, owing to the violence of the floods. The process of spawning is also spread over many months out of the twelve, and angling is impracticable at some of the periods in question, as mahaseer, at any rate, will not take a bait when the water

Reply from the Collector of South Canara, and his draft Fishery Act.

is coloured. The following is the draft Fishery Act proposed by Mr. H. S. Thomas in 1870:—

Whereas it is expedient to provide for the improvement of the fisheries in the Madras Presidency, it is hereby enacted as follows:—

PRELIMINARY.

1. *Short Title.*—This Act may be cited for all purposes as the Madras Fishery Act, 1870.

2. *Application of Act.*—This Act shall apply to all places subject to the authority of the Madras Government, provided that it shall be lawful for the Governor in Council, by notification published in the *Fort St. George Gazette*, to exempt any place from the operation of this Act.

3. *Commencement of Act.*—This Act shall come into operation on the   day of   one thousand eight hundred and seventy .

4. *Definition of terms.*—In this Act, unless there is something inconsistent in the context, the words and expressions hereinafter mentioned, shall have respectively the meanings hereby assigned to them; that is to say—

" Tidal waters" shall include the sea, and all rivers, creeks, streams, canals, and other water as far as the tide flows and re-flows.

" Inland waters" shall mean all waters that are not tidal waters.

" Dams" shall mean all weirs, anicuts, and other fixed obstructions used for the purpose of damming up running water.

" Fishing weir" shall include any artificial structure fixed across the whole or any part of a river for the purpose of catching or facilitating the catching of fish.

" Fixed engine" shall include stake nets, anchored nets, basket traps and all fixed implements or engines for catching or for facilitating the catching of fish.

5. *Penalty on mixing poisonous substances in waters.*—Every person who has poisonous substances in his possession, or who causes or knowingly permits to flow, or puts or knowingly permits to be put into any waters containing fish, or into any tributaries thereof, any liquid or solid matter to such an extent as to cause the waters to stupefy or kill fish, shall incur the following penalties; that is to say—

I. Upon the first conviction a penalty not exceeding fifty rupees.

II. Upon the second conviction a penalty not exceeding one hundred rupees, and a further penalty not exceeding twenty rupees for every day during which such offence is continued.

III. Upon a third or any subsequent conviction a penalty not exceeding two hundred rupees, and a further penalty not exceeding two hundred rupees a day for every day on which such offence is repeated or continued, commencing from the date of third conviction.

6. But no person shall be subject to the foregoing penalties if he satisfy the Court before whom he is tried that the poisonous substances in his possession were intended for some legal purpose.

7. And no person shall be subject to the foregoing penalties if he prove to the satisfaction of the Court before whom he is tried that he has

used the best practicable means within a reasonable cost to render harmless the liquid or solid matter so permitted to flow or to be put into waters.

8. And no person shall be subject to the foregoing penalties if he prove to the satisfaction of the Court before whom he is tried that the poisoning complained of existed before the passing of this Act; that the cost of rendering it harmless would exceed one hundred rupees, or would exceed a reasonable tax on his means; and that he has, prior to the date of the complaint, applied to the Collector of the District for the aid of Government.

9. In the event of the Collector being applied to for Government aid, he shall cause the poisoning to be rendered harmless, and shall proceed in accordance with the provisions of Act   of   (the Arbitration Act) to apportion the share of the expense thereof to be borne by the applicant and the sum to be paid him for any damage done to his property.

10. If the Collector considers that the applicant has no claim under section 8 on the assistance of Government, he shall give notice to the applicant that, unless he himself renders the subject of the complaint harmless within one month or other longer period fixed by the Collector, a complaint will be lodged against him under section 5.

11. *Penalty on destroying Roe.*—No person shall do the following things, or any of them, that is to say—

 I. Buy, sell, or expose for sale, or have in his possession, any spawned roe.

 II. Wilfully disturb any place in which fish have spawned.

And any person acting in contravention of this section shall, for each offence, incur a penalty not exceeding twenty rupees, and shall forfeit all roe found in his possession; but this section shall not apply to any person who uses or has in his possession roe for artificial propagation or other scientific purposes, or gives any reason satisfactory to the Court by whom he is tried for having the same in his possession.

12. *Penalty on using certain nets.*—No person shall take or attempt to take any fish, except shrimps or prawns, with any net having a mesh of less than the following dimensions, that is to say, in the inland waters of less than half an inch in extension from knot to knot (the measurement to be made on each side of the square, or two inches measured round each mesh when wet; or in the tidal waters of less than three inches measured round each mesh when wet); and any person acting in contravention of this section shall forfeit all nets and tackle used by him in so doing, and shall, for each offence, incur a penalty not exceeding rupees fifty; and the placing two or more nets behind or near to each other in such manner as to practically diminish the mesh of the nets used, or the covering the nets used with canvas, or the using any other artifice so as to evade the provisions of this section with respect to the mesh of nets, shall be deemed to be an act in contravention of this section.

13. *Penalty on placing or fixing fixed engines.*—No fishing weir or fixed engine of any description shall be placed or used for catching fish in any inland water; and for the purposes of this section any water flowing to, through, or from irrigated fields shall be included in the term inland water;

(2) and no fixed engine of any description shall be placed in tidal waters between sunset on Saturday and sunrise on Monday: provided that it shall be lawful for the Governor in Council, by notification made in the *Fort St. George Gazette*, to exempt any tidal water from the operation of this clause;

(3) and no fixed engine other than fixed nets of legal meshes shall, for the purpose of catching fish, be set on or near the banks of, or between high and low water marks of, any tidal waters;

(4) and any engine placed or used in contravention of this section may be taken possession of or destroyed; and any engine so placed or used, and any fish taken by such engine, shall be forfeited, and in addition thereto, the owner of any engine placed or used in contravention of this section shall, for each day of so placing or using the same, incur a penalty not exceeding one hundred rupees.

14. When fish or the young of fish are led aside out of a main stream by means of any artificial channel used for irrigation, or for the purpose of supplying towns with water, or for supplying any navigable canal, the revenue authorities shall determine whether it is necessary to place and maintain gratings before such diversions of water, or to make and maintain a free passage therefrom to the main stream, in what manner the same shall be done, and by whom, and at whose cost, in whole or part; and after the expiration of a period of six months from the commencement of this Act, any person or persons failing to put a grating or gratings, or to make a free passage in cases where they are required to do so by this section, shall incur a penalty not exceeding fifty rupees for every day after the expiration of such period of six months, during which he fails to comply with the provisions of this section; and any such person failing so to maintain the same shall incur a penalty not exceeding ten rupees for every day during which such failure continues: provided always that no such grating shall be so placed as to interfere with the passage of boats on any navigable canal.

15. *Penalty on netting near dams.*—No person shall catch or attempt to catch, except by rod and line, any fish within one hundred yards of any dam; and if any person acts in contravention of this provision, he shall incur a penalty not exceeding twenty rupees for each offence, shall forfeit all fish caught in contravention of this section, and all nets or other instruments used or placed for catching the same.

16. *Penalty on taking undersized fish.*—No person shall wilfully take, destroy, injure, buy, sell, or expose for sale, or have in his possession any fish declared, by notification of the Governor in Council in the *Fort St. George Gazette*, to be under-sized fish.

17. *Power to make bye-laws.*—For the better application of this Act, it shall be lawful for the Governor in Council to make from time to time, by notification in the *Fort St. George Gazette*, any bye-law not repugnant to the tenor of this Act.

18. *Power to impose taxes.*—From the date of the commencement of this Act, it shall be lawful to collect the following dues from all persons fishing in waters which are the property of Government:—For every drag or wall net (&c., &c., as in paragraph 139 of the report) not more than nine rupees per annum (and so on as in paragraph 139 of the report), the rates only being trebled.

19. *Recovery of arrears.*—All taxes imposed under this Act shall be recoverable, whether by the Government or by renters under Government, or by such sub-renters as may be thereto authorized by the Collector in a notification in the District Gazette, in the same manner as arrears of land revenue.

20. *Penalty for litigiousness and imposition.*—Every person resisting the recovery of a lawful demand of tax (or interest thereon), or vexatiously and litigiously applying to a Magistrate to stay the recovery thereof, and every person wilfully making an unlawful demand, shall incur a penalty of fifty rupees.

398. In the *Bellary Collectorate,* fifteen *tehsildars* (*see* paragraph 173) compute the fishermen at 7,880, but they also have other occupations: in one tehsil fish are stated to be sold in abundance, but in all the others the supply is insufficient and more could be disposed of, the fish-eating class being set down at 66 per cent. of the people. The amount in the waters is universally considered to have decreased, due to the deficiency of rain, for the last ten or fifteen years. During the monsoon months, small fish are taken in the jungle streams and *nallas* by placing thread and basket nets concavely against the running water. The following are the minimum size of the mesh of nets which are stated to be employed:—One, "as big as a broomstick;" one, "as broad as the ring-finger;" three, as wide "as a 2-anna piece;" one, "as big as half the ring-finger;" one, the "size of a dholl or pigeon pea;" two, "as big as lamp-oil seeds;" two, as small as the circumference of a bodkin; two at $\frac{1}{8}$th of an inch; one at $\frac{1}{8}$th of an inch; and one at less than $\frac{1}{10}$th of an inch between the knots. Fish are said to be trapped in the irrigated fields by three of the reporters. Amongst the various modes of fishing in the Collectorate are the following:—*Idapola,* a drag-net used by two men in tanks; *isara-vala,* a casting-net; *galam,* baited hook: in *nallas* and channels small banks of earth and sand are thrown across running water, leaving a gap, wherein a net is fixed: poison is said to be employed in Alur. Basket nets—fixed nets placed over-night across streams and removed of a morning, and in the irrigation streams nets are likewise fixed.

Bellary Collectorate: opinion of the native officials.

399. In the *Trichinopoly Collectorate,* five *tehsildars* reply (*see* paragraph 175) as before, except that the population numbers about 1,149,801 persons, out of whom 407,068, or upwards of one-third, eat fish. All the *native officials* now report that the amount in waters has decreased of late years (previously one stated they had increased): the use of small meshed nets is universally reported; the minimum size of the mesh is given thus:—One, the "size of the little finger;" one, the "size of a quill;" one, about the "size of a tamarind stone;" one, $\frac{1}{4}$th and one, $\frac{1}{8}$th of an inch. In one talooka only, are fish said to be trapped.

Trichinopoly Collectorate: replies of native officials.

400. In the *Kistna Collectorate,* the *Deputy Collector* observes, as regards prohibiting the sale of fry in the bazar, that any attempt "would be useless. The best way prohibition can, I think, be effected would be by preventing them from being caught in the first instance by regulating the meshes of the nets employed, and by renting out the fisheries with the requisite prohibitory conditions on the subject."

Kistna Collectorate: replies of the native officials.

The *Tehsildars* report as in paragraph 171. The one of *Bezwada* gives the fish-eating population at 70 per cent. of the whole: the minimum size of the mesh of the nets which he previously observed would "admit one finger," he now states "is just large enough to contain a cholum seed." The *Tehsildar of Palnad* now alters his opinion respecting the amount of fish in the waters, which, instead of being "stationary," he now asserts have "decreased." The *Tehsildar of Vinukonda* gives the minimum size of the mesh of nets as equal "to the size of the end of the little finger." The *Tehsildar of Vissanapet* observes—the fishermen have other occupations; the markets are not supplied; more fish could be sold; about 80 per cent. of the people eat fish, whilst the amount in the waters has decreased: half an inch is the minimum sized mesh used: fish traps, snares, and dams are employed; nets are likewise fixed across channels for fishing purposes. The *Tehsildar of Bapatla* states that the markets are supplied; about 80 per cent. of the people eat fish, the amount of which in the waters has decreased; that small ones are captured during the rains, whilst the minimum size of the mesh employed is "just large enough to hold a Bengal gram seed." Waters are dammed, and implements fixed in the current going through a gap where they are taken. In *Bunder*, the fish-eating community is given at 70 per cent.; the amount of fish in the waters has decreased; small ones are captured during the rains; the minimum size of the mesh of the nets is given as "just large enough to hold a Bengal gram seed" (previously he gave it at quarter of an inch). In *Sattenapally*, about 75 per cent. of the people are stated to eat fish, which are "decreasing every year, because the fish in the Kistna River that pass over the weir cannot return:" the smallest mesh used "is of the circumference of a grain of Bengal gram." . The *Tehsildar of Gudewada* considers the amount of fish in the waters to be stationary; 80 per cent. of the people eat fish; numbers of small ones are taken during the rains: the minimum size of the mesh of nets equals that of a 2-anna piece.

401. In the *South Canara Collectorate*, the following are the returns from the native officials:—The *Tehsildar of Udipi* reports the number of fishermen at 1,110; they do not live solely by fishing; they are mostly of the Moger caste; but in one place people of the Karvi caste also follow the same calling. The local markets are supplied; 68 per cent. of the people eat fish; quantities of small ones were formerly destroyed by poison. This is now stopped; "people, therefore, say that the number of fish in such rivers and streams has greatly increased of late and is still increasing," but such fish are taken in freshwater streams and paddy-fields; also by fixed traps and weirs: the minimum size of the meshes of nets employed is $\frac{1}{8}$th of an inch. The *Tehsildar of Uppinangadi* observes that the fisherman have other occupations; everyone catches what he requires, and about 40 per cent. are computed to eat it; the amount in the waters is said to be increased; numerous small fish are trapped in water-courses; the minimum size of the mesh of the nets is $\frac{1}{4}$th of an inch; fish are extensively trapped in paddy-fields. The *Tehsildar of Mangalur's* answers, as applicable to the sea or freshwater fisheries, cannot be accurately sub-divided. The *Tehsildar of*

South Canara Collectorate: replies of Tehsildars.

Cundapur considers that out of 2,000 fishermen 500 are solely thus engaged; they consist of Karu, Moger, Dalji, Karvi, Gabith or Upparcar, and Boyee. About 85 per cent. of the people eat fish; the minimum size of the mesh of nets "is that of a green gram, say $\frac{1}{8}$th of an inch from knot to knot." Small fish are trapped in paddy-fields. The *Tehsildar of Cassergode's* replies refer mostly to the sea fisheries.

BRITISH BURMAH.

(Supplementary Report.) (1)

402. The *Officiating Assistant Secretary to the Chief Commissioner* (October 12th, 1872) observes "that the more the Chief Commissioner enquires into the matter, the more satisfied he is that any attempt to prohibit the capture of small fish would be as impolitic as it is unnecessary"—[an opinion opposed to what he gave April 4th, 1872 (see p. cci) and July 19th, 1872.)]

<small>Final opinion of the Chief Commissioner of British Burma.</small>

403. The *Commissioner of Pegu* (September 25th, 1872) forwards extracts from the opinions of those serving under him. The *Deputy Commissioner of Rangoon* replies that "there is no doubt that in some parts of the district large numbers of breeding-fish are destroyed. This is done at the commencement of the rains, when they go up small streams, and where the water is clear and shallow, for the purpose of spawning: they are at this time easily caught and destroyed, so much so, that the instruments which many persons use are common sticks: very many young fish, too, are no doubt caught where they can be, but this is done chiefly in the small streams which are not rented out, and in the small fisheries. It is the practice in this district in large fisheries to set apart a portion of the fishery for the young fish which may be caught or which pass through the screens, and some of the large fish which are caught are also put into this for purposes of breeding." " I do not think there would be any great difficulty in regulating the size of the mesh. If once the order were given, people would be afraid to use nets with meshes smaller than the regulated size, as the fact could be so easily proved. I am not prepared to say what size of mesh would be advisable, nor am I much in favor of regulating the size. I think that if such a regulation were made, a large number of persons who catch a few fish for their own consumption, and do no harm, would be debarred from doing so." [It is most remarkable that poaching the fry of fish should be held to do no harm if people do not pay for the right, whilst this paragraph ends as follows, showing the loss that such acts must entail on fisheries :]— " I think that those who work them are quite aware of the advantages to be gained by not destroying the small fish, and would protect them *where the fisheries are leased for a term of years.*" " As far as this district is concerned, I would certainly prohibit the capture of breeding-fish, *Nga-vit*, as they are called : their haunts are well known, and *the right to catch these only is rented out in some parts separate from the fishery itself,* which is worked at a different season." [How the fishermen must be astonished at such short-sighted policy. This is the period probably adverted to

<small>Pegu Commissionership: opinions of European Officials.</small>

---

(1) Only received October 23rd, 1872. Replies to questions circulated in 1869 not yet come to hand.

by the Burmese Government when fishing is stopped.] Besides the fishermen, "there are many who, in the parts of the district where the fisheries are worked in the dry season, cultivate lands during the rains." The *Deputy Commissioner of Bassein* reports, that "except the hilsa breeding-fish are not destroyed; [this is erroneous, as I have personally witnessed it to a great extent] but young fish are captured to a considerable extent by traps in the paddy-fields, and in low-lying grounds after the floods have subsided." The minimum sized mesh used is ⅔rds of an inch, and the chief difficulty in regulating such is the small varieties of fish which would thus escape, whilst a fine sized mesh is more expensive than a large sized one. No objections exist to prohibiting the sale of fry in the bazars. "It is very easy to say that it is objectionable to have the young of fish destroyed, a matter which is universally admitted, nor do the fishermen who have a permanent interest destroy the young fish, for they are probably far better acquainted with the habits, breeding season, and of the varieties of fish they catch than more scientific observers, and are not so blind to their own interest as to commit such suicidal acts." [As regards the foregoing, "*scientific observers*" may not be more competent to give opinions than "*Burmese fishermen*," but surely they may be permitted to report upon what they see, and how they think. Destroying fry is denounced by this official to be a suicidal act in *leased fisheries*, but he would permit such unchecked in paddy-fields and in his district by cultivators. Scientific enquirers may have their doubts as to the practical wisdom of such a distinction, and not be prepared to believe that destruction of fry wholesale in paddy-fields does no injury, whilst killing the same in leased fisheries is a suicidal act! In fact, they may perceive a wasteful destruction, not far removed from folly, and which perhaps has escaped the notice of "non-scientific local observers".] "The young fish are, however, destroyed by cultivators in their own paddy-fields, but it is questionable whether the prohibition of this, with the exactions and prosecutions for the breach of the prohibitions, would not entail greater evils than allowing it." The *Deputy Collector of Myanoung* observes that "breeding-fish and very young ones are captured in considerable numbers by means of weirs and traps, the size of the mesh or intervals between the bamboos constituting the trap being so small as to preclude the exit of any fishes however minute:" "baby fish are destroyed in numbers along the banks of the various streams, where they take refuge from the current." In branches of main streams, which are filled only in the floods, all fishes are totally destroyed on the waters falling; but the proportion must be but small to those that escape. [Tradition, always to be received with great caution, and the opinion of the oldest inhabitant, which is generally more or less liable to errors of recollection, as with such "all times are good when old," are adduced to prove the fact that the fisheries have not diminished in productiveness] whilst "the Burmese themselves, on being asked whether they considered the system hitherto in force in Burma had the effect of diminishing to a serious extent the fish food of the province, seemed quite surprised that such a question should be asked." [Doubtless they would have been still more astonished had they been asked whether the present slaughter of young fish in all unleased fisheries and irrigated land was a beneficial or suicidal act. It is, however, stated they were asked if it had diminished to a serious extent the fish food; then by the interrogatory a diminution seems almost conceded, whilst an increase of population is admitted.] But it is continued—"that fish are now as plentiful as ever they were known to be." The smallest interval between the stakes of a weir "was just sufficient to let the water flow through, and of course precluded the exit of fish." If a net, it was of "sufficient size to admit the nail of the little finger of a man's hand." If minute meshed nets were prevented, any regulation " would possibly deprive the poor man, who occasionally gets a few fish for home consumption, of his dinner." So he "recommends that the people be left to use their own nets in their own fashion." If any rules are enforced respecting fry, "it should be imposed on the catchers of fish, and not on the bazar sellers, chiefly women, who would be unable to comprehend or carry out such a rule." The *Deputy Collector of Prome*, whose opinions are so mixed up with the replies of the Myo-okes that some given amongst the latter have been referred to this place instead, observes that especially about Padoung breeding-fish and fry are destroyed. Young fish are also caught in Shway-Lay, but there are very few fisheries there; "Fish are taken indiscriminately, and numerous breeding and young fish must be destroyed. They are taken all the year round in the rivers, and during the rains in the inland or pond fisheries." Is averse to legislation on the minimum size of the mesh of the net which is employed, and there would be difficulties in prohibiting the sale of the fry of fish. The bazar is not fully supplied; more fish could be sold at Padoung; the price is Rs. 45 a viss for large, and Rs. 25 a viss for small fish: at Shwé-doung 1 s. 35 per 100 viss for the former, and Rs. 15 for the latter: during the cold season it is cheaper, but the relative proportions continue. He observes that fish are said to have increased, and "I think that I can confidently assert that, notwithstanding the wanton destruction of young fish, of which Dr. Day saw reason to complain, but which, with all respect, I venture to assert, does not take place, &c." [Really, this is a very remarkable statement: an official, who, I believe, was not in the place, most distinctly denies the statements I made of the destruction of young fish occurring in my presence at Prome when there in 1869, the sorts of which I pointed out, and a few of the very specimens are now in my possession or in the Imperial Museum at Calcutta. He asserts this, although I showed the captures on the spot to Colonel Stoddart and more than one official who were then there, whilst the same destructive proceeding his own answers prove even now to be going on in the paddy-fields and banks of the streams in or near that place. And the next answer is from a contiguous official, who makes, in other words, exactly the same statement as I did, and the accuracy of which is strictly correct.] "Very small fish are taken during the rains in the rice-fields by means of traps called *tsoung*, made of bamboo slips, plaited and tied together in the shape of a basket, the spaces being as small as the spaces between the bamboos of a chick almost. This is carried by the hand, and is suddenly put into the water with the mouth downwards, and pressed down, and the fish caught inside its walls is then collected. Another trap employed for taking small fish on the banks of the streams and in the paddy-fields is called *yek-thai*, which is made of plaited bamboos like a mat, and is shaped somewhat like a shovel." He goes on to describe a lave-net, and remarks upon the *leng-bai*, one of the very nets I complained of, and which in his own words "consists of a very fine meshed net, with two bamboos fastened along each end. It is worked by two men, who take each one end of the bamboo; in fact, it is first taken out at right angles from the bank; the man holding the outer end makes a curve until his bamboo touches the bank * * and the small fish swept up and confined between the bank and the net are caught." He also describes the Chinese dip-net, which he states is a fine net, capturing "any small fish that have been swimming over." The *Deputy Collector of Thyetmyo*, in addition to his former report, observes,—" Very young fish, I fear, are destroyed in great numbers during the rainy season; at this period of the year, they leave the river and ascend any little stream or backwater they can find, and here they fall an easy prey to men, women and children, who pursue them with all sorts of contrivances, which, though generally very simple, are very killing. Two women, for instance, holding a sheet between them, will, in half an hour or so, collect a few pounds of small fry." Were the size of the mesh regulated, one inch is proposed as the minimum.

404. The replies of the *Myo-okes* or *native officials* are thus given:—

Pegu Commissionership. Replies of native officials.

The *Myo-okes of Rangoon* state " tl at as a rule fish, sufficient for one's daily requirements, can always be obtained in the market, but there is a difficulty at times in purchasing large quantities, especially at those seasons of the year in which the fisheries are not being worked." "Opinions differ very much as to whether fish have increased or decreased of late years. The last rainy season was an unusually favourable one, and fish were more plentiful than they had been for years. But I think the general opinion is that fish are not so plentiful as they were some years ago before we took the country." As regards the modes of fishing—one is by putting up bunds and leaving one opening, through which the fish pass and jump into a kind of tray placed to receive them; or by erecting a large thick screen, and having another immoveable one, which is dragged towards the stationary one until the fish are enclosed in such a small space as to be easily caught by bunding off different portions and draining away the water; also by putting up large screens to prevent the fish escaping, and catching them with nets. The *Myo-okes of Prome* reply that by far the larger number of fishermen follow other occupations as well. More fish would be sold in the bazar were it provided: the amount in the waters is said to be increasing. The *Extra Assistant Commissioner of Pantanaw* replies—the number of fishermen as given by the Myo-okes is 791, and they do not pursue any other occupation; they are Taleins and Karens. The local markets are fully supplied. Large fish sell at Rs. 15 per 100 viss, and small at Rs. 7. Fish have slightly increased of late years, considering the rate at which fish was sold last year (*see* answer from Rangoon, that it was an unusually favourable one), I may safely say that the quantity is dependant more on the rise of the waters: if the catching of *Nga-Tit* or fish with spawn is prevented, it will no doubt lead to the increase of fish. The minimum interspace in weirs or between the knots of meshes of nets is $\frac{1}{12}$th of an inch. Fish are trapped in the irrigated fields for home consumption by the cultivators. The modes of fishing enumerated are the same as previously recorded. The *Extra Assistant Commissioner of Myoung Mya* reports that the fishermen generally carry on petty trades during the rains. The amount of fish in the waters remains stationary; some are trapped and otherwise captured in irrigated fields. The *Extra Assistant Commissioner of Theegwen* observes that fish are sold at the fisheries, as there is no proper market: those " obtained in my township sometimes equals former years and sometimes less, but never more." The *Extra Assistant Commissioner of Tsabai Yoon* reports that the fishermen also engage in trade. "The fish in the bazar is neither scarce nor plentiful. I think there is a slight increase in the quantity of fish this year than the previous five or six years." " In using the *gyan,* the fishes are put into a place called *kha-yai-bouk*, whence they are removed to another place termed *win*, whence they are taken to the market." The *Extra Assistant Commissioner of Yay-gyee* observes that out of 768 fishermen in his district 500 exclusively follow this occupation, and 200 employ themselves thus for home consumption. As to the bazar supply of fish, it is " not plentiful every month; scarce in August and September." Small fish obtain half the price per viss that large ones do: the amount in the waters "is rather limited to what it was years ago." Fish are trapped in the irrigated fields. The *Extra Assistant Commissioner of Lay-myet-hna* replies that the bazars are well supplied during the dry weather, but not so in the rains. Of late years the amount in the waters has decreased: they are trapped in irrigated fields. The *Extra Assistant Commissioner of Shwé-loung* reports that "there is no bazar in my township. The fish are carried about and sold in quantities merely sufficient for the people. During the last year fish was carried about and sold sometimes in sufficient quantities, sometimes more, sometimes less." Small fish are taken during the rains, and traps are employed in the fields.

BENGAL.

(Supplementary Report, received November 5th, 1872.)

405. The *Agent to the Governor General, North-Eastern Frontier, and Commissioner of Assam* observes (October, 9th, 1872) that he is "not sufficiently well informed on the subject to have any temptation to be discursive about it," and has to "deplore the absence of the tastes which, either as sportsman or naturalist, would have led me to bestow some attention on the numerous varieties of fishes that are to be found in Assam." No doubt a very unnecessary destruction of freshwater fish goes on at present in Assam; but, on the whole, it may be doubted whether such is a wasteful one, in the sense of injuriously affecting the supply available for legitimate consumption. He observes that "I should be slow to believe that there were fewer fish anywhere in Assam now than there used to be, unless it were demonstrated to me that the actual take of fish anywhere over the same area of water with the same engines and the same skill was less than it used to be; and then, unless the same fact could be proved as to many localities in different parts of Assam, I would not allow the extension of an inference of diminished fish-supply to the whole province." Crocodiles (termed alligators) during the dry season are in extraordinary numbers; the natives assert they have increased, and, as a consequence, that fish have decreased, the Commissioner, considering just the contrary must be the true solution, continuing—" at all events, I have little doubt but that the number of fishes destroyed by the crocodiles on the Brahmaputra is beyond all proportion greater than what is destroyed by man, and it would seem, therefore, that the first duty of a system of fish conservancy for that river would be the killing of the crocodiles." Breeding-fish and their fry and those in all conditions are destroyed by the Assamese by every engine and contrivance that they can command. Owing to a sparse population and a large amount of water, it is surmised that the destruction caused by village populations must be but a small proportion to the whole, consequently that there is not any emergent necessity for attending to the conservancy of its fish, but poisoning the waters is objected to. " Dr. Day will, perhaps, pardon me for suggesting to his objections that the *onus probandi* is with him, and not with those who differ from him, for his is the affirmative proposition, *viz.*, that the supply of fish has diminished, and it is for him to prove it, by showing that the fishermen have improved in their means of capture, have changed their times of fishing, and that the fish-eating population has increased, or in any other way." [Here I must dissent from the statements advanced. *First*, no *onus probandi* lies with me, because I have not wished to prove anything, but impartially carry out an investigation given me by the Government of India, whilst the most satisfactory conclusion would have been that, due to the care of the fisheries by officers in civil employ, they were not deteriorating. *Secondly,*

<small>Opinions of European Officials in North-East Bengal, and Assam.</small>

I would suggest that I could give no opinion respecting Assam until after the receipt of the present reports (as I have never been in the province), and have to observe from such the state of the fisheries until I am able personally to proceed there.] The *Deputy Commissioner of Durrung* (October 9th, 1872) observes—there is good reason to suppose that the supply of fish is falling off. Fish has become of late years much dearer, the fisheries are falling in value, and many of the Dome fishermen are, in consequence, I believe, taking to agricultural pursuits. With, perhaps, the exception of some Marwari merchants and some sepoys, fish would be consumed by all classes in this district could they get it, but, as it is, the supply by no means equals the demand. Fish is neither salted, dried, nor exported, but some is imported. Fish are neither put in tanks nor reared, but on the contrary all means are employed for their destruction and that of their spawn. Everything from a weir to a basket is used, and the meshes of nets are so small that no fry can escape. The fish never have rest, and must decrease in numbers. The only measure for conservation possible would be regulating the smallest size of the meshes permitted. The prevention of the destruction of the fry in the fields is a more serious consideration, as the people for years have procured daily meals from them, and to suddenly withdraw the privilege, even although it would be doubtless much to their eventual advantage, might cause discontent and trouble. "In case of the enactment of fishery laws (and, if the supply of fish is to be kept up, they are most necessary), I am of opinion that they should not come in force all at once, but be tried first in one district and then in another, and even then but partially, going further and further as the people become more accustomed to them. The nets and the regular fishermen might be first commenced with, and when the latter were quieted, and the cry (which would be certain to arise) that Government was going to put a tax on fish got over, other sections of the law might be put in force." The *Deputy Commissioner of Nowgong* replies :—"My own originally acquired knowledge on the subject of fishes is most limited, my study and attention during my Indian career having been devoted principally to ponies, goats, and cats; but from intelligent natives I have been able to glean the following information." There is no reason to suppose that the supply of fish is falling off; it is largely consumed by all classes, except Hindu Marwari traders or kyahs, who entirely eschew fish. The upper classes of Hindus do not preserve, dry, or salt fish at all ; but hill tribes, as the Mikirs, Lalungs, and Cacharies, dry it; also low-caste Hindus, as Domes and Charals, as well as Mahomedans. Dried fish is said to be largely exported to Panimur on the borders of the Naga hills district, where a ready sale is found for it. Fish are neither privately bred nor put into tanks in the district. "I do not think that any measures for conservation of fish seem to be necessary or called for." The *Deputy Commissioner of Seebsagur* observes,—" the supply of fish is not, in my opinion, falling off; not only is every stream well stocked with fish, but at this season of the year, the drains alongside of roads, paddy-fields and ponds all contain an ample supply of fish, and are regularly fished by the people. The Assamese of all classes eat fish, and the consumption is, therefore, very great, and the wholesale destruction which is always going on of the small fry would lead one to suppose the supply would fail, but the River Brahmaputra appears to be sufficient to keep up an ample supply for the numerous streams which communicate with it. Although the people are such large consumers of fish, they do not dry or preserve it, nor is there any trade carried on in fish with distant places. The Nagas, when they come down in the cold weather, purchase or barter cotton for fish, which they dry before taking back to their hills. Nothing whatever is done in the way of breeding fish or stocking tanks, and the only thing, in the way of conservation that is necessary, is to prevent as much as possible the wholesale destruction of fish in small streams, which have run up to spawn. What with dams, traps, baskets and nets, which the villagers use, very few fish escape to the larger streams. But, even with this wholesale destruction, the supply of fish appears abundant, and if this destruction were only partially checked, there would be no fear of the supply running short." The *Assistant Commissioner, Golaghat*, reports:—"I cannot say that I see at present any signs of the fish-supply falling off; but looking at the reckless way in which the young fry are destroyed, it is but reasonable to suppose that, could this habit be checked, the supply would become more plentiful. Many of the river fish, some of which attain a large size, come annually up the smaller streams and deposit their spawn, and the young ones of these are during the rains dispersed over the surface of the country in rice-fields, swamps, drains and ditches. These endeavour subsequently to make their way to the large rivers, but the dangers that beset them on the road are more numerous than those which Bunyan's Pilgrim had to encounter. In the shallow waters in the rice-fields, women and children may be seen in crowds fishing with baskets called *jakai*, through the interstices of which a tadpole could not pass. Those that escape this danger, and, following the flow of the water, arrive at one of the innumerable little bunds separating the various paddy-fields, find their further progress barred by funnel-shaped bamboo traps called *khoka, chapa*, or *ghunee*, through which the water is made to pass, but whose outlets are so small that only the most minute fish can get through. Escaping to the smaller water-courses, their dangers seem to increase. The Assamese divide the channel into sections by erecting bunds, and from one of these they proceed to bale out all the water, capturing every fish, large and small: they then bund off another portion and do likewise. The fish that finally arrive at the smaller rivers find their exit barred by weirs, which will let nothing pass; and not content with this, the Assamese will sometimes resort to poison, employing for this purpose the fruit of a tree called 'Konibehee.' Nearly the entire population consume fish; the only method of preserving it being drying it, and this is only done by Mahomedans and the hill tribes." "Although fish may be occasionally put into tanks, it can hardly be said that they are reared, for within a few months the water in the tank is sure to be carefully baled out and all its inmates destroyed, the net result being the capture of (say) a thousand fish, weighing in the aggregate a couple of pounds." The *Assistant Commissioner of Jorehat* observes that "the numerous streams which run through the country are well stocked with fish, as are the numerous *bheels* and swamps. In the rainy season fish are to be found in every puddle and paddy-field. * * The supply of fish is at present amply sufficient, and, so far as I can ascertain, it is not falling off appreciably. The Brahmaputra, which is never properly fished, is a preserve from which a supply is constantly forthcoming to stock the other waters which communicate with it. Fish is used as an article of diet by all classes of the Assamese, and the consumption is therefore great. The only professional fishermen are Domes, who use boats and nets of large size on the Brahmaputra and the larger streams and *bheels*, and who regularly sell what they catch. Villagers, however, of all classes fish for themselves with baskets, hand-nets and the hook, and also set traps in the streams. In the rainy season numbers of people are continually to be seen at work catching fish in some way or other for their own consumption." They do not preserve it in any way, but use it fresh, or very often half putrid. Fish are not privately bred, nor is any attempt made to stock waters artificially. "The only thing in the way of conservation that I see necessary is to prevent, as far as possible, the wholesale destruction of fish that have run up small streams to spawn, and of their fry. The villagers, if left to themselves, are very fond of damming streams at the end of the rains, when fish, large and small, are running down; this they do in such a way that scarcely anything can escape the traps set in the dam. As long as a fair number of young fish are spared, the supply is not likely to fall off, especially of the better kinds of fish, which, so to speak, have their head-quarters in the Brahmaputra." The *Deputy Commissioner of the Khasi Hills* states that in most of the rivers which drain the high lands, small-scaled and scaleless fishes are found, but not plentifully. Again, in the rivers near the plains, at the lower levels, below the water-falls, the fish are in abundance; they can be seen swimming about in the clear deep pools, and at the foot of the hills. During the dry season, when the rivers are low, a very large quantity of fish, some of them weighing as much as five or six seers, are caught by throwing dams and weirs across the shallows. There are very few tanks in the hills, and in such as exist the fish are very scarce." Sundried fish is a staple for food with the hill people. Fish have not diminished.

406. The *Officiating Collector of Tipperah* (October 18th, 1872)

Opinion of the Collector of Tipperah.

observes that "breeding-fish are undoubtedly destroyed to some extent, as are very young fish, but with respect to these a very sensible practice prevails. Every one who has even a very small tank will put young fish into it for the purpose of creating a fishery. It is said that the greater portion of young fish caught, is disposed of this way." [The native officials of this Collectorate report "very small fish are sold by weight," and again that the minimum size of the mesh of nets is $\frac{1}{12}$th of an inch, and very small fry are trapped.] "I understand that to the north of the district, where fish is far more plentiful than here or in the south, the destruction of breeding-fish is not considered very injurious." They are only caught in rivers by means of nets and a bamboo snare called *parou*, which is baited with shells and insects; the chief months are between May and August. Young fish are also caught in rivers, by means of small-meshed nets, from August to October inclusive. The minimum size of the meshes of nets used is from $\frac{1}{10}$th to $\frac{1}{12}$th of an inch square, and it would be impossible to regulate such, being opposed to public prejudice, and due to the irritation it would cause, although it is our duty to keep up the fish-supply if it can be done. As to prohibiting the sale of the fry of fish in the bazars, such could only be carried out at head-quarters, and it would " interfere with the sensible practice of storing tanks." [I would here suggest that the fry of fish sold dead in the bazars would hardly be adapted for this purpose, whilst live fry for such a use need not be subjected to regulations.] " I am told that natives, when recovering from sickness, eat the young fry as being more delicate in flavour." [This is curious conjoined with the statements made elsewhere in India. In the Panjáb, in the Multan Division, it is a popular belief that fish used as food during the rains occasion sickness (p. xxi) : in the Central Provinces (p. cxxi) that fish eaten at such seasons are the reputed originators of disease.] " I think that the supply is falling off, but very little, if at all, though in the south of the district there is much more difficulty in procuring fish than in the north." Fish are consumed by all classes, except widows of respectable Hindus, and by a man here and there, who objects to eat animal food on principle. The upper and middle classes eat fresh fish, the poorer dried fish; some is dried in the north, but salted in the south of the division. "During the cold season live fish are exported to Calcutta, though this trade is said to have fallen off owing to the opening of the Eastern Bengal Railway. Dried and salted fish are exported to Chittagong in considerable numbers." Young fish that have been reared in tanks are eaten on great occasions in the family, as marriage feasts, *saradhs*, &c. " I do not think that conservation is absolutely necessary here : it would be very difficult to enforce, and would cause a very great deal of discontent, while it seems hardly sufficiently justified by necessity. That is to say, I would not interfere with net or trap fishing, but I think I would prohibit the use of fixed engines, such as bamboo screens and fences in the bed of any river, *khal*, or water channel. Such a mode of catching fish might fairly be put down, while the obstructions are a serious nuisance to passing boats."

407. The *Officiating Commissioner of Dacca* (October 4th, 1872) replies:—" East Bengal, of which this division forms the chief part, is noted for large supplies of fish. In Dacca, Sylhet, and Cachar, the supply is supposed to be falling off, but not to such an extent as to interfere with the ordinary consumption of the people. The causes of this diminution are alleged to be exsiccation of *bheels*, tanks, and other water-courses, reckless destruction of the fry of fish, passing and re-passing of steamers, which are said to drive the river fish to distant quarters, &c. In Backergunge, Mymensing, and Furreedpore, no diminution is reported or supposed to exist." Fifteen-sixteenths of the population may be set down as fish consumers. Fish is salted or dried for home consumption or export, and largely exported to Calcutta and elsewhere by rail or boats. "Everybody in this district, after digging a tank, puts in small fish and fry of various species to be reared, and in every district the number of such tanks is innumerable. Fish is, besides, to be found in abundance in the several rivers, canals, *bheels* and other water-courses with which every district abounds. Under

Opinion of European Officials of Dacca, and Dr. Bose.

these circumstances it does not seem necessary that any measures need be taken for the conservation of fish in this division. On this subject, I beg to submit a very exhaustive and carefully drawn-up report from Dr. Bose, Civil Surgeon of Furreedpore." [The report alluded to doubtless is very creditable, but hardly in accordance with the zoological knowledge of the present half century. Fortunately, however, the native names of most of the fishes are given, by which a few may be recognised; a few more by Hamilton Buchanan's designations, but from whence species of the *Cod* family, *Gadidæ*, could have been procured, it is difficult to understand, as the little sea and estuary *Bregmaceros* is its only representative in India. Others of the Latin terms perhaps have been derived from a dictionary, but certainly not from any zoological work, whilst the last two, excluding the eels, are a *Zeus,* quite an unknown genus in Hindustan, and " a very common fish of the fresh-water, which seldom reaches a foot," *Laceria scincus* is stated to be its scientific name, terms, however, each of which is that of a genus amongst lizards, forms the bases of family designations of reptiles, but becomes unknown amongst fishes!] *Dr. Bose, Civil Surgeon of Furreedpore,* after his list of fish, continues—" the supply is not diminishing here. I can speak from a personal local experience of upwards of fifteen years, and certainly during this time I have never noticed such falling off. On the other hand, the markets always appeared fully as well supplied and sometimes as glutted as ever." All classes consume fish, and even many voishnabs and widows, who usually abstain from it elsewhere. Hilsa are said to be largely salted for Calcutta and other markets; no other fish are preserved, but oil is sometimes taken from this fish as well. Tanks are few, but are generally kept well stocked with fish. In this district, which is annually inundated during the rains, " and where, by the latter means, nature, as it were, by a preconcerted arrangement, undertakes to carry on the breeding of fish on a large scale herself, any artificial culture by the hand of man would appear to me to be almost unnecessary or superfluous," &c. In short, he considers that the inundations occur during the spawning time of fishes, whilst these watery districts are the nurseries for the fry, and admirably adapted for supplying them with food. " Inundations, therefore, far from being a source of great evil, ought to be looked upon as the most beneficent provision in the economy of nature for the breeding and preservation of fish; and such being the case, where these obtain, any other protective measures, which cannot but be of a molecular or liliputian character compared to these gigantic natural operations to the same end, would seem to be hardly called for, or possibly needed." Ignoring how the breeding-fish and fry are destroyed, he considers such destruction as not to be compared with what would accrue were there no inundations or localities where proper pasture could be found by these baby fishes. Breeding-fish are only accidentally caught, and the fry to some extent as inundations recede; but as they are not wantonly so, it is useless to enumerate the machines. If fry were not permitted to be sold, " the effect would be simply to interfere with the food-supply of the people without in the slightest manner helping the cause of pisciculture." The answers given by the Collectors and others are tabulated. In *Dacca* breeding-fish and very young ones are destroyed to a great extent, indiscriminately, in all rivers, *jheels,* water-courses, &c.,

and at all seasons. The minimum mesh of nets is stated to be the size of a grain of gram, interference with which would be unpopular. [In the five districts this one answer is given in the lump, whilst the Commissioner observes " nor is it necessary:" whether this is the opinion of each of the reporters is left to conjecture.] Were the sale of the fry of fish prohibited, a very large amount of food would be taken from the people. The castes of fishermen are Jalooa, Koebarta, Teor, and Mallow. The local markets are generally fully supplied, and fish is eaten, by fifteen-sixteenths of the population: the amount in the waters has decreased by one-fourth from some unknown causes; very young ones are trapped during the rains in irrigated fields; snares are likewise employed. In *Furreedpore*, breeding-fish and young ones are said not to be destroyed to any great extent, but some are taken by the hand and various fish traps. The minimum size of the mesh of the nets equals a grain of gram, interference with which would be extremely unpopular (see remarks above), whilst prohibiting the sale of fry would interfere with the food-supply of the people. In *Backergunge*, breeding-fish and very young ones are not destroyed to any great extent; the minimum size of the mesh of the nets equals a grain of gram, interference with which would be extremely unpopular (see remarks above), whilst prohibiting the sale of fry is not necessary. In *Mymensing*, breeding-fish and very young ones are destroyed to a very great extent, which destruction continually goes on in all parts of the district. The minimum size of the mesh of the nets equals a grain of gram; interference with such would be extremely unpopular (see remarks above). Prohibiting the sale of the fry of fish in the bazars " would be a vexatious and altogether unnecessary interference. It would lead to great abuses and oppression, and the prohibition would be directed against an evil which is altogether imaginary, as there is not the least reason to suppose that the sale of the fry of fish has exercised, or can exercise, any injurious effect upon the fish-supply." In *Sylhet*, breeding-fish and young ones are destroyed to a great extent, and in all parts of the district continually. The minimum size of the mesh of the nets equals a grain of gram; interference with such would be extremely unpopular (see remarks above). No objections exist against prohibiting the sale of the fry of fish in the bazars.

408. The *Commissioner of Chota Nagpore* (October 4th, 1872) forwards replies. The *Deputy Commissioner of Hazareebaugh* (July 23rd, 1872) observes that " there are only three rivers in this district in which fish can be caught, *viz.*, the Barrakur, the Damoodah, and the Soobunrekha." During the rains these rivers are too much flooded to be fished, but as they subside, fish are left in the pools, and are then either netted or taken by angling. As a matter of course, the supply of fish is greater just after the break-up of the rains, and gradually falls off as the pools dry up during the hot weather, and their contents have been almost entirely, if not quite, emptied. The supply of fish is confined to the vicinity of these pools, and consequently is not a common article of diet amongst the people of the district. Fish are never dried or salted; neither are the tanks stocked with young, nor are any privately bred. Basket traps are used which will retain the smallest fry; some tanks near temples, which are perennial, are never

Opinions of European Officials in Chota Nagpore.

netted. "Without interfering with the rights of private property, I cannot suggest any measures, therefore, for the conservation of fish, although I am sure that, if a considerably larger supply could be obtained, it would be eagerly sought for as an article of consumption throughout the district." As the rains subside *nallas* and streams are bunded and emptied of water; thus many small fish are taken; this is generally carried out from February to April inclusive. There would be difficulties in carrying out any order regulating the minimum size of the mesh of nets, as the only people who use nets are the Mullahs, "a very poor tribe who could not pay a fine, if inflicted; while to confiscate their nets would only drive them to commit theft and robbery to keep body and soul together." Fry are not sold in the bazars; "it would be impossible to prevent the villagers catching and eating the fry themselves, if so inclined. The nature of the country is against forming any hope of improving the supply of fish, so as to make it an article of consumption in this district." The *Deputy Commissioner of Singbhoom* (August 6th, 1872) remarks that "all fish are caught and disposed of indiscriminately, without letting go either the breeders or the very young fish. Annually, when the rivers are at their lowest depth, and the pools are low, or in April and May, crowds of persons gather to catch all the fish in these pools, and all is fish that comes to the net with this district people. The tanks are about this time also very low, and are treated in the same way." The smallest mesh of the nets, "I fancy, would admit the little finger;" the difficulties against regulating it "would be those that, in civilized society, are considered and felt as interference with private actions of individuals." The fry of fish are not sold in the bazars. Fish are not captured during the first two months of the monsoon, but just before it: there are few fishermen, and they have other occupations; their castes are Keot or Mullah, Ghooneah, Ghasi, and Dome. The local markets are not fully supplied with fish; the supply is not equal to the demand. The price per seer of fish and mutton is the same: the entire district community eat fish: "reports state that at the annual captures, less quantity is now obtained than before. A large quantity of small fish are not taken during the rains; the minimum sized mesh of the nets would admit the little finger. Fish are trapped in the fields during the rains with *ghoogees*. The modes of fishing are: (1) trapping by *ghoogees, polois, ghoonees,* and *jimrees;* (2) netting by chargoriah, geerájál, *thelá-jál,* and *gentoi-jál,* (3) rod and line, *bungsee.*" In a second letter (August 7th, 1872), the same officer observes—" the supply of fish is not equal to the demand, but the supply at the present time is far greater than formerly. Fish, as a rule, is consumed whenever got, and by all classes of people. The quantity is never so much as to need preserving, but, as a matter of taste, it is consumed both salted and fresh. There is no fish trade to distant places from this district. In a very few instances fish are privately bred and reared in tanks. I do not consider that conservation of fish is of that importance as to call forth any measures, or to form a question of the day in Singbhoom."

The *Deputy Commissioner of Maunbhoom* (June 28th, 1872) replies that the nets in use are (1) *phandi ;* (2) *ganti* (large); (3) *ganti* (small); (4) *pash ;* (5) *donra ;* (6) *chap ;* (7) *chuna.* "Those numbered 3 and 7 have the meshes so small that nothing whatever can escape them, and, as fishing goes on all the year round, immense numbers of small fish are destroyed long before they can come to maturity." The fishing cates are Kewuts, Ghoonas, Matas, Bagtees, and Harees: the supply of fish is very limited, except in the immediate vicinity of large rivers and a few reservoirs, but it is not at all adequate to meet the wants of the people: in some parts of the district the use of fish is almost unknown, and there are no waters to propagate them. " In other parts, if fishing were prohibited during the breeding season, and the use of net with meshes below a certain size forbidden, there is no doubt the supply of fish would increase, and much good be done by adding to the quantity of this very valuable description of food, which would thus be made available to the people at large." " Fish is not largely consumed by the people of this district, simply from the fact of its not being obtainable in sufficient quantities, and none, either salted or dried, is ever imported, whilst exportation is, of course, quite out of the question. The stocking of tanks and reservoirs with young fish is common, and is rendered necessary by the majority of the tanks and reservoirs running dry, or so nearly dry, in the hot season, that all the fish are caught and consumed, when a fresh batch has to be introduced in order to ensure a further supply, but, beyond this, nothing is done for the purpose of conserving it."

409. The *Officiating Commissioner of the Chittagong Division* (October 5th, 1872) forwards a single report from the *Collector of Noakhally*, who remarks that " breeding-fish and very young ones are destroyed, but not to a great extent, in this district. The young ones are destroyed by the villagers in *khlas*, rivers, tanks, ditches, and paddy-fields during the rainy season." The smallest size mesh of the net used is one quarter of an inch; discontent would be caused by regulating such. Fry of fish are not sold in the bazar, but there would be difficulties preventing people catching it for their own use. A close season would cause great inconvenience, and perhaps sickness, whilst it would be almost impossible to enforce. There are 6,310 fishermen in the district, more than two-thirds of whom earn their livelihood entirely by fishing. Nearly all villagers fish for their own use; the Hindu fishing castes are Jâliah, Das, and Jhâlo: the Mahomedans, Myforash. The local markets are not fully supplied with fish; more might be sold; it is consumed to a large extent by about fifteen-sixteenths of the population, in fact by all classes, even by Hindu widows. Small fish are taken in large quantities during the rains; they are caught with nets, hooks, *hoohas*, open baskets, and *chāis*, cages. Fish are trapped during the rains in inundated fields. Spearing is one form of fishing which is employed. There is no reason to suppose that the supply of fish is falling off: it is neither salted nor dried, but some is imported from Sylhet and Chittagong; none is exported; tanks are stocked with fish. " In the dry season fish die largely, owing to the water becoming hot and very shallow: the only measure adopted by the people for the protection of fish is to put a shade over a part of the tank. It would be well if some measures were adopted to deepen the tanks to a certain

Opinions of European Officials of Chittagong.

depth, of at least five cubits of water, in the dry season." [See similar propositions in Dharwar, p. lii, and South Canara, p. xcii, where even a *precedent* will be found, although the originator was a native ruler.] The fishermen of Noakhally are said not to be very expert in their calling. The *Collector of Chittagong* observes—fish, both fresh and dried, is largely used by all classes of the population with the exception of a few Hindu religious mendicants (Boiragis). Fish is often dried; hilsa is salted; none is exported except sharks' fins to Rangoon. Dried fish is imported from Sylhet and Dacca. To the north fish are reared in tanks—not so to the south. No special measures of conservation are considered necessary.

FISH AS FOOD, OR THE REPUTED ORIGIN OF DISEASE.

410. The following notes on fish as food (exclusive of the remarks in the commencement of this report) or medicine, as a cause of sickness or the occasion of accidents, have been collected during the last few years (see *Indian Medical Gazette,* January and February 1871). In investigating the effects of a fish diet upon the population of a district, it becomes necessary first to take into consideration the condition of the people generally, or very erroneous conclusions may be arrived at. Thus, during the Burmese war of 1852-53, the Indian native army suffered severely from scabies and low forms of skin disease, due, it was commonly asserted, to their eating fish conjoined with their poor diet. The European troops had a scorbutic taint, a result, it was argued, of an insufficient supply of vegetables. On the Malabar or western coast of India, leprosy, intestinal worms, and severe skin affections are considered to be consequent upon a fish diet. An important primary consideration should be—what was the condition of the people? Was not impoverished blood, possibly arising from some other cause, the true origin of these various diseases? In olden times we read of leprosy, so common in Europe, being attributed to the consumption of salt pork or fish in an unwholesome state.

General observations on a fish diet.

411. It has been asserted that the Asiatic conquerors of India have all been consumers of a more nourishing food than rice, and that "it may be safely argued that, if the people had been fed upon the simple diet of the inhabitants of the plains, their conquests would never have occurred. The physical powers and moral courage, necessary to the achievements of feats of valour and conquest, have never yet been found in a people who, like the degenerate races in the lowlands, live on grain deficient in nitrogen, and eschew animal food." If this is admitted, how great must be the moral responsibility of legislators, who, living amongst a population such as exists throughout India, more than half of whom would consume fish could they procure it, have permitted the depopulation of the fresh-water fisheries, and allowed the destruction of so great a source for the supply of animal food. Now that it clearly appears millions would eat fish could they obtain it, surely the re-population and future protection of these fisheries will be considered an important subject for consideration as a means of supplying loss of physical powers and nervous energy.

Animal food a necessity. Millions in India, who would eat fish could they obtain it, now prevented by the depopulated state of the fisheries—a good cause for more care of them to be taken in future.

412. Amongst the different races of the Indian Empire, fish as food is held in various kinds of estimation. Commencing at Sind in the extreme west, where the population are chiefly Mahomedans, this diet is almost universally esteemed; even the siluroids are eaten, so long as they have large gill openings: in fact, it is the Shias amongst this race who, following the Koran, appear

The various estimations in which fish is held by the different races inhabiting the Indian Empire.

to reject the scaleless fishes. In the Panjáb, fish (except by Brahmins and a few others) is almost equally relished, as will be seen on turning to the returns from that Administration; but as we examine to the southwards, as Delhi and the upper part of the North-Western Provinces, the Brahmins, high-caste Hindus, and even the Mussulmen who reside amongst them in rural districts, are less addicted to its use, and mostly refuse it entirely, unless they happen to be living on the banks of a large fishing river, as the Jumna. Still in all these districts, unless from some peculiar local cause, 50 per cent. of the urban population may be fairly reckoned as not prohibited by their religion from eating fish. In Lower Bengal it is largely consumed, whilst in Madras, Mysore, Haidarabad and Bombay a very great proportion of the people would eat it could they obtain it; generally the Brahmins, Vysias, Nairs in Malabar, and Jains appear to reject it. In the Central Provinces, from 50 to 95 per cent. are reported as consumers of fish. In hilly districts, fish is almost uniformly eaten when it can be procured, whilst in the extreme east no Burman would consider his meal complete, were it deficient in the odoriferous *nga-pee*. The Andamanese may be said to principally exist on fresh fish, pork, tortoises or turtles, for vegetables are consumed to a very inconsiderable extent, so long as they can procure animal food.

413. Of the foregoing races, an important question is—are any peculiarities noticeable amongst those who eat fish, and those who reject it as food?

General effects of a fish diet on the natives of the East.

When one takes into consideration the wealth or the poverty of these various people, and the differences in climate, I do not think that amongst the Hindu races much distinction can be drawn. We may certainly find such, however, if we compare, for instance, the people of Malabar with the Panjábese or Burmese, but this mode of comparison is useless. The state of the intermediate people and climate must be looked at, and, when this is done, I cannot perceive much differences between the Nairs of Malabar who reject all fish and flesh and the people of Orissa and Lower Bengal who eat the finny tribes. A great and marked change may be observed in Malabar in those who have turned from Hinduism to Mahomedanism, but this generally occurs amongst the fishermen castes, who do not reject animal food. On the other hand, the soil slaves of Malabar are about the most degraded race, except the *Naidis*, wild in the jungles, whilst they all consume fish. The Black Jews, who are in Malabar merely the converted people of the country, or their pure or semi-Jewish descendants, do not appear to be superior to the surrounding population. Neither is any marked difference observable between the native Christian and Hindu, which might not fairly be attributed to greater wealth and a superior mode of living. The Burmese certainly have greater physical powers to the natives of India, than whom they consume more fish, but the diminutive Andamanese are very deficient in these qualities, although the finny tribes form the chief constituent of their diet.

414. It has been asserted that a fish diet has some effect on procreation, and that fish-eating tribes are unusually prolific, concerning which Dr. Pareira (*On Diet, p.* 282) remarks:—" There is, I think, sufficient evidence to prove that ichthy-

Has a fish diet any relationship to the procreative powers of the Asiatic races?

ophagous people are not more prolific than others. In Greenland and amongst the Esquimaux, says Forster, where the natives live chiefly on fish, seals, and oily animal substances, the women seldom bear children oftener than three or four times. Five or six births are reckoned a very extraordinary instance. The Passerais, whom we saw, had not above two or three children belonging to each family, though their common food consisted of mussels, fish and seal flesh. The New Zealanders absolutely feed on fish, and yet no more than three or four children are found in the most prolific families." Amongst the Andamanese, whose chief diet may be said to be fresh fish and pork, it is very rare to find so many as three children in one family; and as they do not indulge in such early marriages as the natives of India, that reason cannot be adduced to account for their paucity of offspring. In Burma, it is sometimes advanced that the chief reason why the Burmese are not more prolific is because they consume so much fish, and they cannot be considered, in comparison with other Asiatic nations, as given to very early marriages. The least prolific races I have personally seen appear to be the Nairs of Malabar, the Burmese, and the Andamanese; the first never touch fish, but their ladies are espoused to the whole of their own and the males of any superior caste. The Burmese wives are faithful to one husband so long as he lives in the neighbourhood, or is only temporarily absent. The Andamanese are reputed to be very particular in only having one, and not changing him so long as they are both alive. The Nairs and Burmese are well off and have good domiciles; the Andamanese live more like wild beasts in the jungles than human beings, are destitute of clothes and houses, and are alternately feasting and pinched with hunger as food is common or the reverse.

415. For the natives of the plains of Asia it appears very questionable whether fresh fish is not more suitable, as food, than the flesh of sheep, pigs and poultry. Anyhow, in certain situations, as the Malabar Coast, the Andaman Islands, and Burma, where sheep deteriorate so rapidly, healthy indigenous fresh fish must be more suitable, as diet for natives, than the exotic sheep. In Europe, mutton appears to be superior to fish; thus, during Lent, persons who change from meat to fish are asserted to complain of debility, which may be due to a sudden alteration in their diet. Jockeys, however, when "wasting" themselves, are said to take fish instead of meat. But fish-eating people in many parts of the world are models of strength, and a fish diet can hardly be asserted as conducing to the deterioration of the *physique* of races. Opinions, however, are divided as to the nutritious qualities of fish in northern climates. Leeuwenhoek (*Select Works*, i., p. 154) observes:—" At a town in my neighbourhood, where the people get their living by fishing, and feed principally on fish, especially when they are on the sea, the men are very robust and healthy even to a great age. * * It is also my opinion that a fish diet is more wholesome than flesh, particularly to those persons who do not use much exercise, because fish is more easily comminuted and digested in the stomach and bowels than flesh."

Marginal note: Fish diet probably more suitable to the inhabitants of the plains of Asia than that of mammals.

416. A great deal has been written and said about the natives of India preferring small fish to large ones; therefore the destruction of fry ought not to be put a stop to, or the poorer classes might suffer. There is no exception throughout the British possessions in India and Burma where small fresh-water fishes obtain so great a value as large ones, taking weight for weight—one maund of large fish realising from 30 to 50 and sometimes 100 per cent. above what a maund of small fish does. The latter have to be sold quickly, because, being usually immature, decomposition sets in rapidly.

Large fish of much more value, weight for weight, than small ones, which putrefy rapidly.

417. Fish as food is employed in many ways in Asia, which it is unnecessary to specify in detail. Fish roes are either salted or dried. Coarse isinglass is prepared from various marine forms, and exported to China from Bombay: towards the Arabian Sea mostly from the percoid forms: in Malabar chiefly from the siluroids: and at the mouths of the Ganges and down the Burmese coasts from both siluroids, polynemi and other genera. Salt and dried fish is largely consumed in the Madras and Bombay Presidencies; also in Sind; but far inland, where the Hindu element is strong, it does not find such a ready sale. Oils of two kinds are obtained—the "medicinal" from the livers of sharks and other chondropterygious or cartilaginous fishes: and the "simple" from either marine or fresh-water species.

Fish as food.

418. Fish employed as food may act injuriously on the system, occasioning poisonous symptoms, and this irrespective of their flesh being diseased or undergoing putrefactive changes. There may be gastro-intestinal irritation, or great nervous depression, with coldness of the body and extremities. Fish may occasion indigestible or poisonous symptoms if eaten, which may be due to their age: thus some, which are eatable when young, have been found to set up irritable or poisonous effects as they become large, as *Caranx fallax*, a horse mackerel, which it is illegal to sell in some places should it weigh above 2¼lbs. Sometimes these results are attributed to the breeding season; thus, on the Indus, in the Central Provinces, and elsewhere such causes have been adduced by local observers in the foregoing reports, and in Europe it has been observed that the eggs and milt act as great irritants. Occasionally some fish in Europe have been found to be unwholesome just before the breeding season, and they have been considered unfit for food. But this is not the case in all; thus the mackerel and other marine fishes are extensively eaten at this season, and in Asia the shad, *Clupea palasah*, and the mangoe fish, *Polynemus paradiseus*, are excellent up to the period they have deposited their eggs, after which they become thin, flabby and positively unwholesome. Thus the unwholesomeness of kelts, or female salmon, which have spawned, but not yet gone to the sea so as to have recovered and become fit for food, has been known from ancient times. Dr. Gerard Boate, Doctor of Medicine to the State in Ireland, observed (1645)—" of the leprosie, which in former times used to be very common, especially in the province of Munster, which was filled with hospitals expressly built for to receive and keep the leprous persons. This horrible and loathsome disease was caused through the fault and foul gluttony of the inhabitants, in the unwholesome devouring of foul salmons

Fish eaten may occasion poisonous symptoms more or less severe, and due to several causes.

when they are out of season, which is after they have cast their spawn, upon which they do not only grow very weak and flabbie, but so unwholesome as it would loathe any man to see them. Nevertheless, the Irish, a nation extremely barbarous in all parts of their life, did use to take them in that very season, and by that means that horrible disease came to be so common amongst them. But the English, having once gotten the command of the whole country into their hand, made very severe laws against the taking of salmons in that unwholesome season, and saw them carefully observed, whereby hindering these barbarians against their will to feed on that poisonous meat; they were the cause that that woeful sickness, which used so mightily to reign amongst them, hath in time been almost abolished." It seems doubtful, however, whether it is not in India more amongst fish which deposit their eggs at one period, as the hilsa, than amongst those who do so more gradually, as the barbels, that the spent condition is most seen in. Although I have heard of mahaseer in this condition, I have not personally witnessed them, and, as they do not deposit all their eggs in one batch, they rarely become very lean and flabby, unless ill from some other cause likewise. Fish may also be unwholesome, due to their having been kept until partial decomposition has set in, or to some substance the fish has swallowed, or to the food which it has eaten. Thus eels often feed upon very foul food, and their flesh has been known to occasion very dangerous symptoms; thus in France, near Orleans, cramps and diarrhœa attacked a whole family who had partaken of some which had been captured from a stagnant castle ditch in the vicinity. Irritation may likewise be occasioned by swallowing fish bones or scales, whilst some persons possess a peculiar idiosyncrasy rendering fish unsuited for their digestive powers. "There can be no form of animal food," observes St. Jules Cyr, " more objectionable than decomposed or putrid fish, and this is especially seen in a season when diarrhœa is prevalent." In India and Burma, where fish in this condition is rather freely consumed throughout the hot season, it does not appear to be proved that semi-putrid fish is more injurious than meat in the same condition, if so much so. During the monsoon months, when the atmostphere is moist, semi-salted fish absorb moisture, and, in Malabar at least, not unfrequently appears to occasion or assist in the production of dysentery and diarrhœa, whilst in Burma such results do not seem to be attributed to *nga-pee*. However, eating fish during the monsoon months often sets up symptoms of indigestion, and even more serious attacks to some persons, due either to partaking of spent fish, or else of the immature, which, having commenced to putrefy, set up derangement of digestive system.

419. It would fill up too much space to detail all the most wholesome species of Indian fresh-water or marine fishes, but a few general remarks may be made upon their general digestibility, premising that certain local peculiarities may exist, altering the otherwise excellent character of a fish. Amongst the *Acanthopterygian* or spiny-rayed families, all that are found in the fresh-waters appear to be adapted for food, without occasioning deleterious effects. Religious prejudices may militate against the employment of some species, but not

Acanthopterygian, or spiny-rayed fish of India as food. Those having accessory breathing organs, whether of this family or siluroids, most esteemed by convalescents.

q

sanitary reasons, unless the last may have been due to any substances swallowed by the fish. Thus at one time the gouramy, *Osphromenus olfax*, taken from a tank in the Mauritius, was found unfit for human food, when it was discovered that they had been consuming the filth from below a latrine which opened into it. Hamilton Buchanan observed of the estuary and marine fish, *Scatophagus argus*, that it is "easy of digestion and excellent flavour, but after death it becomes soft and strongly tasted." This fish, however, is as foul a feeder as the last, and is consequently generally rejected as food. The Indian mackerel, *Scomber kanagurta*, taints very rapidly after death, and not unfrequently sets up gastric irritation, whilst the mullets, *Mugilidæ*, are usually unwholesome, unless eaten when quite fresh. The fishes with accessory breathing organs or cavities are those as a rule most esteemed as nourishing by the natives, whether acanthopterygians or siluroids; thus convalescents in some parts mostly esteem the coie, or climbing perch, or the siluroid magur, *Clarias magur*; next perhaps the singi, *Saccobranchus fossilis*; whilst the spiny-rayed family of *ophiocephalus* likewise hold a high place. In short, it is these families so peculiar to the tropics which are found to be the most wholesome and invigorating. Munier, nearly a century since, informed Sonnerat that fishes of the marine genus *Scarus*, commonly known as "parrot fishes," owing to their brilliant colours and bill-like teeth, were not eaten in Bourbon and the Mauritius between December and April, owing to their unwholesomeness, due, it was supposed, to their consuming large quantities of coral polype. Commerson makes much the same remarks, and observes that it gnaws the coral. It has also been said that fishes which consume the medusæ, commonly termed "Portuguese men-of-war," the *Stephanonia*, appear to be rendered unfit for human food, probably consequent upon their acrid qualities. However, fish are found to be poisonous where these polypes abound; and in other localities where they are also numerous, as the Andaman Islands, the fish appear to be eaten with safety. Dr. Hill (Pro., Scien. Asso., Trinidad, 1868) observes the Formigas constitute a very warren or vivarium of all kinds of fishes, and the fishes there are poisonous. The sea is very shallow, covered with coral reefs, and these again by sea-cucumbers, star-fishes, sea-urchins and sponges.

420. Regarding the *Siluridæ* or scaleless fishes as food, rather diverse opinions are held. The Jews were directed in Leviticus, chap. xi, that "whatsoever hath no fins, nor scales in the waters, that shall be an abomination unto you." They were only permitted to eat "whatsoever hath fins and scales in the waters, in the seas and in the rivers," and this law is likewise generally, but not invariably, observed by the Mahomedans. It is well known that persons of neither of the foregoing religions are to eat the blood which is the life, so they cut the throats of all animals before death, in order to permit it to escape. In Sind, however, the Mahomedans have a tradition that the prophet did this for them in regard to fish, because they die so rapidly after they are removed from the water, and they point to the gill-opening in proof of this having been done, consequently they eat all siluroids which possess well developed gill-openings. In the last paragraph it was observed that the *Clarias* and *Saccobranchus* are much esteemed in India for convalescents, whilst the Burmese have likewise a great partiality for them in their

The siluridæ or scaleless fishes as foo d.

nga-pee. Some of the larger species of *Macrones* and *Arius* which are found in fresh waters are not esteemed, as they consume ordure whenever procurable: perhaps it may be considered questionable whether cholera may not be spread by this agency, if the fish are eaten before being thoroughly cleaned or cooked. This family of fishes, with the exceptions noted, does not appear to be very wholesome, being, as a rule, rather rich, or else hard and indigestible. Their flavour is likewise generally insipid, still the Aor, *Macrones aor*, in some localities is excellent, whilst the absence of bones renders the operation of eating it, not a service of danger, as in many Asiatic fresh-water fishes.

421. The carps, *Cyprinidæ*, which abound in the waters of the plains of India, are all more or less useful as food, although differing widely in their gastronomic value. But as the mountain regions are approached the value of some as food becomes impeached, at least when eaten by strangers, although generally to the residents, and perhaps many of the visitants, no deleterious effects are produced. Dr. McClelland observed of a mountain barbel, *Oreinus progastus*, that "this species is said by the natives of Assam to cause swimming in the head, and temporary loss of reason for several days, without any particular derangement of the stomach. It is the most herbivorous of the barbels," [a statement open to doubt] "and, like some of the gudgeons, tends rapidly to decay after death, and in the abdominal cavity a copious oily secretion is found," [in common with other Indian carps before the breeding season and after they have recovered from such,] "which is probably the cause of its bad effects. * * * Mr. Griffith was informed by the fishermen that, if eaten, it occasions all the symptoms of drunkenness, which coincides with what I have myself heard regarding its effects." (Trans-Asiatic Society, Bengal, xix, page 344.) The late Dr. Jerdon informed me that he had witnessed these symptoms amongst his own servants, produced from eating some species of mountain fishes. When in the Chumba State in the Himalayas, I found another mountain barbel, *Oreinus sinuatus*, very common, but the natives asserted that it never occasioned uncomfortable symptoms, although they were consumed by every class of the community. Some European residents, and others who were visitors, likewise eat them with impunity; however, one of my native servants who tried one declined a second attempt, as he was unwell for 24 hours subsequently. Low down the Ravi, and in some of the other Panjáb rivers, I have heard of deleterious effects being occasioned from partaking of these fishes. Certainly at Chumba the fish were netted and not captured by means of poisoning the water.

Carps in hilly districts may act up deleterious effects.

422. Amongst the *Clupeidæ*, or herring family, which abound in the Indian seas, some being visitants to the fresh-waters for breeding purposes, and a few entirely residing there; several marine forms have been reputed as poisonous, which in some instances appears to be due to the food which they have eaten. *Engraulis boelama*, a small anchovy, has been accused by Dussumier of occasioning death in a few hours, if dressed without its head and intestines having been first removed; they abound, however, at the Andamans, where they are largely eaten, and there is no record in that settlement of any individual having

Herring family: members of it occasionally or always poisonous.

suffered deleteriously from the effects of eating them. They are mostly consumed in a dry state; certainly neither their heads nor intestines are removed. Along the Malabar Coast of India and in Ceylon, eating sardines, either the *Clupea Neohowii* or *C. melanura*, has been thought to occasion poisonous symptoms, but both species abound in the Andamans and are eaten with impunity; still I have personally witnessed many cases of vomiting and purging resembling cholera, especially about the month of October, and which could only be traced to the fact that some unwholesome fish had been the cause. The *Clupea venenosa* was found to be poisonous at the Seychelles by Dussumier, but Colonel Playfair at Zanzibar considered that they "do not appear to possess any such property; on the contrary they form no inconsiderable part of the daily food of the lower orders." (*Alosa venenosa*, Fish, Zanzibar, p. 122.) Dr. Cantor observed, when remarking upon the *Clupea perforata*, that it is found in the Straits, where it is termed a sardine, and most common from June to August. Some specimens procured by Mr. Lewis " were accompanied by the following account of a phenomenon witnessed by that gentleman during his official residence at Bencoolen. In 1822, great numbers of what was supposed to be this identical species presented the appearance of having red eyes. Many natives, after having eaten these fishes, were suddenly attacked with violent vomiting, which, in cases where remedies were not immediately applied, was known within an hour to terminate fatally. At the same time, such of these fishes with the ordinary silver eyes were, as formerly, eaten with impunity." This phenomenon re-occurred the two succeeding years, and he considered it probable that the poisonous fishes were shoals of *C. venenosa*. Any of the foregoing would appear to be poisonous from some local or accidental cause, as the abundance of food which may suit them but renders their flesh poisonous; but in the West Indies, the *Clupea thrissa* is stated to be inherently so. The *Clupea humeralis* is so poisonous at the Antilles, due to feeding on the *Physalia*, that it occasionally causes death in a few minutes; even the common herring, *Clupea harengus*, is sometimes very irritating when eaten, in the North Sea, consequent on living on some minute red worm which are occasionally abundant there. The Indian shad, *Clupea palasah*, when in season, is somewhat rich, and the Burmans do not eat it during sickness, or should they be suffering at the time from skin affections, or have suffered from such during the few preceding months, as they affirm it will aggravate it when present, and reproduce it if only recently recovered from.

423. Amongst the eels, *Murænidæ*, none appear to be reputed unwholesome, still there is no reason they should not become so in India as in Europe (*see* para. 418). The appearance of some is considered repulsive, whilst Jews and Mahomedans reject them.

Eels as food.

424. In the *Sclerodermatous* family, species of the *Balistes* are eaten by the Andamanese, but none of the *Ostracions*, so far as I can ascertain, are employed as food. It is curious that the *Ostracion cornutum* and the *Balistes vetula* are said to be very poisonous

Sclerodermi as food, or poisonous.

off Bourbon and the Mauritius. The frog or puff fishes, *Tetrodons*, are generally reputed to be poisonous, and are rejected as an article of diet by the people of India, but they are highly relished by the Andamanese, and the native doctors in Malabar use them as medicine in phthisical cases. In Burma, where the large yellow *Xenopterus naritus* is found in all the branches of the Irawaddi, the natives bait for them with small fish, and consider their flesh as good for eating. However, at the Cape of Good Hope a spotted *Tetrodon* has caused so many deaths, that the officers of all ships anchoring there are warned against their being used as food. In the Nile, one species is reputed to be very poisonous if eaten. In Japan is found a sort which is used for the purpose of effecting suicide, whilst an edict exists in the army of that country, declaring that, should any soldier die from eating it, his son is prohibited from entering the military service.

425. Sharks, saw-fishes, rays and skates, with the exception of the torpedo, are esteemed as food by many of the Madrassees and the Seedees in Bombay. In Bengal, however, they are rejected by all but the very poorest, some of whom even will refuse them.

<small>Cartilaginous fishes as food.</small>

426. Many diseases have been attributed to the effects of a fish diet. In Bergen, "fish is perhaps more largely used as an acticle of diet than in any other part of the world. * * * There are two large hospitals devoted exclusively to the treatment of patients suffering from a peculiar form of disease, brought on by eating badly cured fish : the disease is a mixture of leprosy and elephantiasis." (*Lancet*, July 1866, p. 83). "A scorbutic taint is considered to ensue in some portions of Europe from a fish diet. Leprosy in the south of Spain is ascribed to this cause." Amongst the Norwegians, phthisis is common and also struma. "Of fresh meat the Norwegians, get but little, and their fish and milk are often used in a state of partial decomposition instead of fresh. * * * Their constitution could rally and get well on a regimen under which an Englishman would sink." (*Medical Times and Gazette*, July 1869). Examining the foregoing statements, one observes that it is not a good fish diet which is accused of producing leprosy, elephantiasis, scurvy and skin diseases, but fish consumed in a state of putrefaction or badly cured; but even this may be open to argument. Natives in some portions of Asia consider that eating fish predisposes to cholera, and many object on that account to its use during epidemics of that malady (*see* ante-paragraph 420 on the *Siluridæ*). Leprosy is a well-marked disease, and has been attributed to an unwholesome fish diet. *Leprosy* is by no means unfrequent in the Panjáb, North-West Provinces, and other districts far inland, amongst people who resolutely refuse ever to eat salt-fish however prepared. The only way in which they consume putrid fish is purchasing the fry during the rainy months, which, prior to being cooked, generally is in a more or less putrid condition. But if we go a little further to the east, we find the Burmese race, who most assuredly are a fish-consuming one (*see* para. 366) and prefer their odoriferous *nga-pee* to fresh fish. In my travels through Burma, I never saw a single instance of leprosy amongst the indigenous population, nor a case of those congenital malformation of the fingers and toes, so

<small>Diseases attributed to a fish diet.</small>

common in India amongst the natives born with a leprous taint. In fact, it has been frequently remarked that this disease does not exist amongst the Burmese. The same remark applies to the fish-and-animal-food-eating Andamanese; whilst on the other hand it is as common in India amongst inland classes who do not eat fish, as those who do so. As regards *Elephantiasis Arabum*, there does not appear to be any stronger reason for attributing its origin to a fish diet, than there is in regard to *E. Græcorum*, or the true leprosy. Hamilton Buchanan observed that this disease, in some parts of India, is attributed by the natives to eating a carp, *Labeo curchius*, and taking large draughts of fresh milk on the same day.

427. *Skin diseases of a low character and inveterate itch* have been considered to be occasioned by this form of diet; this seems in many cases to be thought so, because very poor persons residing along the sea coast, and are unable to procure proper sustenance, consume the refuse of the fish taken, which are either given them gratuitously as worthless, or disposed of at a very cheap rate. This, however, can scarcely be assumed as the sole cause of the low forms of disease (excluding dysenteric diarrhœa, occasionally passing into dysentery) from which these people suffer, which in reality are due to privations, though doubtless badly-cured fish may aggravate diseases, or render the individual more susceptible to the attacks of maladies indigenous to the locality. In the badly nourished, itch or other skin affections, when contracted, are generally severe, and in sea-port towns are mostly perceived amongst the poverty-stricken, who consume the refuse of fish in lieu of more wholesome food, which they are unable to purchase. *Scurvy* has by some been partly attributed to a fish diet. Dr. Gamack, reporting on the Convict Settlement at the Andamans in 1860, observed—"a very limited quantity of fresh meat and fish has been occasionally procurable by the convicts generally, but for the sick the supply has been more liberal, and in the *scurvy* cases was found of the greatest benefit."

Skin diseases and scurvy attributed to a bad fish diet.

428. *Fish wounds*, or those occasioned by their spines, are by no means uncommon. They may set up poisonous symptoms, due to their having a distinctly poisonous character, or severe irritation caused by the jagged nature of the injury inflicted. Severe inflammation, terminating in stiffened joints, have frequently resulted in Europe from wounds caused by the spines of the weever, *Trachinus vipera*. In some cases of injuries caused by siluroids, skates, and ray fishes, one can scarcely resist believing that some species have the power of secreting a direct poison, as the symptoms are often too severe to be attributable to simple inflammation. We perceive some snakes, however, with venomous, others with innocuous, saliva, and it is an interesting question whether the mucous secretions of fishes may not partake of either one or the other of these qualities. Dr. Günther apparently has discovered a poison gland in a fish brought from Guatemala, the *Thalassophryne reticulata*, the secretion from which seems to arise in the mucous system. The effects of some of these injuries from fish spines are doubtless entirely due to the extent of the inflicted wound. Thus, at

Wounds from fish spines, especially of siluroids.

Cochin, a man was brought to one of my hospitals with gangrene of the fore-arm, occasioned by a ray-fish having wound its tail around it, and dragged its armed spine through the muscles down to the bones. Accidents from spines of fishes, especially of the siluroid and ray families, are exceedingly common in the East. In both France and Spain, police regulations require that all spines on fish, which inflict injurious wounds, should be removed prior to their being brought to market. In Orissa, the serrated spine at the base of the tail of the ray-fish is believed to cause fatal wounds. Fishermen invariably remove it, and usually break off the dorsal and pectoral spines from all siluroids.

429. Dr. Jerdon (*Madras Journal, Literature and Science*, 1849) mentioned that wounds from the spiny rays of the *Polyacanthus cupanus* occasion severe pain for a few hours. But it may be generally considered that injuries from these hard rays of most of the *Acanthopterygian* fishes may induce irritation, and even inflammation, lasting for an uncertain time. This irritation may be due to acrid mucus, normally secreted, or rendered irritable, due to excitement in the fish. The severity of the injury will be increased or diminished in accordance with the state of the health of the injured person at the time of the receipt of the injury.

Wounds from spiny rays of fishes.

FRESH-WATER FISHES OF INDIA.

The fresh-water fishes of India. 430. The fresh-water fishes are divisible into those which are strictly so, and marine ones which ascend above tidal influence for breeding or predaceous purposes. The following list enumerates those at present known and described, with their geographical range, their native names (the pronunciation of the latter in accordance with the English language), and the size they attain to:—

Sub-class—TELEOSTEI.

Fishes having an osseous skeleton, completely separated vertebræ, and the posterior extremity of the vertebral column either bony or armed with bony plates. Bulb of aorta simple, with a pair of valves at its origin. Branchiæ free.

Order—ACANTHOPTERYGII.

A portion of the dorsal, anal, and ventral fin-rays unarticulated, forming spines. Air-vessel, when present, completely closed, not having a pneumatic duct.

Family—PERCIDÆ, Cuv.

Percoidei, pt., Cuvier: *Percidæ*, pt., and *Theraponidæ*, pt., Richardson.

Branchiostegals from five to seven: pseudobranchiæ, as a rule, present. Form of body generally oblong. Eyes lateral. All or some of the opercles (except in Apsilus) serrated or armed. Mouth in front of snout, having a lateral cleft, occasionally situated on the lower side. A barbel on the lower jaw in Pogonoperca. Teeth villiform or conical in the jaws, canines occasionally present, the vomer and generally the palatines armed with teeth. Anterior portion of dorsal fin spinous: ventrals thoracic, each having one spine and five rays. Scales ctenoid. Lateral line, when present, continuous, except in some species of Ambassis. Air-vessel usually present, and, when so, simple. Pyloric appendages in varying numbers.

Genus—LATES, Cuv. & Val.

Branchiostegals seven: pseudobranchiæ. Pre-orbital and shoulder bone serrated: pre-opercle with strong spines at its angle, and denticulated along its horizontal limb: opercle spinate. Teeth villiform on jaws, vomer and palatine bones: tongue smooth. First dorsal fin with seven or eight, anal with three spines: caudal rounded. Scales of moderate size. Cæcal pylori few.

1. *Lates calcarifer*, Bloch. This marine, predaceous fish ascends all the large rivers of India and Burma. *Dangara*, Sindee: *Nuddee meen* or *Nair meen*, Malyalim: *Painnee meen*, Tamil: *Pandu kopah* or *Pandu meenu*, Telugu: *Durruah*, Ooriah: *Begti*, Bengal: *Cock-up* of Europeans. D. 7-8/$\frac{1}{11-13}$, A. $\frac{3}{8-9}$, L. l. 52-60, L. tr. 7/12, Cæc. pyl. 3. Of a grey colour. It attains several feet in length.

Genus—AMBASSIS, *Commerson*.

Chanda, Hamilton Buchanan; *Bogoda*, pt., Bleeker.

Branchiostegals six. Body compressed, more or less diaphanous. Lower limb of pre-opercle with a double denticulated edge: opercle without a prominent spine. Villiform teeth on the jaws and palate, generally no canines. Two dorsal fins, the first with seven, the anal with three spines: a recumbent spine directed forwards in front of the base of the dorsal fin. Scales of moderate or small size, frequently deciduous. Lateral line complete, interrupted or absent.

2. *Ambassis nalua*, Ham. Buch., B. vi. D. $7/\frac{1}{10-11}$, A. $\frac{3}{9-10}$, L. l. 30. Lateral line continuous. Lower Bengal to a few inches in length.

3. *Ambassis ranga*, Ham. Buch. *Chandee*, Ooriah and Beng. B. vi. D. $7/\frac{1}{12-14}$, A. $\frac{3}{13-15}$, L. l. 58. Found in Bengal and Madras to a few inches in length.

4. *Ambassis baculis*, Ham. Buch. *Kung-gi*, Panj.; *Nga-koun-ma* or *Nga-zin-zat*, Burm. B. vi. D. $7/\frac{1}{13-15}$, A. $\frac{3}{15-17}$. Scales minute. Found throughout India and Burma, very similar to the last.

5. *Ambassis Thomassi*, Day. *Mullu-cherú*, Mal. B. vi. D. $7/\frac{1}{11}$, A. $\frac{3}{10}$, L. l. 38, L. tr. 6/13. Western Coast of India.

6. *Ambassis nama*, Ham. Buch. *Mucknee* and *Ched-du-ah*, Panjab; *Pud-du* and *Put-to-lah*, Sindee: *Ak-ku-rati*, Telugu: *Buck-ra* and *Pompi-ah*, North-West Provinces; *Cart-kana*, Ooriah. B. vi. D. $7/\frac{1}{14}$, A. $\frac{3}{14}$. Lateral line absent. A small fresh-water fish found throughout India.

7. *Ambassis lala*, Ham. Buch. *Pee-dah*, Sind; *Chandee*, North-West Provinces; *Laal chandee*, Ooriah. B. vi. D. $7/\frac{1}{11}$, A. $\frac{3}{14}$. Scales minute: lateral line absent. Orange with four or five vertical bands, first dorsal nearly black. Found throughout the continent of India except Madras. Only attains a few inches in length.

Family—PRISTIPOMATIDÆ.

Percoidei, pt., *Sciænoidei*, pt., *Sparoidei*, pt., et *Mænides*, pt., Cuv.: *Theraponidæ*, pt., *Hæmulonidæ*, pt., *Sparidæ*, pt., et *Mænides*, pt., Richardson.

Branchiostegals from five to seven. Pseudobranchiæ, usually well developed. Body oblong, compressed. Eyes of medium size, lateral. Mouth moderately or very protractile, placed in front of the snout, and with a lateral cleft. Muciferous system of the head rudimentary or slightly developed. Pre-opercle serrated or entire, barbels absent. Teeth in villiform bands, with conical canines in some genera, but neither molars nor cutting ones in the jaws: palate usually edentulous. A single dorsal fin, the spinous and soft portion being of about equal extent, the first containing strong spines, or continuous with the soft: anal mostly with three spines, its soft portion similar to that of the dorsal: lower pectoral rays branched: ventrals thoracic with one spine and five rays. Scales finely ctenoid or cycloid, extending over the body and head; cheeks not cuirassed. Lateral line continuous. Air-vessel present, more or less simple. Stomach cæcal. Pyloric appendages few, or in moderate numbers.

Genus—THERAPON, *Cuv.*

Datnia, Cuv. and Val.: *Pelates*, Cuv.

Branchiostegals six. Eyes of moderate size. Opercle with spines: pre-opercle serrated. Teeth villiform in both jaws, the outer being sometimes the larger: deciduous ones on the vomer and palatines. Scales of moderate size. Air-vessel divided by a constriction. Pyloric appendages in moderate numbers.

8. *Therapon servus*, Bloch. B. vi. D. 10-11/$\frac{1}{10}$, A. $\frac{3}{8}$, L. l. 80, L. tr. 12/27. Silvery, with three longitudinal dark bands having a slight convexity downwards. Is found in some of the larger rivers as the Hooghly, occasionally above tidal influence. It attains to twelve or thirteen inches in length.

Genus—DATNOIDES, Bleeker.

Branchiostegals six. Pseudobranchiæ. Body somewhat elevated. Eyes of moderate size. Inter-maxillaries very protractile. Pre-opercle serrated; opercle with short spines. One dorsal fin, with a deep notch, having twelve stout spines, anal with three. Caudal rounded. Scales rather small. Air-vessel simple. Pyloric appendages few.

9. *Datnoides polota*, Ham. Buch. *Nga-kya*, Burm. B. vi. D. $\frac{12}{13}\frac{}{14}$, A. $\frac{3}{8}$, L. l. 48, L. r. 70, L. tr. 12/25, Cæc. pyl. 5. Brown, with six or seven narrow black vertical bands on the body, and others radiating from the orbit. Is found throughout the lower portions of the Ganges and Irrawaddi, ascending above tidal reach; it attains about 12 inches in length.

Family—SCIÆNIDÆ, Cuv.

Branchiostegals seven. Pseudobranchiæ sometimes concealed. Body compressed and rather elongate. Eyes lateral, of moderate or small size. Mouth in front of or below snout. Cheeks unarmed: opercles sometimes weakly armed. Muciferous system on the head well developed. Teeth in villiform bands: canines present in some genera, but neither cutting nor molar ones in the jaws: palate edentulous. Two dorsal fins, the second much more developed than the first, or than the anal: spines of first dorsal usually feeble: anal with two spines: pectoral rays branched: ventrals thoracic, having one spine and five rays. Scales ctenoid. Lateral line complete, often continued on to the caudal fin. Stomach cœcal. Pyloric appendages generally few. Air-vessel, when present, as a rule, with branching or elongated appendages.

Genus—SCIÆNA, Cuv.

Johnius, Bloch : *Corvina*, pt., Cuv. : *Leiostomus*, pt., Cuv. & Val. : *Homoprion*, Holb.

Pseudobranchiæ. Body oblong. Eyes of moderate size, and the inter-orbital space rather broad and slightly convex. Snout rounded; the upper jaw longer than the lower, or both equal. Cleft of mouth horizontal or slightly oblique. Barbels absent. The outer row of teeth generally the largest: canines absent. Air-vessel present. Pyloric appendages few, or in moderate numbers.

This genus has been subdivided artificially, in accordance to the length of the second anal spine, as follows:—(1) weak and about half the length of the first ray, *Sciæna*: (2) moderately strong and nearly two-thirds as long as the first ray, *Johnius*: (3) very strong and about equalling the first ray in length, *Corvina*.

10. *Sciæna coitor*, Ham.: Buch. *Vella ketchellee*, Tam.: *Botahl* and *Puttheri-ki*, Ooriah: *Nga-pok-thin*, Burm. B. vii. D. 10/$\frac{1}{27}$, A. $\frac{2}{7}$, Cæc.

pyl. 7-9. Silvery. Ascends all the large rivers of India and Burma for breeding purposes: it attains about 12 inches in length.

Family—SQUAMIPINNES, *Cuv.*

Chætodontidæ, pt., Richardson.

Branchiostegals six or seven: pseudobranchiæ well developed. Body elevated and compressed. Eyes lateral and of moderate size. Mouth generally small, with a lateral cleft, and situated in front of the snout. Teeth villiform or setiform, neither incisors nor canines: in most of the genera the palate is edentulous. Soft portion of the dorsal fin more developed than the spinous, sometimes considerably, more rarely slightly so: anal with three or four spines, its soft portion similar to that of the dorsal: lower pectoral rays branched: ventrals thoracic, with one spine and five rays. Scales cycloid or very finely ctenoid; they extend more or less over the vertical fins, but occasionally are absent from the spinous portion. Air-vessel present, generally simple. Intestines usually much convoluted: stomach cæcal. Pyloric appendages in moderate numbers.

Genus—*TOXOTES* Cuvier.

Branchiostegals seven: pseudobranchiæ. Body oblong, compressed, back depressed. Eyes of moderate size. Snout rather produced; lower jaw the longer. Villiform teeth on jaws, vomer, and palatine bones. A single dorsal fin, having five strong spines situated in the posterior half of the back: anal with three spines. Scales cycloid, of moderate or rather small size, some are extended to over the soft portions of the vertical fins. Air-vessel simple. Pyloric appendages in moderate numbers.

11. *Toxotes jaculator*, Pallas. D. $\frac{5}{11\text{-}13}$, A. $\frac{3}{15\text{-}17}$, L. l. 28, Cæc. pyl. 7-9. Greenish brown, with broad dark bands or blotches. Attains about a foot in length. Found in and above tidal influence in the large rivers of Bengal and Burma.

12. *Toxotes microlepis*, Blyth. *Nga-kya-ma* Burmese. D. $\frac{5}{13}$, A. $\frac{3}{17}$, L. l. 42, Cæc. pyl. 8. Golden, with two to four large black oblong blotches or stripes along its sides. Found in Burma along with the last, attaining about the same size.

Family—CARANGIDÆ, *Günther.*

Scomberoidei, pt., et *Squamipinnes*, pt., Cuv.: *Scombrisidæ*, pt., Richardson.

Branchiostegals usually seven, sometimes less: pseudobranchiæ as a rule present, absent in *Lichia* and *Trachynotus*. Body oblong or elevated, and generally compressed. Eyes lateral, sometimes large. Infra-orbital bones do not articulate with the pre-opercle. Gill-openings wide. Dentition exceedingly varied. The spinous dorsal of less extent than the soft, sometimes even being rudimentary; it is either continuous with, or distinct from, the soft portion: the posterior portion of the dorsal and anal sometimes consisting of detached finlets. The soft dorsal and the anal may be of nearly equal extent, or the latter much the most developed. Ventrals, when present, thoracic, but they may be rudimentary or absent. Scales small, sometimes absent. Air-vessel present. Pyloric appendages usually in large numbers, whilst some genera have but few.

Genus—*EQUULA*, *Cuv.*

Branchiostegals from four to five: pseudobranchiæ. Body elevated and strongly compressed. Eyes lateral. Mouth very protractile. Lower edge of pre-opercle serrated. Minute teeth on jaws; palate edentulous. A single dorsal fin, having less spines (8-10) than rays (15-17) : anal with three spines and less rays than the soft dorsal (13-14) : ventrals thoracic. Scales small, cycloid, and generally deciduous. Lateral line unarmed, usually complete, but in some species terminating below the end of the dorsal fin. Air-vessel ending posteriorly in two horns. Pyloric appendages few.

13. *Equula runconius*, Ham. Buch. *Tunka-chandee*, Ooriah : *Nga-hpee-ma*, Burm. D. $\frac{3}{16\text{-}17}$, A. $\frac{3}{14}$, L. l. 68. Silvery, with short greyish bands descending from the back. This small fish is found in the large rivers of Lower Bengal and Burma.

Family—MUGILIDÆ, Richardson.

Mugiloidei, Bleeker.

Branchiostegals from four to six: pseudobranchiæ. Form of body oblong, compressed, and the anterior portion and head may be depressed. Eyes lateral, with or without adipose lids. Gill-openings wide: gills four. Opercles unarmed. Mouth narrow or of moderate width. Teeth very fine, sometimes absent. Anterior portion of dorsal fins consisting of four stiff spines: anal slightly longer than the second dorsal. Ventrals abdominal, suspended from an elongated shoulder bone; it consists of one spine and five rays. Scales cycloid, rarely ctenoid. Lateral line absent. Pyloric appendages generally few.

Genus—MUGIL, Artedi.

Branchiostegals from four to six: pseudobranchiæ. Eyes with or without an adipose lid. Anterior edge of lower jaw sharp. Teeth, when present, minute. Pyloric appendages generally few (2-10). Upper portion of stomach very muscular.

14. *Mugil cascasia*, Ham. Buch. *Cuck-se* or *Buah*, Panj.: D. 4/$\frac{1}{8}$, A. $\frac{3}{8}$, L. l. 32, L. tr. 16. Silvery: uncovered space on chin, eye, base of pectoral, and centre of base of caudal gamboge yellow. This small mullet is found in the upper parts of the Ganges and Jumna, also in the Indus.

15. *Mugil corsula*, Ham. Buch. *Hurd-wah-re*, Panj.: *Ka-kun-da*, Ooriah; *Corsula* and *In-ge-lee*, Beng.: *Undala*, Hind : *Nga-zen*, Burm. D. 4/$\frac{1}{8}$, A. $\frac{3}{8}$, L. l. 50, L. tr. 15. Ascends all the large rivers east of the Kistna far above tidal influence; it attains a foot in length.

16. *Mugil Hamiltonii*, Day. D. 4/$\frac{1}{8}$, A. $\frac{3}{8}$, L. l. 44, L. tr. 18. Scales ctenoid. Found throughout the large rivers of Burma to nearly 5 inches in length.

Family—GOBIIDÆ.

Pseudobranchiæ present, sometimes rudimentary. Body generally elongated. Eyes lateral, occasionally prominent. The infra-orbital ring of bones does not articulate with the pre-opercle. Gill-opening varying from extremely narrow to wide. Gill membranes attached to the isthmus: four gills. Teeth of various characters, canines sometimes present. A single dorsal fin, sometimes divided into two portions; the spines are flexible, and this part of the fin is not so developed as the soft: anal similar to the soft dorsal: ventrals sometimes united so as to form a disc. Scales and lateral line present or absent. Air-vessel generally absent. Pyloric appendages, if present, few.

Genus—GOBIUS, Artedi.

Branchiostegals five, pseudobranchiæ. Body low and elongated. Gill-openings of moderate width. Opercles unarmed. Teeth in several rows in the jaws; canines sometimes present. Anterior dorsal fin with from five to six flexible spines: the posterior more developed and of the same character as the anal: ventrals united, forming a disc, which is not attached to the abdomen; each has one spine and five rays. Scales present or absent and either cycloid or ctenoid. Lateral line absent. Air-vessel when present generally small. Pyloric appendages usually absent.

17. *Gobius giuris*, Ham. Buch. Goo-loo-wah and Boul-la, Panj.: Gooloo, Sind and N. W. Prov.: Kurdán, Mal.: Oolooway, Tam.: Tsikidundu Tel.: Gulah, Ooriah: Nga-tha-boh, Burm.: Poo-dah, And. D. $6/\frac{1}{8-9}$, A. $\frac{1}{5-9}$, L. l. 26-34. Blotched and spotted with rusty brown. Found in all pieces of fresh water throughout the plains of India, Burma, the Andamans, and occasionally within tidal influence. It attains a foot and a half in length.

18. *Gobius nunus*, Ham. Buch. D. 6/5 (?) A. 7. Greenish, with six black belts. A small goby, found in the lower portions of the Ganges and Irrawaddi Rivers, but ascending above tidal influence.

19. *Gobius Malabaricus*, Day. D. $6/\frac{1}{10}$, A. 11, L. l. 50, L. tr. 10. Brown with a black crescentic white edged mark on the first dorsal fin. It is found in Malabar and Madras, and is only a small species.

Gobius neglectus, Jerdon. D. 6/11, A. 10-11, L. l. ca 50. A moderately sized goby, found along the bases of the Western Ghâts.

Genus—EUCTENOGOBIUS, Gill.

Branchiostegals six. Body elongated. Eyes not prominent. Gill-openings rather narrow, not extending to the lower surface of the head. Teeth in one row in the upper jaw, in several rows in the lower: no canines: palate edentulous. Inferior pharyngeal bones of an elongated triangular shape, having a median longitudinal suture. Two dorsal fins—the first with six flexible spines: ventrals united, not adherent to the abdomen.

20. *Euctenogobius striatus*, Day. Coondallum oolooway, Tam.: Mahturi, if young Naolli, Ooriah: Nga-ka-tha-po, Burm. D. $6/\frac{1}{10}$, A. 11, L. l. 54, L. tr. 20. Buff coloured with some vertical bands. Found throughout the lower districts of Madras, Bengal, and Burma, attaining 6 inches in length.

Genus—PERIOPHTHALMUS, Bl.-Schn.

Branchiostegals five: pseudobranchiæ rudimentary. Body subcylindrical. Eyes placed close together, very prominent, and the outer eyelid well developed. Gill-openings rather narrow. Teeth in both jaws vertical and conical. Two dorsal fins—the first with a varying number of flexible spines: ventrals united in their lower two-thirds: base of pectoral muscular: caudal with its lower edge obliquely truncated. Air-vessel absent. Scales, small or of moderate size, ctenoid, covering body and base of pectoral fin.

21. *Periophthalmus Schlosseri*, Pall. Nga-pyan, Burm. D. $7/\frac{1}{2}$, A. 14. Colours, with blue spots on the body; fins banded with varying colours. Mouths of large rivers in India and Burma, ascending above t'dal influence; rarely exceeds 3 inches in length.

Genus—ELEOTRIS, Gronov.

Philypnus, Cuv. and Val.; *Bostrichthys*, Dum.; *Culius, Butis, Valenciennea, Belobranchus,* and *Eleotrioides,* Bleeker; *Lembus,* Günther. Branchiostegals from four to six, occasionally terminating anteriorly in a spine: pseudobranchiæ present. Gill-openings of moderate width. Body subcylindrical, scaly. Head oblong. Eyes lateral, not prominent, and of moderate size. Teeth small, present or absent on the vomer. Two dorsal fins, the anterior with few (5-8) spines, and these sometimes filamentous: base of pectoral slightly muscular: ventrals placed close together, but not united. Air-vessel large. Anal papillæ distinct. Pyloric appendages generally absent.

22. *Eleotris fusca*, Bl. Poollan, Mal.: *Cul-coondallum* and *Mussoorie*, Tam.: *Kalawishi* and *Bundi-balah-kera*, Ooriah: *Kyouk-ka-tha-bho*, Burm. D. $6/\frac{1}{8}$, A. $\frac{1}{8}$, L. l. 63, L. tr. 16. Of a dark colour. Found throughout the lower districts of India and Burma, also at the Andamans. It does not attain a span in length.

Family—NANDIDÆ, Günther.

Pseudochromides et *Mænoidei*, pt., Müll. and Trosch.

Branchiostegals from five to six: pseudobranchiæ present in marine genera, but sometimes hidden or absent in some of those of the fresh-water. Body oblong and compressed. Teeth feeble, but dentition more or less complete. Dorsal fin single; the spinous portion most developed, or of nearly equal extent to the soft; anal with three spines, and its soft portion resembling that of the dorsal: ventrals thoracic, with one spine and four or five rays. Scales ctenoid, covering the body. Lateral line interrupted, or absent. No superbranchial organ. Air-vessel present. Pyloric appendages few or absent.

Genus—BADIS, Bleeker.

Branchiostegals six: pseudobranchiæ absent. Gills four. Eyes lateral. Mouth protractile. None of the bones of the head armed. Teeth on jaws, vomer, and palatines; none on the tongue. A single dorsal fin, the spinous portion being of much greater extent than the soft: anal with three spines, its rayed portion similar to that of the dorsal. Scales ctenoid, and of moderate size. Lateral line interrupted or absent. Air-vessel large and simple. Pyloric appendages absent.

23. *Badis Buchanani*, Bleeker. *Kala-poo-ti-ah* and *Chi-ri*, Panj.: *Bundei*, Ooriah.: *Pin-lay-nga-ba-mah* and *Nga-mee-loung*, Burm. B. vi. D. $\frac{16-17}{8-7}$, A. $\frac{3}{8-7}$, L. l. 30, L. tr. $\frac{3}{8}$, Cæc. pyl. o. Lateral line interrupted. Purplish black, banded. This small fish appears to be pretty generally distributed through India and Burma, except in Madras.

24. *Badis dario*, Ham. Buch. B. vi. D. $\frac{14}{8}$, A. $\frac{3}{8}$, L. l. 26. Lateral line absent. Colours and size as in the last species. Gangetic Provinces and the Wynaad.

Genus—NANDUS, Cuv. and Val.

Bedula, Gray; *Pristolepis*, Jerdon.

Branchiostegals six: pseudobranchiæ absent (BEDULA), or present (PRISTOLEPIS). Eyes lateral. Body oblong, compressed. Mouth very or *moderately protractile. Opercle with two spines: pre-opercle more or less serrated: preorbital entire. Teeth villiform in jaws, vomer, and palatines, and (in N. marginatus) tubercular on base of the tongue. A single dorsal fin, the spinous portion being of slightly greater extent than the soft: anal with three spines. Scales ctenoid and of moderate size. Lateral line interrupted. Air-vessel large and simple. Pyloric appendages absent.*

25. *Nandus marmoratus,* Cuv. and Val. *Gud-ha, Hool-sa,* and *Mussoas-sah,* Panj.: *Mootaharee,* Mal.: *Septi,* Tel.: *Vaad-hul,* Hind.: *Latha* and *Gud-ha,* Beng.: *Budusi,* Ooriah: *Nga-weh-ma,* Burm. B. vi. D. $\frac{12-14}{11-13}$, A. $\frac{3}{7-9}$, L. l. 46-57. No pseudobranchiæ. Throughout the fresh-waters of India (Sind?) and Burma, attaining 6 inches in length.

26. *Nandus marginatus,* Jerdon. *Chŭtichi,* Mal. B. vi. D. $\frac{14}{12}$, A. $\frac{3}{8}$, L. l. 25, L. tr. $\frac{4}{8}$. Pseudobranchiæ present. Western Ghâts, attaining 4 inches in length.

Genus—CATOPRA, Bleeker.

Branchiostegals six: pseudobranchiæ absent. Eyes lateral. Mouth protractile. Opercle with two flat spines: pre-opercle and pre-orbital serrated. Teeth villiform on jaws, vomer, palatines and the tongue. A single dorsal fin, the spinous portion being of slightly less extent than the soft: anal with three spines. Scales ctenoid, of rather a large size. Lateral line interrupted. Pyloric appendages two.

27. *Catopra nandioides,* Bleeker. B. vi. D. $\frac{13}{15-16}$, A. $\frac{3}{8}$, L. l. 27, L. tr. $\frac{5\frac{1}{2}}{44}$, Cæc. Pyl. 2. Greenish. Burmese rivers and ponds, to 8 inches in length.

Family—LABYRINTHICI, Cuv.

Anabantidæ, pt., Richardson; *Spirobranchidæ,* pt., Swainson; *Osphromenoidei,* Bleeker.

Branchiostegals from four to six; pseudobranchiæ rudimentary or absent. Gills four. Body compressed, oblong, or elevated. Eyes lateral. Gill-openings rather narrow; the membranes united below the isthmus. Above the third or upper portion of the first branchial arch, exists a cavity in which is contained an elaborate apparatus consisting of thin laminæ of bone covered by a vascular mucous membrane, and which is employed for respiratory purposes. Number of dorsal and anal spines variable; ventrals thoracic. Scales ctenoid and of moderate size. Lateral line interrupted or absent. Air-vessel present or absent. Pyloric appendages few or absent.

Genus—ANABAS, Cuvier.

Branchiostegals six: pseudobranchiæ absent. Branchial arches with toothed tubercles. Mouth rather small. Opercles and pre-orbital serrated. Teeth villiform in jaws, and on the anterior and posterior extremity of the vomer; none on the palatines. Dorsal fin single, the spinous portion of greater extent than the soft: anal spines numerous, less than those of the dorsal. Scales rather large, ctenoid. Lateral line interrupted. Air-vessel bifid posteriorly, with either extremity produced. Pyloric appendages few or absent.

28. *Anabas scandens,* Dald. Climbing perch of Europeans. *Undeecollee,* Mal.: *Pauni-eyri,* Tamil: *Coi,* Bengallee and Ooriah: *Nga-byaysma,* Burm.: *Kavaya* or *kawhy-ya,* Singalese. B. vi. D. $\frac{17-18}{8-10}$, A. $\frac{9-10}{8-11}$, L. l. 28-32, L. tr. 5/9-10. Estuaries and fresh-waters of India and

Burma, but most numerous in situations but little removed from tidal influence. Attains to 8 inches in length.

Genus—POLYACANTHUS, Cuv. and Val.

Branchiostegals six: pseudobranchiæ glandular or absent. Body oblong, compressed. Mouth small and but little protractile. Opercles spineless. Teeth small and fixed in the jaws; palate edentulous. Dorsal fin single, the spinous portion of much greater extent than the soft: the anal of a similar character: ventral with one spine and five well developed rays, some of which are usually elongate. Scales rather large, ctenoid. Lateral line interrupted, partially or even entirely absent. Air-vessel simple. Pyloric appendages few.

29. *Polyacanthus cupanus*, Cuv. and Val. *Punnum*, Tam. B. vi. D. $\frac{14-16}{6-7}$, A. $\frac{16-19}{10-11}$, L. l. 29-32, L. tr. $\frac{4}{7-8}$. Greenish, fins barred, with a dark spot at the base of the caudal, and the prolonged ventral ray scarlet. Found in ditches, irrigated fields, and shallow fresh and brackish waters, but slightly above tidal influence, both on the Coromandel and Malabar sides of the Madras Presidency. It rarely exceeds 3 inches in length.

Genus—OSPHROMENUS, Comm.

Trichopus, Lacép.

Branchiostegals six. Body moderately elevated, compressed. Opercle spineless: opercular pieces finely serrated in the immature. Mouth small, protractile. Teeth in jaws fine and fixed; palate edentulous. A single dorsal fin, its spinous portion sometimes in excess, but usually less in extent than its soft part: anal spines in varying numbers. Outer ventral ray long, filiform; the remainder mostly rudimentary. Scales of moderate size, ctenoid. Lateral line interrupted or absent. Air-vessel present. Pyloric appendages two.

30. *Osphromenus nobilis*, McClell. D. $\frac{5-6}{7-8}$, A. $\frac{5}{23}$, L. l. 28-30. Lateral line absent Two white bands along the sides, and a third along the base of the anal fin. A small fish, found in the north and north-east portions of Bengal.

Genus—TRICHOGASTER, Bl. Schn.

Trichopodus, Ham. Buch.; *Colisa*, Cuv. and Val.

Branchiostegals five. Branchial arches with toothed tubercles. Opercle spineless: pre-opercle serrated, as is also usually the pre-orbital. Mouth small and but little protractile. Teeth small, fixed in the jaws; palate edentulous. A single dorsal fin, the spinous of much greater extent than the soft: anal spines similar, but the rayed portion more developed: ventral fin consisting of one long filiform ray. Scales of moderate size, ctenoid. Air-vessel bifid posteriorly, the two ends being prolonged. Pyloric appendages few.

31. *Trichogaster fasciatus*, Bl. Schn. *Kun-gee*, Panj.: *Pich-ru*, Sind: *Kussuah* and *Coilia*, Ooriah: *Ponundi*, Tel.: *Nga-pin-thick-kouk* and *Nga-phyin-thaleb*, Burm. B. vi. D. $\frac{14-17}{8-12}$, A. $\frac{16-17}{13-17}$, L. l. 30-31. Greenish, banded, and some of the fins red-spotted. This little fish extends throughout

the course of large rivers in India and Burma, except Southern and Western Madras.

32. *Trichogaster lalius*, Ham. Buch. *Kung-gee*, Panj. B. vi. D. $1\frac{6}{9}$, A. $\frac{1}{16}$. Banded, owing to every scale being half light-blue and half scarlet; fins spotted with red. Panjáb and Lower Bengal, in the Jumna and Ganges.

33. *Trichogaster chuna*, Ham. Buch. B. vi. D. $1\frac{7}{7}$, A. $\frac{1}{19}$. Caudal fin slightly emarginate. A broad black lateral band. A small species found near Calcutta.

Family—OPHIOCEPHALIDÆ, Bleeker.

Labyrinthici, pt., Cuv.

Branchiostegals five: pseudobranchiæ absent. Gills four. Body elongated, subcylindrical anteriorly, head depressed, and superiorly covered by shield-like scales. Eyes lateral. Gill-openings wide, the membranes of the two sides being connected beneath the isthmus. A cavity exists, which is above and accessory to the true gill-cavity for the purpose of retaining or receiving air, a superbranchial organ is not developed, but some thin bony laminæ are present. Villiform teeth on jaws, vomer, and palate, sometimes with conical ones intermingled. One long spineless dorsal, and a similarly constructed, though shorter, anal. Ventrals thoracic *(Ophiocephalus)* or absent *(Channa)*; when present consisting of six rays, the outer of which is unbranched and articulated at its extremity. Scales of large, moderate, or small size. Lateral line abruptly curved or almost interrupted. Air-vessel present. Pyloric appendages few.

Genus—OPHIOCEPHALUS, Bloch.

As defined in the family. Ventral fins present. Pyloric appendages two.

34. *Ophiocephalus marulius*, Ham. Buch. *Kub-rah, Sawl*, and *Dowlah*, Panj.: *Choaree verarl* and *Cooravoo*, Mal.: *Phool-verarl*, Tam.: *Phoolmurl*, Hind.: *Hoovina-murl*, Can.: *Poola chapa*, Tel.: *Nga-yan-dyne*, Burm. B. v. D. 49-55, A. 33-36, L. l. 59-64. Orange, with vertical bands and white spots. Found throughout the fresh-waters, especially the larger rivers of India and Burma, attaining as much as 4 feet in length.

35. *Ophiocephalus barca*, Ham. Buch. *Bora* and *Burra chang*, Butan. B. v. D. 50-52, A. 35-36, L. l. 62. Dark violet, dotted all over with black. Calcutta, North-Eastern Bengal, and Butan, attaining 3 feet in length.

36. *Ophiocephalus diplogramme*, Day. *Kuch-ki*, Mal. and Canarese. D. 43, A. 27, L. l. 112. Two horizontal black lateral bands. Western Coast of India, attaining a foot and a half in length.

37. *Ophiocephalus striatus*, Lacép: *Chota Sawl* and *Carrodah*, Panj.: *Char-koor*, Sind: *Murl* and *Morrul*, Hind.: *Verarl* and *Wrahl*, Mal.: *Verarlu* and *Curroopoo verarl*, Tamil: *Sowarah*, Tel.: *Sola*, Ooriah: *Koochinda murl*, Can.: *Lolla*, Sing.: *Nga-yan* or *Nga-yan-pa-nan*, Burm. B. v. D. 37-43, A 22-26, L. l. 51-57. Grey above, whitish beneath, striated with black. Found throughout the fresh, preferring the stagnant, waters of the plains of India and Burma, attaining 3 feet or more in length.

38. *Ophiocephalus Stewartii*, Playfair. Brownish black above, lighter below, some black spots on the body. B. v. D. 39-40, A. 27, L. l. 50. Assam, attaining at least 10 inches in length.

39. *Ophiocephalus gachua*, Ham. Buch. *Chub-bu, Dow-lah,* and *Do-ah-ra,* Panj.: *Dheri dhok,* Hind.: *Koravu,* Mal.: *Para korava,* Tam.: *Mar korava,* Can.: *Chenga* or *Chayung,* Ooriah: *Nga-yan-goun-doh,* Burm.: *Chad-dah,* Andamanese. B. v. D. 32-34, A. 21-23, L. l. 40-45. Greenish, pectoral barred, the other fins with orange edgings. Found throughout the fresh-waters of India, Burma, and the Andamans, attaining a foot in length.

40. *Ophiocephalus punctatus,* Bloch. *Gra-e, Dowlah,* or *Dul-loun-ga,* Panj.: *Dhug-gu* or *Muk-koor,* Sind: *Gur-hi-e,* N. W. Prov.: *Phool Dhok,* Hind.: *Korava,* Tam. and Can.: *Gorissa,* Ooriah: *Nga-yan-thin-ohn,* Burm. B. v. D. 29-32, A. 21, L. l. 40. Dirty green, banded and sometimes with numerous black dots over the body. All fresh-waters of India and Burma, attaining a foot in length.

Family—RHYNCHOBDELLIDÆ, *Bleeker.*

Scomberoidei, pt., Cuv. & Val.: *Mastacembelidæ,* Günther.

Branchiostegals six: pseudobranchiæ absent. Gill-opening a slit on side of head: gills four. Body elongated, eel-shaped. Humeral arch not suspended from the skull. Lower jaw long, but without much power of motion. A single long dorsal fin, its anterior portion consisting of free spines: anal with three spines anterior to it: soft dorsal and anal of similar extent: ventral fins absent. Air-vessel present. Pyloric appendages two.

Genus—RHYNCHOBDELLA, *Bl. Schn.*

Mastacemblus, Gronov.

Branchiostegals six. *Cleft of mouth narrow: a long and fleshy snout, inferiorly concave and transversely striated. Minute teeth on jaws and vomer. Dorsal and anal not continuous with the caudal fin. Scales small, cycloid. Lateral line present. Air-vessel elongated.*

41. *Rhynchobdella aculeata,* Bloch. *Aral,* Tam.: *Bommiday,* Tel.: *Gritti* Ooriah: *Nga-maway-doh-naga,* Burm. D. 16-20/48-54, A. 3/44-52. Brownish marbled; a row of from 3 to 9 black ocelli, having buff edges, along the base of the soft dorsal. Throughout the deltas of large Indian and Burmese rivers, but appears to be absent from the northern portions of the Panjáb and the Malabar Coast. It attains about 12 inches in length.

Genus—MASTACEMBLUS, *Gronov.*

Branchiostegals six. *Cleft of mouth narrow: a long and fleshy appendage to the snout, which is not transversely striated inferiorly: pre-opercle generally with spinous teeth at its angle. Teeth in jaws minute. Dorsal and anal fins distinct from, or confluent with, the caudal. Scales small, cycloid. Lateral line present. Air-vessel elongated.*

42. *Mastacemblus Aleppensis,* Bl. Schn. D. 32-35/80, A. 3/80. Bootan, said to attain 18 inches in length.

43. *Mastacemblus zebrinus,* Blyth. *Nga-maway-doh-wettoung,* Burm. D. 29/52, A. 3/56. Yellow with vertical black bands. Found throughout Burma.

44. *Mastacemblus unicolor,* Cuv. and Val. D. 33-34/80-84, A. 3/75-81. Found in the upper portions of the Irrawaddi.

45. *Mastacemblus pancalus,* Ham. Buch. *Chen-da-la, Gürchee,* and *Gro-age,* Panj.: *Ju-gar,* N. W. Prov.: *Par-pa-raul,* Tel.: *Turi*

and *Bah-ru*, Ooriah. D. 24-26/30-40, A. 3/31-44. Throughout India, attaining 6 inches in length.

46. Mastacemblus armatus, Lacép. *Bahm* and *Gro-age*, Panj. and Sind : *Shaa-ta-rah*, Tam. : *Mudi-bom-mi-day*, Tel. : *Bahm* and *Bummi*, Ooriah and Beng. : *Nga-maway-doh-aga*, Burm. D. 35-39/74-87, A. 3/79-87. Marbled and striped, sometimes with round spots. Found throughout India and Burma, even on the Himalayas, attaining 2 feet and upwards in length.

47. Mastacemblus Guentheri, Day. D. 27-28/60-64, A. 3/62-64. Horizontal limb of pre-opercle serrated. Marbled. Malabar, attaining about seven inches in length.

Family—CHROMIDES, *Müller*.

Branchiostegals five or six : pseudobranchiæ absent. Gills four. Body oblong or elevated. Teeth in jaws small, none on the palate: inferior pharyngeal bones triangular, having a median suture. Dorsal fin single, the spinous portion usually of greater extent than the soft : anal with three or more spines, its rayed part similar to that of the dorsal. Ventrals thoracic, with one spine and five rays. Scales generally ctenoid. Lateral line more or less interrupted. Air-vessel present. Pyloric appendages, when present, in small numbers.

Genus—ETROPLUS, *Cuv. & Val.*

Branchiostegals six. Body elevated and compressed. Eyes lateral. Cleft of mouth short. Teeth in two rows in the jaws, compressed and lobate. A single dorsal, the spinous portion being of greater extent than the rayed : anal spines more numerous or of about equal extent to the rays. Scales ctenoid and of moderate size. Lateral line interrupted, or abruptly ceasing. Air-vessel present. Pyloric appendages absent.

48. Etroplus Suratensis, Bl. *Karssar*, Tam. : *Pitul-kas*, Hind. : *Cashi-mara*, Tel. : *Cun-dah-la*, Ooriah. D. $\frac{18\text{-}19}{14\text{-}15}$, A. $\frac{12\text{-}13}{12\text{-}11}$, L. l. 45, L. tr. 21. Green or purple, with eight vertical bands. Malabar and Coromandel Coast, attaining a foot in length.

49. Etroplus maculatus, Bl. *Pul-lut-tay*, Mal. D. $\frac{18}{8}$, A. $\frac{15}{9}$, L. l. 35, L. tr. 21. Canary yellow, with seventeen horizontal rows of golden spots, and three dark blotches along the middle of the side. Found throughout Madras and Malabar, attaining about three inches in length.

Order—ANACANTHINI.

All the rays of the vertical and ventral fins articulated, the latter, when present, being jugular and thoracic. Air-vessel, if existing, not having a pneumatic duct.

Sub-Order—ANACANTHINI-PLEURONECTOIDEI.

Structure of head, unsymmetrical on the two sides.

Family—PLEURONECTIDÆ, *Flem*.

Heterosomata, Bonaparte.

Pseudobranchiæ well developed. Gills four. Body strongly compressed, flattened, with one of its sides coloured, the other being more rarely spotted. Both eyes (except in the very young) placed on the superior or coloured surface. The two sides of the head not equally developed, one continuing almost rudimentary. A single long dorsal and anal fin. Air-vessel absent.

Genus—SYNAPTURA, Cantor.

Achiroides, Bleeker: *Æsopia, Euryglossa,* and *Eurypleura,* Kaup.
Branchiostegals six. Eyes on the right * *side, the upper in advance of the lower. Cleft of mouth narrow, twisted round to the left side. Minute teeth only on the left side : palate edentulous. One of the nostrils on the blind side dilated in some species, not so in others, whilst amongst the latter both pectorals may be present, the right being somewhat the longer. Some have the nasal tube small or simple (Synaptura), or bifid (Euryglossa). Secondly, the left pectoral may be longer than the right (Anisochirus). Thirdly, the left pectoral may be rudimentary (Æsopia). Fourthly, both pectorals may be absent (Achiroides). The vertical fins are confluent. Scales small and ctenoid. Lateral line straight.*

50. *Synaptura pan*, Ham. Buch. *Nga-la-chan*, Burm. D. 59, A. 45, L. l. 75. This species of sole is found in the Ganges and Burmese rivers high above tidal influence.

Order—PHYSOSTOMI, *Müller.*

All the fin rays articulated, except the first in the dorsal and pectoral, which are frequently more or less ossified. Ventral fins, when present, abdominal and spineless. Air-vessel, if existing, having a pneumatic duct.

Family—SILURIDÆ.

Margin of the upper jaw formed by the inter-maxillaries; the maxilla rudimentary often constituting the base of a barbel : no sub-opercle. The rayed or adipose dorsal fins may be present or absent. Skin scaleless, and either smooth or covered with osseous plates. Air-vessel, when present, either free in the abdominal cavity, *(Silurinæ)* or more or less enclosed in bone *(Amblycepinæ)* ; it communicates with the organs of hearing by means of the auditory bones.

Sub-Family—SILURINÆ.

Air-vessel not enclosed in bone.

Genus—AKYSIS, Bleeker.

Body rather elongated : dorsal profile nearly horizontal : neck not elevated. Head depressed, covered superiorly with soft skin. Eyes small, subcutaneous. Mouth terminal, transverse : jaws of unequal length. Nostrils somewhat remote from one another. Gill-openings wide. Barbels eight, their bases slightly dilated. Villiform teeth in the jaws: none on the palate. First dorsal fin having a spine enveloped in skin, and five or six rays: adipose dorsal low: pectoral horizontal, with a spine enclosed in skin : ventral with six rays, entirely behind the dorsal: caudal forked : anal of moderate length (9-11 rays). *Air-vessel not enclosed in bone. Skin smooth or tubercular.*

51. *Akysis Kurzii,* Day. D. $\frac{1}{6}$/0, A. 11. Brown. Pegu hills, only attaining a small size.

---

* NOTE.—The terms right or *dextral*, and left or *sinistral*, are thus employed in these flat fishes. The specimen is placed with its tail towards the observer, the dorsal fin upwards, the anal downwards, and the coloured side is the one referred to.

Genus—ERETHISTES *Mull. & Trosch.*

Hara, Blyth.

Head somewhat depressed, osseous superiorly. Gill-openings narrow, the membrane being confluent with the skin of the isthmus. Mouth small, terminal. Barbels eight, the maxillary ones with broad bases. Villiform teeth in the jaws, and in a band on the palate. First dorsal fin arising anterior to the ventrals, having an osseous serrated spine, and five or six branched rays: adipose dorsal of moderate extent: ventral with six rays; anal of moderate length (10 rays) : *caudal forked. Air-vessel not enclosed in bone.*

52. *Erethistes hara,* Ham. Buch. *Nga-kyouk-pa,* Burm. D. $\frac{1}{6}$/0, A. 10. Brown banded. In the large rivers of Orissa, Bengal, Assam, and Burma, attaining 2½ inches in length.

53. *Erethistes conta,* Ham. Buch. *Nga-thit-to* and *Nga-kouk-thwa,* Burm. D. $\frac{1}{6}$/0, A. 10. Lower Bengal and Burma, attaining 4 inches in length.

54. *Erethistes Jerdoni,* Day. D. $\frac{1}{6}$/0, A. 10. Another small species from Sylhet.

55. *Erethistes elongata,* Day. D. $\frac{1}{6}$/0, A. 10. From the Naga Hills.

Genus—MACRONES. *Dumeril.*

Bagrus, pt., Cuv. & Val.: *Hypselobagrus, Hemibagrus, Pseudobagrus,* and *Aspidobagrus,* Bleeker : *Batasio,* Blyth.

Branchiostegals from about six to twelve. Eyes with free circular margins. A separate inter-neural shield on the nape (Macrones), or no such shield (Hemibagrus). Mouth terminal, transverse: upper jaw generally the longer. Barbels eight, one nasal, one maxillary, and two mandibular pairs. Villiform teeth in the jaws, and in a more or less uninterrupted curved band on the palate. First dorsal fin with one spine, and from five to seven rays: adipose dorsal of varying length: pectoral spine serrated: anal short or of moderate length: ventral with six rays: caudal forked. Air-vessel of moderate or large size, attached to the under surface of the bodies of the anterior vertebræ.

a. *With a separate inter-neural shield on the nape.*

56. *Macrones aor,* Ham. Buch. *Seng-ga-la* and *Sang-go-ah,* Panj.: *Sing-ha-ree,* Sind and N. W. Provinces: *Cumboo kellettee,* Tam.: *Muti jella,* Tel. : *Alli* or *Addi,* Ooriah : *Nga-joung,* Burm. D. $\frac{1}{7}$/0, A. 13. Maxillary barbels extend to the end of the caudal fin. Adipose dorsal with a black spot at its posterior extremity. This large cat-fish is found throughout the plains of India and Burma, attaining several feet in length.

57. *Macrones Lamarri,* Cuv. and Val. *Teng-ga-ra,* Panj. D. $\frac{1}{7}$/0, A. 12. Maxillary barbels extend to the end of the first dorsal fin. A black spot at the posterior end of the adipose dorsal. Found in the upper portions of the Ganges and Jumna, attaining several feet in length.

58. *Macrones affinis,* Blyth. D. $\frac{1}{7}$/0, A. 12. Maxillary barbels do not pass the eye. Body with cross bands. A small species from the Tenasserim Provinces.

b. No separate inter-neural shield on the nape.

59. *Macrones chryseus*, Day. *Manjil yéte*, Mal.: *Pila kuturnee*, Hind. D. ⅐/0, A. 27. Barbels scarcely longer than the head. This and the following species have no separate inter-neural shield on the nape. Body golden, a black blotch behind the opercles. Western Coast of India, attaining upwards of a foot in length.

60. *Macrones batasio*, Ham. Buch. D. ⅐/0, A. 16. Barbels shorter than the head; diaphanous. River Tista, attaining three inches in length.

61. *Macrones gulio*, Ham. Buch. *Nuna tengara*, Beng. D. ⅐/0, A. 14. Maxillary barbels reach anal fin: adipose dorsal short. Brownish. Mouths of large Indian and Burmese rivers, ascending above tidal reach, attaining eight inches in length.

62. *Macrones tengana*, Ham. Buch. *Dum-sah*, Panj. D. ⅐/0, A. 14. Maxillary barbels reach to middle or end of pectoral: adipose dorsal short. Golden with longitudinal stripes. Assam and Panjab, up to 3 inches in length.

63. *Macrones carcio*, Ham. Buch. *Ka-gur* and *Kut-tah-rah*, N. W. Provinces: *Ten-ga-ra*, Beng.: *Kel-let-tee*, Tam.: *Sakujella*, Tel.: *Bi-kun-ti-a*, Ooriah: *Nga-zin-yine*, Burm. D. ⅐/0, A. 12-14. Maxillary barbels reach the caudal fin. Dorsal spine serrated on both sides: adipose fin short. Banded and having a shoulder mark. India, Ceylon, and Burma, to a few inches in length.

64. *Macrones corsula*, Ham. Buch. *Punjah-guggah*, Ooriah: *Nga-ike*, Burm. D. ⅐/0, A. 11. Maxillary barbels reach anal fin: adipose dorsal of moderate length. Brownish, with vertical rows of fine spots. Orissa, Lower Bengal, and Burma, attaining a foot or more in length.

65. *Macrones punctatus*, Jerdon. *Psetta kelletee*, Tam. D. ⅐/0, A. 11. Maxillary barbels reach the base of the ventral fins: adipose dorsal of moderate length. About ten round, black spots along the lateral line. Bowany River in Madras, attaining 18 inches in length.

66. *Macrones cavasius*, Ham. Buch. *Cut-taak kug-ger*, Panj.: *Vella kellettee* and *Cutta*, Tam.: *Muti jella*, Tel.: *Guntea*, Ooriah: *Nga-zin-zine*, Burm. D. ⅐/0, A. 11. Maxillary barbels reach the base of the caudal fin. Dorsal spine entire: adipose fin long. Silvery. India and Burma, to upwards of a foot in length.

67. *Macrones nangra*, Ham. Buch. D. ⅐/0, A. 10-11. Maxillary barbels reach the vent. Dorsal spine entire: adipose fin short. Mud coloured, with three vertical greenish bands. Ganges and Jumna, to about 2 inches in length.

68. *Macrones (?) botius*, Ham. Buch. D. ⅙/0, A. 11. Barbels shorter than the head. Dorsal spine entire. Brown. Northern Bengal, to 6 inches in length.

69. *Macrones leucophasis*, Blyth. D. ⅐/0, A. 11. Maxillary barbels reach the end of anal fin. Dorsal spine posteriorly serrated: adipose fin prolonged. Black, with some white spots. Burma.

70. *Macrones vittatus*, Bloch. D. ⅐/0, A. 8-10. Maxillary barbels reach the middle of the ventral fin: dorsal spine serrated on both sides. Malabar and Coromandel Coast.

71. *Macrones Malabaricus.* D. $\frac{1}{7}$/0, A. 10. Maxillary barbels reach the middle of the ventral fin: dorsal spine short and entire: pectoral serrated on both sides. A round black shoulder mark. Malabar.

72. *Macrones oculatus,* Cuv. and Val. *Cuaree,* Mal. D. $\frac{1}{7}$/0, A. 11. Eye large. Maxillary barbels reach the caudal fin. Occipital process extends to the base of the dorsal fin. Dorsal spine serrated on both sides: adipose fin short. Uniform, with two indistinct, lateral, longitudinal bands. Southern India and Malabar.

73. *Macrones tengara,* Ham. Buch. D. $\frac{1}{7}$/0, A. 10. *Ting-ga-rah* and *Karaal,* Panj.: *Mulleer* and *Kug-ger,* Sind. Maxillary barbels reach the caudal. Dorsal spine entire: adipose fin long. Longitudinal bands and a dark shoulder mark. Upper portions of Jumna and Ganges, Panjáb and Sind, to 6 inches in length.

74. *Macrones keletius,* Bleeker. D. $\frac{1}{7}$/0, A. 9. Maxillary barbels reach the base of anal fin. Dorsal spine entire: adipose fin short. Greyish, with two light longitudinal bands. Jumna and Ganges, also Panjáb, not attaining a large size.

75. *Macrones (?) cavia,* Ham. Buch. *Kanya teng-gara,* Hind. D. $\frac{1}{8}$/0, A. 9. Maxillary barbels as long as the head. Dorsal spine entire: adipose fin short. Brownish, with two transverse bands across the tail. Northern Bengal, attaining 6 inches in length.

Genus—RITA, Bleeker.

Gogrius, Day.

Branchiostegals eight. Eyelids without free circular margins. Mouth transverse: upper jaw the longer. Nostrils on either side contiguous, but the pair on one side widely separated from that on the other. Barbels six, a minute pair at the posterior nostrils, a maxillary and one mandibular pair. Granular or molar-form teeth on the palate. Rayed dorsal fin, with one spine and six rays: the adipose and the anal of moderate lengths: ventral with six or eight rays: caudal forked. Air-vessel large, not enclosed in bone, whilst it may possess posterior elongations.

76. *Rita ritoides,* Cuv. & Val. D. $\frac{1}{6}$/0, A. 12. Humeral process about as long as the head. Air-vessel with posterior horn-like prolongations. Gangetic Provinces, Panjáb, Sind and Burma, attaining a foot in length.

77. *Rita pavimentata,* Val. D. $\frac{1}{6}$/0, A. 12. Humeral process about half as long as the head. Deccan and Bombay.

78. *Rita kuturnee,* Sykes. D. $\frac{1}{6}$/0, A. 12. Humeral process two-thirds as long as the head. Air-vessel without posterior prolongations. Deccan.

79. *Rita (?) rama,* Ham. Buch. D. $\frac{2}{4}$/0, A. 15. Assam.

Genus—ARIUS, Cuv. & Val.

Sciades, sp., et *Ariodes,* Mull. & Trosch.: *Hexanematichthys, Guitinga, Hemiarius, Cephalocassis, Netuma,* et *Pseudarius,* Bleeker.

Branchiostegals from five to six. Head osseous superiorly or covered with very thin skin. Eyes with free orbital margins. Mouth anterior: upper jaw generally the longer. Anterior and posterior nostrils placed close together, the latter being provided with a valve. Barbels six, one maxillary and two mandibular pairs. Teeth in the jaws villiform, always palatine, and sometimes vomerine ones, these may be villiform or granular. First dorsal with one spine and seven rays: the adipose of moderate length or short: pectoral spine strong and serrated: ventral with six rays, situated behind the vertical from the posterior margin of the first dorsal fin: caudal forked or emarginate. Air-vessel not enclosed in bone.

80. *Arius gagora*, Ham. Buch. *Nga-youn* and *Nga-yeh*, Burm. D. $\frac{1}{0}$, A. 18-19. Teeth, palatine, molar form. Silvery. Seas of India and Burma, ascending large rivers above tidal influence, and attaining about a foot in length.

81. *Arius Burmanicus*, Day. *Nga-young*, Burm. D. $\frac{1}{0}$, A. 20-22. Maxillary barbels reach the base of the pectoral fin. Teeth in palate villiform, in two widely set patches. Colours purplish above, silvery below. Rivers of Burma.

82. *Arius sona*, Ham. Buch. D. $\frac{1}{0}$, A. 16-17. Maxillary barbels reach the end of the head. Teeth in palate villiform, in two triangular patches, almost confluent with the vomerine ones. Brownish, becoming white below. Ascends large Indian and Burmese rivers, often above tidal influence.

Genus—PANGASIUS, Cuv. & Val.

Pseudopangasius, pt., Bleeker.

Branchiostegals from about six to twelve. Gill-membranes over-lap the isthmus, but are more or less separate from it. Eyes with free orbital margins. Upper jaw the longer. Anterior nostrils patent and situated in front of snout. Barbels four, slender, one maxillary, and at some distance behind the symphysis, one mandibular pair. Teeth villiform in the jaws, intermixed with conical ones: they are also present in the vomer and palate, the continuity of these two last being usually interrupted. A short first dorsal, with a spine and seven rays situated anterior to the ventrals: adipose fin short: anal long, not confluent with the caudal, which latter is forked: ventrals with six rays. Air-vessel (in P. Buchanani) thick, elongated, extending from the anterior vertebræ to opposite the posterior end of the anal fin, it has a slight contraction between its anterior and posterior two-thirds.

83. *Pangasius Buchanani*, Cuv. and Val. *Jellum*, Ooriah. D. $\frac{1}{0}$, A. 31-34. Large rivers and estuaries of India and Burma, attaining four feet or more in length.

Genus—PSEUDEUTROPIUS, Bleeker.

Schilbeichthys, Bleeker.

Branchiostegals from six to ten. Body elongated and compressed. Abdominal profile more convex than that of the back. Eyes large, generally having broad adipose lids, situated behind and slightly below the angle of the mouth, often partly on the lower surface of the head. Head covered with soft skin. Mouth anterior; upper jaw generally the longer. Nostrils patent, transverse, the posterior being nearer to one another than they are to the anterior ones. Barbels eight, one pair at the posterior nostrils, one maxillary, and two mandibular pairs, these last arising on a transverse line close to the hind margin of the lower lip. Teeth villiform in the jaws, vomer, and palate. Dorsal fin short, with one spine, and six or seven rays; a very small adipose dorsal, which may be absorbed in the adult (Schilbeichthys): pectoral with a serrated spine; anal long, terminating at some distance from a forked caudal: ventral with six, or it may have eight rays. Airvessel heart-shaped, and closely attached to the anterior vertebræ.

84. *Pseudeutropius atherinoides*, Bl. *Put-tul* and *Chel-lee*, Panj.: *Ath-hee*, Sind.: *Put-tah-re*, N. W. Prov.: *Akku jella*, Tel.: *Battuli* and *Bo-potassi*, Ooriah. D. $\frac{1}{6-8}$/0, A. 36-42. Maxillary barbels reach base of anal fin. Three or four longitudinal lateral bands. Throughout the fresh-waters of the plains of India and Burma, attaining about four inches in length.

85. *Pseudeutropius goongwaree*, Sykes. *Nga-myenoke-hpa*, Burm. D. $\frac{1}{6}$/0, A. 43-54. Maxillary barbels reach anal fin. Silvery. Deccan, Bengal and Burma, attaining 10 inches in length.

86. *Pseudeutropius taakree*, Sykes. *Salava jella*, Tel.: *Nga-zin-sap* and *Nga-myin*, Burm. D. $\frac{1}{6-7}$/0, A. 51. Maxillary barbels reach the anal fin. Silvery. Deccan and the Kistna River, also Orissa and Burma, attaining a foot in length.

87. *Pseudeutropius acutirostris*, Day. D. $\frac{1}{6}$/0, A. 46. The maxillary barbels reach the anal fin. Silvery; a black spot on occiput, and a black base to the dorsal fin. Rivers of Burma, mostly in their lower portions. It attains four inches in length.

88. *Pseudeutropius murius*, Ham. Buch. *Ke-raad*, Panj.: *Motusi*, Beng.: *Butchua*, Hind.: *Muri-vacha*, Ooriah. D. $\frac{1}{6}$/0, A. 39-43. Maxillary barbels reach the base of the anal fin. Silvery. Panjáb, Gangetic Provinces, and Orissa, attaining eight inches or more in length.

89. *Pseudeutropius Sykesii*, Jerdon. *Nah kellettee*, Tam. D. $\frac{1}{6}$/0, A. 35-37. Southern Madras and Malabar, to six inches or more in length.

90. *Pseudeutropius garua*, Ham. Buch. *Punia buchua*, Ooriah: *Pultosi*, Beng.: *Buchua*, Beng.: *Dhon-ga-nu*, Sind.: *Buchua*, *Chel-lee* and *Ka-raad*, Panj. D. $\frac{1}{6}$, A. 29-36. Maxillary barbels reach the ventral fin. Adipose dorsal fin becomes absorbed in the adult. Silvery. Larger rivers of India, except Southern Madras, Malabar and Burma, attaining a foot or more in length.

Genus—CALLICHROUS, Ham. Buch.

Kryptopterus, Kryptopterichthys, Micronema, Phalacronotus, Hemisilurus, Silurodes, Pseudosilurus and *Silurichthys*, Bleeker: *Pterocryptis*, pt., Peters.

Gill-membranes overlap the isthmus, but are more or less separated from it. Head covered with skin. Eyes behind and slightly below the cleft of the mouth, lateral, or sometimes partly on the inferior surface of the head; lids without free orbital margins. Cleft of mouth oblique; lower jaw the longer. Nostrils remote from one another. Barbels four or two, one maxillary, and some distance behind the symphysis, one mandibular pair, the latter may be rudimentary or absent. Teeth villiform in the jaws in an uninterrupted band (Silurodes, Bleeker) or interrupted one (Callichrous, Bleeker) on the vomer, none on the palatines. Dorsal fin spineless, short, rudimentary, or absent; when present, anterior to the ventrals: no adipose fin:

pectoral with a serrated or entire spine (sometimes apparently due to sex) : anal long continuous with or terminating close to the caudal, the latter forked or emarginate : ventrals with ten or less rays. Air-vessel in the abdominal cavity not enclosed in bone.

    a. Vomerine teeth in an uninterrupted band.

  91. *Callichrous Gangeticus,* Peters. D. 2, A. 75. Four barbels, the maxillary hardly reach the anal. Vomerine teeth in this species in an uninterrupted band. Anal confluent with caudal. Stated to have been obtained from the Ganges.

    b. Vomerine teeth in an interrupted band.

  92. *Callichrous macrophthalmus,* Blyth. *Nga-noo-than* and *Nga-myin-bouk,* Burm. D. 4, A. 74-76. Eyes, diameter ⅓rd of length of head. Four barbels, the maxillary reaching to the middle of the length of the fish. Vomerine teeth in this, and all the succeeding species, in an interrupted band. Anal not confluent with the caudal; pectoral spine strongly serrated internally in its last half. A round black blotch above the posterior third of the pectoral fin. Irrawaddi and all its branches.

  93. *Callichrous pabo,* Ham. Buch. D. 5, A. 73. Four barbels, the maxillary scarcely reaching beyond the eye. Anal not confluent with the caudal; pectoral spine serrated internally. Assam.

  94. *Callichrous checkra,* Ham. Buch. *Dim-mon,* Sind: *Chelah-wahlah,* Tam.: *Pob-tah,* Ooriah. D. 4, A. 73. Four barbels, the maxillary reaching the end of the pectoral spine. Anal not confluent with the caudal; pectoral spine serrated internally. Sind, Bombay Presidency, Central Provinces, Mysore, and portions of Madras and Bengal.

  95. *Callichrous nigrescens,* Day. D. 5, A. 66-71. Four barbels, the maxillary reach the posterior edge of the orbit. Anal not confluent with the caudal; pectoral spine entire. Finely dotted with black points. Rivers of Burma.

  96. *Callichrous notatus,* Day. D. 4, A. 65-73. Four barbels, the maxillary reach to the middle of the length of the fish. Anal not confluent with the caudal; pectoral spine serrated internally near its end. A round black spot above the middle of the pectoral fin. Burmese rivers, to four inches in length.

  97. *Callichrous bimaculatus,* Bl. *Pob-tah, Puf-ta, Goong-wah,* and *Pallu,* Panj.: *Goong-wah-ree* and *Puf-ta,* N. W. Prov. D. 4, A. 57-66. Four barbels, the maxillary reach the middle of the fish. Anal not confluent with the caudal; pectoral spine internally denticulated near its end. A round black spot above the middle of the pectoral fin. Throughout India and Burma.

  98. *Callichrous latovittatus,* Playfair. D. 4, A. 56-58. Four barbels (stated erroneously only to have two), the maxillary reaching to the end of the pectoral fin. Anal not confluent with the caudal; pectoral spine strongly denticulated internally. Cachar, to 4½ inches in length.

  99. *Callichrous pabda,* Ham. Buch. D. 4, A. 54. Four barbels, the maxillary reaching to the second third of the anal fin. Anal not confluent with the caudal; pectoral spine smooth. A black blotch behind the gill-opening. Ganges.

100. *Callichrous Egertonii*, Day. *Pul-wu-ah* and *Pallu*, Panj.: *Pah-ba-noon*, Sind. D. 4, A. 52-54. Four barbels, the maxillary extend slightly beyond the base of the pectoral fin. Anal not confluent with the caudal; pectoral spine denticulated internally. Numerous brownish blotches cover the body, and a large black one exists over the posterior half of the pectoral fin. Panjáb and Sind.

ϒ 101. *Callichrous anastomus*, Cuv. and Val. D. 4, A. 52-54. Four barbels, the maxillary reach the anal fin. Anal not confluent with the caudal; pectoral spine serrated internally. A round black spot behind the gill-opening. Hooghly.

Genus—WALLAGO, Bleeker.

Branchiostegals from fifteen to twenty-one. Body elongated and compressed, the dorsal profile straight. Eyes above the level of the angle of the mouth. Head covered with skin. Cleft of mouth deep. Snout rather produced: lower jaw slightly the longer. Barbels four, one maxillary and one mandibular pair. Teeth numerous and cardiform in both jaws, and in an oblique patch on either side of the vomer: none on the palatines. A short, spineless dorsal, situated above, or slightly before, the ventrals: no adipose fin: anal long, terminating near the caudal, which last consists of two rounded lobes: ventrals with from eight to eleven rays. Air-vessel heart-shaped, not enclosed in bone.

102. *Wallago attu*, Bl. *Bo-al-le* and *Mul-lee*, Panj.: *Po-i-kee* and *Mul-lee*, Sind: *Vah-lah* and *Wah-lah*, Tam.: *Va-la-ga*, Tel.: *Bo-al-lee*, Ooriah: *Nga-bat*, Burm. D. 5, A. 86-93. Found throughout the Indian Empire, attaining several feet in length; it is esteemed as good eating, but is very voracious, and not a cleanly feeder. Sometimes this fish is termed a fresh-water shark by Europeans.

Genus—OLYRA, McClelland.

Branchiosteus, Gill.

Dorsal profile nearly horizontal. Body low and elongate. Head depressed, superiorly covered with soft skin. Gill-openings wide. Eyes small. Mouth terminal and transverse: jaws of about equal length, or the lower the longer. Nostrils remote from one another. Eight barbels, one to posterior nostril. Villiform teeth in the jaws and on the palate. First dorsal spineless, and having six or eight rays: adipose fin long and low: anal of moderate extent (15 to 23 rays). Ventrals inserted below the dorsal and having six rays. Caudal rounded or lanceolate. Skin smooth. Air-vessel not enclosed in bone.

• 103. *Olyra longicaudata*, McClelland. D. 7/0, A. 23. Jaws of equal length. Caudal lanceolate. Khasya Hills. This, and the following of the genus, are all small fish.

104. *Olyra Burmanica*, Day. D. 8/0, A. 16. Jaws of equal length. Caudal lanceolate. Pegu Hills.

105. *Olyra laticeps*, McClelland. D. 6/0, A. 15. Lower jaw the longer. Caudal rounded. Khasya Hills.

Genus—SILURUS, Artedi.

Dorsal profile nearly horizontal; neck not elevated. Head covered with skin; eyes situated above the level of the angle of the mouth. Gape of mouth transverse. Nostrils remote from one another. Barbels six (Silurus, Bleeker), *or four (Parasilurus,* Bleeker), *one pair being maxillary, and one or two pairs mandibular. Teeth cardiform or villiform in the jaws, in one or two transverse bands on the vomer, none on the palatines. One very short and spineless first dorsal fin, but no adipose one: anal terminates close to, but is not continuous with the caudal: ventral situated posterior to the dorsal, and consisting of eight or more rays. Air-vessel in the abdominal cavity, not enclosed in bone.*

106. *Silurus Wynaadensis,* Day. D. 5, A. 58-62. Six barbels. Leaden colour. Wynaad.

107. *Silurus Cochinsinensis,* Cuv. & Val. D. 4, A. 62. Dark coloured. Darjeeling, Akyab, Tenasserim Provinces to Cochin China.

Genus—CHACA, *Cuv. & Val.*

Head very large, broad and depressed. Gill-membranes confluent, with the skin of a broad isthmus, and the gill-opening somewhat contracted; eyes minute. Gape of mouth very wide, lower jaw prominent. Barbels six, small. Teeth villiform in both jaws, none on the palate. Two rayed dorsal fins, the first with one spine and three or four rays, the second confluent with the caudal: two rayed anal fins, the first with from eight to ten rays, the second longer (8 to 12) and confluent with the caudal: ventral with six rays: air-vessel in the abdominal cavity, not enclosed in bone.

108. *Chaca lophioides,* Cuv. & Val. D. $\frac{1}{4}$/25, A. 10/12. Some short tentacles on head and body. Ganges. Dr. Günther states there is a stuffed specimen in the British Museum of this fish from Nepal, presented by Mr. Hodgson: it is also found in Calcutta.

109. *Chaca Bankanensis,* Bleeker. D.$\frac{1}{3-4}$/22-24, A. 9/11-12. No tentacles; head and body granular. Assam and Burma.

110. *Chaca Buchanani,* Günther. D. $\frac{1}{4}$/18, A. 8/8. Head and body with short tentacles; a ring of them around the eye.

Sub-Family—AMBLYCEPINÆ.

Air-vessel more or less enclosed in bone.

Genus—CLARIAS, *Gronov.*

Macropteronotus, Lacép.

Form of body elongated and compressed. Gill-membranes separated by a deep notch; a dendritic accessory branchial apparatus is attached to the convex side of the second and fourth branchial arches, and is received into a recess behind the place of the usual gill-cavity. Eyes small, the lids having a free circular margin. Superior and lateral portions of the head osseous, and covered with very thin skin. Gape of mouth moderate, anterior, and transverse, its cleft small. Barbels eight, one nasal, one maxillary and two mandibular pairs. Villiform teeth in the jaws, and a similar or granular band across the vomer. Dorsal fin spineless and with an elongated base, extending from the neck to the caudal, with which it may be continuous: no adipose fin: ventrals with six rays: pectoral with a spine. Air-vessel small, transverse, entirely enclosed in a bony cavity, formed across the body and lateral processes of the anterior vertebræ.

111. Clarias jagur, Ham. Buch. D. 53, A. 50. Maxillary barbels slightly longer than the head, vertical fins united. Buchanan does not mention where this species resides, as yet I have not found it; attains 1½ feet in length.

112. Clarias magur, Ham. Buch. *Kug-ga,* Panj.: *Ma-gur,* Beng.: *Nga-khoo,* Burm. D. 64-70, A. 50-53. Maxillary barbels reach nearly to the end of the pectoral fin; vertical fins not united; dirty brown colour. Fresh-waters of the plains of India and Burma; attaining 18 inches in length, and as food considered very nourishing.

Genus—SACCOBRANCHUS, *Cuv. and Val.*

Heteropneustes, Müller.

Branchiostegals seven. Form of body elongated and compressed. Gill-membranes separated by a deep notch: gill-cavity with an accessory posterior sac, which extends backwards on either side of the neural spines, amongst the muscles of the abdominal and part of the caudal regions. Eyes small, the lids having a free circular margin. Superior and lateral portions of the head osseous, and covered with very thin skin. Gape of mouth moderate, anterior, transverse, the cleft small. Barbels eight. Villiform teeth in the jaws, and vomer. Dorsal fin spineless and short: adipose absent: ventral under the dorsal: anal long, confluent with, or separated by a notch from the caudal. Air-vessel placed transversely (in the form of two lobes connected by a tube) across the body of an anterior vertebra, where it is entirely enclosed in bone: a duct passes forwards from either sides, unites and is continued into the pharynx.

113. Saccobranchus fossilis, Bloch. *Sin-gee* and *Noor-i-e,* Panj.: *Lo-har,* Sind: *Thar-lee,* Tam.: *Mar-pu,* Tel.: *Sin-gee,* Ooriah, Beng., and in North-West Provinces; *Bichu ka mutchee,* Hind.: *Nga-gyce* and *Nga-kyee,* Burm. D. 6-7, A. 60-79. Maxillary barbels reach the middle of pectoral or even commencement of the ventral fins. Leaden, sometimes with two longitudinal yellow bands. Throughout the fresh-waters of India and Burma.

Genus—SILUNDIA, *Cuv. and Val.*

Branchiostegals eleven to twelve. Body elongated and compressed. Head covered with soft skin. Eyes lateral, having a free circular orbital margin. Mouth wide, lower jaw the longer. Nostrils wide apart, the anterior pair being in front of the snout, patent, and external to the posterior pair. Teeth in the jaws, and in a crescentic villiform band on the palate. First dorsal fin with one spine and seven rays, the adipose short; anal long: ventral with six rays: caudal forked. Air-vessel lying across the body of an anterior vertebra where there is a groove for its reception, and an osseous process from either side of the vertebra to protect its lateral edges.

114. Silundia Gangetica, Cuv. and Val. *Si-lond,* Panj.; *Wal-la-ke kel-le-tee* (slippery siluroid) and *Poo-nat-tee,* Tam.: *Wan-jou,* Tel.: *Jil-lung* and *Si-lond,* Ooriah and Beng. D. $\frac{1}{7}$/0, A. 40-46. Barbels short. Silvery, fins stained with grey. Estuaries and large rivers of India and Burma; attaining 6 feet or more in length, and is sometimes termed a shark.

Genus—AILIA, Cuv. and Val.

Body elongated and compressed. Head covered with thin skin. Eyes nearly or quite behind the angle of the mouth, and with adipose lids. Upper jaw slightly the longer. Nostrils on either side approximating to one another, the anterior being in front of the snout. Barbels eight—one nasal pair, also one maxillary, the two mandibular pairs arise in a transverse line behind the symphysis. Villiform teeth in the jaws, and in two minute patches on the vomer. A small adipose dorsal fin: ventral with six rays, anal elongated, terminating at a short distance from the caudal which latter is forked. Air-vessel, a transverse tube passing across the body of an anterior vertebra, and more or less enclosed in bone.

115. *Ailia Bengalensis*, Gray. *Pufta*, Panj.: *Mun-glee-ah-nee*, Sind: *Bounce-putti*, Ooriah. D. 0., A. 60-72. The barbels extend to nearly the middle of the length of the fish. Silvery, some of the fins frequently stained with grey at their edges. This small, but well-flavoured fish is found throughout all the large rivers of India and Burma, excluding those of Madras and Bombay. It attains about 7 inches in length.

Genus—AILIICHTHYS, Day.

Differs from Ailia, being destitute of ventral fins.

116. *Ailiichthys punctata*, Day. *Put-tas-si* and *Put-tu-ah*, Panj. D. 0, A. 76-82. Barbels extend to the middle of the length of the fish. Silvery; upper surface of the head nearly black; a large black spot at the base of the caudal fin. Upper portions of the Jumna, the Indus and its affluents. It attains at least 4 inches in length.

Genus—EUTROPIICHTHYS, Bleeker.

Branchiostegals eleven. Body and head compressed; nape slightly elevated. Branchiostegal aperture wide, its membranes not being confluent with the skin of the isthmus. Head covered by skin. Eyes situated above the angle of the mouth, and having broad adipose lids. Cleft of mouth deep, the lower jaw slightly the longer. Nostrils wide. Barbels eight, one nasal, one maxillary, and two mandibular pairs. Teeth in the upper jaw sharp, and in a wide band, also in a broad band on the vomer and palatines. First dorsal fin short, with a spine and seven rays: adipose dorsal also short: ventral with six rays, and situated below the first dorsal: anal having an elongated base, but terminating some distance from the caudal, which latter fin is deeply forked. Air-vessel narrow, tubiform, passing transversely across the body of an anterior vertebra, and all but its central portion received into a bony capsule.

117. *Eutropiichthys vacha*, Ham. Buch. *Chel-lee*, Sind.: *Buchua* and *Nandi-buchua*, Ooriah: *Nee-much*, N.-W. Prov.: *Nga-myen-kouban*, and *katha-boung*, Burm. D. $\frac{1}{7}/0$, A. 47-50. Barbels about as long as the head. Silvery, greyish along the back. Rivers of India and Burma, attaining upwards of a foot in length.

Genus—SISOR, Ham. Buch.

Branchiostegals four. Gill-openings narrow and chiefly lateral. Opercles moveable. Head and trunk rather broad and depressed. Eyes small.

Head osseous and rough in places. A longitudinal row of bony plates along the median line of the back. Mouth small, transverse, inferior. Nostrils round, close together, but separated by a valve. Barbels, one pair of maxillary and several of mandibular. Teeth absent. A single short dorsal fin, without a distinct spine: ventral with seven rays: anal short: caudal with the upper ray prolonged. Air-vessel enclosed in a bony capsule.

118. *Sisor rabdophorus*, Ham. Buch. *Kir-ri-dee*, Sind. D. $\frac{1}{6}$, A. 6. Maxillary barbels reach base of pectoral spine: a species of flap from lower lip with a moderately long barbel on either side, and two more intermediate but shorter ones: between these flaps are several short barbels on a transverse line across the chin, and several more minute ones on the isthmus. Blackish above, lighter below. Upper portions of Ganges, Jumna, and Indus with its affluents, attaining several feet in length.

Genus—GAGATA, Bleeker.

Callomystax, Günther.

Branchiostegals about six. Gill-openings of moderate width, the membrane being confluent with the skin of the isthmus: thorax destitute of plaits. Superior surface of the head with rather rough ridges, and covered by very thin skin. Eyes subcutaneous. Mouth below the snout, small and transverse. Nostrils close together, rounded, the posterior being provided with a small barbel. Barbels eight, the maxillary slightly osseous, and having a broad basal membrane: the two pairs of mandibular ones in a transverse row just behind the lower lip. Small teeth in both jaws; none on the palate. First dorsal having one strong spine and six rays: adipose fin of moderate length: ventral with six rays, situated entirely posterior to the dorsal: caudal deeply forked. Air-vessel in two portions, and enclosed in bony capsules formed from the bodies of an anterior vertebra: these lateral portions, which are globular, communicate with one another.

119. *Gagata typus*, Bleeker. *Puttah-chettah*, Ooriah. D. $\frac{1}{6}$/0, A. 15. Maxillary barbels reach a little beyond the root of the pectoral. Dull grey; the outer two-thirds of the pectoral, dorsal and anal fins black; caudal white. Estuaries and large rivers of Lower Bengal and Burma, attaining about a foot in length.

Genus—HEMIPIMELODUS, Bleeker.

Branchiostegals five or six. Gill-openings infero-lateral, the membranes attached to the isthmus. Upper surface of the head osseous. Eyes subcutaneous. Upper jaw the longer. Nostrils approximating, the posterior being provided with a valve or even with a barbel. Barbels six or eight: if six, consisting of one maxillary and two mandibular pairs: if eight, likewise a nasal pair. Villiform teeth in the jaws: palate edentulous. First dorsal with one spine and six or seven rays: adipose fin short, or of moderate length: pectoral spine strong: anal without an elongated base: ventral with six rays, situated posteriorly to the dorsal: caudal forked. Air-vessel divided into two lobes and enclosed in bone.

a. With eight barbels.

120. *Hemipimelodus itchkeea*, Sykes. D. $\frac{1}{7}$/0, A. 13. Eight barbels, a short nasal pair. Yellowish bronze, three dark blotches on the

head, and four irregular black bands descending from the back as low as the lateral line: a black edging to caudal fin, and a similar mark on either lobe: dorsal fin also with a dark mark. Deccan, to a few inches in length.

b. With six barbels.

121. Hemipimelodus cenia, Ham. Buch. *Pud-du-ah, Chet-wu-ah,* and *Kul-la,* Panj.: *Ce-ni-a,* Sind.: *Jungla* and *Ce-ni-a,* Beng.: *Nganan-joung,* Burm. D. $\frac{1}{6\text{-}7}$/0, A. 13. Six barbels, no nasal pair; otherwise resembles the last species, excepting that its air-vessel is smaller. Large rivers of India (excluding most of Madras) and Burma. It attains 5 inches in length.

122. Hemipimelodus viridescens, Ham. Buch. *Hud-daï,* N. W. Prov. D. $\frac{1}{6}$/0. A. 11. Greenish brown, with two light green bands: a dark mark on the dorsal fin, and each lobe of the caudal with a similar blotch. Jumna River. It is only a small species.

Genus—BAGARIUS, Bleeker.

Branchiostegals twelve. Gill-membranes with their posterior margins free: thorax without any plaits on skin. Superior surface of the head osseous. Eyes small. Mouth anterior: lower jaw the longer. Nostrils close together, divided by a barbel, which belongs to the posterior one. Barbels eight—one nasal, one maxillary, and two mandibular pairs. Teeth in the jaws cardiform and of unequal size. First dorsal fin in advance of the ventral, having one spine and six rays: adipose fin rather short: ventral with six rays: anal of moderate extent: caudal deeply forked. Air-vessel small, consisting of two rounded portions, situated on either side of the body of an anterior vertebra, and partially enclosed in bone.

123. Bagarius Yarrellii, Sykes. Goonch, Panj.: *Rahti-jella,* Tel.: *Sah-lun,* Ooriah. D. $\frac{1}{6}$/0, A. 13-15. Yellowish, with large irregular brown or black markings and cross bands; a black base to the fins; all have likewise a black band, except the adipose dorsal. Large rivers of India, extending to Java. It descends to the estuaries, and attains 6 feet or more in length.

Genus—PSEUDECHENEIS, Blyth.

Body somewhat elongate. Head depressed. Gill-openings small, not extending to the lower surface of the head. An adhesive apparatus, formed of transverse folds of skin, situated between the bases of the pectoral fins, and on the thorax. Head covered superiorly with soft skin. Eyes small, on the upper surface of the head. Mouth small, inferior. Nostrils on either side close together and divided by a barbel. Barbels eight, the maxillary pair having broad bases. Teeth villiform in the jaws, none on the palate. Dorsal fin with one spine and six rays: the adipose one of moderate extent: pectorals horizontal, spine finely serrated: ventral with six rays, and situated under the dorsal: caudal forked. Air-vessel in two rounded lateral portions, entirely enclosed in bone.

124. Pseudecheneis sulcatus, McClelland. D. $\frac{1}{6}$/0, A. 11. Blackish, with some large irregular yellowish blotches (of ground colour): fins yellow with black bands. Rivers below Darjeeling and the Khasya Hills. It attains at least $5\frac{1}{2}$ inches in length.

Genus—GLYPTOSTERNUM, McClelland.

Glyptothorax, pt., Blyth.

Branchiostegals about ten. Gill-opening wide; gill-membranes separated by, and confluent with, the isthmus. An adhesive apparatus formed of longitudinal plaits of skin, situated between the bases of the pectoral fins on the thorax, which frequently become indistinct in old individuals. Head more or less depressed, and generally covered with soft skin. Eyes small, subcutaneous. Mouth inferior. Barbels eight, the maxillary ones having very broad bases. Teeth in the jaws villiform, palate edentulous. Dorsal with one spine and six rays: adipose fin rather short: pectorals horizontal: ventral situated posterior to the dorsal and having six rays: anal rather short: sometimes the pectoral and ventral rays are plaited inferiorly. Air-vessel in two rounded lateral portions, enclosed in bony capsules.

125. *Glyptosternum striatum*, McClelland. *Now-u* and *Nah-he*, if small *Jup-pah*, Panj. D. $\frac{1}{6}$/0,-A. 9-11. Breadth of head nearly equals its length. Maxillary barbels extend beyond the root of the pectoral. Lips not fringed. Occipital process three times as long as broad. Caudal peduncle nearly twice as long as high. Dorsal spine more than half as long as the head. In the young, the outer pectoral and ventral rays are plaited inferiorly. Brown, fins yellow stained with black. Rivers on and along the bases of the Himalayas.

126. *Glyptosternum lonah*, Sykes. D. $\frac{1}{6}$/0, A. 11-12. Breadth of head nearly or quite equal to its length. Maxillary barbels extend to the end of the head. Lips not fringed. Occipital process nearly four times as long as broad. Caudal peduncle twice as long as high. Fin rays not plaited. Dorsal spine not quite half as long as the head. Yellowish brown, banded with blackish, fins yellow. Dorsal, caudal, and anal with black bands. Deccan, attaining at least 6 inches in length.

127. *Glyptosternum trilineatum*, Blyth. D. $\frac{1}{6}$/0, A. 13. Breadth of head about equals its length. Maxillary barbels reach to the end of the head. Lips not fringed. Occipital process nearly three times as long as broad. Caudal peduncle twice as long as high. Fins rays not plaited inferiorly. Dorsal spine rather above half the length of the head. Chestnut brown, with three light longitudinal bands. Burma and Nepal (?), attaining 12 inches or more in length.

128. *Glyptosternum telchitta*, Ham. Buch. *Til-li-ah*, Panj. and N. W. Prov.: *Go-a-che-rah*, Beng. D. $\frac{1}{6}$/0, A. 11. Head longer than broad. Maxillary barbels extend to the posterior edge of the orbit. Lips roughened, but not fringed. Occipital process three times as long as broad. Caudal peduncle twice as long as high. Fin rays not plaited inferiorly. Dorsal spine two-thirds as long as the head. Blackish-brown, fins yellow with black bands. Caudal black, with a yellow edge. From the Panjáb through Bengal and Behar, attaining 5 or 6 inches in length.

129. *Glyptosternum Dekkanense*, Günther. D. $\frac{1}{6}$/0, A. 11. The breadth of the head equals its post-nasal length. Maxillary barbels extend to the base of the pectoral. Lips smooth. Occipital process from five to six times longer than broad. Caudal peduncle about twice

as long as high. Fin rays not plaited inferiorly. Dorsal spine half as long as the head. Blackish, fins yellowish. Dorsal, caudal, and anal banded with black. Jumna, near where it emerges from the Sewaliks, said to be found in the Deccan. Attains 6 inches in length.

130. *Glyptosternum modestum*, Day. D. $\frac{1}{6}$/0, A. 9. The breadth of the head equals its length. Maxillary barbels nearly as long as the head. Lips not fringed. Occipital process slightly longer than broad at its base. Caudal peduncle two-thirds as high as long. Fin rays not plaited inferiorly. Dorsal spine half as long as the head. Uniform brown. Upper portions of Jumna and rivers near Simla. It attains 3 inches in length.

Genus—AMBLYCEPS, Blyth.

Branchiostegals twelve. Gill-opening wide; gill-membranes not confluent with the skin of the isthmus. No thoracic adhesive surface. Head covered with soft skin. Eyes small, subcutaneous. Mouth broad, anterior. Barbels eight. Teeth in jaws villiform: palate edentulous. First dorsal fin enveloped in skin, and having one spine and six rays: pectoral with a short concealed spine: ventrals inserted behind the vertical from the posterior margin of the dorsal, and having six rays: anal rather short: caudal forked. Lateral line absent. Air-vessel almost wholly enclosed in a bony capsule.

131. *Amblyceps mangois*, Ham. Buch. Soock-se, Bil-li, and Su-daal Panj. D. $\frac{1}{6}$/0, A. 11-12. Head as wide as long. Maxillary barbels reach the end of the pectoral spine. Occipital process rudimentary. Caudal peduncle as deep as long. Olive brown, with a dark line commencing opposite the opercles, and dividing into two, one proceeding to the centre of the caudal, the inferior to the base of the anal. Jumna, from its source to Ghazipur on the Ganges, likewise the Kangra valley and hills. It attains 4 inches in length.

132. *Amblyceps cæcutiens*, Blyth. D. $\frac{1}{6}$/0, A. 9. Caudal said to be more sharply forked than in the preceding species. No bands. Burma.

Genus—EXOSTOMA, Blyth.

Gill-openings narrow. Eyes small. Head depressed, covered superiorly with soft skin. No thoracic adhesive apparatus. Mouth inferior, with the lips reflected around it, and mostly covered with glands. Barbels eight or six: when the latter, either one mandibular, or the maxillary pair are absent. Teeth in the jaws in a single or double row: palate edentulous. Dorsal fin with a slender or rudimentary spine and six rays; adipose fin long: pectorals horizontal: ventrals with six rays: caudal cut square, emarginate or forked. Air-vessel in two lateral lobes, both of which are enclosed in bone.

133. *Exostoma Blythii*, Day. D. $\frac{1}{6}$/0, A. 7. Head as wide as long. Six barbels, the maxilla being destitute of any, but terminating in a fleshy appendage. Yellowish brown. Rivers below Darjeeling, to above 3 inches in length.

134. *Exostoma labiatum*, McClelland. D. $\frac{1}{6}$/0, A. 6. Eight barbels, the maxillary extend to the pectoral fin. Lips broad, having a median and lateral lobe on either side with a barbel between. Colour uniform. Mishni Mountain, East Assam.

135. *Exostoma Berdmorei*, Blyth. D. 1/0, A. 6. Eight barbels. Snout pointed. Caudal forked. Tenasserim Provinces.

Family—SCOMBRESOCIDÆ.

Pharyngognathi malacopterygii, Muller.

Pseudobranchiæ concealed, glandular. Margin of upper jaw formed mesially by the inter-maxillaries: laterally by the maxillaries. Barbels present or absent. Lower pharyngeals united into a single bone. Dorsal fin rayed, with or without finlets posterior to it, and situated opposite the anal and in the caudal portion of the vertebral column, no adipose dorsal. Body scaled: usually a keeled row along either side of the free portion of the tail. Air-vessel generally present: sometimes cellular, and destitute of a pneumatic duct. Stomach and intestines in one straight tube, without division, and not having any pyloric appendages.

Genus—BELONE, *Cuv.*

Branchiostegals rather numerous. Body elongated, sub-cylindrical, or compressed. Gill-openings wide. Eyes lateral. The jaws prolonged into a long beak, the upper being formed of the inter-maxillaries. Fine teeth or rugosities in both jaws, with a single row of long, widely set conical ones. No finlets posterior to dorsal fin; caudal usually forked. Scales small. Lateral line on free portion of tail, with or without a keel.

136. *Belone cancila*, Ham. Buch. Kung-gah, Co-wa, Sou-ah and Kahaan, Panj.: Gon-gi-turi, Ooriah: Nga-oh-poung-yoh, Nga-phou-yo, Burm. B. x. D. 16-17, A. 16-17. Lateral line not keeled. Four or five dark blotches between the bases of the pectoral and anal fins. Throughout the waters of the plains of India and Burma.

Genus—HEMIRAMPHUS, *Cuv.*

Hyporhamphus, Euleptorhamphus, Zenarchopterus, and *Oxyporhamphus,* Gill: *Dermatogenys,* (K. and v. Hass.) Peters: *Hemiramphodon,* Bleeker.

Branchiostegals rather numerous. Body sub-cylindrical and elongated. Eyes lateral. Upper jaw, which is formed of the inter-maxillaries, is more or less triangular and short, whilst the lower jaw is elongated far beyond the upper, which prolongation is not so apparent in the immature. Teeth villiform in both jaws. No finlets posterior to the dorsal fin: pectoral may or may not be prolonged: caudal mostly forked or emarginate, sometimes rounded. Scales of moderate or large size. Air-vessel large, sometime cellular. Dorsal and anal rays may be modified. Some viviparous.

137. *Hemiramphus amblyurus*, Bleeker. Nga-phoung-yo, Burm. D. 13-14, A. 10-12, L. l. 48. Viviparous. An indistinct silvery lateral band. Mouths of the Ganges and other large rivers of Bengal and Burma, extending its range to above tidal influence.

Family—CYPRINODONTIDÆ.

Branchiostegals from four to six: pseudobranchiæ absent. Eyes lateral: margin of upper jaw formed entirely by the inter-maxillaries. Barbels absent. Teeth in both jaws, likewise in the superior and inferior pharyngeal bones. One spineless dorsal situated in the posterior half of the body. Stomach without *cul-de-sac.* No pyloric appendages. Air-vessel simple, destitute of connection with the auditory bones.

This family has been sub-divided into those with the mandibles united and intestines short, *C. carnivoræ;* and those with the mandibles disunited and intestines long, *C. limnophagæ.*

Genus—CYPRINODON, *Lacép.*

Lebias, Cuv.: *Aphanius,* Nardo.: *Micromugil,* Gulia.

Gape of mouth small: mandible short, with the bones on either side united. Teeth of moderate size, in a single row, and each being notched. The origin of the dorsal fin anterior to that of the anal, whilst it is largest in the male sex. Scales rather large. Colouration of sexes often different. Intestines rather short.

138. Cyprinodon Stolickanus, Day. D. 9, A. 9, L. l. 27, L. tr. 8. This small species is found in the waters of Cutch.

Genus—HAPLOCHILUS, *McClelland.*

Aplocheilus, McClelland: *Panchax,* Cuv. and Val: *Zygonectes,* Agassiz: *Micristius,* Gill.

Branchiostegals from four to six. Body rather elongated: sides compressed: upper surface of head broad and depressed. Upper jaw protractile. Mandibular bones united at the symphysis. Teeth villiform, in a narrow band on both jaws and sometimes on the vomer. Dorsal fin short, commencing behind the origin of the anal, which latter has an elongated base. Scales of medium size. Lateral line absent. Intestines of moderate length.

139. Haplochilus argenteus, Day. D. 6, A. 14, L. l. 27, L. tr. 11. Found near Madras, attaining 1½ inches in length.

140. Haplochilus lineatus, Cuv. and Val. D. 8-9, A. 15-16, L. l. 32-34, L. tr. 9. An emerald green spot on each scale; eight or ten vertical black bands on the body. Fins tipped with red. Attains 4 inches in length, and is found in Coorg and Malabar.

141. Haplochilus melastigmus, McClelland. D. 7, A. 22, L. l. 29, L. tr. 13. Found near Calcutta and Burma.

142. Haplochilus panchax, Ham. Buch. *Kanakuri,* Ooriah: *Ngacha-loom,* Akyab: *Cho-to-dah,* Andamanese. D. 8-9, A. 15-16, L. l. 32-34. A dark mark at the base of the dorsal fin. Bengal and the Andamans, attaining 5 inches in length.

143. Haplochilus rubrostigma, Jerdon. D. 8, A. 14-15. Numerous brilliant blue spots on the body, alternating with rusty red ones along the sides. Madras and Sind hills. This is a small species.

Family—CYPRINIDÆ.

Branchiostegals three: pseudobranchiæ generally present. Body oblong or elongated: abdomen usually rounded, but if compressed or cutting destitute of ossicles. Margin of the upper jaw formed by the inter-maxillaries. Opercles in four pieces. Mouth toothless, but from one to three rows of teeth in the inferior pharyngeal bones, which latter are strong, free and parallel to the branchial arches. A single-rayed dorsal fin. Head scaleless: body scaled or scaleless, never covered by osseous plates. No *cul de sac* to the stomach, nor pyloric appendages. Air-vessel, if present, large: it may be divided by a constriction into an anterior and posterior portion, neither of which are enclosed in bone (Cyprininæ): or into two lateral portions, partially or entirely enclosed in a bony capsule (Cobitidinæ): or absent (Homalopterinæ).

Sub-Family—CYPRININÆ.

Air-vessel present, not enclosed in bone.

A. Abdomen rounded, not cutting.

Genus—PSILORHYNCHUS, McClelland.

Back somewhat elevated. Head moderately depressed. Snout more or less spatulate. Mouth small, transverse, inferior. Lips entire, not continuous, reflected from off both jaws, and studded with glands. Barbels absent. Dorsal fin with few rays, commencing opposite the ventrals: pectorals horizontal, with their outer rays simple and unbranched: anal short. Scales of moderate size, none on the chest. Lateral line complete, continued direct to the centre of the base of the caudal fin.

144. Psilorhynchus balitora, Ham. Buch. D. 9-10, A. 7, L. l. 33. Reddish brown, irregularly marked with black. North-East Bengal and Assam.

145. Psilorhynchus sucatio, Ham. Buch. D. 9, A. 7. Snout much produced. Greenish, with scattered dots. North-East Bengal.

Genus—MAYOA, Day.

Body anteriorly depressed, posteriorly compressed: snout rounded and smooth. Barbels four, two on the snout, and one at each angle of the mouth. Eyes lateral. Mouth small, transverse, on the inferior surface of the head, and surrounded by a large sucker formed of both lips, which are thick, and have a free posterior edge. Pectorals and ventrals horizontal: dorsal without an osseous ray, and commencing somewhat in advance of the ventrals. Pharyngeal teeth hooked, in three rows, 5, 3, 1/1, 3, 5. Scales of moderate size, none on the chest. Lateral line continued direct to the centre of the base of the caudal fin.

146. Mayoa modesta, Day. D. 8, A. 6, L. l. 35, L. tr. 4½/4½. Greenish brown; a blotch below dorsal fin and another at the base of the caudal. Probably from the Himalayas, to 3½ inches in length.

Genus—DISCOGNATHUS, Heckel.

Garra, Ham. Buch.: *Platycara*, McClell.: *Discognathicthys* et *Lissorhynchus*, Bleeker.

Body elongated, sub-cylindrical. Mouth transverse, semi-circular and inferior: upper and lower lips continuous: no lateral lobes to snout, which projects beyond the mouth. A suctorial disc on the chin, formed by the lower lip: upper lip fringed. Barbels four (Garra), or one pair only at each angle of the mouth (Discognathus). Pharyngeal teeth hooked, in three closely approximating rows, 2, 4, 5/5, 4, 2. *Dorsal fin with few rays, commencing slightly in advance of the ventrals, its base scaleless. pectorals horizontal: anal short. Scales of moderate size, no enlarged anal scales. Lateral line continued to the centre of the base of the caudal fin. Gill-rakers few, short, and widely set. Air-vessel small.*

147. Discognathus lamta, Ham. Buch. *Dho-gu-ru* and *Koor-ka*, Panj.: *Cul-korava*,' (stone ophiocephalus), Tam.: *Pandi pakke*, Can.: *Ko-rafi-kaoli*, Hind. (Mysore): *Putter-chettah*, N. W. Prov.: *Choak-si*, Beng. D. 11, A. 7, L. l. 33-36. Four barbels: a dark spot behind the gill-opening, and generally a band along the side. Throughout India to Burma, attaining 6 inches in length.

Genus—OREINUS, *McClelland.*

Schizothorax, Sect. A., Heckel; *Schizopyge,* sp. Heckel.

Snout rounded. Mouth inferior and transverse: mandibles short, broad, and flat, loosely joined together at the symphysis: margin of the lower jaw having a thick horny covering, thickest internally, and a thick fringed lower lip, which has a free posterior edge forming a sucker. Barbels four. Pharyngeal teeth pointed, hooked, 5, 3, 2/2, 3, 5. *Dorsal fin rather short, with a strong, osseous, serrated ray, and arising opposite the ventrals: anal short. Scales very small, the vent and base of the anal fin in a sheath, covered by enlarged tiled scales. Lateral line passing to the centre of the base of the caudal fin.*

148. *Oreinus progastus,* McClelland. Adoee, Assam. D. 12, A. 7.
• 149. *Oreinus sinuatus,* Heckel. Gool-goolli, and Saul, Panj. D. 10-12, A. 7-8, L. l. 105. Silvery and spotted: sometimes a few of these latter are red, and it is termed a "trout." by some Europeans. Found in the Himalayas and rivers along their bases, attaining 2 feet or more in length.

Genus—SCHIZOTHORAX, *Heckel.*

Racoma, sp. McClelland: *Schizopyge,* sp. Heckel: *Opistocheilus,* pt. Bleeker.

Snout conically rounded, and laterally somewhat compressed. Mouth arched and antero-inferior: mandible neither broad, flattened, nor with a sharp margin, its edge sometimes having a thin, deciduous, horny covering. Barbels four. Pharyngeal teeth pointed, hooked, 5, 3, 2/2, 3, 5. *Dorsal fin rather short, with a strong, serrated osseous ray, and arising opposite the ventrals: anal short. Scales very small, the vent and base of the anal fin in a sheath covered by an enlarged tiled row. Lateral line passing to the centre of the base of the caudal fin.*

150. *Schizothorax Hodgsonii,* Günther. Diu-na-wah, N. W. Provinces. D. 11, A. 7, L. l. 155. Himalayas and head of the Ganges, attaining at least 18 inches in length.

Genus—LABEO, *Cuv.*

Rohita, pt., Cuv. and Val.: *Tylognathus,* Heckel: *Hypselobarbus, Diplocheilus, Diplocheilichthys, Lobocheilus, Rohitichthys, Morulius, Schismatorhynchus* et *Gobionichthys,* Bleeker.

Body elliptical, or moderately elongated. Snout rounded, generally projecting beyond the mouth, and covered with tubercles, and sometimes having a lateral lobe or projection: mouth sometimes anterior, but mostly inferior, transverse and demi-oval. Lips thick, covering the jaws, one or both having an inner transverse fold: a soft horny covering, with a sharp margin on the inner edge of one or both lips. Barbels small, four or two; if only one pair they belong to the maxilla, should there be a second they are on the snout. Pharyngeal teeth hooked, and in three rows, 5, 4, 2/2, 4, 5. *Dorsal fin elongated or of moderate length, destitute of any osseous ray, and arising anterior to the commencement of the* ventrals: anal short. Scales large, moderate, or of small size. Lateral line running direct to the centre of the base of the caudal fin. Gill-rakers short.

151. *Labeo nandina*, Ham. Buch. *Nandin*, Bengal: *Nga-ohn-doh*, *Nga-ne-pyah*, and *Nga-yin-pounsa*, Burm. D. 24-26, A. 7. L. l. 41-44, L. tr. 7½/8. Four barbels. Bengal, Assam, and Burma, attaining three feet in length.

152. *Labeo fimbriatus*, Bl. *Ven-cundee*, Tam.: *Ruchu*, and *Ganda-menu*, Tel.: *Bahrum*, Ooriah. D. 20-21, L. l. 44-47, L. tr. $\frac{9\text{-}10}{8\text{-}9}$. Four barbels. Southern India, to the Deccan and Orissa.

153. *Labeo nancar*, Ham. Buch. D. 20, A. 8. Four barbels. Obtained from small rivers in the Gorakhpur district.

154. *Labeo calbasu*, Ham. Buch. *Kala-beinse*, and *Di*, Panj.: *Di-hee*, Sind: *Nulla ganda-menu*, Tel.: *Kala-beinse*, *Kunda*, and *Kug-ge-ra*, Beng.: *Kala-beinse*, Ooriah: *Nga-nek-pya*, *Nga-noo-than*, and *Nga-ong-tong*, Burm. D. 16-18, A. 7, L. l. 40-44, L. tr. 7½/9. Four barbels. Throughout the fresh-waters of India and Burma, attaining four feet in length.

155. *Labeo curchius*, Ham. Buch. *Cour-sa*, Panj.: *Cir-re-oh*, Sind: *Mo-soo*, Tel.: *Cur-sua*, Ooriah: *Kurchi* and *Goni*, Beng.: *Cursa* and *Cooloose*, Hind.: *Courie*, Assam: *Nga-pay*, Tavoy: *Nga-dane* and *Nga-hoo*, Burm. D. 16-17, A. 7, L. l. 64-80, L. tr. $\frac{14\text{-}15}{16}$. Found throughout India (except the lower parts of Madras) and Burma. It attains nearly five feet in length.

156. *Labeo kontius*, Jerdon. *Currumunnee-cundee*, Tam. D. 16, A. 8, L. l. 38-40, L. tr. 9/8. Barbels four. Cauvery river and its affluents.

157. *Labeo nigrescens*, Day. D. 16, A. 7, L. l. 36, L. tr. 6/7. Four barbels. Each scale with a black spot at its base. South Canara, attaining 18 inches in length.

158. *Labeo Dussumieri*, Cuv. and Val. *Toolee*, Mal. D. $\frac{3}{12\text{-}13}$, A. $\frac{2\text{-}3}{5}$, L. l. 53-55, L. tr. $\frac{8\text{-}9}{0}$. Four barbels. Attains upwards of a foot in length, and is found in Malabar and Ceylon.

159. *Labeo rohita*, Ham. Buch. *Ruhu*, Panj., Beng., and Ooriah: *Dum-bra*, Sind: *Nga-myit-chin* and *Nga-myit-tsan-nee*, Burm. D. $\frac{3}{12\text{-}13}$, A. $\frac{2}{5}$, L. l. 41, L. tr. $\frac{6\frac{1}{2}}{9}$. Four barbels, the rostral sometimes absent. Throughout India, except Madras and Burma, attaining three feet or more in length.

160. *Labeo morala*, Ham. Buch. *Morala*, Beng. D. 13-14, A. $\frac{3}{5}$, L. l. 31. Four barbels. Ganges, attaining 6 inches in length.

161. *Labeo Nashii*, Day. D. 14, A. $\frac{3}{5}$, L. l. 41, L. tr. $\frac{7\frac{1}{2}}{6}$. No barbels. A black lateral band. River at Fraserpett, the foot of the Coorg Hills.

162. *Labeo ricnorhynchus*, McClelland. *Nepura*, Assam.: *Gid*, Panj.: *Kul-ka-batta*, Beng. D. 13, A. 7, L. l. 41-44, L. tr. 8/9. One pair of maxillary barbels. Himalayas and Sind Hills; also in some of the rivers of the plains in Bengal, as the Sone. This will probably turn out to be identical with *Labeo diplostomus*, Heckel, whose name has the priority.

163. Labeo falcatus, Gray and Hard. *Boolla*, Hind. D. 13, A. 7, L. l. 43, L. tr. 8½/7½. One pair of maxillary barbels. Bengal, Assam and Sikkim, attaining three feet in length.

164. Labeo pangusia, Ham. Buch. *Lo-annee*, Beng. D. 13, A. 7, L. l. 40, L. tr. 7½/7. One pair of maxillary barbels. Bengal and Cachar, to eight inches in length.

165. Labeo boggut, Sykes. May prove to be the same as *Labeo striolatus*, Günther. *Kolees*, Mah. D. 12, A. 7, L. l. 60-65, L. tr. 12/14. One pair of maxillary barbels. Central India, Deccan and Cutch.

166. Labeo bicolor, McClelland. *Gid-dah*, Panj.: *Thah-ree*, Sind.: *Mohaylee* and *Gaywah*, N. W. Provinces. D. 12, A. 7, L. l. 43, L. tr. 8½/7½. One pair of maxillary barbels. Himalayas and Sind Hills, as well as contiguous districts in the plains, attaining two feet and upwards in length.

167. Labeo ariza, Ham. Buch. *Coal-arinza-cundee*, Tam.: *Ariza*, Tel.: *Ban-gum-batta*, Beng.: *Morah*, Panj.: *Nga-loo*, Burm. D. 12, A. 7, L. l. 38-40, L. tr. 7½/7. One pair of maxillary barbels. Rivers of India and Burma.

168. Labeo boga, Ham. Buch. *Kyouk-nya-loo*, Burm. D. 12, A. 7, L. l. 40-42, L. tr. $\frac{7\text{-}8}{5}$. One pair of maxillary barbels. Fresh-waters of India and Burma.

169. Labeo mullya, Sykes. D. 11, A. 8. Deccan, to 6 inches in length.

170. Labeo nukta, Sykes. D. 11, A. 7, L. l. 38, L. tr. 8/9. One pair of maxillary barbels. Puna and other localities in the Bombay Presidency.

Genus—OSTEOCHILUS, Günther.

Rohita, sp. Cuv. & Val.

Mouth of moderate width, directed more or less downwards: snout obtusely rounded: lips thickened, continuous, fringed, or crenulated, but the lower is reflected from off the mandible, leaving it uncovered in the form of a sharp and hard transverse prominence. No tubercle inside the symphysis of lower jaw. Barbels four or two. Pharyngeal teeth generally 5, 4, 2/2, 4, 5. *Dorsal fin without osseous ray, having a moderate number of branched ones (10 to about 20), commencing in advance of the ventrals: anal rays few. Scales of moderate or small size. Lateral line passing to the centre of the base of the caudal fin. Gill-rakers short.*

171. Osteochilus rostellatus, Cuv. and Val. *Nga-lah*, Burm. D. 20, A. 8, L. l. 55, L. tr. 9/10. Four barbels; uniform colour. Irrawadi and Salwein Rivers in Burma, to two feet in length.

172. Osteochilus Neilli, Day. D. $\frac{2\text{-}3}{15\text{-}16}$, A. 7, L. l. 34, L. tr. 5½/6½. Four barbels: two dark marks on the body. Sittoung and Billing in Burma, up to 6 inches in length.

173. Osteochilus cephalus, Cuv. and Val. D. 16, A. 9, L. l. 36. One pair of barbels. Pegu, to 1 foot in length.

Genus—CIRRHINA, Cuv. & Val., pt.

Dangila, sp. Cuv. & Val.: *Cyrene*, sp. Heckel: *Mrigala*, sp. Bleeker: *Crossochilus* pt., Günther.

Snout depressed or obtusely rounded, with the soft coverings extremely thin. Mouth broad, transverse. Upper lip fringed or entire. Lower jaw rather sharp, without any, or with a thin lip, generally destitute of any horny covering, but having a small tubercle above the mandibular symphysis. Barbels small, four, two, or none. Dorsal fin rather short, moderate or long, without any osseous ray, commencing in advance of the ventrals: anal fin short and without any row of tiled scales. Pharyngeal teeth 5, 4, 2/2, 4, 5, or 5, 3, 2/2, 3, 5. Scales of large, moderate or small size. Lateral line continuous, passing to the centre of the base of the caudal fin. Gill-rakers short.

174. *Cirrhina Kuhlü*, Cuv. & Val. D. 28, A. 7, L. l. 39-40, L. tr. 7/9. Four barbels: upper lip fringed. Moulmein and Tavoy.

175. *Cirrhina Berdmorei*, Blyth. D. 26, A. 7, L. l. 31, L. tr. 6/? Four barbels: upper lip fringed. Tenasserim Provinces.

176. *Cirrhina Leschenaultii*, Cuv. & Val. *Ven cundee*, Tam.: *Aruzu*, Tel. D. $\frac{3-4}{14-15}$, A. 8, L. l. 42-44, L. tr. 9/9. Four barbels: upper lip entire. Southern India, and as far East as Orissa, attaining at least 1½ foot in length.

177. *Cirrhina mrigala*, Ham. Buch. *Mirrgah* and *Mrigah*, Panj., Beng., and Ooriah: also *Naim*, North-Western Provinces: *Mor-ah-kee*, Sind: *Nga-kyin* and *Nga-gyein*, Burm. Two barbels: upper lip entire. Throughout the fresh-waters of India (except Madras) and Burma, attaining three feet or more in length.

178. *Cirrhina Sindensis*, Day. D. 13, A. 7, L. l. 43, L. tr. 8/8. Two maxillary barbels. Sind Hills, to eight inches in length.

179. *Cirrhina anisura*, McClell. D. 12-13, A. 7, L. l. 38, L. tr. 7½/10½. No barbels: upper lip entire. Bengal and Assam.

180. *Cirrhina dyocheila*, McClell. *Goreah*, Assam. D. 13, A. 8, L. l. 42, L. tr. 8/8. No barbels: upper lip entire. Assam, to two feet and upwards in length.

181. *Cirrhina dero*, Ham. Buch. *Dhengro*, Assam. D. 12-13, A. 7, L. l. 39, L. tr. 7½/7. Two rostral barbels: upper lip entire. Assam, Bengal, Sind and Cutch.

182. *Cirrhina sada*, Ham. Buch. D. 13, A. 7. Four barbels: upper lip fringed. Assam.

183. *Cirrhina gohama*, Ham. Buch. *Behrah* and *Tellarree*, Panj.: *Curru*, Sind.: *Kala-batta*, Beng. D. 10-11, A. 7, L. l. 38-40, L. tr. 6/6. Two rostral barbels: upper lip fringed. Throughout India, except Madras, both on the hills and in the plains, attaining eight inches in length.

184. *Cirrhina latia*, Ham. Buch. D. 11, A. 7, L. l. 39, L. tr. 5½/6½. Four barbels: upper lip fringed. Northern Bengal, Nepal and Assam: it appears to be a small species.

185. *Cirrhina rostrata*, Günther. D. 11, A. 7, L. l. 38, L. tr. 5½/7. Two rostral barbels. Cossye River.

186. *Cirrhina bata*, Ham. Buch. *Dunguda-porah* and *Dommarci-batta*, Ooriah: *Gootellah*, Hind. D. 11-12, A. 7, L. l. 36-38, L. tr. $\frac{5\frac{1}{2}-6\frac{1}{2}}{6-7}$. One pair of maxillary barbels: upper lip fringed. Lower Bengal and Orissa, attaining two feet in length.

187. *Cirrhina mosario*, Ham. Buch. *Herilwa*, Assam. D. 10, A. 7, L. l. 37. No barbels: lower lip fringed. Assam, to six inches in length.

188. *Cirrhina reba*, Ham. Buch. *Soon-nee*, Panj., and Sind: *Felemose* and *Chittahri*, Tel.: *Chetchun-porah*, Ooriah: *Batta*, Beng.: *Rewah*, Hind. D. 11-12, A. 8, L. l. 35-38, L. tr. 7/7. One pair of short rostral barbels: upper lip fringed or entire. Throughout India, attaining a foot in length.

189. *Cirrhina isura*, McClell. D. 10, A. 7., L. l. 36, L. tr. $4\frac{1}{2}/5\frac{1}{2}$. One pair of rostral barbels: upper lip deeply fimbriated. Hooghly at Calcutta.

Genus—SCAPHIODON, *Heckel*.

Capoëta, sp. *Chondrostoma*, sp. Cuv. and Val: *Dillonia, Gymnostomus*, sp. Heckel.

Snout rounded. *Mouth transverse, inferior, with the mandibular edge nearly straight and sharp: the mandibles angularly bent inwards. A horny layer inside the lower jaw, which is not covered by lip: no lower labial fold. Barbels four, two, or absent. Pharyngeal teeth compressed, truncated, 5 or 4, 3, 2/2, 3, 4 or 5. Dorsal fin of moderate extent (up to about 10 branched rays), its last undivided ray being osseous, and serrated or entire, or else it is articulated: anal rather short. Scales large, of moderate or small size, and sometimes irregularly disposed. Lateral line passing to the centre of the base of the caudal fin.*

190. *Scaphiodon Watsoni*, Day. D. 13, A. 7, L. l. 33, L. tr. 6/6. Two barbels: an osseous serrated dorsal ray. Scales regularly arranged. Sind Hills.

191. *Scaphiodon irregularis*, Day. D. 13, A. 7, L. l. 36, L. tr. 9/9. Two barbels: an osseous serrated dorsal ray. Scales irregularly arranged. Sind Hills.

Genus—CARASSIUS, *Nilsson*.

Snout obtuse, rounded. Mouth anterior, arched, and rather narrow: lips thin. Barbels absent. Pharyngeal teeth compressed, in a single row, 4/4. Dorsal fin long, commencing opposite the ventrals, and having its last undivided ray osseous and serrated: last undivided anal ray normally serrated. Scales of moderate size. Lateral line complete, passing to the centre of the base of the caudal fin.

192. *Carassius auratus*, Linn. D. 19-21, A. 8, L. l. 27-29, L. tr. $6\frac{1}{2}/10$. I here place the gold-carp on the authority of the British Museum Catalogue, wherein it is stated that three adult specimens have been received from India through Mr. Masters. I strongly doubt whether this fish exists wild in India or British Burma. Dr. Wright informs me that it has been introduced into the ponds in Nepal. Sykes' species, *C. nukta* (No. 170), is a *Labeo*.

Genus—SEMIPLOTUS, *Bleeker*.

Snout thick and prominent. Mouth wide, transverse, slightly curved, inferior, having a knob at the symphysis. Inter-maxillaries more or less adherent to the maxilla, and but slight powers of motion exist in the upper jaw. Barbels absent. Pharyngeal teeth (in S. modestus) 4, 3, 2/2, 3, 4. Dorsal fin long, its last undivided ray strong, osseous, and either serrated or entire: anal rather short. Scales large. Lateral line passing to the centre of the base of the caudal fin.

193. *Semiplotus modestus*, Day. D. 2|, A. 9, L. l. 32-34, L. tr. 7½/7½. Last undivided dorsal ray osseous and serrated. Hills above Akyab.
194. *Semiplotus McClellandi*, Bleeker. D. 28, A. 9, L. l. 27, L. tr. 6/5. Last undivided dorsal ray osseous and entire. Assam.

Genus—CATLA, *Cuv. & Val.*

Gibelion, Heckel: *Hypselobarbus*, Bleeker.

Head broad: snout with very thin integuments: upper lip absent: the lower moderately thick, having a continuous free posterior margin. The lower jaw with a moveable articulation at the symphysis, but destitute of any prominent tubercle. Eyes with free orbital margins. Barbels absent. Pharyngeal teeth plough-shaped, 5, 3, 2/2, 3, 5. Dorsal fin with rather an elongated base, destitute of osseous ray, and commencing somewhat in advance of the ventral: anal short: caudal forked. Scales of moderate size, no tiled ones along the base of the anal fin. Lateral line complete, continued to the centre of the base of the caudal fin. Gill-rakers long, rather strong, and moderately wide apart in the adult, but fine and closely set in the immature.

195. *Catla Buchanani*, Cuv. and Val. *Bo-assa*, Hind., and *Cutla*, Panj.: *Tay-lee*, Sind: *Catla*, Beng.: *Bar-kur*, Ooriah: *Nga-thaing*, Burm. D. 17-18, A. 8, L. l. 40-43, L. tr. 7½/9. Throughout the freshwaters of India and Burma, so far as the Pegu River: is not found in the southern and western portions of Madras. It attains several feet in length, and is excellent eating.

Genus—MOLA, *Heckel.*

Thynnichthys, pt., Bleeker: *Amblypharyngodon*, pt., Bleeker: *Brachy gramma*, pt. Day.

Pseudobranchiæ present. Head compressed, integuments over snout thin: upper lip absent; only a short labial fold on the side of the mandible. Mouth rather wide, antero-lateral, with the lower jaw somewhat prominent. Eyes in the middle of the depth of the head, and without any adipose membrane. Barbels absent. Pharyngeal teeth molar-form, close together, 5, 3 or 4, 2 or 3/2 or 3, 4 or 3, 5: or 5 or 3, 2 or 3 or 4, 2 or 1/1 or 2, 4 or 3 or 2, 3 or 5. Dorsal fin short, without osseous ray, commencing nearly opposite the ventrals: anal short. Scales small. Lateral line complete, running to the centre of the base of the caudal fin (Thynnichthys): or incomplete (Amblypharyngodon). Intestinal tract narrow, with numerous convolutions. Gill-rakers very short or absent.

196. *Mola harengula*, Cuv. and Val. *Kala-tala* and *Ahku-chappah*, Tel. D. 9, A. 8, L. r. 120, L. tr. 22/25. Lateral line complete. Found in the Godaveri and Kistna Rivers, attaining upwards of a foot in length.

197. *Mola Buchanani*, Blyth. *Talla-maya*, Tel.: *Morara*, Ooriah: *Moah*, Assam: *Mukni*, Panj.: *Nga-beh-byoo* and *Nga-zen-zap*, Burm. D. 10, A. 7, L. l. 55-75, L. tr. 25/28. Lateral line incomplete. Freshwaters of India and Burma, to four inches in length.

198. *Mola melettinus*, Cuv. & Val. *Wumboo*, Mal.: *Oolaree*, Tam.: *Kali-korafi*, Hind.: *Paraga*, Can.: *Muckni*, Panj. D. 9-10, A. 7-8, L. l.

50-57. Lateral line incomplete. Panjáb, Sind, Southern India, and the Malabar Coast, rarely attaining four inches in length.

199. *Mola Atkinsonii*, Blyth. *Nga-pau-ma*, Burm. D. 8, A. 7, L. l. 55, L. tr. 11/11. Lateral line incomplete. Burma; attaining six inches in length.

Genus—BARBUS, Cuv. & Val.

Puntius, pt., Ham. Buch.: *Labeobarbus*, et *Varicorhinus*, pt., Rüppel: *Systomus*, pt., McClell.: *Capoëta*, sp. Cuv. & Val.: *Pseudobarbus*, Bielz.: *Luciobarbus*, Heckel: *Cheilobarbus*, sp. Smith: *Balantiocheilus*, *Hemibarbus*, *Cyclocheilichthys*, *Siaja*, *Anematichthys*, *Hypselobarbus*, *Gonoproklopterus*, *Gnathopogon*, *Hampala*, sp. Bleeker: *Enteromius*, sp. Cope.

Mouth arched. *Eyes without adipose lids. Jaws closely invested by lips, which may have leathery lobes, but no inner fold, nor horny covering. Barbels four (Barbodes), or two (Capoëta): or none (Puntius). Pharyngeal teeth* 5 or 4, 3 or 2, 2 or 2/3 or 2, 2 or 3, 4 or 5. *Dorsal fin rather short, its last undivided ray being either ossified and serrated or entire, or articulated and not osseous: it commences nearly opposite the ventrals: anal rather short, in some species its second ray ossified. Scales large, of moderate or small size. Lateral line complete or incomplete; when the former, continued to opposite the centre of the base of the caudal fin.*

1. *With four barbels (Barbodes.)*
   a. *Last undivided dorsal ray, osseous and serrated.*

200. *Barbus chagunio*, Ham. Buch. *Jerruah*, Beng.: *Chaguni*, Behar. D. 11, A. 8, L. l. 44-47, L. tr. 11/11. Pores on head and snout. India, exclusive of Madras, attaining a foot and a half in length.

201. *Barbus immaculatus*. McClell. D. 11, A. 8, L. l. 32-33, L. tr. 6/6. No pores on snout. Throughout Bengal, North-West Provinces, Assam and Sikkim.

202. *Barbus sarana*, Ham. Buch. *Jundoori*, Panj.: *Poh-pree* and *Kun-nah-nee*, Sind: *Munduttee*, Mal.; *Pungella*, Tam.: *Giddi kaoli*, *Durhie* and *Potah*, Hind.: *Gid-pakke*, Can.: *Kannaku*, Tel.: *Sarana*, Ooriah and Beng.: *Nga-khou-mah-gyee* and *Nga-chong*, Burm. D. 11-12, A. 8, L. l. 29-31, L. tr. 5½/5½. Fresh-waters throughout India and Burma; it attains upwards of 2 feet in length.

203. *Barbus pinnauratus*, Day. D. 11, A. 8, L. l. 27-29, L. tr. 6/5. A black lateral blotch. Sind, portions of Bombay, Malabar, and in the Kistna River, up to 5 inches in length.

204. *Barbus goniosoma*, Bleeker. D. 11, A. 7, L. l. 24, L. tr. 4½/4½. Mergui in Burmah, up to 6 inches in length.

205. *Barbus roseipinnis*, Cuv. & Val. D. 11, A. 7, L. l. 22. Fins red. Pondicherry, to 4½ inches in length.

206. *Barbus rodactylus*, McClell. D. 10. Lower Assam, to 5 inches in length.

   b. *Last undivided dorsal ray, osseous and entire.*

207. *Barbus dubius*, Day. D. 13. A. 7, L. l. 42, L. tr. 9/7. Bowany River at the foot of the Neilgherry Hills.

208. *Barbus Mysorensis*, Jerdon. *Coatee cundee*, Tam. D. 13, A. 7-8, L. l. 40, L. tr. 7/7. Rivers along the bases of the Wynaad and Neilgherry Hills, up to several feet in length.

209. *Barbus Carnaticus*, Jerdon. *Poaree cundee, Saal cundee* and *Shellee*, Tam.: *Giddi kaoli*, Hind.: *Gid-pakke*, Can. D. 12, A. 7-8, L. l. 30-32, L. tr. 5/5. Rivers along the bases of the Wynaad and Neilgherry ranges of hills, attaining to 25 lbs in weight.

210. *Barbus Jerdoni*, Day. D. 12, A. 8, L. l. 28, L. tr. 6/4. Rivers of South Canara.

211. *Barbus hexastichus*, McClell. *Lobura* and *Bokar*, Assam. D. 12-13, A. 7-8, L. l. 24-27. Rivers on and around the Himalayas, and also in Assam, attaining $2\frac{1}{2}$ feet in length.

212. *Barbus mosal*, Ham. Buch. *Burapatra*, Assam. D. 12, A. 7-8, L. l. 25-27, L. tr. $\frac{24 \cdot 4}{4}$. No lobed lip. Mountain streams and rivers along the bases of the eastern range of the Himalyas, also Canara, attaining 3 feet or more in length.

213. *Barbus tor*, Ham. Buch. *Kukkiah*, Panj.: *Kurreah*, Sind: *Poo-meen-cundee*, Tam.: *Naharm*, Hind.: *Mahaseer*, by Europeans. D. 12, A. 7, L. l. 23-27. Lips lobed. Throughout the hill ranges of India and rivers around their bases, extending their migrations to long distances, attaining several feet in length.

214. *Barbus sophore*, Ham. Buch. D. 12, A. 7, L. l. 25, L. tr. $3\frac{1}{2}/4\frac{1}{2}$. Khasya Hills.

215. *Barbus Neilli*, Day. D. 13, A. 8, L. l. 24-16, L. tr. $4\frac{1}{4}/4$. Kurnool in Madras, stated to attain to 60 lbs. weight.

216. *Barbus compressus*, Day. D. 12, A. 8, L. l. 22, L. tr. 4/5. A specimen in the Calcutta Museum, its locality doubtful, perhaps Cashmere.

217. *Barbus Himalayanus*, Day. *Chit-rah-too*, Panj. D. 11, A. 7, L. l. 32-34, L. tr. $5\frac{1}{2}/6$. Ussun and Girri Rivers near Simla on the Himalayas.

218. *Barbus microprogon*, Cuv. & Val. D. 10, A. 8, L. l. 38, L. tr. $4\frac{1}{2}/5$. Stated to be from Mysore.

219. *Barbus chilinoides*, McClell. D. $\frac{3-4}{7}$, A. 7, L. l. 32-35, L. tr. $5\frac{1}{2}/5$. Himalayas and Ganges, to 8 inches in length.

220. *Barbus Stracheyi*, Day. D. 11, A. 7, L. l. 23, L. tr. $3\frac{1}{2}/5$. Akyab and Moulmein, growing to a large size.

c. *no osseous dorsal ray.*

221. *Barbus pulchellus*, Day. D. 13, A. 9, L. l. 30, L. tr. $6/5\frac{1}{2}$. Upper half of body dark coloured. South Canara in inland streams, attaining at least 18 inches in length.

222. *Barbus Stevensonii*, Day. D. 12, A. 8, L. l. 27, L. tr. $4\frac{1}{2}/5$. Akyab.

223. *Barbus Blythii*, Day. D. 12, A. 8, L. l. 22, L. tr. 4/5. Tenasserim Provinces, to 2 inches in length.

224. *Barbus melanampyx*, Day. D. 11, A. 7, L. l. 20, L. tr. $3\frac{1}{2}/3\frac{1}{2}$. Red, with three vertical black bands. Western Ghâts and Neilgherries, up to 3 inches in length.

2. *With two barbels (Capoëta).*

a. *With osseous serrated dorsal ray.*

225. *Barbus hampal*, Günther. D. 12, A. 8, L. l. 26, L. tr. 5/5 Tavoy, up to 9 inches in length.

b. *Osseous dorsal ray entire.*

226. *Barbus dorsalis*, Jerdon. D. 11-12, A. 8, L. l. 24, L. tr. 4½/4. *Lambi kaoli*, Hind.: *Saal cundee*, Tam.: *Mar-pakke*, Can. Southern India, extending to the Malabar Coast and Ceylon, not attaining a large size.

227. *Barbus chola*, Ham. Buch. *Karoon*, Tam.: *Kerrundi*, Beng.: *Pittha kerrundi*, "bitter carp," Ooriah: *Chaddu paddaka*, Tel.: *Katcha karawa*, Hind.: *Nga-khon-ma* and *Nga-lowar*, Burmese. D. 11, A. 7, L. l. 26, L. tr. 5½/5. India and Burma generally, except the Panjáb and Sind. It attains 5 inches in length.

228. *Barbus amphibius*, Cuv. & Val. D. 10-11, A. 7, L. l. 23, L. tr. 4½/4. From Poona down the coast of Canara.

229. *Barbus parrah*, Day. *Parrah perlee*, Mal.: *Katcha karawa*, Hind. D. 11, A. 8, L. l. 25, L. tr. 5/4. Malabar, Mysore and Madras, to 6 inches in length.

230. *Barbus titius*, Ham. Buch. *Tit pungti*, Beng.: *Pet-toh-ee*, Sind: *Borajalee*, Assam. D. 10, A. 7, L. l. 25. Two black spots. Throughout India, except its more southern portions.

231. *Barbus thermalis*, Cuv. & Val. D. 11, A. 8, L. l. 25, L. tr. 5½/5½. Mysore, Cachar and Ceylon, to 3 inches in length.

232. *Barbus lepidus*, Day. D. 11, A. 7, L. l. 21, L. tr. 5/3. Some of dorsal rays elongated. From Canara down the Western Coast along the base of the Neilgherries, also in Ceylon, attaining 6 inches in length.

c. *No osseous dorsal ray.*

233. *Barbus kolus*, Sykes. *Nilisu*, Tel. D. 12-13, A. 8, L. l. 40-42, L. tr. 10/8. Deccan and throughout the Kistna River, attaining upwards of a foot in length.

234. *Barbus curmuca*, Ham. Buch. D. 11, A. 8. Southern India, to 3 feet in length.

235. *Barbus Denisonii*, Day. D. 10-11, A. 8, L. l. 28, L. tr. 4½/3½. Body longitudinally banded. Hill ranges of Travancore, to 6 inches in length.

236. *Barbus arulius*, Jerdon. D. 11, A. 7, L. l. 23, L. tr. 5/3½. Body vertically banded. Wynaad and Neilgherry Hills, as well as the rivers at their bases.

237. *Barbus Puckelli*, Day. D. 9, A. 8, L. l. 24, L. tr. 4/3. Mysore, up to 3 inches in length.

3. *No barbels (Puntius).*

a. *With osseous serrated dorsal ray.*

238. *Barbus apogon*, Cuv. & Val. *Nga-ta-zee* and *Nga-lay-toun*, Burm. D. 12, A. 8, L. l. 36, L. tr. 8/7. Burma.

239. *Barbus ambassis*, Day. *Bunkuai*, Ooriah. D. 11, A. 7, L. l. 36, incomplete. Bengal, Orissa and Madras, attaining about 3 inches in length.

240. *Barbus conchonius*, Ham. Buch. *Kunchon pungti*, Beng. D. 11, A. 7, L. l. 26, incomplete, L. tr. 5½/6½. A black spot on side over anal fin. North-West Provinces, Behar and Lower Bengal, attaining 5 inches in length.

241. *Barbus gelius*, Ham. Buch. *Cutturpoh*, Ooriah: *Geli pungti*, Beng. D. 11, A. 3/5, L. l. 25, incomplete, L. tr. 9. A black band over tail: a spot across bases of the first 6 dorsal rays, another over base of anal. Bengal and Orissa, to 2 inches in length.

242. *Barbus ticto*, Ham. Buch. *Kaoli* and *Kotree*, Hind. D. 11, L. l. 23, incomplete. Throughout India, except the Malabar Coast. It rarely exceeds 4 inches in length.

243. *Barbus punctatus*, Day. *Putter perlee*, Mal. D. 11, A. 7, L. l. 23, complete, L. tr. 6/4. Two black spots, one below commencement of lateral line, the other near its termination. Malabar, attaining to 3 inches in length.

244. *Barbus phutunio*, Ham. Buch. *Kudji kerundi*, Ooriah: *Phutuni pungti*, Beng. D. 10-11, A. 8, L. l. 20-23, incomplete, L. tr. 8-10. Four vertical black bands on a brown body, and a dark one down the centre of dorsal fin. Bengal, Orissa and Ceylon, up to 3 inches in length.

245. *Barbus guganio*, Ham. Buch. *Gugani*, Beng. D. 10, A. 7, L. l. incomplete. Gangetic Provinces and Assam.

246. *Barbus Stoliczkanus*, Day. D. 10, A. 7. L. l. 25, complete, L. tr. 5/6. Two black marks on lateral line. Eastern Burma.

247. *Barbus pyrrhopterus*, McClelland. D. 9, A. 7, L. l. 22-24, complete, L. tr. $4\frac{1}{2}/4\frac{1}{2}$. A dark spot near posterior end of lateral line. Upper Assam.

b. Osseous dorsal ray entire.

248. *Barbus stigma*, Cuv. & Val. *Po-ti-ah*, *Chiddu* and *Paandra*, Panj.: *Katcha karawa* and *Pottiah*, Hind.: *Katch-karawa*, Can.: *Chadu perigi*, Tel.: *Pattiah-kerundi*, Ooriah: *Nga-khoon-ma*, Burm. D. 11, A. 8, L. l. 25, L. tr. 5/4. A dark spot near posterior end of lateral line, another across the base of middle dorsal rays. Found throughout India and Burma, attains 5 inches in length.

249. *Barbus chrysopterus*, McClelland. *Pot-ti-ah* and *Door-kah*, Panj.; *Durru*, Sind: *Bo-ah-re*, North-West Provinces. D. 11, A. 7, L. l. 23, complete L. tr. 5/5. Fins black tipped. Assam, North-West Provinces, Panjáb and Sind.

250. *Barbus unimaculatus*, Blyth. D. 11, A. 7, L. l. 24, incomplete, L. tr. $4\frac{1}{2}/4\frac{1}{2}$. A black mark at base of each dorsal ray. A number of fry from the Tenasserim Provinces are in the Calcutta Museum.

251. *Barbus filamentosus*, Cuv. & Val. D. 8, A. 7, L. l. 21, complete L. tr. 5/3. Branched dorsal rays elongated. Southern India and the Western Coast, attaining 6 inches in length.

252. *Barbus terio*, Ham. Buch. *Doordah*, Panj.: *Kakatchia kerundi*, Ooriah: *Teri pungti*, Beng. D. 11, L. l. incomplete. A black mark at side of anal fin, a second under posterior end of dorsal. Panjáb, Gangetic Provinces and Orissa, attaining 3 or 4 inches in length.

253. *Barbus Duvaucellii*, Cuv. & Val. D. 10, A. 7, L. l. 27, complete. Bengal.

254. *Barbus Waagneri*, Day. D. 10-11, A. 7, L. l. 23-24, incomplete, L. tr. 4/7. One black spot. Salt range.

c. Without osseous dorsal ray.

255. Barbus Punjaubensis, Day. D. 11, A. 5, L. l. 43, incomplete. Lahor, attaining 2 inches in length.

256. Barbus cosuatis, Ham. Buch. *Koswati*, Beng. D. 11, A. 7, L. l. 22, incomplete, L. tr. 6. Gangetic Provinces and Lower Bengal, also Bombay, attaining 3 inches in length.

257. Barbus vittatus, Day. *Kaoli*, Hind. D. 10, A. 7, L. l. 20-22, incomplete, L. tr. 4/3. Four black spots on side and a black streak down the dorsal fin. Mysore, Western Coast, and Cutch, attaining about 2 inches in length.

258. Barbus presbyter, Cuv. & Val. D. 11, A. 7, L. l. 26. L. tr. 6/2. Bombay.

259. Barbus puntio, Ham. Buch. D. 11, A. 7, L. l. 23, incomplete, L. tr. 4/4. A black spot encircles the free portion of the tail. Bengal and British Burma, attaining about 3 inches in length.

Genus—NURIA, Cuv. & Val.

Esomus, Swainson.

Pseudobranchiæ present. Mouth narrow, directed obliquely upwards, sub-orbitals broad. Barbels four, the rostral shorter than the maxillary pair. Pharyngeal teeth, crooked, pointed 5/5. Dorsal fin without osseous ray, and with few branched ones, it is inserted posterior to the ventral but not to over the anal, the latter having but few or a moderate number of branched rays. Scales of moderate size. Lateral line, when present, passing to the lower half of the base of the caudal fin. Gill-rakers short.

260. Nuria albolineata, Blyth. D. 9, A. 13, L. l. 31, incomplete. A silvery lateral band. Moulmein.

261. Nuria danrica, Ham. Buch. *Chid-dül-lu*, Panj.: *Soom-a-rah, Mola*, and *Mah-wa*, North-West Provinces: *Danrica* and *Jongja*, Beng.: *Kurriah dahwiee*, Hind.: *Nga-zin-byoon*, Burm. D. 8, A. 8, L. l. 30-34, complete, L. tr. $\frac{5-6}{3}$. A black lateral band. Throughout India, Ceylon, and Burma, attaining 5 inches in length.

262. Nuria Malabarica, Day. D. 9, A. 7, L. r. 32, L. tr. 7. Lateral line absent. A silvery band along the sides, which occasionally has a narrow black edge superiorly. The coast districts of India, Burma, and also the Nicobars, attaining 3 inches in length.

Genus—RASBORA, Bleeker.

Leuciscus, sp. Cuv. & Val.

Pseudobranchiæ present. Eyes with free orbital margins. Cleft of mouth oblique, lower jaw slightly prominent, having one central and on either side a lateral prominence, fitting into corresponding depressions in the upper jaw. Barbels two (rostral) or none. Pharyngeal teeth 5, 3 or 4, 2/2, 4 or 3, 5. Dorsal fin without osseous ray, and but few branched ones, inserted posterior to the origin of the ventral, but not extending to over the anal, which latter is short. Scales large or of moderate size. Lateral line concave, continued to the lower half of the caudal fin. Gill-rakers short, lanceolate.

a. With a pair of barbels.

263. *Rasbora elanga*, Ham. Buch. *Dahwiee*, Hind. D. 9, A. 7-8 L. l. 40-42, L. tr. 7/6. One pair of rostral barbels. Gangetic Provinces, Assam, and Burma, attaining 8 inches in length.

b. Without barbels.

264. *Rasbora daniconius*, Ham. Buch. *Mile-lo-ah, Chin-do-lah Raan-kaal-le* and *Charl*, Panj.: *Mile-lo-ah*, North-West Provinces: *Kokanutchee*, Mal.: *Jilo*, Ooriah: *Danikoni* and *Angjani*, Beng.: *Nga-doungzee*, and *Nga-nauch-youn*, Burm. D. 9. A. 7, L. l. 30-32. No barbels, mostly a black lateral stripe. Throughout India, Ceylon and Burma, attaining 5 inches in length.

265. *Rasbora Neilgherriensis*, Day. *Ovaree cundee*, Tamil. D. 9, A. 7, L. l. 34, L. tr. 6½/5. A light lateral band. Rivers on or contiguous to the Neilgherry Hills; it attains 8 inches in length.

266. *Rasbora Buchanani*, Bleeker. D. 9, A. 7, L. l. 26-29. No lateral band. Gangetic Provinces, Mysore, Madras and Burma.

Genus—ASPIDOPARIA (Heckel), Bleeker.

Morara, Bleeker.

Mouth small, inferior: lower jaw having a sharp crescentic edge, destitute of lip. Sub-orbital ring of bones, of moderate width or broad. Pharyngeal teeth 4, 4, 2/2, 4, 4. Dorsal fin without osseous and with very few branched rays, commencing opposite to or behind the origin of the ventrals, but not extending to above the anal, which latter has a moderate number (10 to 12) of rays. Scales of medium size. Lateral line concave and passing along the lower half of the base of the caudal fin.

267. *Aspidoparia morar*, Ham. Buch. *Pa-o-char, Chilwa*, Panj.: *Kareer-ee*, Sind: *Chippuah* and *Chel-lu-ah*, North-West Provinces: *Amlee*, Dec.: *Morari* and *Morar*, Beng.: *Bayi*, Ooriah: *Nga-hpyen-boo*, and *Yenboung-za*, Burm. D. $\frac{2-3}{7-8}$, A. 11-12, L. l. 38-42, L. tr. 5½/5. Continent of India (except the Western Coast and to the south of the Kistna River), Assam and Burma, attaining 6 inches or even more in length.

268. *Aspidoparia jaya*, Ham. Buch. *Pah-ru-ah*, N. W. Prov.: *Chola*, Assam. D. 12, A 10, L. l. 58, L. tr. 7/10. Upper portions of Gangetic Provinces in the plains, and Assam.

Genus—ROHTEE, Sykes.

Osteobrama, Heckel: *Smiliogaster (?)*, Bleeker.

Body compressed and elevated. Pseudobranchiæ present. Mouth anterior: lips thin. Barbels absent. Pharyngeal teeth 6 or 5 or 4, 4 or 3, 2 or 3/3, or 2, 3 or 4, 4 or 5 or 6. Dorsal fin short, having its last undivided ray osseous and serrated, and commencing opposite the interspace between the bases of the ventral and anal fins, the latter of which has many rays. Scales small. Lateral line passing nearly to the centre of the base of the caudal fin. Gill-rakers short.

269. *Rohtee cotio*, Ham. Buch. *Goord-ha, Duh-riee*, and *Put-too*, Panj.: *Duh-riee*, Sind: *Goord-ha, Chen-da-lah, Muck-nee*, N. W. Provinces; *Koti*, Beng.: *Nga-hpan-ma*, Burm. D. 11-12, A. 29-32, L. l. 71, L. tr. $\frac{15\text{-}17}{21}$. Continent of India and Burma.

270. *Rohtee Alfrediana*, Cuv. and Val. *Goonta*, Beng. D. 10-11, A. 31-36, L. 1. 42-60, L. tr. $\frac{8\cdot10}{14\cdot17}$. Lower Bengal, Assam and Burma, to 6 inches or more in length.

271. *Rohtee Vigorsii*, Sykes. *Gollund*, Ooriah : *Khira*, Tel. D. 11, A. 25-26, L. 1. 75, L. tr. 18/19. Deccan, Kistna and Mahanuddee Rivers, attaining 8 inches in length.

272. *Rohtee microlepis*, Blyth. *Nga-hpeh-oung* and *Nga-net-pya*, Burm. D. 11-12, A. 21, L. 1. 71-73, L. tr. 18/22. The Godaveri River, also throughout Burma ; it attains 15 inches and more in length.

273. *Rohtee Ogilbii*, Sykes. D. 11, A. 16, L. 1. 55, L. tr. 13/11. Deccan, and Kistna River, to 6 inches or more in length.

Genus—*BARILIUS*—(*H. B.*) *Bleeker*.

Opsarius, sp. McClelland : *Pachystomus*, sp. Heckel : *Chedrus*, (Swains.) Bleeker : *Opsaridium*, Peters : *Pteropsarion*, sp. *Schacra*, sp. *et. Bola*, sp. Günther.

Pseudobranchiæ present. Mouth anterior, sometimes oblique, and having a moderate or deep cleft : lower jaw with a knob above the symphysis, and a corresponding depression in the upper jaw for its reception. Sub-orbital ring of bones generally broad, more especially the third, which may even extend entirely behind the vertical from the posterior edge of the orbit. Barbels four (Pachystomus, " Heckel," Bleeker) or two (Bendilisis, Bleeker), or none (Barilius, Ham. Buch.) Pharyngeal teeth hooked, 5, 3 or 4, 2 or 1/1, or 2, 4 or 3, 5 : *or else* 5, 2 or 4/4 *or* 2, 5. *Dorsal fin without osseous ray, of moderate length, inserted posterior to the ventrals, sometimes extending to above the anal, which latter has a somewhat elongated base. Scales of moderate or small size. Lateral line concave continued on to the middle or lower half of the caudal, or incomplete or absent. Gill-rakers very short or absent.*

1. *With four barbels (Pachystomus).*

274. *Barilius rerio*, Ham. Buch. *Poncha geraldi*, Ooriah. D. 9, A. 15, L. 1. 26-28, L. tr. 6. Blue horizontal bands. Gangetic Provinces, Orissa and Madras, to two inches in length.

275. *Barilius piscatorius*, McClell. *Charl* and *Lo-har-ree*, Panj. D. 9, A. 13-14, L. 1. 42, L. tr. 8/4. Ten vertical bars. Panjáb and rivers in the Sub-Himalayan range : Nepal, and Sikkim, also the Gangetic Provinces, attaining 5 inches in length.

276. *Barilius radiolatus*, Günther. D. 10, A. 12, L. 1. 56, L. tr. 5/6. Central India.

277. *Barilius modestus*, Day. D. 9, A. 12-13, L. 1. 43, L. tr. $5\frac{1}{2}/4\frac{1}{2}$. Back dark, sides silvery. Panjáb, to 4 inches in length.

278. *Barilius Bleekeri*, Day. D. 9, A. 12-13, L. 1. 43, L. tr. $7\frac{1}{2}/5\frac{1}{2}$. Seven vertical bars. Sub-Himalayan range in the Panjáb, up to 3 inches in length.

279. *Barilius shacra*, Ham. Buch. *Gürha*, Panj. D. 9, A. 10, L. 1. 53, L. tr. 11/9. Twelve vertical bars. Jumna, Gangetic Provinces, and Assam, also Behar, not attaining above 5 inches in length.

280. *Barilius bendelisis*, Ham. Buch. D. 9, A. 11, L. 1. 43, L. tr. 8/4. Short vertical bars. Mysore and Southern India, to $4\frac{1}{2}$ inches in length.

281. *Barilius cocsa*, Ham. Buch. *Pah-tah, Puk-wah-re, Kun-nul, Dahrah,* and *Bur-re-ah,* Panj.: *Khoksa,* Beng.: *Johra,* Mah. D. 9-10, A. 9-10, L. l. 42, L. tr. $\frac{8\frac{1}{2}\text{-}9}{5}$. Vertical bars. Continent of India, especially on and near mountain ranges; not recorded from the Malabar Coast or Sind. It attains 6 inches in length.

2. *With two barbels (Bendilisis).*

282 *Barilius vagra*, Ham. Buch. D. 9, A. 13-14, L. l. 42-45, L. tr. $6\frac{1}{2}/4\frac{1}{2}$. Indistinct vertical bars. Gangetic Provinces, to 5 inches in length.

283. *Barilius barila*, Ham. Buch. *Gilland* and *Caedra,* Beng.: *Persee,* Hind. D. 9, A. 13, L. l. 43-46, L. tr. $6\frac{1}{2}/5$. Fourteen or fifteen vertical bars. Sind, Gangetic Provinces and Orissa, attaining 4 inches in length.

284. *Barilius nigrofasciatus*, Day. D. 9, A. 13, L. l. 30, L. tr. 7. Dark lateral bands. Pegu and Salwein Rivers. Does not appear to attain an inch in length.

3. *Without barbels (Barilius).*

285. *Barilius Bakeri*, Day. D. 13, A. 16-17, L. l. 38, L. tr. 9/4. A row of large spots. Hill ranges of Travancore to six inches in length.

286. *Barilius Canarensis*, Jerdon. D. 12, A. 15, L. l. 38, L. tr. 9/4. Two rows of spots. Canara, attaining 6 inches in length.

287. *Barilius gatensis*, Cuv. and Val. *Aart cundee,* "river carp," Tam. D. 10-11, A. 15-16, L. l. 40, L. tr. 8/5. With fifteen vertical bars. Western Ghâts, Neilgherry Hills, and rivers around their bases.

288. *Barilius tileo*, Ham. Buch. *Tilei,* Assam. D. 10, A. 14, L. l. 70, L. tr. 14/5. Two rows of spots. Eastern portion of the Himalayan range and rivers in Assam, attaining 8 inches in length.

289. *Barilius papillatus*, Day. D. 10, A. 13-14, L. l. 39, L. tr. $\frac{7\frac{1}{2}\text{-}9\frac{1}{2}}{6\frac{1}{2}}$. From seven to nine vertical bands. Orissa and neighbouring provinces in Bengal, attaining 3 inches in length.

290. *Barilius bola*, Ham. Buch. *Gool-lah,* Panj. and N. W. Prov.: *Buggarah,* Hind.: *Korang,* Assam: *Bola,* Beng.: *Bugguah,* Ooriah. D. 10, A. 13, L. l. 88, L. tr. $\frac{12\text{-}15}{9\text{-}11}$. Two rows of blotches. Panjáb, North-West Provinces, Bengal, Orissa and Assam, attaining a foot in length.

291. *Barilius guttatus*, Day. *Nga-la-wah,* Burm. D. 9, A. 14, L. l. 44, L. tr. 9/5. Two rows of spots. Irrawaddi River, to 7 inches in length.

292. *Barilius barna*, Ham. Buch. *Balisundree,* Assam: *Bahri,* Ooriah. D. 9, A. 13, L. l. 42; L. tr. $\frac{8\text{-}9}{5}$. Nine vertical bands. Gangetic Provinces, Assam and Orissa, attaining 4 inches or more in length.

293. *Barilius borelio*, Ham. Buch. *Boreli* and *Soli,* Beng. D. 9, A. 11, L. l. 39, L. tr. 7/7. Silvery. Gangetic Provinces, to 4 inches in length.

294. *Barilius hoalius*, Ham. Buch. *Hayali,* Beng. D. 9, A. 10. Uniform. Rivers of Northern Bengal, to 6 inches in length.

Genus—DANIO, Ham. Buch. sp.

Perilampus, sp. McClell.: *Paradanio*, et *Devario*, Bleeker.

Body compressed. Pseudobranchiæ present. Mouth narrow, directed obliquely upwards. Sub-orbitals broad. Barbels four, or two, or none: not invariably constant in species. Pharyngeal teeth hooked, 5, 3, 2/2, 3, 5. Dorsal fin with a moderately elongated base: its posterior rays being opposite to the anal, which is long. Scales of moderate size. Lateral line concave, passing to the lower half of the caudal fin. Gill-rakers short.

295. *Danio devario,* Ham. Buch. *Khan-ge, Maal-le, Pur-ran-dah,* Panj.: *Chay-la-ree,* Lower Sind: *Da-bah* and *Duh-ri-e,* N.-W. Prov.: *Debari,* Beng.: *Bonkuaso,* Ooriah. D. 15-17, A. 17-19, L. l. 41, L. tr. 11/5. No barbels. Throughout India, except the Panjáb and south of the Kistna; it attains 4 inches in length.

296. *Danio spinosus,* Day. D. 15-16, A. 20, L. l. 52, L. tr. 15/4. No barbels, or only a short rostral pair. One or two spines on edge of orbit. Pegu: to 4 inches in length.

297. *Danio aurolineatus,* Day. D. 14, A. 18, L. l. 34-40, L. tr. 8/4. One pair of rostral barbels. South Malabar, to 3 inches in length.

298. *Danio lineolatus,* Blyth. D. 13, A. 17, L. l. 33, L. tr. 7½/3. Rostral and maxillary barbels. Sikkim and Darjeeling.

299. *Danio dangila,* Ham. Buch. D. 12-13, A. 17-18, L. l. 38, L. tr. 7/4½. Two pairs of long barbels. Darjeeling, Bengal, and Behar, attaining 5 or 6 inches in length.

300. *Danio chrysops,* Cuv. and Val. D. 13, A. 20, L. l. 45. No barbels. Bengal.

301. *Danio, Neilgherriensis,* Day. *Cowlie,*Tam. D. 12-13, A. 13-14, L. l. 35, L. tr. $\frac{6-7}{4}$. Rostral and sometimes maxillary barbels. Rivers on Neilgherry Hills, to 3½ inches in length.

302. *Danio osteographus,* McClelland. D. 13, A. 16-17, L. l. 35-37, L. tr. 7½/3. Rostral and usually maxillary barbels. India and Ceylon, to 6 inches in length.

303. *Danio æquipinnatus,* McClelland. D. 12, A. 14-16, L. l. 32-34, L. tr. 7/3½. Rostral and maxillary barbels. Base of Garrow Hills, Assam.

B. A portion or the whole of the abdominal edge cutting.

Genus—PERILAMPUS, McClelland.

Paradanio, sp. Day: *Cachius* et *Eustira,* Günther.

Pseudobranchiæ present. Body oblong, compressed, with a cutting abdominal edge. Mouth obliquely directed upwards. Barbels absent. Pharyngeal teeth hooked, and in three rows, 5, 4 or 2, 2 or 1/1 or 2, 2 or 4, 5. Dorsal fin rather short, without any osseous ray, and commencing opposite or behind the origin of the anal, which last has many rays. Scales of moderate size. Lateral line concave, passing to the lower half of the base of the caudal fin.

304. *Perilampus atpar,* Ham. Buch. *Mor-ri-ah,* Panj.: *Bi-dah,* Sind.: *Bonkuaso,* Ooriah: *Kachhi,* Beng.: *Nga-man-dan, Ya-paw-nga,* and *Nga-phyin-gyan,* Burm. D. 9. A. 22-24, L. l. 55, L. tr. 11/4. Greenish with a silvery lateral band. Throughout India and Burma, attaining 4 inches in length.

305. *Perilampus laubuca*, Ham. Buch. *Coon-che-li-e*, North-West Provinces: *Dunnahrah*, Hind.: *Laynbuka* and *Dankena*, Beng.: *Bankoe*, Ooriah: *Nga-me-loung*, Burm. D. 11, A. 19-22, L. l. 34, L. tr. 7/5. A black mark above base of pectoral fin. Gangetic Provinces, Orissa and Burma, attaining 3 inches in length.

Genus—CHELA, Ham. Buch.

Oxygaster, v. Hass.: *Leuciscus*, sp. Cuv. & Val.: *Laubuca*, *Macrochirichthys* et *Paralaubuca*, Bleeker.

Body rather elongated and compressed: abdominal edge cutting. Pseudobranchiæ present. Mouth directed somewhat upwards, with the lower jaw prominent, and generally having a knob above the symphysis. Barbels absent. Pharyngeal teeth hooked, slender, and in 2 or 3 rows. Dorsal fin short, without any osseous ray, situated principally or entirely opposite the anal, which latter has an elongated base: pectorals long: caudal forked. Scales of moderate or small size. Lateral line concave.

306. *Chela Sladoni*, Day. D. 10, A. 21, L. l. 68, L. tr. 10/8. The Irrawaddi River.

307. *Chela argentea*, Day. D. 9-10, A. 17-18, L. l. 43-45, L. tr. $6\frac{1}{2}/3$. Bowany and Cauvery Rivers in Madras, to 6 inches in length.

308. *Chela bacaila*, Ham. Buch. *Pur-rund*, Panj.: *Cun-da-lah*, *Vounche*, and *Phar-ba-dan*, Sind: *Chel-liah* and *Charl*, North-West Provinces: *Jellahri*, Ooriah. D. 9, A. 14-15, L. l. 90-110. Throughout India except Malabar, attaining 6 inches in length.

309. *Chela novacula*, Val. D. 9, A, 17, L. l. 60, L. tr. 15/3. India.

310. *Chela flavipinnis*, Jerdon. D. 9, A. 17-19, L. l. 65, L. tr. 9/5. Cauvery and its branches.

311. *Chela untrahi*, Day. *Untrahi*, Ooriah. D. 9, A. 20, L. l. 52, L. tr. 7/5. Mahanuddee, to 5 inches in length.

312. *Chela phulo*, Ham. Buch. *Bung-ka-charl*, Panj.: *Muk-ka*, Sind: *Phul-chela*, Beng.: *Dunnahree*, Hind. D. 9, A. 20, L. l. 87, L. tr. 12/6. India, extending downwards to the Kistna River; it attains 4 inches in length.

313. *Chela sardinella*, Cuv. & Val. *Nga-koon-nyat*, Burm. D. 9, A. 21, L. l. 48, L. tr. $7\frac{1}{2}/4$. Irrawaddi River, attaining 6 inches in length.

314. *Chela Panjábensis*, Day. *Took*, Panj. D. 9, A. 17, L. l. ca. 110, L. tr. 12/9. Ravi River in the Panjáb.

315. *Chela alkootee*, Sykes. D. 10, A. 10. Deccan, to 1 inch in length.

316. *Chela jorah*, Sykes. D. 10, A. 11. Beema River near Pairgaon in the Deccan.

317. *Chela teekanee*, Sykes. D. 10, A. 14. Beema River, attaining $2\frac{1}{2}$ inches in length.

318. *Chela gora*, Ham. Buch. *Boun-chi* and *Kundul*, Panj.: *Phar-ri-e*, Sind: *Chel-li-ah*, North West-Provinces: *Chel-hul*, Hind.: *Gora chela*, Beng.: *Hum-catchari*, Ooriah. D. 10, A. 15, L. l. 140-160. Panjáb, Gangetic Provinces, Assam, Orissa and Sind, attaining 8 inches in length.

319. *Chela clupeoides*, Bloch. *Netteli*, Tam. D. 9-10, A. 14-15, L. l. 80, L. tr. $13\frac{1}{2}/6\frac{1}{2}$. South of the Kistna River, attaining 6 inches in length.

Sub-Family—HOMALOPTERINÆ, *McClelland*.

(Air-vessel absent).

Pseudobranchiæ absent. Branchial aperture vertical and narrow. Body elongated and anteriorly depressed, having a broad smooth abdomen. Snout prominent, before the mouth, which latter is small, transverse, central, inferior, and with fleshy lips. Barbels present. Pharyngeal teeth in a single row, conical. Pectoral and ventral fins horizontal, forming half discs. Body scaled. Air-vessel absent.

Genus—HOMALOPTERA, *v. Hass*.

Balitora, Gray: *Platycara*, McClell.

Head and anterior part of body depressed: snout more or less spatulate. Mouth small, inferior, with two pairs of rostral barbels, and one at either angle of the mouth. Pharyngeal teeth small (from 5 to 15), and in one row. Pectoral and ventral fins with many rays, the outer of which are simple: dorsal short, situated opposite to the ventral: anal likewise short.

320. *Homaloptera Brucei*, Gray and Hard. *Cul cundee*, stone carp, Tam. D. 11. A. 7. L. l. 70. Brown, blotched with darker. This fish is found in the rivers of the Wynaad, attaining at least $3\frac{1}{2}$ inches in length.

321. *Homaloptera maculata*, Gray and Hard. D. 11, A. 7. L. l. 70, L. tr. 10/7. Found in the Eastern Himalayas, from about Darjeeling, through Bootan, Assam and the Khasya Hills.

Sub-Family—COBITIDINÆ.

Air-vessel present, partially, or entirely enclosed in a bony capsule conghina.

Pseudobranchiæ absent. Body elongated, oblong, compressed or cylindrical, but not depressed. Eye with or without an erectile spine near the orbit. Snout and lips fleshy. Mouth small, inferior, and furnished with from six to twelve barbels. Pharyngeal teeth few and in one row. Vertical fins spineless; dorsal with a varying number of rays (8-30): anal with few (7-8): ventrals absent in one genus. Scales small and cycloid when present, usually immersed in mucus. Lateral line single, sometimes incomplete or absent. Air-vessel present, entirely or partially enclosed in a bony capsule.

A. With an erectile spine near the orbit.

Genus—APUA, *Blyth*.

Body elongated and compressed. A small, erectile, bifid, sub-orbital spine. Eight barbels—one rostral, one maxillary, and two mandibular pairs. Dorsal fin in the posterior third of the body, but anterior to the anal: ventral fins absent.

322. *Apua fusca*, Blyth. D. 8, A. 8. Pegu.

Genus—ACANTHOPHTHALMUS, *v. Hass*.

Body elongated and compressed. A small erectile, bifid, sub-orbital spine. Six barbels—one rostral, and two maxillary pairs. Dorsal fin situated in the posterior third of the body, anterior to the anal, but behind the ventrals.

323. *Acanthophthalmus pangia*, Ham. Buch. *Pangya*, Beng.: *Ngatha-lay-doh*, Burm. D. 8, A. 7. Light cinnamon colour. North-East Bengal and northern portions of Burma.

Genus—ACANTHOPSIS, *v. Hass*.

Prostheacanthus, Blyth.

Body very elongated. Snout long and compressed. Barbels eight, two being mandibular. A small bifid, erectile spine situated in advance of the orbit. Dorsal fin opposite to the ventrals: caudal forked.

324. Acanthopsis choirorrhynchus, Bleeker. *Nga-tha-lay-doh*, Burm. D. 12, A. 8. Upper portions of the Irrawaddi.

Genus—COBITIS, *Artedi*.

Somileptes, Bleeker.

Body elongated and compressed: dorsal profile nearly horizontal. Six barbels, on the snout and upper jaw. A small, erectile, bifid, sub-orbital spine. Dorsal fin inserted opposite to the ventral: caudal truncated or rounded.

325. *Cobitis gongota*, Ham. Buch. D. 10, A. 8. Barbels short. Assam.

326. *Cobitis guntea*, Ham. Buch. *Kondaturi*, and *Gup-kari*, Ooriah : *Nga-tha-lay-doh*, Burm. D. 8-9, A. 7. Barbels long. From Orissa, through Bengal and Burma, also in the Bombay Presidency, attaining 4 inches in length.

Genus—LEPIDOCEPHALICHTHYS, Bleeker.

Platacanthus, Day.

Body elongated and moderately compressed. Eight barbels, two of which belong to the mandible. A large, erectile, bifid, sub-orbital spine. Dorsal fin short, commencing opposite or nearly so to the ventral: the internal ray of the pectoral fin may be modified into a flat osseous spine: caudal truncated or slightly emarginate.

327. *Lepidocephalichthys thermalis*, Cuv. and Val. *Assaree*, Tam.: *Jubbi cowri*, Ooriah: *Bálu*, Hind. D. 9, A. 7. Dorsal slightly in advance of ventral. Southern India, the Malabar Coast and Ceylon.

328. *Lepidocephalichthys balgara*, Ham. Buch. *Jubbi cowri*, Ooriah. D. 8, A. 7. Dorsal not in advance of ventral. India generally.

Genus—BOTIA, Gray.

Hymenophysa, McClelland.

Body oblong, compressed, with the dorsal profile more or less convex. Eyes with a free circular eyelid: a bifid, erectile, sub-orbital spine. Barbels six to eight: when six, all are on the snout and upper jaw: if eight, the extra pair are on the mandible. Dorsal fin commences anterior to the root of the ventral: caudal forked. Air-vessel in two divisions, the anterior being partially enclosed in a bony capsule, whilst the posterior portion is free in the abdominal cavity.

329. *Botia nebulosa*, Blyth. D. 15, A. 7. Barbels six. Darjeeling.

330. *Botia dario*, Ham. Buch. *Sahinga*, Panj.: *Buctea*, Hind.: *Shee-uharo*, Sind. D. 13, A. 8. Barbels eight. Generally throughout the rivers of India, except those of Madras: even in the Sind Hills.

331. *Botia hymenophysa*, Bleeker. *Nga-tha-lay-doh* and *Shoay-zagay*, Burm. D. 11-15, A. 8. Barbels six. Upper portions of the Irrawaddi.

332. *Botia Almorhæ*, Gray. D. 12, A. 8. Barbels eight. Almorah. The Revd. W. Carleton informs that he has also procured it from a stream at Kalka, 40 miles from Simla.

333. *Botia rostrata*, Günther. D. 12, A. 8. Barbels eight. Bengal and Assam.

334. Botia Berdmorei, Blyth. D. 12, A. 7. Barbels eight. Tenasserim Provinces.

335. Botia histrionica, Blyth. D. 10, A. 7. Barbels eight. Pegu.

Genus—JERDONIA, Day.

Platacanthus, sp. Day.

Body elongated and moderately compressed. Eight barbels, two of which are mandibular. A free, erectile, bifid, sub-orbital spine. Dorsal fin long (27 branched rays), commencing before the ventrals: the internal ray of the pectoral fin modified into a flat osseous spine: caudal slightly emarginate.

336. Jerdonia maculata, Day. D. 30, A. 9. Madras.

B. No erectile spine near the orbit.

Genus—NEMACHEILUS, v. Hass.

Acoura et *Acourus,* Swain.: *Acanthocobitis,* Peters.

Body elongated. Dorsal profile nearly horizontal. Barbels eight or six: when the former, the extra pair belong to the posterior nostrils: none on the mandibles. No spine on the head. Dorsal fin of moderate length, or short, situated opposite the ventrals.

a. *With eight barbels.*

337. Nemacheilus Evezardi, Day. D. 17, A. 7. Greenish, with small dark blotches. Poona.

b. *With six barbels.*

338. Nemacheilus pavonaceus, McClelland. D 15-17, A. 7. Body with cross bands: caudal emarginate, with rounded angles. Assam and Tenasserim Provinces.

339. Nemacheilus botia, Ham. Buch. *Bil-turi,* Assam: *Soon-da-lee,* Panj.: *Gool-lu-ah,* North-West Provinces. D. 14, A. 7. Body irregularly blotched. Caudal emarginate. Throughout India, except its most southern portion.

340. Nemacheilus Rüpelli, Sykes. D. 12-13, A. 8. Short bars on body. Caudal emarginate. Poona.

341. Nemacheilus moreh, Sykes. D. 12, A. 7. Caudal wedge-shaped. Deccan.

342. Nemacheilus monoceros, McClelland. D. 12, A. 6. Caudal rounded. Assam.

343. Nemacheilus aureus, Day. D. 12, A. 7. Body blotched. Caudal and dorsal fins barred. Caudal forked. Jubbulpur in the Central Provinces.

344. Nemacheilus rupicola, McClelland. *Larreah, Gur-dun,* and *Chi-tal,* Panj. D. 10-11, A. 7. Eleven to seventeen brown bands wider than the ground colour. Caudal forked. Himalayas, and from the Panjáb through the North-Western Provinces, Bengal and Assam, attaining 3½ inches length.

345. Nemacheilus semiarmatus, Day. D. 11, A. 7. Irregular spots and bars on body and fins. Caudal forked. Rivers along the base of the southern slopes of the Neilgherry Hills in Madras.

346. Nemacheilus zonalternans, Blyth. D. 11, A. 7. Ten or eleven vertical bands, with intermediate ones superiorly. Caudal entire. Tenasserim Provinces.

347. Nemacheilus zonata, McClelland. D. 10, A. 6. Eleven to thirteen dark zones encircle the body, not half the width of the ground colour. Caudal forked. Upper Assam, Bengal and North-West Provinces.

348. Nemacheilus subfuscus, McClelland. D. 10, A. 7. Ten brown zones encircle the body, wider than the ground colour. Caudal forked. Upper Assam and Burma.

349. Nemacheilus sinuatus, Day. D. 10-11, A. 7. Vertical brown bands, with shorter intermediate ones. Dorsal and caudal barred, the latter fin cut square. Wynaad and Sind Hills.

350. Nemacheilus chlorosoma, McClelland. *Wattara*, Tel. D. 9, A. 7. A spotted dark line along middle of body. Caudal square. Kistna River and Upper Assam.

351. Nemacheilus phoxocheila, McClelland (?). D. 11, A. 7. Assam.

352. Nemacheilus serpentarius, Day. D. 10, A. 7, L l. 64. A dark band from eye to dorsal fin. Some specimens in the Calcutta Museum.

353. Nemacheilus striatus, Day. *Cul-irum* and *Cul-nakura*, Tam. D. 10, A. 7. Numerous yellow bands. Caudal slightly forked. Wynaad, attaining 3½ inches in length.

354. Nemacheilus mugah, Day. *Mugah*, Beng. D. 9, A. 7-8. Fifteen brown bands, one-third as wide as the ground colour. Caudal forked. Midnapur, to 2 inches in length.

355. Nemacheilus notostigma, Bleeker (?). D. 10, A. 7-8. Blotched. Caudal forked. Cauvery River above Trichinopoly, also (?) Ceylon.

356. Nemacheilus montanus, McClelland. *Saant-al* and *Laal mutche*, Panj. D. 9-10, A. 7. Twelve vertical brown bands. Caudal forked. Himalayas.

357. Nemacheilus spilopterus, Cuv. and Val. D. 9, A. 7. Eleven to fifteen irregular bands. Caudal slightly emarginate. Himalayas and Assam.

358. Nemacheilus savona, Ham. Buch. *Savon-khorka*, Beng. D. 10-11, A. 7. Ten to twelve very narrow white bands. Caudal slightly emarginate. Bengal.

359. Nemacheilus Beavani, Günther. D. 10, A. 7. Dark bands wider than interspaces. Caudal forked. Cossye River, to 2 inches in length.

360. Nemacheilus Denisonii, Day. D, 10-11, A. 7. Nine to twelve yellowish zones. Caudal forked. Neilgherry and Coorg Hills, and rivers along their bases.

361. Nemacheilus triangularis, Day. D. 10, A. 7. Seven black-edged bands. Caudal emarginate. Travancore Hills.

362. Nemacheilus Griffithii, Günther. D. 10, A. 7. Marbled. Caudal emarginate. Probably from Assam.

363. Nemacheilus corica, Ham. Buch. *Khorika*, Beng.: *Chould-hi* and *Taal-la-nah*, Panj. D. 10, A. 7. About thirteen blotches along the side. Caudal forked. Panjáb, North-East Bengal and Assam.

364. Nemacheilus Guentheri, Day. D. 10, A. 7. Reticulated with brown. Caudal lobed. Rivers along the southern slopes of the Neilgherry Hills in Madras.

365. Nemacheilus Blythii, Day. D. 9, A. 7. Brownish. Caudal forked. Two specimens in the Calcutta Museum.
366. Nemacheilus Butanensis, McClelland. D. 9, A. 7. Caudal rounded. Bootan, to 5 inches in length.
367. Nemacheilus rubripinnis, Jerdon. D. 8, A. 7. Nine vertical bars. Caudal emarginate. Malabar.
368. Nemacheilus turio, Ham. Buch. D. 8 (10?), A. 7. Blotched. Caudal emarginate. Assam.
369. Nemacheilus guttatus, McClelland. D. 8. Blotched. Caudal entire. Upper Assam.

Genus—MISGURNUS, Lacép.

Cobitichthys, Bleeker.

Body elongated and compressed. No sub-orbital spine. Ten or twelve barbels, four being on the mandible. Dorsal fin arising opposite the ventrals. Caudal rounded.

370. Misgurnus lateralis, Günther. D. 10, A. 8. Barbels ten. Body longitudinally banded, a black spot on base of caudal. Attains above 3 inches in length. Bengal.

Family—CLUPEIDÆ, *Cuv.*

Gill-openings usually very wide. Pseudobranchiæ large (except in Megalops). Abdomen compressed into a serrated edge or else smooth. Opercular pieces four. Margin of the upper jaw formed mesially by the inter-maxillaries, laterally by the maxillaries, which are composed of three pieces, these are sometimes moveable. Barbels absent. Dorsal fin with a few or moderate number of rays, no adipose fin; anal sometimes with an elongated base. Scales on body, none on the head. Stomach with a blind sac. Pyloric appendages numerous. Air-vessel more or less simple.

A. **Abdomen with a compressed, serrated edge.**

Genus—CLUPEA, sp. *Artedi.*

Sardinella, Harengula, Rogenia, Clupeonia, Spratella, Kowala, Meletta, et Alausa, Val.: *Clupalosa,* Bleeker: *Alausella, Pomolobus, Opisthonema, Brevoortia,* Gill: *Sardinia,* Poey.

Body compressed: the serrature of the abdomen extending forwards into the thoracic region. Upper jaw not projecting beyond the lower. Teeth, when present, deciduous and rudimentary. Dorsal fin situated opposite the ventral: anal of moderate or long extent: caudal forked. Scales large, of moderate and more rarely of small size.

371. Clupea variegata, Day. *Nga-la-bee,* Burm. D. 15, A. 29, L. l. 90. Anterior scales irregularly, posterior regularly arranged. A dark humeral spot. A row of about 18 bars across the back. Dorsal with a black band in the lower portion of its posterior half: caudal black-tipped. Irrawaddi and its branches, up to 7 inches in length.

372. Clupea chapra, Ham. Buch. *Sou-e* and *Hilsa,* Panj.: *Pul-looree, Chu-chee,* Sind. D. 15, A. 21-22, L. l. 80. Scales regularly arranged, except over the abdomen. A dark humeral spot. Rivers and tanks in their vicinity throughout India as low as the Kistna. It attains 6 or 7 inches in length.

373. Clupea palasah, Cuv. and Val. *Pulla* throughout the Indus *Oolum,* Tam.: *Pulasa,* Tel.: *Hilsa* and *Ilisha,* Ooriah and Beng.

Nga-tha-louk, Burm.: "sable fish" Trichinopoly. D. 18-19, A. 19, L. l. 45-49, L. tr. 17. This fish, a shad, ascends all the large rivers of India and Burma during the S. W. or N. E. monsoons for breeding purposes.

Genus—CORICA, Ham. Buch.

Clupeoides, Bleeker.

Body oblong, moderately compressed. Abdominal serrature generally commences behind the ventral fins. Lower jaw longer than the upper. Teeth rudimentary and deciduous. Dorsal fin situated opposite the ventral: anal of moderate extent, its last rays may be detached.

374. *Corica soborna*, Ham. Buch. *Cutwal-alise* and *Godhaee*, Ooriah. D. 16, A. 13+2, L. l. 40, L. tr. 9. Mahanuddee River, up to 2 inches in length.

Genus—PELLONA, Cuv. & Val.

Branchiostegals six. Body rather elongate and strongly compressed: thoracic and abdominal edges serrated. Mouth of moderate size: upper jaw generally emarginate and shorter than the lower. Fine teeth in the jaws, palatine and pterygoid bones, also on the tongue, but none on the vomer. Dorsal fin medial: ventrals small, inserted anterior to the dorsal: anal elongated. Scales large, or of moderate size, rarely small.

375. *Pellona Sladeni*, Day. *Nga-zen-bya*, Burm. D. 13, A. 44, L. l. 48, L. tr. 10. Caudal black edged. Irrawaddi River, certainly above Mandalay, attaining 7 inches in length.

Genus—ENGRAULIS, Cuv.

Clupea, sp. et *Stolephorus*, Lacép.: *Thrissa*, Cuv.

Branchiostegals short, rather numerous. Gill-openings wide, the membrane connecting them short, leaving the isthmus uncovered. Body oblong or elongated and compressed. Cleft of mouth lateral, snout conical as a rule, the upper, but as an exception the lower jaw may be the longer. Intermaxillaries small, concealed: maxillaries of varying length, but always long, and with a membranous attachment to the cheeks. Teeth small, sometimes of unequal size, usually present on the jaws, vomer, palatine and pterygoid bones. The dorsal fin may be in advance of or posterior to the origin of the anal: the upper pectoral rays may or may not be prolonged: anal of moderate or great extent. Scales large or of moderate size.

376. *Engraulis purava*, Ham. Buch. *Pussai*, Ooriah. D. 13-14, A. 43-50, L. l. 46, L. tr. 12. This fish ascends tidal rivers, and frequently is found in fresh-water tanks to which inundations have extended.

377. *Engraulis taty*, Ham. Buch. D. 13-15, A. 51-56, L. l. 42-46, L. tr. 12. Found in the same localities as the last, but not so commonly.

378. *Engraulis telara*, Ham. Buch. *Tampara*, Ooriah: *Pencha*, Beng.: *Nga-hta-yawet*, Burm. D. 13, A. 70-78, L. l. 52-55, L. tr. 14. Found in the whole extent of the Ganges, Jumna, Brahmaputra, Mahanuddee and Irrawaddi Rivers.

Genus—CHATOËSSUS, Cuv. & Val.

Branchiostegals from four to six. Body oval, short, deep, and moderately compressed, with a cutting serrated abdominal edge. Eyes with lateral adipose lids. Snout overhanging a narrow transverse mouth. The superior combs of the first branchial arches unite with those of the opposite side forming two angles, one pointing forwards, the other backwards, the fourth branchial arch having an accessory respiratory organ. Teeth absent. A single-rayed dorsal fin, having the posterior ray prolonged in some species: ventrals in front of or below dorsal fin: anal posterior to the dorsal, elongated: caudal forked.

379. Chatoëssus modestus, Day. D. 16, A. 28, L. l. 47, L. tr. 17. Last dorsal ray not prolonged. Uniform colour. Scales regularly arranged. Irrawaddi and its branches, to $5\frac{1}{2}$ inches in length.

380. Chatoëssus manmina, Ham. Buch. *Mackundi*, Ooriah. D. 14, A. 21-24, L. l. 58-60, L. tr. 22. Large rivers and tanks of Assam, Orissa and Gangetic Provinces, attaining 8 inches in length.

B. Abdomen without a serrated edge.

Genus—MEGALOPS, (Commers), Lacép.

Branchiostegals numerous: pseudobranchiæ absent. Body oblong, compressed. Abdomen rounded. Snout obtusely conical. Mouth anterior, lower jaw prominent. A narrow osseous lamella adherent to the symphysis of the mandibles, covering the intermediate part, between the two bones. Gill-membranes separated. Villiform teeth on the jaws, vomer, palatine and pterygoid bones, likewise on the tongue and on the base of the skull. A single dorsal opposite the ventrals.

381. Megalops cyprinoides, Brouss. *Cunnay*, Mal,: *Punnikowu* and *Naharm*, Ooriah: *Nga-tan-youet*, Burm. D. 18-20, A. 24-27, L. l. 37-42, L. tr 6/6. Throughout tanks along the coasts of India and Burma.

Family—NOTOPTERIDÆ.

Pseudobranchiæ absent. Body compressed. Tail prolonged, tapering. Margin of the upper jaw formed by the inter-maxillaries mesially, and the maxillaries laterally. Barbels absent. Opercular apparatus incomplete. A parieto-mastoid cavity on either side, leading into the interior of the skull. A single-rayed dorsal fin, belonging to the caudal portion of the vertebral column: anal very long. Head and body scaled. Stomach without blind sac: two pyloric appendages. Air-vessel present, and divided in its interior. The ova fall into the cavity of the abdomen before exclusion.

Genus—NOTOPTERUS, (Lacép.), Cuv. & Val.

Mystus, sp. Ham. Buch.

Branchiostegals from three to nine. Gill-membranes partly united. Snout obtuse, convex. Muciferous channels on head well developed. Cleft of mouth lateral, not deep. Maxilla formed of a single bone, and articulated to the inter-maxillary. Lower margin of pre-opercle serrated, likewise some of the other bones of the head. Sub-opercle absent. Teeth in both jaws of irregular sizes, also on vomer, palatines, pterygoid, and sphenoid bones, and in two rows on the tongue. A dorsal fin present (Notopterus), *or absent* (Xenomystus): *anal fin long, united to the caudal. Ventrals, when present, rudimentary and united together. Scales small. Abdomen serrated along its margin. Lateral line distinct. Muciferous channels on head well developed. Air-vessel sub-divided internally, and ending in front in two horns, the anterior of which is in immediate connection with the auditory organs: posteriorly it ends in two branches divided from one another by the hæmal spines. Intestines short. Cæcal pylori long.*

382. Notopterus kapirat, Bonn. *Moh, But,* and *Pur-ri*, Panj.: *Moh*, N. W. Prov.: *Ambutan-wahlah*, "Barber's knife," Tam.: *Wallak tattah*, Mysore: *Pulli*, " a slice," Ooriah: *Nga-hpeh*, and *Nga-phe*, Burm. D. 9, A. 100-108, L. r. 225. Throughout the fresh-waters of India and Burma, attaining 2 feet or more in length.

383. Notopterus chitala, Ham. Buch. *Gundun,* Sind: *Chitul*, Ooriah: *Chitala*, Beng. D. 8-10, A. 110-125, L. l. 180. Upper profile of head concave. Rivers and tanks of Sind, Lower Bengal, and Orissa, attaining several feet in length.

Family—SYMBRANCHIDÆ.

Symbranchii, Müller.

Gill-openings confluent into a single slit, which is situated on the abdominal surface. Body elongated. Margin of the upper jaw formed by the inter-maxillaries, the maxillaries being internal and parallel to them. Barbels absent. Vertical fins as mere folds of the skin, and no paired ones. Scales, if present, minute. Vent far posterior to the head. Air-vessel absent. Ribs present. Stomach destitute of blind sac. No pyloric appendages. Ovaries with ovi-ducts.

Genus—AMPHIPNOUS, Müller.

Pneumabranchus, McClelland.

Gill-membranes almost entirely adherent to the isthmus. Three branchial arches having rudimentary laminæ, and with narrow slits between them. An air-sac communicates with the gill-cavity. Palatine teeth in a single row. Scales on body small, longitudinally arranged.

384. Amphipnous cuchia. Ham. Buch. *Cuchia,* Ooriah and Beng.: *Nga-sheen*, Burm. Found in the Lower Provinces of Bengal, Orissa, Burma, and along the coast, attaining 2 feet or more in length.

Family—SYMBRANCHUS, *Bloch.*

Unibranchapertura, Lacép.: *Ophisternon*, McClelland: *Tetrabranchus*, Bleeker.

Gill-membranes not adherent to the isthmus. Four branchial arches with the gills well developed: no air-sac accessory to the gill-cavity. Palatine teeth in a band Scales absent.

385. Symbranchus Bengalensis, McClelland. Lower Provinces of Bengal, and coast districts of India.

Family—MURÆNIDÆ.

Body elongated, cylindrical or band shaped. Margin of the upper jaw formed anteriorly by the inter-maxillaries, which are more or less coalescent with the vomer and ethmoid, whilst laterally the sides of the jaw are formed by the maxillaries Vertical fins, when present, confluent or separated by a projecting tail: no ventrals. Scales rudimentary or absent. Vent far posterior to the head. Stomach with a blind sac. No pyloric appendages. Ovaries destitute of ovi-ducts.

Genus—ANGUILLA, *Cuv.*

Muræna, sp. Artedi: *Torpolepis*, pt., McClelland.

Gill-openings narrow, situated near the base of the pectoral fins. Upper aw not projecting beyond the lower. Teeth small, in bands. Dorsal fin commences at some distance from the head: pectorals present. Scales small and imbedded in the skin.

386. *Anguilla labiata*, Peters. *Pa-lug-dah*, Andam. Fresh-waters of Andaman Islands.

387. *Anguilla Bengalensis*, Gray. Generally distributed throughout India, attaining a large size.

388. *Anguilla bicolor*, McClelland. Lower Provinces of Bengal, Orissa, and Madras.

389. *Anguilla virescens*, Peters. *Jee-tah-dah*, Andam. Fresh-waters of Andaman Islands.

Order—LOPHOBRANCHII, Cuv.

Fishes possessed of a dermal, segmental skeleton, with the opercular pieces reduced to a single plate. Gill-opening small. Muscular system very slightly developed. Gills composed of small rounded tufts attached to the branchial arches. Snout produced. Mouth terminal and small. Teeth absent. Air-vessel stated to be destitute of a pneumatic duct.

" In most of the species the males perform the function of hatching the eggs, which for that purpose are deposited, up to the time of the evolution of the young, either between the ventrals *(Solenostomus)*, or in tail pouches *(Hippocampus)*, or in pouches on the breast and belly *(Doryrhamphus)*, or in rows on the breast and belly *(Nerophis)*, and are thus carried about by the fish. The egg-pouches may be compared to birds' nests, or to the skin-fold in which the wandering Penguin *(Aptenodytes Patagonicus)* transports its eggs: and remind one of the Marsupials amongst the mammals."—*Kaup*.

Family—SYNGNATHIDÆ.

Gill-openings round, small, and situated at the posterior-superior angle of the gill-cover. A single dorsal fin: ventrals and occasionally one or more of the other fins absent.

Genus—ICHTHYOCAMPUS, Kaup.

The edges of the concave back and tail are continuous, and are continued, although sometimes very indistinctly, to the caudal fin. Dorsal fin opposite or nearly so to the vent: pectorals and caudal present. Egg-pouch in the males on the tail, having a cutaneous covering.

390. *Ichthyocampus carce*, Ham. Buch. D. 23-26. Rings 15-16 + 38-40. This pipe-fish ascends rivers of Malabar and Bengal; it attains 5 inches in length.

Genus—DORYICHTHYS, Kaup.

Doryrhamphus, Chæroichthys, et Microphis, Kaup.: *Belonichthys*, Peters.

Ridges well developed on the body. Humeral bones firmly united. Dorsal fin of moderate extent or long, situated opposite the vent. Lateral line interrupted or continued to the lower edge of the tail.

391. *Doryichthys cunculus*, Ham. Buch. *Kunnur-dant*, "Crocodile's tooth," Ooriah. D. 50. Rings 17-18 + 25-27. Found ascending the rivers of Malabar and Bengal.

392. *Doryichthys Bleekeri*, Day. D. 41-45, Rings 20+23. Malabar, ascending rivers.

Order—PLECTOGNATHI.

Fishes with the bones of the head completely ossified, whilst those in the remainder of the body are incompletely so: vertebræ few. Gill-openings narrow, situated in front of the pectoral fins: gills pectinate. Head generally large. Mouth narrow: the bones of the upper jaw mostly united, sometimes produced into the form of a beak. Teeth may be distinct in the jaws, or absent. There may be a single soft dorsal appertaining to the caudal portion of the vertebral column and situated opposite the anal: in some a rudimentary spinous dorsal is also present: ventrals, when existing, being in the form of spines. Skin smooth, with rough scales, or ossified in the form of plates or spines. Air-vessel destitute of a pneumatic duct.

Family—GYMNODONTIDÆ.

Bones of upper and lower jaw form a beak, having a cutting edge, and covered with a layer of ivory-like substance, in which a median suture may be present or absent. A soft dorsal, caudal, and anal exist, but no spinous dorsal: pectorals present: ventrals absent.

Genus—XENOPTERUS, Bibron.

Chonerinus, Bleeker.

Jaws divided by a median suture. Nostrils funnel-shaped, having fringed margins. Dorsal and anal fins long. Body more or less covered with fine dermal spines having a double or treble root. They are able to inflate their bodies with air, and float on the water, abdomen uppermost.

393. *Xenopterus naritus*, Richardson. D. 25-26, A. 23-25. Of a yellow colour. Found throughout the Burmese rivers far above tidal influence. It attains a considerable size, and is used as food.

Genus—TETRODON, Linn.

Back broad or compressed into a ridge. Jaws divided by a median suture. When a conspicuous nasal organ exists, there may be two on either side in a papilla (Tetraodon, Bleeker): or only a single tubular nasal opening on either side (Crayracion, Bleeker): or an imperforate nasal cavity with a fringed margin (body spiny) (Chelonodon, Müller): or a simple round nasal cavity (body smooth) (Monotretus, Bib.); or two imperforate nasal tentacles on either side (Arothron, Müll.): or if invisible, and back is compressed into a keel (Anosmius, Peters). Dorsal and anal fins short. Body wholly or partially covered by fine dermal spines, which, however, may be entirely absent. There may be a more or less distinct fold along the lower part of the tail (if nasal organs are very distinct) (Gastrophysus, Müller): if there is no such fold (but distinct nasal organs and spiny body) (Cheilichthys, Müller): or should the fold be absent and the skin smooth (Liosaccus, Günther).

394. *Tetrodon cutcutia*, Ham. Buch. *Teepah-benki*, Ooriah. A simple round nasal cavity. Body smooth. Brownish lines forming a net-work on the sides of the body, whilst a large black ocellus margined

with white exists on the side. Mouths of the Ganges, Irrawaddi, and other large rivers, ascending far above tidal influence.

395. *Tetrodon fluviatilis*, Ham. Buch. Two imperforate nasal tentacles on either side. Body nearly smooth. Superiorly greenish-yellow, with vermiculated blackish lines, becoming white below: there are also irregular black spots and blotches. Large rivers of India and Burma, far above tidal influence.

396. *Tetrodon patoca*, Ham. Buch. *Bheng-pulli*, Ooriah: *Nga-boo-din*, Burm. An imperforate nasal cavity with a fringed margin. Body spiny. Light brown above with whitish spots, becoming silvery below. Large rivers of India and Burma, far above tidal reach.

Sub-class—CHONDROPTERYGII.

Skeleton cartilaginous: no cranial sutures. Rarely a single gill-opening, as the gills by their outer edges are attached to the skin, and there exists an intervening gill-opening between each: no gill-cover. Three series of valves at the bulbus arteriosus. Optic nerves although united do not decussate. Body with vertical and paired fins, the posterior pair abdominal: caudal with an upper lobe, which is elongated. Intestines with a spiral valve. Male sex with prehensile organs attached to the vertical fins. Ovaries containing large ova which are fertilised, and in some likewise developed internally. Embryo with external deciduous gills. No air-vessel.

Order—PLAGIOSTOMATA.

Body more or less cylindrical, or depressed: the trunk may or may not pass into the tail. From five to seven gill-openings, which may be lateral or inferior. Jaws distinct from the skull.

Sub-Order—SELACHOIDEI, OR SHARKS.

Body more or less cylindrical, gradually merging into the tail. Gill-openings lateral.

Family—CARCHARIIDÆ.

The snout may be produced longitudinally (Carchariinæ or true sharks): or laterally (Zygænina or hammer-headed sharks). Spiracles absent or present. Eye with a nictitating membrane. A small pit may or may not exist above the root of the tail, and a second behind the angle of the mouth may be present or absent. Mouth crescentic, inferior. Teeth may be erect or oblique, with a single cusp, having sharp, smooth, or serrated edges: or they may be small, the cusps being obsolete: or with one in the centre, or one or two lateral ones: or even obtuse. The first dorsal fin, destitute of a spine, is placed opposite the interspace between the pectoral and ventral: anal fin present.

Genus—CARCHARIAS, Müll. and Henle.

No spiracles. A pit above the root of the caudal fin. Snout longitudinally produced. Mouth crescentic: the labial fold or groove rarely extends beyond the angle of the mouth. Teeth with a sharp triangular cusp, sometimes dilated. The first dorsal fin, destitute of a spine, is placed opposite the interspace between the pectoral and ventral: caudal with a distinct lower lobe.

397. *Carcharias Gangeticus,* Müll. and Henle. Teeth $\frac{27\text{-}30}{27\text{-}30}$. Of a grey colour. This savage ground-shark ascends all the large rivers of India and to above tidal influence; it attains 5 feet in length.

Sub-Order—BATOIDEI, OR RAYS.

Body depressed, forming, due to largely developed pectoral fins, a more or less flat disc, and having a thin and slender tail. Spiracles present. Gill-openings in five pairs, inferior. Dorsal fin, when present, on the tail: anal absent.

Family—PRISTIDÆ.

Snout much produced, flattened, and having a saw-like appearance, due to large teeth existing along its lateral edges.

Genus—PRISTIS, Latham.

Body elongate and depressed. Gill-openings inferior and of moderate width. Spiracles wide and posterior to the eye, which latter has no nictitating membrane. Nostrils inefrior, without tentacles. Teeth minute. Dorsal fins spineless: the first quite or nearly opposite to the ventrals: front edge of pectoral free.

398. *Pristis cuspidatus,* Latham. Mahanuddi and Irrawaddi Rivers, ascending far above tidal influence.

Family—TRYGONIDÆ.

Body flattened and disc-shaped, with a long and slender tail. Pectoral fins are continued forwards anteriorly and laterally to the end of the snout. No lateral longitudinal folds to the tail. Vertical fins, if present, in the form of a serrated spine.

Genus—TRYGON, Adanson.

Nasal valves coalesce and form a triangular flap. Teeth flattened. Pectorals continued forwards to the lateral edge of the snout. Tail long, whip-like, either destitute of any fin, or with cutaneous folds, which do not extend its entire length: armed superiorly with one or two serrated, lanceolate spines. Body smooth or tuberculated.

399. *Trygon uarnak,* Forsk. *Sankush,* Ooriah. Ascends rivers, often above tidal influence.

400. *Trygon sephen,* Forsk. This species is also frequently captured above the influence of the tides.

ON PRESERVING SPECIMENS OF FISH.

431. The best mode of preparing specimens of fish for scientific purposes is in spirit,* having the following advantages over stuffing—that they are more adapted for examination, are carried with greater ease, and are less subject to injury whilst *en route*.

On making preparations of fish.

432. For preserving fish in spirit, the following five considerations should be attended to—(1) the spirit; (2) the receptacles for the specimens; (3) the selecting and preparing the fish; (4) the treatment of the specimens as regards how they are to be placed in spirit, their labelling, and their packing; (5) what fish there are for which this process is unsuited.

Preserving fish in spirit.

1st.—*The spirit.*—I prefer the methylated alcohol, it being unsuited for drinking, and consequently less chance of being tampered with. But bazar arrack, or any spirit which will burn on the application of fire, and be entirely consumed, is of sufficient strength for the preservation of fish. On this spirit becoming too impure for use, it can be re-distilled.

2nd.—*The receptacle for the specimens.*—These for collectors (in contradistinction to the glass jars or bottles required in museums) are of two kinds:—tins with screw lids, and glazed earthenware jars with cork bungs, each having its advantages and disadvantages. *Tin cans* are made at Calcutta of any size, fitting wooden collecting boxes. The following I have found useful:—a strong iron-bound wooden box, with a lid having hinges and a hasp for a padlock, 16 inches high, 14 broad, and 12 wide (inside measure), receiving two cans which accurately fit it. Each of these cans has an opening into which is soldered a brass female screw of 4 inches in diameter; a moveable top screws into this orifice (cost about Rs. 30). The disadvantage of the cans are that no means of evaporation existing, the spirit is liable to become much heated during the hot weather, to the great injury of the specimens whilst travelling. The advantages are that there is no leakage, whilst each tin, if so desired, can be singly carried by a cooly without any chance of breakage. The *glazed earthenware jars* with cork bungs are very well adapted for specimens, and spirit keeps much cooler in them than in tin cans. The disadvantages are that the bungs may leak, or the jars become broken; they require bladdering, and also painting or varnishing over the bladder to render them secure. *Small bottles* well wrapped up in rag are exceedingly useful, put inside tins or jars for the

---

* I omit weak solutions of carbolic acid, as we have yet to ascertain what proportions will be most suitable for them to stand the rough usage of Indian transit, as well as how long they will keep.

purpose of protecting small specimens, or small perforated tin boxes would answer the same purpose.

3rd.—*Choosing and preparing the specimens.*—Fish need not be above 6 or 8 inches in length, unless of an eel-like shape, when they should be twice that length; care must be taken to obtain them fresh; a long slit should be made up their abdomens, the intestines, except the air-bladder, removed, and the abdominal cavity well washed out. If it is desired to preserve the intestines, they should be carefully and gently smeared over with a thin layer of arsenical paste. Sharks, rays, and skates should never be less than 10 inches in length excluding the tail, whilst larger ones should be skinned, care being taken not to injure the jaws or the teeth.

4th.—*The treatment of the specimen after it has been prepared.*— The first thing to be done to every specimen, whilst moving about, is to attach a distinguishing mark to it. This may be accomplished by appending a piece of tin having a number scratched upon it, or a bit of parchment on which one has been inscribed in indelible ink (or even in common dark ink if allowed to thoroughly dry previous to being put in the spirit). The locality where taken, and the native name when procurable, should be invariably recorded. The specimens may now be placed inside the first or soaking jar, or tin can full of spirit, being careful that the fish should not fill up above half of the receptacle in hot weather, or two-thirds in the cold season. Here they may be left to soak for six or eight days, and then be removed, washed, and placed in a second or intermediate jar of clean spirit, from whence they may be finally removed after ten days' soaking. Each must now (about 16 or 18 days after capture, according to their size) be rolled up securely in rag, and packed tightly in a case of fresh spirit. In rolling specimens up in rag, no two should touch each other. Unless thus secured, their fins will be destroyed when marching, their scales rubbed off, and most probably they will be irretrievably ruined. The spirit in the first and second jars can be used several times over for the first process in fish-soaking; when it becomes cloudy and dirty, it should be re-distilled.

5th.—*The specimens for which this process is unsuited* are the larger fish, as it is presumed the collector will not carry a cask of spirits in order to secure them. Large sharks, rays, and skates it is intended to keep, should be skinned and preserved by means of arsenical soap, and well soaked in turpentine. The mode of skinning fish is too well known to require detailing here.

FINIS.

www.ingramcontent.com/pod-product-compliance
Lightning Source LLC
Chambersburg PA
CBHW020535300426
44111CB00008B/670